the organization
and administration of
physical education

the organization and administration of physical education

FOURTH EDITION

EDWARD F. VOLTMER

ARTHUR A. ESSLINGER
University of Oregon

New York
APPLETON-CENTURY-CROFTS
Educational Division
MEREDITH CORPORATION

preface

It is estimated that there are as many as 40,000 men and women serving in administrative capacities in the field of physical education in the United States. They serve as chairmen of secondary school or college departments of physical education, as athletic directors, city or state supervisors, intramural directors, or have various other administrative positions in the field of physical education.

The success of these organizations depends in no small measure upon the skill and insight of the administrators. This, in turn, is based to a considerable extent upon the specialized preparation that they have received in this area. It has become recognized in the fields of business, industry, and government, as well as in education, that special courses in administration are invaluable in the preparation of personnel for this type of service.

A course in administration of physical education is of value not only to those who eventually become administrators; every teacher must know how to operate within the framework of an organization under the direction of an administrator. A teacher is expected to conform to certain standards of behavior and his success and advancement are dependent upon his proper adjustment in his organization. In addition, virtually every teacher must carry out certain administrative responsibilities in connection with his teaching assignment.

Every effort has been made to make this textbook inclusive and practical. The basic problems of organization and administration were ascertained by job analyses. Surveys of the duties of physical education administrators in secondary schools, colleges, and universities have provided the basis for the administrative assignments treated. This approach has resulted, we hope, in a balanced text including all important phases of organization and administration.

The authors are indebted to many individuals without whose assistance this volume would not have been possible. They owe a particular debt of gratitude to the many students and teachers whose reactions, criticisms, and suggestions have greatly strengthened the book. They are also grateful to the publishers, organizations, schools, and individuals who generously permitted use of various materials.

A. A. E.

contents

PREFACE v

1. THE NATURE AND PHILOSOPHY OF ADMINISTRATION 1

The meaning of administration. Importance of administration. Justification for study of administration. Essential skills of administration. Teaching versus administration. Qualifications of the administrator. Types of administrators. Values related to democratic administration. Misconceptions of democratic administration. A PHILOSOPHY OF ADMINISTRATION. Meaning of philosophy. Importance of a philosophy. Sources of philosophy. Democratic administration favored in democracy. An administrator's prayer. Duties of physical education administrators.

2. THE OBJECTIVES OF PHYSICAL EDUCATION 17

The necessity of having objectives. Physical education defined. Physical education objectives derived from educational objectives. The purposes of education. THE OBJECTIVES OF PHYSICAL EDUCATION. Recapitulation. THE PHYSICAL DEVELOPMENT OBJECTIVE. Importance of physical development objective accentuated by automation. Values of physical fitness. Role of physical education emphasized by automation. DEVELOPMENT OF MOTOR SKILLS. DEVELOPMENT OF KNOWLEDGE AND UNDERSTANDING. THE SOCIAL DEVELOPMENT OBJECTIVE. Contribution to the social development objective. Most important objective in physical education. Physical education, an integral part of education.

3. THE PROCESSES OF ADMINISTRATION 47

The basic processes of administration. PLANNING. What is planning? Types of plans. Administrative policies for a physical education organization. Guiding policies. Standard procedures and methods. Strategic considerations in planning. ORGANIZING. Grouping activities in physical education. Departmentation. Organization for physical education in public schools. Organization for health and physical education in colleges and universities. Delegation. Administrative staff. Committees.

DIRECTING. *Meaning and importance of direction. Ways of directing. Characteristics of good direction. Standard operating procedures. Indoctrination. Silent direction. Creating the desire to follow directions.* COORDINATING. *Nature and importance of coordination. Causes of poor coordinating. Facilitating coordination.* CONTROLLING. *Controlling related to other administrative processes. Maintain close contact with operations. Functions involved in control. Instruments of control.*

4. THE PHYSICAL EDUCATION SERVICE PROGRAM   91

The scope of the physical education program. The inadequacy of present-day programs. Evidences of inadequate programs. Causes of inadequate programs. Technique of curriculum development. Steps involved in curriculum construction. Principles for selection of activities. How sex differences affect the program. Time allotment. THE ELEMENTARY SCHOOL PROGRAM. *Importance of physical education in the elementary schools. The core of the elementary school physical education program.* THE PHYSICAL EDUCATION PROGRAM IN THE PRIMARY GRADES. *Characteristics of primary grade children. Implications for the physical education program in the primary grades.* THE PHYSICAL EDUCATION PROGRAM IN THE INTERMEDIATE GRADES. *Importance of physical education in the upper elementary grades. Characteristics of intermediate grade children. Implications for the physical education program in the intermediate grades.* THE JUNIOR HIGH SCHOOL PROGRAM. *Characteristics of junior high school students. Implications for the junior high school program.* THE SENIOR HIGH SCHOOL PROGRAM. *Characteristics of senior high school students. Implications for the senior high school program. The physically educated high school graduate. The block program. Homogeneous classes. Flexible scheduling. Substitutions for physical education. Preparation of curriculum outline. Summer session physical education programs.* THE COLLEGE PROGRAM. *Should physical education be required? Nature of the requirement. Time requirement. Proficiency requirement. Orientation programs. Survey course in activities. Waiver of the physical education requirement. Characteristics of college students. The program of activities. Coeducational physical education. Criteria for appraisal of instructional programs.*

5. THE PHYSICAL EDUCATION STAFF   156

Significance of staff. Qualifications. Selection of staff. Training load. Training in service. STAFF MORALE. *Nature of morale. Factors affecting teacher morale.*

6. SCHOOL HEALTH EDUCATION   176

Relationship of health education and physical education. Health education responsibilities of physical educators. Changing outlook on health. The objectives of the school health program. Organization of the school health program. The scope of the school health program. HEALTHFUL SCHOOL LIVING. *Meaning. Wholesome school environment. The Organization of a healthful school day. School food services. Teacher-pupil relationships. The teacher's health.* SCHOOL HEALTH SERVICES. *Nature and scope of health services. Health appraisal. The follow-up program. Communicable disease control. Emergency care procedures. Health supervision of the school personnel. Excuses.* HEALTH INSTRUCTION. *Meaning and purpose of health instruction. Importance of health instruction. The health teacher. Time allotment. Basic principles of health instruction. Scope of health instruction program. The conceptual approach. Methods of teaching health.*

7. THE PHYSICAL EDUCATION PLANT   214

Need for familiarity with the problem. Importance of teaching stations. INDOOR PHYSICAL EDUCATION FACILITIES. The main gymnasium. Auxiliary gymnasium. Location of building. Room dimensions. Arrangement. Traffic control. Materials and construction. Indoor surface materials. Locker unit. Apparatus. THE SWIMMING POOL. Indoor versus outdoor pool. Preliminary planning considerations. Major construction features. Factors increasing construction cost. Water circulation. Water treatment. Pool supervision. OUTDOOR ACTIVITY AREAS. Site selection. Play areas for secondary schools. General features. Athletic field and court layouts.

8. INTERSCHOOL ATHLETICS   255

BACKGROUND OF INTERSCHOOL ATHLETICS. Colleges and universities. Interscholastic athletics. The relationship of athletics to physical education. Objectives of athletics. Standards in athletics for boys in secondary schools. CONTROL OF ATHLETICS. Control of intercollegiate athletics. Control on a national level. Regional control of intercollegiate athletics. Local control of intercollegiate athletics. Control of interscholastic athletics. Control on the national level. Achievements of the National Federation. Control of interscholastic athletics by state high school athletic associations. Local administration of interscholastic athletics. MEDICAL SUPERVISION OF ATHLETICS. Protecting the health of athletes. Athletic accident benefit plans. ELIGIBILITY REQUIREMENTS. Importance of eligibility requirements. The amateur rule. High school eligibility regulations. Awards. Value of awards. Major and minor awards. Requirements of awards. THE ATHLETIC DIRECTOR. Athletic directorship usually a part-time position. Responsibilities of the athletic director. Administration of athletic contests. PROBLEMS OF INTERSCHOOL ATHLETICS. The serious athletic problems. Desirable trends in athletics.

9. INTRAMURAL ATHLETICS   335

Development of intramural athletics. The relationship of intramural athletics to required physical education and interscholastic athletics. Organization of the intramural department. Intramural finances. Units of competition. The program of activities. Eligibility for intramural competition. Medical examinations. Accident insurances. Preliminary training periods. Time periods. Officials. Protests. Forfeits. Intramural publicity. Intramural coaching. Intramural awards. Intramural statistics. Methods of organizing competition. Elimination tournaments. Round robin tournaments. Combination tournaments. Challenge tournaments. The funnel tournament. The tombstone tournament. Point systems. Intramural trends.

10. STUDENT LEADERS IN PHYSICAL EDUCATION   382

Educational values of student leadership. Student leaders in class work. Student leaders in intramural activities. Student leaders in varsity athletics. Leaders corps.

11. BUDGET MAKING AND FINANCE   390

Importance of efficient financial management. THE PHYSICAL EDUCATION BUDGET. Source of financial support. Steps in preparing the physical education budget. THE ATHLETIC BUDGET. Support of interschool athletics. Sources of athletic income in high schools. Procedure in preparing the athletic budget. Type of student tickets. Sources of athletic income in colleges and universities. Concessions. Increasing gate receipts. *The control of finances. Special procedures in large cities. Budget making. Procedure in making a budget. Administering the budget. A practical budget. The accounting procedure. Expense reports. Interschool financial agreement. Handling school funds. Game reports. Petty cash fund.*

12. PURCHASE AND CARE OF EQUIPMENT   420

Importance. Provision of equipment by school. Purchasing equipment. Purchasing policies. Official equipment. How to buy. Local dealers. Purchasing in a small school. Approval of equipment by the national federation. Ordering equipment. Considerations in selecting athletic equipment. Purchasing specific items of equipment. The care of equipment. Equipment room management. Care of specific types of equipment. Cleaning uniforms. Repairing equipment. School laundry.

13. PUBLIC RELATIONS IN PHYSICAL EDUCATION   450

What is public relations? Purposes of public relations in education. Purposes of public relations in physical education. Need and importance of public relations in physical education. Responsibility for public relations. Principles of public relations in physical education. Planning and organizing the public relations program. Multiple publics. The teacher's role in public relations. Public relations techniques and media. Public relations by national, district, and state organizations. Public relations in interscholastic and intercollegiate athletics. Public relations with the general public. Public relations with newspapers, radio, and television personnel. Public relations with alumni and parents. Public relations with opponents. Athletic publicity. Radio and television.

14. LEGAL LIABILITY FOR INJURY   478

Importance of knowledge concerning legal liability. Administrative responsibility. Negligence. School board liability. Trends in regard to governmental immunity. Statutory imposition of responsibility of school districts. Liability of private institutions. Liability of teachers. Liability insurance. Defenses against negligence. Sources of suits in physical education. Liability in first-aid and medical treatment. Value of releases and waivers. Policies and procedures to reduce accidents. Accident reports.

15. OFFICE MANAGEMENT   494

Importance of efficient office management. Office unit orientation. Office functions and practices. Office management in a small high school. Office management in a medium-sized high school. Office management in a large institution. The secretary.

16. EVALUATION   511

Importance of evaluation. Aspects of evaluation. Knowledge of standards essential. Purposes of evaluation. Evaluation must be continuous. EVALUATION OF STUDENT ACHIEVEMENT. The physical development objective. The motor skill development objective. The knowledge and understanding objective. The social development objectives. EVALUATION OF STAFF. Criteria of an effective staff. Appraising staff members. PROGRAM EVALUATION. Evaluative instruments. SELF-EVALUATION. Criteria for self-evaluation.

contents

Appendix A. STANDARDS IN ATHLETICS FOR BOYS IN SECONDARY
SCHOOLS   526

Appendix B. WISCONSIN INTERSCHOLASTIC ATHLETIC ASSOCIATION
MEDICAL ALLOWANCES   531

Appendix C. CRITERIA FOR EVALUATING THE PHYSICAL EDUCATION
PROGRAM IN SENIOR HIGH SCHOOLS   535

Appendix D. CRITERIA FOR APPRAISAL OF COLLEGE INSTRUCTIONAL
PROGRAMS   542

Appendix E. COMPETITION FOR GIRLS AND WOMEN   546

Appendix F. ATHLETIC FIELD AND COURT LAYOUTS   551

INDEX   563

1

the nature and philosophy
of administration

The meaning of administration

One of the characteristics of our modern way of life is the great prevalence of organizations. While there have been organizations for thousands of years, only in recent decades have they multiplied with such spectacular speed. We have only to contrast the living conditions of today with those of a century ago to appreciate how much more our lives are influenced by organizations. Wherever one turns there are organizations of varying sizes and purposes.

Organizations are created when a group of people come together to accomplish certain objectives that as individuals they could not do for themselves or could not do as well. It is immediately apparent that such organizations as schools, hospitals, factories, banks, churches, department stores, and governmental departments can render a quality of service that could never be offered by individuals working independently.

Organizations do not automatically function smoothly and efficiently. Their success depends largely upon a specialized type of leadership which is known as administration. In common usage the term "administration" is synonymous with "management." Administration "is conceived as the necessary activities of those individuals (executives) in an organization who are charged with ordering, forwarding and facilitating the associated efforts of a group of individuals brought together to realize certain defined purposes." [1] Thus, administration is mainly

---

[1] Ordway Tead, *The Art of Administration* (New York, McGraw-Hill Book Company, 1951), p. 3.

concerned with guiding human behavior in the service of some goal. Whatever the nature of the organization it is through human behavior that necessary tasks are accomplished. *The crux of administration is managing human behavior.*

Concerning the field of physical education, the administrator is expected to accomplish the purposes of his organization with the human and material resources that are available to him. Whether he be the chairman of a high school department or a director of a college department, division, school, or college of physical education his responsibility is to lead, guide, direct, and control those individuals who are members of his unit in order to achieve to the maximum extent the objectives for which the organization was created.

Importance of administration

The importance of administration in general is well expressed by Dimock: [2] "I believe that institutions largely determine the kind of life society is going to have and that administrators as a class largely determine the quality of the institutions." Tead [3] further elaborates this point:

Indeed, so pervasive in influence, so valuable, so adroitly constituted is this skill that it (administration) deserves to be recognized as a fine art. If work with paints or clay, with combinations of sounds in music, with combinations of words and ideas in literature—if these are fine arts, we are certainly entitled to call that labor also a fine art which would bring closer together in purpose the organized relationships of individuals and groups to each other. It is indeed, an art of the highest order to be able to bring about the most fruitful collaboration in a world where associated effort is the typical expression of individuals who seek to be productively alive. And this art becomes in all good sense a social undertaking of fundamental public importance.

The quality of the physical education program in an institution depends more upon the administration than any other factor. It is true that what can be accomplished depends appreciably on the facilities, equipment, personnel, and time allotment that are available but in any given situation a good administrator produces a substantially better program than a poor one. Many examples of physical education departments are available which, despite excellent resources, are considered weak because of poor administration. Likewise, many departments that have inadequate facilities, equipment, and manpower do surprisingly well because of the ability of their administrators. It has been demonstrated repeatedly that it is the administrator who makes the difference between a successful and unsuccessful program.

---

2 Marshall Dimock, *A Philosophy of Administration* (New York, Harper & Row, Publishers, 1958), p. 2.

3 *Op. cit.,* p. 4.

The administrator achieves the goals of his department to the extent that he is familiar with the recommended standards and practices in all aspects of his program and can obtain optimal performance from all of his personnel toward those standards and practices. Two variables are involved here. The administrator must have a target at which to shoot. In other words, he must be familiar with the best practices in the various aspects of his program. He must have in view the standards that he and his staff are to try to achieve. In addition, he has the responsibility of achieving results with those who are associated with him. This role becomes more difficult as the size of the organization increases. Likewise, problems are frequently encountered because individuals do not always work together harmoniously. In fact, jealousies, frictions, and antagonisms frequently prevail. The administrator must direct, guide, coordinate, and control these variable human factors. He must be able to relate himself to his staff in such a way as to elicit the best efforts of every member. Morale and teamwork are essential if the objectives of the department are to be realized.

Justification for study of administration

In virtually all programs of professional preparation in physical education one or more courses in administration are required. These courses have come to be regarded as essential in the preparation of physical educators for several reasons. In the first place, all physical educators find themselves working in an organization under the direction of an administrator. In the elementary and small secondary schools their immediate superior is likely to be the principal. In larger secondary schools, colleges, and universities a departmental organization exists in which the departmental chairman or director is the administrator.

In either case, physical educators must know how to operate within an organization and under the direction of an administrator. It is important for them to understand how organizations operate in order that they may function more effectively. They are expected to fit into the organization and to conform to the administrative pattern that exists. The administrator assigns the staff member's duties, works out his schedule, supervises his performance, provides the necessary supplies and equipment, requires that he conform to existing policies, evaluates his work, determines whether salary increases and tenure are to be recommended, and the like. This relationship of the administrator and teacher bears heavily upon the success and satisfaction that the latter experiences. Consequently, it is incumbent upon him to understand the nature of administration and his role in relation to it.

In the second place, many physical educators eventually become administrators themselves. This assignment cannot be undertaken and discharged successfully unless the individual has had considerable professional preparation for it. It is possible for an individual to be a very successful teacher and coach and yet be quite unprepared to become an administrator. Administration is a large, involved field of specialization with its own philosophy, principles, and techniques; these must be acquired before one can become a skilled administrator. The rapid development of special courses in executive development, management, and the like indicate the growth and importance of this field of study.

Essential skills of administration

Katz [4] has indicated that the skills of effective administrators are: (1) technical skill, (2) human skill, and (3) conceptual skill.

Technical skill. Katz [5] defines technical skill as ". . . an understanding of, and proficiency in, a specific kind of activity, particularly one involving methods, processes, procedures, or techniques. Technical skill involves specialized knowledge, analytical ability within that specialty, and facility in the use of the tools and techniques of the specific discipline."

The technical skills of a physical education administrator include a wide variety of items such as budget making, equipment purchase and care, facilities maintenance, scheduling athletic contests, drawing up and running of tournaments, certifying the eligibility of athletes, establishing policies and the like.

Human skill. Katz [6] defines human skill as: "The executive's ability to work effectively as a group member and to build co-operative effort within the team he leads." This involves understanding other people and being able to work effectively with them. As the term implies, it signifies skill in human relations. Implicit in this skill is a realistic understanding of self.

Conceptual skill. This is defined as: [7] "The ability to see the enterterprise as a whole; it includes recognizing how the various functions of the organization depend on one another, and how changes in any one part affect all the others."

Conceptual skill increases in importance with the size of the staff and the scope of the operation. For the physical education administrator of a very large secondary school, of a city-wide program, or of a department or school in a large college or university conceptual skill is essential. Little conceptual skill is required in a small school in which the physical education department includes only three or four individuals.

---

[4] Robert Katz, "Skills of an Effective Administrator," *Harvard Business Review*, Vol. 33, No. I (January-February, 1955), pp. 33-42.

[5] *Ibid.*, p. 34.

[6] *Ibid.*

[7] *Ibid.*, p. 35.

Griffiths [8] refers to a study of the differences between successful and unsuccessful school administrators in which it was discovered that there were very little differences between the two groups in their technical skills. The difference between the successful and unsuccessful administrators in their human skills was very great. The difference between the two groups in those practices called conceptual was even greater. He concludes that "it is evident that success in administration is related to the degree of human and conceptual skill the individual brings to the job."

Teaching versus administration

Ordinarily newly graduated staff members devote their efforts largely to teaching. After they have had some years of teaching experience many will have an opportunity to assume some administrative responsibilities. They will be confronted eventually with the decision whether or not to go into administration and devote increasing amounts of time and energy to it. They will need to evaluate all aspects of this type of service because administration has its disadvantages as well as advantages.

In a position in which at least half of the responsibilities are administrative in nature the individual should understand the following limitations.

1. Administration is more time-consuming than teaching. The task of the administrator is never finished. His responsibilities are so numerous that it is a rare occasion when there is nothing more to be done. He is concerned with every aspect of his department's operation and he is obligated to see that everything functions smoothly.

2. Administration is involved with countless details. The individual who abhors details should not consider being an administrator. In a large organization the administrator may be able to delegate details to some other staff member but this is not ordinarily possible in the great majority of school situations.

3. Because of the heavy demands upon his time the administrator does not have as many opportunities for close associations with students. For many individuals such relationships represent one of the most rewarding aspects of teaching.

4. The responsibilities of the administrator are great. He is never without them. He is the person responsible for the attainment of the purposes of the department. He is blamed whenever anything goes

[8] Daniel Griffiths, *Human Relations in School Administration* (New York, Appleton-ton-Century-Crofts, 1956), p. 12.

wrong. In addition the problems that his staff members are unable to handle finally come to him for solution. In the large administrative setups there is frequently much tension and pressure on the administrator.

5. If an individual enjoys teaching, research, or writing, he must recognize that his administrative responsibilities will probably make it necessary to curtail these activities. The extent to which this is necessary depends upon the percentage of his total load which is devoted to administration.

6. At times the administrator must make decisions that affect others adversely. Inevitably, he will have to deny promotions, merit salary increases and tenure to some staff members who, in his opinion, do not deserve them. These actions usually result in disappointment, criticism, and at times embitterment on the part of those concerned. Disciplinary action must be taken at times when staff members require it. This is usually an unpleasant occasion. There is no way to avoid such problems.

7. The administrator must relate himself to all staff members in such a way that each serves with maximum effectiveness. This requires much tact and diplomacy at times. He must adjust to the peculiarities and idiosyncrasies of his associates. Some excellent teachers may be unreasonable and demanding. Tolerance and patience are usually necessary to handle such individuals.

8. Administration is frequently a lonely assignment. Because of his relationship to his staff members, the administrator cannot be partial to any one of them. If he shows preference for various staff members, socially as well as professionally, others will feel discriminated against.

These points represent an imposing list of unfavorable factors. What then are the favorable aspects of the administrator's assignment? They can be enumerated as follows:

1. Ordinarily, the administrator receives a higher salary than any member of the teaching staff. This is in recognition of the importance of the leadership of the chairman or director.

2. The position of the administrator affords greater security than that of any of his staff members. He is less likely to be released or transferred. For some individuals, this is an important consideration.

3. One of the greatest satisfactions of the administrator is the opportunity to help young staff members grow and develop into professional leaders. Through his guidance, direction, and supervision he can play an important role in their future success. He must provide the climate in which his staff members advance, otherwise, his organization will not succeed.

4. The satisfaction of achieving the purposes of his organization is a very rewarding feature of the administrator's work. He is able to make a larger contribution to these purposes than any other of his staff mem-

bers. He has the power and authority to make his influence felt more than if he were a teacher.

Qualifications of the administrator

Most authorities on administration have described the personal characteristics that are essential or helpful to administrators. Many desirable attributes of personality and character have been listed. In fact, the number of such qualities is almost endless. It is possible to conclude that virtually all positive, wholesome, commendable human qualities are assets to prospective administrators.

Bucher [9] recommends the following qualifications for the physical education administrator: (1) administrative mind, (2) integrity, (3) ability to instill good human relations, (4) ability to make decisions, (5) health and fitness for the job, (6) willingness to accept responsibility, (7) understanding of work, (8) intellectual capacity, and (9) command of administrative techniques.

Dimock [10] describes the qualifications of the successful administrator in the following statement:

Administration is outstanding individuals. Individuals who, in their personalities and character, exhibit an integration of universal values, such as wisdom and reverence, honesty and integrity, devotion to human interests, as well as those traditions which are favored in the cultural stream of a particular civilization, such as the American, where dynamism and decisiveness, logic and objectivity are given attention.

Ordway Tead,[11] a foremost authority on administration, recommends the following administrative qualities as essential:

My own studies of personnel administrative qualities stress the need for (1) sheer physical and nervous vitality and drive, (2) ability to think logically, rationally, with problem-solving skill that "gets to the point" more quickly than average, (3) willingness to take the burdens of responsibility for executive decisions and actions, (4) ability to get along with people in a sincerely friendly, affable, yet firm way, and (5) ability to communicate by voice or pen in effective ways.

Residually, then, we are talking about intellectual capacity which is in some considerable measure innate and unlearned, about high-level purposiveness, about a contagious enthusiasm for goals and methods needed to achieve them, about a total glamour of personal drive that catches others up into group loyalty, persistent striving, and gratification simultaneously obtained for personal desires and for those satisfactions realized through one's creative institutional contributions.

9 Charles Bucher, *Administration of School Health and Physical Education Programs* (St. Louis, The C. V. Mosby Co., 1963), pp. 66-70.

10 *Op. cit.,* p. 5.

11 Ordway Tead, *Administration: Its Purpose and Performance* (New York, Harper & Row, Publishers, 1959), p. 59.

Types of administrators. Administrators may be categorized by their conception of the power and authority they possess and how they will employ it. Griffiths [12] has classified administrators into four types, namely, the laissez-faire administrator, the hard-boiled autocrat, the father type, and the democratic administrator. Each of these types represents a different philosophy of administration.

1. The laissez-faire administrator. This type of person is really not an executive at all. He makes little use of the formal power of his position and makes no effort to obtain informal power. He never exerts any leadership—never takes a stand. Faculty members do what they want. Complete abdication of authority and direction by the administrator is characteristic of this type of executive. The consequence of this type of leadership is an attitude of hopelessness and very low morale on the part of the individual staff members.

2. The hard-boiled autocrat. This type of administrator relies solely upon the formal power of his position. He is arbitrary, inconsiderate, coercive, and employs close and continuous supervision and tight and inflexible controls over individual and group behavior. He acts upon the concept that inasmuch as the teacher is being paid, he should do everything he is told to do and do it unquestioningly. He is not interested in the opinions of his subordinates and never solicits their suggestions. Someone has said: "Administrators hold power, and where humans hold power, there is temptation to tyranny; and where there is temptation there is yielding." The autocratic administrator is one who has yielded to the temptation.

Such administrators are rarely successful in a democratic society. Staff members have a smoldering resentment, lack of morale, and loss of initiative and enthusiasm. Staff turnover is high. The abuse of power which characterizes such an administrator is the cause of more administrative failures than any other single factor.

3. The father-type or benevolent dictator. This type of administrator is friendly, approachable, and understanding. He looks after the needs of his staff members and he wants them to bring their problems to him. He manifests interest in each individual and he never forgets to praise excellent work. Morale and productivity under such an administrator are excellent.

The negative aspect of such executive leadership is the loss of initiative and creativity on the part of staff members. So much reliance is placed upon the administrator's judgment and wisdom that faculty members lose their independence. Also, because such an administrator believes that he is wiser and more experienced than the members of his

12 *Op. cit.*, pp. 148-154.

staff, he makes the important decisions and establishes the policies. He does not take advantage of their experience and insight.

4. The democratic administrator. This type of administrator makes the fullest possible use of the formal power of his position and the informal power of his personal leadership. The democratic administrator respects the personalities of his subordinates and relates himself to each staff member to obtain his maximum contribution to the objectives of the organization. He solicits the opinions of staff members and involves them in decision making on certain issues. Group participation is encouraged. Freedom of action prevails. Regular staff meetings are scheduled. Periodic evaluation of programs and progress toward goals is made. Effective communication is provided. Good human relations are stressed.

Values related to democratic administration

The values associated with democratic administration have been well described by Grieder and Rosenstengel.[13] While the reference is to a school administrator the statement is applicable to any administrator.

1. The democratic process enriches the thinking of all parties concerned. If two persons give one another a dollar, each has still only a dollar. But if two persons exchange ideas, each then has two ideas and, from these ideas may emerge, or an integration which, in effect, is different from either of the original ideas may be created. The comparison and combination of points of view and the arguments and suggestions of many minds are infinitely richer than those of one mind or only a few minds.

2. When individuals have a voice in arriving at decisions and engaging in the study and thinking that precedes the making of a decision, they are more likely to accept the result than if they had no part.

3. *Esprit de corps* or staff unity is more likely to develop when members share in attacking problems. Agreement on common purposes is essential to the success of an undertaking, and such unity can be achieved better by widely diffused participation than any other means. Unity, it is true, can be achieved by "beating people into line," by cracking the whip, but these methods cannot be adopted as administrative procedures in the schools of a democratic nation no matter how genteely applied.

4. The democratic process fosters self-realization through freedom to express one's ideas and to participate in research or study. It affords a channel for the fulfillment of human potentialities to a striking degree which contrasts strongly to the bottling up of such resources in an authoritarian regime.

5. Tensions among individuals and groups are more likely to be dissipated as persons work together and get to know each other's qualities. Face to face conference on a basis of equality tends to break down animosities, suspicions, and misunderstandings.

[13] Calvin Grieder and William Everett Rosenstengel, *Public School Administration*, copyright 1954, The Ronald Press Company, New York, pp. 91-92.

6. The efficiency with which an enterprise is conducted is, in the long run, improved, although the time required for democratic methods may sometimes appear to make for inefficiency. A "smooth-running school system," the goal of some administrators, is not easily attained except by totalitarian methods. But the price that must be paid for mechanical operating efficiency is seen to be too high when one considers the denial of expression, the waste of human resources, the quality of service, and the submergence of the fundamental objectives of public education. Both the processes and the outcomes of education must be considered in a nation which subscribes to democratic principles. Efficiency must be measured by how well processes and out-comes reflect these principles, and how they affect people, not how well everything is kept on an even keel. Human nature being what it is, a vital school system can hardly be a model of placidity.

7. Persons who participate regularly in policy-formulation and decision making are more likely to be enthusiastic about their department and their work than persons who have limited opportunity or none at all to participate. A recent study by Chase [14] on teacher morale shows that nearly two thirds of the teachers who reported regular and active participation were enthusiastic about their work in the schools, contrasted with only one third of those reporting no participation. A small amount of participation seemed to yield less enthusiasm than no participation.

Misconceptions of democratic administration

A great deal of misunderstanding exists about what democratic administration actually is. Many individuals believe that it means that staff members vote on all issues that arise. Some believe that the administrator acts autocratically if he ever makes a decision alone. These are erroneous concepts of the nature of democratic administration.

The administrator has the prerogative of deciding to what extent he will involve his staff members in decision making. He is entitled to administer in the way he believes will produce the best results. The responsibility for the success of the organization is his and his superior holds him accountable for results. He has the authority to make decisions but if he chooses, he may delegate this authority to his staff members. It should be understood that the use of the democratic method does not relieve the administrator of his responsibility. If the decision should have a disastrous result, the administrator cannot escape his responsibility by claiming that "it was a group decision." Responsibility must be centered upon one individual and not an entire group.

The administrator must decide within what areas "group decisions" will be permitted and to what extent he will be bound by such decisions. Griffiths [15] recommends that decisions which affect the professional behavior of teachers should be made at the faculty level. This would include such considerations as (1) curriculum, (2) teaching methods, (3)

14 Francis S. Chase, *Administration and Teacher Morale* (Chicago, University of Chicago Press, 1954), pp. 1-4.
15 *Op. cit.,* p. 230.

grading, (4) instructional materials, (5) audio-visual aids, and (6) classroom descipline. Griffiths [16] adds:

In areas which do not affect the professional behavior of teachers the administrator should consult with those people who have information which will be of help, but he must make the decision himself, regardless of the attitude of the faculty. There are times when he can and should use the veto. This should be clearly understood, and the areas in which the administrator assumes authority to make decisions should be familiar to all of the staff.

The areas in which the administrator should make the decisions include (1) budget, (2) promotions, (3) tenure, (4) nonreappointment, and (5) salary increases. The administrator should consult with staff members in regard to these areas for the purpose of being aware of as many of the alternatives as possible.

A PHILOSOPHY OF ADMINISTRATION

Meaning of philosophy

The word "philosophy" has been defined in many ways. Its simplest definition is "the pursuit of wisdom," or "the eternal search for truth." A fuller definition is "the love of wisdom; a science which investigates the facts, principles and problems of reality in an attempt to describe, analyze and evaluate them."

Importance of a philosophy

The philosophy of the administrator is of crucial importance. It is significantly related to the kind of administrator he is. It serves as a directional post to guide his steps. All administrators become involved in philosophical problems. They can never become successful unless they can formulate a valid philosophical foundation for their actions.

The importance of a philosophy of administration has been expressed by Dimock: [17]

The busy executive needs such a philosophy because it is the indispensable tool of decision making, and the administrator's life is filled with daily decisions, some small and relatively insignificant, others large and momentous. But every decision, no matter how seemingly small and insignificant, needs to be related to an overall strategy, which is built on the bedrock of philosophy.

Every administrator has a philosophy whether or not he realizes it. His decisions are based upon the beliefs and values that constitute his

[16] *Ibid.*
[17] *Op. cit.*, p. 5.

philosophy. His philosophy is the result of all of his experiences. It may be mature or immature, consistent or inconsistent, logical or illogical, rational or irrational.

Sources of philosophy

The philosophy of the physical education administrator grows out of at least three factors, namely, (1) his philosophy of life, (2) his philosophy of education, and (3) his philosophy of physical education. Perhaps other considerations are also involved but the administrative philosophy of the executive in physical education will be strongly affected by each of these aspects.

Philosophy of life. It would be impossible to have a philosophy of administration entirely disassociated from one's philosophy of life. The life purposes, the ideals, the values an individual holds, his reactions to people and their reactions to him are all part of his personal philosophy, which inevitably exerts a powerful influence upon his philosophy of administration.

A philosophy of life relates significantly to the manner in which an individual works with his subordinates. Administrators have power. It comes from two sources, namely, that which is ascribed to his office and that which he achieves by the manner in which he relates to his staff members. Formal power or authority is delegated and vested in the office regardless of the person who happens to fill it. Informal power or influence is earned or achieved irrespective of the office held. It depends upon the personality and character of the administrator and the manner in which he works with his staff members.

It is apparent that the administrator who supplements the formal authority of his position with the informal power or influence that he earns by his personal leadership is the better executive. Experience has demonstrated that the administrator must earn the respect and cooperation of his subordinates. For him to rely solely upon the authority that is vested in his office is to court certain failure.

The administrator's relationship to students is also governed largely by his philosophy of life. He may regard his associations with his superiors, with other faculty members, and with his own staff members, and his responsibilities for budget, equipment, facilities, office management, and the like as far more important than his relationships with students. As a consequence, he becomes virtually inaccessible to them. On the other hand, he may regard the students as having a high priority. In this case, his point of view is well expressed by the following statements:

1. A student is the most important person in our business.

2. A student is not dependent upon us—we are dependent upon him.
3. A student is not an interruption of our business—he is the purpose of it.
4. A student does us a favor when he calls—we are not doing him a favor by serving him.
5. A student is part of our business, not an outsider.
6. A student is deserving of the most courteous and attentive treatment we can give him.
7. A student is one who brings us his wants—it is our job to fill them.
8. A student is the lifeblood of any school.

Philosophy of education. A philosophy of education is of crucial importance to the individual who serves as an educational administrator. The beliefs he entertains concerning the aims, objectives, and principles of education will govern his attitudes and decisions regarding school matters. Every educational executive's thinking and action receive their purpose and direction from his philosophy of education.

Philosophy of physical education. A philosophy of physical education grows out of one's philosophy of education. While the ultimate aim is the same, the approach and the program of physical education are different. The administrator's philosophy of physical education undergirds his thoughts and actions concerning such matters as outcomes, standards, methods, curriculum, evaluation, and the like. His philosophy enables the administrator to evaluate what he is doing as opposed to what he is supposed to do. It gives direction to his actions and keeps him on the track.

Democratic administration favored in democracy

It would be logical to expect that in a democracy democratic administration would naturally prevail. Certainly our people are accustomed to democratic procedures and resent any other type of treatment. Despite this, however, many administrators do not operate in a democratic manner. Tead's statement [18] is a strong endorsement of democratic administration:

The consensus of study and experience is well-nigh conclusive that where friendly appeals are made by congenial and trusted leaders, where the attractiveness and importance of group goals are made clear, where the group pride is built up, where the personal stake of each person in the group outcomes is clearly grasped by all, where the leader has a personal concern and solicitude for the integrity and promise of each member of his group—where this whole body of conditions is being realized, the resulting group behavior will be productive and happy to an optimum degree.

[18] Ordway Tead, *The Art of Administration* (New York, McGraw-Hill Book Company, 1951), p. 52.

The administrator's objective is to obtain the fullest use of each individual's best talents in behalf of his organization. This is a difficult and challenging task particularly in a large organization and over a prolonged period of time. Dimock's philosophy [19] of administration is pertinent to this objective:

Finally, I would have a rule to test every policy or preference or action of mine: What does it do to the dignity of the individual and to his potential for growth? Not, what does it do for my institution; not, what does it do for my power; not, what does it do for my wealth and ability to indulge myself? None of these. Rather, what does it do for the individual?

The reason is that the growth of the individual is the chief satisfaction of management and, in addition, it is the surest safeguard that freedom and enterprise will be the most valued aspects of our business and governmental system. For when growth can truly be called creative, then it partakes of the highest power known to the divine or to the mundane.

An administrator's prayer [20]

Many of the concepts involved in a philosophy of administration are expressed in the following administrator's prayer.

Grant me the self-awareness to know honestly what I am, what I can do, and what I cannot;

Grant me the judgment to channel my energies into those avenues which best utilize my abilities and do not require talents which I do not possess;

Grant me the humility to learn from others, even though they be younger, less experienced, or of humbler station than I;

Grant me the wisdom to cheerfully admit error and learn from my experiences, that I may grow and develop and avoid repetition of mistakes;

Grant me the courage to make decisions whenever they are necessary and to avoid rashness when they are not;

Grant me the sensitivity to judge the reactions of others that I may modify my actions to meet the needs of those affected;

Grant me the consideration to recognize the worth of each individual, and to respect all those with whom I have contact, neither stifling their development nor exalting myself at their expense;

Grant me the perspicacity to acknowledge that I can be no more effective than my subordinates enable me to be, and to deal with them so that they can help me by helping themselves;

Grant me the tolerance to recognize mistakes as a cost of true learning, and to stand by my subordinates, accepting my responsibility for their actions;

19 *Op. cit.,* p. 171.
20 Robert Saltonstall, *Human Relations in Administration* (New York, McGraw-Hill Book Company, 1959), p. 450.

Grant me the insight to develop a personal philosophy, that my life may have more meaning and satisfaction and that I may avoid capricious action under pressures of expediency;

Grant me the patience to live realistically with my circumstances, striving always for the better, but recognizing the perils of too rapid or too drastic change;

Grant me all these things, dear Lord, that I may live a more useful life, through serving my fellow men, and through them, serve Thee.

Duties of physical education administrators

The duties of physical education administrators vary greatly according to the size of the department they administer. In the great majority of secondary schools and small colleges and universities the physical education administrator spends most of his time teaching or coaching or both. In such instances the administrative aspects of his position are not as varied and time-consuming as they would be in a larger institution.

The administrative duties of physical educators who have such responsibilities include the following:

1. Establishing departmental policies
2. Personnel administration
3. Program administration
   (a) Basic instructional program
   (b) Health educational program
   (c) Interschool athletic program
   (d) Intramural athletic program
4. Relationships with facilities
5. Purchase and care of equipment
6. Budget and finance
7. Public relations
8. Office management
9. Evaluation
10. Legal liability relationships

Each of the above duties will be considered in detail.

SELECTED REFERENCES

Dimock, Marshall, *A Philosophy of Administration* (New York, Harper & Row, Publishers, 1958).

Tead, Ordway, *Administration: Its Purpose and Performance* (New York: Harper & Row, Publishers, 1959).

Tead, Ordway, *The Art of Administration* (New York, McGraw-Hill Book Company, 1951).

2

the objectives of
physical education

The necessity of having objectives

In order to proceed efficiently and with dispatch toward any goal it is essential that the goal be known. Nothing is more important for the physical education administrator to know than the objectives he is expected to achieve. He has been provided with certain human and material resources with which he is expected to accomplish various purposes. These purposes—or objectives—dictate everything he does. They give direction to his efforts and those of his staff and they provide the basis for evaluating the success of the department.

Physical education defined

Physical education is the process by which changes in the individual are brought about through his movement experiences. Physical education aims not only at physical development but is concerned with the education of the whole man *through* physical activity. It would be erroneous to believe that only physical responses are involved in physical education activities. The whole organism interacts in any experience and this involves mental, emotional, and social, as well as physical reactions. Such behavior provides the physical educator with an exceptional opportunity to guide the responses of students so that valuable mental, emotional, social, and physical learnings accrue.

Spranger emphasizes the broader aspects of physical education in these words: [1]

[1] F. Duras, "Some Thoughts About Physical Education," *The Australian Physical Education Journal* (March, 1965), p. 3.

17

And we shall not be satisfied with a teacher of physical education who doesn't know anything but how to teach physical activities or, even worse, can only perform them. Teachers of physical education as we see them, must be part of the spirit and meaning of the cultural tasks with which they are confronted.

Whether or not all of the potentialities are realized depends upon the leadership. Unfortunately, some physical educators concern themselves only with the physical outcomes and ignore these other valuable aspects of development. All of the results are important and should be constantly sought. If physical education is to make its maximum contribution to the optimum development of the child the physical educator must use *all* his opportunities.

Physical education objectives derived from educational objectives

Physical education as part of the school curriculum must share the function of education. That function is related to helping individuals grow, develop, and adjust to the problems of individual happiness, to competent membership in the family, to constructive citizenship in a democracy, and to appreciative understanding of the ethical values that undergird our world society.

As a member of the educational family physical education subscribes to educational objectives and endeavors to make its best contribution to their realization. The only justification for physical education—or any other subject in the school curriculum—is that it contributes in an important way to educational objectives. The criterion applied to every school subject or activity is that it be in harmony with educational goals. Physical education is not peculiar in the objectives it strives to attain but it is unique in the opportunities that its activities provide both because of their nature and the methodology inherent in them.

The purposes of education

Over the past half century many writers, committees, and commissions have given expression to statements of educational objectives. By all odds, the best known and most influential were those formulated in 1918 and 1938 and described below. The Commission on the Reorganization of Secondary Education spent three years preparing the *Cardinal Principles of Secondary Education,* which was published in 1918. This publication proposed a set of seven cardinal objectives for the school. These were (1) health, (2) command of the fundamental processes, (3) worthy home membership, (4) vocational competence, (5) effective citizenship, (6) worthy use of leisure, and (7) ethical character.

This statement of educational objectives has been extensively used by educators. Even today, after four decades, they are still quoted frequently. It is worth noting in this connection that the Educational Policies Commission,[2] a high-level committee of the National Education Association, had this to say about the *Cardinal Principles of Secondary Education:* "It is probably the most influential educational document issued in this country."

In 1938 the Educational Policies Commission [3] in its *The Purposes of Education in American Democracy* developed four objectives, each with various subobjectives. These were:

1. The objectives of self-realization
 (a) The inquiring mind
 (b) Speech
 (c) Reading
 (d) Writing
 (e) Number
 (f) Sight and hearing
 (g) Health knowledge
 (h) Health habits
 (i) Public health
 (j) Recreation
 (k) Intellectual interests
 (l) Esthetic interests
(m) Character

2. The objectives of human relationship
 (a) Respect for humanity
 (b) Friendships
 (c) Cooperation
 (d) Courtesy
 (e) Appreciation of the home
 (f) Conservation of the home
 (g) Home-making
 (h) Democracy in the home

3. The objectives of economic efficiency
 (a) Work
 (b) Occupational information
 (c) Occupational choice
 (d) Occupational efficiency
 (e) Occupational adjustment
 (f) Occupational appreciation
 (g) Personal economics
 (h) Consumer judgment
 (i) Efficiency in buying
 (j) Consumer protection

2 Educational Policies Commission, *Purposes of Education in American Democracy* (Washington, D.C., National Education Association, 1938).
3 *Ibid.*

4. The objectives of civic responsibility

  (a) Social justice
  (b) Social activity
  (c) Social understanding
  (d) Critical judgment
  (e) Tolerance
  (f) Conservation
  (g) Social applications of science
  (h) World citizenship
  (i) Law observance
  (j) Economic literacy
  (k) Political citizenship
  (l) Devotion to democracy

To a considerable extent these objectives represented a restatement or reclassification of the seven cardinal principles. They have been extensively used and have largely superseded the seven cardinal principles.

In 1961 the Educational Policies Commission listed the development of the rational powers of man as the central purpose of American education. The following quotation contains the Commission's concluding statement: [4]

Individual freedom and effectiveness and the progress of the society require the development of every citizen's rational powers. Among the many important purposes of American schools the fostering of that development must be central.

Man has already transformed his world by using his mind. As he expands the application of rational methods to problems old and new, and as people in growing numbers are enabled to contribute to such endeavors, man will increase his ability to understand, to act, and to alter his environment. Where these developments will lead cannot be foretold.

Man has before him the possibility of a new level of greatness, a new realization of human dignity and effectiveness. The instrument which will realize this possibility is that kind of education which frees the mind and enables it to contribute to a full and worthy life. To achieve this goal is the high hope of the nation and the central challenge to its schools.

This latest statement by the Educational Policies Commission should not be construed as a rejection of or lack of support for the 1918 and 1938 statements of educational objectives. Rather it represents a reemphasis upon the central purpose of education. This reemphasis does not negate the previous statements of educational objectives. That the seven cardinal principles or the four objectives enunciated by the Educational Policies Commission in 1938 are still valid educational purposes can be seen by the statement from *The Central Purpose of American Education* [5] that "The American school must be concerned with all

    [4] Educational Policies Commission, *The Central Purpose of American Education* (Washington, D.C., National Education Association, 1961), p. 21.
    [5] *Ibid.,* p. 2.

these objectives if it is to serve all of American life. That there are desirable educational objectives is clear."

In summary, the educational purposes that have had special significance for physical education for the past fifty years still have validity. Such objectives as health, good citizenship, ethical character, wise use of leisure, self-realization, human relationships, and civic responsibility are no less important today than they were previously.

The objectives of physical education

There is no dearth of statements of the objectives of physical education. Down through the centuries various authors have given expression to the values which, they believed, were inherent in physical education programs. Despite the fact that the educational philosophy of the time and place does exert an influence upon physical education objectives it is amazing how consistent these statements have been over a span of hundreds of years. Today in scores of textbooks there are found statements of physical education objectives in the context of modern educational philosophy.

Stoodley [6] has analyzed the physical education objectives as they are stated by 22 different authors. Altogether 493 different items were listed. These have been summarized under these headings, (1) health, physical, or organic development, (2) mental-emotional development, (3) neuromuscular development, (4) social development, and (5) intellectual development.

In addition to the objectives stated by various authors there are also available the objectives as formulated by professional organizations. Publication of objectives by professional organizations has the advantage of being prepared by a group of carefully selected individuals. They represent the opinion of more than one individual. Because of their influence and value official statements of the objectives of physical education by the American Association for Health, Physical Education and Recreation and its antecedent—the American Physical Education Association—will be presented.

Report of the Committee on Objectives. In 1934, the results of several years of work were reported by the Committee on Objectives of the American Physical Education Association.[7] This report represented an important contribution to the literature on this topic.

[6] Agnes Stoodley, *The Stated Objectives of Physical Education for Women.* Ed.D. dissertation, Stanford University, 1947, p. 37.

[7] "Report of Committee on Objectives," *Research Quarterly* (December, 1934), p. 29.

THE OBJECTIVES OF PHYSICAL EDUCATION

1. Physical fitness. Knowledge, skills, and attitudes re:

(a) Normal growth and development

(b) Organic vigor and efficiency; fitness of the vital organs to maintain the functions of circulation, respiration, digestion, elimination, nutrition, and heat regulation, and to adopt effectively and economically to the varied demands made upon them

(c) Neuromuscular efficiency, including physical alertness, agility, speed, accuracy and facility of movement (motor skills), rhythmic activity, optimum muscular strength and endurance

(d) Vitality and control of the nervous system, for vigorous action and for prompt relaxation and rest

(e) Body postures and mechanics, that are efficient for the activity at hand and favorable to health

(f) Knowledge of one's own health requirements, and ability to adjust personal health practices to meet the demands of unusual situations

(g) Absence of defects causing drain on physiological resources

(h) Objectives under other categories contribute to physical fitness

2. Mental health and efficiency. Knowledge, skills and attitudes re:

(a) Power to think and will body movements

(b) Quick perception and power to analyze a situation and see its essential elements

(c) Power to discriminate and weigh evidence bearing upon alternative courses of action; straight thinking; sound and rapid judgment and decision; problem solving; orderliness in thinking and acting; and ability to organize

(d) Mental alertness; power of sustained attention and concentration of thought

(e) Broad, wholesome interests and skills in physical education activities and related recreational pursuits; curiosity

(f) Comparison and evaluation of results; sane attitudes toward "winning" and "losing"; recognition of the true function of recreative sports

(g) Sense of rhythm

(h) Wholesome mental attitudes; mental "stance" and integrity; habits of recognizing, weighing, and facing facts squarely

(i) Knowledge of one's own powers and limitations

(j) Knowledge of a variety of healthful activities, rules of games, health practices, qualifications for leadership, etc.

(k) Objectives under other categories contribute to mental health and efficiency.

3. Social-moral character. Knowledge, skills, and attitudes re:

(a) Sympathy; due consideration of, and respect for, the rights (including property rights), abilities, feelings, opinions, experiences, limitations, and responsibilities of others; unselfishness; helpfulness to others

(b) Courtesy; good manners and speech; conformity to wholesome social customs; promptness

(c) Honesty; truthfulness; sincerity (earnestness)

(d) Sense of justice; "fair play"; treat all as we would be treated; democracy

(e) Active cooperation with others toward a common goal for the satisfaction and welfare of the group

(f) Sane attitudes toward sex and the social obligations of the two sexes

(g) Wholesome aggressiveness; disciplined ambition

(h) Self-discipline; control of personal and social conduct

(i) Reliability; trustworthiness; sense of honor and duty

(j) Respect of rules and properly constituted authority; obedience to law; respect for sound principles

(k) Perseverance toward worth-while goals of achievement; not easily discouraged; "stick-to-it-ive-ness"; industry

(l) Self-direction and self-reliance; ability to see, accept, and meet social responsibility

(m) Effective and wholehearted leadership or followership according to the demands of the situation

(n) Loyalty to principles which one believes to be right

(o) Disciplined initiative and the "courage of one's convictions"

(p) A friendly play spirit; companionability

(q) A proper sense of self-respect, but absence of conceit or self-importance; due confidence in self and others

(r) A pleasing personal appearance; hygienic practices as a social obligation

(s) Objectives under other categories contribute to social-moral character.

4. Emotional expression and control. Knowledge, skills, and attitudes re:

(a) Sane standards for the experience of satisfaction; disciplined ambition in relation to successful performance; proper ratio between "winning" and "losing," etc.

(b) Facility of feeling and expressing pleasure, happiness, kindness, courage, enthusiasm, cheerfulness, love of companionship, fairness, and other traits suggested in preceding categories; skill in dramatization of beneficial emotions

(c) Mental poise; self-control ("keep your head!"); patience

(d) Avoidance of emotional strains, such as worry, fear, overtension, control of excitement; control of reactions to unpleasant, unavoidable circumstances ("the enjoyment of unpleasant places")

(e) The emotional experience of relaxation; "resting points of satisfaction" and "periods of constructive composure"

(f) The impersonal or objective attitude toward situations likely to disturb emotional balance; control of egoistic tendencies

(g) Redirection of impulses to anger, pugnacity, jealousy, into constructive channels; substitution of constructive intellectual reactions for unconditioned ("out-of-the-clear-blue-sky") motor tendencies; deliberation; postponement of reaction until validated by reason and harmonized with one's own social-moral standards

(h) Wholesome standards of "likes" and "dislikes"

(i) Objectives under other categories that contribute to wholesome emotional expression and control.

5. Appreciations. Knowledge, skills, and attitudes re:

(a) Rhythm and music (sympathetic interpretation and expression, forms of rhythms, national moods and ideals, relaxation, harmony, etc.)

(b) Nature (fields, streams, woods, skies, fresh air; forms, colors, and activities of nature; man's place in nature; etc.)

(c) Personality (cheerfulness, poise, manners, companionship, etc.)

(d) Freedom (respect for law, emotional expression and control, joy, etc.)

(e) Physical laws (reaction of physical forces, gravity, momentum, etc.)

(f) Enjoyment (of effort, accomplishment, creative and imitative activities, etc.)

(g) Value of making correct choices (discrimination, taste, judgment, etc.)

(h) Bodily vigor (fullness of bodily powers, fitness, etc.)

(i) Objectives under other categories contribute to appreciations.

A platform for physical education. A joint committee of the American Association for Health, Physical Education and Recreation and the Society of State Directors of Health, Physical Education and Recreation [8] was appointed to develop a platform for physical education. This statement was approved by both organizations in 1950. It includes the following statement of the objectives of physical education:

1. Develop and maintain maximum physical efficiency. A physically efficient person enjoys sound functioning of the bodily processes, is free of remediable defects, possesses such qualities as strength, endurance, speed, a sense of balance, agility, and good posture and efficient body mechanics, and exercises these qualities according to his age and physical condition, maintaining a balance of activity, rest, work, and recreation. One who has unremediable defects learns to adjust to and compensate for his infirmities and develop his capabilities in order to live a happy, useful life.

2. Develop useful skills. In this sense, a skillful person is proficient in many fundamental skills, such as walking, dodging, gauging moving objects, and lifting, which are essential to living safely and successfully, and has abilities in a variety of activities, such as team and individual sports, swimming, and dancing, that contribute to physical and social efficiency at each stage of life.

3. Conduct himself in socially acceptable ways. A person who behaves desirably, among other things, acts in a sportsmanlike manner, works for the common good, and respects the personalities of his fellows (team games and other group activities offer many opportunities to practice these qualities). He enjoys, contributes to, and is at ease in a variety of wholesome social situations (co-educational sports, dancing, swimming and other such activities help to provide learning experiences in such cases), exercises self-control in activities which are mentally stimulating and often emotionally intense, reacts quickly and wisely under pressure, is courageous and resourceful. Games, contests, and other competitive sports help to bring out these qualities when there is good leadership.

4. Enjoy wholesome recreation. A person who engages in wholesome recreation includes in his daily living activities that bring deep satisfaction, that are often creative, relaxing or stimulating, and draws upon a fund of recreational interests, knowledges, appreciations, and skills.

Physical education division statement. This Is Physical Education,[9] prepared by a committee of the Division and subsequently approved by the Division, was published in 1965. The objectives of physical education recommended in this statement are:

---

[8] "The Platform for Physical Education," *Journal of Health, Physical Education, Recreation* (March, 1950), p. 136.

[9] Physical Education Division, AAHPER, *This Is Physical Education* (Washington, D.C., American Association for Health, Physical Education, and Recreation, 1965), p. 3.

1. To help children learn to move skillfully and effectively not only in exercises, games, sports, and dances but also in all active life situations.

2. To develop understandings of voluntary movement and the ways in which individuals may organize their own movements to accomplish the significant purposes of their lives.

3. To enrich understandings of space, time, mass-energy relationships, and related concepts.

4. To extend understandings of socially approved patterns of personal behavior with particular reference to the interpersonal interactions of games and sports.

5. To condition the heart, lungs, muscles, and other organic systems to respond to increased demands by imposing progressively greater demands upon them.

Recapitulation

In the review of physical education objectives that has just been made it is apparent that certain variations exist. Some statements include a greater number of objectives than others. Certain objectives are included in some listings but not in others. Such variations should be expected because of differences in terminology. Some terms are more inclusive than others. However, the impressive feature is that so much similarity exists in the expressions of objectives. An adequate summary of physical education objectives as formulated by various authors and professional organizations can be listed as, (1) the physical development objective, (2) the motor development objective, (3) the knowledge and understanding objective, and (4) the social development objective. The recreation objective has not been omitted. Rather, it has been included as part of the motor development objective. Each of the objectives will be considered in some detail.

THE PHYSICAL DEVELOPMENT OBJECTIVE

This objective—also known as physical fitness, physical conditioning, organic development or biological development—is concerned with increasing the capacity of the body for movement. It is involved with such characteristics as strength, stamina, cardiorespiratory endurance, agility, flexibility, and speed. This objective has been basic for physical education for thousands of years. Even in primitive times it was recognized that physical exercise was capable of increasing the physical fitness of individuals. Military leaders particularly were conversant with the role of physical activity in improving the effectiveness of their military personnel.

Plato was among the first to recommend the careful plannng of the physical education of youth. In his *Protagoras* of about 350 B.C. he said: ". . . send them to the master of physical training so that the bodies may better minister to the virtuous mind, and that they may not be compelled through bodily weakness to play the coward in war or any other occasion."

Socrates also emphasized the importance of the physical development objective in these words: "No citizen has a right to be an amateur in the matter of physical training . . . what a disgrace it is for a man to grow old without ever seeing the beauty and strength of which his body is capable." [10]

Down through the ages similar expressions have been made. Goethe, for example, said: "Take thought for thy body with steadfast fidelity. This soul must see through these eyes alone, and if they be dim, the whole world is clouded."

Browning expressed similar sentiments in his poem, "Rabbi Ben Ezra": "Thy body at its best. How far can that project thy soul on its lone way!"

Basic to the physical development objective is the optimum development of the vital organs. Today, we are aware of the important role of physical education in the development of organic power. It is a well-known fact that increased physical activity results in increased activity of vital organs. When an individual exercises vigorously the bulk of the muscles involved and the amount of combustion are so great that the demand for oxygen and the need for elimination of waste products stimulates a greatly increased functional activity of the circulatory, respiratory, excretory, and heat-regulating mechanisms, and eventually of the digestive system.

Hetherington [11] points out:

Although we have, generally speaking, no volitional control over the organic functions, by controlling the intensity and the duration of big-muscle activity we can control indirectly and to a fine degree the heightened functional activity or exercise of the organic mechanisms and nutritive processes. In this way, we control the development of organic power.

Hetherington observes that "activity is the *only source of the development of the latent powers* that are planted in the organism by heredity." Proper sleep, rest, and nutrition are favorable to the proper functioning of the organism but they have no power to develop latent resources. Only physical activity is capable of doing this.

The benefits of vigorous physical activity are not restricted to the vital organs. The skeletal and muscular systems are also improved. Some of the beneficial effects are: [12]

10 E. N. Gardiner, *Greek Athletic Sports and Festivals* (London, Macmillan & Co. Ltd., 1910), p. 130.

11 Clark W. Hetherington, *School Program in Physical Education* (New York, Harcourt, Brace & World, Inc., 1922), p. 37.

12 The Athletic Institute, *Report of the National Conference on Interpretation of Physical Education* (Chicago, The Athletic Institute, 1961), p. 10.

1. Structural development of bones, ligaments, and cartilage by furtherance of ossifications, the toughening of the ligaments, and thickening of articular cartilage.

2. Functional adaptation of all structures in skeletal muscles including muscle fibers, the tendons and related connective tissue and the capillaries.

It is this involvement of the muscular system that leads to the development of strength and muscular endurance, which are such important aspects of physical fitness.

Hetherington [13] also points out that the development of a strong, stable, healthy nervous system depends largely upon much vigorous physical activity during childhood and youth. The optimum development of the nervous system is highly related to the strength, health, and stability of the less complex, larger, and phylogenetically older nerve centers as contrasted with the younger, smaller centers controlling the finer integrations of the fingers, and vocal and sensory mechanisms. The only way that the nerve centers can be reached and developed is by exercising them, by exercising the muscles that they control. Consequently, thorough development of the big, fundamental muscle groups will bring about a corresponding development of the important nerve centers controlling these muscles. As Hetherington puts it: "Natural muscular development is a symbol of nervous development and functional power."

Importance of physical development objective accentuated by automation

While the physical development objective always has been highly regarded throughout man's recorded history, events of the past several decades have enormously accentuated its importance. The events alluded to are the rapid development of automation and mechanization. Mechanical slaves have largely eliminated the physical effort involved in most work activities. This, in turn, has had profound effects upon our people.

Automation and mechanization represent the latest stages of the Industrial Revolution. For the past 150 years there has been a steadily increasing replacement of human effort by mechanical devices. Modern Western civilization represents the climax of this development by combining maximum technical perfection of labor-saving gadgets with their maximal mass distribution. These developments are dramatically substantiated by Dewhurst: [14]

Even more striking changes have taken place in the relative importance of the energy sources accounting for total work output. In the middle of the nine-

13 *Op cit.*, p. 33.
14 Frederick Dewhurst and Associates, *America's Needs and Resources* (New York, The Twentieth Century Fund, 1955), p. 908.

teenth century more than one-eighth of all the work was done by human beings and more than half by horses, mules and oxen. Animate energy—muscle power—thus accounted for slightly less than two-thirds of the work, and inanimate sources for a little more than one-third. By 1900 the work-animal share had dropped to 22 percent of the total and that of human workers to five percent. Fifty years later muscle power was all but eliminated, and inanimate energy accounted for nearly 99 percent of our much larger work output.

.   .   .

Sources of Energy in Total Work Output

	1850	1900	1950
Human	13.0%	5.3%	0.9%
Animal	52.4	21.5	0.6
Inanimate	34.6	73.2	98.5

Labor-saving devices have greatly reduced the physical effort involved in work of every conceivable type even including that of the housewife and the children about the home. Our children have also been relieved of most of the exercise in other aspects of their lives. The running and walking that boys and girls have engaged in for countless generations have been greatly curtailed by our modern modes of transportation. We ride everywhere—even around the block to the store.

Television has also played havoc with the exercise practices of our children and youth. The following statement by Wilbur Schram [15] indicates the dimensions of the problem: "The average child spends on the television in his first 16 years of life as much time as he spends on school." Another estimate that has been made is that the average child spends eighty-two minutes per day viewing television.

Automation and mechanization, while providing many blessings, have had a disastrous effect upon the physical fitness of our children, youth, and adults. Many data to this effect are available (see pages 92 to 95). It is clear that our extensive technological developments in America brought widespread sedentarianism, which in turn has resulted in the serious deterioration of the physical fitness of our people. This situation should occasion no surprise because a fundamental biological principle is that disuse results in deterioration. What we do not use we lose. Thousands of years ago Hippocrates, Father of Medicine, said: "That which is used, develops; that which is not used, wastes away."

Values of physical fitness

Of what consequence is physical fitness? Why should we be concerned about the declining levels of physical fitness of our children, youth, and adults? In our automated age what need do we have for such qualities as strength, endurance, agility, vitality, and vigor? There are

15 Wilbur Schram, *Phi Delta Kappan* (June, 1961).

two reasons why the physical erosion of our people is a matter of serious concern. These are that (1) physical fitness increases the functional efficiency of the human organism, and (2) physical fitness is significantly related to health.

Increased functional efficiency. Physical fitness is necessary for a successful and enjoyable life because it increases the functional efficiency of the human organism. People who are physically fit can do more things and do them more efficiently than the physically unfit. The stronger the muscles, the more one can experience with less fatigue. The weaker one's muscles, the more quickly does fatigue discourage activity, whether physical or mental. Fatigue reduces the service one may render. The individual who builds up greater resistance to fatigue comes to the end of the day and the end of the week much less exhausted. He can enjoy life more and his disposition is better. As Montaigne says: "The stronger the body the more it obeys; the weaker, the more it commands."

According to Ruskin: "There is no wealth but life." Yet life without health, energy, stamina, zest, and satisfaction is sterile. The essence of living is action. If people are too weak or too tired to act, they really are not living. Weakness makes us slaves; strength sets us free. What choice shall we make? Emerson, in his "Essay on Education," advises:

Let us have men whose manhood is only the continuation of their boyhood, natural characters still; such are able for fertile and heroic action; and not that sad spectacle with which we are too often familiar, educated eyes in uneducated bodies.

The following statement by Lee and Wagner emphasizes the importance of physical fitness:

No matter what the arena of life, physical fitness increases materially the opportunities for living fully. Many people live at a level of fitness far below their capacities, making drudgery both of work and play. Others, although living more nearly at their fitness level, do not experience a rich, full life through sheer lack of what it takes physically to reach the heights. Those who in the growing years attained the heights of physical capacity and, in later years, have had the determination to maintain those heights experience a fullness of life that is a closed book to the weak of spirit.[16]

Much evidence is available to show the effects of physical fitness on the functional efficiency of individuals. According to Dr. Hollman: [17]

Males, who do not practice any kind of sport, have lost, on an average, one-third of their former performance capacity of heart and circulation by the time they reach the age of 55. On the other hand, physical trained persons between 50 and 60 years old, were as fit as the average person between 20 and 30 who take no physical exercise. Exercises and sports training act as a brake element

16 From Mabel Lee and Miriam Wagner, *Fundamentals of Body Mechanics and Conditioning* (Philadelphia, W. B. Saunders Co., 1949), p. 1.

17 Wildor Hollman, "The 'Hufeland' Prize Essay," *Sport* (Hamburg, West Germany, Broschek and Company, 1964), p. 47.

against biological aging and the resulting decrease in fitness. At the same time, lack of movement activity, for instance, leads to a reduction of an average of 18 per cent of the performance capacity coupled with functional disorders of the circulation, as if a healthy person spends about a week in bed. The same applies in principle also to female persons.

A low level of physical fitness affects functional efficiency in a number of ways. Various investigations have revealed significant relationships between lack of physical fitness and academic performance and social adjustment. A very impressive long-range study has been done at the United States Military Academy [18] at West Point. Over a period of fifteen years, 9942 entering cadets have taken the physical aptitude test. In the following data the inferior group consisted of the lowest 7 percent and the superior group the highest 7 percent on the physical aptitude test. It should be kept in mind that the poorest candidates were not admitted to the Academy. In 1951-1955 the rejection rate was the bottom 5 percent, in 1956-1960 it was the bottom 10 percent and in 1961-1963 it was the bottom 15 percent. Thus, in the data presented in Table 2-1,

Table 2-1.

	INFERIOR GROUP			SUPERIOR GROUP		
	1951 to 1955	1956 to 1960	1961 to 1963	1951 to 1955	1956 to 1960	1961 to 1963
1. Failure to Graduate	50.8%	45.0%	48.3%	25.7%	26.0%	18.8%
2. Cadet Discharge for Any Reason	29.8	24.1	29.8	13.7	13.2	11.3
3. Cadet Resignation	21.7	21.0	18.5	10.5	13.5	7.5
4. Leadership Ability	8.2	5.8	6.6	34.5	41.3	40.0
5. Low Aptitude for Military Service	17.8	14.0	19.2	2.7	2.2	1.2
6. Academic Failure	16.5	17.2	17.2	13.6	11.4	8.1

Source: Office of Physical Education, United States Military Academy, West Point, New York, *A Fifteen—Year Summary of the Application of Physical Aptitude Examination for Selection of West Point Cadets, 1964.*

the lowest 7 percent really represented a group from which the very lowest had already been eliminated.

Other studies have shown that low physical fitness is often associated with poor academic performance. Coefield and McCollum [19] at the

18 Office of Physical Education, United States Military Academy, West Point, New York, *A Fifteen Year Summary of the Application of Physical Aptitude Examinations for Selection of West Point Cadets, 1964.*

19 John R. Coefield and Robert H. McCollum, *A Case Study Report of 78 University Freshmen Men With Low Physical Fitness Indices.* Master's thesis, University of Oregon, 1955.

University of Oregon found that seventy-eight male freshmen with lowest Physical Fitness Indices were definitely low in scholastic achievement even though they were above average in scholastic aptitude. Page [20] found that 83 percent of the freshmen male students dismissed from Syracuse University because of academic deficiencies had Physical Fitness Indices of less than 100; 39 percent had PFI's below 85. Jarman [21] investigated the academic achievement of boys at ages, nine, twelve, and fifteen years, who had high and low scores on various physical fitness and strength tests. For each age and for each test, the high and low groups were equated by Intelligence Quotients with the means and standard deviations being comparable. Quite generally, the boys with the high scores on the various physical tests had significantly superior grade-point averages in their class work and significantly higher means on standard scholastic achievement tests.

Former President John F. Kennedy's convictions [22] about the relationship between physical fitness and intellectual performance are pertinent:

For physical fitness is not only one of the most important keys to a healthy body; it is the basis of dynamic and creative intellectual activity. The relationship between the soundness of the body and the activities of the mind is subtle and complex. Much is not yet understood. But we do know what the Greeks knew: that intelligence and skill can only function at the peak of their capacity when the body is healthy and strong; that hardy spirits and tough minds usually inhabit sound bodies.

Physical fitness is highly related to successful participation in play activities. This relationship plays a very important role in the social adjustment of children. A study designed to show the relationship between physical fitness and social acceptance and academic success was made by Popp.[23] He administered the Physical Index test to 100 sophomore boys. The twenty boys with the highest Physical Fitness Indices (102-135) and the twenty boys with the lowest indices (56-79) were chosen for contrast through case studies. All forty boys selected were arranged in a single alphabetical list. Five teachers and administrators without knowledge of the boys' test scores independently chose boys they would most and least like to have for sons. Ten boys were selected by each judge in each of the two categories. Sixteen boys were named by at least one judge in the "desirable" classification. Eleven of these or 69 percent

20 C. Getty Page, *Case Studies of College Men with Low Physical Fitness Indices.* Master's thesis, Syracuse University, 1940.

21 Boyd Jarman, *Academic Achievement of Boys Nine, Twelve and Fifteen Years of Age as Related to Physical Performances.* Master's thesis, University of Oregon, 1959.

22 From "The Soft American" by John F. Kennedy, *Sports Illustrated,* December 26, 1960, © 1960 Time Inc.

23 James Popp, *Comparison of Sophomore High School Boys Who Have High and Low Physical Fitness Indices Through Case Study Procedures.* Master's thesis, University of Oregon, 1959.

were from the high PFI group and five or 31 percent had low PFI's. Sixteen boys were also chosen in the "undesirable" group. Twelve of these or 75 percent were from the low PFI group. Other comparisons made are shown in Table 2-2. The boys in the high fitness group checked only half as many fatigue problems on the Health Habit Questionnaire as did the boys in the low fitness group.

Table 2-2.

	High Group	Low Group
Overweight	None	10 or 50%
Intelligence Quotient	108.7	104.5
Grade Point Average (C = 2; D = 1)	2.22	1.86
Failure to Graduate with Class	1 or 5%	8 or 40%
Rank of Entire Group of 20 in Graduating Class of 200	88th	108th
Entered College	8 or 40%	7 or 35%
Number and Percentage Graduating from College	8 or 100%	2 or 15%

Source: James Popp, *Comparison of Sophomore High School Boys Who Have High and Low Physical Fitness Indices Through Case Study Procedures.* Master's Thesis, University of Oregon, 1959.

Jones, in a study in which he compared boys high in strength and physical ability with those low in these qualities, found a positive relationship between strength and physical ability and good physique, physical fitness, early maturing, social prestige, popularity, emotional buoyance, self-confidence, and an apparently satisfactory level of personal adjustment.[24] Similarly, those low in strength and physical ability showed a pronounced tendency toward an asthenic (thin) physique, late maturing, social difficulties, lack of status, feelings of inferiority, and personal maladjustment in other areas. He concludes that "Competitive athletic skills are among the chief sources of social esteem in the period preceding maturity. This is attributable not merely to the high premium which adolescents place upon athletic proficiency, but also to the fact that strength and other aspects of physical ability are closely joined to such favorable traits as activity, aggressiveness and leadership."

Contributions of physical fitness to health. The second reason why physical fitness is so important is that it is highly related to health and well-being. The detrimental effects of physical inactivity have reached such alarming proportions that it has been found necessary to coin a

24 Harold E. Jones, "Physical Ability as a Factor in Social Adjustment in Adolescence," *Journal of Educational Research* (December, 1946), pp. 287-301.

new term—hypokinetic diseases, i.e., diseases produced by lack of activity —to designate them.

In the past fifteen years there has been a great deal of research that demonstrates conclusively the dangers of a sedentary existence to health. Hein and Ryan [25] made an intensive survey of clinical observations and research literature concerning the contributions of physical activity to physical health. The conclusions of the 117 research studies reported were:

1. Regular exercise can play a significant role in the prevention of obesity and thereby influence the greater incidence of degenerative disease and shortened life span associated with this condition.

2. A high level of physical activity throughout life appears to be one of the factors that inhibit the vascular degeneration characteristic of coronary heart disease, the most common cause of death among cardio-vascular disorders.

3. Regular exercise assists in preserving the physical characteristics of youth and delaying the onset of the stigmata of aging and probably exerts a favorable influence upon longevity.

4. Conditioning the body through regular exercise enables the individual to meet emergencies more effectively and so serves in turn to preserve health and to avoid disability and perhaps even death.

The following comments by Kraus, Prudden, and Hirschborn [26] emphasize the important contributions that physical fitness can make to health:

Coronary heart disease is twice as frequent in the sedentary as in the active; other diseases more frequent in the sedentary than in the active are diabetes, duodenal ulcer, and other internal and surgical conditions; 80% of low back-pain is due to lack of physical activity; lack of physical fitness goes parallel with emotional difficulties; the physically active show better adaptability to stress, less neuromuscular tension and less fatigability; active individuals age later, do not tend to absolute and relative overweight, have lower blood pressure, are stronger and more flexible, and have greater breathing capacity and lower pulse rate.

Further evidence that emphasizes the significant relationship of physical education to health is the following resolution that was passed by the House of Delegates of the American Medical Association in June, 1960:

Whereas, the medical profession has helped to pioneer physical education in our schools and colleges and thereafter has encouraged and supported sound programs in this field; and

25 Fred V. Hein and Allan J. Ryan, "The Contributions of Physical Activity to Physical Health," *Research Quarterly* (May, 1960), p. 263.

26 Hans Kraus, Bonnie Prudden, and Kurt Hirschborn, "Relation of Inactivity to Production of Hypokinetic Diseases," *Journal of the American Geriatrics Society* (May, 1956), pp. 463-470. Reprinted from the *Journal of the American Geriatrics Society* by the kind permission of Doctor Edward Henderson, Editor-in-Chief.

Whereas, there is increasing evidence that proper exercise is a significant factor in the maintenance of health and the prevention of degenerative disease; and

Whereas, advancing automation has reduced the amount of physical activity in daily living, although the need for exercise to foster proper development of our young people remains constant; and

Whereas, there is a growing need for the development of physical skills that can be applied throughout life in the constructive and wholesome use of leisure time; and

Whereas, in an age of mounting tensions, enjoyable physical activity can be helpful in the relief of stress and strain, and consequently in preserving mental health; therefore be it

Resolved, that the American Medical Association through its various divisions and departments and its constituent and component medical societies do everything feasible to encourage effective instruction in physical education in our schools and colleges.[27]

Role of physical education emphasized by automation

Troester [28] observes:

We must face the fact that in this modern technological society man is no longer required to move vigorously to meet his daily needs. Few activities demand his speed, strength, endurance and agility. He can let machinery provide his needs and choose whether he wishes to move or to be relatively inactive. In short, man now possesses the freedom to be weak.

From the beginning of time until the past several decades man had no such choice. The normal requirements of living insured an adequate amount of physical activity. The extreme degree of sedentarianism with the attendant effects upon health and efficiency was rarely a problem.

The consequences of automation have given new dimensions to physical education and have enormously increased its place and significance in our schools. Everything that our elementary and secondary schools, colleges, and universities hope to accomplish with students is related to their health and vitality. Students who graduate from our educational institutions will need bodies worthy of their minds, if they are to assume the difficult and important tasks that will increase their usefulness to mankind. Consequently, the school that fails to provide excellent physical education is jeopardizing all of its aims and aspirations. It is inconsistent and illogical to put so much effort and resources into preparing fine scientists, doctors, engineers, lawyers, musicians, poets, philosophers, journalists, businessmen, and the like who cannot achieve

27 Reprinted with the permission of the American Medical Association, Chicago, Illinois.
28 Carl Troester, *Journal of Health, Physical Education, Recreation* (February, 1961), p. 14.

to their full potential because they lacked the strength, stamina, health, and vitality to do so. As Willgoose [29] expressed it: "The noblest thoughts in the minds of men are but wishful thinking in a body physically unable to put the thoughts in action."

The lack of physical fitness has assumed such proportions that it has serious implications for the nation. Our soft, easy life is undermining not only the vitality, strength, and health of our people but of our nation as well. "On the other hand, if there is a tendency to shun the toil essential to the development of excellence, to choose the easier role of the spectator, to shrink from the shock of the conflict, to prefer the inactive life, there is grave danger that biological and spiritual deterioration may become so general as to threaten the continued existence of that civilization."

As advances in technology provide more leisure, as the machine further lifts from the backs of men the necessity for manual labor, as the standard of living rises to ever greater heights, can the prosperity, the ease, and the luxury that go with it be survived? Will this new leisure be used constructively or will dissipation increase? No other civilization has been able "to withstand the combination of time and money in the hands of its masses." All history is a story of peoples going uphill in wooden shoes and coming down on the other side in silk stockings. Durant presents the possible approaching crisis in these words:

The life of thought endangers every civilization that it adorns. In the earlier stages of a nation's history there is little thought; action flourishes; men are direct, uninhibited, frankly pugnacious and sexual. As civilization develops, as customs, institutions, laws, and morals more and more restrict the operation of natural impulses, action gives way to thought, achievement to imagination, directness to subtlety, expression to concealment, cruelty to sympathy, belief to doubt; the unity of character common to animals and primitive man passes away; behavior becomes fragmentary and hesitant, conscious and calculating; the willingness to fight subsides into a disposition to infinite argument. Few nations have been able to reach intellectual refinement and esthetic sensitivity without sacrificing so much in virility and unity that their wealth presents an irresistible temptation to impecunious barbarians. Around every Rome hover the Gauls; around every Athens some Macedon.[30]

In the light of all of the evidence that emphasizes the paramount importance of the physical development objective of physical education, the concern of Presidents Eisenhower, Kennedy, and Johnson is understandable:

Recent studies, both public and private, have revealed disturbing deficiencies in the fitness of American youth. Since the youth of our Nation is one of our

29 Carl Willgoose, *Evaluation in Health Education and Physical Education* (New York, McGraw-Hill Book Company, 1961), p. 104.

30 From *The Life of Greece,* copyright 1939 by Will Durant, reprinted by permission of Simon and Schuster, Inc., New York, p. 470.

greatest assets, it is imperative that the fitness of our youth be improved and promoted to the fullest possible extent.

President Eisenhower [31]

But the harsh fact of the matter is that there is an increasingly large number of young Americans who are neglecting their bodies—whose physical fitness is not what it should be—who are getting soft. And such softness on the part of individual citizens helps to strip and destroy the vitality of the Nation.

President Kennedy [32]

The fitness of our Nation for the tasks of our times can never be greater than the general physical fitness of our citizens. A people proud of their collective heritage will take pride in their individual health, because we cannot stay strong as a country if we go soft as citizens.

President Johnson [33]

DEVELOPMENT OF MOTOR SKILLS

This objective of physical education is as old and as highly esteemed as the physical development objective. It refers to learning to move skillfully and effectively in all types of situations including games, sports, and dances. The synonym—neuromuscular skills—is frequently used since the mechanisms of behavior involved are muscle-nerve structures.

Very early in life the child begins to combine simple bodily movements into a pattern for some purpose. This process of pattern forming is what is termed motor skill learning. It continues in a sequential hierarchical development with each skill made up of and built on the base of such skills as the individual already possesses.

During the first few years of life the child gradually acquires the skills of crawling, sitting, standing, and walking. His immediate problems are those of postural and balance control and space orientation. After many repetitions these actions become automatic and the child is ready for the more difficult coordinations of running, jumping, kicking, bending, throwing, and climbing. These are all basic, fundamental movements upon which complex motor skills are eventually built.

The degree of the development of motor skill depends upon the variety, amount, and intensity of participation in motor activities during the years of growth. Nature gives the impulses for the proper amount

[31] The White House Executive Order establishing the President's Council on Youth Fitness and the President's Fitness Advisory Committee on the Fitness of American Youth (July 16, 1956).

[32] From "The Soft American" by John F. Kennedy, *Sports Illustrated*, December 26, 1960, © 1960 Time Inc.

[33] The President's Council on Physical Fitness, *Physical Fitness Facts* (Washington, D.C., U.S. Government Printing Office, 1965).

of activity in the repetition of play. A boy throws a baseball many thousands of times in order to throw it effectively. So it is with each activity. Through infinite repetition the harmonious coordination of the nervous and muscular systems is achieved and motor skill is the result.

At the beginning stages of learning motor skills the child must give attention to the detailed movements. With much practice, however, the skill can be performed automatically. This is of great advantage because the individual can now devote his attention to other considerations such as meeting the exigencies and contingencies of the game. His higher brain centers are now free to concentrate on relating his efforts to those of his teammates and on strategic maneuvers. Skilled performance would be impossible if the performer found it necessary to give conscious attention to all the detailed movements he was executing.

Neuromuscular skill must be gained through continuous activity during the period of childhood and youth. It is difficult to gain after maturity. In an unpublished report entitled "Motor Learning at the High Skill Level," John Lawther points out:

This quantitative aspect of early motor learning has been overlooked in much of the motor-learning research. Without an extensive variety of childhood motor experiences as a background, the adolescent and the adult skill learning will be very slow and discouraging; and perhaps will not be persisted in, until efficient levels are attained. The adult who is the so-called motor illiterate has not the patience, the desire but, more importantly, no longer either the time or the energy to build such motor skill bases as were skipped over because of a childhood of relative inactivity.

Importance of motor skills. The attainment of all of the objectives of physical education depends to a large extent upon the development of a wide variety of motor skills. We know that individuals will not continue to participate in sports, games, or dances unless they possess some reasonable measure of skill. Individuals become frustrated and embarrassed when, after considerable practice and effort, their motor performance is still inept. There is no joy or satisfaction in participating in a physical activity if the result is always failure and defeat.

The attainment of the physical development objective depends heavily upon participation in physical activities in out-of-school hours and throughout the period of adult life. The limited time available in the physical education program will pay much greater dividends insofar as physical fitness is concerned if it is used to develop interest and skill in sports, dance, and other activities in which the individual will participate after school. A high relationship exists between the level of skill developed and future participation in that activity.

High among educational objectives is the development of desirable leisure-time activities. Man now has unprecedented amounts of leisure at his disposal and with the advent and rapid spread of automation the prospects for the future indicate that much more free time will become available to everyone. That this is not an automatic blessing is one of the tragic lessons we have learned from our experience. Because leisure has such great potentialities for enriching or degrading life its proper use has become a major concern of society. As a consequence recreation has assumed increasing significance as an educational goal.

The contributions that physical education is capable of making to wholesome recreation cannot be equaled by any other school subject. Participation in sports is a preferred form of recreation not only during youth but throughout the period of adult life. Sports represent particularly desirable leisure-time activities because they are interesting, wholesome, healthful, adventurous, and truly re-creative. Inherently youth desires physical activity, competition, cooperation, fellowship, and many of the other elements of the physical education program. It is well to note that adequate provision for the leisure time of adolescents is more important than is the preparation for their leisure time when they will be adults. If the problem is adequately handled in youth, there will be little cause for anxiety about it during the time of adult life.

To make a major contribution to the recreational aspects of physical education two conditions must prevail. In the first place activities should be included in the program which have high potentialities for carrying over to present and future leisure. Secondly, at least a fair degree of skill in these activities must be developed. A high relationship exists between the level of skill attained in a sport and the extent of recreational participation in that sport. Many physical educators adhere to the belief that physical education objectives are better served by teaching fewer activities but developing a higher level of skill in them than by offering twice as many activities that would be learned only half as well.

Motor skills play an important role in the social adjustment of children and youth. No single factor means so much to a boy's status as to be able to play well with his age group. Children live on a different level from that of adults. In play situations the good performer is the hero and the poor performer is pushed into the background. Much of child life is play life, and a large share of it deals with physical skills; whereas, only a small part of adult life is play, and good performance is not stressed so much. If an adult loses at golf or does poorly in a softball game at a picnic, it matters little, for success in those areas is not particularly vital; there are many other things that influence happiness so much more. The child does not have these numerous other phases of endeavor to which he can turn for success if he fails miserably in his physical skills. He must master the fundamental motor skills or suffer the consequences of loss of standing and recognition among his fellows in one of the major fields of youthful endeavor. That is one of life's most severe punishments, and it can be avoided by improving physical abilities. The child who lacks skill loses status with his group and all too often retreats, becomes bookish, or vents his discontent in unsocial behavior.

Much evidence is available to show the impact upon a child who lacks physical skills. Breckenridge and Vincent [34] point out the fact that much social contact evolves from physical skills and activities. "The boy who cannot throw a ball or run fast becomes a group liability. The girl who does not roller skate or ride a bicycle with skill is likely to have a lonely time." Studies by Kuhlen and Lee [35] and by Tryon [36] disclosed that the seventh grade boy who lacks skill and has a distaste for organized games is frequently ridiculed and shunned by his age group; at the twelfth grade, outstanding athletic skill can maintain the prestige of a boy even though he has few other assets. Gutteridge [37] states: "Skill in bodily activity is to be ranked first among the factors that lead to the child's acceptance among his peers." Rarick and McKee [38] report: "Proficiency in gross motor activity assumes greater importance (as children grow older) as is evidenced by the prestige placed upon skillful performance by the child's peers."

After a careful summary of many research studies, Cowell [39] stated: "Studies reveal that socially well-adjusted persons tend to be more successful in athletics, physical fitness, and physical education activities than are persons who are less well adjusted socially."

DEVELOPMENT OF KNOWLEDGE AND UNDERSTANDING

The physical educator is concerned with teaching knowledge-type as well as skill-type subject matter. While this objective does not ordinarily receive the emphasis and attention to which it is entitled it is, nevertheless, a vitally important aspect of physical education.

One type of subject matter that is invariably taught in physical edu-

34 Marian E. Breckenridge and E. Lee Vincent, *Child Development* (Philadelphia, W. B. Saunders Co., 1955), p. 272.

35 Raymond Kuhlen and Beatrice J. Lee, "Personality Characteristics and Social Acceptability in Adolescence," *Journal of Educational Psychology*, 34:321 (1943).

36 Caroline Tryon, *Evaluation of Adolescent Personality by Adolescents*, Society for Research in Child Development, IV, No. 4 (1939).

37 M. Gutteridge, *Child's Experiences in Bodily Activity*, Forty-sixth Yearbook of the National Society for the Study of Education (Chicago), Pt. 2, pp. 208-222.

38 Lawrence Rarick and Robert McKee, "A Study of Twenty Third-Grade Children Exhibiting Extreme Levels of Achievement on Tests of Motor Proficiency," *Research Quarterly* (May, 1949), p. 142.

39 Charles Cowell, "The Contributions of Physical Activity to Social Development," *Research Quarterly* (May, 1960), p. 293.

cation is the knowledge of rules, techniques, and tactics of the various activities included in the program. This content is indispensable. Much of it is presented in the form of outside reading assignments. There is a great deal of intellectual activity involved in physical education activities and successful performance is directly related to it.

A considerable body of related health information is taught in connection with physical education classes. Such health considerations as warm-up, conditioning procedures, safety measures, desirable sanitary practices, and the like can be effectively covered. Students become acquainted with various physiological factors such as muscle soreness, hypertrophy, and second wind. A wide variety of exercise precautions are naturally presented as a part of physical education instruction.

In recent years there has been increasing trend particularly in colleges and universities to include in physical education classes the reasons why it is important to participate in physical education activities. Logan and McKinney [40] support this practice:

Physical educators by their nature are a group action-oriented people. Consequently, most of the teaching in physical education takes on the *how-to syndrome.* Many physical educators believe that the student must be in action all of the time to derive the potential values of neuromuscular activity. It is hoped by the physical educator that, by some strange osmotic process, current action will diffuse into a habit pattern for future action on the part of the student. Students do need to be taught the *how-to* of skill, but this is not enough for our current, *thinking* student. He also needs to know the *why-of* participation in neuromuscular activities. He needs to know what the neuromuscular activity means to him in terms of his own physiologic, anatomic, psychological, and philosophic requirements. The combined *how-to* and *why-of* approaches to teaching physical education may help motivate the students to participate in an activity throughout their lifetimes. The college physical education class should be the beginning of so-called physical fitness, not the end. We are basically interested in a gallon of perspiration distributed over a lifetime, not a thimbleful distributed over two years of college physical education.

When the *why* of physical education is included in classes such topics as the following are presented:

1. Physiological aspects of physical activity
2. Anatomical aspects of physical activity
3. Psychological aspects of physical activity
4. Physical fitness evaluation
5. Relationship of physical activity to physical and mental health
6. Meeting future physical activity needs
7. Importance of proper use of leisure
8. Sociological aspects of exercise and sports

[40] Gene A. Logan and Wayne C. McKinney, "The Service Program: A Challenge to the Intellect," *The Annual Proceedings of the College Physical Education Association* (December, 1962), p. 18.

Another type of knowledge which results from physical education is the understanding of other individuals which it provides. While the physical education teacher does not formally present such materials to his students the activities of physical education offer an exceptional opportunity to understand human nature. In the close, intimate, face-to-face contacts in physical activities the real person is revealed. Particularly in competitive sports students throw off self-consciousness, formality, artificiality, and restraints and their fundamental character and personality are displayed. Under the pressures, excitement and emotional tension of competition such qualities as honesty, loyalty, teamwork, determination, dependability, resourcefulness, leadership as well as their opposites can be observed. In ordinary relationships in school or out, such insights are rarely possible.

Finally, a valuable part of the knowledge that comes through physical education is not easily expressed in words. Musicians and artists have called the sensory experiences associated with their disciplines as "non-verbal communication." In physical education the sensory perceptions identified with kinesthesia are in the same category. Some of the most valued meanings in the lives of people come from the perceptions identified with movement. This idea is well described in the following statement: [41]

The experiences in the physical education class also provide specialized opportunities for developing ideas about how space is organized, how time is related to space, and how gravity acts on all material objects. These understandings result in many specific concepts about what it means to pull, to push, to lift, to carry, to run, to jump, to swim, to be strong, to exert force, to resist force, to play, to fight, to cooperate, to compete. Dictionary definitions of these concepts show how difficult it may be to express their full meanings in words, but they become meaningful within the context of the physical education experiences. The concept of rhythm, for example, can be understood and acted out long before it can be verbalized. Other concepts such as balance, equilibrium, motion, up, down, circle, round, parallel, vertical, horizontal, spiral, twist, turn, and juggle can all be demonstrated by moving in appropriate ways. These lists suggest only a few of the complex concepts that may be understood by organizing the sensory data available within the movement-oriented experiences of physical education.

THE SOCIAL DEVELOPMENT OBJECTIVE

Students acquire social development when they become familiar with the ways of the group, become active members of it, adjust to its standards, accept its rules, and, in turn, become accepted by the group.

[41] Physical Education Division, AAHPER, *op. cit.*, p. 5.

There is much for the youth to experience, to learn and to incorporate as part of his behavior before he becomes truly socialized. A variety of social habits, attitudes, and ideals must be acquired by one in order to adjust to his family group, his peers, his classmates, and to the wider social relationships involved in his community, state, nation, and the world.

Character and personality are intrinsic aspects of the social objective. This is so because the behavior of an individual usually affects other people who assess it as good or bad, moral or immoral, socially acceptable or unacceptable. The assessment by others of one's behavior reflects the character of an individual. Character, in turn, is the basis for personality. Since personality is the sum total of an individual's responses to the social situations in which he finds himself, it, likewise, has social implications.

Basic to the development of a strong character and desirable personality is a set of values which gives purpose, meaning, and dedication to life. Everything we are and do and say reflects our basic values. Thus it is that character, personality, and values are all involved in the social development objective. Likewise, citizenship, which is concerned with desirable attitudes and behavior toward organized society and its institutions, is a part of this objective.

Specifically, the social objectives mean that the boy or girl acts in a sportsmanlike manner, works for the common good, and respects the personalities of his fellows. He enjoys, contributes to, and is at ease while participating now and in the future in physical education activities with those of his own and the opposite sex. The boy or girl should be able to exercise self-control in activities that are mentally stimulating and often emotionally intense, to react quickly and wisely under pressure, to be courageous and resourceful. He should be able to take defeat graciously and without rancor or alibi and victory with modesty and dignity. Students appreciate their obligations and responsibilities as leaders and followers in group situations. They have respect for the rules and properly constituted authority.

In summary, the specific qualities involved in the social objective include sportsmanship, cooperation, teamwork, tolerance, loyalty, courtesy, justice, friendliness, service, unselfishness, integrity, dependability, helpfulness, and thoughtfulness.

Contribution to the social development objective

Physical education is one phase of school work that lends itself particularly to the development of character. Student interest prevails, activity is predominant, and relatively great authority and respect are accorded those in charge. The physical education class provides more than just a place to discuss character education theory; it furnishes a laboratory for actual practice. We develop character much more surely through experience than we do by hearing about what should be done or should not be done. It is one matter to decide upon the correct response to a tense situation when merely looking on, and an entirely different proposition to decide and act correctly when in the midst of heated combat. One contestant may foul another, unnoticed by the official, near the end of a close game and thus prevent an opportunity to score. The player fouled cannot get advice about his ensuing action and decide some time later what to do. He must decide at once and provide an immediate answer through action. This splendid educational laboratory demands actual responses to tense situations just as much as life in general does. The whole setup provides real rewards and punishments, which with proper guidance will serve to encourage sportsmanship, cooperation, sociability, self-control, leadership, and other qualities of character and citizenship.

The competitor is an active citizen, not a passive one. It is the acting citizen who receives training. There are laws or rules that must be obeyed as he drives on toward his major ambition of winning the contest or performing well. There are penalties imposed immediately upon any infraction of the law. Opportunities to give, to take, to obey, and to cooperate are numerous. Here is the ideal setting for developing the good citizen, the socially adjusted and ethical individual, provided, of course, that the situation is well handled and well regulated. In no school situation are the goals adequately attained if those in charge are incapable or indifferent.

The dominant drive for a winning team or good performance leads to the development of good habits. Sane character habits, such as controlled sex life and abstinence from the use of alcohol, are steps in the direction of good citizenship that can be prompted by athletic competition. In order that he may be a better player, the youngster will practice these and other habits of good citizenship. In the long run as well as in the immediate situation, clean living builds for success. Habits of clean living and good citizenship tend to carry on just the same as do undesirable habits. Enough good ones crowd out some bad ones. Our personality with its basis of character is, after all, the sum total of our responses to the social situations in which we find ourselves. We establish characteristic reactions to familiar situations. Pursuit of interesting, desirable goals during the period of habit formation will help to develop desirable reaction patterns. It may be unreasonable to contend that the boy who displays cooperation and consideration in game situations will ask a tired mother to permit him to do the dishes in the evening: it is probable that he sees no common elements in these situations. All good traits certainly will not carry over completely from one situation to another; but, if there are many, at least a few may be expected to carry over to similar situations. When all other phases of school life contribute their bit toward good citizenship and ethical character, *generalizations* of fairness, sportsmanship, and the like can be built up which will have some carry-over value. The identical elements involved should also carry over to similar home and community situations.

Much research data can be used to demonstrate the important contribution that physical education is capable of making to the social development objective. The studies by Popp and Jones (see pp. 31-32) are examples that demonstrate the importance of physical fitness in furthering the socialization of our youth. The value of motor skills was shown in the research by Kuhlen and Lee, Tryon, Gutteridge, Rarick and Mc-Kee, and Cowell (see p. 39). These are only a few of the many studies which provide convincing evidence that physical education under good leadership is capable of making a major contribution to the social activities.

Obligation of physical education to contribute to social objectives. The fact that physical educators are able to develop such qualities as strength, endurance, agility, and a wide variety of physical skills imposes an obligation upon them to develop in their students a sense of direction and a framework of values consistent with the purpose of the school. When a high level of physical fitness has been developed in an individual, he is more effective for good or bad, depending upon his attitudes and ideals. It is just as easy to develop a more effective antisocial individual as it is to produce a person who uses his superior physical endowments for social benefit. Accordingly, it is essential that physical educators stress the social and moral values of their activities as well as the physical. This point is expressed exceptionally well by Williams: [42]

This emphasis upon the education of the whole person runs the risk that the physical may be neglected because of the pressing demands of the intellectual and because of the high compensation that an industrial society pays for mental skills. Nevertheless, that risk should be run. Force and strength without humane direction are too terrible to contemplate. All persons should know that vigor and vitality of peoples are dependent mainly upon muscular exercise for their development and entirely for their maintenance, and that, aside from the conditioning influences of heredity and favorable nutrition, vigorous physical education is the indispensable means today for national strength. But it should never be forgotten that vitality that is ungenerous, beastly and knavish is no proper objective for any division of education. Let the sponsors of physical education have deep convictions about the tremendous importance of vigor and vitality in peoples; let them assert, time and again, and everywhere, the strategic and imperative role of muscular activity in development, but let them guard against an unworthy exclusiveness that leaves them devoted to strength with no cause to serve, skills with no function to perform, and endurance with nothing worth lasting for.

42 Jessie Fiering Williams, *Developing Democratic Human Relations*, Section on Physical Education (Washington, D.C., Association for Health, Physical Education, and Recreation, 1951), pp. 83-84.

Most important objective in physical education

Which of the four objectives, namely, physical development, motor skills, knowledges, and understandings and social adjustment is the most important insofar as the physical educator is concerned? It is immediately apparent that each of these is a highly valid objective, which makes a significant contribution to our educational programs. Over a long period of time each has become recognized as deserving appropriate emphasis in our schools.

From the standpoint of American society, the social objectives are undoubtedly the most important. No one would question that the character, personality, citizenship, and values of our students deserve a higher priority than physical fitness or motor skills. Certainly, qualities such as ideals of justice, truth, duty, personal integrity, self-discipline, sportsmanship, cooperation, and the like, deserve emphasis ahead of strength, endurance, coordination, and game strategy.

However, it must be pointed out that the social objectives are not the sole province of the physical educator. The responsibility for these important outcomes is shared with other areas of education. Every teacher, regardless of his teaching specialty, has the responsibility for guiding his students into emotionally, socially, and ethically approved behavior.

Moreover, it is necessary to point out that any course of study in the school curriculum must justify its existence in some special way beyond the generalized contribution it might make. Our schools cannot afford the time or expense of school subjects that cannot demonstrate a distinctive contribution to educational purposes.

The unique objectives of physical education are physical development, motor skills and knowledges and understandings about physical education and related activities. If these purposes are not accomplished in physical education, they will not be achieved elsewhere in the school. Consequently, they deserve a high priority insofar as the physical educator is concerned. To give these objectives a priority does not represent an attempt to set up an order of value, but rather an order of approach.

Physical education, an integral part of education

Physical education is that part of education which proceeds by means of, or predominantly through, movement; it is not some separate, partially related field. This significant means of education furnishes one angle of approach in educating the entire individual, who is composed of many component, interrelated functional units, rather than of several distinctly compartmentalized faculties. The physical, mental, and social aspects must all be considered together. *Physical education, when well taught, can contribute more to the goals of general education than can any other school subject;* not more to each goal than any other subject but more to all goals than any other school subject. This is made possible, in part, by the fact that participation in physical education is very largely on the level at which the youngsters live. They grant their coaches and teachers great authority; the instructors in physical education have less need to demand it than do most other teachers. Opportunity for excellent achievement knocks continually at the door of the physical educator, making physical education one of the keenest-edged tools in the educational kit. With it he may sculpture beautiful figures or hack to pieces and multilate the already partially shaped raw material that comes to him. In discussing contributions, we assume that a reasonably skilled teacher is in charge, for even the most perfect system or machine will not function without competent direction.

SELECTED REFERENCES

The Athletic Institute, *Report of the National Conference on Interpretation of Physical Education* (Chicago, The Athletic Institute, 1961), p. 10.

Bucher, Charles A., *Foundations of Physical Education,* 4th ed. (St. Louis, The C. V. Mosby Co., 1964), Chaps. 1, 4-8.

Committee on Objectives of the American Physical Education, "Report of the Committee on Objectives," *Research Quarterly* (December, 1934), p. 29.

Educational Policies Commission, *Purposes of Education in American Democracy* (Washington, D.C., National Education Association, 1938).

Educational Policies Commission, National Education Association and American Association of School Administrators, *The Central Purpose of American Education* (Washington, D.C., National Education Association, 1961).

Hetherington, Clark W., *School Program in Physical Education* (New York, World Book Company, 1922).

Oberteuffer, Delbert, and Celeste Ulrich, *Physical Education,* 3rd ed. (New York, Harper & Row, Publishers, 1962), Chaps. 1-7.

Physical Education Division, AAHPER, *This Is Physical Education* (Washington, D.C., American Association for Health, Education and Recreation, 1965).

Research Quarterly (May, 1960).

Streit, W. K., and Simon McNeely, "A Platform for Physical Education," *Journal of Health, Physical Education, Recreation* (March, 1950), p. 186.

3

the processes of administration

The basic processes of administration

The methods or procedures that the administrator employs to perform his various duties and thus accomplish his objectives are known as processes. These processes are almost universally applied by administrators as they perform their assignments regardless of the field or level in which they operate. They are basic to the physical education administrator as he performs his functions.

These processes have been described by many writers on administration. There is much similarity in the listings although some authors employ terms that are more inclusive than those used by others. Newman [1] lists five processes as follows: (1) planning, (2) organizing, (3) assembling resources, (4) supervising, and (5) controlling. Cowell and France [2] categorize the components of administration as: (1) planning, (2) organizing, (3) directing, (4) coordinating, and (5) evaluating. Sears [3] classifies these processes as: (1) planning, (2) organizing, (3) directing, (4) coordinating, and (5) controlling. This latter categorization will be employed in the subsequent treatment of this subject.

[1] William H. Newman, *Administrative Action: the Techniques of Organization and Management*, 2nd ed. (Englewood Cliffs, N.J., Prentice-Hall, Inc., 1963), p. 4.

[2] Charles C. Cowell and Wellman L. France, *Philosophy and Principles of Physical Education* (Englewood Cliffs, N.J., Prentice-Hall, Inc., 1963), p. 162.

[3] Jessie B. Sears, *The Nature of the Administrative Process* (New York, McGraw-Hill Book Company), 1950, p. 32.

PLANNING

What is planning?

Planning is deciding in advance what is to be done. It is a method or technique of looking ahead to devise a basis for a course of future action. It is an intellectual activity involving facts, ideas, and principles. Knowledge, logical thinking, and good judgment are, or should be, involved in planning if it is to be effective.

Administrative planning necessary. It is apparent that every teacher must do considerable planning in connection with every course he teaches. Coaches must spend much time in planning practice sessions as well as actual contests. The intramural director must develop plans for the various aspects of his program. In short, every staff member must spend an appreciable amount of time every day in planning in connection with his duties.

Over and beyond the planning for which each staff member is personally responsible there must be organizational planning. It is the administrator's responsibility to plan for his department. Behind virtually everything that happens in a physical education department there is or should be a plan. There are, of course, unexpected occurrences for which no plan has been made but these are the exceptions that prove the rule. Every action of every staff member should be based upon a plan. The activities that are taught, the regulations that govern participation such as absences, tardiness, uniform, make-ups, the way in which students are classified, scheduled, tested, and graded should all be part of an overall plan. The relationship between staff members must be planned so that coordination and harmony prevail. Behind every committee meeting, staff meeting, conference, telephone call, letter, and interview there should be a plan.

It is the administrator's responsibility to see that planning occurs. This is why planning has been called "the nucleus of the administrative process." The administrator is concerned that staff members do adequate planning for their teaching and coaching duties. Unless a staff member does he will not be of much value to the department. These plans should harmonize with the overall plan of the organization. There will be a variety of plans for different segments or parts of the organization. These must be consistent with each other and lead to the achievement of the objectives of the department.

Importance of planning. The success of a department of physical education depends largely upon good planning. It is true that poor execution might spoil an effective plan; in most cases, however, it is the lack of planning or poor planning that results in failures, mistakes, and shoddy performances. This applies equally to the teacher, coach, or administrator. It has been proved repeatedly that those succeed best who form definite ideas of what they are going to do before they start to do it.

The term "too little and too late" referring primarily to lack of manpower and materials is due to lack of planning. Crises and embarrassing delays usually can be traced back to lack of foresight. Failure to take full advantage of opportunities to improve the program or to obtain additional facilities stems frequently from the failure to plan. Expedient actions and hurried decisions could be avoided by careful planning. How many times after a poor performance has the expression "If I had only thought of that" been used. Careful planning will facilitate problem solving, eliminate random work, and decrease the trials necessary, the false reactions, and the time used per problem.

Who plans? It is, as stated above, the administrator's responsibility to see that careful planning occurs. He must plan for planning. He usually does a great deal of the planning himself but he almost invariably consults with a number of other people. The executive seeks advice on what might be done, obtains facts from many sources, checks his tentative plan with those who will be affected, and before he is done probably will modify his original plan considerably.

The administrator frequently delegates certain types of plans to a committee or to a particular individual. Certain individuals within the department might be specialists in an area and be better qualified to plan than the administrator. Because the soundness of the plan depends upon the accuracy of the data and facts employed a research specialist might be called upon for help.

If a permissive climate prevails within the organization individual staff members might initiate and submit plans themselves. No person has a monopoly on good ideas and many valuable suggestions may be forthcoming if all staff members are encouraged to suggest plans to improve the work of the department. Businesses and industries have improved their operations immeasurably by encouraging employees to submit suggestions or ideas. It is vitally important to give appropriate credit and reward to those staff members who come up with excellent plans.

When to plan? From what has already been said about planning it is apparent that it is or should be going on constantly. It is not something that the executive reserves for the occasional interval when he is not up to his ears in work. There will be, of course, occasions that develop which demand planning at definite periods. For example, the budget is due at a specific time annually and planning is necessary prior to its submission.

Most administrators find it necessary to be free from disturbance in order to do creative planning. Constant interruptions from the telephone, staff members, and students make it extremely difficult to do the reflective thinking so essential to sound plans.

Short-, intermediate-, and long-range plans. Plans are differentiated on a temporal basis. There are short-, intermediate-, and long-range plans. Short-range plans are those designed for the very near future. They may involve consideration of the agenda for a faculty meeting on the next day or the details of a teaching schedule that is due next week. While no precise time limitations are established for short-range plans anything within a period of a month or two would be considered a short-range plan. An intermediate-range plan would be, for example, for a budget for the next fiscal year. A long-range plan would be in excess of a year. It might involve the construction of a new facility, the development of a new curriculum, or the creation of a new staff. Some long-range plans may extend to as much as ten years.

Short-range planning is generally carried on much more effectively than long-range planning. The latter type is more difficult and less imminent. Many of the variables involved cannot be pinned down in a precise manner. Yet, if plans for the distant future are not developed the years pass and no significant improvement occurs. To obtain a new gymnasium may require changing the climate in the community by graduating many classes of students who have been sold upon the necessity of the new facility. In one example, it took a chairman 16 years to bring to fruition a long-range plan for a new gymnasium.

Types of plans

Single-use plans. In general two types of plans may be identified. The first of these is the single-use plan, which, as its name implies, is used only once for a specific situation. These plans are used for occasions such as the dedication of a new building or the sponsoring of a special conference.

Standing plans. Standing plans are used by virtually all organizations. Such plans are available to use when a given situation develops. Advantages of standing plans are described by Newman: [4]

1. Executive effort is economized. Once the standing plan is established it is unnecessary for the executive to redecide the same issue. The plan is applicable, of course, only under a given set of conditions.
2. Delegation of authority to act is greatly facilitated.
3. Widespread use of the "one best way" is possible. If an operation is to be repeated a large number of times, considerable effort to ascertain the most effi-

[4] William H. Newman, *Administrative Action: the Techniques of Organization and Management 2nd.* © 1963. Reprinted by permission of Prentice-Hall, Inc., Englewood Cliffs, N.J., p. 51.

cient way of performing it is warranted. And, having discovered this method, it is made standard practice for all those who perform that activity.

4. Significant personnel economies are possible. The establishment of standing plans for a large part of the duties of a given position allow such positions to be filled with persons of less experience and all-round ability than would be needed if the incumbent made the plans himself.

5. Control is made easier. Standing plans, especially standard methods and procedures lead to uniformity of action and relatively definite performance standards can be established for such activities.

6. Coordination of activities is greatly aided by a preliminary coordination of plans.

Three types of standing plans are described by Newman [5] as follows:

1. Policies. A policy is a general plan of action that guides members of the enterprise in the conduct of its operation.

2. Standard procedures. Standard procedures are a series of steps, often taken by different individuals.

3. Standard methods. A single operation—the "one best way" to perform an operation.

Administrative policies for a physical education organization

Any department that is to function adequately must have sound, well-established administrative policies as a basis on which to operate. It is not enough to struggle along solving problems as they arise. Conditions may make it possible to go through the motions of conducting a department by this resorting to lame expedients but sound administration demands a positive planned procedure rather than a floundering makeshift. It is essential that all staff members as well as the director, know the policies that are to serve as guides. Staff friction often arises when there is a difference of opinion as to the manner in which an operation is to be performed. When all persons concerned know that one way rather than another is the accepted policy, conflicts will be reduced to a minimum.

It should be evident to any student of administration that local conditions will influence policies, and that under certain circumstances administrative policies will be called for which differ materially from equally sound policies found applicable under other conditions. The policies presented below and discussed at length later in this chapter purport to cover the field adequately but not to condemn similar fundamental ideas stated in a different manner. Although presented from the viewpoint of a larger departmental organization, the following policies can be modified without much difficulty to apply to smaller schools. It is readily apparent that a number of the policies do not apply in situations where one member constitutes the entire department. Generally, admin-

5 *Ibid.*, p. 40.

istrative problems increase as the size of the department increases, or, starting with a large department, decrease as the department decreases in size. This means fewer policies for smaller departments. Policies are developed through experience of both the policy maker and others. In any case, trial application in the local situation may eliminate, modify, or establish prospective policies.

Guiding policies

There are six major policies under which are grouped the more specific explanatory policies. The director should:

1. Insofar as possible operate on the basis of facts.
   (a) Before setting up a policy, secure the facts that will provide a defensible basis.
   (b) When he performs an executive act, take steps immediately to collect facts that will enable him to appraise the effect of the act.
   (c) Ask for support of a policy only if facts point toward the desirability of the procedure; one should not ask for support on a personal basis.

2. Be just to his staff.
   (a) Reward and encourage the contribution of ideas and service by the staff.
   (b) Require all members to be qualified for their positions.
   (c) Stress staff selection rather than dismissal as a way out of staff troubles.
   (d) Delegate authority and responsibility clearly.
   (e) Meet with the staff to discuss policies and procedures, especially any tentative plans affecting them.
   (f) Inform staff members concerning openings in other institutions.
   (g) Provide a reasonable teaching load.

3. Be just to his students.
   (a) Provide for student leadership and responsibility.
   (b) Provide the most adequate and workable scheme of classification of students possible.
   (c) Give grades for work in physical education.
   (d) Teach skills and games useful in school and in later life to non-athletes as well as athletes.
   (e) Provide for an extensive rather than an intensive program.
   (f) Require a medical examination of all participants in physical activities.
   (g) Take care of injuries suffered in athletic competition.
   (h) Keep the gymnasium, service units, and play areas clean and sanitary.

(i) Provide towels and adequate protective equipment for rugged activities.

4. Be just to the public.

(a) Keep the public continually informed about the educational work that is being done.

(b) Keep the department well represented in all worthwhile civic organizations.

(c) Operate on a sound financial basis; have a budget and follow it.

5. Be just to his opponents and competitors.

(a) Seek the advice of opponents.

(b) Join an athletic conference.

(c) Regulate the crowds at athletic contests so that both teams may compete under favorable conditions.

6. Be just to the educational system.

(a) See to it that pursued aims and objectives are in accord with those of education.

(b) Refrain from embarrassing faculty members by asking special favors for athletes.

(c) Cooperate rather than contend with other departments.

In view of the fundamental importance of these major policies and subpolicies, they are discussed in greater detail in the following paragraphs:

1. Insofar as possible operate on the basis of facts.

(a) It may be necessary from time to time to modify or even replace established policies, but there will be little need of this if the supporting facts for each policy are at hand before it is adopted. If policies are formed predominantly on the basis of trial and error, more modifications and replacements will be found necessary. This limitation need not eliminate the use of hunches or inspirations; it merely insists upon a thorough checkup on the idea before trying to put it into practice. Time and effort spent in collecting information on a proposed policy are usually well-invested. Too often a prospective procedure, apparently sound upon preliminary consideration, will prove to be undesirable after a more thorough investigation of its implication. For example, a subpolicy concerning insurance of football players might be proposed, but before the wisdom of such a procedure can be determined many facts must be collected. The cost of insurance, the size of the squad, the cost of caring for injuries without insurance, and the amount paid through insurance in event of injury will all help to provide the answer. Until those facts are known, the administrator cannot justifiably accept or reject the proposal. At times, temporary policies must be established before the facts concerning them are available; however, such cases are infrequent. Except in those rare cases the facts should be collected first and the policies should be based on them.

(b) Every administrator must make some decisions on the spur of the moment and others after but cursory consideration. After the decision has been made or the executive act has been performed, steps should be taken immediately to collect the facts that will enable one to appraise the consequences of the act. At times it is necessary to go beneath the surface to find the real facts, for things may be apparently satisfactory but actually undesirable. The sublime confidence that all is well may be rudely shaken by the jarring of harsh facts. Since it is better to find out for one's self before too much damage has been done than to wait for complaints or friction to call mistakes to one's notice, it is necessary to get the evidence concerning the results of significant executive acts.

(c) It is difficult, but necessary, because of the unreliability of judgment when strongly flavored with emotional content, to eliminate or reduce to the minimum the personal prejudices or desires that influence policy formation. Cursory observation of the display of parental fondness, bordering on ecstasy, at the normal actions of an average, firstborn baby offers evidence of the power of emotions over calm judgment. To illustrate further, the old home place is often beautiful to those who have many pleasant memories built around that cherished spot, but only ordinary to the stranger. It is fortunate indeed that feelings of appreciation can make the commonplace beautiful and extremely worthwhile. However, those unacquainted with the personal feelings which have influenced policy formation will note only the mediocrity that results and will judge accordingly. At best, a weak policy is still weak in spite of personal preference for it, and it is generally recognized that a policy can serve only according to its strength.

2. Be just to his staff.

(a) One of the well-established principles of applied psychology is succinctly stated in the law of effect. This law declares that other things being equal, the individual tends to repeat those responses that are satisfying and to avoid those that produce annoyance. Every member of a staff has many possibilities for service to the department that can be stimulated into usefulness if he is given sufficient incentive to exert himself. The law of effect applies in this situation as in ordinary learning situations; stimulation and encouragement will bring about valuable suggestions and outstanding services. By the same token, indifference and destructive criticism will as certainly limit or eliminate valuable suggestions and additional services. No outstanding department can be maintained without the helpful suggestions and volunteer services of most of its members. The enthusiasm that comes when individuals feel they are significant parts of the organization often prompts heretofore neglected members to rise from mediocrity to excellence. Appreciation of suggestions and efforts made by members helps to create the feeling of "really belonging."

(b) One of the most severe, yet justifiable, condemnations of physical education today is the contention that those who teach it are not adequately prepared. Most states have special physical education certification requirements and the remainder are adopting them. This fact will help decidedly in putting the physical education program into the hands of prepared personnel. In the absence of specific certification requirements (a condition that exists in some states), each school system should require ample preparation of prospective candidates for the positions to be filled. For instance, if there is an imperative need for a coach who can win games, a well-prepared prospect should be selected, for there are men of that type available. In many, although not all, smaller communities, teachers are selected because of their ability to teach academic subjects or to coach some sport, and then the most likely person is assigned to teach the remainder of the physical education program. Poorly taught physical education classes are almost certain to result, since the one selected may have little or no training for this additional work. As the community becomes aware of this inefficiency there is a loss of faith in physical education classwork and, consequently, an unwillingness to support it. In this way physical education maintains a position of insignificance in many communities because of untrained personnel. Even in larger communities no staff member should be hired just for the sake of friendship, for that is unfair to the department and to the trained members of the staff. If physical education is to progress, it must do so under the guidance of well-trained personnel.

(c) There is no more important phase of administration than that of selecting a staff, for it is the staff that puts the program into operation and maintains its proper functioning. That portion of a director's budgeted time and effort which is to be devoted to personnel replacements should be expended very largely before actual hiring takes place. Ultimately, this procedure requires less time and is decidedly more pleasant, because it reduces the number of replacements by decreasing dismissals, with their accompanying unpleasantness and implied condemnations. Wise selection requires a thorough understanding of the general and specific qualifications for each staff position, plus the ability to detect those qualifications, or their absence, in prospective members. This presupposes a competent department head who has thought through the entire program. It is hardly possible for a director who does not know just what he seeks to accomplish to select the proper staff to carry out efficiently a program to be determined at some later time. Each staff member employed and later dismissed by the same superior officer is to a certain extent a condemnation of the person who discharges him. He is also apt to be an enemy of the official who must make the decision that deprives him of his position, even though an honest effort is made to place him in a new position. The emphasis should be decidedly upon selection rather than dismissal.

(d) The director should delegate authority and responsibility clearly. In order that misunderstandings may be reduced to the minimum, it is absolutely necessary to delegate clearly. The administrator who permits or encourages two different staff members to believe that they each have complete authority over one phase of the work, in order to avoid the unpleasantness that may result from telling one that he is subordinate to the other, is building toward discord and future trouble. The evil day may be postponed temporarily by this expedient, but it will be all the more violent when it does arrive. Lack of clear delegation of responsibility will provide an excuse for someone to avoid a portion of the unpleasant or arduous tasks, while other conscientious members will do more than their share. It should be pointed out particularly that delegation of responsibility should always carry with it delegation of authority. Anyone who is to be held accountable for a phase of the program must in all fairness have authority to act on matters concerning that unit. It would be no more unfair to hold a coach responsible for a team without granting him authority to conduct practice than it would be to expect any other staff member to produce results without authority to proceed adequately in his area of operation.

(e) It is important to meet with the staff to discuss policies and procedures; to meet each member in private conference from time to time and to meet all as a group at regular intervals. Morale is developed, in part at least, by getting together and developing a unity of purpose. Many possible minor difficulties can be forestalled by working out different angles of problems together. Builders of enthusiasm know the value of group meetings. Several thousand supporters of a team while in their respective homes could not develop the enthusiasm or unity of purpose that comes from getting together in a pep meeting. A truly great staff must have enthusiasm and unity of purpose, although of a somewhat different type from that of a football crowd. The director who becomes one of the staff, rather than someone apart from it, during the group meetings is building general staff support for the time when he may need it.

(f) Although but a small percentage of physical education staff members are teaching merely for the financial rewards connected with it, practically all of them need money in order to live in a society such as ours, and for that reason they are looking for positions that pay better salaries. Many are also looking for opportunities to rise in the profession even though the salary may not be increased. In order to be just to the staff members, the director should pass on to those who might be interested beneficial information concerning openings in other schools. This may at times deprive his staff of the services of a good instructor, but there are plenty of others who would be glad to work for that type of director. At any rate, staff members should be held through payment of adequate salaries and through their enthusiasm for the department that employs them, rather than by attempts to keep them in the dark concerning possible opportunities for advancement elsewhere. The practice of increasing wages only because some other institution will take an employee away unless it is done, is a political procedure and is hardly worthy of an educational institution.

(g) Policies concerning teaching load are discussed in Chapter 5.

3. Be just to his students.

(a) If the science instructors of any school blessed with a splendid laboratory for physics or chemistry were to make no provision for student use of it, they would be justly criticized. Because of the nature of its program and the instinctive urges of the pupils the physical education department has a splendid laboratory for developing social qualities, especially leadership. Those in charge are under as much obligation to use it as are the instructors in charge of a science department to use their laboratory. Such use should provide opportunities for students to assume responsibility and to share leadership in a number of the activities on the program under competent guidance. As has been pointed out in Chapter 2, the incentives to achieve are fundamental and strong, the rewards are satisfying, and action predominates. The leader is the man of action—one who can command in critical situations. Physical education can easily provide many of these situations for developing leadership and responsibility. Any department that fails to do this is not fulfilling its obligations to its students.

(b) There are very definite limits established in most schools beyond which the classification of students for physical education purposes cannot profitably be employed. The present practice of classifying students on the basis of academic ability is the major factor that limits schoolwide classification for physical education purposes, because groups cannot be broken down and re-formed for each type of activity; this would involve insurmountable schedule-making difficulties. A wide variety of abilities in different activities and relatively few easily applied good tests also limit the scope of classification. It is possible, however, to classify within the actual class in most schools, and within the same grade in some schools. This should be done where possible because in this way physical education can be made more truly educational.

(c) Physical education is an academic subject, and its standing can be established and maintained more adequately by offering the same academic rewards that are offered in other departments for the same excellence of achievement. There will be more incentive to achieve if rewards are commensurate with achievement, than if the students who really work get the same meaningless "Cr." as other students who merely put in an appearance. Grading will make for better teaching situations and provide a means of interesting better qualified personnel. As the instructors and students improve, the program will appeal more to the taxpayers, and they will be more willing to support it. By giving grades, a department of physical education puts itself in a position to offer better service.

(d) The physical education course should include activities that are useful during the time that participants are in school as well as after their school days are over. It is entirely possible that a number of activities can serve both purposes well. There are some, however, that will serve better during school days, such as football and basketball, and others that customarily, although not of necessity, serve more generally at a later time. Handball and volley ball are games of this type. Some departments overemphasize the games most interesting and useful during school days, others "go to seed" by sponsoring predominantly those activities that will serve better later in life. Both must be included in a balanced program.

(e) Every normal student in school has the right to expect that interesting physical activities and facilities for enjoying them will be provided for him or her. It is a mistake to expect all students to fit into the mold formed by a few popular physical activities. It is also impossible to provide facilities for every type of activity that any student might desire; but it is entirely possible and reasonable to provide a variety of activities, rather than to concentrate on a few. Inclusion of as large a sampling as the institution can afford and direct should be a goal for every department. By means of this comparatively extensive offering each student has the opportunity of selecting the activities that he enjoys. This policy is in direct opposition to the regulation, not uncommon in colleges and universities, that all students must learn to swim. This old fallacy seems to be built on the supposition that those who can swim will be able to save themselves from drowning when the emergency arises. The facts, often overlooked, are that many good swimmers drown, that a goodly number of people are never put in the position where they need to swim, that swimming (during the winter months particularly) may increase sinus and ear infection in certain cases, and that it is often decidedly unpleasant for those who have difficulties in learning. This unpleasantness may create a dislike for physical education. This is not a condemnation of swimming, which is a splendid activity, but a condemnation of the policy of requiring it of all students. There is no one sport or other activity in which proficiency should be required of all;

choice rather than specific requirement marks the progressive activity program. It should be pointed out here that the instructor should give the best he has to every student, whether or not he is a varsity athlete or ever has a chance to become one.

(f) There are many youngsters as well as adults who are not aware of their own serious ailments. There are still others who will try to keep any information about such a weakness a secret if they have reason to believe that its discovery will deprive them of participation in some favored activity. There is still a third group that will feign illness or an abnormality in an attempt to avoid physical exercise which they probably need very badly. In order that a department may operate with accurate knowledge of the condition of the pupils and thus reduce permanent injuries or even fatalities, a medical examination is necessary. This examination should be given before activity classes or groups meet. Only the careless or inefficient instructor will be satisfied with the examination given at just any time during the semester. The preliminary inspection may be made by the school nurse or some instructor, but the examination proper should be made by a doctor of medicine. It is unwise and may even be dangerous for the coach or physical education instructor to assume a doctor's duties unless he is a physician.

(g) Certain types of athletic competition are apt to result in injuries, such as breaks, bruises, abrasions, sprains, and dislocations. Since some of the participants will not receive treatment unless the school provides it, it is the responsibility of each educational institution to furnish this service. Lack of funds, carelessness, a false belief in the virtue of being able to endure injuries, or fear of parental disapproval of the activity through which this injury was sustained may lead to nontreatment of the injury if the matter is left to the student's initiative. Since the school sponsors interesting, although rigorous, activities, it must take care of the accidents that happen as a result of participation, if only to those who engage in them.

(h) No school has a right to expect or require students to engage in activities or to dress for and bathe after the activities, under dirty and unsanitary conditions. If physical education is to maintain and promote health, the least that can be expected of the department is cleanliness and sanitation sufficient to prevent the spread of disease and infection. That meager minimum is not really adequate, for education at its best is conducted in pleasant surroundings; it even gains in effectiveness because of an excellent environment. Respect and appreciation are instilled most thoroughly through example. When those in charge show by the condition in which they keep the plant that they respect and appreciate it, then those who come to learn will have similar feelings for the physical equipment and the program that is offered there.

(i) In some situations it is not possible to provide adequate equipment for certain rugged activities. When that condition exists, those activities should not be sponsored by the institution, for severe injuries often result because of inadequate protective equipment. There will be pressure at times from some community groups for certain activities. If the activities are acceptable, those in charge should work toward providing the necessary equipment and even let the community sponsors help secure the equipment, but should refrain from engaging in the activities until it is provided. It is often difficult to keep individually furnished towels clean or even available when they are needed; for that reason it is advisable for the school to furnish towels whenever possible. In many situations it is easier to renounce any responsibility in this matter than it is to plan and carry through a campaign to secure towels, a place to keep them, and an individual to care for them. However, the entire program will function more satisfactorily as a general rule if this service is provided.

4. Be just to the public.

(a) The director should keep the public continually informed concerning the educational work being done. By this means those in charge may be able to remain long enough in a situation to carry out an educational program that is planned and partially under way. The parents of a community will cooperate in promoting a worthwhile program for their children if they know about it. They cannot know as much as they should unless they are regularly informed concerning the program. Experience teaches us that the public will support a star about whom it is constantly informed; it will do the same for a good program about which it knows. Any parental or general community support for an educationally sound physical education program for its boys and girls is a step in the direction of justice for the community.

(b) The school is one of the significant units in the socioeconomic life of any community, and the physical education department is one of the school units that has the most contact with the public. If the school, through its physical education department, is to serve the public best, its members must be acquainted with the other individuals in the community and have some common interests with them. (An educational agency that wins more valuable services from the community because of its close contact with it is in this very way serving the community, for it is helping the public to help itself.) As the individuals who comprise a community learn to know those in charge of the physical education program better, they will be more sympathetic to it and thus provide an opportunity for physical education to serve the community as a whole. Friendship offered a useful institution or part of an institution enables that institution to render more clearly its optimum service. There will be times when worthy community projects need the assistance that the physical education department can provide, and connection with community organizations will provide a knowledge of the needs as they arise.

(c) Until quite recently it has been common practice for many departments of physical education to spend money according to the day-by-day, or week-by-week demands and then to turn to the school board at the end of the year to make up the not infrequent deficit. That method of handling funds is not only inadequate, because those in charge hardly know where they stand financially, but also unfair to the public. The community has a right to expect that money devoted to conducting the physical education program will be provided for and spent according to a well-worked-out plan. Justice to those who pay the bills demands that there be a budget and that it be followed closely. Planned spending is usually more careful and conservative spending.

5. Be just to his opponents and competitors.

(a) Since the public is more generally interested in the physical education program, which includes athletics, than in any other phase of school work, a greater number of individuals in the community will develop strong emotional attitudes toward parts of this program and toward those who conduct it. Some of these attitudes will be favorable and some will be unfavorable. Those who attack are the opponents of those who sponsor and direct the program. The wise director will ask the advice of his opponents so that he may know more clearly what his own weaknesses are and how he can correct them. Some of our greatest benefactors are our most severe critics, if we will but profit by their suggestions. Advice from critics is only advice, just as is advice from personal friends—it is to be followed or ignored according to the wishes of the one who receives it. The wise director will also ask the advice of his critics in order that he may discover their weaknesses. He will avoid arguing with them on their weak points because points of difference are seldom cleared up through arguments, but he may explain certain points upon which they are apparently misinformed. Finally, the wise director will ask the advice of his opponents in order to give them an opportunity to explode their ammunition in a rather harmless way or to decide that they don't care to use it at all. It satisfies some persons simply to "get it off their chests" or at least to have an opportunity to do so.

(b) Each school that participates in interschool contests should join an athletic conference. Conference membership promotes understanding through developing acquaintance and establishing rules and regulations. Much of the petty quarreling concerning some phases of Olympic competition could be eliminated if all nations had the same rules and regulations concerning the disputed points. Conference membership improves officiating through common interpretation of rules and established policies concerning the selection of officials. It simplifies the matter of schedule making and helps maintain an interest in the contests. All in all, it makes membership convenient and serviceable to one's competitors and one's own school.

(c) As physical education becomes more educational, visiting teams will be accepted as guests and accorded the treatment due guests. This condition prevails quite generally now among the players themselves, but the spectators, who really have less at stake, are more inclined to exhibit antagonism toward visiting teams. This is due almost entirely to the lack of spectator education. It requires effort and persistence to control crowds, but they can usually be controlled, if those in charge want to control them and will put forth an honest effort to do it. Much improvement has been made in spectator control, but booing is still prevalent enough in many situations and decreases the educational value of the whole procedure. The first step toward general improvement is to put one's own house in order; then others may be influenced to correct their unsatisfactory practices. This reform is certain to come; we must hasten the approach of that day.

6. Be just to the educational system.

(a) There are few civic organizations, institutions, or departments within institutions in the United States that do not have reasonably sound, forward-looking objectives. However, there are many that have such objectives but fail to attain them with any marked degree of success. Physical education departments are sometimes listed among this group; in fact, physical educators have been accused of having one set of objectives in theory and another in practice. This charge is due in part to the fact that the most interesting and exciting phases of the program are displayed "in the front window," where all may see. The activities of other more protected and secluded departments are thus apt to continue unnoticed while their more evident theories are compared with physical education practices. It is unfair to compare one group's theory with another group's practice. However, in order that the disparity between theory and practice, which does exist in many situations, may be reduced to a minimum, physical education must see to it that the pursued aims and objectives are identical with the stated aims and objectives, which, as presented in Chapter 2, are in accord with the goals of education.

(b) Physical education is not a weak and sickly child in the academic family that needs special care and protection. Instead, it is a healthy, well-nourished member and can better maintain that position by living on a regular diet than by being pampered with sweets and tidbits, in the form of gift grades and special privileges to athletes. This does not mean that the athlete should not have the same opportunities as other students; he certainly should, but he is not entitled to more. Real men are developed by meeting the tests of school and life squarely rather than by depending on special privilege. In considering his future life the student who is passed because he belongs to a certain group is handicapped rather than benefited. For that reason those in charge of an educational unit will not ask for favors but for equal treatment. This will substantiate the principle that a department should make clear to its students—that no academic immunities are in order, since others have not received them. Although this may mean the loss of a few games now and then, it will mean a definite gain in the matter of developing men and women, which is the true justification for any unit of an educational system.

(c) It is important to be a good member in the school family, to give as well as take in the matter of sharing facilities. By sharing within reason, a director will build general faculty good will, which will help, especially in times of stress, in keeping the department functioning. Other departments will have certain scheduled events that are significant to them, and the director should, insofar as possible, avoid conflicts with those events and their purposes. It is advisable to attend faculty meetings, even though they are not particularly thrilling. By demonstrating that "cooperation" rather than "contention" characterizes the physical education department, the other school departments will be led to respond more readily with the same attitude. The entire school can educate more thoroughly if harmony prevails.

Standard procedures and methods

It is highly desirable for the staff members of a department of physical education to employ standard procedures and methods in handling many of the operations in connection with their duties. It is extremely confusing for students to find that different staff members use entirely different methods and procedures. Consistency in many of the operations will not only bring about more efficient operations but will definitely lead to better public relations. Standard procedures and methods may be adopted for the following items:

1. Absence and tardiness
2. Accidents
3. Use of audio-visual aids
4. Keys
5. Telephones
6. Staff meetings
7. Drops and adds
8. Examinations

9. Make-ups
10. Grading standards
11. Rainy weather procedures
12. Program change
13. Office supplies
14. Secretarial service
15. Office hours
16. Symbols used in roll books
17. Time of starting and dismissing classes
18. Uniform for activity classes
19. Tutoring students
20. Excuses
21. Procedure on first class meeting
22. Procedure when instructor is ill

Standing plans in areas such as those listed above should be thoroughly discussed by all staff members before being adopted. Once adopted they should be included in a departmental manual. Such a manual aids in the orientation of new staff members and serves to remind the older staff members of the standard method or procedure to be employed.

Strategic considerations in planning

Newman [6] discusses at some length various strategic considerations in planning. He points out that it is highly desirable to adjust a plan to the anticipated reactions of those who will be affected by the plans. Many a plan will encounter difficulty if consideration is not given to the responses of those who are involved in one way or another with the enterprise. Newman recommends that the skillful executive should "be aware of alternative strategies he might use (or be subjected to)," and "recognize key factors in choosing a particular strategy for a specific situation." Newman describes the following strategies:

1. Strategies for initiating change
   (a) Mass concentrated offensive. An all-out effort is made to accomplish the objective.
   (b) Fabianism—avoid decisive engagement. This strategy favors a gradual rather than revolutionary approach to carry out the plan.
   (c) Make a quick showing. An initial and prompt favorable result on some aspect of the plan can gain acceptance of the entire project.
   (d) Camel's head in the tent. Sometimes a small beginning can be made when a total program would be unacceptable.

[6] *Ibid.*, pp. 87-99.

(e) Boring from within. When an executive has an emotional antagonism toward a project his attitude might be changed by enlisting the cooperation of one of his staff members.

2. Joint action strategies

(a) Strength in unity. This strategy consists of securing allies to join in promoting a change.

(b) Unwilling ally. Often an individual who is disinterested in a plan can be made an active ally by assigning him some important role in connection with its execution.

(c) You scratch my back, I'll scratch yours. This involves an exchange of favors.

3. Defensive strategies

(a) Keep on sawing wood. Have faith in the plan and despite criticism continue to exert maximum effort to achieve success.

(b) Red herring across the trail. This strategy aims to confuse the issue by deliberately endeavoring to divert attention to another matter.

(c) Counter-invasion. This technique involves responding to a proposal with a counter proposal.

(d) Divide and rule. This approach endeavors to weaken the opposition by creating a split within it.

4. Cautious strategies

(a) Passing the buck. This technique involves transferring blame to someone else.

(b) Let someone else pull your chestnuts out of the fire. A desirable action may more appropriately be taken by someone other than the one who will benefit from the action.

(c) Conserve your gunpowder. Use only as much pressure as is necessary to accomplish the desired result and keep in reserve sufficient power for future emergencies.

5. Negotiating strategies

(a) Haggling. This strategy involves bargaining about terms in which one party offers less than he is willing to pay and the other asks for more than he actually is willing to accept.

(b) Lay all cards on the table. This approach involves a frank revelation of the entire situation.

(c) Surprise. As its name implies this strategy refers to an unexpected maneuver.

6. Timing strategies

(a) Strike while the iron is hot. This technique calls for prompt action when the situation is propitious.

(b) Things must get worse before they get better. Even though he recognizes the need for improvement the executive must realize that at times the situation must degenerate further before others are convinced that the desirable action is necessary.

(c) Time is a great healer. Some plans will have a better chance for success after a cooling-off period.

(d) Keep one jump ahead. This strategy involves keeping ahead of competitors.

ORGANIZING

Bartky [7] defines organizing as "the process or state of being in which two or more people coordinate their efforts and pool their resources to achieve given purposes." Newman [8] provides further understanding of the nature of organizing by his statement: "The administrative process of organizing an enterprise or any of its parts consists of (1) dividing and grouping the work that should be done (including administration) into individual jobs, and (2) defining the established relationships between individuals filling these jobs."

Organizing involves consideration of such subjects as grouping of activities, departmentation, delegation, administrative staff and use of committees. Each of these topics will be reviewed.

Grouping activities in physical education

There are a variety of ways of grouping activities. However, in physical education the grouping is almost invariably done on the basis of *functions*. In public schools and colleges and universities the major functions performed in connection with physical education include:

1. Teaching physical education activities
2. Coaching different interschool athletic teams
3. Conducting an intramural athletic or girl's athletic association program
4. Administering the physical education program
5. Administering the interschool athletic program
6. Teaching undergraduate and graduate professional courses
7. Administering a program of professional preparation
8. Teaching health education classes

[7] John Bartky, *Administration as Educational Leadership* (Stanford, California, Stanford University Press, 1956).

[8] *Op. cit.*, p. 143.

Departmentation

Because physical education and interschool athletic programs have been operating in secondary schools, colleges, and universities for over one hundred years an organizational pattern has gradually evolved. The major functions mentioned above are usually grouped and performed in a departmental setup in secondary schools and in a department, division, or autonomous college or school in institutions of higher education.

Organization for physical education in public schools

The state is the authority for all education in the public schools within its jurisdiction. Education is a state function in the United States and to a large extent the state determines the type and quality of education, including health and physical education, which prevails in the public schools within its boundaries.

This authority of the state in regard to public education is discharged in most states through a state board of education. This organization is empowered to develop, regulate, and supervise the educational system within the state. By means of school laws and codes the state board of education exercises control over teacher certification, the prescribed curriculum, and appropriation of state funds to local school districts.

On the local level the board of education plays a very important role in the educational program of its school district. The local boards of education are organized and operated in accordance with state regulations. They are the policy making body and they have the power to levy taxes and support the schools. While the board of education must assure that the local schools comply with state educational regulations it is free to go far beyond these if it so desires. Thus, in connection with the health and physical education program the state requires minimum standards but if the local school board wants to exceed these it is perfectly free to do so. This explains why some communities require a daily program of physical education even though the state law requires only three days per week.

School boards exercise their authority through the superintendent. He is responsible for carrying out all state regulations as well as the local regulations and policies established by the board of education of his school district. He works through the principals of the various elementary and secondary schools. The principals have the responsibility of administering the educational program within their own schools.

The administrative setup for health and physical education within a community may involve (1) the city director or supervisor, (2) the chairman of the department of physical education within a junior or senior high school, and (3) the director of athletics for the school.

In most cities a city-wide director of health and physical education has the overall administrative responsibility for the program in all of the schools of the school district. He is very much involved in curriculum development and the improvement of instruction. He plays a leading role in the planning of new facilities when they are being considered.

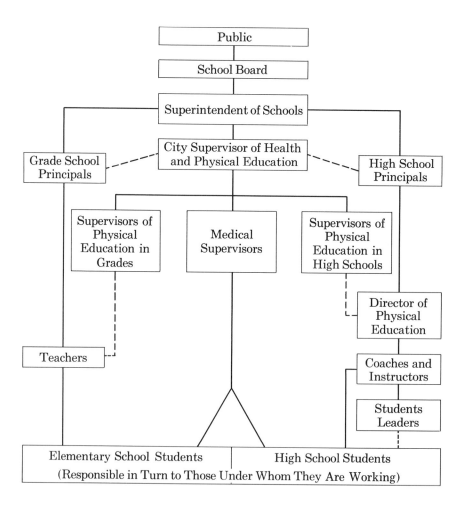

Figure 3-1. Public School Departmental Organization. The physical education organization setup for a moderate-sized city system in which one person supervises the health, interscholastic, and required physical education and intramural units.

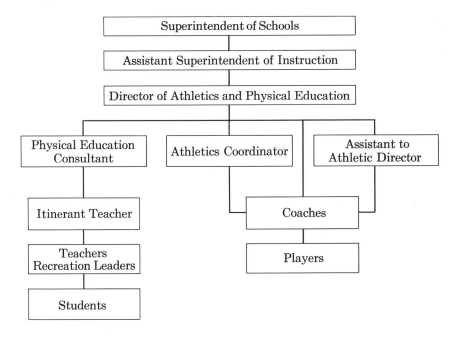

Source: Athletic Department, Dallas Independent School District, Dallas.

Figure 3-2. School System Organization. The organization for a large city in which the size of the physical education and interscholastic athletic programs is such that the director requires full-time assistants for physical education and athletics.

He usually participates, along with the principal, in the selection of new staff members within his area of responsibility. He might also consolidate all equipment requests and submit orders for all the schools under his jurisdiction. The supervisors of the elementary school teachers usually come under his direction.

The city-wide administration of interscholastic athletics may or may not be the responsibility of the city director of health and physical education. Usually, the larger cities have a separate athletic director to coordinate all interschool athletic competition. The athletic director and the city director of physical education must work closely together because the two programs are so closely related and involve many of the same personnel and facilities.

The great majority of junior and senior high schools have a departmental setup for health and physical education under the direction of a departmental chairman. The exceptions to this pattern are found in the very small secondary schools. The chairman is responsible for the administrative direction and supervision of the programs of health education and physical education. (In some secondary schools health education may be set up separately or it might be handled in the biology department.) He is directly responsible to the principal. His duties may include the administration of interschool athletics although many of the larger secondary schools have a separate director of athletics. Where this situation prevails the two administrators must coordinate their work very closely.

The plans of departmental organization showing administrative relationships are presented in Figures 3-1 to 3-3.

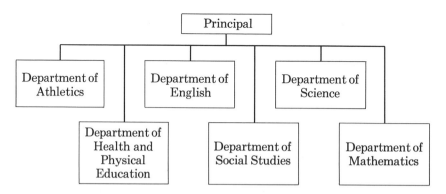

Figure 3-3. Departmental Organization in a Large High School. The organization for health education, physical education, and interscholastic athletics in a large senior high school where the athletic program is administered separately from the health education and physical education program. It is essential that the chairman of physical education and the athletic director closely coordinate the use of personnel, facilities, and equipment.

Organization for health and physical education in colleges and universities

Colleges and universities both public and private are subject to state control just as the public schools are. They are chartered by the state to conduct various types of programs. The state authorizes the different certificates, diplomas, and degrees that the institution offers for successful completion of a program of study. Such authorization is not granted by the state until the resources of the institution are carefully evaluated and the state is satisfied that desirable standards of faculty, facilities, curriculum, library, and the like can be met.

In a study of recent trends in the organization of college physical education Donnelly [9] discovered that the structural unit reported in the 239 institutions surveyed was 6 colleges, 7 schools, 51 divisions, and 175 departments. Seventy-six or 32% of the institutions maintained completely separate men's and women's departments. In 58 or 24%, the department or division head of physical education was responsible to the dean or director of education. Twenty-one of the intramural departments were administered by the athletic department while in most of the remaining institutions the intramural director reported to the

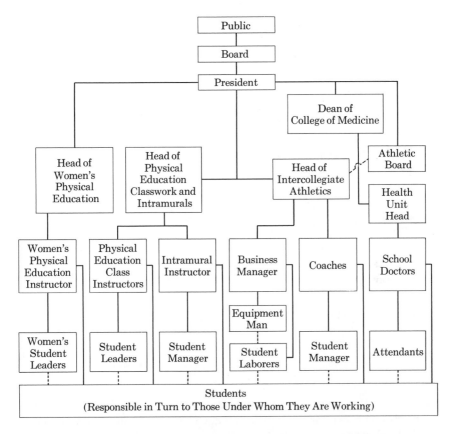

Figure 3-4. University Departmental Organization. It is assumed that intercollegiate athletics is separate from other physical education work, that conduct of the health unit is a function of the college of medicine, and that the women's department is also a separate unit.

9 Rich Donnelly, "Recent Trends In Organization of College Physical Education Departments for Men," *66th Proceedings of the National College Physical Education Association,* 1962, pp. 148-156.

head of the physical education unit. Seventy-five percent of the athletic directors were directly responsible to top level college administrative personnel while 21 percent were responsible to the director of physical education. Figures 3-4 and 3-5 are examples of two different organizational setups on the higher education level.

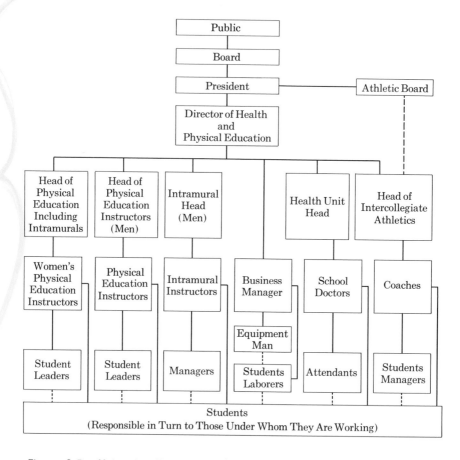

Figure 3-5. University Departmental Organization. One individual should head this entire department, which includes five major units: health, women's physical education, men's physical education class work, intercollegiate athletics, and intramural athletics.

The organizational setup of a college or school is usually found only in very large universities. The status of a college or school is attained when the scope of operations is quite extensive. Usually included in such an organization are the basic instruction program for men and women, the intramural athletic program, women's recreation association program, and undergraduate and graduate professional programs in health education, physical education, and recreation. In some institutions the program of intercollegiate athletics is also a part of a school or college.

An independent college or school of health education, physical education, and recreation represents the ultimate in such organizations in higher education. (Figure 3-6 presents the organization of an autonomous school in a state university.) It possesses many advantages the chief of which are:

1. Autonomy:
   (a) Curriculum
   (b) Budget
   (c) Facilities
   (d) Personnel
   (e) Requirements for professional students
2. Economy of operation
3. Staff can be selected for more clear-cut and better defined services in specialized areas
4. Better control of equipment and buildings
5. Avoids the possibility of an unfavorable intermediary

Delegation

Whenever an administrator has more to do than he can handle by himself one solution is to seek the assistance of one of his subordinates. When the executive assigns some of his duties to a member of his staff it is known as delegation. While the physical education administrator in most secondary schools does not carry such a heavy administrative load as to require additional help this is not the case with city directors and in large secondary schools, and colleges and universities.

Delegation is a very desirable procedure for the overloaded administrator to follow. His efficiency is reduced and his organization suffers the consequences unless his load can be lightened. Many administrators are hesitant to delegate because they lack confidence in their subordinates, because they think they are more capable of handling the situation themselves and because they are not cognizant of the harm that is being done by their overloaded condition. Of all the practices of administrators which are detrimental to their organization failure to delegate is one of the most pronounced.

Newman [10] suggests that delegation has three aspects:

[10] *Op. cit.*, p. 185.

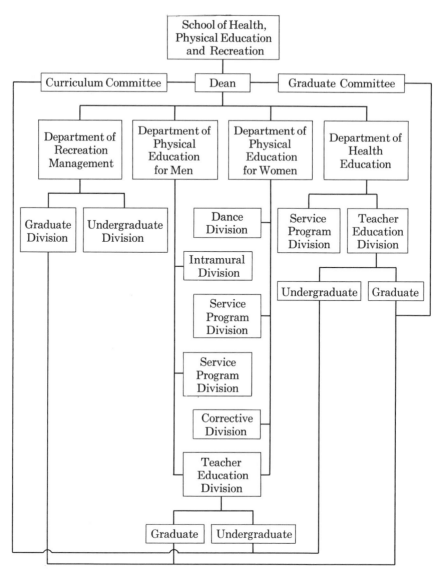

Figure 3-6. Organization of an Autonomous School. All graduate programs must be conducted under the policies of the University Graduate Council and the School of Health, Physical Education and Recreation Graduate Committee. All undergraduate professional curricular matters are referred to the faculty of the School of Health, Physical Education and Recreation through the Curriculum Committee. The supervision of student teaching is coordinated with the School of Education. However, all of the supervision is performed by staff members of the School of Health, Physical Education and Recreation. Some staff members from the Athletic Department are used to teach service and undergraduate professional classes. They are partially on the budget of the School of Health, Physical Education and Recreation. Their services are provided during terms when their sport is not in season. The Athletic Department is an autonomous unit and the Athletic Director reports directly to the President.

1. The assignment by an executive of *duties* (planning and doing of specified activities) to his immediate subordinates.
2. The granting of permission (authority) to make commitments, use resources, and take other actions necessary to perform the duties.
3. The creation of an obligation (responsibility) on the part of each subordinate to the executive for the satisfactory performance of the duties.

Principles of delegation.

1. No member of an organization reports to more than one supervisor. This principle is frequently violated in health and physical education organizations. A staff member's work load may be divided between two or three programs in each of which he is responsible to a different supervisor. He might have duties in the basic instructional, the professional preparation, and the intercollegiate athletic programs. This situation creates a variety of problems. Each supervisor might assign more duties to the staff member than that to which he is entitled. This results in an overloaded teacher. At times, also, the requirements of one supervisor may be in conflict with those of another and the staff member is in a dilemma about which course of action to take. Finally, the staff member may have difficulty in giving his best efforts to the various programs to which he is related. This happens frequently to the individual who has coaching responsibilities. Because of the competitive nature and pressure of interschool athletics many coaches neglect other aspects of their responsibilities in order to give more emphasis to their coaching duties.

Because it is virtually impossible in many schools to avoid dual subordination the administrator must recognize the problems that are created and do what he can to minimize them. One of the most effective approaches is for the various supervisors to come together and agree upon the load and schedule each will impose upon the staff member. By working closely together they can eliminate some of the problems inherent in this type of situation.

2. Responsibility for a function is matched by the authority necessary to perform that function. This principle has been recognized for centuries. The individual who has been assigned the responsibility for a function must be given the authority commensurate with that responsibility. If the responsibility is for a minor function then only a small amount of authority is needed. But if the function is a large, significant one then the staff member must have the authority that is required to perform the function successfully. If an individual is assigned the responsibility of administering the state track and field championship meet he must have the authority over manpower, materials, facilities, and funds to accomplish the objective successfully. It is not fair to hold

an individual accountable for results that he has not been permitted to guide according to his own best judgment.

3. Responsibility cannot be delegated. An administrator of a physical education department is not relieved of his responsibility when he delegates a duty to one of his staff members. Accountability is not removed by delegation. The administrator cannot excuse himself when failure results from the actions of an incompetent subordinate.

4. Definite and clear cut responsibilities should be assigned. The failure to delegate definite and clear-cut responsibilities to each executive and staff member results frequently in confusion, indecision, and poor performance. When two individuals believe that the same responsibility or assignment is theirs hard feelings are frequently generated.

5. Orders should never be given to subordinates over the head of a responsible executive. The chain of command should not be violated. To do so is to encourage the subordinate's disrespect for his supervisor and to damage the morale of the executive.

Administrative staff

A second way in which an overworked executive can lighten his load is to appoint a staff assistant. Such a position would probably rarely exist in a secondary school physical education department but it is found in colleges and universities and in the central offices of city directors. The city director is himself a staff assistant but he may have one or more assistants himself. For example, some city directors have staff assistants who, because of their specialization, assume responsibility of certain programs such as health education, interscholastic athletics, or the supervision of elementary education teachers.

Administrative staff personnel do not have a command function and they are not in a position to give orders to faculty members of a school. Staff personnel are differentiated from "line" personnel such as the superintendent of schools, the building principal, and the chairman of the physical education department. Line officers have been delegated power by the board of education, which is manifested by the authority inherent in their positions.

In light of this situation neither the city director nor any of his staff assistants is in a position to direct the chairman of a physical education department or any of his staff members to take any specific action. As staff personnel, they must endeavor to accomplish their purposes by suggestions, persuasion, and discussion rather than by commands.

Committees

Most physical education organizations make use of committees. Under certain circumstances they perform very useful functions and they are an asset to the unit. The advantages and disadvantages of committees according to Newman [11] are given in the following points.

Advantages of committees:

1. Provide integrated group judgment
2. Promote coordination
3. Secure cooperation in execution of plans
4. Train members and obtain continuity of thinking

Limitations of committees:

1. Slow and expensive action
2. Divided responsibility
3. Danger of compromise decision.

Newman [12] also describes the conditions that are favorable to the use of committees:

Committees are likely to be particularly useful:

1. When a wide divergence of information is necessary to reach a sound conclusion
2. When the decision is of such importance that the judgment of several qualified individuals is necessary
3. When successful execution of decisions depends upon full understanding of their ramifications
4. When activities of three or more divisions need to be adjusted frequently to secure coordination

Committees are usually not desirable:

1. When speed is vital
2. When the decision is not particularly important
3. When qualified personnel are not available
4. When the problem is one of execution rather than decision

DIRECTING

Meaning and importance of direction

Direction initiates action. It occurs when the executive "gives the signals to act, orders or empowers others to act, indicates what the action is to be and when it is to start and stop. In its essence, direction is authority on the move, guided and controlled by the will of the officer." [13] It occurs after the preparation stage, which involves planning, organizing, and assembling personnel and other resources.

[11] *Op. cit.*, pp. 240-245.
[12] *Ibid.*, pp. 242-248.
[13] Jesse B. Sears, *The Nature of the Administrative Process* (New York, McGraw-Hill Book Company, 1950), p. 127.

Direction is important because when it is done effectively it enhances the chances of a successful operation. When it is done poorly it threatens the progress and success of the enterprise. The manner in which direction is conducted has a marked effect upon the behavior of those being directed. Both the quantity and quality of their performance depends upon their reaction to the directions they receive.

Ways of directing

Directing may be done orally or in written form. Oral direction should be used only when the order is simple and will be acted upon immediately. It is also more in order when the individual has performed the task previously. Verbal directions are also indicated when the supervisor is present to check the execution of the assignment. Emergencies may also necessitate the use of spoken orders.

Verbal directions have the advantage of communicating the speaker's feelings to his listeners. His intensity, enthusiasm, and emotions are capable of strongly motivating his co-workers. However, depending upon his personality and voice, the opposite reaction could also be produced.

Written directions are indicated when the task is complex and involves many details, when a considerable number of people at different times and places are involved, and when misunderstanding could result in serious consequences. Written materials also have the advantage of being available for reference at a later date.

Characteristics of good direction

The purpose of the direction is to communicate the desired instructions. There should be no doubt in the minds of the subordinates just exactly what they are to do, how they are to do it and when the assignment is to be completed. Poor performance is the result of directions that are not clear or complete. Likewise, the directions should be reasonable and within the capacity of the individual to follow.

The execution of directions is facilitated when the subordinates understand their purpose. When they know why they are performing an assignment they are in a better position to make necessary adjustments when unexpected developments occur. To explain the why of a direction is particularly important with school personnel who are professionally prepared for their responsibilities. In addition, such a practice is conducive to better morale.

Standard operating procedures

Virtually all organizations have standard operating procedures. These methods have been found to be the best way of accomplishing a task. The use of standard operating procedures not only assures that the best method of doing the task will be employed but it also avoids the necessity of the administrator giving detailed explanations. When staff members know how to proceed in certain situations the administrator is relieved of the necessity of giving directions. This is a desirable situation.

Indoctrination

Indoctrination is another valuable concept related to direction. It involves instilling in all staff members the beliefs, ideals, and attitudes that the administrator believes are essential to the success of the organization. This is more difficult to accomplish than to obtain adherence to standard methods and procedures. Likewise it is more important. The administrator's goal is to have all staff members give their loyalties and best efforts to the enterprise. This can only be accomplished when the individuals are imbued with a commitment to the organization's philosophy and objectives. This will not happen accidentally. The indoctrination of staff members with the desired beliefs and attitudes represents one of the administrator's most important responsibilities.

Silent direction

By "silent direction" is meant the example set by the administrator. His actions are more influential than his words; his personal example can influence his staff members either positively or negatively. If his example is consistent with his aims for his staff members his leadership is accentuated. If the physical education executive directs his staff members to proceed in a manner that he himself does not follow they will not have respect for him and their morale will deteriorate.

Creating the desire to follow directions

The administrator should understand that the best results are obtained when the staff members being directed have both the ability and the desire to carry out the instructions. Association with staff members over a period of time enables the department chairman to assess the abilities of the various individuals. A much more difficult proposition is to create the desire on the subordinate's part to give his best efforts to the task. What makes this assignment particularly difficult is the necessity of maintaining this desire at a high level year in and year out.

Indoctrination and silent direction are important considerations in developing and maintaining the desire—or morale—of staff members at a high level. The administrator's personality and character are crucial in attaining this objective. His understanding of his staff members and the manner in which he works with them are vital elements. He should know that free people resent excessive bossing. Constant commanding is poor direction. Excellent advice to administrators was offered several thousand years ago by the Chinese philosopher, Lao-Tse: [14]

> A leader is best when people
> barely know he exists,
>   Not so good when people obey
> and acclaim him,
>   Worst when people despise him.
>   "Fail to honor people, they fail
> to honor you."
>   "When his work is done, his aim
> fulfilled,
>   They will all say, "We did it
> ourselves."

COORDINATING

The problems of coordination multiply as the size and complexity of the organization increases. The close and constant contact of individuals in a small department simplifies the organizational setup, promotes communication among staff members, and facilitates supervision and control. While all of these factors make coordination easier it would be incorrect to assume that the physical education administrator of a small high school or college department need not concern himself with coordination. It has been pointed out that even two individuals who are lifting a heavy log need to coordinate their efforts.

Nature and importance of coordination

By the term "coordination" is meant the pulling together, unifying and integrating all of the diverse elements of an organization toward the accomplishment of its objectives. It involves making a smoothly working, harmonious team out of all the human resources at the administrator's command. The efforts of all personnel must be synchronized and dovetailed in the team effort. There is always the tendency of some individuals to give priority to their personal and selfish interests. The administrator must combat these divisive developments by obtaining the full support and teamwork of everyone concerned in behalf of the organization's objectives.

Many instances of poor coordination in physical education organizations are available. The following examples are typical:

1. The administrator did not make clear which of two staff mem-

[14] Lao-Tse, *Tao-Teh-King*, translated by Paul Carus (La Salle, Illinois, The Open Court Publishing Company, 1927), p. 84.

bers was to supervise the noon-hour recreation program. As a consequence neither appeared. Without leadership, the program was completely disorganized and bordered on chaos.

2. A staff member worked under three different supervisors. Two of the supervisors gave him assignments that required him to be in two different places at the same time.

3. An outstanding speaker had been secured to come to the campus to speak to the physical education majors. At a staff meeting arrangements for this presentation were announced. All staff members were to bring their students to the lecture hall for the presentation. However, one staff member was absent from the meeting and the administrator failed to remember to notify him of the arrangements. As a consequence neither he nor his students attended the lecture.

4. During registration the enrollment for one class was so great that a change in teaching stations was necessitated. The shift involved three different instructors and their classes. One instructor was not notified and as a consequence he and another staff member appeared at the same teaching station.

5. The football coach and the athletic director had failed to coordinate the details of a forthcoming trip of the squad. As a consequence the squad members were confused because of the conflicting statements concerning certain aspects of the trip.

6. A staff member had secured approval to attend a conference of his professional organization. He was under the impression that the departmental chairman would make arrangements to have his classes covered. The chairman assumed that the staff member had made these arrangements. As a result no instructor was available to teach the classes.

It is apparent from these examples that the failure to coordinate frequently leads to embarrassment, friction between staff members, a poor public image of the organization and, worst of all, a lack of efficient use of human resources. Coordination is a necessity for a smoothly functioning organization that obtains maximum effectiveness from its personnel.

Causes of poor coordinating

At the root of most of the coordination problems is the failure to perform various of the other administrative processes properly. The absence of or poor planning, faulty organizing, poor directing, and ineffective controlling either singly or in combination produces poor coordination in an organization. The following statement amplifies this point: [15]

15 United States Department of Agriculture, *Essentials of Good Management* (Washington, D.C., 1956), p. 25.

In management, coordination deals with synchronizing and unifying the actions of a group of people. Basically, coordination should flow or result from effective planning, organizing, directing, and controlling. Continued need for special coordinating devices may, in fact, be an indication of poor planning and organization. It is certain that far too much time will be consumed in coordinating efforts if the other functions of management are not well performed.

Another cause of coordination problems is poor communication within the organization. Operations fail to function smoothly because some individual was not informed or was improperly informed concerning his role. No team can work together as a unit if some members are in the dark as to what the plans are.

Facilitating coordination

A number of procedures may be employed to improve coordination in a health education and physical education organization. Some of the more effective of these are:

Organizational charts and statements of duties and relationships. Problems of coordination arise when:

1. Individuals in the organization do not know to whom they report and who reports to them.
2. A staff member reports to two or more superiors.
3. When two administrators or staff members believe they are responsible for the same activity.
4. Lack of clear understanding of exactly who does what.

These problems are minimized when organizational charts and statements of duties and relationships are available to all staff members. They help to eliminate the twilight zones where no one feels responsible. They should also point up and thus reduce areas of overlapping responsibility.

An adequate system of formal communication. A frequently made statement in organizations is: "The left hand doesn't know what the right hand is doing." Such a comment arises when the communication within the department breaks down. Changes in policies, plans, schedules, and procedures must be transmitted to all the individuals involved. Emergency conditions may necessitate a variety of temporary changes. The administrator must consider all ramifications of the situation and see that the proper information gets to everyone concerned.

Regular staff meetings provide an excellent means of disseminating much information. Minutes of such meetings should be distributed to all staff members. In this way those who were unable to attend will still obtain the needed information. Committee meetings also facilitate an exchange of information, particularly if the minutes of the meeting are made available to others.

In schools with small departments most of the communication can be done verbally. In larger departments memos, letters, and special reports distributed to all staff members will be helpful. A bulletin board that is readily available to staff members and is regularly consulted by them is also a valuable aid to communication.

Adequate supervision. Effective supervision will disclose misunderstandings and problems of coordination and thus enable corrective action to take place. It is when the administrator is unaware of what is happening in his organization that difficulties in coordination develop. When he is in close contact with his personnel he can clarify relationships and correct misunderstandings before much harm has been done.

Voluntary coordination. Voluntary coordination will contribute appreciably toward an effectively coordinated organization. Newman [16] recommends several factors that aid in voluntary coordination:

1. Instill dominant objectives. Coordinated action is easier to attain when all members of a department have high morale and a strong esprit de corps. When the individuals concerned have pride in their organization and are willing to subjugate their selfish interests for the welfare of the group coordination is simplified. When the personnel are so anxious that their team effort prosper that they are mutually helpful to each other and go beyond the bounds of what is expected of them the ideal attitude prevails.

2. Develop generally accepted customs and terms. Voluntary coordination is enhanced when various staff members understand each other and know what to expect. The use, within an organization, of customary ways of working and a common terminology facilitates working relationships.

3. Encourage informal contacts. Informal contacts at coffee breaks, luncheons, in the locker room, and in recreational activities provide an opportunity to supplement formal communications. Such friendly relations between staff members promote voluntary adjustments which improve coordination.

CONTROLLING

The controlling process is concerned with determining whether everything is proceeding in accordance with the plan that was developed, the orders that were issued, and the principles that were established. In

[16] *Op. cit.,* pp. 410-413.

a health education and physical education department controlling means checking whether suitable progress is being made toward the objectives, whether the duties and responsibilities are being properly discharged, and whether everything is operating according to plan.

Controlling related to other administrative processes

Controlling is closely related to the other administrative processes of planning, organizing, directing, and coordinating. After the plans have been made, the organization developed, the action started, the efforts coordinated, it is logical and natural to check to see that the operations are proceeding according to plan. If the first four processes are all effectively executed the problem of control will be greatly simplified.

Maintain close contact with operations

An important consideration in control is for the administrator to know what is going on. By close personal contact with the staff members as they perform their duties he can observe deviations from desirable procedures. In this way he can control the situation before a major crisis develops. He must have a realistic mental picture of the program in operation or his planning, organizing, coordinating, and directing may be based upon faulty premises. Some administrators err by spending all of their time in their offices. After a time they lose touch with reality.

Functions involved in control

Koontz and O'Donnell [17] point out that "control involves three basic functions: (1) setting standards of satisfactory performance, (2) checking results to see how they compare with the standards, (3) taking corrective action where actual results do not meet the standards."

Setting standards of satisfactory performance. In setting performance standards the members of the health and physical education department should be involved. They must be familiar with the standards that their students are expected to attain. Likewise, they will be in an advantageous position to know what standards are realistic and could reasonably be attained. Finally, they must be enthusiastic about bringing their students up to the expected levels of achievement. The most effective way of accomplishing these various objectives is to have the staff members participate in the determination of the standards.

---

[17] Harold Koontz and Cyril O'Donnell, *Readings in Management* (New York, McGraw-Hill Book Company, 1959), p. 434.

The physical education administrator would be interested in standards of three types, namely, (1) standards of instruction, (2) standards of professional ethics and responsibility, and (3) standards of student achievement. Standards of instruction are concerned primarily with methods of teaching, handling students, and the like. Standards of professional ethics and responsibility refer to the ideals of the profession. This area also would involve participation in professional organizations.

Insofar as standards of student achievement are concerned there never have been available previously so many objective standards. Through the support of the American Association for Health, Physical Education and Recreation nationally standardized tests of physical fitness, motor skills, and knowledge in a wide variety of physical activities are available for boys and girls from 10 through 16 years of age (see Chapter 16). A number of states have also developed physical fitness test batteries and standards for children and youth of various ages.

Checking results to see how they compare with the standards. Standards of instruction of various staff members are readily checked by observation, written and oral reports, and consultation with staff members. It does not take the administrator long to assess the teaching performance of his staff members.

Likewise the professional attitudes and ethics of staff members are readily determined. Membership in and support of professional organizations is clearly discernible.

Insofar as student achievement is concerned it is a simple matter to compare the performance of one's own students with national standards. There never has been a time previously when the administrator of a physical education program could so readily assess the level of attainment of his students in physical fitness, skill development, and knowledge as he can today.

Taking corrective action where actual results do not meet the standards. When the results do not come up to expectations the administrator must correct the situation. This, of course, assumes that the standards are realistic and attainable by his organization. What steps he takes will depend upon his analysis of why the expected results were not forthcoming. In a health and physical education organization the major factors to be considered are: (1) environmental factors, (2) qualifications of staff members, and (3) disciplining personnel.

1. Environmental factors. The equipment and facilities available, time allotment, class size, and classification of students are the major physical considerations that may hamper the physical educator from reaching desired standards of performance. Even under the best of circumstances it is difficult to accomplish much in two 30-minute periods of physical education per week. When to this is added the further handi-

caps of inadequate facilities and equipment, class size from fifty to eighty students and freshmen, sophomores, juniors, and seniors all combined in the same class the obstacles facing the instructor are formidable.

Some of the above factors can be corrected much more readily than others. The scheduling of students into homogeneous classes can be done by the principal of the secondary school if he is convinced that this is a desirable procedure. The procurement of additional items of equipment is not a major expense item but would be a budgetary problem in some schools. A more serious financial problem is an increase in time allotment and a decrease in class size. In either case this means additional staff members which, in comparison to equipment items, is far more expensive. From the standpoint of the cost factor the most expensive item is additional facilities. A new athletic field, tennis courts, swimming pool, or gymnasium are difficult to procure because cost runs into many thousands of dollars.

2. Qualifications of staff members. If the failure to attain the desired standards is due to one or more incompetent staff member, the administrator's first step is to try to eliminate the incompetence. This might be done via an in-service training program. Another possibility is to take additional courses in extension or in summer school. Still another alternative is to reassign the staff member to other duties in which he is more competent.

If the administrator's efforts to bring the staff member up to a satisfactory level of ability are unavailing the latter should be dismissed. This is easy to do if the staff member does not have tenure. It goes without saying that tenure should not have been granted to a staff member unless he had clearly demonstrated his ability.

3. Motivation. Very frequently, staff members about whose competence there is no question are not performing up to expectations. This situation is usually due to a lack of motivation. The administrator's aim is to secure maximum performance from all staff members throughout the year and every year. This is a very difficult assignment, which cannot be achieved unless all staff members are adequately motivated. If any staff members are not putting forth their best efforts the administrator must discover why.

The primary incentives to motivate staff members as described by Newman [18] are:

1. Higher financial status
2. Social status and respect
3. Security
4. Attractive work
5. Opportunity for development
6. Worth-while activity

[18] *Op. cit.,* p. 391.

7. Personal power and influence
8. Treatment of each subordinate as an individual person
9. Voice in his own affairs for each man
10. Just and diligent supervision

Once he determines the factor or factors involved in the lack of motivation of a staff member the administrator will be in a position to know how to proceed. In some situations, however, he will find that he is unable to correct the problem.

4. Disciplining personnel. Fortunately, in educational institutions it is only infrequently that the imposition of disciplinary measures becomes necessary. Such disciplinary action often fails to correct the problem and leads to resentment and poor morale. However, occasions will arise when the administrator must take disciplinary action for violation of rules. Failure to do so would likely cause other staff members to ignore the regulations.

The resort to disciplinary action is an important matter that must be properly handled by the administrator. The following check list suggests some of the factors which should be considered: [19]

DISCIPLINARY ACTION

1. Have I secured the necessary facts?

   (a) Did the employee have an opportunity to tell fully his side of the story? _____
   (b) Did I check the employee's immediate supervisor? _____
   (c) Did I investigate all other sources of information? _____
   (d) Did I hold my interview privately so as to avoid embarrassing the interested employee or employees? _____
   (e) Did I exert every possible effort to verify the information? _____
   (f) Did I check the employee's past record? _____

2. Have I considered all the facts in deciding upon the disciplinary measure?

   (a) Have I found out what has been done in similar cases in my unit? _____
   (b) Have I found out what has been done in similar cases in other units? _____
   (c) Have I shown any discrimination toward an individual or group? _____
   (d) Have I let personalities affect my decision? _____
   (e) Does the measure fit the violation? _____
   (f) Will the measure prevent a recurrence? _____
   (g) Will the measure maintain morale? _____
   (h) Will the measure encourage the employee's initiative? _____

[19] Training Bulletin No. 3, Civilian Training Branch, Office of the Surgeon General, U.S. Army, War Department (Washington, D.C., 1945).

(i) Will the measure create a desire on the part of the employee to do what is right? _____

(j) Have I checked this decision with my immediate supervisor? _____

3. Have I administered the corrective measure in the proper manner?

(a) Did I consider whether it should be done individually or collectively? _____

(b) Am I prepared to explain to the employee why the action is necessary? _____

(1) The effect of the violation on the office, fellow employees and himself. _____

(2) To help him improve his efficiency and also that of the unit. _____

(c) Am I prepared to tell him how he can prevent a similar offense in the future? _____

(d) Am I prepared to deal with any resentment he might show? _____

4. Have I made the necessary follow up?

(a) Has the measure had the desired effect on the employee? _____

(b) Have I done everything possible to overcome any resentment? _____

(c) Is the employee convinced that the action was for his best interest? _____

(d) Have I endeavored to compliment him on his good work? _____

(e) Has the action had the desired effects on the other employees in the unit? _____

Instruments of control

A variety of instruments of control are available to the administrator. Some of the most important of these are:

1. Releasing or reassigning personnel. This has already been discussed (see p. 86). It represents an effective means of exercising control when unsatisfactory results are due to poor leadership.

2. Policies and standard procedures. One of the most effective of all control devices is the use by all staff members of departmental policies and standard procedures. Since they represent the best ways by which staff members can perform their various duties the administrator can exercise control through such policies and procedures. It is apparent that the organization that has all staff members using well-designed policies and procedures will operate at maximum efficiency.

3. Budget. It is recognized in any organization that the budget is a powerful instrument of control. Many of the things that the administrator or staff members want to do cannot be done because funds are not available. The administrator can, by the manner in which he chooses to employ his financial resources, control many of the activities within his organization. For example, he can eliminate activities in the basic in-

structional program by not purchasing the equipment that is necessary. The quality of the intramural program can be strongly influenced by the funds that are available for equipment, officiating, awards, secretarial help, and the like. By making funds available for an additional staff member, class size or teacher load or both may be reduced. A good testing program can be started when funds are available to purchase the necessary equipment.

4. Professional standards and ethics. Desirable professional conduct, as recommended by the profession, strongly influences and controls the actions of some staff members as well as administrators. The American Association for Health, Physical Education and Recreation has developed a code of ethics. In addition, it has developed recommended standards for every aspect of our school programs. Many members of the profession have accepted these ethics and standards and they are strong guides to action.

5. Facts and principles. The control that is exercised over the behavior of staff members should be based upon facts and principles. Certainly, there are no better guides to action. For example, class dismissal time should be based upon the length of time required by students to get to their next class. An instructor should not be scheduled for more than three consecutive classes because he will become overfatigued. A staff member should not be scheduled to teach too many sections of the same activity because he will be likely to lose his enthusiasm.

6. The program of instruction. Staff members are not free to teach whatever they choose. They are expected to follow the curriculum that has been developed. They will spend the prescribed time on the various units that are to be covered. For each unit there should be a course outline or syllabus that should be followed. These materials should have been carefully worked out in advance and all staff members should have been involved in the process. Consequently, the course of instruction should reflect the best thinking of the staff. As such it exercises control over staff members.

7. Institutional regulations and policies. Over and beyond the departmental policies and standard procedures are the institutional regulations and policies. The school system as a whole and the school will have certain rules and regulations that the departmental chairman must observe. He, in turn, must see that his staff members conform to these various levels of regulations and policies.

SELECTED REFERENCES

Donnelly, Rich, "Recent Trends in Organization of College Physical Education Departments for Men," *66th Proceedings of the National College Physical Education Association,* 1962, pp. 148-166.

Newman, William H., *Administrative Action: the Techniques of Organization and Management,* 2nd ed. (Englewood Cliffs, N.J., Prentice-Hall, Inc., 1963).

Pfiffner, John M., and Robert V. Presthus, *Public Administration,* 4th ed. (New York, The Ronald Press Company, 1960).

Sears, Jessie B., *The Nature of the Administrative Process* (New York, McGraw-Hill Book Company, 1950).

Simon, Herbert A., *Administrative Behavior* (New York, The Macmillan Company, 1957).

Urwick, L., *The Elements of Administration* (New York, Harper & Row, Publishers, 1943).

4

the physical education
service program

The scope of the physical education program

The total physical education program with which all schools are concerned consists of three aspects, namely: the service, intramural, and interschool programs. Each phase is important, and no physical education program is complete unless each of these aspects is well developed, coordinated, and integrated. The service program (also known as the required program or the basic instruction program) is that which is ordinarily required by state law or local regulation. The classes are scheduled during the school day, and all students are expected to participate unless excused. The emphasis is instructional, and the objective is to provide each student with the minimum essentials of physical education. The intramural program is concerned with the provision of athletic competition for all students within a school. Ordinarily, this competition is over and above that which occurs in the service program. The intramural program is important because it gives all students an opportunity to develop the athletic skills they have been taught in the service program. The interschool program is that phase which is concerned with the provision of competition for the most highly proficient students in the various sports with teams from other institutions. This chapter will be devoted to a discussion of the service program.

The inadequacy of present-day programs

It is unfortunate that in most communities physical education practice lags far behind current physical education philosophy. The curriculum, especially, has not kept pace with the best thought in the field. From the elementary school through the university, the great majority of programs are inadequate and haphazard. There are a number of notable exceptions in the more progressive schools, but for the most part, the programs are not so soundly conceived and well organized as other courses of study within the school.

This is well illustrated by the most comprehensive survey that has ever been made in physical education.[1] This survey encompassed 2,648 different high schools in twenty-five different states. It involved the evaluation of the indoor and outdoor facilities, locker and shower rooms, supplies, remedial program, health examination, aquatics, service program, organization, and the athletic and intramural programs. The median national score was only 28 percent of possible. The various states ranged from 41 percent of possible (Connecticut) to 17 percent (Tennessee and Mississippi). Remedial programs (4 percent) and aquatics (5.8 percent) were the lowest areas. The next lowest was the area of service program with only 28.7 percent of possible. The two highest in attainment were organization and administration (43.6 percent) and athletics (42.1 percent).

Evidence of inadequate programs

There is a great deal of evidence extending over several decades that our physical education programs have not been particularly successful in achieving their objectives. Data are available from many sources that the record of physical education in accomplishing the physical development objective is far from impressive. One of the major revelations of World War II was the lack of physical fitness of a large percentage of men inducted into the military service. Physical fitness testing programs in the Army, Navy, and Air Force revealed an appalling lack of strength, endurance, agility, and coordination of inductees. Karpovich and Weiss,[2] in a study of inductees into the Army Air Forces, found that 48 percent were in poor or very poor condition. Larson[3] discovered that it was necessary to improve the physical fitness status of Army Air Forces personnel as much as 90 percent beyond entrance condition in order to meet minimum physical fitness standards. What is particularly distressing about these data is that they represented

1 Karl W. Bookwalter, "A National Survey of Health and Physical Education for Boys in High Schools, 1950-54," *Professional Contributions,* American Academy of Physical Education, No. 4 (1955), pp. 1-11.

2 Peter V. Karpovich and Raymond A. Weiss, "Physical Fitness of Men Entering the Army Air Forces," *Research Quarterly* (October, 1946), p. 186.

3 Leonard A. Larson, "Some Findings Resulting from the Army Air Forces Physical Training Program," *Research Quarterly* (May, 1946), pp. 144-146.

the performance of the group of men in America from ages eighteen through thirty-eight who were generally considered the most fit.

From the book *Educational Lessons from Wartime Training* [4] the following statements concerning the physical abilities of men entering the Armed Services during World War II are revealing:

In a standard test of endurance, 67% of newly inducted soldiers failed to pass *minimum* standards. In a standard test of strength of torso, the percentage was 56.5%, in a standard test of agility, 76.5%, and in a standard test of speed, 47% of newly inducted soldiers failed to pass minimum requirements. In a different, but highly correlated standard test of endurance, 52% of the newly inducted soldiers and 52% of the air-crew trainees from seven widely scattered Army Air Forces basic training centers received ratings of "poor" or "very poor." The percentages of incoming servicemen unable to swim were: Army and Navy, 20-50% whites; 50-80% Negroes; Army-Air Forces personnel, 20-30%.

When the vast majority of men came into the armed forces, they lacked the endurance to walk long distances (without packs), or run half a mile, or perform heavy physical work throughout a day, without becoming excessively fatigued or quitting before the assignment was completed. Most new men in the service lacked the muscular strength to lift or carry reasonably heavy objects, "pull their weight"; thousands of them could not chin themselves once. Most incoming servicemen showed marked inability in such basic skills as falling, throwing, jumping, crawling, pushing, carrying, pulling, pivoting, dodging and lifting.

Little wonder that Colonel Rountree, Chief of the Selective Service Medical Division, said in 1943: "The greatest internal problem of the American people, after complete victory in World War II concerns the health of the American people, their physical and mental fitness for their present and postwar responsibilities."

How have we done since the end of World War II? The evidence is clear that the physical fitness of our school population is far from what it should be. Testing programs in our colleges and universities have revealed that a large percentage of entering freshmen were seriously deficient in various aspects of physical fitness. This, of course, reflects adversely upon the public school physical education programs. In 1957-1958 Hunsicker [5] made a national survey by testing 8,500 boys and girls in twenty-eight states with a seven battery physical fitness test. The sample was carefully drawn so as to represent a true cross section of our school children from ten through seventeen years of age. This testing program provided convincing evidence of the unfitness of American youth. In every aspect of physical fitness and at every age level the average performances were unbelievably low. Weakness in the arms and shoulder girdle and lack of endurance were the most glaring deficiencies.

[4] *Educational Lessons from Wartime Training*, Alonzo G. Grace, et al., copyright 1948, American Council on Education, Washington, D.C., used by permission, p. 66.

[5] Paul Hunsicker, "AAHPER Physical Fitness Test Battery," *Journal of Health, Physical Education, Recreation* (September, 1958), pp. 24-25.

Confirmatory evidence of the low level of physical fitness of our children and youth has become available by comparisons with children of other countries. In 1954 Kraus and Hirschland [6] using the Kraus-Weber test found that 56.6 percent of Eastern seaboard children failed one or more items on a six battery test of minimum physical fitness. Only 8.3 percent of Swiss, Austrian, and Italian children failed it. Kraus indicated that on the basis of performance on this test American children were almost twenty times weaker and five times less flexible than European children.

In a study of 8,000 Danish boys and girls Knuttgen [7] found that they possessed virtually twice the endurance as compared to our children when measured by the 600 yard run. Eighty-nine percent of the boys and 91 percent of the girls scored beyond the American means in the standing broad jump, which is a measure of leg power. In speed and agility 95 percent of the Danish girls and 90 percent of the Danish boys exceeded the American means. In overall physical fitness, the Danish girls were far superior to our girls and the Danish boys were substantially more fit than ours were.

Means [8] reports substantially the same results in a comparison between British and American pupils. In overall physical fitness for girls the British mean was the same as the American 73rd percentile. For British boys, the average on all the tests was at our 64th percentile. In speed and endurance, the British girls at ages ten, eleven, and twelve performed better than American boys.

Means [9] reported a comparison of performance of 20,000 Japanese children as compared to American pupils. Japanese children excelled American youth in almost every basic component of physical fitness—in many cases by alarming margins. Only in abdominal endurance were American children and youth superior. In tests of arm strength, speed, agility, leg power, and endurance Japanese children and youth showed to far better advantage.

In 1965 Hunsicker made another national survey of youth fitness similar to the one he made in 1957-1958. Using the same procedures and basically the same test batteries (in the girl's test the flexed arm hang was substituted for the modified pull-ups) 9,627 boys and girls from 110 schools were tested. In comparison to the 1957-1958 data marked improvement was shown. Statistically significant differences at the 5 per-

[6] Hans Kraus and Ruth Hirschland, "Minimum Muscular Fitness Tests in School Children," *Research Quarterly* (May, 1954), p. 178.

[7] Howard Knuttgen, "Comparison of Fitness of Danish and American School Children," *Research Quarterly* (May, 1962), pp. 190-196.

[8] Louis Means, "British Youth Take Fitness Test," *Journal of Health, Physical Education, Recreation* (January, 1961), p. 75.

[9] Louis Means, "Are Japanese Youth More Fit Than American Youth?" *Journal of Health, Physical Education, Recreation* (February, 1960), p. 61.

cent level were found for practically all the test items at all age levels for boys. The girls also showed statistically significant differences in most of the tests.

This gratifying upswing is attributed to a number of factors. Undoubtedly some of the improvement was due to the greater familiarity of students with the test battery. At the same time the national concern that has been aroused about the physical unfitness of children, youth, and adults has led to an increased awareness of parents, teachers, administrators, and medical personnel that physical education programs needed to be strengthened. This has led to increased time allotments, added supervisory and teaching personnel, and improved facilities. In addition, many physical educators have given increased emphasis to the physical development objective.

Despite this encouraging report by Hunsicker there is no reason to believe that the problem is solved. The gains that have been made represent only limited progress where large advances are necessary. The average performances of children and youth, while improved, are still low. In reference to the improved performance of American children as shown by Hunsicker's study the following comment by the President's Council on Physical Fitness [10] is very appropriate: "This is a good beginning, but it should not be mistaken for more than that. A physical fitness profile of the United States still reveals glaring gaps and weaknesses, and stubborn problems of programing implementation and improvement remains."

How successful has physical education been in accomplishing its other objectives? World War II revealed that school physical education programs have not been successful either in accomplishing the motor skill objective—particularly as related to recreational activities. Many inductees were found to have limited athletic skills. For example Larson [11] discovered that from 40 to 50 percent of inductees did not have a sufficient degree of skill in any sport to desire participation. Only 3 to 5 percent had participated in varsity athletics in secondary schools or colleges. Approximately 30 to 40 percent were unable to swim. Only a small percentage of servicemen were able to qualify as expert swimmers. The great majority had never participated in golf, tennis, badminton, handball, archery, and bowling prior to their entry into the armed forces.

Many colleges and universities administer physical fitness and skill tests to entering students. These testing programs, plus subsequent experience with these students, substantiate the disclosures during World War II that physical educators still have a long way to go in the achieve-

[10] President's Council on Physical Fitness, *A Report to the President* (Superintendent of Documents, U.S. Government Printing Office, Washington, D.C., 1965), p. 22.
[11] *Op. cit.,* p. 146.

ment of their objectives. The evidence from all sources lends support to Bookwalter's evaluation of secondary school physical education programs.

In summary, data from World War II and the intervening years have provided convincing evidence that our physical education programs have not made an impressive record in achieving at least two of its objectives, namely, the physical development and the motor skills objectives. Unquestionably, physical education programs have improved appreciably over the past several decades. Personnel are better prepared and facilities are generally better. However, the problem is that the need for physical education has become accentuated. Improvement in programs has not kept pace with the tremendous decrease in physical activity in our daily lives coupled with a growing culture of abundance, ease, and comfort. In other words, the need for physical education has developed more rapidly than has program improvement.

Causes of inadequate programs

Inadequate time allotment has been one of the factors which has made it difficult to accomplish the objectives of physical education. Although several states make a daily period mandatory in all elementary and secondary schools, most states do not begin to approach such a requirement. The minimum time allotment required in the various states is indicated on p. 111. In this connection, an extensive study by the United States Office of Education [12] showed that in the 1943-1944 school year only 50 percent of all boys in the eleventh and twelfth grades were provided with any organized instruction in physical education. This was an amazing revelation in the midst of World War II. That conditions have not improved in the postwar years is evident from the statement by Vice President Richard Nixon [13] at the Annapolis Conference on Fitness in 1956: "Less than 50 percent of our boys and girls in high school have physical education."

Another factor that has adversely affected physical education programs is inadequate facilities. Physical education activities, involving as they do vigorous activity, require considerable space, which is usually expensive. In addition, certain activities such as swimming, bowling, golf, handball, and tennis require specialized facilities, which are extremely costly. Because of the high expense of many physical education facilities, they are often not provided, and many worthwhile activities cannot be included in the program. Probably more than any other single factor, the limitations imposed by inadequate facilities restrict the type of program that might be offered.

12 U.S. Office of Education, *Education for Victory*, Vol. 3, No. 1 (July 3, 1944), p. 7.
13 *Journal of Health, Physical Education, Recreation* (September, 1956), p. 9.

A final reason for the existence of so many inferior programs lies in the fact that educationally sound methods of curriculum construction have not been applied in physical education. The physical educator usually builds his own program. The activities that he teaches will depend upon his training and philosophy. Whether the program is good or bad it is usually accepted. School administrators are usually alert to deficiencies in other aspects of the curriculum but have a lack of critical judgment in regard to physical education, which has led to the acceptance of very inadequate service programs. This opportunity for physical educators to construct their own programs has often been exploited. If it is desired to build up the varsity athletic teams, the entire program may be shaped toward this end with no consideration for educational outcomes. This has been a common practice. It is an unfortunate fact that too often the physical education program is organized and conducted for purposes other than the best interests of youth.

Technique of curriculum development

Until comparatively recently, the development of the physical education program involved only the director or supervisor of physical education. This individual was presumed to be the expert on curriculum building, and he planned the course of study which the various instructors were expected to follow. In many cases, particularly in large cities, the course of study was worked out in great detail with each day's lesson prescribed, even to the sequence in which the activities were to be presented and the number of minutes that were to be spent on each. The task of supervision involved comparing the course of study with what the teacher was doing to ascertain whether he was teaching the lesson in the prescribed manner.

For several reasons this approach to curriculum development proved unsatisfactory. In the first place, no sequence of meaningful experiences can be planned in absentia for any given group of pupils; to be meaningful these experiences must be planned with a full knowledge of the individuals in question. Not only do the students differ, but the facilities and equipment also vary from school to school. For this reason, teachers on the scene can frequently make more accurate judgments than can the administrator who is not familiar with the specific situation. Certainly, there is something to be gained by involving them in the process of curriculum revision. In the second place, teachers cannot conduct their activities intelligently unless they can perceive the purposes or objectives of the activities. The prescribed curriculum approach gave teachers no opportunity to discuss with the curriculum expert the results that they were expected to attain and the best procedures for accomplishing them. Finally, this approach soon robbed teaching of all its satisfactions and rewards. It was too mechanical and inflexible to provide opportunity for the teacher to use his initiative, to express himself, to explore, and to experiment. It ignored the very obvious fact that teachers are more enthusiastic and interested in teaching a program that they have helped to develop.

Curriculum construction and revision today is done on an entirely different basis in most schools. If one individual constitutes the department, he must do most of the planning himself. However, in larger departments all staff members participate in evaluating and revising the curriculum. In very large departments a curriculum committee works continuously on curricular matters and reports its recommendations to the entire physical education faculty. In all cases all staff members have ample opportunity to express their views in regard to the curriculum. Modern curriculum development programs are postulated upon the assumption that only as the teacher plays an active and intelligent role in the development of the course of study materials can the curriculum be effectively revised.

The principal may be invited to participate in the curriculum revision prorgam. If the school system has a curriculum specialist, he will invariably be invited to work with the physical education staff. In some schools carefully selected students are included on the committee. Finally, a board member or some prominent individual in the community who has special qualifications might also be invited to participate. In other words, all groups who have a stake in the physical education curriculum or who can contribute to the deliberations are asked to work on the committee.

Steps involved in curriculum construction

A vast amount of literature on curriculum construction and curriculum revision has become available in recent years. Definite procedures are recommended to be followed in developing a school curriculum or a course of study within the total curriculum. These steps usually involve:

1. Social philosophy. Any consideration of the nature and purposes of physical education must inevitably be based upon the social and educational philosophy of the time and place in which it operates. Physical educators frequently want to start the curriculum construction process with a consideration of the objectives of physical education and the selection of activities which will attain the objectives. However, prior considerations are involved. Since physical education is a part of the entire system of education, its philosophy and objectives must be consistent with the philosophy that prevails in education. Educational philosophy

in turn arises out of the social philosophy of the society in which it functions. Physical education does not exist in a vacuum. It obtains its direction and purpose from the society in which it exists and the educational system of which it is a part.

In America our social philosophy is based upon the belief that the total well-being of each person is a primary and controlling consideration. As Tead [14] expresses it: "It [that is, a democracy] involves the effort of people to live together in ways which assure that for the conduct of all phases of the common life they have necessarily to share, there is a responsibility assumed by all in behalf of all."

The basic tenets of a democracy include:

(a) Worth of the individual. Democracy holds that the individual and the society of which he is a part have common purposes, namely, bringing about through effective cooperation the highest and fullest development of each individual.

(b) Belief in the equality of opportunity for the optimum development of each individual's potentialities.

(c) Reciprocal individual and group responsibility for promoting common concerns.

(d) The free play of intelligence in the solution of common problems. In a democracy common problems are to be solved through the free play of intelligence rather than through force, appeal to authority, or uncritical acceptance of the value of any one group or individual.

2. Educational philosophy. The basic purpose of education during all periods of civilization, from the primitive to the present, has been and is to enable the individual to become a better citizen of the society in which he lives. No society would tolerate for long a school system whose purposes were not in harmony with the welfare of that society. An educational program is successful only when in all of its aspects it contributes to the purposes of the society in which it lives and has its being. Thus, in America the aim of education is to assist each individual to achieve his optimum development in meeting effectively the continuous demands of living in a democratic society and in a closely interdependent world.

Educational objectives implement educational philosophy. They are the steps that lead to the aim. The seven cardinal principles and the educational objectives of the Educational Policies Commission have been stated in Chapter 2.

3. Statement of objectives. Objectives express needs as seen by the person or persons who formulate them. Education—and therefore physi-

cal education—exists to meet the needs of children. These needs are of two types: individual and societal. Individual and societal needs blend in objectives toward which the school sights are set.

The objectives of physical education are of two types: the ultimate and the immediate. The ultimate objectives are the educational objectives expressed above, that is, the seven cardinal principles or the objectives of the Educational Policies Commission. The immediate objectives have been expressed in Chapter 2 (see p. 25).

4. The nature of children. Although the needs of children determine the direction of development for which the school shall strive, it is the nature of the child which determines what is appropriate for education at each stage of development. The best conceivable forms of adult behavior represent goals toward which the education of the child must proceed, but the steps necessary in moving toward these goals are dictated by the character of the child's interests, urges, and capacities. It is evident that a thorough understanding of the nature of the child is an essential prerequisite for the physical educator when he builds a program.

The characteristics of children are rarely given the consideration they merit by physical educators when they organize and develop their courses of study. Considerable physiological and psychological harm has been done by the selection of activities which were not suited to the capacities and interests of the students. Before any program of activities is provided, the demands of those activities on the one hand and the interests, desires, urges, strength, endurance, motor ability, and skills of the students on the other hand must be known. These are outlined for pupils of different grade levels throughout this chapter.

5. Selection of activities to attain objectives. This is the most difficult of all aspects of curriculum construction. The activities which are of greatest value in meeting the needs of children are obviously the ones that should be given priority. However, certain activities satisfy the needs of children better in one area than others. For example, some activities are outstanding from the standpoint of developing physical fitness but may be of little value from the recreational standpoint. Other activities may contribute appreciably to the recreational needs of students but have little value insofar as physical fitness is concerned. This poses a difficult problem to those who are developing the program.

To assist in the selection of activities various principles are indicated below (see p. 101).

6. Administrative provisions to implement program. Once the activities of the program are selected and an appropriate sequential arrangement worked out, various administrative provisions must be made to facilitate the program. Several sections of this volume are devoted to a description of the provisions.

7. Evaluation of the program. The program needs to be periodically evaluated to determine if it is accomplishing the intended results. If it is not, the proper corrective procedures should be employed. Chapter 16 includes a consideration of evaluative procedures.

Principles for selection of activities

In order to select from the many activities of child and adult life those more likely to attain the objectives of physical education, certain guiding principles will be set up. All of the activities of the program will not satisfy all of these criteria, but those that conform to the majority of them are of greatest value. The program based upon the following physiological, psychological, and sociological principles is a practical one, although lack of facilities and inadequate training of teachers may eliminate some of the activities. These practical considerations vary so widely that any modification of the program must be made locally.

PHYSIOLOGICAL PRINCIPLES

1. The physical education program should provide ample opportunities for a wide range of movements involving the large muscles.
2. The facts related to the growth and development of children should guide in curriculum construction.
3. Provision should be made in the program for the differences in physical capacities and abilities that are found among students.
4. The physical fitness needs of students must be met by the physical education program.

PSYCHOLOGICAL PRINCIPLES

5. The physical education program should consist predominantly of natural play activities.
6. The activities should be selected in the light of the psychological age characteristics of the child as well as the physiological.
7. Activities that are valuable in arousing and expressing emotions should be chosen.
8. In the selection of activities some provision should be made for progression.
9. In the selection and placement of activities sufficient time should be provided so that the skills may be learned reasonably well.
10. Activities that best meet the seasonal drives of the students should be selected.

SOCIOLOGICAL PRINCIPLES

11. The curriculum should be rich in activities adaptable to use in leisure time.
12. Activities should be selected for their possible contributions to the youth's training for citizenship in a democracy.
13. The curriculum should be suited to the ideals of the community as well as its needs.
14. Activities that are particularly rich in possibilities for individual character training are especially desirable.

Inasmuch as these principles form the basis upon which a successful program may be built, the following points concerning each should be noted:

1. The physical education program should provide ample opportunities for a wide range of movements involving the large muscles. Physical education is primarily concerned with big-muscle activities. The big muscles are those of the trunk, shoulders, hips, and neck and are used in running, jumping, throwing, striking, climbing, and pushing and pulling activities, and the small muscles are those of the face, throat, fingers, and toes. The small muscles are used in writing, drawing, typing, piano playing, and other like activities. In man's evolution, the big muscles are the older, fundamental muscles, and the small muscles are the newer accessory ones. Most of the values attributed to physical education arise from the fact that the activities are big-muscle activities. For example, the development of health has already been mentioned as a prominent objective of physical education. There is little development of health by the action of the smaller muscles because very little organic activity is involved. But when the big muscles of the body are used, they burn up more energy, which results in a greatly increased functional activity of the circulatory, respiratory, excretory, and heat-regulating mechanisms and, later, the digestive mechanism. It is this organic activity that develops organic power, vigor, vitality, resistance to fatigue, and health. The only known way to reach and develop the vital organs is through vigorous total body activities.

Moreover, the big-muscle activities contribute to the development of character. To quote from Hetherington: [15]

The worth of any activity for character discipline is determined primarily by the nature of the instincts and the emotions exercised. . . . The values of physical education in character training bulk large, because natural big-muscle activities are the outcroppings of the most fundamental instincts and emotions in human nature.

[15] C. W. Hetherington, *School Program in Physical Education* (New York, Harcourt, Brace & World, Inc., 1922), p. 27.

The character development values of activities involving the use of the smaller muscles are not nearly so great because such activities do not call into play the strongest instinctive tendencies.

2. The facts related to the growth and development of children should guide in curriculum construction. In order that the best educational results may be obtained, those activities that are best adapted to the strength, endurance, and coordination of each age group should be selected. From the standpoint of the readiness of the organism to assimilate physical education activities, there is a best time for each activity. There is also an optimum degree of exercise that is beneficial at the various stages of development. This principle is recognized somewhat by the modified playing regulations of junior and senior high school sports as compared with college regulations. But much more needs to be done in interscholastic athletics as well as in physical education classwork.

Growth and development take place according to a definite and continuous pattern that depends upon hereditary and environmental factors. Growth and development do not proceed evenly and do not occur in the same manner in both sexes. The appearance of new teeth, the slow development of the heart, the physiological changes brought on by adolescence, and sex differences are only a few of the factors that greatly affect the program of physical education. All of these factors will be discussed in more detail when the activities for each age group are selected.

3. Provision should be made in the program for the differences in physical capacities and abilities that are found among students. Special provision must be made in the physical education program for the great physical differences that exist among students. In order to avoid a program that would make excessive demands upon any individual, it is necessary to know what his physical capacities and abilities are. The medical examination will discover the physical defects that would handicap or prevent students from engaging in the regular program. For these students other activities must be provided. These activities must be within the capacities of each individual and selected with a view to remedying the defect, if possible.

There are also in every group, those who are appreciably below normal in coordination, speed, strength, agility, and balance. Rather than to permit such students to participate in the regular activities, a special program should be arranged to give special attention to their deficiencies. When these students have developed a suitable level of physical fitness, they should return to the regular program.

4. The physical fitness needs of students should be met by the physical education program. Automation, by drastically reducing the vigorous exercise involved in work of all types, has accentuated the importance of physical education's contribution to physical fitness. The physical

aspects of fitness of each individual should be periodically assessed, and proper activities to meet individual and group needs should be scheduled.

One aspect of physical fitness in which our youth is particularly lacking is strength of the arm and shoulder girdle. This deficiency is serious because it affects successful performance in so many different sports. Unfortunately, some of these sports are not, in and of themselves, particularly good developers of arm and shoulder girdle strength. For this reason, teachers must be alert to this situation, and if a need exists they should provide appropriate activities. Among the better activities to develop strength in the upper extremities are wrestling, apparatus and tumbling, rope climbing, weight training, and selected conditioning exercises.

5. The physical education program should consist predominantly of natural play activities. Natural play activities are those that are based essentially on racial activities organized and integrated into games and sports. These racial activities developed thousands of years ago in response to the situations that confronted primitive man. He had to run, jump, throw, strike, chase, flee, pounce upon, dodge, and climb to get food, provide goods, and preserve his life. From time immemorial man has performed these racial activities so that today there is a powerful inner drive in every individual to do these things. But the twentieth century offers few opportunities for their expression except perhaps through physical education activities. Football, basketball, baseball, in fact all of our popular sports, are popular largely because they are composed of natural racial activities. It might well be said that the most interesting activities are those that include most of these instinctive drives. Football is extremely popular because it satisfies so many racial urges, such as running, jumping, throwing, kicking, dodging, chasing, striking, and fleeing. On the other hand, calisthenics and marching have seldom been popular because they include very few of the racial activities. Expression through these natural play activities is inherently satisfying, for each individual is prepared in his nervous system to respond in the required way. The program, in order to utilize these inner drives to the fullest extent, should consist predominantly of play activities based on them.

6. The activities should be selected in the light of the psychological age characteristics of the child as well as the physiological. This is one of the most important factors to be considered in constructing a physical education program. There are rather clearly defined age stratifications in regard to play interests, and the content of the curriculum should be in harmony with them. As a general rule, boys of nine to twelve have developed different play interests from those they had at the six-to-nine-year level. College students usually have different play interests from

those in the junior high school. Most men and women can readily recall their own changing interests in their youth. These changes do not appear and disappear at exactly the same time for all children; nor do the latter all desire to express the same play interest in the same way. Individual differences do exist, but there is a striking similarity in the play interests that children manifest at various ages. The good curriculum will be guided by these natural tendencies that appear spontaneously at different ages.

The significance of this for the curriculum builder is that the program should contain a variety of activities from which each individual may select those that interest him most. Of course, the activities of the program must be in harmony with the age level of the group. The election of physical education activities should begin in the senior high school, which is the place where the election of academic activities begins. Such a wide variety of play activities is presented in the elementary school that election is hardly necessary. It is important that students should have exploratory experiences in a wide variety of activities before they are permitted to elect. Unless they are familiar with all the activities available the privilege of election will be almost meaningless.

7. Activities that are valuable in arousing and expressing emotions should be chosen. The development of the intellectual capacities has so engrossed educators that they have devoted little thought and attention to the emotions, which are the generative forces behind most conduct. Man's behavior has sprung from emotions and instinct for so many thousands of years that we cannot expect our conduct today to be based entirely upon intelligence. What is needed in our schools, as much as anything else, is provision for the education of the emotions.

Physical education occupies a strategic position among the school subjects for guiding and modifying the emotions. Latin, rhetoric, and mathematics neither arouse the emotions nor offer the opportunities for emotional expression that physical education activities do. Man craves sports and games that are dramatizations of situations that exercise the old racial instincts and emotions. If expression rather than repression were the rule, the mental health of our nation would present a much less serious problem. Emotional stability is only achieved through practice in controlling and modifying the feelings released. Physical education makes a most substantial contribution to education in providing a laboratory setting in which emotional control is practiced. In view of this fact, the curriculum of physical education should include those activities which are particularly valuable in arousing and offering an outlet for emotional expression. Body-contact activities, such as football, basketball, soccer, and wrestling, are very effective in this respect, because they exercise deeper, more powerful emotions than many of the noncontact activities. The contact sports are even of benefit to spectators, who experience them vicariously and give expression to their aroused emotions by cheering.

8. In the selection of activities some provision should be made for progression. The physical education program should show progression from the kindergarten or first grade through the twelfth grade. This requires that the elementary and junior and senior high school physical education programs be carefully integrated. Unfortunately, in many instances, the programs at these different school levels are completely unrelated. This results in overlapping and duplication in certain areas and in complete neglect in others. A program that is well integrated will accomplish significantly more results than one that is not.

Every school system should determine what qualities, skills, and attitudes it desires its high school graduates to possess as a result of their experiences in physical education. These qualities, skills, and attitudes thus become the objectives of the entire school system, and the program at the various grade levels should be developed to accomplish these objectives. All of the activities of the elementary and junior high school should be planned with reference to the senior high school program. (See p. 138 for the attributes of the physically educated high school graduate.)

9. In the selection and placement of activities sufficient time should be provided so that the skills may be learned reasonably well. Far better results will be secured from a physical education program that provides a few activities to be learned well than from one that offers many activities that are learned only partially. Everyone enjoys doing that which he can do well. There is far more value in acquiring a fair degree of skill in several sports than in becoming a jack of all sports and a master of none.

Under this principle, more time will be provided for the more difficult skills. The backward handspring is a more complex skill than the forward roll, and the "full gainer" is more difficult to perform than a "front header" dive. Similarly, the fundamentals of softball are much less difficult to master than those of hard baseball. If a skill is worth acquiring, it should be well acquired. This does not necessarily mean that every skill must be thoroughly mastered by every student in the class. It suggests, rather, that sufficient time be allowed in order to enable the average student to perform the activity with a fair degree of skill.

10. Activities that best meet the seasonal drives of the students should be selected. Students have a readiness for seasonal activities. When professional, college, and high school teams are playing football, students have a desire for this sport. When the football season is over, they anticipate basketball and other indoor activities. The spring of the year is time for baseball, track and field, golf, and tennis. There is far more

readiness for indoor activities in disagreeable weather than on warm, sunny days.

11. The curriculum should be rich in activities adaptable to use in leisure time.

The new and growing leisure represents one of America's greatest social problems because of its extent and almost universal possession; because it may be said that his sense of time is the measure of man; because misuse of this gift can destroy health, reduce efficiency, break character and degrade life while wise use can enhance health, increase efficiency, elevate character, and enrich and glorify life. Civilization itself can be advanced or destroyed according to the use of it by people as a whole.[16]

The solution to this great social problem that leisure presents lies with education. Our schools have been slow to realize their responsibilities in this respect, but since the advent of the depression in 1929, more and more attention has been devoted to the activities with which people occupy their leisure time. This concern is not solely with the leisure-time activities of adults, for children of all ages have been emancipated from many of the chores and duties that diminished their available leisure time.

The increased emphasis on avocational activities in the schools is of considerable significance to physical education. Americans, young and old, spend countless leisure hours either playing or watching sports and games. Preparation for all these leisure hours spent in the realm of sports is one of the major objectives of the program of physical education. The practice of postponing until adulthood the education in golf, tennis, handball, volleyball, swimming, squash rackets, and other big-muscle play activities of adults has always failed and will continue to fail to produce satisfactory results. The vast number of college graduates who have very little or no skill in these sports, and will never develop any, is ample evidence of the weakness of the physical education program of the past. Moreover, in order to produce the most favorable educational results, some preparation for the leisure activities of the child should be provided throughout his school life. It would be a mistake to select the activities entirely on the basis of adult needs. One of the outstanding criticisms directed against education today is that the activities are too far removed from the student's present needs and interests and, therefore, are not significant to him. Although it is doubtful that this criticism would be true for play activities to the extent that it is true of academic activities, nevertheless the program of physical education should be adaptable for use in both present and future leisure time.

12. Activities should be selected for their possible contribution to the youth's training for citizenship in a democracy. One of the most fundamental objectives of our educational system is the development

---

[16] Eugene T. Lies, "The New Leisure Challenges the School," *Journal of Health, Physical Education, Recreation* (November, 1934), p. 18.

of the civic and social virtues desired in a democratic society. These virtues are best developed by practicing them in natural situations. This is possible in physical education activities. Team sports under capable leadership can develop cooperation, loyalty, leadership, followership, sportsmanship, respect for the rights of others, and other qualities essential in the citizens of a democracy. In athletics, the dominating drive to win stimulates the development of these qualities, for youth soon finds out that they are necessary for success. Furthermore, provincialism, which is contrary to democratic principles, is reduced by team sports. Regardless of the diverse nationalities that may be represented in a team, the players are teammates, and all barriers between them cease to exist as they cooperate for a common purpose. In team competitions, the only measure of a man is what he does as a member of the team—his race, creed, wealth, and class are all forgotten. No better training for citizenship in a democracy is available anywhere in the school system.

13. The curriculum should be suited to the ideals of the community as well as its needs. What may be a perfect physical education program in one community might prove to be an utter failure in another. Social dancing is a physical education activity that is readily accepted in certain schools, but which in others would not be tolerated by the community. Boxing and wrestling are extremely popular activities in some communities, but in others they are taboo because of the stigma attached to professional boxing and wrestling. Communities with a large foreign population often prefer soccer to all other activities. Although these foreign communities may prefer their native games, these are not their greatest need in this country. The program of physical education should seek to acquaint the newcomers gradually with American games and sports and American ideals of sportsmanship. Thus, the ideals of the community are powerful factors to be considered in the selection of the content of the program. Likewise, the needs of the community must be reckoned with. In the northern states winter outdoor activities can hold a prominent position on the program, but they may be utterly out of place in the south.

When the physical educator finds himself in a community that is hostile to certain valuable activities, he should hold them in abeyance until public opinion has become favorable to them. Nothing is gained by attempting to force a physical education program that is unacceptable. The best procedure is to change gradually the attitude of the students and public in favor of the new activities.

14. Activities that are particularly rich in possibilities for individual character training are especially desirable. The development of character as an objective of physical education has already been discussed. Because physical education activities exercise the most fundamental emotions and instinctive tendencies, they are powerful factors in

developing good character. The skilled teacher, by his teaching, by his suggestions, and by his own example, will utilize the possibilities inherent in sports and games for developing desirable traits of character that will operate in these activities and may even carry over into other life situations.

Considering the great importance of character development and the splendid opportunities that play activities present for developing it, those activities that are of greatest value in this respect should be included in the program. Certainly, football and basketball offer far more opportunities for character education than horseshoe pitching or badminton does. As was pointed out before, the "worth of any activity for character discipline is determined primarily by the nature of the instincts and emotions aroused." [17]

Most forms of athletic competition, particularly contact sports such as football and basketball and combat activities such as wrestling, are of greatest value for character training because they exercise the deep fighting, attacking, fleeing, and egotistic emotions. Football, basketball, soccer, speedball, baseball, water polo, and wrestling all present wonderful opportunities for character development. Whether or not character is developed in these physical education activities and is transferred to other activities depends upon the leadership.

How sex differences affect the program

The differences between the sexes are so important that they deserve special consideration even though they have been provided for by the principles set up for the selection of activities. These differences are anatomical, physiological, and psychological; and in order that the program may best serve its purpose they must be carefully considered. The differences are not sufficiently pronounced until the beginning of the fourth grade to warrant the separation of the sexes in play activities. After that, girls cannot compete equally with boys in running activities. The assumption has been that the pelvis of the girl becomes wider, and this causes a greater obliquity of her thigh bones which handicaps her running ability. A recent investigation at the University of Iowa reveals, however, that the pelvis of the girl is not particularly wider than that of the boy. Lack of practice and less marked arm and upper-body strength are probably important modifying factors. In addition to this disadvantage the girl is not as strong as the boy; nor does she have the endurance that he has. She is particularly underdeveloped in her upper body. This is demonstrated by the fact that the width of her knee approaches that of the boy much closer than does the width of her elbow.

[17] Hetherington, *op. cit.*

The measurements of her lower extremities compare much more favorably with those of the boy than do those of her upper extremities. Baldwin [18] made a comparison of the strength of the right and the left arm and the upper back of boys and girls from seven through seventeen years of age, and he found that the girls were inferior at every age. Her smaller heart, chest measurements, and lung capacity naturally do not permit the girl to have the endurance that the boy possesses.

These handicaps of strength, endurance, and speed are not the only factors that make the separation of the sexes desirable. The menstrual period of girls, which frequently commences in the elementary school, presents a problem that is best handled by the separation of boys and girls. Most medical men agree that moderate exercise is desirable during these periods; consequently, there are many girls who partake in a modified amount of activity if they partake in any at all at these times. Puberty also brings various psychological differences between the sexes which make separate programs desirable. Boys and girls show greater differences in play activities from eight and a half to ten and a half years than at any other period. Girls become greatly interested in social dancing, an interest that is not shared by boys to a marked degree for a number of years. Boys are interested in personal combat activities, in which girls are seldom interested. Boys develop a keen competitive spirit in their games and play hard and aggressively to win. Girls do not demonstrate these traits in their activities because, from the present viewpoint of society, they are undesirable for them. However, both sexes have a common interest in many activities. There is not so much difference in the kind of activity as in the manner in which the activities are engaged in by the two sexes.

Because of these differences it is desirable to separate the sexes in their play activities beginning with the fourth grade. But by the time they reach senior high school and college, they are becoming more interested in the same activities and tend to play together much more. In some junior and senior high schools boys and girls are brought together in certain of the milder physical education activities. The valuable social lessons justify much more coeducational physical education than our schools have heretofore provided.

The high school and college girl needs physical education activities, and it is fortunate that she is not bound by the social taboos that fifty and more years ago restrained her predecessors from engaging in vigorous sports and games. Her greatly increased interest and participation in sport activities have made her far superior in physical skills to

18 Bird T. Baldwin, *The Physical Growth of Children from Birth to Maturity*, State University of Iowa Studies in Child Welfare, Vol. 1, No. 1 (Iowa City, State University of Iowa), p. 94.

girls of fifty years ago. That such traits as sportsmanship, loyalty, co-operation, and emotional control have been underdeveloped in the girl and are not foreign to her nature is shown by the big improvement in these qualities since the girl has had the chance to engage in big-muscle play activities, particularly play competitions. As the woman is entering more and more into the social, political, and economic life of the world, she needs the opportunities for developing these desirable social characteristics that the false social standards of the past kept her from doing.

Time allotment

The matter of time allotment is of great importance because no program of activities can operate successfully unless a proper amount of time is allotted to it. Unfortunately, the time required by most state physical education laws is totally inadequate for a well-balanced program. The minimum requirement for the different states, based on a careful survey for the school year 1965-1966, is shown in Table 4-1.

The amount of time which should be devoted to physical education in the various grades depends upon the needs of children for physical activity. Under the present circumstances the meager time allotted to physical education is best utilized by devoting it predominantly to instructional purposes, with the hope that there will be sufficient carryover in the leisure-time activities of children to satisfy their needs for big-muscle activity. Physical education leaders believe that approximately an hour a day would be a desirable allotment of time, but few schools ever realize this ideal. Several states require a daily program, but the large majority require only two or three periods per week.

What portion of the allotted time should be devoted to each of the activities in the program must also be carefully considered. The program should be systematically organized and graded in order that the limited time may be used to the best advantage. The practice of devoting the bulk of the time year after year to the same activities is indefensible and reflects an outworn philosophy of physical education. Even the best activity becomes relatively less valuable after several years of regular exposure to it. To offer basketball for three years in the senior high school physical education program to the exclusion of other important activities is as unjustifiable as to offer the same students the identical course in ancient history for three years. Of course, the more important and complicated activities require greater time than some of the simpler, less important ones. The first appearance of an activity in the program should call for instruction in the fundamentals; later appearances of the same activity call for instruction in the more complicated skills and strategic maneuvers.

Table 4-1. Required time allotment for physical education.

State	Elementary School	Secondary School
Alabama	Not Specified*	1 Period Every Other Day
Alaska	K-1-2-3—50-100 Minutes Weekly; 4-5-6—75-150 Minutes Weekly; 7-8—100 Minutes Weekly	1 Year of Daily Attendance
Arizona	Grades 1-3—10% of School Day; Grades 4-8—14% of School Day	Not Specified*
Arkansas	120 Minutes Weekly	80 Minutes Weekly
California	20 Minutes Daily	1 Period Daily
Colorado	Not Required	Not Required
Connecticut	Not Required	Not Required
Delaware	150 Minutes Weekly	2 Periods Weekly
Florida	30 Minutes Daily	3 Periods Weekly in Grades 7 and 8; 2 Units Required in Grades 10-12
Georgia	30 Minutes Daily	30 Minutes Daily in Grades 7 and 8
Hawaii	90 Minutes per Week	90 Periods or ½ Unit† per Year for Each Year
Idaho	Not Specified*	90 Periods or ½ Unit† for 1 Year Only
Illinois	A Daily Period	A Daily Period
Indiana	75 Minutes Weekly	120 Minutes Weekly
Iowa	50 Minutes Weekly	50 Minutes Weekly
Kansas	Not Required	1 Unit† Required within Grades 9-12
Kentucky	120 Minutes Weekly	A Period Every Other Day
Louisiana	120 Minutes Weekly	120 Minutes Weekly
Maine	2 Periods Weekly	2 Periods Weekly Except in Grade 12
Maryland	135 Minutes Weekly	180 Minutes Weekly
Massachusetts	Not Specified*	Not Specified*
Michigan	Not Specified*	Not Specified*
Minnesota	Grades 1 and 2—Daily 25-Minute Period; Grades 3-6—Daily 30-Minute Period	2 55-Minute Periods per Week in Grades 7-10
Mississippi	Not Required	Not Required
Missouri	90 Minutes Weekly	2 Periods Weekly
Montana	Not Specified*	1 Unit† of Health and Physical Education Required for Graduation
Nebraska	Not Required	2 55-Minute Periods Weekly
Nevada	Not Required	3 Years Required Either on a Daily Basis or on Alternate Days
New Hampshire	Not Specified*	Not Specified*
New Jersey	150 Minutes Weekly	150 Minutes Weekly

Table 4-1. (cont'd).

State	Elementary School	Secondary School
New Mexico	30 Minutes Daily	1 Unit† of Physical Education Required for Graduation
New York	120 Minutes Weekly	300 Minutes Weekly
North Carolina	150 Minutes Weekly	A Daily Period in Grade 9
North Dakota	30 Minutes Daily	80 Minutes Weekly
Ohio	90 Minutes Weekly	1 Unit† of Health Education and Physical Education Required for Graduation
Oklahoma	Not Required	1 Year with 5 Periods Weekly Required in Junior High School
Oregon	Regular Class Period Daily	Daily Period through Grade 10; 25% of Time Must be Devoted to Health Education
Pennsylvania	120 Minutes Weekly	2 Periods Weekly
Rhode Island	100 Minutes Weekly	100 Minutes Weekly
South Dakota	Required 2 Periods Weekly in Grades 7 and 8	Required 2 Periods Weekly for 2 Years from Grades 9-12
South Carolina	Daily 15-20 Minute Period	1 Unit† of Physical Education Required for Graduation
Tennessee	Not Specified*	2 Periods Weekly
Texas	150 Minutes Weekly	120 Minutes Weekly
Utah	Grades 1-6 Not Specified;* 90 Periods Yearly in Grades 7, 8, and 9	1 Unit† of Physical Education Required for Graduation
Vermont	Not Specified*	1 Unit† of Physical Education Required for Graduation
Virginia	30 Minutes Daily from Grades 1-7	2½ years Required for Graduation; Periods Per Week Not Specified
Washington	20 Minutes Daily	90 Minutes Weekly‡
West Virginia	150 Minutes Weekly	2 Periods Weekly
Wisconsin	150 Minutes Weekly	3 Periods Weekly
Wyoming	Not Required	Not Required

*Physical education is required but the time per week is not specified.
†A unit is equivalent to a daily program for one year. This amounts to a total of 180 periods. This time allotment may be spread over more than one year.
‡Unless excused upon a written request of parents or guardians.

Source: W. Earl Armstrong and T. M. Stinnett, *A Manual on Certification Requirements for School Personnel in the United States* (Washington, D.C., National Education Association, 1964), p. 40.

THE ELEMENTARY SCHOOL PROGRAM

In addition to the general objectives of education each division of the school has a purpose that is peculiar to itself. The unique function of the elementary school is to provide preparation for the child in the tools of education or, as expressed in the seven cardinal principles, "command of the fundamental processes." It is the place where the child acquires the basic knowledge, skills, habits, and the ideals of thought, feeling, and action that are essential for everyone, regardless of sex, occupation, or social status.

Importance of physical education in the elementary schools

Unquestionably, the weakest aspect of physical education is the program in the elementary schools. This six-year period is likewise more important than any other similar span of time because this is when a strong foundation for physical and motor fitness must be established. The basis must be laid for the development of such factors as strength, endurance, agility, coordination, balance, flexibility, power, and skill in a wide variety of motor activities. In fact, if the proper beginnings are not made during this period, adequate adjustment may be impossible at a later date. Unquestionably, the elementary school years represent "the golden years" from the standpoint of developing the physical and motor potentialities of our people.

The accumulation of evidence concerning the alarming lack of physical fitness of the American people and the consequent results upon their effectiveness, health, and well-being has given rise to much speculation about what must be done to solve the problem. Many proposals have been made and it is almost unanimously agreed that the *single most important consideration is the improvement of the elementary school physical education programs.* The facts are that the manner in which physical education is conducted in most of our elementary schools does not even begin to approach adequacy.

Time allotment for physical education in elementary schools. The two most vulnerable aspects of elementary physical education are time allotment and leadership. Concerning time allotment, a daily period of thirty minutes is the standard recommended by the American Association for Health, Physical Education, and Recreation, as well as by many other professional organizations. In Schneider's survey [19] of 523 school systems she found that only about one-fourth of these schools had such a time allotment. The number and percentage of school systems offering a daily physical education period of at least thirty minutes are shown in Table 4-2.

Even though only about 25 percent of the elementary schools now meet the recommended time allotment, the contention is made here that this amount is inadequate. The changed conditions of living call

[19] Elsa Schneider, *Physical Education in Urban Elementary Schools,* Bulletin 1959, No. 15 (U.S. Office of Education, Department of Health, Education, and Welfare, Washington, D.C.).

Table 4-2.

Grade	Number	Percent
1	114	22
2	120	23
3	122	23
4	145	28
5	151	29
6	145	28

Source: Elsa Schneider, *Physical Education in Urban Elementary Schools*, Bulletin 1959, No. 15 (U.S. Office of Education, Department of Health, Education and Welfare, Washington, D.C.).

for an appreciably greater amount of time to be devoted to physical education from the first through the sixth grades than has been traditionally scheduled. The fifteen to thirty minutes per day may have been enough in the past but this amount does not suffice in our highly mechanized, automated existence. The amount of physical activity which the boy and girl from six to twelve partakes in outside of school does not remotely compare to that which children fifty and even twenty-five years ago had. The work activities and chores that formerly provided the vitally needed physical development have been virtually eliminated.

These changed living circumstances greatly accentuate the importance of physical education in our schools. We must now rely almost solely on our school physical education programs to provide the physical activity that is essential to the well-being of our children. However, if physical education is to compensate for the effects of automation and technology and particularly the automobile and television, it must be at its best. More time and attention must be devoted to it. Elementary school physical education is incapable of meeting its greatly increased responsibilities with the traditional allocation of time. No less than sixty minutes per day from first grade through sixth grade is necessary.

Leadership for physical education in elementary schools. With respect to leadership for physical education in the elementary schools, Schneider's survey, given in Table 4-3, shows that classroom teachers are still used in the majority of schools.

Classroom teachers are rarely capable of handling elementary school physical education classes in an acceptable manner. They have a very superficial professional preparation for such an assignment if they have any at all. Further, many of them are not interested in assuming the responsibility for this program. A major reason for their attitude is that they do not feel properly qualified for such teaching. Certainly, they cannot begin to approach the performance of a professionally prepared

Table 4-3.

	Grades 1-3	Grades 4-6
Physical education taught by classroom teachers without help from a consultant or specialist	26%	16%
Physical education taught by classroom teachers with help from a consultant or specialist	62	54
Physical education taught by a special physical education instructor	12	29

Source: Elsa Schneider, *Physical Education in Urban Elementary Schools*, Bulletin 1959, No. 15 (U.S. Office of Education, Department of Health, Education and Welfare, Washington, D.C.).

teacher. Rodgers [20] found that the special teacher did a significantly better job of teaching the skills of soccer, volleyball, and softball than classroom teachers.

The time has arrived when a truly professional performance is necessary in the physical education program of the elementary schools. When life outside of school was meeting some of the exercise needs of children, the quality of leadership was not as crucial as it is today. We can no longer afford the myth that a nonprofessionally prepared teacher can do a professional job. Physical education has now become so important in our schools, it is so significantly related to the health, adjustment, happiness, and attitudes of children that it can no longer be relegated to untrained leaders.

It is an interesting fact that in most of the countries that have long-standing, well-established educational systems specialists are used for the physical education program in the elementary schools. For example, in most of the European countries it is considered so essential to get elementary school children started properly that specialists teach the physical education classes. The attitude prevails that physical education in the elementary schools is much more important than it is in the secondary schools and should be given priority.

The core of the elementary school physical education program

Nixon and Jewett [21] describe what they regard as the core of the physical education program in the elementary schools:

[20] Elizabeth Rodgers, *An Experimental Investigation of the Teaching of Team Games* (New York, Teachers College, Columbia University, 1936).

[21] John E. Nixon and Ann E. Jewett, *Physical Education Curriculum*, copyright © 1964, The Ronald Press Company, New York, p. 110.

The authors maintain that the core of the physical education curriculum in the elementary school should become movement exploration, leading to the development of flexibility, strength, endurance, and rhythmic accuracy. As a part of carefully planned experience in movement exploration, every child should receive expert instruction and ample guided practice in developing efficient movement patterns for all those basic activities that are characteristically human —walking, running, throwing, and the like. His physical education classes should make extensive use of games and gamelike activities; but the selection of content should be determined by his need to extend the movement possibilities of his own body, and to learn specific movement patterns repeatedly demanded by common human activities, rather than by a concept of learning games.

THE PHYSICAL EDUCATION PROGRAM
IN THE PRIMARY GRADES

Characteristics of primary grade children

Before the activities for the physical education program in the primary grades are selected it is necessary to know the nature of the child physically, psychologically, and socially. The child is usually five or six years of age when he starts in the elementary school. His preschool years have been spent mainly in getting control of the fundamental movements of his body and in familiarizing himself with his environment. His chief characteristics are:

PHYSICAL CHARACTERISTICS
(Ages 6-8)

1. Stature: in the period of slow but steady increase.
2. Weight: in the period of steady growth.
3. Health: susceptibility to disease is somewhat higher than it was before the child started school. The child does not have many antibodies in his blood when he enters school because he has not come into daily contact with large groups of other children. Furthermore, the appearance of permanent teeth may have the effect of lowering resistance somewhat.
4. Pulse rate: higher than in adults.
5. Blood pressure: lower than in adults.
6. Red blood cells: fewer in number; 4,000,000 per cc. of blood is normal for children of this age group, and 4,500,000 to 5,000,000 per cc. is normal for adults.
7. Oxygen debt: the child can accumulate less oxygen debt than adults.

8. Hemoglobin: 85 percent is normal for adults, and 70 percent is normal for children of this age group.

9. Heart: smallest in comparison to body size of any age. The heart at the age of seven is one-third adult size, but it must supply a body that is nearly one-half adult size.

10. Endurance: poor, as would be expected from the red blood cell count, small heart, and hemoglobin content of blood.

11. Strength: not well developed at this period. Arm and shoulder girdle strength are particularly lacking.

12. Eyes: not sufficiently developed to focus on fast-moving, small objects.

13. Coordination: child is just getting control of gross movements; not much skill in fine movements yet; kinesthetic control improving.

14. Skeleton: bones are soft and easily deformed. Postural emphasis is needed in these grades because it is difficult to remedy poor posture after the ossification of bones has occurred.

15. Reaction time: not well developed.

Much data are available to show that children of elementary school ages today are taller, heavier, and more mature than their counterparts of several decades ago. Hale [22] reports:

Since 1880, a period of only 75 years, the average 14-year-old boy has gained five inches in height and 24 pounds in weight. In weight alone this represents a 25 per cent increase. In the same period, the average 10-year-old girl has gained four inches in height and 14 pounds in weight. In the last 25 years, the average 12-year-old boy and girl has gained three inches in height and 15 pounds in weight, and the average 14-year-old boy of today has grown to the size of the 16-year-old.

The accelerated rate of maturation of children is due to advances in medicine, nutrition, and control of our environment. Antibiotics and vaccines have eliminated or lessened many childhood diseases. The vitamin-fortified and balanced diets that are now within the financial means of most families provide for more optimum growth.

PSYCHOLOGICAL CHARACTERISTICS

1. Imitation is strongest characteristic.
2. The child has hunger and drive for exercise and activity.
3. Short interest span. The child needs a considerable number and variety of activities rather than a few.
4. The child is egocentric. He is not interested in team games.
5. Curiosity is a strong characteristic.

[22] Creighton Hale, "Changing Growth Patterns of the American Child," *Education* (April, 1958), p. 467.

6. The child is very assertive.
7. Interest in activity is for its own sake rather than any future outcome of it. The child does not like to drill on a skill.
8. The child does not demonstrate leadership qualities.
9. Interest is chiefly in large-muscle rather than small-muscle activity.
10. Approval of adults is more important than that of peers.
11. Sex differences are insignificant.
12. Interest is great in stories, rhythms, swimming, chasing, being chased, hiding and finding, and hunting games.

Implications for the physical education program in the primary grades

The physical capacities of the child in the first and second grades develop slowly and steadily. Coordination gradually improves, and by the time the child is in the third grade he may have developed surprising skill in various motor activities. After a great deal of research Cureton [23] has shown that elementary school children are capable of far greater physical and skill development than has been supposed. Their potentialities as well as their interests have been seriously underestimated.

All children need much participation in various play activities, both in school and out, to develop their potentialities adequately. Exploration of movement should be a major emphasis in the primary grades. This is the only way that the child can learn the movements of which the body is capable.

Long-continued strenuous activity is not desirable for children of the early elementary grades. These children are exceedingly active and crave physical activity, but they need frequent changes in type of activity as well as occasional rest periods.

Rhythmic activities deserve a prominent place in the physical education program for the primary grades. Not only do children enjoy these activities but they are unusually well adapted to their needs. From them children acquire skill in fundamental body movements that are basic to future skill performance. They learn to appreciate music and to express their ideas and feelings through movement. Coordination, balance, graceful movement, and a sense of rhythm are also acquired from rhythmic activities.

The fundamentals of various sports and games of low organization involving sport skills can be introduced in the latter part of the second and in the third grades. Years ago, sports were usually reserved until the

[23] Thomas Cureton, *Improving the Physical Fitness of Youth,* Monographs of the Society for Research in Child Development, Vol. 29, No. 4 (Yellow Springs, Ohio, The Antioch Press, 1964, Serial No. 95, 1964).

upper elementary grades or the junior high school period. However, in their out-of-school play young children exhibited an interest and ability in various popular sports. This practice was accentuated by the radio and particularly the television. The child could not help developing a strong interest in the traditional sports at a very early age. All of these factors have encouraged the inclusion of sports activities and elements earlier and earlier in the elementary grades. This does not imply that children of these ages should be taught the highly organized sports like baseball and basketball. It does mean that boys and girls in the primary grades have a readiness and ability to participate in activities that involve the elements of these sports.

Children in the first and second grades are not interested in practice drills for the purpose of improving their skills. However, by the third grade they are ready to practice for skill development if the periods are not very long.

The ball plays a very important role in the sports and recreation of the American people. Success in many sports is dependent upon the possession of ball-handling skills. Such skill development can be started as early as the first grade. Balls of varying sizes are available for children of these ages.

In the first grade, story plays and mimetics have great appeal because of the strong imitative and dramatic characteristics of young children. This interest drops off rapidly, however, so that by the third grade further inclusion of these activities in the program is hardly justified. In addition, various games of low organization which involve imitations of familiar objects are also very popular.

In the first and second grades boys and girls are not ready for team activities. However, by the third grade they can engage in group play where teamwork is not heavily involved.

No specific time allotment is recommended for relays. Beginning in the third grade relays can be a valuable activity if they are used properly. Ordinarily, relays would not be used for an entire period or even a major part of a period. One or two carefully selected relays can provide a change of pace which is very popular with students. Excellent physiological benefits can come from relays. In addition, students can gain practice in some of the skills that are being currently emphasized in the program.

Swimming can be very successfully carried on in the primary grades. In schools with adequate facilities this activity should be included. However, so few schools have facilities or access to facilities that this activity cannot be considered for the ordinary elementary school program.

In the program of activities suggested in Table 4-4 the total allotted time is divided among the general types of activity rather than among

Table 4-4. Program for girls and boys, grades 1-3.

RECOMMENDED TIME ALLOTMENTS

	Grade 1	Grade 2	Grade 3
1. Rhythms (Including Movement Exploration, Fundamental Rhythms, Singing Games, Story Plays, Folk Dances)	50%	40%	30%
2. Stunts, Tumbling, and Self-Testing Activities	15	15	20
3. Games of Low Organization	25	25	30
4. Basic Skills and Lead-Up Games	10	20	20

RECOMMENDED ACTIVITIES

Grade 1	Grade 2	Grade 3
1. Rhythms	1. Rhythms	1. Rhythms

(a) Movement Exploration:
  Movement in Stationary Position
  Locomotion Exploration
	(a) Movement Exploration:
	  Exploring Locomotion
	  Moving to Music
		(a) Fundamental Rhythms:
		  Sliding
		  Running
		  Hopping
		  Skipping
		  Galloping
		  Marching
		  Jumping
		  Trotting

(b) Fundamental Rhythms:
  Walking
  Running
  Hopping
  Jumping
  Skipping
  Sliding
  Galloping
	(b) Fundamental Rhythms:
	  Walking
	  Running
	  Hopping
	  Skipping
	  Galloping
	  Marching
	  Jumping
	  Trotting
		(b) Singing Games:
		  Carousel
		  Looby Lou
		  Thread Follows the Needle
		  Jolly is the Miller
		  A-Hunting We Will Go

(c) Singing Games:
  A-Hunting We Will Go
  Muffin Man
  London Bridge
  Did You Ever See a Lassie?
  How Do You Do My Partner?
	(c) Singing Games:
	  Oats, Peas, Beans and Barley
	  Hippity Hop to the Barber Shop
	  Very, Very Tall
	  Pop Goes the Weasel
	  Pussy Cat
		(c) Folk Dances:
		  Tantoli
		  Ace of Diamonds
		  Bridge of Avignon
		  Old Dan Tucker
		  Hansel and Gretel

(d) Folk Dances:
  Shoemaker's Dance
  Danish Dance of Greeting
  Chimes of Dunkirk
  Turn Around Me
	(d) Folk Dances:
	  The Crested Hen
	  Bleking
	  Children's Polka
	  Seven Jumps
	  Shoemaker's Dance
	(e) Story Plays:
		2. Stunts, Tumbling, and Self-Testing Activities
		  Foot Clap
		  Knee Dip
		  Forward and Backward Rolls

Table 4-4. (cont'd).

Grade 1	Grade 2	Grade 3
I See You	Modes of Travel	Elbow Balance
(e) Story Plays:	Indians	Beam Walking
Circus	George Washington	Situps
Firemen	Going to the Store	Pullups
May Queen	The Eskimo	Pushups
Brownies	2. *Stunts, Tumbling, and*	Squat Vault
2. *Stunts, Tumbling, and*	*Self-Testing Activities*	Bar Snap
Self-Testing Activities	Forward Roll	Hand Walk (on
Bear Walk	Backward Roll	Parallel Bars)
Blind Balance	Beam Walking	3. *Games of Low Orga-*
Forward Roll	Wheelbarrow	*nization*
Stoop and Stand	Rocking Chair	Three Deep
Duck Waddle	Rope Skipping	Black Tom
Measuring Worm	Skin the Cat	Bull in the Ring
Lame Dog	Seal Walk	Soccer Dodge Ball
Camel Walk	Crab Walk	Circle Dodge Ball
Elephant Stand	Follow the Leader	Signal Chase
Rope Climbing	Rope Climbing	4. *Basic Skills and Lead-*
Log Rolling	3. *Games of Low Orga-*	*Up Games*
Rope Skipping	*nization*	(a) Basic Skills:
3. *Games of Low Orga-*	Midnight	Ball Throw for
nization	Dodge Ball	Distance
Cat and Rat	Cheese It	Ball Throw for
Fox and Geese	Spider and Flies	Accuracy
Crows and Cranes	Poison Tag	Soccer Kick for
Black Tom	Center Base	Distance
Old Mother Witch	4. *Basic Skills and Lead-*	Running Broad
Follow the Leader	*Up Games*	Jump
Caged Tiger	(a) Basic Skills:	(b) Lead-Up Games:
4. *Basic Skills and Lead-*	Ball Skills	Keep It Up
Up Games	Throwing, Catching,	Kick Ball
(a) Basic Skills:	Bouncing, Rolling	Boundary Ball
Throwing and	Travel Ladder	Corner Ball
Catching Large	Standing Broad Jump	
Ball	(b) Lead-Up Games:	
Standing Broad Jump	Dodge Ball	
Balancing on Line	Distance Throws	
Kicking and Striking		
Rolling Ball		
(b) Lead-Up Games:		
Call Ball		
Ball Toss		
Target Ball		
Catch Ball		

the specific activities. This is done to permit greater flexibility of the program. The specific activities suggested under each general type of activity are merely illustrative of the kind that should be offered.

THE PHYSICAL EDUCATION PROGRAM
IN THE INTERMEDIATE GRADES

Importance of physical education in the upper elementary grades

It is very important that children in the upper elementary grades experience an excellent physical education program. This three-year period is a time when they are capable of developing surprising skill and ability. They are "skill-hungry" and their desire to participate in sports and games is a dominant one. If good leadership is available they will make extremely rapid progress. Those students who are unfortunate in not having a good program during this period will fall so far behind in their development that it will be exceedingly difficult ever to catch up.

The consequences of children falling appreciably behind their group in strength, coordination and skills in the popular activities are serious. Play is the major concern of these children and repeated failure in this important realm produces social and emotional disturbances that often have detrimental and unfortunate results in later years (see p. 39). Children now attach great importance to their peer group and if they do not perform well in physical activities their peers will reject them. Eventually this results in the withdrawal of the weak, awkward child from the group.

Characteristics of intermediate grade children

In the upper elementary grades the boys and girls are separated for part of the physical education program. They should continue to participate in rhythms together to the extent possible, although girls will spend more time on these activities than the boys. It is desirable also to carry on certain of the games and relays coeducationally, although these must be well suited to both girls and boys.

The chief characteristics of children in the upper elementary grades are indicated below. It is necessary to point out that children do not suddenly change when they reach a certain age. The fact is that considerable individual differences exist in children at all school levels. In the fourth grade there will be those who are as advanced as some sixth graders physically and psychologically. The converse is also true.

PHYSICAL CHARACTERISTICS
(Ages 9-11)

1. Height and weight: there is a steady increase in height and weight.
2. Skeleton: the bones are still soft, but ossification is progressing.
3. Endurance: quite improved.
4. Heart: the child is stronger and better able to undergo considerable hard work.
5. Eyes: children can now focus better on fast-moving objects.
6. Coordination: many skills are now automatic. The child no longer needs to devote his higher brain powers to his own body movements and he can now think of the play and strategic measures that he might employ to effect his activities.
7. Health: excellent; resistance to illness is high.
8. Strength: improved; but the child is still surprisingly weak, particularly in the upper extremities.
9. Reaction time: excellent.
10. Children have boundless energy. They are very active.

PSYCHOLOGICAL CHARACTERISTICS

1. Beginning of gregarious spirit—gangs, teams, clubs.
2. Cooperation and teamwork are more developed.
3. The child is less individualistic and self-assertive.
4. Interest in competitive and fighting activities is developing.
5. Interest span is gradually lengthening, and fewer activities are engaged in.
6. There is love of excitement and adventure. The child likes to dare.
7. Interested in practicing to develop skills.
8. Children are ready to assume leadership responsibilities at the end of this period.
9. Girls are very much interested in rhythms, but boys lose interest unless the teacher is very skillful.
10. In the latter part of this period the standards and approval of the peer group become of paramount importance.
11. Boys like to imitate sport heroes.
12. There is a marked interest in the popular American sports.

Children from ten to twelve years of age are predominantly pre-adolescents. This stage of development is distinguished by two outstanding characteristics. The first of these involves an emancipation of the child from his primary identification with adults. Up to this time he has lived in submission and obedience to adults. The dependence upon adults now gives way to a developing individuality with its normal desire for self-direction. The child, in the latter part of this school level, exhibits a growing independence and self-reliance. An attitude of hostility to parental and adult standards frequently develops. The child demands the right to make his own choices.

Secondly, as the child begins to loosen his ties with adults he must turn elsewhere for the security that is so essential for his healthy development. He finds this in his peer group. This is a difficult but essential adjustment to make. This is where the boy and girl obtain important lessons in getting along with others, in give and take, in modifying their desires and actions in terms of other persons. This is also where they acquire another code of behavior—the peer code. Unfortunately, all too often this code is diametrically opposed to that of adult society. Adults must realize that the child is undergoing inner conflicts as a result of his efforts to live up to the standards of both his parents and his peers.

Implications for the physical education program in the intermediate grades

Children in the upper elementary grades desire more highly organized activities than they have had previously. They are more competitive and they begin to want to play in teams. Sports are a dominant interest for both girls and boys. They live in a sports-minded culture and it is inevitable that they would have a strong preference for the sports that are popular in their community. Organized programs on the local or higher levels in baseball, football, basketball, track and field, swimming, tennis, badminton, golf, gymnastics, ice hockey, and wrestling have demonstrated that boys and girls from nine through twelve years of age are not only highly interested in these sports but also are capable of developing remarkable skill in them. This ability is frequently accompanied by a high degree of strength, endurance, agility, and coordination.

Such considerations call for a program (see Table 4-5) that emphasizes sports. Girls are enthusiastic about rhythms but sports appeal to them also. Both sexes have now reached the stage of development when they enjoy drilling on specific skills to improve their ability. Movement accuracy and good form should be stressed.

Folk, social, and square dancing are important activities in the fourth to sixth grades. They should be taught on a coeducational basis. Aquatic activities are very popular where facilities for such instruction

Table 4-5. Program for girls and boys, grades 4-6.

RECOMMENDED TIME ALLOTMENTS

	Grade 4		Grade 5		Grade 6	
	Girls	Boys	Girls	Boys	Girls	Boys
1. Rhythms	30%	20%	25%	15%	25%	15%
2. Gymnastics (Including Stunts, Self-Testing Activities, Tumbling, Apparatus, Trampoline)		25	25	25	25	25
3. Basic Skills and Lead-Up Games	25	30	25	30	25	30
4. Team Sports	10	15	15	20	15	20
5. Aquatics	10	10	10	10	10	10

RECOMMENDED ACTIVITIES

Grade 4

1. Rhythms
   (a) Fundamental
       Rhythms:
       Polka
       Slide
       Schottische
       Minuet
   (b) Folk Dances:
       Seven Steps
       Virginia Reel
       Broom Dance
       Children's Polka
       Coming Through the
         Rye
2. Gymnastics
   (a) Tumbling:
       Forward Roll
       Backward Roll
       Shoulder Roll
       Elbow Balance
       Head Stand
   (b) Trampoline:
       Seat Drop
       Knee Drop
       Forward Roll
       Backward Roll
   (c) Apparatus:
       (1) Parallel Bars
           Hand Walk

Grade 5

1. Rhythms
   (a) Fundamental
       Rhythms:
       Polka
       Slide
       Schottische
       Waltz
   (b) Folk Dances:
       Csebogar
       Ace Diamonds
       Captain Jinks
       Varsovienne
       Troika
   (c) Square Dances:
       Irish Washerwoman
       Grand March
       Old Arkansas
       Birdie in the Cage
2. Gymnastics
   (a) Tumbling:
       Cartwheel
       Handstand
       Round Off
   (b) Trampoline:
       Seat-hand and
         Knee-seat Drop
       Jumping
       Jumping with Half
         Twists

Grade 6

1. Rhythms
   (a) Folk Dances:
       Kerry Dance
       Little Man in a Fix
       Road to the Isles
       Cotton Eyed Joe
       Jesse Polka
   (b) Square Dances:
       Dive for the Oyster
       Grapevine Twist
       Star by the Right
       Texas Star
2. Gymnastics
   (a) Tumbling:
       Review
       Handspring
   (b) Trampoline:
       Review
       Knee Drop
       Two Seat Drops-
         Back Drop
   (c) Apparatus:
       (1) Parallel Bars
           Review
           Rear Vault
           Dismount
           Support and
             Travel
       (2) Rings

Table 4-5. (cont'd).

Grade 4	Grade 5	Grade 6
Seat Travel	(c) Apparatus:	Review
Swing	(1) Parallel Bars	Grip and Hang
(2) Rings	Upper Arm Swing	(3) Horizontal Bar
Swinging	Front Vault	Review
Kip Position	Dismount	Knee Circle
(3) Horizontal Bar		Back Circle
Bar Snap	(2) Rings	(4) Vaulting
3. *Basic Skills and Lead-*	Hang and Tuck	Review
Up Games	(3) Horizontal Bar	Rear Vault
(a) Basic Skills	Hip Pullover	Thief Vault
Softball Throw for	Skin the Cat	3. *Basic Skills and Lead-*
Distance and	(4) Vaulting	*Up Games*
Accuracy	Straddle Vault	(a) Basic Skills
Standing and Running	Front Vault	Sprints
Broad Jump	Side Vault	Six Pound Shot-Put
25-Yard Dash	Squat Vault	Basketball Dribble
Softball Catching	3. *Basic Skills and Lead-*	Basketball Pass for
Base Running	*Up Games*	Accuracy
Chinning	(a) Basic Skills	Basketball Pass for
Pushups	(b) Broad Jump	Distance
Situps	High Jump	Free Throwing
(b) Lead-Up Games	40-Yard Dash	(b) Keep Away
End Ball	Football Kick for	Hand Tennis
Long Ball	Distance and	Deck Tennis
Pin Soccer	Accuracy	Aerial Darts
Circle Dodge Ball	Catching Forward	Net Ball
Bat Ball	Pass	Paddle Tennis
One Old Cat	Serving Volleyball	4. *Team Sports*
Six-Hole Basketball	Passing Volleyball	Soccer
Bounce Basketball	(b) Lead-Up Games	Softball
Keep Away	Captain Ball	Touch Football
Captain Basketball	German Bat Ball	Volleyball
4. *Team Sports*	Corner Kick Ball	Basketball
Soccer (Modified)	Rotation Soccer	5. *Aquatics*
Softball	Punt Back	Diving
5. *Aquatics*	Cage Ball	Elementary Crawl
(a) Aquatic Skills:	Newcomb	Stroke
Bobbing	4. *Team Sports*	Elementary Breast
Prone Float	Soccer (Modified)	Stroke
Trick Float	Softball	Elementary Back
Prone Glide and	Touch Football	Stroke
Recovery	Volleyball	Side Stroke
Horizontal Float	5. *Aquatics*	
Finning	(a) Aquatic Skills	
Sculling	(b) Elementary Crawl	
	Stroke	

Table 4-5. (cont'd).

Grade 4	Grade 5	Grade 6
Treading (b) Elementary Crawl Stroke	(c) Elementary Back Stroke (d) Elementary Breast Stroke	

are available. Children of these ages also are attracted to gymnastics, particularly the trampoline.

THE JUNIOR HIGH SCHOOL PROGRAM

The junior high school period is one in which all the students are undergoing marked changes physically, psychologically, and socially. In fact, these adolescent changes were important factors in the development of the junior high school system. At no other age level do such profound changes occur and such wide individual differences exist as during this period.

Characteristics of junior high school students

It is obvious that the physical education program for boys and girls of this age level must be geared to accommodate these radical adolescent changes. Before he can successfully set up a program adapted to the needs of these boys and girls, the curriculum planner must be familiar with their various physical and psychological characteristics.

PHYSICAL CHARACTERISTICS

1. Puberty: reached first by girls from one to two years in advance of boys. A small percentage of girls have their first menstruation between ten and eleven years of age; the typical girl starts in her thirteenth year; about 10 percent do not start until after their fifteenth birthday.
2. Anatomical age: the union of the epiphyses of the metacarpal bones and phalanges of the female hand is completed at the age of sixteen. In the majority of boys this union occurs between eighteen and nineteen, indicating a sex difference in anatomical age of from two to three years.
3. Skeleton: bones grow rapidly, especially the long bones of the arms

and legs. This causes posture to become poor unless an effort is made to prevent it.

4. Height and weight: the most rapid acceleration in rate of growth of height and weight is at the age of twelve for girls and fourteen and a half for boys. Prepubescent boys grow 1.8 inches and increase in weight 7.6 pounds in one year. Postpubescent boys grow 3.3 inches and gain 16.6 pounds in one year. Great differences exist among pupils. Some are as much as five years apart physiologically.

5. Strength: develops rapidly after puberty begins in boys. However, the greatest acceleration takes place *after* the rapid increase in height.

6. Motor ability: continues to improve but at a slower rate. Some boys appear to have a lower motor-ability score during the most rapid increase in growth. Awkwardness is more likely to accompany the rather sudden beginnings of growth than the later and more rapid growth.

7. Circulatory system: the heart increases greatly in size and volume.

8. Endurance: reduced during the junior high school period.

PSYCHOLOGICAL CHARACTERISTICS

1. Age of loyalty—of teams, clubs, gangs.
2. The peer group assumes great importance.
3. Increasing power of attention. Narrowed interest to fewer games.
4. Power of abstract reasoning developing.
5. Desire for excitement and adventure.
6. Hero worship and susceptibility to adult leadership.
7. Fighting tendency strong in boys.
8. Great interest in dancing by girls, but a loss of interest by boys.
9. Desire of both sexes for competitive activities.
10. Strong interest in personal appearance on part of girls.
11. Confidence in oneself frequently lacking.
12. Tendency to become moody and unstable.

Implications for the junior high school program

These characteristics of junior high school students call for a program (see Table 4-6) that includes activities sufficiently strenuous to challenge but not overtax the circulatory system. Competition between girls and boys in body contact sports at this time is out of the question because the physical differences between them are greater than when they were younger. However, the fine opportunities for social training

Table 4-6. The junior high school program.

RECOMMENDED TIME ALLOTMENTS

	Grade 7		Grade 8		Grade 9	
	Girls	Boys	Girls	Boys	Girls	Boys
1. *Rhythms*	25%	15%	25%	15%	25%	15%
2. *Team Sports*	25	30	25	30	25	30
3. *Individual Sports*	20	20	20	20	20	25
4. *Gymnastics*	20	25	20	25	20	20
5. *Aquatics*	10	10	10	10	10	10

PROGRAM FOR BOYS

Grade 7

1. *Rhythms*
   (a) Folk Dances:
       Little Brown Gal
       Swedish Polka
   (b) Square Dances:
       Arkansas Traveler
       Sentimental Journey
   (c) Social Dances:
       Waltz
       Conga
       Fox Trot
2. *Team Sports*
   Basketball
   Soccer
   Softball
3. *Individual Sports*
   Track and Field
   Archery
   Bowling
4. *Aquatics*
   Intermediate Crawl
     Stroke
   Intermediate Breast
     Stroke
   Intermediate Back
     Stroke
5. *Gymnastics*
   (a) Tumbling and Free
       Exercises:
       Back Extension
         Roll
       Forward Roll
         Variations
       Scales

Grade 8

1. *Rhythms*
   (a) Folk Dances:
       Highland Schottische
       Irish Lilt
   (b) Square Dances:
       Red River Valley
       The Girl I Left
         Behind Me
   (c) Social Dances:
       Waltz Combinations
       Conga
       Rumba
2. *Team Sports*
   Touch Football
   Volleyball
   Softball
3. *Individual Sports*
   Track and Field
   Wrestling
   Badminton
4. *Aquatics*
   Advanced Crawl Stroke
   Advanced Breast Stroke
   Advanced Back Stroke
5. *Gymnastics*
   (a) Tumbling and Free
       Exercises:
       Backward Roll
         Variations
       Shoulder Balance
       Hand and Shoulder
         Spring
       Forearm Balance

Grade 9

1. *Rhythms*
   (a) Folk Dances:
       Military Schottische
       Road to the Isles
   (b) Square Dances:
       Oh, Johnny
       Sioux City Sue
   (c) Social Dances:
       Conga
       Rumba
2. *Team Sports*
   Speedball
   Basketball
   Baseball
3. *Individual Sports*
   Track and Field
   Tennis
   Handball
4. *Aquatics*
   Diving
   Butterfly Stroke
   Side Stroke
5. *Gymnastics*
   (a) Tumbling and Free
       Exercises:
       Neck Spring
       Back Hand Spring
       Foot Pitch Back
         Somersault
   (b) Side and Long Horse
       Vaulting:
       Stoop—Far End
       Straddle—Near End

Table 4-6. (cont'd).

Grade 7	*Grade 8*	*Grade 9*
(b) Side Horse Vaulting: Neck Spring Head Spring Thief	(b) Side and Long Horse Vaulting: Hand Spring Straddle—Far End Squat—Far End	Squat—Near End
(c) Parallel Bars: Cross Rest Spring Forward Roll Shoulder Roll	(c) Parallel Bars: Swing Dip Front Upper Arm Swing "L" Hold	(c) Parallel Bars: Back Roll Short Kip Swing Forward Roll
(d) Horizontal Bar: Short Underswing from Stand Bar Vault—Front Bar Vault—Side	(d) Horizontal Bar: Short Underswing from Support Grip and Hang Back Circle	(d) Horizontal Bar: Cast Swing and Rear Dismount Hock Swing Dismount Back Hip Circle
(e) Trampoline: Hand and Knee Half- Twist Seat Drop Knee Drop—Front Drop Front Drop (from Stand)	(e) Trampoline: Bouncing (Tuck) Seat Drop—Front Drop Kip-up—Snap Up Back Drop (Flat)	(e) Trampoline: Back Drop (Pike) Bouncing (Pike) Jump with Half-Twist Seat Drop Hand and Knee—Back Drop
(f) Still Rings: Hang—Chin—Tuck Hand—Chin—Pike Inverted Hang	(f) Still Rings: Kip Position Skin Cat Cast and Swing	(f) Still Rings: Muscle Up Forward Roll "L" Hold
	(g) Side Horse: Single Leg Swings Single Leg Cuts	(g) Side Horse: Feint—Side Vault Feint—Front Vault Feint—Rear Vault Single Leg Full Circles

PROGRAM FOR GIRLS

Grade 7	*Grade 8*	*Grade 9*
1. *Rhythms* (a) Folk Dances: Little Brown Gal Oxen Dance Swedish Polka	1. *Rhythms* (a) Folk Dances: Highland Schottische Troika Irish Lilt	1. *Rhythms* (a) Folk Dances: Military Schottische Gypsy Wine Road to the Isles
(b) Square Dances: Arkansas Traveler Sentimental Journey	(b) Square Dances: Red River Valley The Girl I Left Behind Me	(b) Square Dances: Oh, Johnny Sioux City Sue
(c) Social Dances: Waltz Fox Trot Conga	(c) Social Dances: Waltz Combinations Conga **Rumba**	(c) Social Dances: Rumba Conga
(d) Modern Dance		(d) Modern Dance

Table 4-6. (cont'd).

Grade 7	Grade 8	Grade 9
2. *Team Sports*	(d) Modern Dance	2. *Team Sports*
Basketball	2. *Team Sports*	Basketball
Soccer	Volleyball	Field Hockey
Softball	Softball	Fieldball
3. *Individual Sports*	Speedball	3. *Individual Sports*
Track and Field	3. *Individual Sports*	Track and Field
Archery	Track and Field	Archery
Bowling	Badminton	Tennis
4. *Aquatics*	Paddle Tennis	4. *Aquatics*
Intermediate Crawl Stroke	4. *Aquatics*	Diving
Intermediate Breast Stroke	Advanced Crawl Stroke	Butterfly Stroke
Intermediate Back Stroke	Advanced Breast Stroke	Side Stroke
	Advanced Back Stroke	5. *Gymnastics*
5. *Gymnastics*	5. *Gymnastics*	(a) Tumbling and Floor Exercises:
(a) Tumbling and Floor Exercises:	(a) Tumbling and Floor Exercises:	Handstand
Forward Roll Variations	V-Seat—Free	Round Off
Cartwheel	Swedish Fall	Handspring
Backward Roll Variations	Headstand	Walk Over Backward
Arabesque	Modified Dive Roll	Cartwheel (Step Out)
V-Seat—Hand Support	Back Extension Roll	(b) Trampoline:
(b) Trampoline:	(b) Trampoline:	Back Drop (Pike)
Knee Drop—Front Drop	Bouncing (Tuck)	Bouncing (Pike)
Front Drop (from Stand)	Seat Drop—Front Drop	Hand and Knee Back Drop
Hand and Knee Half-Twist Seat Drop	Kip-Up—Snap-Up	Jump with Half-Twist Seat Drop
(c) Uneven Parallel Bars:	Back Drop (Flat)	(c) Uneven Parallel Bars:
Jump Support Mount	(c) Unever Parallel Bars:	Pendulum Mount
Thigh Rest Mount	Single Cut Mount	Crotch Seat Mount
Rear Dismount	Front Dismount	Hip Circle Dismount
Hip Roll	Cast Dismount	Angel Balance
Scissors Circle	Hip Circle	(d) Balance Beam:
(d) Balance Beam:	Scale	Wolf Rest Mount
Jump and Mount	(d) Balance Beam:	Pirouette Turn
Positions (Knee, Seat, Thigh, Stand, Squat)	Scales	Arabesque
Walk (Vary Stride and Rhythm)	Hitch-Kick Step	Body Waves
	Thigh-Rest Mount	Candle Hold
	Squat Rest Mount	(e) Vaulting:
	Pivot Turn	Squat Vault
	Jump and Turn	Straddle Vault
	(e) Vaulting:	Flank Vault
	Squat without Push	
	Front Vault	
	Rear Vault	

Table 4-6. (cont'd).

Grade 7	Grade 8	Grade 9
Run (Vary Stride and Rhythm) Jump and Skip Jump Off (e) Vaulting: Jump to Stand-Jump Jump to Squat-Jump Courage Vault		

that coeducational games offer should be utilized by bringing the sexes together occasionally in dancing and in the less vigorous sports.

A program emphasizing team games of higher organization is consistent with the nature of junior high school boys and girls. Team activities should predominate in this school level. This is not to suggest that individual and dual sports should not be included in the program. It has been well established that junior high school students enjoy badminton, tennis, archery, bowling, and golf when they are well taught under favorable circumstances, i.e., adequate facilities and appropriate equipment. It is also desirable to include these activities because some students terminate their school career at the end of the ninth grade. These individual and dual activities will be much more likely to be used during adult recreation than team sports.

THE SENIOR HIGH SCHOOL PROGRAM [24]

Senior high school students are usually from fourteen to nineteen years of age. They have continued to mature physically, mentally, emotionally, and socially. Their capacities are such that few activities are contraindicated. Their activities represent the peak of the public school program.

Characteristics of senior high school students

Characteristics that will influence the physical education program planned for the young people of this group are as follows:

PHYSICAL CHARACTERISTICS

1. Height and weight: the girl has passed through the period of rapid growth. Her height remains comparatively constant, although she

[24] See Appendix C for evaluative criteria for the secondary school physical education program.

will increase in weight. Some boys are pubescent and in the period of most rapid growth. Others are postpubescent and will increase little in height. Boys increase rapidly in weight.

2. Strength: increases greatly in boys during this period, although arms and shoulder girdle strength is deficient. The strength of girls reaches its peak at the age of sixteen and declines or remains stationary after this age.
3. Coordination: gradual improvement.
4. Skeleton: well calcified, but posture is poor.
5. Circulatory system: at age sixteen it is 82 percent of adult efficiency. At seventeen it is 90 percent of adult efficiency. At eighteen it is 98.5 percent of adult efficiency. Thus, from age sixteen the heart is capable of strenuous activities.
6. Endurance: endurance is better than at any previous age. With proper conditioning, endurance no longer represents a problem except, perhaps, in a few pubescents who are still in the stage of very rapid growth.
7. Reaction time: better than it has ever been.
8. Motor ability: rate of motor learning increases; greater ability to handle the body. Pupils are eager to perfect skills.

PSYCHOLOGICAL CHARACTERISTICS

1. Further narrowing of interests and trend toward specialization.
2. Still an age of loyalty and cooperation, but the desire to belong is tempered by consideration of personal interests and advantages. Still an age of team games.
3. Marked development of self-confidence.
4. Greater powers of attention and reasoning. Increase in ability to participate in group planning and problem solving.
5. Strong interest in grooming and personal appearance by both sexes. Boys are much interested in their physical development.
6. Hero worship is still a strong influence.
7. Fighting tendency is strong in boys. They are highly competitive.
8. Girls have an inclination to be attracted by passive social activities.
9. Strong interest in opposite sex.
10. Increased interest and ability in leading.

Implications for the senior high school program

The physical education program (see Table 4-7) in the senior high school should emphasize team and individual and dual sports. Sports are a dominant interest for both sexes. Team sports still have a

Table 4-7. The senior high school program.

RECOMMENDED TIME ALLOTMENTS

	Grade 10		Grade 11		Grade 12	
	Girls	Boys	Girls	Boys	Girls	Boys
1. Rhythms	25%	10%	25%	10%	25%	10%
2. Team Sports	25	30	25	30	25	25
3. Individual Sports	25	25	25	25	25	35
4. Gymnastics	15	25	15	25	15	20
5. Aquatics	10	10	10	10	10	10

PROGRAM FOR BOYS

Grade 10

1. *Rhythms*
   (a) Folk Dances:
   Csardas
   Oyda
   Rheinlander
   (b) Square Dances:
   Lili Marlene
   Alabama Jubilee
   (c) Social Dances:
   Samba
   Conga
2. *Team Sports*
   Soccer
   Basketball
   Baseball
3. *Individual Sports*
   Track and Field
   Tennis
   Handball
4. *Aquatics*
   Life Saving and
   Water Safety
5. *Gymnastics*
   (a) Tumbling and Floor
   Exercises:
   Stand on Shoulder
   Back Somersault
   Head Spring
   (b) Side and Long
   Horse Vaulting:
   Stoop—Rear End
   Back Straddle—Far
   End
   Stoop—Half-Turn

Grade 11

1. *Rhythms*
   (a) Folk Dances:
   Tarantella
   La Jesucita
   Reap the Fox
   (b) Square Dances:
   Wagon Wheels
   Five Foot Two
   (c) Social Dances:
   Samba
   Jitterbug
2. *Team Sports*
   Touch Football
   Volleyball
   Baseball
3. *Individual Sports*
   Wrestling
   Badminton
   Golf
4. *Aquatics*
   Life Saving and
   Water Safety
5. *Gymnastics*
   (a) Tumbling and Floor
   Exercises:
   Leg Pitch Back
   Somersault
   Arm to Arm Balance
   Two Arm Elbow
   Balance
   (b) Side and Long
   Horse Vaulting:
   Hand Stand—
   Quarter Turn

Grade 12

1. *Rhythms*
   (a) Folk Dances:
   Highland Fling
   Hull's Victory
   Old Dan Tucker
   (b) Square Dances:
   Oklahoma Star
   Spanish Circle
   (c) Social Dances:
   Waltz, Foxtrot
   Combinations
   Cha-Cha-Cha
2. *Team Sports*
   Speedball
   Basketball
3. *Individual Sports*
   Golf
   Tennis
   Badminton
4. *Aquatics*
   Life Saving and
   Water Safety
5. *Gymnastics*
   (a) Tumbling and Floor
   Exercises:
   Round Off Back
   Hand Spring
   Round Off Back
   Somersault
   Front Somersault
   Valdez
   (b) Side and Long
   Horse Vaulting:
   Cartwheel

Table 4-7. (cont'd).

Grade 10	*Grade 11*	*Grade 12*
(c) Parallel Bars:	Cartwheel	Handspring
Hand Stand	Handspring	Hecht
Cast	(c) Parallel Bars	Handstand—
Back Uprise	Front Uprise	Quarter Turn
Double Leg Cut Off	Kip—End of Bars	(c) Parallel Bars:
(d) Horizontal Bar:	Drop Cast	Glide Kip
Front Hip Circle	Back Shoulder Roll	Back Kip
Swing Half-Turn	(d) Horizontal Bar	Drop Kip
Seat Circle—Back	Seat Circle—Front	Windy
(e) Trampoline:	Back Kip	(d) Horizontal Bar:
Front Drop—Back	Free Hip Circle	Back Uprise
Drop	(e) Trampoline	Baby Flyaway
Swivel Hips	Back Over to Front	Sale Circle Backward
Jump with Half Twist	Drop	(e) Trampoline:
To Back Drop	Cradle	Front Somersault
(f) Still Rings:	Back Rollover to Feet	to Feet
Shoulder Balance	Swivel Hips—Back	Back Rollover to
Double Leg Cut Off	Drop	Back Drop
Inlocate	(f) Still Rings:	Jumping with Full
(g) Side Horse:	Dislocate	Twist
Scissors—Front	Kip	(f) Still Rings:
Needle Dismount	Back Uprise	Front Uprise
Moore Mount	(g) Side Horse:	Back Lever
	Back Scissors	French Lever
	Double Rear Dismount	(g) Side Horse:
		Keire-In
		Triple Rear Dismount
		Double Leg Circle

PROGRAM FOR GIRLS

Grade 10	*Grade 11*	*Grade 12*
1. *Rhythms*	1. *Rhythms*	1. *Rhythms*
(a) Folk Dances:	(a) Folk Dances:	(a) Folk Dances:
Csardas	Tarantella	Highland Fling
Oyda	La Jesucita	Hull's Victory
Rheinlander	Reap the Fox	Old Dan Tucker
(b) Square Dances:	(b) Square Dances:	(b) Square Dances:
Lili Marlene	Wagon Wheels	Oklahoma Star
Alabama Jubilee	Five Foot Two	Spanish Circle
(c) Social Dances:	(c) Social Dances:	(c) Social Dances:
Samba	Samba	Cha-Cha-Cha
Conga	Jitterbug	Waltz, Fox Trot
Rumba	(d) Modern Dance	Combination
(d) Modern Dance	2. *Team Sports*	(d) Modern Dance

Table 4-7. (cont'd).

Grade 10	Grade 11	Grade 12

2. *Team Sports*
   Soccer
   Basketball
   Softball
3. *Individual Sports*
   Track and Field
   Tennis
   Archery
4. *Aquatics*
   Life Saving and
     Water Safety
5. *Gymnastics*
   (a) Tumbling and Free
     Exercises:
     Tour Jet
     Scales
     Walk Over Front
     Pas Chasse Steps
   (b) Trampoline:
     Front Drop—Back Drop
     Swivel Hips
     Jump with Half
       Twist to Back Drop
   (c) Uneven Parallel Bars:
     Push Stem Mount
     Forward Roll Dismount
     Forward Roll to Layout
     Rear and Front Swing
     Thigh Rest Handstand
   (d) Balance Beam:
     Straddle Seat Mount
     Alternate Foot Leap
     Kip Position
     Front Vault Dismount
     Side Seat Dismount
   (e) Vaulting:
     Stoop Vault
     Wolf Vault
     Neckspring

Fieldball
Speedball
Basketball
3. *Individual Sports*
   Badminton
   Golf
   Bowling
4. *Aquatics*
   Life Saving and
     Water Safety
5. *Gymnastics*
   (a) Tumbling and Free
     Exercises:
     Splits
     Back Handspring
     Pirouettes
     Hitch Kicks
   (b) Trampoline:
     Back Over to Front
       Drop
     Swivel Hips—Back
       Drop
     Cradle
     Back Rollover to Feet
   (c) Uneven Parallel Bars:
     Cast Mount
     Back Touch Dismount
     Knee Hook Dismount
     Double Leg Circles
     Cast Swing
   (d) Balance Beam:
     Straddle Mount
     Hitch Kick Leap
     V-Seat
     Forward Roll
     Cartwheel Dismount
     Squat Seat With
       Forward Extension
   (e) Vaulting:
     Cartwheel
     Thief Vault
     Scissors Vault

2. *Team Sports*
   Field Hockey
   Volleyball
3. *Individual Sports*
   Golf
   Tennis
   Badminton
4. *Aquatics*
   Life Saving and
     Water Safety
5. *Gymnastics*
   (a) Tumbling and Free
     Exercises:
     Tinsica
     Split Leaps
     Stride Leap
     Round Off Back
       Handspring
     Lunge with Turns
   (b) Trampoline:
     Back Rollover to
       Front Drop
     Front Somersault to
       Feet
     Back Rollover to
       Back Drop
     Jumping with Full
       Twist
   (c) Uneven Parallel
     Bars:
     Hip Circle Mount
     Flank Dismount
     Handstand Layout
       Dismount
     Hip Circle
     Leg Circle
   (d) Balance Beam:
     Fence Mount
     Needle
     Split
     Backward Roll
     Handstand Arch-
       over Dismount
   (e) Vaulting:
     Cartwheel Quarter
       Turn
     Headspring
     Handspring

strong appeal but interest is also high in the individual and dual sports such as tennis, golf, badminton, bowling, and handball (boys). Skiing is popular in those schools where it can be scheduled. Interest still remains strong in aquatic activities. Boys and girls respond well to folk, square, and social dancing when it is provided on a coeducational basis. Girls are partial to modern dance when good instruction is available. Tumbling, trampoline, and apparatus activities are well received by both sexes when good instruction and facilities are provided. Wrestling and weight training are popular activities among the boys. There is interest in fencing by both sexes when it is scheduled.

Coeducational activities should be scheduled on occasions. Schools that have a daily program should endeavor to have a coeducational program once per week. In addition to the various forms of dancing boys and girls can participate together in tennis, golf, badminton, bowling, and skiing.

If possible some provision for a choice of activities should be made in the eleventh and twelfth grades. Many high schools provide several alternatives from which the students may make a choice. Where it is possible to do this the students respond favorably to it.

The physically educated high school graduate

The elementary and secondary school physical education programs should be articulated to produce the best results. The objective should be to attain to the maximum extent the objectives of physical education. At the National Conference on Fitness of Secondary School Youth [25] the attributes of the physically educated high school senior at graduation were spelled out. These were:

Attitudes:
1. A strong desire to be healthy
2. Acceptance of the need to exercise daily to maintain physical fitness
3. An awareness of the value of safety procedures in and on the water
4. Appreciation of "change of pace" from work to recreational activities (an essential part of healthy living)
5. A desire to achieve a high degree of excellence in skills to enjoy participation
6. Appreciation of one's strengths and limitations
7. Acceptance of the concept of one's role as a member of a team
8. Positive attitudes and desire for personal cleanliness and safe practices in physical activities
9. Appreciation of wholesome intergroup relationships and respect for the rights of others

[25] Report of the National Conference on Fitness of Secondary School Youth, *Youth and Fitness* (Washington, D.C., American Association for Health, Physical Education, and Recreation, 1959), pp. 28-29.

10. Appreciation of the values in good sportsmanship and of its fullest application to total living
11. Appreciation of the value of the creative aspects of correct body movements

Knowledge:

1. Knowledge of what constitutes body mechanics (acceptable posture) and how this relates to good health
2. Knowledge of the proper functioning of the body and of their responsibility to maintain personal fitness
3. Knowledge of the rules of water safety (swimming, rescue, artificial respiration, boating, etc.)
4. Understanding of the nature and importance of physical fitness and knowledge of how to develop and maintain it throughout life
5. Understanding of the rules, strategies, backgrounds, and values of sports and other physical activities
6. Knowledge of proper selection and care of school and personal athletic equipment
7. Understanding and appreciation of the role of physical education in the total education program
8. Knowledge of the proper mechanics of sports and activities
9. Understanding of the importance and the role of physical fitness in successful academic achievement (sound mind, fit body)
10. Knowledge of the scientific and health reasons for proper hygiene and safety practices as applied in physical activities
11. Understanding of one's physical capacities and limitations
12. Knowledge enabling them to be intelligent spectators of the popular American sports
13. The ability to distinguish between sound and unsound commercial health and exercise practices and programs

Skills:

1. Ability to assume good posture and maintain it while sitting, standing, walking
2. Development of skills in at least four seasonal team sports, the level of skill attained being such that there is enjoyment in participation
3. Ability to swim well enough to feel at home in the water (involves mastery of the different strokes and survival skills)
4. Development of skills in at least four indoor and outdoor single or dual sports, the level of skill being such that there is enjoyment in participation
5. Development of proper rhythmic response to music, including basic skills in folk, square, modern, and/or social dance
6. Development of skill in one combative activity (boxing excluded) for boys, the level of skill being such that there is enjoyment in participation
7. Ability to apply skills in fundamental body movements—in running, throwing, jumping, lifting, carrying, etc.—to other physical activities
8. Achievement of an adequate level of skill in self-testing activities such as track and field, calisthenics, tumbling, apparatus, etc.
9. Good habits of cleanliness, personal appearance, and safety practices in all physical activities

The block program

In junior and senior high schools the use of the block program of scheduling physical education activities is recommended. In the block program the time allotment for an activity is concentrated rather than distributed. For example, if it were determined that thirty periods were to be allotted to basketball in the senior high school program this entire period of time would be utilized in a block. Thus, if physical education were scheduled daily, basketball would be scheduled for six consecutive weeks before another activity were scheduled. The most popular block of time is four weeks. Blocks of three, five, and six weeks are also extensively used.

A widespread practice is to schedule the same program each year without change. In this type of program, each student repeats in the eleventh and twelfth grades what he had in the tenth grade. This procedure is defended on the basis that students have a readiness for seasonal activities and that they should have them when their interest is so great. This is contrary to the block program.

The use of the block system is preferred for several reasons. In the first place, there is no educational justification in repeating the same activities in the same way, year after year. New material should be presented each class period (excepting, of course, an occasional period during which an examination is given or the previous material is reviewed), just as it is in the class meetings for every other subject. The expectation prevails that in an educational institution, the children will grow in understanding, skills, and attitudes. The instructor is expected to start where the instruction terminated the previous period and to carry on from that point.

Secondly, the block program is favored because it facilitates learning. If the time allotment for an activity is spread out over a considerable period of time, with other activities intervening, students will forget what they have been taught in previous lessons. Finally, students are better able to develop the skills and the physical condition for a particular activity when the instruction is concentrated. If thirty-six periods are allocated to wrestling for the three years of the junior high school, more skill, understanding, and physical fitness will be developed if all the periods are concentrated during one year than if twelve periods are scheduled for each of three years. Eighteen periods for each of two years is preferable to twelve periods each year.

An advanced course in an activity is very much to be desired if it is really advanced. The elementary course should definitely be a prerequisite to the advanced course. In reply to the contention that students want seasonal activities, this is certainly a fact but there is a variety of seasonal activities. Wrestling, gymnastics, badminton, and volleyball are just as seasonal during the winter months as basketball. Also, when students want additional participation in a sport, they may obtain it in the intramural program. For example, if an adequate unit on basketball were provided in the tenth grade, students could participate further in this sport in the eleventh and twelfth grades in the intramural program.

Homogeneous classes

Teaching is greatly facilitated in junior and senior high schools if students are scheduled for physical education homogeneously insofar as their grade in school is concerned. When the teacher has a class with sophomores, juniors, and seniors in it, his teaching becomes as difficult as it would be for the English instructor who is confronted with the same situation. In fact, it might be more difficult, because the seniors are two years advanced in size, strength, endurance, and skill over the sophomores. When the administrator schedules students of different grades in the same classes, he is making it much more difficult to achieve the educational objectives of the program.

In the majority of secondary schools, students are not scheduled for service classes on a homogeneous basis. However, a sufficient number of schools follow this practice to indicate that it can be done if the principal wants to do it, and the physical education administrator should urge scheduling on this basis. In many cases, it has been successful to present a plan in writing to demonstrate the feasibility of homogeneous scheduling. In other instances, physical educators have volunteered to set up the entire schedule of classes for the high school to demonstrate that it might be done.

No problem of maintaining homogeneous groups would be created if three instructors and adequate facilities were available. In the event that only one instructor were available, the different grades could be taught separately if student leaders were used. In such a stiuation, the instructor would serve as supervisor of the students. Another solution to the problem is to offer alternating programs. With this plan, the instructor would provide a different program each year for three years. However, this is a poor substitute for scheduling by classes.

Flexible scheduling

By flexible scheduling is meant that the classes will be of varying lengths and sizes and will not necessarily meet on a daily basis. Flexible scheduling is contrasted with the traditional set schedule in which all classes were of the same length and size and usually met on a daily basis. This new approach to scheduling is more applicable to secondary schools because elementary schools and colleges and universities have always had more variation and flexibility in the length, size, and number of periods per week.

The pattern of flexible scheduling most frequently found involves fewer periods per week but of greater length. As an example, a school which previously had allotted a daily 45-minute period for physical education changed to two double periods and one single period per week. This really benefits physical education because more time will be available for activity. Assuming that 20 minutes per period were needed for changing and showering the daily period would provide 125 minutes per week for instruction and participation. On the other hand, each double period would permit 70 minutes for physical education. Thus, two double periods and one single period would provide 165 minutes of actual class time contrasted to 125 minutes in the daily program. If three double periods per week replaced the daily schedule—as is done in some schools—the advantage would be even greater.

The longer periods have an additional advantage. In many secondary schools it is necessary at times to use facilities that are located at some distance from the school. Such facilities may be athletic fields, swimming pools, tennis courts, bowling alleys, and golf courses. Double periods greatly facilitate the use of such facilities. In fact, double periods are advantageous for classes held at the school. Physical educators have complained for years about the difficulty of accomplishing their objectives in a 25- to 30-minute activity period. To have 70 or 80 minutes available for instruction, practice, and participation would seem a more favorable situation.

In addition to varying the number and length of the class meetings each week flexible scheduling also involves variations in class size. The students from three or four classes may be combined on regular occasions. Such an arrangement is advantageous when it is desired to present the same material to the students in several classes. It may be that the same lecture or film is planned. The economy of staff time under this system is apparent. Such an arrangement also facilitates the use of visiting speakers.

Flexible scheduling in secondary schools is still in its early stages. It seems safe to predict that virtually all schools will adopt some of these procedures. What the ultimate effect will be on health education and physical education programs is difficult to forecast. At the present time the advantages seem to bulk larger than the disadvantages. The chief disadvantage appears to be the reduction in number of class meetings per week. However, if this is offset by *more minutes of activity* per week it does not appear to be a serious disadvantage.

Substitutions for physical education

In some school systems the substitution of band or ROTC for physical education is permissible. This practice is based on the assumption that physical activity is involved in military drill and in the marching band. It is immediately obvious that this is not a valid justification and that it should be resisted by the physical education administrator as strenuously as possible. A proper substitution occurs when the outcomes of the different programs are approximately identical. The results of band practice and ROTC are worthwhile, but they are different from those in physical education. The small amount of vigorous exercise involved in these activities would never develop organic vigor, vitality, strength, and stamina. Nor would band practice or military drill develop the neuromuscular skills in motor activities or the social and moral values that can be achieved through physical education.

Still another type of substitution is found in many secondary schools. This involves the acceptance of participation on an interschool squad in lieu of participation in the service program. This practice is based upon the assumption that the values of interschool athletics are synonymous with those of the service program. Proponents of this system point out that the physiological outcomes of athletics are greater than those found in the instructional program. Also, the social and character values are at least equivalent. In addition, it is argued that members of varsity squads, if they also participate in the required physical education program, will get more physical activity than is good for them. Moreover, these athletes could make valuable use of the period normally devoted to physical education classes for study purposes.

The opponents of this point of view point out that instruction is given in a wide variety of activities and that varsity squad members will miss important units of activity if they are excused. It is clear that to excuse those on the football squad from instruction in swimming, lifesaving, tennis, dancing, golf, and the like is to deprive them of exceedingly valuable instruction. These opponents are also skeptical of the claim that participation in the service program will overly fatigue varsity candidates. For these reasons, many leaders do not recommend the substitution of the varsity program for the service class activities.

A middle ground is taken by those who recommend that interschool squad members be excused from the service program when the service course activity is identical to or closely related to the varsity sport in which they are participating. Thus, members of the football squad might be excused from the instructional program when a touch football unit was being covered. They would not be excused from any other activity. Members of the basketball squad might be excused from participating in basketball service classes.

Preparation of curriculum outline

It is a standard practice in secondary schools (and in colleges and universities) to require each instructor of academic subjects to prepare a curriculum outline for all the courses for which he is responsible. This outline is ordinarily prepared in accordance with specifications that have been established in the particular school. A copy of the curriculum outline is filed in the principal's or superintendent's office.

Such a practice is recommended for physical education. The advantages of this procedure have been proved over the years. Yet, in many schools, the physical educator is not required or expected to provide a curriculum outline. Relatively few school administrators have such outlines from the physical education department on file. This is unfortunate and casts a reflection upon the quality of the physical education program and the training and ability of the physical education administrator.

Summer session physical education programs

One of the most recent and promising trends is the provision of physical education programs for elementary and secondary students during the summer. These may be designed for several objectives. One purpose is remedial. This program could be particularly beneficial to the students who are poorly skilled or are in the low fitness category. Another purpose is to provide activities such as tennis, golf, and swimming, which cannot be made available during the academic year.

THE COLLEGE PROGRAM

When high school graduates enter a college or university in America they almost invariably discover that like English composition a certain amount of physical education is required for graduation. Although the number of years or terms of the requirement, the hours required per week, and the nature of the program may vary, the great majority of college students must register for some physical education. This practice of requiring physical education is of many years' standing. It originated nearly a hundred years ago because college administrators and faculty members considered that a certain amount of participation in physical education activities was essential to the health and well-being of students and, accordingly, should be required.

Should physical education be required?

In recent years the validity of the requirement has been debated in many institutions. The arguments in favor of the requirement can be summarized as follows:

1. The health and well-being of the students, both now and in the future, is dependent upon regular exercise. Such activity is a health practice universally endorsed by the medical profession.
2. Unless physical education is required, those who need it most will evade it. The weak, flabby, poorly coordinated students have little desire to engage in activities that are difficult for them and in which they were previously unsuccessful. No one enjoys participating in an activity in which he appears to poor advantage.
3. Most high schools provide such poor programs that their graduates are not adequately prepared to elect activities in college. To elect intelligently requires a knowledge of the alternatives.
4. Unless there is a requirement, many students who do elect physical education will elect only their favorite sport. Most students will avoid activities with which they are not familiar.
5. A certain amount of regular physical activity is necessary in a college or university to provide respite from the academic pursuits. Students cannot study advantageously all the time. After several hours of concentrated intellectual effort any individual will find himself refreshed after a period of vigorous, enjoyable physical activity.
6. College and university students also need a certain amount of recreation to balance their intellectual regimen. It is to their benefit when their recreation is obtained in wholesome activities, such as sports and games.
7. The physical education requirement does not limit the student to a specific activity but to a field or area of activities. The university requires a certain number of hours for graduation. Practically all of these hours must be intellectual activities. But a small part of this total requirement is to be in the area of movement.

The common arguments against the requirement are:

1. It encourages poor teaching. The students are required to attend; thus the instructor finds little incentive to be a superior teacher.
2. College students are sufficiently mature that they can be depended upon to do the things that are best for them. They will take physical education voluntarily if they need it.
3. College students resent requirement. As a consequence they are not likely to continue participation after the requirement has been fulfilled.

4. The requirement is undemocratic. It provides a "captive audience," which defeats the very objectives of the program.
5. The requiring of participation is the wrong approach to get people to participate voluntarily throughout their adult life.

At the present time the advocates of the elective program are very much in the minority. Fundamentally, the elective program has little chance of operating successfully unless the following essential conditions prevail:

1. Strong, effective physical education programs in the public schools are experienced by all high school graduates. In other words, an elective program would be feasible if all the students who enter colleges and universities came with the knowledge, skills, and attitudes that are the results of excellent public school physical education.
2. Adequate numbers of superior physical education teachers are available.
3. Superior facilities and equipment exist in the institutions of higher learning.
4. The entering students are, in some way, made aware of the opportunities that are available to them in the physical education department. To accomplish this all faculty members in the institution must understand the physical education program and publicize its advantages among their students. An alternative would be to require each freshman to consult with a member of the physical education department who could explain the opportunities the program offers.

It is clear that it will be many years before the above conditions are realized. Even in those states where physical education is most advanced public school physical education is far from ideal. By the same token, only a very small percentage of the institutions of higher learning meet the above stipulations. Under these circumstances it is understandable that most physical educators favor retention of the requirement.

Nature of the requirement

As has been indicated, most colleges and universities have some sort of requirement in physical education. Oxendine,[26] in a survey of 259 colleges and universities found that physical education was required of all students in 83 percent of the institutions and part of the students in 12 percent. Of these, 24 percent required one year of physical education for graduation; 60 percent two years; 3 percent three years; and 5

[26] Joseph Oxendine, "The Service Program in 1960-61," *Journal of Health, Physical Education, Recreation* (September 1961), p. 37.

percent four years. In the majority of institutions the required classes meet three times per week. A small percentage meet four or five periods per week. The usual length of period is fifty minutes (out of which must come time for dressing and showering), but a recent trend is to have double periods. This is a desirable development because a single period really makes available only thirty minutes for the program.

In Oxendine's study it was revealed that in 16 percent of the schools ROTC could be substituted for part of the physical education requirement. In 64 percent participation on a varsity squad was accepted in lieu of part of the requirement. Marks in physical education were given in 19 percent of the schools on the pass or fail basis. In 67 percent physical education grades were counted in the computation of grade point averages.

Time requirement

Most institutions appear to require only that each student accumulate a certain amount of credit or successfully complete physical education courses for a prescribed number of semesters or terms. It is not uncommon to specify that within the time requirement each student must either take a course in swimming or pass a proficiency test. Oxendine's survey showed that in 46 percent of the colleges and universities a proficiency test in swimming was required. In 27 percent a physical fitness proficiency test was required.

A common practice is to administer a physical fitness test to all entering freshmen. Those who fail to meet the established standard are required to register for a special course that is designed to improve their physical fitness. Once they complete this course, they are free to elect their remaining activities.

Also within the time requirement a number of institutions specify areas from which courses must be taken. For example, each student might be required to pass one course in each of the categories shown in Table 4-8 for graduation.

Table 4-8.

Aquatics	Combative Activities	Gymnastics	Rhythmic Activities	Team Sports	Individual Sports
Elementary Swimming	Boxing	Tumbling	Square Dancing	Basketball	Handball
Advanced Swimming	Wrestling	Apparatus	Ballroom Dancing	Volleyball	Badminton
Water Safety and Lifesaving	Fencing	Trampolining	Modern Dancing	Soccer	Tennis
				Speedball	Bowling
				Touch Football	Archery

A few institutions permit students to substitute intramural participation for part of the required work.

Proficiency requirement

Some colleges and universities make extensive use of proficiency or achievement tests. By passing such a test, which is equivalent to the final examination in a service course, the student is relieved of one term or one semester of the requirement. In other words, if he possesses the skill and knowledge that the average student possesses at the end of a service course, part of the requirement is waived. No credit is granted. In some institutions a skilled, versatile athlete might be able to pass enough achievement tests to have the entire service requirement waived.

It is likely that the future will see a much greater use of proficiency tests. With the predictions of a doubled enrollment in the next ten years most colleges and universities, with their present facilities and staffs, will be unable to handle the volume of students. It is quite unlikely that sufficient additional facilities will be made available. Under the circumstances, physical educators will be inclined to concentrate upon those who most need physical education. It is also to be expected that public schools will graduate students with better backgrounds in physical education than they have heretofore. Certainly the pressure of heavy enrollments will cause many schools to refrain from requiring a student to take a course in which he is already highly skilled.

Orientation programs [27]

Some colleges and universities make use of orientation programs. Such programs are predicated on the conviction that physical education should have purposes over and beyond the development of physical fitness and motor skills. Proponents of orientation courses argue that college students need to know something about the philosophy of physical education, its importance in modern life, why it is part of the curriculum, the outcomes that may be expected. They emphasize the value of understanding the origin, backgrounds, development, and significance of sports in our society. Many other areas of knowledge are important, such as sports etiquette, the laws of training and conditioning, safety precautions, physiology of exercise, first aid, purchase of athletic equipment, and the nature and significance of sportsmanship. Certainly, from the standpoint of public relations, the accomplishment of these intellectual objectives would be invaluable.

[27] The material in this section has been adapted from Hubert McCormick, *Enriching the Physical Education Service Program* (New York, Teachers College Bureau of Publications, 1942), pp. 58-101.

There are three types of orientation programs. The first type is generally conducted during the freshmen orientation week. This usually involves only one period during which all freshmen are given pertinent information, which they need to relate themselves properly to the physical education, intramural, and intercollegiate athletic programs offered by the institution.

The second type of orientation program is a part of the regular service program. Part of the time is devoted to lectures, movies, discussions, and demonstrations pertaining to related material. This may be done at regular or irregular intervals. For example, one period per week in which the students meet in an academic classroom may be devoted to orientation materials. In some instances outside reading assignments are required.

The third type is an entirely separate academic course. This may be an elective course or it might count as part of the physical education requirement. A textbook is employed which is specifically designed to give the students an understanding and appreciation of physical education.

Survey course in activities

In some institutions the physical education program during the first term or first year is devoted to giving all freshmen students an opportunity to participate in a wide variety of activities. For example, ten or twelve activities may be surveyed, with from six to ten periods devoted to each. The purpose is to familiarize students with the most important activities so that their subsequent choices will be made intelligently. It is felt that such a procedure is necessary because of the narrow, ineffective programs in high schools.

Waiver of the physical education requirement

In the majority of schools, both World War II and Korean War veterans have been routinely excused from physical education. In addition, in other schools ROTC is accepted in lieu of physical education. In 1949 the College Committee on Physical Education and Athletics,[28] representing the College Physical Education Association, the National Collegiate Athletic Association, and the American Association for Health, Physical Education, and Recreation, issued the following statement in regard to this matter:

1. It should be clear to all in college physical education and in colleges gen-

[28] The College Committee on Physical Education and Athletics, "College Physical Education for Peace and Defense," *Fifty-second Annual Proceedings of the College Physical Education Association* (Chapel Hill, N.C., 1949), p. 134.

erally that military science and physical education are not synonymous. They are two different programs employing different techniques, seeking different outcomes, and existing for different purposes. Leaders in both areas recognize these differences. One seeks preparation for defense through military skills and techniques, the other seeks adjustment to democratic ways through recreational skills taught to secure outcomes in total personal development. Confusion remains only in the minds of those who believe that physical fitness is the sole, or at least the principal, outcome of both. Obviously, both military science and physical education (including athletics) have a place in twentieth century society. They are not, however, mutually inclusive.

2. On campuses where both programs are offered there should be developed a spirit of cordiality and cooperation without infringement, precedence, or domination of one over the other.

3. The College Committee fully subscribes to the recommendation of many other groups to the effect that a course in military science is not a proper substitution for physical education.

4. Likewise, the College Committee strongly urges faculties to establish the principle of equivalence when accrediting military experience with reference to physical education. This problem loomed large following VJ Day, and the Committee feels that some considerable injustice was done many veterans by eliminating them from recreational or therapeutic physical education so necessary to their continuing adjustment to the college or community environment. The best results were obtained on those campuses where credit was given for physical education as it was for other areas of learning; that is, on the basis of experience in the services equivalent to the kind and quality of instruction receivable on the campus. The committee recommends that where blanket or indiscriminate credit for physical education was given just because the student was in military service, the practice be now discontinued and experience in physical education from any future military service be evaluated for quality the same as experience in other fields.

Characteristics of college students

PHYSICAL CHARACTERISTICS

1. Height and weight: growth nearly complete. There may be a gain in weight.
2. Strength: approaching period of greatest strength which is reached about the age of twenty-four.
3. Skeleton: ossification complete; more difficult but not impossible to improve posture.
4. Coordination: reaches its peak at this stage. If the college student has had a good background in physical education he will be excellently coordinated.
5. Endurance: the college student is capable of great endurance. If a proper period of training is undergone, endurance will not limit participation in any activity.
6. Reaction time: best at this age.

1. Specialization in a few preferred activities.
2. Preference by girls for individual and dual activities. These are also popular with boys.
3. Great interest in opposite sex. Coeducational activities, such as social dancing, golf, tennis, badminton, volleyball, archery, and bowling are popular.
4. Boys continue to be interested in combative and team sports, although there is a decline in the number and variety engaged in.
5. Strong tendency for many to give up sport participation if they are not required or motivated to continue.
6. Great interest in personal appearance. Boys are anxious to be well-developed physically.

The program of activities

If boys and girls have been given the proper physical education program in their precollege careers, they will be prepared to continue in several activities in which they have some skill and which they have learned to enjoy before entering college. They will now be more concerned with their future leisure-time recreational activities than they have been heretofore, and, consequently, there will be an increased interest in adult play activities. This preparation for leisure is in harmony with the purpose of the college, which is to prepare students for their adult life. Unfortunately, however, very few students enter college with an adequate background in physical education, and in the past far too many have graduated from college with the same disadvantage. The wide difference in the secondary school preparation of college students presents a problem in setting up the physical education curriculum. It necessitates as extensive a program of activities as it is possible to provide with existing facilities.

The play interests of college men carry over well from the last years of high school. There is a marked interest in team sports, and there is a greater tendency to specialize in a particular position in a single sport. Individual sports are also popular, although guidance is necessary to bring some freshmen and sophomores to a consideration of their future sports participation. There is a definite trend toward specialization and concentration of interests toward life ambitions, development of talents, and pursuit of hobbies. In addition to the strong interest in basketball, softball, volleyball, touch football, soccer, speedball, and baseball, there is a marked desire for tennis, swimming, golf, handball, bowling, and badminton. Where good facilities are available winter sports are very popular.

Kenney [29] conducted an evaluative study of the service program for men at the University of Illinois in which questionnaire data were obtained from graduates for the years 1939, 1940, 1941, 1942, 1951, and 1952. Swimming was the most popular sport activity among the graduates, with 72.7 percent reporting that they engaged in this activity. Ballroom dancing was second, with 71.35 percent reporting participation. Basketball, baseball, softball, and volleyball are the only team sports that appear among the first twenty sports activities.

Other percentages for this group are as follows:

1. Those who participate in sports and physical exercise nearly every day of the year.   14.0%
2. Those who participate in some sport or exercise activity about once a week or more on a year-round basis.   42.6%
3. Those who do not participate in any of the sports or activities they took while attending the university.   34.0%
4. Those who report that "to have fun" is one of their most important motives for participation in sports.   76.6%
5. Those who report that "to maintain health and vigor" is one of their principal motives for participating in sports.   47.5%
6. Those who give as the reason for failure to participate "the greater appeal of sedentary recreational activities."   16.0%
7. Those who participate in conditioning exercises at home (this being the most popular of physical activities that graduates engage in daily on a year-round basis).   18.0%

These data indicate the desirability of stressing recreational activities in the college service program. Some provision should be made to insure that each college student has some activities that he can use in later life. Certainly activities such as golf, tennis, swimming, dancing, handball, bowling, badminton, archery, skiing, and fly casting, which will provide recreation and enjoyment for thirty or forty years to come, are essential to all college men. Moreover, all men should be equipped

29 Harold Kenney, "An Evaluative Study of the Required Physical Education Program for Men at the University of Illinois," *Fifty-ninth Annual Proceedings of the College Physical Education Association* (Chapel Hill, N.C., 1956), p. 205.

with activities that they can use at home to maintain their health and vigor.

The list of activities in Table 4-9 is based on the interests and needs of college men. Beginning courses in all of these activities are necessary for those students who lack fundamental training in the sports that interest them. Likewise, advanced courses should be offered for those with an adequate background who desire to go further.

Table 4-9. Program for college men.

Team Sports
Basketball
Softball
Volleyball
Soccer
Speedball
Touch Football
Lacrosse
Field Hockey
Ice Hockey
Rugby
Flickerball

Aquatics
Swimming—Beginning
Swimming—Intermediate
Swimming—Advanced
Diving
Lifesaving
Water Polo

Rhythmics
Folk Dancing
Square Dancing
Ballroom Dancing
Modern Dancing
Clog and Tap Dancing

Individual Gymnastics

Individual Sports
Archery
Boating and Canoeing
Tennis
Golf
Handball
Badminton
Squash Racquets
Fly Casting
Bowling
Ice Skating
Table Tennis
Hiking
Camping Activities
Horseshoes and Quoits
Skiing

Combative Activities
Wrestling
Fencing
Judo

Gymnastics
Tumbling
Apparatus
Trampolining
Weight Training

The play interests of college men and women are more similar than they have been since the early elementary grades. There is a strong tendency for them to play together during the college years in some of the milder activities, such as golf, badminton, swimming, tennis, and volleyball. Unfortunately, however, many girls cease their participation in sports once they are no longer required to take physical education. Undoubtedly, much of the blame for this situation can be placed on the formal program of the past. Certainly, formal activities would hardly attract the interest of the girl, particularly at a time when she had so many other things to do. Besides being uninteresting to the girl, the formal program contributed very little to her needs. This situation is changing today. The program for girls and women (see Table 4-10) includes more recreative sports and games, and, with the lifting of social

Table 4-10. Program for college women.

Team Sports
Basketball
Field Hockey
Softball
Volleyball
Soccer
Speedball
Fieldball

Rhythmics
Folk Dancing
Ballroom Dancing
Square Dancing
Clog and Tap Dancing
Modern Dance

Gymnastics
Tumbling
Trampolining
Body Conditioning
Body Mechanics

Aquatics
Swimming—Elementary
Swimming—Advanced
Diving
Water Safety and Lifesaving
Synchronized Swimming

Individual Sports
Archery
Badminton
Bowling
Canoeing
Golf
Deck Tennis
Hiking
Table Tennis
Horseback Riding
Camping Activities
Skiing
Fencing
Ice Skating

taboos, there will be increasing participation in sport activities.

A good program of physical education is vitally important for college women. It can go far toward correcting the deficiencies of the previous programs that she has had. Her chief needs are various types of dance activities and individual and dual sports. What has been said regarding the need of college men to specialize in one or more sports that will carry over to adult leisure time applies equally to college women. They have as much leisure as men, if not more, and they have spent it chiefly in passive amusements, such as card parties, teas, and the like. To her dancing activities the college girl needs to add skill in golf, tennis, swimming, badminton, canoeing, equitation, table tennis, archery, hiking, skiing, and bowling. Fortunately, these activities appeal to college girls, who are enthusiastically entering into them. Surprisingly, judo or personal defense has proven a popular activity for girls in some schools.

Coeducational physical education

More and more provision is being made on the college and university level for coeducational physical education. It has taken a long time to break down the resistance to coeducational activities, but the trend is definitely in this direction. The joint classes may be taught by either a man or woman—whoever is best qualified to teach the activity in question. Dancing activities—ballroom, square, folk—are the best courses to start on the coeducational basis. However, golf, archery, fencing, tennis, badminton, skiing, and bowling can readily be taught to mixed groups.

Criteria for appraisal of instructional programs

In a conference on physical education for college men and women a list of criteria was developed for appraising the physical education programs in colleges and universities. These criteria summarize very well the important considerations involved in the instructional programs and are presented in Appendix D.

SELECTED REFERENCES

AAHPER, *Physical Education for College Men and Women* (Washington, D.C., American Association for Health, Physical Education, and Recreation, 1954).

Andrews, Gladys, Jeannette Saurborn, and Elsa Schneider, *Physical Education for Today's Boys and Girls* (Boston, Allyn & Bacon, Inc., 1960).

Cowell, C. C., and H. W. Hazelton, *Curriculum Designs in Physical Education* (Englewood Cliffs, N.J., Prentice-Hall, Inc., 1955).

Dauer, Victor P., *Fitness for Elementary School Children Through Physical Education* (Minneapolis, Burgess Publishing Co., 1963).

Fait, Hollis F., *Physical Education for the Secondary School Child* (Philadelphia, W. B. Saunders Co., 1964).

Nixon, John, and Ann Jewett, *Physical Education Curriculum* (New York, The Ronald Press Company, 1964).

Vannier, Maryhelen, and Hollis F. Fait, *Teaching Physical Education in Secondary Schools* (Philadelphia, W. B. Saunders Co., 1957).

Vannier, Maryhelen, and Mildred Foster, *Teaching Physical Education in the Elementary Schools* (Philadelphia, W. B. Saunders Co., 1963).

5

the physical education staff

Significance of staff

James A. Garfield, former President of the United States, said, "Give me a log hut, with only a simple bench, Mark Hopkins on one end and I on the other and you may have all the buildings, apparatus, and libraries without him." Possibly this quotation comes closer to over-emphasizing the importance of the faculty in the total school setup than it does to presenting all the factors in correct proportion. However, it points to a significant truth that has at times been overlooked: *no school can be greater than its staff, nor can a program advance beyond the vision of those who administer it;* the program must rely upon the staff to put it into efficient operation. Any philosophy that dictates the selection of staff members on the basis of friendship or politics rather than upon adequate qualifications can only fulfill its program in a mediocre way.

Before 1925 well-trained people in the field of physical education were comparatively scarce. Except for a brief decline during the depression years, the supply of men graduating from college with majors in the field rose gradually from 1925 to 1941, then dwindled to just a few during the war years. From 1946 to 1951 or 1952 the number increased rapidly, after which there was a noticeable decline followed by a slight rise in 1956. Calls from the armed forces temporarily removed from teaching many of the graduates of the past few years. However, the supply of men with a bachelor's degree has recently met and is meeting the demand quite well. The situation concerning women with bachelor's degrees in physical education is entirely different. There has been a marked shortage for years, and indications are that the shortage will continue. This situation provides excellent employment opportunities for women who major in the general area. The supply of both men and women with as much as two years of graduate training was inadequate in the late forties. By 1967 the supply of men with doctor's degrees was almost adequate, but the supply of women with even as much as a master's degree was very limited and of those with doctor's degrees was still less. Indications are that the situation will remain much the same for the next several years.

Since requirements for majors vary widely from school to school, it does not follow that all of those who receive degrees are equally trained. Semester hours required in physical education for a major vary from sixteen to more than sixty, and the type of instruction given also varies considerably from school to school. Out of this varied training come many well-prepared graduates, as well as some who are less so. However, the administrator who really desires a well-prepared physical education staff can have it, provided he has even mediocre tact and selecting ability. It costs little more to secure good instructors than to secure poor ones. It is a matter of knowing adequate qualifications and being able to determine which of the candidates have those qualifications. The administrator, in making staff selections, often relies upon recommendations of reliable people about whom he knows, or he may compare recommendations received from those about whom he does not know. In many cases he knows quite well some outstanding prospective faculty member to whom he can offer the position. Some administrators keep a file of excellent people for use when an opening occurs. Those who do the selecting may also provide opportunities for the prospective candidate to exhibit his qualifications by inviting him to participate in informal activities when he visits the local region. By these and other means excellent staff members can be selected.

Qualifications

What, then, are the chief considerations in selecting a physical education instructor? There are four of major importance, which can be ranked according to their bearing upon one's success as a teacher: (1) personality, (2) training, (3) experience, and (4) health. The perfectly qualified instructor has all four in abundance. However, over 99 percent are not perfect. We must, then, choose among the various important phases.

Personality the most important. As formerly defined, personality is the sum total of an individual's responses to the social situations in which he finds himself. This means that there are many phases of personality, for personality is as wide and as inclusive as life. There is no such thing as a personality perfect in all situations, for there are no persons who are never angry, never frightened, or never ill at ease at some time in their lives. Each individual shows different aspects of his personality in different situations. The outstanding athlete may exhibit superior personality traits in game situations but may appear to considerable disadvantage in the ballroom or in speaking before the assembly. The son who has been dominated at home by his father becomes almost a different person when he is entirely removed from his father's influence. Situations modify personality traits. The wild enthusiasm loosed by scoring an important touchdown would be out of place in a mathematics class, even if expressed over the solution of an extremely difficult problem. Since personality is extremely wide and inclusive, a list of personality attributes would have to be very long if it were to approach completeness.

The fundamental basis of personality is character. The two are not synonymous, but basic character traits are sure to crop out occasionally; and if not restrained, they will be prominent in the customary flow of one's reactions. Personality with its fundamental basis of character is most important in a teacher because it is most important in life. It is more important in the physical education teacher-coach than in other instructors because he or she will be imitated most frequently by the students. There will be exceptions to this, of course, but one thousand teachers who handle the physical education activities in various schools will be imitated more often by students than will one thousand teachers of English, mathematics, history, or the other academic subjects in the same schools. Character qualities and acceptable reactions are caught more than they are taught. Yet the teaching of important character traits, even though they are learned indirectly, must be planned. It should be true that those who are better educated have personalities based on sound character rather than upon superficial mannerisms that can be brought to the fore upon demand and then discarded. The mother who has preached truthfulness to her boy for years can nullify all her efforts by trying to get him into a circus at reduced admission when he is just over the age limit. In the same manner a coach can discredit all his teaching about rule observance by coaching from the side lines, when both he and the players know that such procedure is contrary to the rules. In each case the boys will draw the obvious conclusion that standards are to be lived up to except when there is a personal advantage to be gained by disobeying them. These teachings must be avoided for they do not constitute a defensible type of character education. Since character is the fundamental basis on which personality is built, the physical education instructor must be a person of sound character.

In attaining success in a position, one's personal reaction to young-sters and adults will be of first importance. Professional preparation, past experience, health, and all other factors are secondary to this. It is less difficult to teach a new coach the fundamentals and the strategy of a game he has never played than it is to change his personality from one that does not fit to one that does fit his coaching situation. Conduct-ing the class or handling the squad so that morale, with its elements of enthusiasm, cooperation, and determination, is sustained is just as im-portant as teaching skills and strategy. Personality is the prime essential in the morale builder.

The importance of personality and character in the teacher is no-where better expressed than by Pullias, et al: [1]

All of this is to say that the most fundamental principle of all we have consid-ered about excellence in teaching is that if the teacher would effectively fulfill his role as a teacher, he must constantly grow in greatness as a person. In deep-est essence, a teacher can be no greater as a teacher than he is as a person. The aphorism "What you are speaks so loud I cannot hear what you say" is no more applicable anywhere in life than in teaching.

Preparation is second in importance. From the standpoint of success as a teacher of physical education an adequate professional preparation is more significant than experience or health. Granted equivalent per-sonality qualifications, the teacher with a thorough preparation and little or no experience is worth much more than the one with much experience, but poor professional preparation. Experience is a valuable asset but it is doubtful that it can compensate for a weak professional preparation.

Table 5-1 indicates the basic and minimum requirements in the dif-ferent states for authorization to teach physical education in public schools. An analysis of these data immediately reveals appreciable dif-ferences in certification requirements. The range is from sixteen to fifty-four semester hours. Assuming equivalence in such factors as the quality of teaching, equipment, facilities, and library in teacher educa-tion institutions, it is apparent that some states require a much higher standard of professional preparation than others.

What constitutes a strong undergraduate professional preparation? At the Professional Preparation Conference [2] this question was carefully considered. The curricular areas that were *strongly recommended* to develop the competencies needed by the beginning teacher follow.

[1] Earl Pullias, Aileene Lockhart, Marjorie Bond, Marguerite Clifton, and Donna Mae Miller, *Toward Excellence in College Teaching* (Dubuque, Iowa, William C. Brown Company, Publishers, 1963), p. 44.

[2] American Association for Health, Physical Education and Recreation, *Professional Preparation in Health, Physical Education and Recreation* (Washington, D.C., 1962), pp. 65-70.

Table 5-1. Basic and minimum requirements in semester hours for authorization to teach physical education.

STATE	MEN		WOMEN	
	Basic	Minimum	Basic	Minimum
Alabama	24	18	24	18
Alaska	16	–	16	–
Arizona	30	18	30	18
Arkansas	21	21	21	21
California	24	20	24	20
Colorado	18	–	18	–
Connecticut	35	35	35	35
Delaware	41[ab]	41	41[ab]	41
District of Colombia	30[c]	30	30[c]	30
Florida	30	–	30	–
Georgia	30	30	30	30
Hawaii	36[d]	24	36[d]	24
Idaho	30	20	30	20
Illinois	20	20	20	20
Indiana	40	24	40	24
Iowa	30	15[e]	30	15[e]
Kansas	24	15	24	15
Kentucky	24	18	24	18
Louisiana	33	33	33	33
	20[f]	20	20[f]	20
Maine	B[g]	B[g]	B[g]	B[g]
Maryland	30	30	30	30
Massachusetts	18	9	18	9
Michigan	24	15	24	15
Minnesota	Major	Minor	Major	Minor
Mississippi	30	30	30	30
Missouri	24	24	24	24
Montana	30	20	30	20
Nebraska	24[h]	18[i]	24[h]	18[i]
Nevada	Major	–	Major	–
New Hampshire	30[l]	12	30[l]	12
New Jersey	40	40	40	40
New Mexico	36	36	36	36
New York	54	54	54	54
North Carolina	36	–	36	–
North Dakota	16	16	16	16
Ohio	–	24[k]	–	24[k]
Oklahoma	30	18	30	18
Oregon	24	24	24	24
Pennsylvania	36	36	36	36
Puerto Rico	30	30	30	30
Rhode Island	40	40	40	40

Table 5-1. (cont'd).

	Basic	Minimum	Basic	Minimum
South Carolina	24	24	24	24
South Dakota	15	–	15	–
Tennessee	24[bl]	24	24[bl]	24
Texas	24[m]	24	24[m]	24
Utah	40	40	40	40
Vermont	36	18	36	18
Virginia	30	30	30	30
Washington	Major	Minor	Major	Minor
West Virginia	33[b]	24	33[b]	24
Wisconsin	22	22	22	22
Wyoming	24	18	24	18

a. Plus 21 semester hours in professional education.
b. Grades 1-12.
c. Thirty semester hours for authorization to teach in senior high school, 24 in junior high school.
d. Minimum of 12 semester hours in health and 16 in physical education and a course in the teaching of physical education.
e. Fifteen semester hours for teaching half time or less, 30 semester hours for more than half time.
f. Thirty-three semester hours gives authorization in health, physical, and safety education; 20 semester hours gives authorization only in physical education (including coaching).
g. B means a bachelor's degree.
h. Twenty-four semester hours in the field, with 6 or equivalent in each subject taught.
i. Eighteen semester hours in the field, including preparation in each subject taught.
j. Thirty semester hours in the area of preparation, plus 6 in methods of teaching the specialty on the elementary and secondary school levels.
k. Forty semester hours for a special certificate.
l. Including 12 semester hours of health, 12 of physical education.
m. All-level endorsement requires 34 semester hours.

Source: W. Earl Armstrong and T. M. Stinnett, *A Manual on Certification Requirements for School Personnel in the United States*, National Commission on Teacher Education and Professional Standards, Washington, D.C., 1964, p. 40.

General education:

1. English Composition
2. Physical Science
   (a) General Chemistry
   (b) General Physics
3. Biological Sciences
   (a) General Biology
   (b) Human Anatomy
   (c) Human Physiology
4. Social Science
   (a) History

(b) General Psychology

(c) General Sociology

5. Humanities

(a) Literature (English, American, or Foreign)

(b) Philosophy

(c) The Arts (Art, Music, Theater Arts)

At the Professional Preparation Conference it was recommended that 50 percent of the undergraduate program be devoted to general education courses.

General professional education:

1. Social and Philosophical Foundations of Education
2. Educational Psychology (growth and development)
3. Educational Curriculum and Instruction
4. Directed Teaching

The amount of credit hours to be devoted to course work in general professional education is from 15 to 17 percent of the total required for graduation.

Specialized professional preparation:

1. Introduction and Orientation to Physical Education
2. Administration and Supervision of Physical Education
3. Curriculum and Instruction in Physical Education
4. History, Philosophy, and Principles of Physical Education
5. Measurement and Evaluation in Physical Education
6. Kinesiology
7. Physiology of Activity
8. Adapted Physical Education
9. Health Education and Safety Education
10. Recreation
11. Physical Activities

(a) Fundamental skills and exercise:

(1) Conditioning exercises

(2) Fundamental movements

(3) Exercise with apparatus

(4) Marching tactics

(5) Posture and body mechanics

(6) Weight training

(7) Individual self-testing events

(8) Stunts and tumbling

(b) Sports and games:

(1) Aquatics, including life saving and water safety

(2) Combatives—wrestling

(3) Team sports

Men	*Women*
Baseball	Basketball
Basketball	Soccer
Football	Speedball
Touch football	Softball
Softball	Volleyball
Speedball	
Volleyball	

(4) Individual and dual sports

Men	*Women*
Archery	Archery
Badminton	Badminton
Golf	Golf
Gymnastics	Gymnastics
Tennis	Tennis
Track and field	Track and field
	Bowling

(5) Mass or group games

(6) Individual and group contests

(7) Relays

(c) Rhythms and dance activities:

Men	*Women*
Social dance	Folk dance
Square dance	Fundamental rhythms
	Modern dance
	Social dance
	Square dance

No specific recommendations were made in regard to the amount of time and credit that should be allocated for the various courses recommended. However, the total hours for the specialized professional preparation area should represent about one-third of the total. Thus, if 120 semester hours were required for graduation, 40 should be devoted to this area.

The academic courses listed under *Specialized Professional Preparation* are nearly always included among the requirements for major students in those institutions that are recognized for their strong programs in physical education. In regard to the area of physical activities a conference of representatives of the institutions in the Northwest District,

AAHPER,[3] recommended that sixteen semester hours or twenty-four quarter hours be required of physical education majors.

In many small secondary schools the amount of physical education and coaching to be handled does not constitute a full teaching load. Consequently, school administrators must assign academic courses to the physical education teacher. It is preferable in this situation to employ a physical education major who is also qualified in an academic area. Such candidates are available and are to be preferred to those with a physical education minor. A minor possesses only a second-rate preparation and the best that can be said of it is that such a staff member is better qualified than the one with no preparation.

The preparation for a physical education minor which was recommended at the Professional Preparation Conference [4] includes the following courses:

1. Introduction and Orientation to Physical Education
2. Administration and Supervision of Physical Education
3. Curriculum and Instruction in Physical Education
4. History, Philosophy, and Principles of Physical Education
5. Measurement and Evaluation of Physical Education
6. Skills for Teaching and Coaching
7. Health Education and Safety Education

At the Professional Preparation Conference [5] the following recommendation was made: "Five years of professional preparation are essential for the basic preparation of personnel in each of the areas of health education, physical education, and recreation education."

Many school districts, particularly the larger ones, require a fifth year or a master's degree for all staff members. Ordinarily a master's degree is the minimum requirement for personnel in institutions of higher education. The doctorate is quite generally required of physical education administrators and those who have responsibilities at the graduate level. In fact, many colleges and universities require staff members with doctorates to teach undergraduate professional courses.

The discussion of professional preparation thus far has been largely in terms of *quantitative* considerations. The hours required for certification and the courses recommended for the physical education major program do not involve *qualitative* factors. A professional student could have all of the courses recommended at the Professional Preparation

3 Northwest District, American Association for Health, Physical Education and Recreation and The Athletic Institute, *Proceedings of the Menucha Conference* (1964), p. 88.

4 American Association for Health, Physical Education and Recreation, *Professional Preparation in Health, Physical Education and Recreation* (Washington, D.C., 1962), pp. 65-70.

5 *Ibid.*, p. 23.

Conference and still not be as well prepared as another who had only 50 percent of the recommended curriculum. The difference is due to the quality of programs offered.

Quality is involved in a number of factors. Of major importance are the standards for admission and retention of the physical education professional students. Some physical education departments refuse to permit the admission of candidates of doubtful quality and academic ability. In some colleges and universities with high academic standards such students could not make the grade.

The quality of the teaching staff is another vitally important consideration. In certain institutions highly trained specialists are available to teach each professional course. There is a great difference between what students get out of courses taught by well-prepared teachers as compared to the same courses taught by instructors who have only a superficial background in the area. It is an unfortunate fact that in many institutions the professional courses are taught by staff members who lack the background and mastery of the subject matter. This applies equally to the activities as the classroom courses.

Another critical item is the pride that the department takes in the quality of its products. Some physical education organizations are proud of the reputation that has been gained of graduating superior professional students. All of the faculty members are dedicated to producing quality products and no stone is left unturned to accomplish this objective.

Finally is the matter of sufficient resources for a superior operation. Such factors as the adequacy of the equipment, facilities, library, and number of faculty are all related to quality programs. The number of available faculty members is an important consideration. If the number of staff members is inadequate they are either overloaded or their classes are overly large.

Experience. From the viewpoint of producing a supply of better teachers, experience has two values: (1) it may improve those who participate, and (2) it will help select from prospective instructors those who have the basic qualifications for success in teaching.

The word "may" is used advisedly in connection with the first statement above, because all experience is not beneficial. Some is positively harmful. One is not sure to learn how to succeed through failure. A failure may teach one what to do and what not to do in a specific position, or it may discourage one. That experience which teaches one how to succeed better another time can be extremely valuable although it makes for failure in the present situation. It may be a decidedly helpful experience for a pitcher to throw a ball that is hit for a home run and thus learn what not to do the next time. Individual failures are no particular handicap and do not really make much difference. It is what the one who fails does about it that really counts. The true value of experience from the viewpoint of improving teachers is that it be genuinely successful and that it lead to better future performances. To be valuable, it should also be varied. Ten years in the same position doing the same things is less valuable than the same excellence of experience in several positions doing varied tasks. In terms of experience repetition of the same thing soon yields a rapidly diminishing return.

Experience serves as a testing device for those who select teachers. By applying pressure from various directions, strong boxes can be selected out of a group of boxes varying in strength. The pressure does not make the strong boxes strong; rather, it provides a method of determining which ones are strong. Experience does the same thing and more for teachers. It furnishes a practical means of selecting the good ones, while giving all a chance to improve to a limited extent. Many good teachers have the essentials at the start, as do the strong boxes, and experience helps classify them.

Two years in a position should familiarize an instructor with the new techniques and try him out sufficiently to meet most experience requirements. It is not correct, however, to assume that the instructor is poor because his efforts do not meet with approval in one situation. At least another two-year period of failure is necessary before the experience rating can justly be "poor," and even then the individual may succeed, although he is more apt to fail, in a third position.

Health. It is readily apparent that the entire absence of health would make it impossible for one to teach just as would the entire absence of personality or training. However, health is the least important of the four significant factors that make for success in teaching. One may teach more acceptably while enduring *some* illness than with health and a very poor personality or inadequate professional preparation; though, of course, he will be less happy than if he were enjoying health. Even experience, third among the four significant factors, contributes more to teaching success than does health. Lack of mental health is more of a handicap than lack of physical health.

Certain forms of illness—some mental, others physical—are of such a nature as to make the one afflicted with them a positive detriment in the school room or gymnasium. Tuberculosis and extreme nervous or emotional instability (which might be included under personality) are each contagious enough to condemn their possessor as unfit to teach. Still there are many instructors, afflicted with one or the other, who are teaching acceptably enough to be allowed to remain in teaching positions. Some diseases do not have enough apparent effect on teaching success to cause dismissal, even though they are liable to be harmful to the pupils. Certain diseases are apt to be harmful to pupils without becoming an immediate cause of loss of present or prospective teaching positions. To protect the health of the pupils, then, a medical examination should be required of all teachers, and those with contagious diseases should not be employed.

Selection of staff

Bates [6] made a comprehensive survey of the practices employed in the selection of men teachers for positions in high school physical education. The sources and kinds of information ranked by superintendents and placement directors in the order of importance were:

1. Personal interview
2. Observation in a teaching situation
3. Reference letters
4. College transcripts
5. Record of participation in sports
6. Statement of philosophy of physical education
7. Professional and civic activities
8. Written examinations
9. Performance of physical education skills

The personal interview. The personal interview is undoubtedly the most important of all procedures employed to select new staff members. It is exceptional that candidates are selected without being interviewed. When the expense of bringing the candidate to the community is prohibitive he may be interviewed at a convention or in his own community by a designated staff member who is traveling in that vicinity.

The interview should be carefully planned. It is designed to evaluate such factors as manner and appearance, poise, personality, verbal expression, personal philosophy of physical education, recreational interests, professional attitudes, and aspirations. The candidate should be encouraged to ask questions about any matters of concern. In addition to the formal interview impressions may be obtained at luncheon and dinner meetings or during participation in a recreational activity.

It is standard procedure to involve a committee in the interview. In addition to the physical education administrator several staff members should participate. These should be the staff members who will be most closely associated with the new staff member. In secondary schools the principal usually participates in the interview. If there is a city director he frequently is also involved. In the higher education level a dean or even the president may participate in the interview.

Observation in a teaching situation. This is a very desirable procedure but it is not extensively employed because of the problems of

[6] Aubrey Bates, "Selection of Men Teachers of Physical Education," *Research Quarterly* (May, 1954), p. 129.

implementing it. It is so advantageous, however, to see candidates in action that the efforts to arrange for them to teach one or two classes are justified.

Reference letters. Reference letters are invariably involved in the selection of new teachers. They may be assets or liabilities. When they accurately portray the weaknesses as well as strengths of the candidates they are invaluable. When weaknesses and undesirable characteristics are not mentioned where they exist a letter of recommendation has little validity. It has happened occasionally that some administrators, in order to get rid of a weak or undesirable staff member have not represented him in a true light in a letter of recommendation.

In this situation the reputation of the writer is of major importance. The integrity of many individuals is so well-established that complete reliance may be placed on their recommendations. The same confidence cannot be felt in a recommendation when the writer's integrity is unknown. In this latter case one's confidence in a written recommendation is improved when the author holds a responsible position in an institution that has a professional program of recognized standing.

The crucial importance of the character of candidates has been pointed out. The best way to determine this factor is from individuals who have been closely acquainted with the candidate. This information can be obtained via a letter of recommendation or a discussion either personally or by telephone. Of all considerations that must be evaluated fully and accurately none compares to the character of the individuals being considered.

College transcripts. Some employing officers are interested in examining transcripts of candidates; others are not. They do provide certain insights that may prove helpful. Indications of strengths and weaknesses may be revealed. Also, the academic ability of the candidates may have some significance.

In this connection it should be pointed out that the institutions attended by the candidates is an important consideration. Some colleges and universities are quality institutions and their physical education graduates are superbly prepared. Physical education departments in such institutions make every effort to eliminate weak candidates. While professional preparation is only one of the criteria to be assessed in employing new staff members its quality can be readily evaluated by determining the institution where the preparation was obtained.

Record of participation in sports. This is an important consideration where coaching is involved. It can be easily determined.

Statement of philosophy of physical education. The philosophy of candidates is invariably requested. Ordinarily it is determined in the personal interview. At times a written statement is requested.

Professional and civic activities. Information about the professional and civic activities of candidates is sought in personal interviews. Such participation is an asset to candidates.

Written examinations. Many school systems use the results of the National Teacher Examinations to evaluate the candidate's general professional background and his competence in the field of physical education. These are standard examinations, which are available at various centers.

Performance of physical education skills. A few school systems require candidates to demonstrate their activity skills. This has proven a valuable procedure for many years. It is not extensively used because of various problems in administering the tests.

Teaching load

Sound administration requires thorough consideration of the amount of work assigned to each staff member, just as it does careful staff selection.

Extremes in teaching assignments are undesirable. It is a worse administrative procedure to assign heavy loads to some staff members and only half loads to others than it is to assign too much work to all; for a general overloading may have the defense of necessity, while the partiality evident in grossly unequal assignments has no defense. Even though necessity demands temporary overloading in some cases, the efficient administrator will work persistently for a normal load for his staff. An excellent, but overworked staff, may produce only mediocre results. If physical education is worth teaching at all, it is worth teaching well.

Teaching loads in secondary schools are reasonably well standardized. Five periods per day plus a study hall or preparation period will approximate the teaching load in most secondary schools. In small schools in rural areas the teaching load will generally be greater. Departmental chairmen are usually relieved of part of the regular teaching load, usually one period per day. A similar arrangement is made for athletic directors. In many school systems the chairman and athletic director also receive extra compensation for their administrative duties.

It should be recognized that teaching load involves more than the number of classes taught per day. Conferences with students, grading papers, various clerical duties such as recording physical fitness test scores and preparation are all involved. All of these factors are related to the total number of students handled by the teacher. It is possible for a teacher to have a heavier teaching load than a colleague even though the latter may teach one less class per day. This is due to differences in class size. For this reason another standard is frequently employed, namely, one teacher for every 190 pupils.

On the higher education level twelve hours per week of undergraduate academic teaching is a widely prevalent standard. From eighteen to twenty-four hours of physical activity classes represents teaching loads in many colleges and universities. In small institutions the academic and activity teaching loads are appreciably larger.

No standard work load exists for administrators in institutions of higher education. In addition to their administrative assignment most will teach and many will coach. He must spend whatever time it takes on his administrative duties to make the department run efficiently. He must do that whether it requires ten to sixty hours a week.

Proper class size depends on such factors as space and equipment available, type of activity, degree of classification of pupils for activity, and grade level. Even though there are many modifying factors, certain general conclusions regarding class size may prove valuable. Generally a class of from thirty to forty pupils is not too large to provide an excellent teaching situation. Under favorable conditions a good teacher can produce acceptable results with classes ranging in size from fifty to sixty pupils. Favorable conditions include ample facilities and certain specific activities that lend themselves well to use by large groups. It requires a very good teacher to produce even mediocre results with a class of one hundred or more. Necessity usually demands simply riding herd, instead of teaching, when the group is that large.

Training in service

The supervisory phase of staff improvement is included here because it fits well rather than because of the assumption that the supervisor is an administrative officer. Customarily, the supervisor is not an administrative officer, although the same person may be responsible for both phases of the work. Training in service is particularly important for the beginning teacher or coach. This phase of improvement of instruction is largely a problem for high schools and elementary schools, since most instructors start there. Some of the better organized college and university physical education departments provide for supervision of instruction, especially for the new and inefficient members. Three significant obstacles prevent others from doing it: (1) the staff members who need it may resent the implication behind proffered assistance; (2) those in charge may be poorly trained in general supervision or in the specific activity under consideration; and (3) the need for supervision may not be recognized.

After the staff has been selected and is ready to be put to work the following means of improvement are suggested:

1. Developing the learning attitude

2. Encouraging additional study
3. Providing reading material
4. Providing good examples
5. Conducting meetings
6. Rewarding improvement and alertness

It is essential first of all that the various staff members desire to improve or learn during their period of employment; otherwise efforts to apply the means of improvement suggested above will fail. Lack of sufficient interest in personal advancement to prompt the effort necessary to improve, and false dignity, which puts the instructor above being a student, are sure to contribute to mediocre performance. Attitudes favoring learning can be built up. Those in charge must be students; they must admit, by deed as well as word, that they do not know the answers to all the problems that may arise and that they are willing to learn. The spirit of improvement can become contagious enough that the whole staff accepts the attitude of wanting to learn. Then pursuit of the other phases of improvement will bring significant results.

More and better opportunities to study during the period of employment are being offered by colleges and universities. Credit courses are offered by means of extension and Saturday classes. A few hours can be earned by this means each semester. Radio lectures and university-owned moving pictures provide further means of education, customarily without credit. Although not truly training while in service, summer schools might well be mentioned in this connection. The summer school offerings of many institutions are now sufficiently extensive to meet the needs of advanced study in any recognized field.

It is not enough to provide just any reading material. Certain types are worth more than others. Three of these are suggested as particularly valuable: (1) an occasional good background book to help give perspective, (2) mimeographed or typed material, from the supervisory officer, dealing with sources of information, methods, plans, and the like, and (3) specific references dealing with the topic upon which additional information is desired or needed. An enthusiastic faculty will locate much of this material and pass it around to those who can use it. However, the supervisor will need to provide additional sources even in the better situations.

Many approaches are possible in providing good examples: (1) the supervisory officer may well demonstrate a certain lesson or procedure, preferably with some other group than that of the instructor for whose benefit the demonstration is given, in order to avoid undermining the students' confidence in the instructor; (2) each staff member should have an opportunity to demonstrate his or her specialty or some well-developed technique; (3) moving pictures of excellent performers can be shown; (4) opportunities should be provided to visit excellent teachers in neighboring cities—a day or two each year spent in this manner can be extremely valuable; (5) coaching clinics contribute their bit; and (6) short two-day coaching schools, with demonstrations, during the Christmas vacation season, are valuable.

Two types of meetings are essential in supervisory work: (1) the group meeting, and (2) the private conference. The one in charge must take care to avoid dominating the situation too thoroughly. If the purpose in mind is that of giving information or expressing the supervisor's views, this can be accomplished almost as well through written material, and thus much of the individual instructor's time can be saved. Questions and discussions are essential elements in both group and private sessions. These features are readily promoted by providing for free expression. This should be the place where each one may say what he thinks; and, incidentally, many of the statements made should not be repeated outside. It is wise to allow criticisms and suggestions to be made in open meetings, for if they are not countenanced in the group conferences, they are apt to be expressed elsewhere. Each supervisor must guide the trend of the discussion and decide quite largely the topic to be introduced, but any staff member should have an opportunity to raise questions and make suggestions. An occasional correction of an administrator's or supervisor's mistake through discussion in a staff meeting may be a healthy procedure. It certainly should not be avoided at the cost of free expression.

By employing the last of the six suggested methods of improving instructors in service, the administrator promotes the first essential procedure listed. When there are rewards for alertness, cooperation, and service, then the staff will strive to improve. Some of the common methods of improving instruction through rewarding efficient, cooperative service are: (1) increasing salary, (2) giving a little well-directed praise, (3) increasing rank and authority, (4) providing educational publicity concerning meritorious service, and (5) passing on information concerning better positions that have opened or are about to open.

STAFF MORALE

The maintenance of high staff morale is as important as any other responsibility the administrator has. Morale is an extremely critical factor because it affects the performance of staff members so decisively. An individual with high morale will contribute 100 percent of his potential while one with low morale will do just enough to get by. In any given set of circumstances a staff with high morale will be much more effective in achieving the purposes of the program than one with low morale.

Even with the best of facilities, equipment, time allotment, class size, teacher load, salaries, and curriculum poor staff morale will affect progress toward departmental objectives adversely.

Nature of morale

Morale is synonymous with esprit de corps or élan of a group. Pride is another characteristic of morale. The morale of the U. S. Marines exemplifies both esprit de corps and pride. A fuller concept of morale is provided by French:[7]

Morale refers to the condition of a group where there are clear and fixed group goals (purpose) that are felt to be important and integrated with individual goals; where there is confidence in the attainment of these goals, and subordinately, confidence in the means of attainment, in the leaders, associates, and finally in oneself; where group actions are integrated and cooperative; and where aggression and hostility are expressed against the forces frustrating the group rather than toward other individuals within the group.

Factors affecting teacher morale

Many studies have been made of the factors that affect teacher morale. It is recognized that morale develops from a multitude of interrelated variables and dimensions and rarely results from one or two isolated factors. Among the more important of considerations are:

1. Good communications
2. Adequate salary scale
3. Appropriate facilities and equipment
4. Assignment in which teacher is interested and for which he is prepared
5. Pupil, parent, and community respect for teachers
6. Congenial colleagues
7. Reasonable fringe benefits
8. Quality program
9. Participation in policy decisions
10. Excellent administration

Each of these factors will be briefly reviewed.

1. Good communications. It is frustrating for staff members to be kept uninformed concerning matters that are important to them. They become resentful when they learn from students or local citizens items of information that should have come to them through normal channels of communication. At times they are embarrassed by their lack of in-

[7] John R. French, "The Disruption and Cohesion of Groups," *Journal of Abnormal and Social Psychology* (July, 1941), p. 376.

formation. Their performance may be adversely affected by their failure to be adequately informed.

Another aspect of communications involves the opportunity of staff members to discuss common concerns with each other and with the administrator. They appreciate the freedom to raise questions and to contribute ideas. This means much to them and makes them feel a part of a team. It definitely contributes to their morale.

2. Adequate salary scale. An adequate salary is an important consideration in developing morale. It is not the most significant item but is included among the major factors. Staff members become particularly sensitive about their salary when they believe they have been discriminated against. When they believe they were entitled to an increase and they fail to get it, and other staff members do, they feel that their efforts are not appreciated.

3. Appropriate facilities and working conditions. Physical educators are eager to achieve results in their teaching and they chafe when they are markedly handicapped by poor working conditions. They want to take pride in their program and when the facilities and equipment make a good program impossible their morale is affected, particularly if there is no prospect in the immediate future to remedy the situation.

4. Teacher is prepared and interested in his assignment. The teacher's preferred assignment is usually in his teaching major. Here he is best prepared and will probably do his most effective teaching. Teachers are ordinarily dissatisfied when they are required to teach a subject for which they are not prepared and in which they are not interested. They must spend a great deal of time in preparation and even then they do not feel the confidence that they would in their major field.

5. Pupil, parent, and community respect for teachers. No teacher can be satisfied in an environment where respect and courtesy for him and the profession are absent. In communities where public attitudes toward schools are wholesome and constructive and teachers are accepted into community and social life they will much more likely be accorded cooperation and respect from the students.

6. Congenial colleagues. This includes colleagues outside the physical education department as well as within it. A friendly and congenial atmosphere within the department and the school contributes much to job satisfaction. This is particularly pertinent to physical educators because some academic colleagues may not regard physical education as a bona fide discipline.

7. Reasonable fringe benefits. Suitable provisions for retirement, sick-leaves, sabbatical leaves for travel or study are made in virtually all colleges and in many secondary schools. It has not been until recently that secondary schools have granted sabbatical leaves for travel or study but the practice is growing rapidly.

8. Quality program. It contributes to the morale of a teacher to feel

that he is a member of a staff that has the reputation within the area, state, or region of having an excellent program. The majority of individuals take pride in being members of acknowledged first class organizations. Physical educators believe that they can render a valuable service to the students, the school, and the community but this cannot be done with a poor or indifferent program.

9. Participation in policy decisions. Teachers like to be consulted before decisions are made which directly affect them or their immediate environment. They prefer the democratic administrator who respects their opinion. Their participation in policy decisions gives them a sense of security.

10. Excellent administration. Many studies of teacher morale agree that the administrator himself is the crucial factor in the development and maintenance of morale. Griffiths [8] states: "The administrator is the key to the morale problem. He sets the climate for morale in his school."

Physical education staff members look to their departmental chairman to improve their circumstances and to solve their problems. They look to his leadership to reduce class size, to lighten teacher loads, and to secure good facilities and appropriate equipment. They expect him to support them in their disciplinary problems. He should recognize, and reward meritorious service. They want him to be fair and impartial to all staff members and to respect their opinions.

The administrator's responsibility for morale is a heavy one. There are certain variables over which he has little or no control. But those factors that he can partially or wholly control he should employ for the best interests of the morale of his staff.

SELECTED REFERENCES

AAHPER, *Professional Preparation in Health, Physical Education and Recreation* (Washington, D.C., American Association for Health, Physical Education and Recreation, 1962).

Griffiths, Daniel, *Human Relations in School Administration* (New York, Appleton-Century-Crofts, 1956), Chap. 7.

Howard, Glenn W., and Edward Masonbrink, *Administration of Physical Education* (New York, Harper and Row, Publishers, 1963), Chap. 13.

Pullias, Earl, Marjorie Bond, Marguerite Clifton, Aileen Lockhart, and Donna Mae Miller, *Toward Excellence in College Teaching* (Dubuque, Iowa, William C. Brown Company, Publishers, 1963).

[8] Daniel Griffiths, *Human Relations in School Administration* (New York, Appleton-Century-Crofts, 1956), p. 156.

6

school health education

Relationship of health education and physical education

Many people regard health education and physical education as synonymous or one as being part of the other. This is an entirely erroneous impression. Health education and physical education are separate and distinct, though closely allied, fields. Physical education is that phase of education which comes about through or in connection with vigorous muscular activities. Health education, on the other hand, comprises all of the experiences that contribute in any way to the individual's health knowledge, health habits, and health attitudes. Health education differs from physical education in subject matter, methods, and in some purposes.

Physical education has important contributions to make to health education, and vice versa. Inherent in physical education are exceptional opportunities to develop health knowledge, health habits, and health attitudes. On the other hand, the emphasis in health education on such areas as exercise, nutrition, recreation, rest, and desirable health practices has important implications for physical education. However, a lecture in health education or a trip to the local dairy is not physical education, nor is a unit in basketball or wrestling health education.

Health education responsibilities of physical educators

The majority of physical educators in secondary schools and colleges and universities have important responsibilities in the school health education program. They must cooperate fully with the school doctor, nurse, or other medical personnel. Many physical education teachers participate in the administration of the medical examinations. Studies have shown that more physical educators teach the separate health courses than do any other teachers. A survey by the Federal Security Agency [1] revealed that in forty-two different states physical education and health education are taught by the same certified teacher. All physical education teachers have the responsibility in their physical education classes for teaching health habits, health attitudes, and health knowledge whenever a favorable opportunity presents itself. Because of their excellent background, many physical educators serve as health counselors, particularly in the smaller schools. Finally, physical education and health education are combined into one department in many schools, and the physical education director has the responsibility for administering both programs.

Because of these important and varied relationships to the health education program the physical educator must be familiar with this important area. This is particularly true for the administrator in physical education who bears the responsibility for implementing all of the health education obligations of the department.

Changing outlook on health

Schools have broadened the scope of their programs considerably in the last half century. Modern philosophy considers that an educational institution is concerned with more than the intellectual development and vocational preparation of youth. Experience has clearly shown the inadequacy of an education that has been limited to only these objectives. Health has come to be considered one of the most important of the objectives of education. Health is too important to be trusted to individual or family initiative. Educators realized that whatever other objectives are sought, health aids in progress toward them. Health is basic to learning, to happiness, to success, to effective citizenship, and to worthwhile living. Without health, the individual is less effective than he might have been and is handicapped in everything he does. Some persons with poor health have made significant contributions to society, but these contributions have come in spite of their handicaps.

World War II greatly increased the importance of the health objective. The lack of health and physical fitness of American men and women was one of the major revelations of the war. The selective service medical examinations revealed all too clearly that insufficient attention

[1] Federal Security Agency, *Health Instruction in the Secondary Schools* (Washington, D.C., U.S. Government Printing Office, 1951), p. 17.

has been given to health. Although some progress had been made, the nation was shocked that we had profited so little from our experience in the previous war. Public opinion was aroused, and all health agencies accelerated and expanded their activities. The schools have responded to the challenge and are emphasizing health to a degree never before approached.

Modern concept of health. When educators first made a place in the curriculum for health, they regarded it only as physical soundness. An individual was ill when confined to his bed—otherwise, he was well. The emphasis was on freedom from disease and physical defects. As time passed, more and more was read into the meaning of health. It was found that a psychosis or neurosis was more detrimental to the health of an individual than flat feet and that emotional breakdowns were as serious as physical breakdowns. This broadened concept of health is expressed in the definition: *Health is considered that condition, mental and physical, in which the individual is functionally well adjusted internally as concerns all body parts and externally as concerns his environment.* This definition of health is positive; it means more than merely keeping out of the hospital. It implies a healthy organism and a healthy personality.

The objectives of the school health program

The aim of the school health program is the development of optimum physical, mental, emotional, and social health among all pupils. The specific objectives that lead to the accomplishment of this aim are outlined by Anderson: [2]

1. A continuing appraisal of each child's health status
2. An understanding of each child's health needs
3. Supervision and guidance of the health of the children
4. Development of the highest possible level of health for each youngster
5. Prevention of defects and disorders
6. Detection and correction of all defects and disorders
7. Special health provisions for the exceptional child
8. Reduction in the incidence of communicable and noncommunicable diseases
9. In each youngster a positive health awareness and a desire for a high level of health
10. Development of wholesome health attitudes
11. Development of healthful personal practices
12. Acquisition of scientific and functional knowledge of personal and community health
13. Development of an appreciation of aesthetic factors related to health
14. Development of a high level of self-esteem in each youngster
15. Effective social adjustment

[2] C. L. Anderson, *School Health Practice* (St. Louis, The C. V. Mosby Co., 1956), pp. 33, 34.

16. Mentally hygienic school environment
17. Establishment and maintenance of sanitary practices and surroundings
18. Provision of emergency measures

Organization of the school health program

Since health is so educational in function, it is very important that its supervision and control be centered in the board of trustees or board of education. In the past, many communities placed the responsibility for the public health work in the board of health. The board of health has the machinery for the control of communicable disease and can administer this phase of the program better than the board of education. Considering the educational aspects of the school health education program, the control should reside in the board of education, but there should be cooperation with all local groups interested and concerned with health.

The best way of bringing about school and community coordination and cooperation in matters relating to the health of the school population is through a community health council. This council should be composed of representatives of the schools, the local board of health, the county medical and dental associations, and all other public and private agencies concerned with health. The community health council concerns itself with broad policies and problems and mobilizes all the health resources of the community behind the school health program.

A health council or health committee should be organized, where possible, in each school. The function of the health council is to give guidance and leadership to the health education program within the school and to cooperate with the community health council through duly appointed representatives. Membership on the health council should include the principal, the school medical adviser, the health coordinator, various teachers, and student and parent representatives. If a school psychologist, nurse, nutritionist, and dentist are available, they should also be included.

Every school must have a physician who will function as a school medical adviser. Small schools will be unable to afford a full-time medical adviser, but it will be possible for them to obtain one on a part-time basis. It is essential that every school have recourse to a physician to advise upon the many health problems that require medical judgment. In many communities where the school is unable to afford a paid medical adviser, the county medical society will frequently cooperate by contributing the part-time services of several physicians without charge.

There must be someone in each school who has a definite responsibility for the total school health program. This individual is known as the health counselor or health coordinator. In the smaller schools and colleges the coordinator may be any instructor, head of department, or, in the case of high schools, the principal or superintendent. Regardless of the size of the institution, the best qualified individual should be in charge of the health program. The director of physical education is frequently the health coordinator. Educators have associated physical education closely with health values and objectives. Unless the physical educator is well trained for health education there is no justification for placing him in charge of the health education program. If he has been well-prepared, however, he is in a strategic position to perform excellent service. Students usually esteem him highly and grant him great authority, particularly if he is the coach. He comes into close informal contact with the boys and thus gains a better understanding of their health problems and needs. The woman physical educator, too, can get closer to the girls than any other teacher. Innumerable opportunities occur in the physical education classes and intramural and interscholastic sports to protect, promote, and teach health. In the smaller institutions the physical examination is usually conducted by the physical education department. For these reasons the physical educator makes an excellent health coordinator in the small schools if he or she is well-trained. Teacher-training institutions are providing much more adequate preparation in health education than hitherto, and in the future physical educators will be better qualified as health coordinators. In the large institutions the task of administering the physical education department requires so much of the director's time and effort that it is inadvisable for him to undertake the additional responsibilities involved in directing the health education program.

The health coordinator. The success of the school health program depends to a great extent upon the health coordinator. He should have the following qualifications and training:

1. A strong basic science background, including physics or chemistry, biology, physiology, and bacteriology
2. A strong preparation in education, including educational psychology, principles of education, educational methods, curriculum construction, and tests and measurements
3. Thorough preparation in the field of health, including personal health, nutrition, mental hygiene, first aid, health and physical diagnosis, and communicable disease control
4. An understanding of the purpose and functions of all health agencies in the community, particularly the local public health organization
5. An understanding of the nature and functions of the total school health program

6. An appreciation of the potential contribution of all subject-matter fields and all other phases of school life to the total health program
7. Training in special skills required in health education, including the methods and materials in health education, the evaluation of sources of material and information, the nature, preparation, and use of visual aids, public relations and publicity methods and techniques, and the nature of the printing and duplicating processes and their use

The duties of the school health coordinator usually involve the following activities:

1. To assume the responsibility for developing and supervising the total school health program
2. To coordinate the school health program with all pertinent agencies and individuals, including parents, public health agencies, family physicians, and the local medical society
3. To interpret to teachers the results of physical, medical, dental, and psychological examinations of their students
4. To assume the responsibility of the follow-up of medical and dental examinations
5. To ascertain that the school physician's recommendations for special programs for certain students are implemented
6. To help secure the most effective utilization of the school physician's time
7. To see that students needing special attention are referred to the school physician
8. To assist teachers who have pupils or advisees with health problems
9. To determine that students who participate in extracurricular activities can do so without adverse effects upon their health
10. To check students who return to school after illness or injury and to assist in their readjustment
11. To assume the responsibility for checking the sanitary environment of the school
12. To analyze the health factors involved in truancy and excessive absence and to take appropriate action
13. To maintain all health records of students
14. To make arrangements early in the school year for screening tests for vision, hearing, and posture
15. To secure publicity for the school health program and to see that all staff members are aware of the services available to them
16. To give leadership to the health instruction program. This involves curriculum revision with all those who teach special health courses; preparation of syllabi; assistance in obtaining films, books, and health instruction materials; and provision of in-service training

where necessary. It also means coordinating the efforts of all teachers whose courses offer excellent possibilities for correlating instruction

17. To work out detailed procedures to be followed when accidents occur
18. To assume the responsibility for the school safety program
19. To set up procedures for the evaluation of the school health program

Personnel. Health cannot be effectively taught in two or three periods a week. The entire staff of the school must protect, promote, and teach health every day in every way if a genuine contribution to the health of the child is to be made. A health-conscious staff is essential to a successful program.

The health personnel may include physicians, dentists, dental hygienists, psychologists, psychiatrists, nurses, oculists, nutritionists, other specialists, and visiting teachers. There are no accepted standards as to the size of the staff, although physicians, dentists, and nurses are considered necessary. The size of the staff is dependent upon what the school board and the community want and are willing to pay for. It is desirable that all of the health staff have some educational training in order that they may have an educational viewpoint.

The scope of the school health program

The major phases of the total school health program are: (1) healthful school living, (2) health service, and (3) health instruction. Although each of these major areas is discussed separately, it should be emphasized that all are so closely related as to form parts of one coordinated whole, and only by such coordination can a worthwhile program be developed. The relationships can readily be perceived in Figure 6-1.

HEALTHFUL SCHOOL LIVING

Meaning

Healthful school living is a more inclusive term, to be preferred to those that formerly designated this phase of school health education. This term refers to the entire environment that surrounds the pupil. It not only involves safe and sanitary facilities but also includes careful planning of the school day for study, play, and rest. Since teachers are also part of the school environment, the establishment of healthful teacher-pupil relationships is an important aspect of healthful school living.

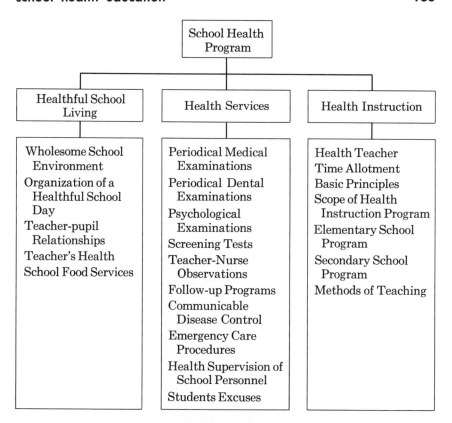

Figure 6-1.   Coordinated Phases of School Health Program.

Wholesome school environment

Every school is obligated to surround its students with a healthful environment: physical, social, and emotional. Intelligently planned, hygienically arranged, well-equipped school plants kept in a sanitary and safe condition are essential in the development and protection of child health. Construction and maintenance of the school building should be in accordance with standards established by law and by official building and health regulations. Adequate and well-arranged lighting and seating, properly functioning heating and ventilating systems, reliable equipment for fire protection, approved plumbing, suitable acoustics, adequate toilet facilities, and sanitary drinking fountains are some commonly recognized requirements for a healthful school environment. Furthermore, adequate handwashing facilities, hot and cold water, liquid or powder soap, and paper towels are all necessary for pupils as well as for teachers.

Standards for school sanitary facilities are established in building codes of state education departments and sanitary regulations of state health departments. These standards were determined by experts, and if they are up to date and adhered to within a school, the proper physical environment for children will be assured. The responsibility for sanitary inspections may be that of the school nurse, school doctor, health officer, or sanitary inspector, principal or superintendent. In smaller schools, the health coordinator or superintendent may make the inspections.

The organization of a healthful school day

The health educator has more control over the organization of a healthful school day than he has over the environmental conditions of the children. Any organization of the school day must be considered unhygienic if it overtaxes school children mentally or physically. Some of the factors that must be regarded by the health counselor are these:

1. The length of the school day
2. The number and the length of the periods
3. The student load
4. The number and kind of study periods
5. The placement of the activities
6. The amount and kind of homework and the importance attached to it
7. The number, length, and kind of rest and relaxation periods
8. Extracurricular activities

More high school and college students have had their health affected adversely by poor organization of the school day and unsatisfactory teacher-pupil relationships than by unhygienic surroundings. High school and college students need guidance in the scholastic load they are carrying. They are frequently prone to undertake a heavy extracurricular load as well as other outside work. Some supervision is necessary to prevent them from undertaking too much. The extracurricular participation may be restricted, the scholastic schedule may be lightened, or, if possible, the outside work may be reduced if the student demonstrates that he is carrying too great a load.

The daily schedules of high school and college students should be such as to establish a regular program of work and insure sufficient time for meals, sleep, rest, exercise, and recreation. The college scholastic work should be limited to approximately eight hours per day or forty hours per week. The scholastic load should be about six hours per day in the high schools. Six periods of from 55 to 60 minutes are preferable to eight 45-minute periods. When the long period is used, there should be a "mid-period stretch" for several minutes. Part of the 60-minute period is used for supervised study, which tends to reduce the amount of homework. Five or six hours of home study per week is all that can be expected of high school students. When the 45-minute period is used, two of the eight periods should be devoted to study or activity periods.

School food services

An important feature of healthful school living is the school food service program. This program has two objectives: (1) to improve the health of children through serving more nutritious, well-balanced meals at minimum cost, and (2) to use the lunch period as an educational experience.

The food service program really cuts across all aspects of the total school health program. The provision of good nutrition is a part of healthful school living. Nutrition education belongs in the area of health instruction. The supervision of the diets of students who are suffering from malnutrition is an aspect of the school health services program.

The principal and ultimately the superintendent of schools is responsible for the total food services program. Whenever possible this responsibility is delegated to a qualified director of food service.

In connection with food services the sale of candy and carbonated beverages in the school lunchroom or anywhere else in the school should be eliminated. The American Medical Association, the American Dental Association, and the National Congress of Parents and Teachers are opposed to these products. Their opposition is based upon available evidence that these products affect the health of students adversely.

Teacher-pupil relationships

Every teacher in the school has a contribution to make to the health of the pupil. In addition to instructing and supervising the health of the students, the teacher can do much to promote health by his teaching methods. The latter are particularly important from the standpoint of mental hygiene. Too much stress should not be placed upon term examinations as a basis for promotion or final grades. The policy of rewards and punishments should be considered carefully. Imprudent disciplinary measures may have serious mental hygiene implications. The instructor should use fear only as a last resort to motivate desirable attitudes and conduct. Insofar as possible he should so conduct his classes that fear of failure, ridicule, sarcasm, or embarrassment may not result. He must recognize that constant failure invariably causes poor mental hygiene. The instructor is confronted with many different personalities, and he cannot treat them all alike. Teachers who understand the principles of mental hygiene and put them into daily practice make an indispensable contribution to the health education program.

The teacher's health

The highest attainable health of the body, the mind, and the personality of every school child is the aim of the health education program. Such an aim could hardly be attained by unhealthy teachers. For years teachers were assumed to be healthy when, in reality, many were not. The school has as much right to demand physical fitness from its teachers as intellectual and moral fitness. Not only is it incompatible for a teacher in poor health to teach, but such an individual may even prove a source of contagion to the students. An unhealthy instructor is a health liability to an educational institution.

High schools and colleges have been giving more and more attention to the matter of the health of the instructional staff. In the past, the school itself was responsible for many of the factors that impaired the teacher's physical fitness. The heavy teaching load, the unhygienic lighting and ventilation of the school room, inadequate salaries, lack of rest rooms and rest periods, and dogmatic, destructive criticism were factors unfavorable to health. Other causes of ill health include hurried eating, insufficient recreation, poor living conditions, and lack of exercise.

The teacher's health may be promoted and safeguarded in a number of ways. Following are some recommended procedures for maintaining and improving teacher health:

1. Periodic physical examination, including a tuberculin test and a chest X-ray for positive reactors
2. Health qualifications for new teachers
3. A reasonable teaching load
4. Rest periods and rest rooms
5. Recreational facilities for teachers
6. Adequate salaries
7. Insurance of salaries during illness
8. Sanitary and healthful teaching environment
9. Medical and hospital care for teachers
10. Desirable, healthful living quarters for teachers
11. Provision for health instruction for teaching staff
12. Retirement fund for teachers
13. Health insurance
14. Teacher tenure

SCHOOL HEALTH SERVICES

Nature and scope of health services

This service program embraces the various protective measures assumed by the school to conserve and improve the health of children. The highest attainable physical, mental, and emotional health of every school child is the goal of the school health services program. The health services vary considerably in different institutions, but the minimum essentials of a good program include the following activities:

1. Health appraisal:
   (a) The periodic medical examination
   (b) The periodic dental examination
   (c) Psychological examinations
   (d) Screening tests
   (e) Teacher-nurse observations
2. The follow-up program
3. Communicable disease control
4. Emergency care procedure
5. Health supervision of school personnel
6. Student excuses

The scope of the school health services is limited in the curative and remedial field because of the noneducational aspects of this type of activity.

Health appraisal

The total assessment of the health status of the school child is called *health appraisal.* Health appraisal is defined as "the process of determining the total health status of a child through such means as health histories, teacher and nurse observations, screening tests, and medical, dental, and psychological examinations." [3] Not only do the physician, dentist, and nurse play a part in the health appraisal but the parent, teacher, and psychologist are also involved. The term *health appraisal* is a broader and more comprehensive one than physical examination, health examination, or medical examination.

The periodic medical examination. The medical examination is that phase of health appraisal which is performed by the physician. A

[3] National Education Association and American Medical Association Joint Committee on Health Problems in Education, *School Health Services* (Washington, D.C., and Chicago, 1953), p. 7.

periodic medical examination is the very foundation of the entire health program, as health protection, health instruction, and health promotion are all dependent upon it. By determining the health status of every student, the medical examination may be used as the basis on which to plan the student's curricular and extracurricular activities or as a yardstick to measure improvement in health and to guard against impairment of health. Cases of communicable disease must be discovered in order that their transmission may be checked and treatment obtained.

The ideal program is one in which the examination is done by the family physician and the results reported to the school. The parents and pupils are thus taught that medical care and supervision are their responsibilities and not those of the community. In addition, the family physician is better acquainted with the pupil, and more time and opportunity are available for a thorough examination. Then if any therapy is needed it can be done immediately. Family physicians should employ the same examination record form that the school system uses.

The students who are not regularly subjected to an examination by their family physicians should receive one from the physician serving the school. If a school physician is not available there are usually some local agencies such as a welfare or health department clinic, which can arrange to take care of children from underprivileged homes.

The recommended standard for the number of medical examinations includes one that is a preliminary to entrance to the kindergarten or first grade, one in the intermediate grades, one in the junior high school, and one before leaving school. Additional examinations should be arranged whenever there are suspicious indications. Previously, the recommended standard was an annual examination. Experience has shown that this standard was impractical. Those schools that were attempting to meet this standard were often providing such a superficial examination as to invalidate the procedure. Less frequent but more thorough examinations produce better results.

When examinations are given at school, qualified physicians and nurses should give them, although the faculty and reliable students may assist in some of the routine details, such as weighing and measuring. The time of the physician should be devoted as much as possible to those aspects of the examination which cannot be done by anyone else. Women physicians should examine the girl students. A satisfactory examination requires from twenty to thirty minutes for each student. A minimum of fifteen to twenty minutes of the physician's time should be given to each individual. The child should be stripped to the waist or clothed in a slipover. Privacy is essential if the fullest confidence of the student is to be secured.

Preliminary to the examination, all available health records of the student should be brought up to date and reviewed. Each pupil should have a cumulative health record throughout his school career. Excellent forms have been developed for this purpose. In addition to the data from the periodic medical and dental examinations, the cumulative record should include the family health history, the health history of the individual, his health habits and complaints, symptoms and signs of health disturbances that he reports, teachers' and nurses' observations of health, attendance record, and the results of all psychological tests.

During the examination, the physician should attempt to secure the confidence and the cooperation of the student. It is desirable, particularly in the elementary grades, to have the parents attend the medical examination. Every effort should be made to schedule the examination when parents can attend. They can help the examiner to obtain a better understanding of their child and his health habits. The parents will discover the health status of their child, and they can ask questions that have been troubling them. The educational aspects of the examination should be interpreted to the students and to the parents. The examiner will lose an invaluable opportunity if he fails to commend the student upon the favorable aspects of his health and his good health habits.

The medical examination should be quite complete. If a blood test or urinalysis is needed, it should be done privately. Both these tests are too expensive for most schools to provide routinely. Some provision should be made for detecting tuberculosis. Many schools administer the tuberculin test and x-ray the positive reactors. Schools can obtain specialized assistance from local, state, and national organizations devoted to tuberculosis control.

Participation in interscholastic or intercollegiate athletics should be contingent upon passing an adequate medical examination. The recommended standard is an examination of the participants prior to the beginning of each sport. The minimum standard is an examination once each year with a reexamination for those who have suffered a disabling injury or illness. The general examination that is ordinarily given to students is not thorough enough for athletes. The medical examination of athletes should include an examination of the heart, pulse, and blood pressure before and after exercise, the lungs, bones, joints, and the inguinal and umbilical region for hernia. A urinalysis is strongly recommended. A tuberculin test, followed by an X ray for the positive reactors, should be required.

The periodic dental examination. The periodic dental examination is another essential aspect of the health appraisal program. The fact that dental decay is the most prevalent physical defect among school children emphasizes the necessity of providing such a program. The great majority of school children experience some dental decay, which could readily be prevented by the application of proper procedures.

Basic to the accomplishment of the objectives of the dental health program is an annual visit to the dentist for an examination and correction of defects that are found. This procedure will enable the dentist to discover and correct conditions before they become serious.

The school's responsibility in regard to dental health involves the encouragement of children and their parents to see their dentist at regular intervals. Every parent should be made aware of the child's dental defects and the possible consequences if not corrected. It also includes, in many communities, the conduct of dental inspections. A dental inspection is not as complete as a regular dental examination in the dentist's office, but it does serve the purpose of discovering dental conditions that require correction. Many schools routinely provide dental inspections, but others do not. Dental hygienists often administer the dental inspections. The trend is definitely to place the responsibility for dental treatment upon the parents. Special arrangements are usually possible for the children of destitute families.

Psychological examinations. Another important aspect of health appraisals is related to the mental and emotional health of the pupils. This is a significant aspect of health and one that must not be neglected. Tests of intelligence, reading, social adjustment, personality, and attitudes toward school and other children are very helpful in providing additional data that relate to the health of children. In addition, the classroom teacher is able to report anecdotes, particularly of those children who deviate from the normal. The school administrator, psychologist (if one is available), counselor, guidance teacher, social worker, health educator, physician, and nurse may have valuable data to add to the cumulative health record in regard to the mental and emotional aspects of health.

The mental health program is concerned with the discovery and prevention of mental and emotional illness. In the discovery of such conditions the classroom teacher plays a vital role. His close association with students throughout the school year gives him an exceptional opportunity to understand them. If the teacher has a good preparation in child growth and development and understands child behavior, he will be able to detect children who depart from the normal. A knowledge of the factors that lead to mental and emotional illness is important in the prevention program. One of the most important considerations is that the child experience some success in his school activities. Constant failure is damaging to anyone's mental and emotional health. Providing an opportunity for each pupil to be creative in ways natural to him is another important factor. Satisfying relationships with classmates are also indispensable for the well-adjusted child.

Screening tests. Screening tests are so-called because they "screen out" pupils who may be in need of further examination and diagnosis by specialized health service personnel. Such tests are utilized particularly for height, weight, vision, and hearing. The screening process is usually done by the classroom teacher or nonmedical personnel, thus saving the valuable time of the school physician or nurse.

The classroom teacher should measure the height and weight of his pupils at stipulated intervals, preferably, at the beginning, middle, and end of each school year. The weighing and measuring should be done under constant conditions. Children who lose weight, show no gain, or gain excessively over a period of three months, should be examined by a physician to determine the reason.

The Snellen test is the most extensively used screening test for vision in the schools. Whichever test is used, it should be administered by the classroom teacher. It should be given annually to all elementary and secondary school pupils and more frequently when visual defects are suspected. A screening test for color deficiency should also be administered once in the upper elementary grades.

The screening test for hearing should be administered annually in the elementary schools and every two years in the secondary schools. The audiometer is used for this test. It should be administered by a technician, nurse, or the classroom teacher. If the teacher does it he should have special training.

Teacher-nurse observations. Teacher-nurse observations are also an important part of health appraisal. The teacher, particularly, comes into constant contact with the students; he may, therefore, readily observe changes in their behavior or appearance. Frequently, teachers are not qualified to detect deviations that may be significant but they may easily be prepared to do this. Teachers may be taught what to look for by the school nurse, health coordinator, or physician.

Among the conditions that the teacher should note as he observes his pupils are the following: [4]

1. Eyes:
(a) Sties or crusted lids
(b) Inflamed eyes
(c) Crossed eyes
(d) Repeated headaches
(e) Squinting, frowning
(f) Protruding eyes
(g) Watery eyes
(h) Rubbing of eyes
(i) Excessive blinking
(j) Twitching of the lids
(k) Holding head to one side

[4] Joint Committee on Health Problems in Education of NEA and AMA *Health Appraisal of School Children* (National Education Association, Washington, D.C., 1957), pp. 13-15.

2. Ears:

(a) Discharge from ears
(b) Earache
(c) Failure to hear questions
(d) Picking at the ears
(e) Turning the head to hear
(f) Talking in a monotone
(g) Inattention
(h) Anxious expression
(i) Excessive noisiness of child

3. Nose and throat:

(a) Persistent mouth breathing
(b) Frequent sore throat
(c) Recurrent colds
(d) Chronic nasal discharge
(e) Frequent nose bleeding
(f) Nasal speech
(g) Frequent tonsilitis

4. Skin and scalp:

(a) Nits on the hair
(b) Unusual pallor of face
(c) Eruptions or rashes
(d) Habitual scratching of scalp or skin
(e) State of cleanliness
(f) Excessive redness of skin

5. Teeth and mouth:

(a) State of cleanliness
(b) Gross caries
(c) Irregular teeth
(d) Stained teeth
(e) Gum boils
(f) Offensive breath
(g) Mouth habits such as thumb sucking

6. General condition and appearance:

(a) Underweight—very thin
(b) Overweight—very obese
(c) Does not appear well
(d) Tires easily
(e) Chronic fatigue
(f) Nausea or vomiting
(g) Faintness or dizziness

7. Growth:

(a) Failure to gain regularly over 6-month period
(b) Unexplained loss in weight
(c) Unexplained rapid gain in weight

8. Glands:

(a) Enlarged glands at side of neck
(b) Enlarged thyroid

9. Heart:

(a) Excessive breathlessness
(b) Tires easily
(c) Any history of "growing pains"
(d) Bluish lips
(e) Excessive pallor

10. Posture and musculature:

(a) Alignment of shoulders and hips
(b) Peculiarity of gait
(c) Obvious deformities of any type
(d) Alignment of spine on "standing tall"
(e) Muscular development
(f) Coordination
(g) Muscle tone
(h) Use of the feet in standing and walking

11. Behavior:

(a) Overstudious, docile, and withdrawing
(b) Bullying, overaggressive, and domineering
(c) Unhappy and depressed
(d) Overexcitable, uncontrollable emotions
(e) Stuttering or other forms of speech difficulty
(f) Lack of confidence, self-denying, and self-censure
(g) Poor accomplishment in comparison with ability
(h) Lying (imaginative or defensive)
(i) Lack of appreciation of property rights (stealing)
(j) Abnormal sex behavior
(k) Antagonistic, negativistic, continually quarreling

If the teacher observes some signs of disease or health defect, he should take the case to the school physician, the school nurse, or the principal. Every school should have some individual who can make a more thorough examination of the suspected cases and authorize them to be sent home or to remain in school. The teacher should never be expected to make the decision of whether or not the pupil should be excluded from school. When the individual is sent home from school, the parents should be notified of the reason. They should be urged to secure medical attention, and the nurse or visiting teacher should ascertain whether the services of a physician have been obtained. When the student is able to return to school, he should have a certificate to that effect from his doctor. It is recommended that the students be examined also by the school physician or nurse before being readmitted to class. The control of communicable disease is made more difficult in schools where undue emphasis is placed upon perfect attendance. The real tribute belongs to the child who protects his classmates by staying home when he does not feel well.

The follow-up program

The value of a medical examination depends in a large measure on the follow-up program. In too many institutions the results of the examinations are recorded, filed, and forgotten. The number of defects which are corrected after the examination is far more important than the number of defects discovered by the examination. Concerning the correction of defects there are two principles that must be recognized: (1) no school health service must take away the fundamental responsibility of the parent; and (2) any corrective work must be made an educational procedure.

The school is an educational institution, not a hospital or clinic. The school is not prepared for curative or remedial services and should minimize its activities in this field. The responsibility for the treatment of defects and disease rests upon the family. The school staff should render first aid in emergencies and then call for the services of the family physician if further attention is needed. The only corrective work to be undertaken by the school must be educational in nature. Adapted or corrective physical education falls into this category. The department of physical education provides corrective classes in which those individuals with physical defects and organic disturbances that are amenable to correction by physical modalities are given certain exercises or activities to remedy their condition. Instruction and practice in various recreative activities in keeping with the individual's defect are also given.

If the parents are unable to be present at the medical and dental examinations, they should be notified by letter of the findings, and suggestions should be made concerning future examinations, treatment, and care. It is advisable to invite the parents to visit the school and confer with the school physician or nurse on the examination results. Instead of sending a letter, the school nurse may visit the home and report and interpret the results of the examination and the recommendations of the examiner. At school, the results should be interpreted to the students and their individual needs pointed out.

The teachers should be informed of the health status of their pupils and the steps that should be taken to remedy the defects. Teacher-nurse conferences should be regularly scheduled. They are usually most valuable if devoted largely to review and exchange of information regarding specific cases of children who seem to be in serious need of medical care, follow-up, or special study. The fully informed teacher can be most helpful both in adjusting the classroom program to the student's needs and influencing him and his parents to obtain correction of the remediable conditions as recommended by his family or school physician.

The correction of all remediable defects found on the medical and dental examinations is the chief purpose of the follow-up program. When the family cannot or will not assume the responsibility for correcting the defects, the school should bring the fact to the attention of public health authorities and social agencies. All agencies contributing to child health should be coordinated and their services brought to the attention of those families that are unable to pay for the attention of a physician. The school nurse or the visiting teacher is usually in the best position to make the arrangements between the family and the welfare organization.

Communicable disease control

The local health officer is the legal representative of the state board of health, which has full power in the control of communicable disease. He consults with the private physician when the illness affects the community or school. He informs the schools concerning the current rules, regulations, and policies for the control of communicable disease. He plans jointly with the school administrator for the immunization and testing program, in cooperation with the private physicians in the community. He advises school officials concerning the exclusion from school of pupils or teachers because of exposure to or presence of communicable disease.

The superintendent or principal is responsible for giving the school staff adequate interpretation of the most recent public health practices and for developing for their guidance procedures that are based on these practices. Written and printed instructions with reference to the teacher's role in communicable disease control should be placed in the hands of every teacher in the school. The school administrator collaborates with the private physicians and public health officials in formulating plans for the schools. He also keeps parents informed about the school's policies and procedures, usually by letter and group meetings.

One of the most important considerations in communicable disease control is the immunization procedures that are employed. It is a recognized fact that artificial immunization through vaccination is highly effective against smallpox, diphtheria, tetanus, measles, whooping cough, and polio. Despite this fact, a large portion of the school population is unprotected against these diseases. If the immunization program operated as it should in the preschool years and in the elementary schools, the problem of immunization in high school and college would be reduced considerably.

Parents should be encouraged by every means possible to have their children immunized by their family physician in their preschool years. It is recommended that the smallpox vaccination be administered to children before their first birthday. The diphtheria, whooping cough, and tetanus immunization is recommended for children from three to six months of age. This can be done at one time by means of the triple antigen, which provides protection against all three diseases simultaneously.

The practice of postponing these protective procedures until the children enter elementary school should be strongly discouraged. The public must be educated to the value of artificial immunization and the necessity of having it done early. The real facts should be placed before the public through the newspapers, school publications, letters, visits by the school nurse, and parent-teacher meetings. Religious objections and ignorance are the chief foes to be combated. The schools should cooperate with the public health program of promoting immunization.

As each child enters the elementary school his needs for immunization should be determined. The necessary information is obtained from the family physician on a form that is sent to the parents. Some children will not have had any previous immunization. Those children who have been previously immunized will require booster injections. Whatever the needs of the children, follow-up procedures will be necessary for proper immunization. Parents are expected to assume this responsibility through their family physician. When the family cannot afford this expense public health or social agencies are available to handle it. Some colleges and universities give vaccinations as part of the service for the student health fee. Others make no charge for it and vaccinate those who need it as part of the entrance examination. During epidemics the public health agencies or the school usually furnish emergency inoculations.

The common cold. The common cold is a communicable disease that presents special problems. No difficulty is presented when the student actually has a severe cold. Such a student should be excluded from school. Also, when it becomes clear that a severe cold is impending, the student should be discouraged from remaining in school. However, it would not be feasible to exclude from school all students who manifest symptoms of a cold. Often the student has an allergy rather than a cold. Probably the best procedure is to delay action until the evidence justifies exclusion from school.

Overemphasis upon attendance. Another problem of communicable disease control is the unwarranted emphasis upon perfect attendance. The motivation to obtain an award or recognition for perfect attendance has brought many children to school when they were ill and should have remained home. It is ironical that they should be honored while they are actually exposing their classmates to a communicable disease and neglecting proper care of their own health.

Emergency care procedures

All schools should be prepared to render first-aid treatment in the emergency situations that occur so often. The school doctor should prepare detailed instructions and standing orders for the guidance of the teachers and nurse with reference to the procedure in handling common school emergencies. The school doctor or nurse should administer first aid if it is needed. If they are not available, first aid should be given by some member of the teaching staff who is qualified to do it. All teachers of physical education, shop, health, driver-training, and safety education classes should be certified in Red Cross first-aid training. In the event of a serious accident, the school doctor or any other physician easily and quickly obtainable should be called immediately. The names, addresses, and telephone numbers of nearby physicians who may be called in emergencies should be posted in the principal's office.

After first aid has been given, the parents should be tactfully notified of the child's accident. The parent should indicate the hospital, physician, or home address to which the sick or injured child should be taken if the parent himself cannot promptly call for the child. The sick or injured child should never be sent home unaccompanied by a responsible person. If the parents cannot be reached, the family physician should be called. There should be on file in the school the name of each pupil's family physician, whose notification in case of emergency has been authorized by the child's parent. The best-qualified individual should be prepared to help an uncertain parent decide what is to be done next for the child. All school personnel should clearly understand that they should not go beyond first-aid treatment of an accident or illness. They should not diagnose or administer medication of any kind unless prescribed by a physician.

Health supervision of the school personnel

The importance of a healthy school personnel has already been pointed out. The school health service has the responsibility for supervising the health of the teachers, the custodians, the secretaries, and others who come into contact with the students. The medical examination should be given annually for the school officials as it is for the students. The follow-up program for the correction of defects should be carried on among the teachers and custodians as vigorously as among the students. A complete medical examination should be a prerequisite to a position in any educational institution. It is of particular importance to inspect carefully for signs of tuberculosis. The school personnel must be closely supervised during any illness and should be prevented from coming into contact with the students as long as there is danger to them.

Excuses

The problem of excuses arises chiefly in connection with physical education classes. A written excuse by a physician should be the customary method of excusing students from classes. Whenever possible, the school physician should be the only individual authorized to grant excuses. Many unjustifiable excuses have been requested by family physicans. In order to reduce unwarranted excuses to a minimum, the family physician should be requested to write out the reasons why the students should be excused. The school physician should then review the validity of the excuse and in case of doubt require the family physician to prove his point. When family physicians know that their excuses are subject to the approval of the school physician, they will hesitate to grant unjustifiable excuses. Whenever excuses are granted, their duration should be indicated.

When the problem of excuses develops, the cause may be that the program is so poor that it does not deserve the support of the physician.

Another reason may be that many physicians do not understand the nature and purposes of the program. If this situation prevails it should be rectified. The physicians can be readily approached through the local medical society. The orientation of the physicians should preferably be made by the school medical adviser if one is available.

HEALTH INSTRUCTION

Meaning and purpose of health instruction

The third phase of the school health program is health instruction. Students learn a great deal about health from the health service and healthful school living phases of health education, but the term *health instruction* is used to define the effort to promote understanding of health and the observance of desirable health practices. The fundamental purpose of health instruction is to equip the student with sufficient knowledge about health to enable him to attain and maintain, both in attitude and practice, the highest possible level of health.

Importance of health instruction

Health instruction is an important means of bringing about healthful behavior among all people. A healthful environment and excellent health service in themselves will not solve all our health problems. Every individual must make countless decisions that affect not only his own health but the health of others about him. Many health objectives depend upon the understanding cooperation of all people. Thus, every individual should be capable of intelligent self-direction in matters related to personal and community health. As far as possible everyone should possess a scientific attitude toward health and conduct himself in accordance with recognized scientific knowledge.

Ignorance, indifference, and prejudice need to be combated as vigorously as sickness and disease. The outstanding problem in the prevention of disease at the present time is not the accumulation of more knowledge about disease but the putting into practice of the now available knowledge of disease prevention and control. The failure of many people to employ immunization procedures is an example. Many physical defects developing during childhood, such as those involving hearing, sight, posture, nutrition, and dental decay, could be prevented in large part by intelligent health behavior. A scientific attitude toward health is needed to break down superstitions and fads and to counteract the misleading advertisements in newspapers, in magazines, and over radio and television.

Sliepcevich [5] has aptly summarized the importance of health instruction in the following:

If the health and well-being of school age children can be considered a priceless commodity, and if this is essential to the realization of other educational and social goals, then the time for action in the area of health education is now. Billions of dollars are being spent annually for hospital and home nursing care, medical and paramedical services, and other efforts to restore and rehabilitate the ill back to health. These activities are commendable and humanitarian, and no one can deny that they are essential and important. But even the success of these programs depends on an educated population for support and understanding. The time seems long overdue for comparable efforts, through the educational process, directed at the maintenance and conservation of good health.

In the schools is found an age group in its developmental stages of growth and maturity and habit forming years. Given the necessary climate for learning, health instruction can provide young people with scientific evidence so

[5] Elena Sliepcevich, *School Health Education Study: A Summary Report* (Washington, D.C., School Health Education Study, 1964), p. 12.

they can think critically about health problems, weigh alternate choices and make sound decisions, achieve self-direction and self-discipline for their own health, and acquire a sense of responsibility for health problems of the immediate and worldwide community. In what better place and at what better time can an individual acquire these skills and attitudes than within the framework of our educational system? The solution of health problems confronts every individual throughout his lifetime. Every day he must make choices that may adversely or favorably affect his health. No one can escape these decisions.

The health teacher

According to the definition given of health instruction, this term is to be used to define that time and effort given in class to promote an understanding of health and the practice of health habits. Obviously, in a broader sense, the child learns of health through other classes. In this sense, health instruction is a responsibility of the entire faculty.

Health instruction in the elementary school grades is usually considered as best left with the classroom teacher. He should be as well prepared for this task as he is prepared for arithmetic, social studies, reading, or any other subject he teaches. This is rarely the case. In some states certification requirements insure some preparation but they are minimal. In larger school districts supervisory assistance is usually provided. Under present circumstances supervisory assistance is indispensable because the background in health education of elementary school teachers is unequal to the responsibility.

It was revealed in the School Health Education Survey [6] that "two-thirds or more of the health classes in grades 7, 8, and 9 and 90 percent or more in grades 10, 11, and 12 were taught by the teacher with a combined major in health and physical education, or with specialization in physical education only." The predominance of physical educators as health education teachers raises the question of their qualifications. Many physical education teachers—probably most—are not adequately prepared to teach health education. While the great majority have had some preparation in health education, it usually consists of two or three courses which, at best, provide a very superficial background.

The following comments of Sliepcevich [7] on this subject are pertinent:

The time has come when health education and physical education should be regarded as two *separate* fields of specialization—regarded as such within our own professional circles as well as to our colleagues in other fields and the public

---

[6] *Ibid.*, p. 26.

[7] Elena Sliepcevich, "Implications of the School Health Education Study for Professional Preparation of Teachers." Address given at annual convention of American Association for Health, Physical Education, and Recreation, Dallas, Texas, March 21, 1965.

at large. Both fields have as their long-range goal—the health and well-being of the individual—but there the similarity ends. These two fields have different content, different methodology, different problems, different organizational relationships, are taught in different environments and require a different set of competencies and skills from the teacher. They are *not* synonymous in any sense. To provide for one of these areas in the curriculum does not fulfill responsibility for the other.

Their ultimate goal may be to foster the health of the individual, but art and music also have as their long-range goal, the enhancement of culture.

Yet there is no expectation that if an individual has musical skills he should also have artistic skills—nor is a teacher generally employed to teach art, and then expected to teach music also.

In our professional preparation programs where realistically a second field of competency is an asset for the beginning teacher, the student should not have to buy the "health and physical education" package. He should select one or the other for his specialized field of concentration and then be free to choose a second field in *which* he has *interest,* for *which* he has *enthusiasm,* and in *which* he has a *chance* of *succeeding.* The second field may well be the other area of our concern, but a *choice* has been made, rather than an ultimatum issued. The profession of physical education should recognize the fact that physical educators have been the scapegoats for many of the inadequacies in health education and poor health instruction and consequently their public image has not been helped. Far too many physical educators have been expected to become health teachers because they had no choice in the matter. *Confronted* with heavy and energy-consuming teacher assignments in physical education, *burdened* by additional responsibilities in coaching or intramurals, they have had the additional pressures of teaching and preparing for a subject which requires time to prepare, and time to teach; a willingness to read extensively and continually; and which demands a strong conviction about the values of health education for all students.

Time allotment

In the first three grades the teaching of health in carried out largely through a correlation of health with the other subjects in the curriculum. However, an average of at least two periods per week should definitely be devoted to health instruction. In the upper elementary grades this correlation is continued, but, in addition, three periods a week should be devoted specifically to this subject. Specific health courses should be required in the secondary schools with a minimum time allotment of a daily period for one semester either in the ninth or tenth grade and a similar amount of time in the eleventh or twelfth grade. The minimum time devoted to health in colleges and universities should not be less than two or three semester hours. Most institutions of higher education require such a course.

Many schools are not giving proper emphasis to health instruction. One of the most pernicious practices is to use part of the time allotted to physical education for health instruction. This is sometimes done when inclement weather prevents outdoor physical education activities. In some schools one period per week of the physical education time is given over to health instruction. Other schools do not have a specific time allotment but attempt to teach this subject entirely through the use of special speakers. The speakers used are mostly physicians, dentists, nurses, or public health personnel. Although these talks may have value, health instruction, if it is to take its rightful place in the school program, should be made part of the regular curriculum with a specially prepared teacher in charge.

Basic principles of health instruction

Anderson [8] has recommended the following basic principles, which are recognized as fundamental to sound, effective health instruction.

1. Emphasis is on the positive aspect of health, not the negative aspects. That is, the aim is to build up and maintain as high a level of health as possible in each child.

2. Health is an end to be gained, not an academic subject.

3. Instruction is directed to the well, or normal, child. Children temporarily below par will be benefited by the health practices acquired by the whole class.

4. Throughout school life, health promotion should be one of the objectives of the whole school program.

5. Learning experiences must be adapted to the physiological, psychological, and social development of the children.

6. Instruction must be based on the child's interests, needs, abilities, and backgrounds.

7. Learning results from experience, and opportunities must be provided for experience through participation, doing things, and reacting to situations.

8. Problem solving provides the most effective learning situation but only when the problems are real and meaningful to the learner.

9. The objectives of any activity must be specified in terms of learner outcomes and must be recognized as personal goals by the child if learning is to be effective.

10. Instructional activities must always be related to the actual experiences of the learners.

11. Learning experiences are most effective when the child sees the relationship of one experience to the whole of experience.

12. Learners should be helped in making generalizations and in applying these generalizations to various new experiences.

13. Integrated learning is most effective, and only as it becomes unified, will learning be lasting. Both fragmented learning and isolated facts are ineffective and soon forgotten.

[8] C. L. Anderson, *School Health Practice* (St. Louis, The C. V. Mosby Co., 1956), pp. 274, 275.

14. Repetition, or drill, is justified when the learning must be precise and is useful as a tool or skill.

15. Each child is unique, learns at his own rate and in his own way, and thus a variety of activities and materials is essential.

16. Accompanying, incidental learning always takes place, and teachers should be alert for opportunities to make each learning experience yield greater returns in learning.

17. Health work in the school cannot be fully effective unless integrated with the life of the home and the community and the forces in which both can contribute to the child's education.

Scope of health instruction program

The health instruction program should not be thought of as being limited to the formal health course. Two other aspects of health instruction are recognized as important. These are the incidental instruction and the correlated teaching. The incidental health instruction is that which arises naturally in various contacts with students. In such associations situations develop which enable the instructor to give guidance relative to health matters. The student may come to the physical educator with a personal health problem about which he solicits advice. As a result of his close, informal relationships with students the physical education teacher frequently discovers students who need health advice. The report of each student's medical examination provides an exceptionally good opportunity for incidental health instruction.

Correlation. Interest can be aroused and health habits motivated by the ways in which health is taught. In addition to being taught in a definite course devoted to the subject, health should be presented in all of the other school subjects. When health is taught daily in connection with the sciences, the social studies, physical education, and other fields, with definite objectives to achieve and precise content to cover, the process is known as correlation. The practice of teaching various aspects of health in other school subjects has been long advocated by leaders in the field of health education. In addition to the value of increased interest, it offers an opportunity to present essential health information in what might be a more natural setting and thus give the student a better understanding and appreciation of it. If the faculty member directly responsible for the health program is well trained and is given proper cooperation by the entire teaching staff, a large amount of factual health knowledge can be presented through established subjects in the curriculum. Health instruction is to be looked upon not as a responsibility of the health teachers alone but as a joint responsibility of the entire faculty. Too many times no practical application to the field of health is made by the other teachers.

In the junior and senior high school the health coordinator is usually responsible for the direct instruction if there is a separate time allotment and for the integration of health with the other subjects in the curriculum. In colleges and universities the health administrator or health coordinator is responsible for the correlations, but he may assign this task to one of his assistants.

There are obvious criticisms of the attempt to teach health only through this correlation method. The courses with which health is chiefly correlated may not be elected by the student. The general science teacher, the home economics teacher, and other instructors are interested chiefly in their subject and may not be particularly interested in emphasizing the material relating to health. The health coordinator should be able to show the various other members of the faculty how these correlations can be made in a perfectly normal way, and the program should be worked out so that duplication of factual material is minimized as far as possible.

The health course. On the junior and senior high school levels and in colleges and universities formal courses in health are essential. Even though some health may be effectively taught through incidental and correlated instruction, invariably important areas will be omitted. In addition, such a course is needed to provide students with a unified, integrated presentation of the health materials that are related to their needs.

Health instruction in the elementary schools. In the elementary grades, health instruction is the responsibility of the classroom teacher. In the primary grades a daily period of health instruction is not essential, but a minimal time allotment would be two 30-minute periods per week. In the intermediate grades three periods of substantial length are needed. It should be stressed that incidental and correlated instruction, of which there is a good deal in the elementary grades, should be over and beyond this time allotment. Another important consideration is that when teachable moments arise the teacher may spend considerably more time on health instruction than usual.

In the elementary grades, the emphasis is placed upon the development of desirable habits and attitudes toward healthful living. The scientific facts upon which habits and attitudes are based should not be stressed. The instruction should be informal and should grow out of the daily experiences of the children. In the upper elementary grades the development of health practices and attitudes should continue, but the children need to know reasons for acceptable health behavior. They are interested in factual information and are eager to discover answers for themselves.

A number of studies have provided insight into the health needs and interests of elementary school children. These indicate that the major emphasis in the primary grades should be given to such aspects as developing habits of personal cleanliness, caring for teeth, eyes, ears, and nose, proper eating habits and choice of foods, developing proper attitudes toward physical and dental examinations, preventing colds, skin disease, and other infections, wearing appropriate clothing, and acquiring habits of safety. In the intermediate grades instruction can be continued on many of the above items but on a more advanced level. Other aspects that may be covered include prevention of infections, nutrition, fire prevention, traffic safety, safety measures in school, home, and playground, rest, getting along with adults, simple first-aid procedures, and purification of water and milk.

In the School Health Education Study [9] the strengths and weaknesses of the health content areas were determined for sixth grade students. Exercise, sleep, and relaxation, cleanliness and body care, and food ranked as the three strongest areas while the weakest were dental health, mental health, and safety education.

The importance of the health coordinator has been previously discussed. Such a person is particularly needed in the elementary schools because the teachers are not as well prepared for their health education responsibilities as they are on the secondary school level. Someone must plan a program with sequential, steadily more advanced learning experiences at each succeeding grade. Teachers need assistance in articulating what they teach with what has been taught before and with what will be taught later. In planning what is to be taught in the separate health class the health content that has been taught through correlation and incidental teaching must be taken into consideration. It is apparent that without such coordination the elementary school health education program will be conducted on a hit-or-miss basis, which will inevitably result in needless repetition of content on the one hand and omission of essential material on the other.

Health instruction in the secondary schools. In the secondary schools, an increasing emphasis should be given to health knowledge. The development of proper health habits, attitudes, and knowledge should proceed concurrently. Experience has clearly shown that the relationship between health knowledge and health behavior is not high. Most people with unhealthy habits really know better. The problem is one of proper attitudes. The correct feelings and emotions must be taught along with the health facts. The teacher who knows his students and his health materials can guide the learning experience so that the feeling and ideas become appropriately associated in the learner. When satisfaction accompanies proper behavior and dissatisfaction the improper behavior, correct attitudes will be developed, particularly if the satisfaction and dissatisfaction come immediately.

Three important considerations involved in determining the con-

[9] Sliepcevich, *School Health Education Study: A Summary Report,* p. 56.

tent of the secondary school health instruction program are: (1) health interests of students, (2) strengths and weaknesses in health content areas, and (3) needs of students as revealed by research. Each of these items will be discussed in turn.

1. Health interests of secondary school boys and girls. A number of studies of health interests of secondary school students have been made. Lantagne, in a study of the health interests of 10,000 secondary school boys and girls, reports the leading health interest as shown in Table 6-1. This survey revealed that most of the items of greatest interest to boys were also of greatest interest to girls. Girls were more interested in problems such as menstruation, childbearing, personal appearance, and nutrition. Boys were more interested in driver safety and physical activity.

2. Strengths and weaknesses of secondary school students in health content areas. In developing the health instruction program on the sec-

Table 6-1.

BOYS		GIRLS	
Health Interest	*Percent Interested*	*Health Interest*	*Percent Interested*
1. Sex Instruction	65	1. Sex Instruction	70
2. Safety in Water	64	2. Juvenile Delinquency	67
3. Tobacco and Human Health	61	3. Cancer	64
4. How to Use a Gun Properly	60	4. Causes of Suicide	64
5. Sports vs. Apparatus Activity	58	5. Preparation for Marriage	64
6. Atomic Warfare	58	6. Safest Age to Have a Baby	64
7. Juvenile Delinquency	58	7. Causes of Mental Illness	64
8. Speed and Accidents	58	8. Jealousy	60
9. Cancer	56	9. Sunburn	58
10. Causes of Suicide	55	10. Pregnancy and Health	58
11. Problems of Tooth Decay	54	11. Deaths of Mothers in Childbirth	57
12. How to Report Accidents	51	12. Problems of Tooth Decay	57
13. Hit-and-Run Drivers	51	13. Lifelong Care of the Eyes	56
14. Drunken Driving	50	14. Communicable Diseases	55
15. Lifelong Care of Eyes	50	15. Ability To Have Children	54
16. Problems of Alcohol	48	16. Cancer Is Inherited	54
17. War and Disease	47	17. Tobacco and Health	54
18. Causes of Mental Illness	45	18. How to Report Accidents	51

Source: Joseph Lantagne. "Health Interests of 10,000 Secondary School Students," *Research Quarterly* (October, 1952), pp. 342,343.

ondary school level it is extremely helpful to know the strengths and weaknesses of the students in the various areas. The data in Tables 6-2 and 6-3 have been made available by Sliepcevich after an extensive national survey.

Table 6-2 shows that the areas in the ninth grade in need of more emphasis are habit-forming substances, consumer health, fatigue, sleep

Table 6-2. Comparison of percentage of correct responses by health content area and by practices, attitudes, and knowledge for males and females within district groups on the ninth grade Health Behavior Inventory.

| Category | LARGE | | MEDIUM | | SMALL | | TOTAL |
| | Male | Female | Male | Female | Male | Female | for |
	(270)	(270)	(430)	(430)	(300)	(300)	Group
1. Care of Special Senses	76.9	82.4	68.0	70.5	72.4	78.8	77.5
2. Community Health	78.4	82.6	79.1	82.1	73.2	83.8*	80.0
3. Consumer Health	48.8	49.6	44.3	47.5	44.8	46.6	46.8
4. Defense Against Disease	66.4	71.5	66.2	69.0	61.1	68.5	67.2
5. Dental Health	71.3	75.8	68.2	71.3	62.9	68.9	69.7
6. Exercise and Body Mechanics	78.8	78.5	65.3	66.9	71.8	71.8	74.6
7. Fatigue, Sleep, and Rest	65.6	69.6	55.4	59.5	60.2	64.2	64.6
8. Habit Forming Substances	59.7	64.5	53.1	58.2	59.6	68.3†	62.7
9. Mental Health	63.5	74.7*	65.1	70.1	59.8	70.9*	67.4
10. Nutrition	75.6	78.7	72.5	77.7	67.6	72.0	75.2
11. Personal Health and Grooming	75.9	81.1	76.3	80.4	71.3	76.6	77.4
12. Safety and First Aid	66.9	72.6	69.3	71.7	66.0	70.4	69.7
Practices	46.2	51.6	44.6	49.1	40.0	46.1	46.3
Attitudes	76.6	81.3	72.1	77.8	74.2	78.9	77.2
Knowledge	77.7	83.3	70.7	73.0	73.2	79.7	77.9

*Significant at the .01 level.
†Significant at the .05 level.

Source: Elena Sliepcevich, *School Health Education: A Summary Report* (Washington, D.C., School Health Education Study, 1964), p. 58.

and rest, defense against disease, mental health, safety, and first aid. For the students in the twelfth grade the weakest areas were nutrition, community health, chronic diseases, consumer health, exercise, sleep and relaxation, and family health (see Table 6-3).

Table 6-3. Comparison of percentage of correct responses by health content area for males and females within district groups on the twelfth grade Health Behavior Inventory.

	LARGE		MEDIUM		SMALL		TOTAL
Category	Male (270)	Female (270)	Male (430)	Female (430)	Male (300)	Female (300)	for Group
1. Chronic Diseases	57.1	60.0	54.0	62.0*	52.3	61.8*	57.9
2. Communicable Diseases	68.0	73.1	70.0	74.5	64.7	71.4	70.6
3. Community Health	56.0	57.3	54.4	61.6†	49.9	61.6*	57.0
4. Consumer Health	55.3	70.0†	59.2	63.8	53.3	61.7*	59.5
5. Dental Health	70.0	74.2	69.4	75.2	66.1	71.5	71.3
6. Exercise, Sleep and Relaxation	64.1	70.7	67.9	74.5*	61.0	70.4*	68.6
7. Family Health	62.3	74.6†	64.2	75.5†	60.0	74.0†	68.7
8. Mental Health	71.2	80.1*	71.5	81.1†	65.6	77.9†	74.8
9. Nutrition	42.5	47.5	43.1	49.4	40.5	46.4	45.2
10. Personal Health	72.8	80.6†	73.0	82.0†	70.6	81.4†	76.9
11. Safety Education	70.5	71.6	69.1	69.9	64.7	71.8	69.6
12. Stimulants and Depressants	82.9	87.7	80.0	88.0†	74.4	86.6†	83.3

* Significant at .05 level.
† Significant at .01 level.

Source: Elena Sliepcevich, *School Health Education Study: A Summary Report* (Washington, D.C., School Health Education Study, 1964), p.60.

3. **Problem areas revealed by research.** In developing the content for the secondary school health instruction program the health interests and the assessment of strengths and deficiencies in the various health areas are important considerations. In addition, research shows critical problem areas that represent student needs. Sliepcevich [10] observes:

Other research data support the need to emphasize the following areas as a part of health instruction and, in some instances, provide reasons for earlier grade placement.

Alcohol education: Studies indicate that the majority of teenagers will have experimented with alcoholic beverages prior to graduation from high school; personal use tends first to occur at ages 13 to 14 in the home or under adult supervision. In some communities six out of ten young people use alcohol; in other communities a minority are users. Intelligent choices about use of alcoholic beverages must be based on objective data which allow for an understand-

[10] Sliepcevich, *School Health Education Study: A Summary Report*, pp. 38, 39.

ing of the physiological, psychological, cultural, social, and economic aspects of drinking.

Community health programs: Billions of dollars are spent annually for the medically indigent, construction of hospitals and clinics, and training of personnel. Official and private health agencies rely on the informed citizen to support such services.

Consumer health education: In 1959, teenage expenditures amounted to ten billion dollars and were expected to be twice that amount by 1970. Health products are widely advertised through mass media. A billion dollars a year is invested by the public in medical quackery.

Environmental hazards: Emerging health problems such as water and air pollution, radiation, pesticides, and food additives require an enlightened population to bring about necessary preventive and corrective action.

Health careers: One of every 30 persons employed in the United States works at maintaining the nation's health. There is an increasing shortage of health personnel. Young people have a tendency to choose careers early in their secondary school experience or even before.

International health activities: More than one-half of the world's population has an income of less than $100 a year; two-thirds of the world's people live in underdeveloped areas. Such factors as malnutrition and disease may affect the choice of political ideologies. World health problems cannot be ignored.

Nutrition and weight control: Dietary practices become increasingly worse throughout the teenage years especially for girls. There is evidence that the overweight child is more likely to become the overweight adult. Eating habits are affected by a complex of social pressures and emotional factors.

Sex education, family life, parenthood and child care: Questions about sex asked by fifth and sixth grade children in anonymous surveys reflect distorted facts and a need for accurate information. Recent statistics show that more women marry in their eighteenth year than in any other, and more have their first child in their nineteenth year. Nearly 40 percent of unwed mothers are between the ages of 15 and 19; illegitimacy is on the increase.

Smoking: Reportedly, about one in three high school seniors smoke; in some communities the estimate is as high as one in two. The greatest number of smokers begin between the ages of 10 to 15 years. More than a million of today's school-age children will die of lung cancer before the age of seventy, if present smoking patterns and death rates for smokers continue.

Venereal disease education: Venereal disease infects more than 250,000 young persons (15 to 19) annually according to recent estimates. An increase of 56 percent in syphilis among teenagers was reported between 1960 and 1961.

The conceptual approach

A new approach to the health education curriculum has grown out of the School Health Education Study.[11] What is known as "the

[11] The materials relating to the School Health Education Study have been abstracted from: School Health Education Study, *Health Education: A Conceptual Approach* (Washington, D.C., School Health Education Study, 1965).

conceptual approach" has been designed to solve such problems as the needless repetition of subject matter, the memorization of facts, the failure to produce behavioral change, and the difficulty of selecting what to teach out of the extraordinary amount of knowledge that has developed in recent years. The conceptual approach emphasizes concepts or generalizations about related data rather than facts. This approach has been undertaken in other curriculum areas.

This approach involves setting up a framework for health education from kindergarten through twelfth grade. An outline of this framework includes:

1. Three key concepts which are the unifying threads that characterize the process underlying health.
2. Ten concepts emerging from the key concepts and viewed as the major organizing elements of the curriculum or indicators for the direction of the learning experience.
3. Thirty-one substantive elements, which serve as guides to select and order the substances of health education in its physical, mental, and social dimensions.
4. A set of long-range student *goals* categorized under three domains: cognitive, affective, and action.

The project concerned with the conceptual approach to health education is continuing. Considerable experimental work has been done and more will be done in the future. While it is still too early to evaluate these developments there is every reason to believe that they will have profound effects upon health education in our schools in the future.

Methods of teaching health

One of the most common criticisms of health teaching is that the subject lacks interest. This criticism has been made by elementary and junior and senior high school groups, as well as by freshmen in college. It has been due, no doubt, in the past in large part to insufficient preparation of the health instructor and too much duplication of teaching material. Many school principals, superintendents, and other faculty members still think of health in terms of washing the hands before eating, brushing the teeth three times a day, and drinking six or eight glasses of water daily. Although some of these facts have some value, one can hardly expect interest if they are taught in the elementary grades and again in the junior and senior high school and college. If the health course is to appeal to students, their interests and needs must be considered in the selection of subject matter. These needs and in-

terests are constantly changing; and unless the health instruction is modified and adapted to them at the different school levels, this subject will
always prove distasteful and uninteresting. There is also the tendency
to base the instruction predominantly on adult needs and interests.
While these are important, it is extremely difficult to interest students
in health problems that are thirty to forty years away. The best procedure is to follow the middle path and to consider both present and
future needs and interests.

In the past the lecture method was used predominantly in health
education courses, but the trend at present seems to be a combination
of the lecture and textbook method. The use of the textbook is a highly
desirable method of teaching health education, for it results in greater
student activity and application. One of the drawbacks to using a textbook has been the scarcity in the past of good publications in this field.
Health texts not only must be well written, interesting, and nontechnical, but they must include the latest developments in all phases of
health. There are constant changes occurring in the subject matter
covered in health education, and regardless of how good a book may be
today, it may be soon out of date. Fortunately, there are available at
present a number of excellent publications, and with the increased interest in this field it appears likely that there will be no lack of good
health textbooks in the future.

The use of group discussion in conjunction with the lecture method
is strongly recommended; students find it more enjoyable and they are
more highly motivated to adopt desirable health practices. In addition,
studies have substantiated that students felt that when opportunities
fc: discussion were provided learning was more effective.

Through the use of well-selected health films, slides, and posters an
otherwise uninteresting health course may be made interesting and certainly much more valuable. There are health films available at the present time for elementary, junior, and senior high schools presenting material in an interesting way and including material that many times
would be impossible or at least very difficult to present by ordinary class
methods. Health films and slides, however, are not to be looked upon as
a teaching method but as a teaching aid. Most state boards of health
have extensive film libraries. At very little cost schools from the state may
procure these films. Slides are available from the same source. The teacher
sufficiently interested, with a small amount of training and very little
material, should be able to make his or her own collection of slides.
Posters are available from most of the national associations, such as the
National Safety Council, the National Tuberculosis Association, the National Society for the Prevention of Blindness, or the National Society
for the Control of Cancer. The materials presented by these associations
are authentic, and the teacher should not neglect these sources.

The use of class demonstrations is a very effective means of presenting health facts. The teacher should have received sufficient training in health to be able to carry out various simple experiments. The growth requirements of bacteria, their wide distribution, the effects of drying, sunlight, boiling, and pasteurization on them can be easily demonstrated. A comparison can be made of the bacterial count of raw milk with that of pasteurized milk or of river water with tap water. The size and the shape of various types of bacteria can be shown easily by the staining of these organisms and by the use of the microscope. Simple feeding experiments carried out as a class project would be an interesting and worthwhile method of presenting certain facts in this field. There are many other simple, inexpensive demonstrations that may be made. There are on the market various health workbooks and laboratory guides that should be of value to the teacher for class demonstrations.

In every community there are various class trips that can be taken which should add interest and value to health instruction. A visit to the sewage-disposal and water plants will create more interest in municipal health problems than will ordinary classroom instruction. A visit to some good dairy to show modern sanitary methods of processing milk and to a farm where precautions are not taken should be interesting and valuable. The health teacher should take every opportunity of utilizing those facilities available in the community.

Graphic materials, such as wall charts, are great aids in teaching health. Some universities and colleges are able to use human cadavers and specimens to facilitate instruction. Many departments use health habit inventory charts as a means of bringing the desirable and undesirable habits before the students. In junior and senior high schools an excellent device is to put on a health exhibit.

Teaching by television is being used increasingly. It has been frequently employed to teach health education. Research has shown that television instruction is as effective as or significantly more effective than conventional methods of teaching. Evidence is also available to show that television is a valuable teaching aid when used in conjunction with other methods of teaching.

In summary, it is apparent that the health education teacher has a variety of teaching methods at his disposal. The considerable research that has been done to evaluate the different procedures indicates that no one method is clearly superior for all situations. A variety of methods is preferable to the exclusive use of one method. The teacher must consider the age and background of his students, class size, student interests and goals, and the nature of his subject matter in determining the method he will finally select.

SELECTED REFERENCES

Anderson, Carl, *School Health Practice* (St. Louis, The C. V. Mosby Co., 1956).

Byrd, Oliver, *School Health Administration* (Philadelphia, W. B. Saunders Co., 1964).

Grout, Ruth, *Teaching in Schools* (Philadelphia, W. B. Saunders Co., 1953).

Irwin, L. W., J. H. Humphrey, and W. R. Johnson, *Methods and Materials in Health Education* (St. Louis, The C. V. Mosby Co., 1956).

Joint Committee on Health Problems in Education of National Education Association and The American Medical Association, *Health Appraisal of School Children* (Washington, D.C., National Education Association, 1957).

Lantagne, Joseph, "Health Interests of 10,000 Secondary School Students," *The Research Quarterly* (October, 1952), pp. 342, 343.

Oberteuffer, D., *School Health Education* (New York, Harper & Row, Publishers, 1954).

Report of Joint Committee, NEA and AMA, *Health Education,* 5th ed. (Washington, D.C., National Education Association, 1961).

Sliepcevich, Elena, *School Health Education Study: A Summary Report* (Washington, D.C., School Health Education Study, 1964).

Walker, Herbert, *Health in the Elementary School* (New York, The Ronald Press Company, 1955).

7

the physical education plant

Need for familiarity with the problem

There are very few principles of physical education administration that have been less adequately applied than have those that deal with the planning and construction of buildings to house the program. The large number of inadequate physical education buildings, even on university campuses, is material evidence of this fact. Several factors have contributed to this condition. One of the most significant has been the practice of copying a building in a neighboring city or state, mistakes and good points alike. This practice has been employed because it has proved to be temporarily less troublesome than making a survey of local conditions, a study of building construction, and evaluating the results by a sound educational philosophy, before starting to build. Another factor has been a change in educational philosophy and a consequent shift in emphasis from a formal to a more natural activity program. The newer program demands more and different activity rooms, which tends to make the older type of plant obsolete. In some situations there has been an unwillingness on the part of those in authority to seek and utilize the advice of informed staff members, and in others physical education people have proved unable to advise judiciously when consulted.

Wise and efficient planning and construction of a physical education plant can obviate many administrative, financial, and functional difficulties. A few examples of this are presented here and again later, since they deserve to be emphasized by repetition. Elimination of permanent seats in the gymnasium will increase space insofar as the service program is concerned; well-placed activity rooms will make supervision relatively easy; properly recessed radiators will reduce the number of accidents; reduction of unnecessary hall space will save money; properly placed drinking fountains and lavatories will make the building a more efficient service unit; properly sloped cement floors will be easier to clean; a sloping roof will shed water much better than a flat one; louver-type windows will provide good ventilation, even in rainy weather; cement locker bases will make the cleaning of the locker room easier; and the concentration of showers, lavatories, and drinking fountains in a comparatively small area will reduce the plumbing bill. Any effort spent in planning will pay large dividends in the future to those who are responsible for the physical education unit. It is not enough to hire an architect and leave all matters of arrangement to him, for he does not have the background or philosophy that the competent physical educator has. The one who is to plan an efficient unit must understand the program it is to house. In addition, it is erroneous to assume that architects and engineers are in a position to keep abreast of all the new concepts, designs and materials relative to physical education facilities. Certainly, an architect is necessary, but he must be guided in order that the finished building may be supremely functional, as well as attractive.

It is the responsibility of the physical education administrator to make sure that adequate planning is done for the new facility. Due to the magnitude of this task all staff members should be involved in the planning. Since a gymnasium, for example, is built for from fifty to sixty years, the needs and requirements of the department must be projected that far into the future. The plan entails a detailed listing of the various areas required—gymnasiums, special activity areas, classrooms, conference rooms, swimming pool, offices, locker and shower areas, home and visiting team rooms, supply room, training room, storage facilities, and the like—with their dimensions and desirable features indicated.

It is particularly important that the administrator himself be familiar with the up-to-date literature relating to the specific facility being contemplated; there are many instances where they have been very influential in getting a better facility because of their knowledge. When a major new facility is being planned the administrator should visit outstanding facilities in his region, preferably accompanied by the architect, with the aim of getting ideas for the best facility for the available funds.

Importance of teaching stations

For nearly a century physical education has been plagued by the lack of facilities which has led to the curtailment of the required program in a variety of ways. The shortage of teaching stations has resulted in a time allotment of two or three days per week instead of daily, and in the reduction of the years of the required program. Programs of intramural athletics and girls' athletic association activities have also been woefully inadequate due mainly to the unavailability of facilities in the afternoons immediately after the last class period.

The total number of teaching stations required depends upon:

1. Number of students
2. Number of days per week the program is required
3. Number of years program is required
4. Class size
5. Nature of the program
6. Number of periods in the school day
7. The climate in the area
8. The requirements of the intramural and interschool programs

The number of teaching stations required in a school can readily be determined by the following formula:

$$\frac{\text{Number of students}}{\text{Average class size}} \times \frac{\text{Number of meetings of class per week}}{\text{Total number of class periods per week}}$$

In planning physical education facilities the anticipated enrollment in ten years should be the basis for determining the number of teaching stations required. It is a deplorable fact that many physical education plants are too small the day they are completed.

In the great majority of schools in the country the total number of teaching stations required must be provided in the indoor facilities because the outdoor teaching stations cannot be used during the winter months. If the outdoor facilities can be used throughout the year a smaller number of indoor teaching stations are required.

The greatest mistake in providing facilities for physical education has been the failure to make space available for intramural and girls' athletic association activities as well as for interschool squads immediately after school. Experience has shown that these are the best times for the intramural and girls' athletic program. Unfortunately, in most secondary schools and colleges and universities facilities are not adequate at these favorable hours.

INDOOR PHYSICAL EDUCATION FACILITIES

The types of indoor physical education teaching stations include the gymnasium, wrestling room, apparatus room, weight room, dance studio, corrective gymnasium, and swimming pool. Colleges and universities also have handball and squash courts, bowling alleys, and many have field houses.

The main gymnasium

The main gymnasium is the largest area and accommodates the most students. The size of the gymnasium is affected by the requirements of interschool basketball plus provisions for spectators. The number of teaching stations desired also affects the ultimate size of the gymnasium. Figure 7-1 may serve as a guide for determining the size of the gymnasium. Suggested sizes and seating capacities for gymnasiums at the various school levels are shown in Table 7-1.

A commendable practice has been to build a very large gymnasium and to create two teaching stations by means of folding partitions. Balconies on both sides of the main floor can also provide two additional teaching stations. Such balconies can have folding bleachers to supplement the seating capacity of the gymnasium for interschool athletic competition. These bleachers can be located at the front of the balconies and fold back when opened. In this way they can serve as a wall between the teaching stations on the balconies and those on the main floor.

Another factor governing the size of the main gymnasium is the space requirements of the different activities that will be carried on in that teaching station. Courts for badminton and volleyball are invariably laid out in the main gymnasium in addition to those for basketball. It is desirable to plan for sufficient courts to handle a class of appropriate size. An instructor can handle 36 students adequately on three volleyball courts. If he teaches 24 students on two courts it is obvious that the instructional cost is appreciably greater.

It may be necessary to conduct fencing, dancing, wrestling, and gymnastics in the main gymnasium. However, separate areas for these activities are preferable. This is particularly true of gymnastics and wrestling, which require so much specialized equipment that must be moved both before and after the class. If separate rooms are not provided for these activities storage space for the equipment should be provided in the main gymnasium. The failure to provide adequate storage

Table 7-1. Suggested gymnasium sizes and types.

RECOMMENDED TYPE OF SCHOOL	Type	DIMENSIONS AS RELATED TO FIGURE 7-1.										CEILING HT.	NO. AND SIZE OF TEACHING STATIONS PROVIDED THAT MOVABLE PARTITIONS ARE USED	APPROX. SEATING WITH FOLDING BLEACHERS‡	NUMBER TIERS OF SEATING
		A	B	C	D	E	F	G	H	I	J				
Elem.	I	86'	54'	74'	42'	6'	6'	6'	6'	0'	0'	20'	2-43'x54'	0	0
Jr. H.S.	II	86'	65'	74'	42'	6'	6'	6'	6'	11'	0'	22'	2-43'x65'	350	6†
Jr. H.S.	III	96'	72'	84'	50'	6'	6'	6'	6'	11'	0'	22'	2-48'x72'	385	6†
Community Use*															
H.S. Girls	IV	96'	70'	84'	50'	6'	6'	6'	6'	8'3"	0'	22'	2-48'x70'	320	5†
H.S. Boys	V	96'	78'6"	84'	50'	6'	6'	6'	6'	8'3"	8'3"	24'	2-48'x78'6"	640	5
H.S. Boys	VI	100'	93'5"	84'	50'	6'	6'	8'	8'	13'8"	13'8"	24'	2-50'x93'5"	1070	8
H.S. Boys	VII	100'	104'5"	84'	50'	6'	6'	8'	8'	19'3"	19'3"	24'	2-50'x104'5"	1500	11

*Larger basketball court where adult community use is anticipated.
†Bleachers on one side only.
‡Figures in this column assume that seating on side walls is continuous. If there are breaks in continuous seating, higher seating must be provided to maintain these seating capacities. For each added tier of folding bleachers, add 22' to dimensions B, I, and J. Figure 7-1.

Note: Table 7-1 shows suggested sizes and seating capacities for gymnasiums at the various school levels. The lettered dimension columns are related to Figure 7-1. In addition to the basketball courts shown, the space will provide for other standard court games such as volleyball, badminton, and paddle tennis. The recommended ceiling heights are all acceptable for these games, and the use of folding bleachers will make maximum space available.

Source: The Athletic Institute, *Planning Facilities for Health, Physical Education and Recreation* (Chicago, The Athletic Institute, 1956).

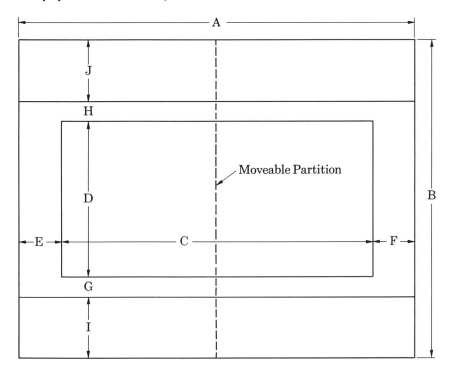

Key to Dimensions—A and B: Overall size of gymnasium, inside measurements; C and D: Basketball court size, 74' × 42'—junior high and elementary schools, 84' × 50' —high school boys and girls; E and F: End safety zones 6' minimum, 8' preferred for added safety; G and H: Side-court safety clearance areas 6' minimum, 8' preferred for added safety; I and J: Space devoted to folding bleachers set on the main floor. The amount of space will vary according to needed seating. Folding bleachers should be recessed if feasible. If not recessed, the depth of the folded bleachers should be added to the overall dimensions. It is strongly recommended that seating be provided through the use of folding bleachers rather than built-in permanent seating. No structural supports should be in front of bleachers. Seating calculations should be made on the basis of 18" per seat.

Source: The Athletic Institute, *Planning Facilities for Health, Physical Education and Recreation* (Chicago, The Athletic Institute, 1956), p. 57.

Figure 7-1. Recommended Gymnasium Floor Space with Choice as to Size of Teaching Station and Amounts of Seating.

areas has been a major error in constructing gymnasiums for the past seventy-five years. When appropriate storage is not available, the equipment interferes with other activities, creates congestion, and frequently results in damage to the equipment.

Physical education programs have been greatly benefited by three developments that have made more activity space available and have permitted a more varied program. These developments are: (1) folding bleachers, (2) swing-up basketball backboards, and (3) folding partitions.

Folding partitions are invaluable in dividing a large area into two or more separate teaching stations. Some schools use nets to divide a large gymnasium but the folding partitions are much to be preferred because they provide acoustic and visual separation from the other teaching station. The partitions should extend from floor to ceiling and move on an overhead track. Floor tracks are not recommended. The partitions should be electrically operated and recessed when closed. They should be insulated in order that sound is not transmitted from teaching station to teaching station. The walls should be sturdy enough in order that balls may be thrown against them by students who are practicing various skills.

Many secondary schools have combined a gymnasium with an auditorium or cafeteria. This practice never works out satisfactorily. Conflicts in the use of the area inevitably occur. The combination appears attractive from the standpoint of economy but over a period of years much more satisfactory results are obtained from a separate gymnasium.

Auxiliary gymnasium

A large number of high schools and colleges and universities find it necessary to construct an auxiliary gymnasium. This is a multi-purpose area and could be used for a variety of activities such as fencing, dancing, calisthenics, games of low organization, tumbling, badminton, and volleyball. Such a facility could be used for intramural and recreational activities when the main gymnasium is occupied by the basketball squad.

Location of building

For small communities this is determined at the time the site of the school is selected, for there is often but one building to house the entire school. For somewhat larger schools, where the buildings must all be placed in a limited area, the matter of placement of the physical education building is of relatively small significance; but for large schools, especially colleges and universities, the location of the building or buildings often quite definitely sets the limits of their serviceability. At some universities the fieldhouse, physical education plant, or playing areas are so far removed from the major concentration of classrooms that in many instances students must rush to and from academic and activity classes. This need to hurry tends to make physical education an unpleasant experience for the student. When the activity areas are far removed from the living quarters students who lack transportation are handicapped in their efforts to participate in intramural competition because it is a workout to travel to and from the area. Since the participant must take two workouts or none, quite a number of them will choose none rather than two, especially on those occasions when the weather is bad or there are other events competing for their time. These absences can be a major cause of forfeitures of intramural contests, and the anticipation of the problems involved in traveling back and forth may account for failure to sign up for participation in the first place. Since the physical education plant is a service unit, it should be located in a pleasant environment on a properly drained site near the center of the campus where all students may find it readily accessible when they have an hour or two for physical activity. A well-constructed physical education plant does not mar a landscape, but instead enhances it. Beautiful grass and shrubs are poor substitutes for normal, healthy students in any case. If the school does not provide a convenient recreational unit, outside interests will replace recreation with commercialized amusement, which is socially and financially less valuable.

The deciding factor in the location of many elementary and secondary schools is the accessibility to outdoor athletic facilities that are controlled by the park and recreation department. In recent years the trend has been for school districts and park and recreation departments to work out arrangements for joint use of facilities. Such arrangements have resulted in many more physical education areas than would otherwise have been possible. Likewise, the school facilities are available for use by park and recreation departments during after-school hours. Such joint planning benefits everyone in the community.

Room dimensions

The size, shape, and height of rooms will vary according to the purposes for which they will be used; consequently, it is not possible to determine the optimum dimensions without knowing the local conditions that will affect them. However, there are general limits that should be observed, except in rare cases when some specific modifying factor dictates different proportions. In case of doubt moderation rather than extremism is a sound policy to follow in planning size of rooms.

This is particularly true of size, since too large a room is proportionately more expensive in terms of the service it can render per unit cost. There are but few occasions when such a room can be used to capacity, and all idle, enclosed space represents an unwarranted financial burden. Then, too, more teaching stations can be provided if the enclosed space is broken into smaller units. Except for ticket booths, toilets, closets, offices, and rooms of that type, very small rooms are not particularly serviceable, for they must, of necessity, remain idle much of the time. Those smaller than 12 by 15 feet are hard to justify. The building should be constructed in such a way that it will contribute greatly to the entire educational system. Sliding walls will provide for varying room sizes. This point of view will limit extravagant expenditure of funds for construction of extra-large seating accommodations for basketball crowds, which will be needed on only a night or two a year when a particular rival plays on the home floor. The chief function of the plant should not be that of providing seats for spectators but of providing a laboratory for training citizens.

Odd-shaped, many-sided rooms with projections are costly to construct and are limited in their uses; consequently, they should be eliminated as much as possible in the planning. The main gymnasium room or basketball court should be approximately one and a half times as long as it is wide. This shape lends itself well to use for common activities, and it can be spanned more economically than a square room of the same floor area. The smaller activity rooms and academic classrooms should be longer than they are wide with a ratio of about five to three respectively.

Each room should have sufficient height of ceiling to accommodate the activities that are to take place in it. Any additional height is unnecessary and costly, and any reduction in desirable height cramps the activity program. The recommended standards for gymnasium ceiling heights are: elementary schools, 20 feet (if the gymnasium is to be used by the recreation department the ceiling height should be raised to 22 feet), junior high schools, 22 feet; senior high schools, 22 to 24 feet. Where there is a balcony, however, the ceiling may need to be 30 feet or higher. Locker, shower, and classrooms need not be more than 10 to 12 feet in height.

Arrangement

It is in regard to arrangement that a great many mistakes in building planning are made, for a comparatively large share of planning has to do with the relationship of rooms to each other and the placement of the various service fixtures within the rooms. The placing of service fixtures will be considered under the discussion of each fixture. The following points should be kept in mind when considering the matter of correct room, hall, and stair arrangement within the building:

1. Place units that are to be used together close to each other.
   (a) The medical supervisor's room should be adjacent to the locker room.
   (b) The shower room should adjoin the locker room.

(c) The swimming pool should be close to the shower room.

(d) The supply and equipment room should be contiguous to the locker room.

(e) The storeroom should be conveniently near the supply room.

(f) The drying room should be near the equipment and shower rooms.

(g) The apparatus room should be adjacent to the gym floor and it should be provided with large doors.

(h) The toilets and lavatories should be near the locker room.

(i) The director's office should be in a location convenient for supervision of activities.

(j) The waiting room should be close to the director's office.

(k) The janitor's room should be close to his work center.

(l) The locker room should be adjacent to the gymnasium if the two are on the same floor.

2. Limit halls to the very minimum. It costs money to enclose, heat, and clean hall space. The hall is not particularly a service unit if adequate pupil circulation within the building can be provided without it. Some halls are necessary and must be provided, but in general the space enclosed by the outer walls should be used for service units rather than for unnecessary halls. If possible, passage should be directly outdoors from the locker room. The line of traffic to the outdoors should not cross the line of traffic to the showers.

3. Have stairs lead directly from the locker room to the gymnasium and wide enough for a line of traffic to go down while another line is coming up, provided the gymnasium is on the floor above, as is customary. This avoids the necessity of passing through cold halls, helps keep students with street shoes off the gym floor, and saves space.

4. Provide outdoor exits and stairs, if necessary, from main gym floor. These serve particularly well when crowds use the gymnasium.

5. Avoid placing another room over the swimming pool, if possible. If this cannot be avoided, the floor of the room above should be damp-proofed.

Traffic control

One of the common mistakes in gymnasium construction is the failure to make adequate provisions for the circulation of the various individuals who will use the facilities. The main objectives in planning for traffic circulation are: [1]

1. Providing for minimum travel distances.

[1] The Athletic Institute, *Planning Facilities for Health, Physical Education and Recreation* (Chicago, The Athletic Institute, 1956), p. 135.

2. Reducing travel congestion.
3. Minimizing the disturbance of classwork.
4. Increasing the comfort and safety of occupants.
5. Facilitating supervision.
6. Separating different groups.
7. Reducing maintenance problems.

In planning for traffic control a flow chart should be prepared to show the movement of all the different types of individuals who will be involved with the facility. While students will be the main users, consideration must also be given to spectators at athletic contests and intramural events, as well as to various groups under the auspices of the recreation department who will use the facilities in the evenings and during the summer months. In addition, consideration must be given to personnel who deliver supplies, equipment, laundry, and the like.

Spectator traffic should be routed in such a way that travel across the pool decks, gymnasium floor or locker rooms is avoided. Direct access from outdoors or from the main school corridors to the bleachers should be provided. Spectators also should be able to get to toilets, drinking fountains, and the refreshment stand without crossing the floors of activity areas.

Insofar as the students are concerned provisions must be made to handle the volume coming to and from the locker and shower room areas. The movement of students from their lockers to and from the activity area (swimming pool, gymnasium, or athletic fields) to the equipment room, shower room, drying room, and back to their lockers must be carefully planned to avoid congestion and unnecessary loss of time. Figure 7-2 illustrates some of the traffic flow involved.

Materials and construction

The funds available, the materials at hand, the use to which the constructed part is to be put, the attitude of the community toward types of construction and materials, and the workmen available at the time will largely determine the quality and type of material and construction that will contribute to each finished unit in the building. If funds are ample and the community desires to use them, there can be relatively great freedom of choice in materials and construction. However, most communities must build economically, if at all, and they consequently wish to select serviceable, reasonably priced materials and put them together in a comparatively inexpensive but substantial manner. In economizing, it is best to use materials of a good standard grade; it is false economy to use cheap materials. The cost and availability of fireproofed material should be considered by those who plan to

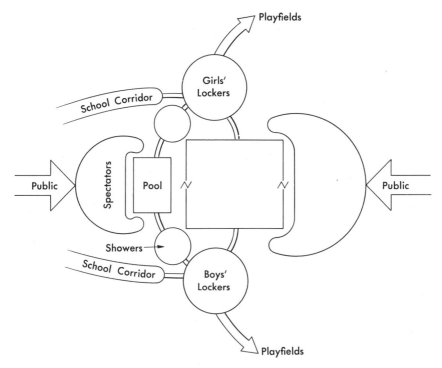

Source: John H. Herrick, Ralph D. McCleary, Wilfred E. Clapp, and Walter F. Bogner, *From School Program to School Plant* (New York: Holt, Rinehart and Winston, Inc., 1956), p. 325.

Figure 7-2. Space Relationships in the Physical Education Suite.

build. The various major parts of a building, including fixtures, will be considered in turn from the viewpoint of materials and construction. The placement or arrangement of fixtures will also be discussed. In the construction of all building parts the first important step is to secure reliable contractors or workmen, and the next is to provide for inspection of the work as it is being done.

Indoor surface materials

In the Report of the Third National Facilities Conference various indoor surface materials were recommended. These are indicated in Table 7-2.

Floors. The floors for activity rooms, classrooms, and offices are generally high grade hard maple. This type of flooring has stood the test of time and hard use and, therefore, is generally preferred. Hard

Table 7-2. Suggested indoor surface materials.

ROOMS	FLOORS — Asphalt, Rubber Linoleum Tile	Cement, Abrasive and Nonabsorbent	Maple, Hard	Terrazzo Abrasive	Tile, Ceramic	LOWER WALLS — Brick	Brick, Glazed	Cinder Block	Concrete	Plaster	Tile, Ceramic	Wood Panel	Moisture-Proof	UPPER WALLS — Brick	Brick, Glazed	Cinder Block	Plaster	Acoustic	Moisture-Resistant	CEILINGS — Concrete or Structure Tile	Plaster	Tile, Acoustic	Moisture-Resistant
Apparatus Storage Room	2	1	2			1		2	1	C		2				2	1			C	C	1	
Classrooms	2		1					2		1		2				2	1			C	C	1	
Clubroom			1					2		1		2				1	2				C	1	
Corrective Room		1	1	2		2	1								2					C	C	1	
Custodial Supply Room	2	1			2																	1	
Dance Studio			1		2	1	2	1	1	1		2				1	2	*		C		1	
Drying Room (Equip.)					2	2	1					2				1	1					1	
Gymnasium			1	2		2	1	2			1	C	*	1	2	2	2	*	*	C		1*	*
Health-Service Unit	1		1				1	2		3	1		*	2			1				C	1	*
Laundry Room	2	2			1		1	2	2	1	1		*	1		1			*		C	1	
Locker Rooms	2	3			1	2		3	2	1				2		1						1	
Natatorium		3		2	1		1	2	2	2	1		*	2	2	2	2					1	
Offices			1				1	2		1		1		2	1	1	1				C	1	
Recreation Room			1			2				3		1				2	2	*				1	
Shower Rooms		3		2	1		2				1		*	1		1			*			1	
Special-Activity Room	2		1							2		1				1	2					1	
Team Room		3		2		2	1	2	2	2				2		1	1				C	1	
Toilet Rooms		3		2	1		1	2	2	3	1		*	1		1	2				C	1	
Toweling-Drying Room (Bath)		3			1		1			2	1		*	1	1	2	2				C	1	*

Note: The numbers in the table indicate first, second, and third choices. "C" indicates the material as being contrary to good practice. An * indicates desirable quality.

Source: The Athletic Institute, Planning Areas and Facilities for Health, Physical Education and Recreation (Chicago, The Athletic Institute, 1965), p. 155.

maple is a dense, strong, heavy, remarkably hard, exceptionally durable wood. It is free from slivering and splintering, extremely resilient, polishes under friction, thus increasing its wear resistance, and, because of its close grain, is very sanitary.

Standard lengths are recommended in preference to the special long lengths. The long lengths are much more expensive, without compensating benefits.

Four grades of hard maple flooring are available but only grades one or two should be used for activity areas. The flooring should be seasoned and dry when it is installed. It is recommended that when the finished floor is laid the temperature should not be more than 70° F. or less than 50° F.

The steps in laying the floor in the gymnasium are:

1. A base of 4 inches of crushed rock should be laid. This should be rolled.
2. A concrete slab from 4 to 6 inches should be placed on top of the crushed rock.
3. A ¼ to ½ inch covering of asphalt mastic (tar) should be applied to the concrete slab.
4. A good grade roofing paper should be placed on top of the asphalt mastic.
5. Sleepers (2 by 3 inches or 2 by 4 inches) should be laid on edge above the roofing paper.
6. A 1 by 4 inches or 1 by 6 inches subflooring (usually pine, fir, hemlock, or spruce) should be laid diagonally over the sleepers. The subfloor should be dry with not more than 14 percent moisture.
7. A layer of saturated, perforated felt paper should cover the subflooring.
8. The maple flooring should be nailed to the sleepers. To provide for expansion a 2-inch space between the flooring and the walls should be provided.

Once the floors are in, they should be sanded, and cleaned by dry mopping with a cloth slightly dampened with turpentine. One or two coats of floor seal should be applied and buffed with fine steel wool. Lines in different colors and widths for three and four different games should then be painted on the gym floor. The sealing process should then be repeated after which the finish dressing is applied. An additional coat of finish should be applied annually.

Walls. Concerning the walls of the gymnasium a variety of factors should be considered. These are:

1. It is decidedly advantageous to have the walls smooth up to 12 feet in order to have them serve as rebounding surfaces for balls.

2. No wall should constitute a hazard because of its rough or uneven surface. The inner wall surface should be smooth, especially where students are to come in contact with it, to reduce the number of abrasions.
3. The lower portion of the walls should be able to take hard usage and should be resistant to marking and scarring.
4. The lower walls should be finished with materials that can easily be cleaned without affecting the finish.
5. Light-colored walls reflect light better and provide a more cheerful atmosphere.
6. Fastenings for equipment and apparatus should be placed in the wall before the finish surface is applied.
7. There should be no projections from the walls into the playing area. Roll-away bleachers should be recessed. Drinking fountains should not be located in the gymnasium area.
8. Above the 12-foot level acoustical materials should be emphasized.
9. Angle irons screwed to the floor where the floor meets the wall will round the corner and facilitate cleaning.
10. A dead air space between the inner and outer walls will provide insulation against sound, cold, and heat.

Ceilings. Ceiling materials vary considerably according to the room. For offices, standard classrooms, and high gymnasium rooms acoustical tile is recommended. If apparatus is to be fastened to the ceiling, all necessary clamps and fasteners should be installed before the ceiling is finished. To prevent condensation of moisture, ceilings should be insulated. A light ceiling will have the same general lighting advantages as light walls.

Doors. Wood, glass, reinforcing wire, copper, brass, and iron or steel are commonly combined to make satisfactory doors for any part of the physical education building. The specific purpose to be served will dictate the proper combination of the above materials. The funds available and the use and treatment the door can be expected to withstand should influence its selection. If light must enter through the door or vision is to be unobstructed, a section of glass is necessary; translucent glass is desirable if only light is to enter. If the door is to be subjected to alternate wetting and drying, as in the shower room, a covering of copper will reduce expansion and contraction. However, the copper may add more to the cost than funds will permit. If the door is to receive rough usage, rugged construction, brass kick plates, nonshatter glass, and protective bars over the glass are desirable features. If the door is to span a large space, strong but comparatively light construction is essential.

Other significant points to consider in selecting and installing satisfactory doors are these:

1. All exit doors should open outward and be equipped with panic bolts, so that crowds may not be trapped by a locked or blocked door.
2. Doors should be fastened to expansion bolts rather than wooden plugs driven into the wall since the wood is apt to work loose.
3. Door stops should be provided to keep doors from being "banged" to pieces.
4. Doors should open out from, rather than into, main gym or activity rooms, even though a little vestibule is necessary at the head of a stairway.
5. Folding doors should be used to separate the gymnasium into halves, if use of it for two classes at a time is planned.
6. Strong, efficient locks should be provided for doors that need to be kept closed.
7. Large doors should be provided to gym room for use by visitors or spectators and for use in moving apparatus and materials in and out.
8. Doors should be placed in the most convenient locations to facilitate circulation of traffic within the building.

Lighting. Lighting in physical education areas is provided by natural and artificial means. Natural lighting is that which comes through windows. When windows are used they should be elevated from 10 to 14 feet above the floor on the two long sides of the gymnasium. If windows are used in dressing rooms they should be located above the lockers and as high as possible. The amount of window space should be equivalent to 20 to 25 percent of the total floor area.

When natural light is available it should be used; when it is not, artificial lighting becomes necessary. The intensity of light in any part of the area can be regulated by adjusting the intensity of the source and by placing light bulbs and reflectors correctly. Semidirect light causes less glare and eyestrain. Satisfactory intensity for general physical education activity is from 20 to 30 foot candles; for more exact vision greater intensity is desirable. A foot candle is a measurement of illumination equivalent to that produced by a standard candle at a distance of one foot.

Ventilation. Ventilation can be provided either by means of open windows or via mechanical means. Mechanical ventilation is necessary in swimming pools, wrestling rooms, and locker and shower areas. It is also desirable in gymnasiums to remove odors, reduce humidity, and at times to remove heat. Ventilation aims to produce four changes of air per hour without creating drafts.

Ventilation via windows is not feasible in swimming pools or locker and shower areas. In large gymnasiums ventilation by means of windows will not be adequate by itself but it may supplement mechanical ventilation. In general, ventilation in physical education areas is largely provided by a mechanical fan system with exhausts.

Plumbing. In selecting plumbing equipment it is wise to purchase good standard materials from a reliable dealer. Durability, strength, simplicity of design, and a good finish are the marks of satisfactory equipment.

All pipes for water, heat, gas, or other purposes and all sewage and drain pipes should be laid before the walls and the foundation are built. Care should be taken to mend the damp-proofing in the event that pipes are laid after the walls are in. Toilets, showers, lavatories, cuspidors, and drinking fountains should be placed conveniently, of course, but in such position that a minimum of approach and disposal pipes are necessary. That is, if some of these service units must appear in each fourth of the building, it is more economical to place

them near each other thus ⊞ or even thus ⊞ than thus ⊞ .

This cannot be arranged in all cases, but it can in many. Girls' showers, for instance, might as well be on the opposite side of the walls from boys' showers as in some other corner of the room or section of the building. Fewer pipes need be used, too, if the unit on the floor above is directly above the unit on the floor below. Hot and cold water pipes should be far enough apart so that the cold water remains cold, especially at the drinking fountains. The cleaning problem is simplified, the appearance is improved, and the danger of accident is reduced if pipes are enclosed in the walls. Those factors sufficiently outweigh the increased cost of installation and the greater difficulty of getting at pipes when something goes wrong, so that enclosing in the walls is recommended if provision is made for access when necessary.

Specific suggestions for each of the following service units are presented under the unit concerned.

1. Radiators and heating:

   (a) Sufficient radiation should be provided to furnish adequate heat on cold days—about 60° F. for the activity rooms, about 70° F. for the locker rooms, and about 80° F. for the shower and swimming pool rooms.

   (b) Proportionately fewer heating units are needed to heat large rooms than to heat small ones, because as rooms get larger the volume increases more rapidly than the area of exposed outer surface through which heat passes off. A 1-inch cube has a height of 1 inch, a volume of 1 cubic inch, and a surface of 6 square inches; a 2-inch cube has a height of 2 inches, a volume of 8 cubic inches and a surface of 24 square inches; and a 3-inch cube has a height of 3 inches, a volume of 27 cubic inches, and a surface of 54 square inches. In the above, the ratio between volume and surface decreases from 1 to 6, to 1 to 3, to 1 to 2.

(c) Radiators should be recessed into walls and placed above the heights of pupils. If recessed, a few protecting bars or grates should be used. It is probably best to suspend them from the ceiling in locker rooms.

(d) Heat pipes should be insulated to conserve heat, to prevent burns, and to prevent overheating of some rooms and halls.

(e) Radiators should be distributed so that they provide a comparatively even temperature throughout the room.

2. Showers:

(a) Sufficient showers to care for the peak load should be provided. Fourteen square feet for each shower should be allowed, with one shower for five boys and one shower for four girls. If girls are to have individual showers and dressing booths, one shower can serve only two conveniently. The recommended standard for showers for girls is 90 percent of the group type and 10 percent of the individual type. The shower heads should be spaced at least 4 feet apart.

(b) A large drain pipe from the showers is necessary to prevent the danger of overflow to other rooms.

(c) Showers should be arranged so that water flowing from one shower does not interfere with the use of another.

(d) Shower heads should be higher than the heads of the boys and men who are to use them, but they should be set to discharge diagonally downward so that those who use them may avoid getting their heads wet if they so choose. Girls' shower heads should be shoulder high.

(e) Shower heads with removable faces can be cleaned easily.

(f) Individual control of showers is advocated. Although central control is more economical, individual control under supervision is not particularly expensive and is much more satisfactory to the shower takers. Younger children may have to be taught how to take showers, and that can be done at school with little effort.

(g) At each shower head there should be a liquid soap dispenser.

(h) The recommended lighting is 20 foot candles.

3. Drying rooms:

(a) The drying room should be located between the shower and locker rooms, with entrances to each.

(b) The drying room should be approximately the same size as the shower room.

(c) The floor and the walls (up to 6 feet) should be similar to those in the shower rooms.

(d) Towel racks adequate to accommodate the peak load should be installed.

4. Lavatories:

(a) Lavatories should be near the toilet room.

(b) White porcelain finish is preferred to colored finish.

(c) Paper towels and liquid soap should be provided near the lavatories.

(d) Faucets that turn off automatically when left on are practical.

5. Toilets:

(a) Enough toilets to take care of peak load classes should be provided—approximately one urinal for twenty boys and one stool for fifteen girls, and one stool for thirty boys.

(b) The type of toilet that flushes readily with a small amount of water is practical.

(c) A foot release for flushing is much more sanitary than a hand release.

(d) The height of the urinals should be regulated for the convenience of the boys who are to use them.

6. Cuspidors:

(a) The type of cuspidor that will flush easily with a little water is practical.

(b) The foot flush type is preferable.

(c) At least one cuspidor should be placed in the main gym room, recessed in the wall with bars to keep balls out of it. This is essential since some players must expectorate during activity periods, and if no proper place is provided the floor or wall will have to suffice.

(d) To facilitate cleaning, the bars should be removable or should swing back.

(e) The finish should be of a different color from that of the drinking fountain.

7. Drinking fountains:

(a) There should be one drinking fountain just outside the main activity room and another in the locker room. Drinking of water should be encouraged by providing a convenient supply; consequently, additional fountains may be necessary.

(b) The cold-water pipe leading to the fountain should be insulated if it is close to a hot-water pipe.

(c) A foot release should be provided.

(d) A type of drinking fountain that is not apt to squirt water out on the floor should be chosen.

(e) The type of fountain that throws water toward one side rather than straight up is preferable.

8. Lockers and baskets:

(a) Two or three small locker rooms rather than one large room are recommended. One of the rooms can then be kept at a lower temperature for those who like to dress in a cooler room. Also, one small room can be used for the visiting team's locker room when visitors come to compete. This is an essential courtesy that should be extended to visitors because they are guests of the institution and should be given a guest room, with the privacy it affords.

(b) Cement bases should be built for the lockers.

(c) Aisles about 5 feet wide should be provided when lockers are placed in rows.

(d) Lockers should be arranged so that light from the windows falls between the rows.

(e) In small rooms lockers should be arranged around the walls.

(f) Metal lockers used to store equipment should be ventilated by sucking warm, dry air through them and discharged out of doors.

9. Locker rooms:

(a) The locker room should be large enough to provide 20 square feet for each occupant during the peak load.

(b) The recommended standard for lighting is 20 foot candles.

(c) The recommended temperature is 70° F.

(d) Adequate ventilation and acoustical treatment are vitally important.

10. Team rooms:

(a) Full-length lockers large enough to permit storage of practice equipment should be available for all squad members.

(b) It is desirable to locate lockers around walls in order to leave center area open for squad meetings.

(c) The team room should be available to squads in season.

(d) A bulletin board and a chalk board should be installed.

(e) The training room should be adjacent to the team room.

11. Custodial facilities:

(a) Custodial closets should be located appropriately to facilitate custodial operations.

(b) A storage area for custodial supplies is necessary.

(c) A service sink in or adjacent to the custodial closets is a necessity.

Locker unit

Lockers and baskets vary greatly in size, materials used in construction, and methods of handling. The wire type allows clothes to dry much better than the metal louver type but admits more dust and water. Larger, full-length lockers are more convenient and adequate than the small 12 by 12 by 36-inch type but also more expensive. The problem, then, is to provide that combination of lockers and baskets that most adequately meets the needs of the various groups concerned without entailing too great expense.

It is generally agreed that the varsity athletes should have individual lockers placed in the varsity locker room. Full-length lockers are recommended, but if funds will not permit them, half-length lockers can be made to do. Each locker should have a good strong lock on it. The master-key-combination type is recommended. The inside of the door should be painted white to improve visibility.

Some schools provide half-length lockers for all students who use the locker rooms, and a few provide full-length lockers for all. This is very convenient but too expensive to be recommended for general use. Some combination of basket and locker systems is much better. There are three reasonably good systems: two with attendants on duty during class time, and one without. In all three systems there are enough full-length lockers provided to care for the peak load. This includes class members, going and coming, recreational activity people, and intramural competitors. These lockers might be distributed in two or three smaller locker rooms or, in the event locked basket compartments are used, around the walls of the room which contains the baskets. In one of the systems requiring an attendant, two rows of baskets are situated back to back. Each basket is locked in its compartment with a master-key-combination lock. The student gets his basket and changes his clothing, putting his street clothes in an adjacent full-length locker provided for that purpose and locking it with the padlock that was on his basket compartment. An equipment exchange window is maintained at which the student can get clean clothes at the end of his exercise period. In the other system requiring an attendant, as in the one above, each person using the locker room has a basket with his assigned number on it. The baskets are placed on shelves in the basket room; those for each class in the same section of the basket room. When a student desires his basket, he calls out his number and the attendant slides the basket along a chute to him. The wire basket, about 15 by 10 by 20 inches, contains his gym clothes, a clean towel, and the padlock for the locker in which he is to keep his street clothes. He selects his locker and uses it. When he has taken his shower and is ready to leave, he slides his basket into the chute. The attendant puts in a clean towel and places the basket back on the rack in the stall containing its number.

The third basket-locker system recommended here does not require an attendant on duty during the time baskets are used. The locker arrangement is the same as above, but the basket arrangement differs. The same type of baskets, with numbers on them and corresponding numbers on their individual compartments, is recommended; but these baskets are placed around the outside of a series of hollow oblong cages. The cages project outward somewhat like the spokes from a hub but more like the fingers of four hands crossed at the wrists. In the central, or wrist, area is the equipment room. Above the total basket setup is heavy wire fencing to provide ventilation and safety for equipment. Each cage is about 20 to 30 feet in length, 8 feet in width, and 6 feet in height, exclusive of the wire fencing above it. Heavy wire compartments around the outer part of the cage are arranged in five tiers to contain the students' baskets. The passageway down the center of the hollow cage is wide enough to permit servicing the individual baskets from two large baskets on rollers, one for used clothes and one for clean clothes. The student's basket is constructed low enough in the back, toward the inside of the cage, to permit the attendant to exchange towels and clothing issued by the department and to check equipment. A tray is provided in the upper part of the back of the student's basket to contain the clothing that is to be exchanged. Two bars extend across the basket on which to put damp clothing so that it will dry better. A metal door on the front of the compartment, toward the outside, is provided with a good master-key-combination padlock. This lock can also be used on the locker when the student leaves his street clothes there. The student may take his basket from its compartment when he needs it and return it when he is through with it. This system is economical, convenient, and sanitary.

The following locker room accessories are desirable:

1. Benches for all lockers. Long benches fastened to the floor by steel posts serve very well.
2. Mirrors for both girls and boys. One in each small locker room, and at least one at each end of the large locker room, if there is a large locker room.
3. Dressing booths for girls. It is satisfactory to provide booths for only a part of the class, since some will not care for them. More and more girls are accepting the type of dressing facilities and showers used by boys.
4. A bulletin board near the entrance to locker room or rooms.
5. Hair dryers for the girls' locker room.

Apparatus

Apparatus should be selected on the basis of its prospective usefulness in furthering a modern physical education program rather than because of traditional support of the activity for which it will be used. Traditional support does not condemn it, but in itself is not sufficient to determine the selection of apparatus. Rugged, simple, standard pieces should be chosen. Even though the original cost may be greater, the difference will be compensated for in reduced repair bills. Since shipping costs for heavy pieces are relatively high, it may be more economical to purchase from some dealer close at hand.

Mobile pieces that can be fastened to floor or wall catches or thrown off rollers by means of a lever are recommended. When the apparatus has been used, it can then be swung back against the wall, raised to the ceiling, or rolled off to the apparatus room, leaving the main floor available for other activities. Mats and smaller pieces that require no fastening should be stored out of the way on a platform on wheels and in boxes on wheels.

THE SWIMMING POOL

The swimming pool is a very important physical education facility. Swimming contributes more than all the other activities to the physical education objectives. As a recreational activity for people of all ages it is unsurpassed. Students find swimming to be one of the most popular activities in the curriculum, and parents are always eager to have their children learn to swim for its safety aspects. Finally, the ability to swim opens the door to many other aquatic activities, such as water-skiing, scuba diving, boating and canoeing, fishing, and sailing.

All of these factors justify an important place for swimming in the physical education curriculum. The problem in the public schools is to obtain the facilities. The great majority of colleges and universities have swimming pools but secondary schools do not. In elementary and junior and senior high schools swimming is usually taught in pools that belong to other agencies. Only a small percentage of public schools have their own swimming pools; there has, however, been a rapid increase in such facilities in the past two decades. School boards are now much more amenable to granting approval for the construction of swimming pools but it will still be a long time before the majority of secondary schools have one.

The attitude of the American public has become increasingly favorable toward the provision of aquatic facilities from public funds. Many secondary schools have been able to acquire such facilities on the understanding that they would be available for total community use in the evenings, on weekends, and during the summer months. It would be far more difficult to sell the idea of a pool that would be used exclusively by a school.

Indoor versus outdoor pool

Because the outdoor pool is much less expensive than the indoor one many communities have built outdoor swimming pools. Unfortunately, this restricts the use of the pool largely to the summer months in most communities. From the standpoint of a school facility an indoor pool is far more preferable. While some people are not enthusiastic about swimming indoors during the summer months the other advantages decidedly favor the construction of an indoor pool that is to be used as part of the physical education program of a school.

The dilemma of whether to build an indoor or an outdoor pool, both with advantages and drawbacks, has been solved in recent years by the construction of combination indoor-outdoor pools. By the use of high glass sliding doors ample sunlight may be available. During warm weather the doors can be opened for outdoor sunbathing. Such facilities when properly designed and constructed have proven very popular. Likewise, there is increasing use of plastic covers over outdoor pools in order to permit swimming for most of the year.

Preliminary planning considerations

Knowledge and experience must be involved in the planning of swimming pools. Throughout the country examples of poorly designed and constructed facilities are easy to find. New concepts, materials, and processes have developed so rapidly in swimming pool construction that it would be a mistake to undertake the construction of aquatic facilities without consulting a knowledgeable individual. If the architect is not an experienced, up-to-date pool builder he should consult an expert. A consultant is very frequently engaged when a large facility is being contemplated. The guidance of specialists in heating and ventilation, acoustics, plumbing, water purification, and lighting is necessary. Finally, those who will conduct the various programs in the pool should be involved in the planning. Unfortunately their experience with the practical problems in using the pool is frequently not solicited.

In planning a new pool the various uses that will be made of it are a prime consideration. School pools are used for more than instructing nonswimmers. They include programs for water safety instruction, intramural and interschool competition, synchronized swimming, pageants, water polo, scuba diving, recreational swimming, and hydrotherapy. The requirements for each of these activities must be incorporated in the planning.

Virtually every State Department of Public Health has various regulations pertaining to swimming pools. Compliance with these regulations is a must. These laws usually cover such factors as water circulation, filtration, water treatment practices, sanitary standards, safety features, and the like.

Design. Because of the construction costs most indoor pools are rectangular in shape. A few schools have constructed L or T shaped pools, which have significant advantages. In such pools the divers are separated from the swimmers; this not only reduces accidents but makes swimming more enjoyable. In addition, since a larger shallow area is made possible an increased number of beginning swimmers can be handled. Some rectangular pools have movable bulkheads to separate the diving area from the remainder of the pool.

The ultimate in indoor swimming facilities is to have, in addition to the rectangular pool, separate instructional and diving pools. The instructional pool is small (30 by 42 feet) and shallow (3 to 4 feet) and is designed to teach beginning swimmers. The diving well is provided exclusively for diving. This eliminates the diving boards in the main pool. These two additional pools are strongly recommended if funds are available to pay for them. They not only enable more swimmers to be accommodated, but they also provide more satisfying conditions for everyone concerned. However, the single, multiple-purpose pool will be the type that will prevail in most of those schools fortunate enough to possess a pool.

The customary length of an indoor pool is 75 feet, 1 inch. The width is usually a multiple of 7 feet. Thus, many schools have pools of 35, 42, 49 or 56 feet in width. It should be noted that in recent years there has been a trend to depart from a width that is a multiple of seven. This is due to the desire to have a buffer zone of 1 or 2 feet along each side. This is helpful for competitive swimmers in the outside lanes because it contributes to smoother water.

Table 7-3. Minimum recommended occupancy design factors.

Activity	Indoor Pools	Outdoor Pools
Shallow-Water Area (Under 5'-0"):		
Recreational Swimming	14 sq. ft./capita	15 sq. ft./capita
Advanced Swimming Instruction	20 "	25 "
Beginning Swimming Instruction	40 "	45 "
Deep-Water Area (Over 5'-0"):		
Recreational Swimming	20 "	25 "
Advanced Swimming	25 "	30 "
Diving (Based on Area Within 30 ft. of Deep-end Diving Wall)	175 "	200 "
Minimum Walk Width*	6 ft.	12 ft.
Sum of walk dimensions,* on either side of the pool length or width, shall not be less than	18 ft.	30 ft.

*Walk dimensions shall be horizontal clear deck width, not including any portion of the coping or interior gutter sections.

Source: The Athletic Institute, *Planning Areas and Facilities for Health, Physical Education and Recreation* (Chicago, The Athletic Institute, 1965), p. 173.

The number of occupants of the pool depends upon the nature of the activity. Recommended standards are given in Table 7-3.

For secondary school and college students the pool depth at the shallow end should range from 3 feet 6 inches to 4 feet. At the deep end the depth is determined by the diving boards. The 1-meter board requires a minimum depth of 9 feet and the 3-meter board a minimum depth of 12 feet. The slope of the pool bottom from the shallow end should not exceed a 1-foot drop to every 20 feet. To provide adequate overhead clearance for diving, 15 feet above the highest springboard is needed.

The decks of the pool should provide sufficient space for land drills, lifesaving activities, and physical conditioning. It is also possible to put folding bleachers on the decks. For these reasons at least one deck should exceed the minimum width. At least 6 feet should be provided on one side and 12 feet or more (depending upon the number of spectators to be accommodated) on the other. The width of the deck at the shallow end should be not less than 10 feet and 15 feet at the deep end. It is a recommended minimum standard that the total amount of deck space be equivalent to the water surface area.

Major construction features

Location. An indoor pool can be constructed anywhere in the building but the preferred location is on the ground level. This location is not only the most economical form of construction but it also provides ready access from the outside. In the past the location of the pool directly underneath the gymnasium created serious problems. It is difficult to control the moisture from the pool, which will, of course, damage the gymnasium floor.

The pool should be accessible from both the girls' and boys' locker rooms. If separate locker and shower areas are available for the general public access to the pool is necessary. Also, the pool should be located so that spectators at swimming events have direct access to the seating area.

Materials. A wide variety of materials may be used for the construction of the swimming pool shell. Steel, plastic, and aluminum may be used, but concrete in various forms is utilized most extensively. The decks, sides, and basin of the pool are usually constructed of reinforced, form-poured concrete. Precast, prestressed concrete or concrete block may be used for the pool walls. Pneumatically applied concrete may also be employed for the entire pool shell.

Tile is the favored swimming pool finish. The advantages of tile are that it can be readily cleaned, slipping is rendered less likely, it is durable and attractive in appearance. Its disadvantage is its cost although over a period of years this factor is not excessive. Abrasive tile is usually used at the ends of the pool to reduce slipping on turns in competitive swimming. The lanes, which are marked on the pool floor, are made of black tile.

A wide variety of other pool finishes are available. Rubber-base paint is the least expensive. Water-resistant oil vehicle paints are much more costly, but they are more serviceable. Various chemical coatings have been developed. Plaster finishes have some advantages. Precast-stone terrazzo construction has been used successfully.

Ladders. Ladders should be available at each corner of the pool. They should be recessed into the side walls.

Coping. The coping is a slightly elevated area from 12 to 18 inches wide which extends around the entire pool. It prevents the return of water from the deck to the pool. The coping also facilitates cleaning the deck without getting dirty water in the pool. It also serves as a slightly elevated platform that swimmers use to dive into the pool.

The coping is usually made from precast-concrete sections. It is essential that it not be slippery when wet.

Overflow gutters. Most state boards of health require overflow gutters for sanitary reasons. They serve a useful purpose in carrying waste materials and debris off the surface of the water. They are helpful to many swimmers who wish to climb out of the pool. In addition, they also serve as a place for swimmers to hold on to while resting. The recommended standard is that the overflow gutters extend completely around the pool.

Several different types of overflow gutters are available. The "roll-out" and "deck-level" gutters are popular. The gutters should be constructed so that they can be cleaned and maintained easily. They should be deep enough to prevent the waste water from washing back into the pool. The drain openings inside the gutters should be located every 10 feet.

Markings. Water depth markings should be located at critical points on the deck. They should be permanent, preferably set in tile. For swimming competition, distances should be marked in 5-yard increments. These markings should be permanent both on the face of the pool and the deck.

Acoustics. Noise will be a problem in indoor pools unless provisions are made to counteract it. Any indoor area with smooth, hard walls and ceiling will be noisy. Moisture-proof acoustical material on the ceiling and on at least two of the side walls will solve the problem.

Heating. The water temperature for instructional classes should be 80° F; for competitive swimming it should range from 76° F. to 78° F. The air temperature should be 5° F. warmer than the water temperature. Radiant heating in the deck has proven successful in controlling air temperature. The unit heater with attached blower also serves the purpose well. Air temperature should be thermostatically controlled.

Ventilation. Ventilation is important in order to reduce humidity and condensation. It is best provided by a mechanically operated ventilation system. The most important consideration is the location of air intakes. They must be high enough to avoid drafts for those using the pool. The comfort of both swimmers and spectators depends upon temperature and ventilation.

Lighting. Much sentiment exists for completely artificial lighting. If a good system is available uniformity of lighting is assured; glare and shadows are eliminated, and the growth of algae inhibited. Another advantage is that with the elimination of outside windows it is easier to maintain proper air temperature, humidity, and ventilation.

Some natural lighting is available in many pools. Sunlight is desirable if the rays do not cause interference to the swimmers or spectators. This can be controlled by the proper location of windows and the use of glass block or tinted fiberglass.

The recommended standard for lighting is 50 foot candles at the surface of the water or at deck level.

Underwater lighting. Underwater lighting is a desirable feature even though it adds to the expense of construction. Such lighting is invaluable for pageants and water shows but it also facilitates cleaning and promotes safety. Lights are not recommended at the shallow end of the pool. At the deep end the recommended location is halfway between the surface and the bottom. The sidewall lights should be 2 feet below the surface at the shallow end and gradually lower as the pool depth increases.

Access tunnel. An access tunnel around the outside of the pool basin, while not absolutely necessary, is a desirable feature of a pool. Such a tunnel makes it much simpler to inspect and repair much of the plumbing. Underwater lighting is facilitated, and windows for viewing and taking films can be readily provided.

Factors increasing construction cost

The cost of a pool is a factor of major importance for most schools. Many communities do not have swimming facilities because of cost considerations. Swimming pools are expensive yet perhaps not as costly as might be expected. There are many features that while desirable are not absolutely necessary. Some of these are:

1. Extensive use of tile on the floor and walls of the basin of the pool and on the decks
2. Underwater windows and lights
3. Access tunnel
4. Greater height, width, and length of building than necessary. This is a major expense item

5. Greater pool depth, particularly at deep end, than is necessary. The recommended standard is that 75 to 85 percent of the total water area should be less than 5 feet deep
6. Expensive heating and ventilation systems
7. Windows are more expensive than solid walls
8. Expensive acoustical arrangements

Water circulation

The purposes of water circulation are to keep it clear, clean, and pure. The size of the filters and the capacity of the pump should be such as to recirculate the water four times every 24 hours. In this manner the various processes through which the water passes can be accomplished. The flow of the water can be readily perceived in the schematic diagram in Figure 7-3.

Water treatment [2]

A school swimming program requires the best quality of water. This is water that (1) has maximum visibility, (2) provides maximum protection against disease, and (3) eliminates the factors that cause discomfort to swimmers.

Maximum visibility is a necessity for swimming instruction and lifeguarding. At all times when the pool is in use the water should have such a degree of clarity that a disc, 2 inches in diameter, which is divided into quadrants in alternate colors of red and black, shall be clearly discernible through 15 feet of water with its different colors readily distinguishable.

To protect swimmers from infectious disease is an obligation of all pool operators. Water readily transmits various pathogenic organisms, which, if not countered, could make swimming a dangerous and undesirable activity. Concerning the comfort of the swimmer certain water conditions are known to produce irritation of eyes, ears, and skin.

The following four factors are involved in water treatment: (1) filtration, (2) pH control, (3) alkalinity control, and (4) disinfection.

Each of these considerations will be discussed.

1. Filtration. The purposes of filtration are to remove suspended matter and a substantial percentage of bacteria from the water. (The hair strainer also removes some of the debris and foreign particles from the water.)

A variety of filters are available. Those most commonly used are:

[2] The data concerning water treatment comes from The Athletic Institute, *Planning Areas and Facilities for Health, Physical Education and Recreation* (Chicago, The Athletic Institute, 1965), Chap. 13.

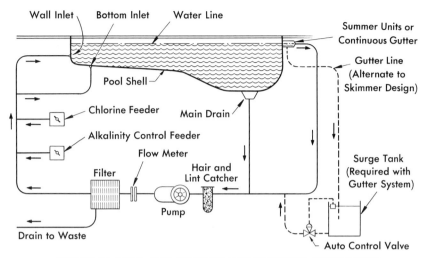

GRANULAR MEDIA AND PRESSURE DIATOMACEOUS EARTH FILTERS

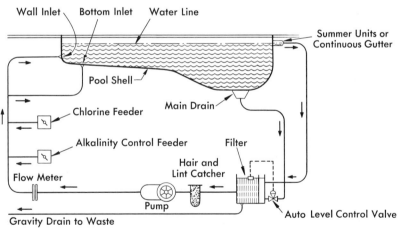

VACUUM TYPE DIATOMACEOUS EARTH FILTERS

Note—Pool overflow and vacuum lines have been omitted for clarity.

Prepared by Milton Costello, Consulting Engineer, Wantagh, New York 11794.

Source: The Athletic Institute, *Planning Areas and Facilities for Health, Physical Education and Recreation* (Chicago, The Athletic Institute, 1965), p. 176.

Figure 7-3. Typical Pool Hydraulic Schematics.

(1) gravity sand and gravel, (2) pressure sand and gravity, (3) pressure diatomaceous earth, and (4) vacuum diatomaceous earth. Each type possesses certain advantages, and local conditions should determine which to select.

2. pH control. The term pH refers to the relative amount of acidity or alkalinity of the pool water. The pH of water varies from 0 to 14 with 7 representing the point where there is a balance of acid and alkaline ions. A pH from 7 to 14 indicates an increasing alkaline condition of the water while from 7 to 0 represents an acid condition. For a pool that uses a chlorine disinfectant the recommended standard is a pH of from 7.2 to 7.6.

The pH of the water should be checked daily and a record maintained of the readings. Because chlorine and body acids have the effect of increasing the acidity of the water this is the condition that usually must be combatted. This is done by adding an appropriate amount of soda ash. To reduce excessive alkalinity the addition of sulfamic acid to the water is recommended.

3. Alkalinity control. While the pH reveals the relative amount of alkalinity present in the water it fails to indicate the actual, total amount of alkalinity. It is necessary to determine the quantity of the carbonate and bicarbonate alkalinity. The recommended standard is that the alkalinity should never be permitted to drop below 50 parts per million. Water that is naturally hard contains sufficient carbonates and bicarbonates to maintain proper alkalinity. These counteract the effects of acid-producing substances such as chlorine. Soft water will probably require the addition of suitable chemicals to maintain proper alkaline balance. Water need not be tested on a daily or weekly basis for alkalinity.

4. Disinfection. Disinfection is the chemical process of killing disease-producing bacteria as well as other types of microorganisms. In a swimming pool this is accomplished by maintaining a uniformly dispersed residual of some chemical capable of killing bacteria. A variety of chemical agents have been used to disinfect the water but chlorine, bromine, and iodine come closest to meeting basic specifications. Of these chlorine is the most widely used largely because it is readily available, fast acting, easy to store and use, is nontoxic to humans when used properly, and kills bacteria faster than any other disinfectant. When properly employed, chlorine can be depended upon to keep both the bacterial and algae populations within proper limits at all times.

The chlorinator should have the capacity to maintain from 3 to 5 parts per million of residual chlorine at all times of operation. The free chlorine residual should not fall below 0.4 nor exceed 0.6 parts per million. This amount of chlorine not only destroys the bacteria in the water before it enters the pool but it also provides a hostile environment for those that are introduced into the water by the swimmers. This amount of residual chlorine represents the normal standard. However, there is another approach to chlorination which is known as superchlorination. By maintaining 1 to 2 parts per million of chlorine and increasing the pH to 7.4 to 7.8 the disinfecting action against bacteria is markedly increased.

Tests for residual chlorine should be made and recorded hourly throughout the period the pool is used and a permanent record of all tests should be kept.

Pool supervision

In operating the pool the following practices should be observed:

1. Use a suction cleaner to clean the bottom and sides of the pool. This should preferably be done early in the morning after the sediment has had time to settle to the bottom. It will be necessary to clean the pool daily if it is being heavily used.
2. Test daily for air and water temperature and the pH of the water. The chlorine residual should be tested hourly when the pool is in use. These data should be recorded.
3. All persons using the pool should be required to take a shower bath before using the pool. The bath should be in the nude and involve warm water and soap. Those using the toilet should do so prior to taking the shower.
4. A lifeguard who is qualified as a Water Safety Instructor should be on duty. At no time should individuals be permitted in the water unless the lifeguard is available.
5. All persons entering the pool should be inspected. Those having skin disease, rash, open lesions, nasal or ear discharge, or a communicable disease should be denied admission.
6. Objects that may carry contamination or endanger the safety of bathers must not be brought into the pool.
7. Girls should be required to wear swimming caps.
8. Discourage the practice of dangerous stunts and pushing and shoving in and around the pool. Running on the pool decks should be prohibited.
9. Doors to the pool should be locked when the pool is not in use.
10. Prohibit blowing of the nose and spitting in the water.
11. Maintain water temperature of 80° F. for instructional classes and recreational swimming. The air temperature should be 5° F. warmer than the water temperature.

12. Pool decks should be scrubbed at least daily. Disinfection with chlorine solution or other germicides should be done daily.
13. Individuals should not be permitted to walk on the decks with street shoes.
14. Tobacco, food, and drink should be completely banned from the enclosure of the pool.

OUTDOOR ACTIVITY AREAS

Approximately 50 percent of the total physical education program in public schools and colleges and universities takes place on outdoor facilities. Consequently it is necessary that these facilities be as carefully planned and designed as the indoor activity areas. Ordinarily, these areas in elementary and secondary schools are planned as part of the total school facilities.

The major error in the past regarding outdoor facilities was the failure to provide sufficient space. Unfortunately, this mistake cannot be rectified when the area surrounding the school is built up. To obviate such errors school planners are today giving much more consideration to the total area available when new schools are being contemplated. The National Council on Schoolhouse Construction [3] has recommended the following standards for total acreage for different types of schools:

1. Elementary schools—ten acres plus one additional acre for every 100 pupils
2. Junior high schools—twenty acres plus one additional acre for every 100 pupils of estimated enrollment
3. Senior high schools—thirty acres plus one additional acre for every 100 pupils of estimated future enrollment

With such acreage available adequate space for indoor and outdoor physical education facilities can be provided.

A major factor that has contributed to school boards and administrators endeavoring to acquire more land for school sites is the expectation on the part of the people of the community that the facilities would be available to other groups when not required for school use. The trend is definitely in the direction of joint use by the school and community. In particular, the recreation department can take advantage of outdoor play areas. In this way the public receives maximum returns from the money expended.

[3] National Council on Schoolhouse Construction, *Guide for Planning School Plants* (East Lansing, Mich., Michigan State University, National Council on Schoolhouse Construction, 1964).

Site selection

When sites for schools are being considered the area to be used for athletic fields should be analyzed from the standpoint of suitability. Such considerations as drainage, subsurface water conditions, need for fill or rock excavation should be reviewed. It is desirable that the outdoor areas be close to the locker rooms but not so close that noise will interfere with academic classes. It is generally accepted that students should not be required to cross a street to get to the play areas.

Play areas for secondary schools

Sufficient outdoor play areas are needed to accommodate service classes for girls and boys, intramural athletics for boys, girls' athletic association activities, and interscholastic athletics for boys. It is quite possible in the larger secondary schools that as many as four or five outdoor teaching stations are necessary for service classes. It is apparent that several outdoor athletic fields are necessary, supplemented, if possible, by tennis courts.

Facilities for spectators for football, baseball, and track and field contests will probably not be needed in most junior high schools. To avoid the expense of constructing expensive facilities for spectators at each senior high school many communities have provided one stadium where the competitive sports of all schools can be played. If possible it is desirable to hold football practice on a field other than the one on which the games are played.

Junior and senior high schools need athletic fields that can accommodate football, touch football, soccer, baseball, softball, track and field, field hockey, speedball, and archery. A hard-surfaced area, which can be used for outdoor basketball and volleyball, is an asset. The recommended dimensions for game areas are indicated in Table 7-4.

General features

Drainage. This is an important consideration on unpaved areas. With adequate drainage various athletic fields dry out more rapidly after periods of wet weather and thus permit more usage. There are two types of drainage, namely, surface and subsurface.

Surface drainage is accomplished by grading in such a way that the middle of the activity area is slightly elevated, thus resulting in a slope toward the sides of the field. The recommended slope is 2 percent, i.e., 2 feet in every 100 feet. The water drains off the field into catch basins or natural water collectors. Subsurface drainage is accomplished by means

Table 7-4. Recommended dimensions for game areas.*

Games	Elementary School	Junior High School	High School (Adults)	Area Size (Including Buffer Space)
Basketball	40' x 60'	50' x 84'	50' x 84'	7,200 sq. ft.
Basketball (College)			50' x 94'	8,000 sq. ft.
Volleyball	25' x 50'	25' x 50'	30' x 60'	2,800 sq. ft.
Badminton			20' x 44'	1,800 sq. ft.
Paddle Tennis			20' x 44'	1,800 sq. ft.
Deck Tennis			18' x 40'	1,250 sq. ft.
Tennis		36' x 78'	26' x 78'	6,500 sq. ft.
Ice Hockey			85' x 200'	17,000 sq. ft.
Field Hockey			180' x 300'	64,000 sq. ft.
Horseshoes		10' x 40'	10' x 50'	1,000 sq. ft.
Shuffleboard			6' x 52'	640 sq. ft.
Lawn Bowling			14' x 110'	1,800 sq. ft.
Boccie			15' x 75'	1,950 sq. ft.
Tetherball	10' circle	12' circle	12' circle	400 sq. ft.
Croquet	38' x 60'	38' x 60'	38' x 60'	2,200 sq. ft.
Roque			30' x 60'	2,400 sq. ft.
Handball (Single-wall)	18' x 26'	18' x 26'	20' x 40'	1,200 sq. ft.
Handball (Four-wall)			23' x 46'	1,058 sq. ft.
Baseball	210' x 210'	300' x 300'	400' x 400'	160,000 sq. ft.
Archery		50' x 150'	50' x 300'	20,000 sq. ft.
Softball (12" Ball)†	150' x 150'	200' x 200'	275' x 275'	75,000 sq. ft.
Football			160' x 360'	80,000 sq. ft.
Touch Football		120' x 300'	160' x 360'	80,000 sq. ft.
6-Man Football			120' x 300'	54,000 sq. ft.
Soccer (Men) Minimum			165' x 300'	65,000 sq. ft.
Maximum			240' x 360'	105,000 sq. ft.
Soccer (Women)			120' x 240'	40,000 sq. ft.

*Table covers a single unit; many of above can be combined.
†Dimensions vary with size of ball used.

Source: The Athletic Institute, *Planning Areas and Facilities for Health, Physical Education and Recreation* (Chicago, The Athletic Institute, 1965), p. 18.

of drain tiles that convey the water to a storm sewer or other outlet.

Surfacing. The criteria for surfaces of physical education activity areas outlined at the Third Facilities Conference [4] are:

1. All-year usage
2. Multiplicity of use
3. Dustless and stainless

[4] The Athletic Institute, *Planning Areas and Facilities for Health, Physical Education and Recreation* (Chicago, The Athletic Institute, 1965), p. 78.

4. Nonabrasiveness
5. Pleasing appearance
6. Durability
7. Resiliency
8. Low maintenance cost
9. Reasonable initial cost
10. Ease of maintenance

No surface is ideal for every type of activity area. Turf comes the closest to being the best all-around surface. However, it does not hold up well under heavy use. It is somewhat expensive to maintain properly. Likewise, problems are created in wet weather. Three other types of surfacing are:

1. Bituminous or blacktop. This type of surface has greatly increased in popularity in public schools and colleges and universities. An up-to-date assessment of this type of surface was reported at the Third National Facilities Conference: [5]

The common bituminous surface has many of the advantages which are sought in any surfacing material. It provides a durable surface which can be used on a year-round schedule. The maintenance of bituminous surface is comparatively easy and inexpensive. Such a surface can also be used for many different activities. When properly installed, the surface is dust-free and drains quickly. Asphalt surfaces can be marked easily and with a relatively high degree of permanence. Asphalt also provides a neat-appearing, no-glare surface that will blend well with the landscape.

The disadvantages of bituminous surfaces are their relatively-high installation costs and lack of resiliency as compared to some other types of surfaces. However, the high installation cost will be offset by low maintenance costs.

Bituminous surfaces will vary as to firmness, finish, resiliency, and durability in direct relation to the kinds and proportions of aggregates and other materials used in their mixture.

Asphalt can be combined with a variety of other materials to provide a reasonably resilient or extremely hard surface. The use of such materials as cork, sponge, or rubber in combination with asphalt will yield a fairly-resilient surface. Aggregates such as slag or granite will produce an extremely hard surface when combined with asphalt.

2. Concrete. Concrete has fewer advantages and more disadvantages than blacktop. As a consequence its use has declined.

3. Synthetics. Considerable research is being carried out with various types of synthetic surfaces. Experimentation has been done with such synthetic compounds as chlorinated butyl-rubber, rubber asphalt, synthetic resins, mineral fiber, asphalt, plastics, and vinyl. Some of these materials show great promise. They are resilient, durable, nonabrasive,

[5] *Ibid.*, p. 80.

require little maintenance, come in a variety of colors, and are excellent for year-round use.

Orientation of fields and courts. For the safety of the participants as well as equitable playing conditions fields and courts should be laid out to reduce the effects of the sun's rays. In rectangular fields and courts the flight of the ball is usually parallel to the long axes of the playing area. At the time of the day and year when the sport is being played the direction of the sun's rays should be determined. The playing field or court should then be laid out so that its long axis is perpendicular to the sun's rays. If these directions are followed the play on football, soccer, and rugby fields will be in a north-south direction. In baseball the rays of the late afternoon sun should be perpendicular to a line drawn from home plate through second base.

Fencing. Most play areas should be fenced. A suitable fence for many locations consists of 11 gauge woven wire 10 feet high. This will protect property, provide privacy, reduce supervising problems, and keep balls and other play materials from rolling, flying, or being carried into the streets. Fencing is particularly necessary for tennis courts. If a number of courts are constructed side by side complete fencing between courts is not necessary. A partial fence—extending in about 20 feet from the rear fence—will eliminate a great deal of ball chasing.

Lighting. Outdoor athletic areas have been lighted for night use primarily for interschool athletics. In colleges and universities night lighting has been frequently used for intramural athletics and for student and faculty recreation. Much greater use of all outdoor areas could be obtained, however, if more extensive use of night lighting were made. Not only would the use be appreciably extended but such use would be much more enjoyable when the heat is excessive during the day.

The assistance of lighting engineers should be sought whenever a project involving outdoor athletic areas is contemplated.

Baseball fields. A considerable problem arises in orienting baseball diamonds so that both the players and the spectators will be handicapped as little as possible. For professional games the spectators often receive more consideration than they do for school contests. The school diamonds should be laid out to favor the players, for they are of prime importance and often they play without spectators. For schools it is satisfactory to have the base line from home to first base run directly west. This will considerably reduce interference with vision by the afternoon sun. Adequate backstops should be provided to reduce lost balls and ball chasing in general and to protect spectators. The distance from home plate to the backstop should be 60 feet. This same distance should separate the base lines and the stands or fence.

The construction and care of the diamond is important. The area should be approximately level, with adequate provision for drainage.

The pitcher's plate may be elevated on a gradually sloping mound not higher than 18 inches above the surface of the infield. The ground should be rolled in the spring, and the grass should be kept mowed in both the infield and outfield. If the sod is removed from the base paths and other sections of the infield, those areas need care before each game. If water is available, they are customarily wet down, raked, and rolled, after which, first and third base lines are extended, and the boxes at home plate are marked with lime. Permanent markers on the foul lines in deep right and left field are valuable aids in judging fair and foul balls.

Football fields. The football field should be laid out and constructed in such a manner that it will be the most adequate playing area possible. In order that the team defending the least favored goal may be handicapped as little as possible by the sun and the wind the layout must be considered carefully. Since the prevailing winds in most sections of the country blow from the west, and since the sun shines from the west in the late fall afternoon it is often best to lay out the field north and south if possible. Other factors may make this undesirable but, in general, it is well to keep this in mind.

The field and adjacent territory should be well drained. This is especially important if it is located on low ground. Coarse gravel a couple of feet under the surface soil, which is composed of 8 to 10 inches to 1 foot of loam, with well-placed tile will aid materially in quick drainage. Most fields are already constructed without a gravel base and cannot be rebuilt. Tile alone may help considerably in such cases.

The field should be about 8 inches higher in the center than at the sideline and should slope gradually and evenly to the sides of the playing area to allow water to drain off quickly rather than be left to stand in pools any place on the field.

The four common faults in the construction of turfed athletic fields are:

1. Poor subsurface drainage.
2. Inadequate surface drainage.
3. Improper texture of the soil. The topsoil should consist of a mixture of sand and loam. The amount of clay should not exceed 15 percent.
4. The wrong type of grass. Expert advice should be sought before the type of grass is selected. Weather and soil conditions in different parts of the country favor certain types of grass. The assistance of the local agricultural agent or a nearby agricultural college or experimental station should be sought in order to select the best variety of grass for the football field.

Tennis courts. For school use a battery of from six to eight tennis courts is recommended. One or two courts cannot be used for class instruction because they could not accommodate the number of students in a class.

The dimensions of the doubles court are 78 by 36 feet. The recommended size of the area for a court is 120 by 60 feet. This provides a space of 21 feet from the base line to the backstop and 12 feet from the sideline to the edge of the court surface. Fencing 12 feet high should enclose the courts.

Perhaps the most satisfactory layout position for tennis courts would be from northwest to southeast. However, courts as a rule are not placed at an angle, so the north and south position is most common.

Tennis court surfaces are classified as porous and nonporous. The porous surfaces permit some seepage of moisture while the nonporous surfaces are impervious. Porous surfaces include grass, clay, and various types of crushed materials. Concrete and various bituminous combinations are the types of nonporous surfaces in most frequent use.

For secondary schools and colleges and universities the porous type surfaces are not practical. They require too much maintenance and they cannot be used after rainy weather for too long a period of time. There are many regions in the United States, especially in the northern part, where hard surface courts are almost essential if tennis is to be played in the spring of the year.

Cement is one of the most satisfactory surfacing materials. The cost is high, but if properly laid, a cement court will last a long time. Proper laying includes good drainage around the edge and under the court, coarse gravel and rock base to a depth of 12 to 18 inches, then coarse cement, and finally a finish surface of fine cement. The surface must not be too smooth, or players will experience difficulty in keeping their footing. Asphalt is much more economical than cement but needs repair and replacement in a comparatively short time.

There are a number of specific tennis court surface preparations that are also good. Thousands of tennis courts have commercially prepared surfaces such as Grasstex, Lay-Kold, Pave-coat, and the like. These courts possess the advantages of cement courts but none of the disadvantages. They are resilient, do not radiate heat, glare is eliminated and they are not hard on the legs and feet. They are, however, more expensive than cement courts.

Track. The running track requires a 440-yard oval with a straightaway of a minimum of 140 yards but preferably 240 yards in order that 100- and 220-yard races could be run without the necessity of traversing a curve.

The track should contain at least six lanes. The minimum lane width is 36 inches but 42 to 48 inches is preferred.

A convenient arrangement for most schools is that of placing the track around the football field. This is economical of space and places the performers in both sports in positions where they can be observed from the same bleachers.

The traditional cinder track was constructed by excavating from 2 to 3 feet. The bottom layer should consist of 10 to 12 inches of coarse cinders or crushed stone. This should be rolled. The next layer should consist of 6 to 8 inches of medium cinders. The upper layer should consist of from 3 to 6 inches of fine cinders and clay in the proportions of four parts of cinders to one part clay.

In the past decade a rapid development of all-weather tracks has occurred. These are constructed of different materials such as: (1) fibrous asphalt composition, (2) rubber, sand asphalt hot mix, (3) rubberized asphalt cold mix, (4) synthetic resin material, and (5) rubber-cork asphalt composition.

The advantages of such tracks include:

1. Their resiliency prevents shin splints.
2. The footing is always good.
3. The maintenance cost is reduced or eliminated.
4. The lane markings are permanent.
5. The condition of the surface is always uniform.
6. The appearance of the surface is enhanced.
7. Inclement weather causes fewer cancellations or postponements of meets.
8. Rubber-soled shoes can be used as readily as spiked shoes.
9. The performances of athletes are not adversely affected by wet weather.
10. Spike openings close and heal immediately.

The chief disadvantage of these all-weather tracks is their initial cost. However, because of the reduced maintenance cost the expense over a period of a decade or two is probably not greater than the traditional track surfaces.

Athletic field and court layouts

For detailed specifications of athletic field and court layouts for various physical education activities see Appendix F.

SELECTED REFERENCES

The Athletic Institute, *Planning Facilities for Health, Physical Education and Recreation,* 3rd ed. (Chicago, The Athletic Institute, 1965).

Gabrielsen, M. Alexander, and Caswell M. Miles, *Sports and Recreation Facilities for School and Community,* 3rd ed. (Englewood Cliffs, N.J., Prentice-Hall, Inc., 1964).

Scott, Harry A., and Richard B. Westkaemper, *From Program to Facilities in Physical Education* (New York, Harper & Row, Publishers, 1958).

8

interschool athletics

BACKGROUND OF INTERSCHOOL ATHLETICS

Colleges and universities

As far back as anthropologists can go in man's history they find evidences of his participation in sports and games. But despite the fact that man has always wanted to play, and has played when possible, only recently has he ventured to play in the schools. The traditional philosophy of education, with its emphasis on scholarship and intellectual development, could conceive of no place for play in an educational institution. Naturally, this powerful urge could not be entirely throttled, and despite the unsympathetic and frequently hostile attitude of the faculty, the students indulged in various sports and games in their leisure moments. It was not until the nineteenth century that students dared form teams for interschool contests. Organized athletics appeared in England as early as 1822 when the first Eton-Harrow cricket match was played. Oxford and Cambridge met for the first time in 1827. In the United States, the first interschool contest was a rowing race between Yale and Harvard in 1852. In 1859 the first baseball game was played between Williams and Amherst.

Despite these sporadic contests prior to the Civil War, the real development came afterward. Up to this time the impromptu type of play on campus predominated. But the war, as all wars since have done, greatly stimulated interest in sports. This fact, plus the greatly expanded enrollments, gave such impetus to athletics that the informal, intramural type of program developed a new facet, namely, interinstitutional competition. The better teams within institutions began to challenge similar teams in nearby schools. This form of extramural competition proved immediately popular. Participants and student bodies were extremely enthusiastic and supported this new development wholeheartedly. Faculty members were undoubtedly aware of these student activities but took no action to control or curtail them.

At first, the captain was the coach of the team. As interest in intercollegiate athletics increased, it became obvious that more experienced leadership was necessary. The practice developed of employing on a seasonal basis an alumnus who had been an outstanding performer. Alumni coaches eventually gave way to professional coaches. In the days before gate receipts, coaches were paid by the students, alumni, or friends of the institution. Since colleges and universities had no facilities for athletics, it was necessary for students to obtain, prepare, and maintain the playing areas. Originally, all the playing equipment and uniforms were furnished by the players, but as the importance of the contests grew, parents, alumni, or friends contributed to their purchase.

For a number of years after the Civil War this student-initiated and -conducted program flourished. But as it grew many problems developed. In the first place, the amount of work which was necessary to conduct a program of athletics became too much for students who were expected to carry a normal academic load. Secondly, the constantly changing student population prevented any stability in leadership and continuity in policy. Thirdly, due to both of these factors many undesirable practices occurred. Business matters were not efficiently handled, and financial irregularities resulted. A fierce struggle was waged within the institution when the different sports competed with each other for players, financial support, and facilities. Many questionable practices were engaged in to recruit athletes. Eligibility rules were nonexistent; travel was unrestrained. Students with injuries did not receive proper medical care. Student leadership proved incapable of meeting the many problems that developed.

The athletic situation deteriorated to such an extent that the faculty was finally forced to take steps to eliminate the problem. Two major changes in the conduct of the program resulted:

1. At the insistence of college administrators, the students were forced to establish an organization that would give more stability to the management. These organizations were called student athletic associations, which were directed by an alumnus called a graduate manager.
2. Institutional control was exercised through an athletic committee, which was constituted in some cases entirely of faculty members and

in others by a combination of faculty, alumni, and students. The graduate managers were to administer the athletic program under the policies established by the athletic committees.

Although these two measures brought intercollegiate athletics much more under institutional control, they did not involve the acceptance of athletics as a legitimate educational activity. The entire financial support of the athletic program was the responsibility of the student athletic association. The college administrators and faculty were determined to eliminate the evils that had developed, but they had no intention of recognizing athletics as a function of higher education.

For a time this new arrangement seemed to solve the problems that had proved so objectionable to the faculties and administrations. Certainly, the graduate manager arrangement was an improvement over the student-directed program. The pressures on students were relieved, and the graduate manager brought efficiency and businesslike methods into operation. However, graduate managers were not educators. They were closer to the alumni and coaches than to the faculty. As intercollegiate athletics became a lucrative enterprise, managers became more concerned about financial rather than educational outcomes.

Inevitably a conflict arose between the faculty members on athletic committees and graduate managers on matters of policy. In many athletic committees the alumni, students, or both gained control over the faculty members, and, in effect, the institution no longer had any jurisdiction over the program. As evil practices mounted and problems multiplied a meeting of college presidents was held in 1905 which led to the formation of the Intercollegiate Athletic Association of the United States. This later became the National Collegiate Athletic Association, whose purpose was to eliminate the evils and raise the standards of intercollegiate athletic competition.

When it became clear that the leadership of graduate managers left much to be desired, college administrators came to the conclusion that the only way to conduct intercollegiate athletics along educational lines was to appoint a faculty member to administer them. The most logical person in the majority of institutions was the director of physical education or some member of his staff. These individuals were already concerned with the physical phase of the student's life. Many had participated in intercollegiate athletics and had coaching experience. When increasing numbers of these individuals received professional preparation in physical education, they were well qualified to direct the athletic program.

As time went on, more and more colleges and universities gradually eliminated the student athletic associations and delegated this responsibility to physical education departments. Along with this change in organizational setup colleges and universities accepted the financial responsibility of the program. The great majority of institutions provided and maintained the facilities and employed the personnel from the institutional budgets. Generally, the intercollegiate program was expected to be self-supporting insofar as the current operating expenses were concerned.

With these developments athletics, at long last, were accepted as an integral part of the educational programs. Even though they were partially self-supporting and still included some type of athletic committee setup, they were organizationally and philosophically a legitimate phase of the educational life of the institution. To be sure there were exceptions, primarily among the larger institutions, where the graduate-manager and student-athletic-association type of organization persisted. But in the smaller colleges and universities and some of the larger ones the athletic program had evolved through the stages of the impromptu intrainstitutional competition, the student-sponsored and conducted programs, and the graduate-manager and athletic-association setup to the place where it was regarded as within, rather than without, the institutional curriculum.

Interscholastic athletics

The development of interscholastic athletics followed and paralleled that of intercollegiate athletics in many respects. It is quite likely that many features of high school athletics were copied from the intercollegiate patterns. The interscholastic movement began ten or fifteen years after the Civil War, when athletics in institutions of higher learning were already well underway. Like intercollegiate athletics, high school athletics were initiated by students without the support and sympathy of school administrators and faculty members. The students received more encouragement and assistance from the community than from the school. The early physical educators were uncooperative and, in many cases, hostile to the program because it was contrary to their philosophy and practice. Just as in colleges and universities, many problems and uneducational practices developed under student sponsorship and leadership. When conditions became intolerable, school administrators were forced to assume control. This led eventually to the acceptance of interscholastic athletics as an essential part of the school curriculum.

The relationship of athletics to physical education

While athletics were springing up without the encouragement or guidance of school authorities, physical education classwork was being increasingly emphasized in the schools. The growing number of students with nervous breakdowns and otherwise impaired health finally forced school administrators to recognize that steps must be taken to safeguard the health of students. Confronted with this problem, educators turned to Europe again and borrowed the most popular systems of physical education then in vogue, which, together with hygiene, were added to the curriculum to assist in the digestion of the already heavy intellectual diet. In colleges, physicians, because of their medical background, were placed in charge of the hygiene and physical education classes. Physical education usually consisted of American modifications of German or Swedish formal gymnastics. This form of physical education was unpopular with both high school and college students, who endured it only because it was required. At the same time, the students in their leisure moments were vigorously and enthusiastically promoting various sports and contests among themselves and with students of other schools.

When school administrators decided to accept interschool athletics and introduce it into the school curriculum, they logically located it in the physical education department. It proved to be an unwelcome guest. Physical educators viewed this foundling with suspicion and reluctantly accepted it as a necessary evil. A bitter struggle was waged for the leadership of the combined department. Little harmony and cooperation existed between athletics and physical education, and considerable jealousy and antagonism developed. This was to be expected, because, at that time, the two areas were so far apart in philosophy, activities, and methodology that they could never be harmoniously reconciled.

A new philosophy of education, emerging about the beginning of the twentieth century, had profound implications for physical education. This new philosophy exploded the ancient theory of the dualism of the mind and the body and accepted the concept of the unity of the human organism. It also conceived of the function of the school as that of directing children and youth in learning the activities that constitute socially efficient conduct. No longer was the purpose of the school the development of the mental capacities only. No longer was the classroom the "brain factory" and the gymnasium the "muscle factory." The structural, analytical concept of education, which dismembered the child into his mental, physical, social, and moral attributes and then attempted to develop each independently, was rejected. The school existed for the purpose of preparing each child for the finest kind of living possible for him to achieve, given his capacities.

Out of this new philosophy of education a new philosophy of physical education evolved gradually. It conceived of physical education as education by means of the physical rather than education of the physical. In other words, fine living became the aim of physical education just as it became the aim of every phase of school life. The emphasis shifted from the purely physical to the mental and social as well. This new conception revolutionized traditional practices in physical education. In 1910, because of the influence of Wood and Hetherington, a new era of physical education began. They advocated the elimination of the formal systems of gymnastics and the substitution of natural play activities. This new movement gathered impetus, and today it is accepted as the American system of physical education. It has largely replaced the German and Swedish systems and their variations, which were not acceptable to American youth.

The broadened educational philosophy also gave athletics a new significance in the educational setup. Here were great potentialities for developing in youth desirable knowledge, skills, habits, and attitudes. It was found that athletics, under proper guidance and leadership, could become a powerful educational force, particularly in the development of social and moral, as well as physical, qualities. The dramatic nature of interschool athletics made them even more valuable in some respects than the physical education activities of the curriculum. But the regrettable fact remained that the administration of interinstitutional athletics left much to be desired. Although the conduct of athletics has been improved immeasurably since their inclusion within the school program, certain practices still exist which can hardly be called educational in nature.

This new conception of education and physical education, plus the changes that have occurred in interschool athletics, has profoundly altered relations between the two areas. Most of the causes of conflict have disappeared, so that, today, the athletic program is considered an essential phase of the total physical education program. With similar aims, objectives, activities, personnel, and facilities there is much more reason to combine the interschool, intramural, and service programs into one integrated unit, rather than separate departments. When these three programs are coordinated they aid and abet each other. In addition, a unified department is much less expensive than separate departments, which duplicate personnel, equipment, and facilities. For the great majority of colleges and universities and all secondary schools the most effective educational outcomes are obtained when all the big-muscle play activities—curricular as well as extracurricular—are coordinated in one department under the leadership of a well-qualified individual.

Objectives of athletics

The objectives of interschool athletics should be identical with those of physical education (see Chapter 2). The opinion is well established in educational circles that the only justification for interscholastic and intercollegiate athletics is their contribution to educational and physical educational objectives. The great majority of school administrators and faculty members still evaluate athletics upon this basis, although the programs in some schools are conducted for purposes that could never be construed as educational.

Coaches of interschool teams have the opportunity to achieve physical education objectives to a greater extent than the leaders of service and intramural activities. They have significant advantages in the greater time and better facilities that are available. In addition, they are concerned with a smaller number of students, all of whom are highly motivated. Under the circumstances, participants in interschool competition attain a greater measure of physical fitness and motor skills than is possible in the service and intramural programs. Insofar as the mental, emotional, and social objectives are concerned, the potentialities for developing them are greater in the interschool program, but the extent to which these opportunities are realized depends upon the leadership.

Standards in athletics for boys in secondary schools

Interscholastic athletics have been conducted in America for a period of approximately eighty-five years. In this long period of time many valuable lessons have been learned. Gradually, desirable standards for the conduct of athletics have evolved. Such standards have done much to improve interscholastic athletics. They represent ideal practices and policies, which, if extensively adhered to, would raise the quality of athletic programs. (See Appendix A for the "Standards and Athletics in Secondary Schools" which were developed by a joint committee of the Association of Secondary School Principals, the National Federation of State High School Athletic Associations, and the American Association for Health, Physical Education, and Recreation.)

CONTROL OF ATHLETICS

Control of intercollegiate athletics

Once school administrators arrived at the stage where they endeavored to control and supervise athletics, they soon found that however well one school might conduct its own program, other schools did not necessarily do likewise. The need of some organized body to direct and control intercollegiate athletic competition was soon felt, and this gave birth to our present athletic associations and conferences.

Another factor was also involved in the development of athletic conferences. In the early days of intercollegiate athletics, administrators who wanted to raise standards found it very difficult to do alone because of the pressures of alumni, students, supporters, and townspeople who did not always have the best interests of the institution and participants in mind. They found, however, that this objective was much easier to accomplish with a group of like-minded administrators. Pressure groups had difficulty in opposing the new standards because each institution in a league or conference had to comply or lose its natural rivals.

Control on a national level

The National Collegiate Athletic Association is a national organization, which has as its primary purpose "the regulation and supervision of college athletics throughout the United States in order that the athletic activities of the colleges and universities may be maintained on an ethical plane in keeping with the dignity and high purpose of education." Membership in the National Collegiate Athletic Association, originally organized in 1905 as the Inter-Collegiate Athletic Association, is open to all colleges and universities in the United States. It is divided into eight geographic districts, each under its own vice president, who acts upon charges involving eligibility and who advises upon the conduct of intercollegiate athletics in his own district. He reports to the annual convention of the association on the strictness with which the rules have been enforced during the year, changes in eligibility requirements by institutions, local conferences, leagues, district competitions, if any, and any other facts or recommendations that might be of interest to the association.

Membership in the National Collegiate Athletic Association is voluntary. In 1966 a total of 626 institutions were members. It has a College Division of smaller institutions. Dues are based upon the size of the institutions. Each member institution is entitled to one faculty representative. Thus, the association represents faculty control on a national level.

Until 1947, the National Collegiate Athletic Association had never attempted to force compliance to its regulations and standards. Prior to this time it had attempted to control intercollegiate athletics by persuasion and appeal to reason. In 1948 legislation was adopted to curb the rapidly developing abuses and evils. This legislation, which became known as the "Sanity Code," made the National Collegiate Athletic Association an accrediting association, which forced compliance to its regulations under pain of expulsion from the organization. The controversy over this new role was so great that the "Sanity Code" was rescinded in 1951. In 1952, however, enforcement machinery was established to implement the Association's regulations. Since that time the legislation of the Association, particularly in regard to illegal recruiting, has been enforced.

The National Collegiate Athletic Association [1] performs the following services:

1. Serves as an over-all national discussion, legislative, and administrative body for the universities and colleges of the United States on matters of intercollegiate athletics

2. Represents the colleges before the Congress of the United States in legislative matters pertaining to elimination of the federal admissions tax on college athletic events, antibribery and gambling laws, sports, television, and federal aid to education affecting sports and physical education

3. Maintains a 12-person national headquarters staff in Kansas City, Missouri, and a 10-person service bureau (National Collegiate Athletic Bureau) staff in Forest Hills, New York

4. Publishes annual "Official Guides" in nine sports through the National Collegiate Athletic Bureau. The NCAB also collects, compiles and distributes to the press and college officials the official statistics of college football, baseball, track and field, and basketball, and generally performs other functions commonly associated with a records-keeping agency.

5. Conducts 21 National Collegiate Championship events in 13 sports—baseball, basketball (college and university divisions), cross-country (college and university), fencing, golf (college and university), gymnastics, ice hockey, skiing, soccer, swimming (college and university), tennis (college and university), outdoor track and field (college and university), indoor track and field, and wrestling (college and university). This historic series dates back to 1883, when the first National Collegiate Tennis Championships were held. Over this 83-year span more than 53,000 student-athletes have competed in these events, with 3,372 earning the coveted title, "National Collegiate Champion."

6. Conducts studies as a means of developing solutions to athletic problems, such as surveys on television, postseason events, athletic and recreational facilities, sports injuries and safety, recruiting and financial aid, length and time of playing and practice seasons

7. Participates in the U.S. Olympic and Pan American movements as the administrative agency for the colleges in fund-raising, sports organization, and the providing of coaches and athletes for the United States teams. Three of the United States' most successful teams (basketball, swimming, track and field) were directed by coaches of NCAA member institutions in 1964 at Tokyo.

8. Enacts legislation to deal with athletic problems when they spread across regional lines and member institutions concur that national action is needed

9. Administers group travel and medical insurance programs whereby member institutions can provide catastrophe coverage for student-athletes when they are engaged in practice, play, or transport. More than 85,000 persons are enrolled annually in these two programs.

10. Maintains a central clearing and counseling agency in the field of college athletic administration

[1] The National Collegiate Athletic Association, *The Story of NCAA* (Kansas City, Mo., 1965), p. 3.

11. Provides financial and other assistance to various groups interested in the promotion and encouragement of intercollegiate and intramural activities; actively assists the various national coaching associations in projects which provide better teaching, better competition and sounder administration.

12. Provides a large film library, covering play in national meets and tournaments. This library of more than 300 titles includes films on baseball, basketball, boxing, football, gymnastics, ice hockey, swimming, track and field, and wrestling.

Regional control of intercollegiate athletics

Athletic conferences have assumed much responsibility for controlling the athletic programs of member institutions. Most colleges and universities belong to some type of conference. Institutions of similar types, curriculum, philosophy, entrance requirements, size, and financial resources tend to join together in athletic conferences. Sometimes these institutions are all within one state, but frequently they are located on a regional basis.

These conferences exist for the purpose of regulating athletic competition between like-minded institutions. The member institutions want to compete with schools that have similar standards. The National Collegiate Athletic Association necessarily must be general in its rules and regulations and allow the conferences to equalize competitive opportunities on a state or regional basis.

A conference facilitates scheduling, builds a more friendly spirit between schools, promotes proper publicity, stimulates more ethical practices, standardizes eligibility, and provides a convenient means of discussing and solving problems. Conferences definitely stimulate interest on the part of alumni, students, and supporters. The competition for the conference championship against traditional rivals is invariably conducive to good attendance.

The athletic conferences are controlled by faculty representatives of member institutions. The athletic directors, coaches of various sports, and publicity directors have separate organizations of their own which ordinarily meet at the same time as the faculty representatives. These different groups may make recommendations to the faculty representatives, but in the last analysis, the latter group establishes the policies, rules, and regulations of intercollegiate competition of member institutions.

A number of the larger athletic conferences employ a full-time commissioner who discharges stipulated duties. Usually, these duties involve the enforcement of the conference regulations, particularly those relating to eligibility, subsidization, and recruiting. Institutions that are found to violate conference regulations may be fined, obliged to forfeit contests, placed on probation, or expelled from the conference.

Local control of intercollegiate athletics

The third and final phase of controlling intercollegiate athletics resides within each institution itself. This form of control complements those of the National Collegiate Athletic Association and the athletic conferences. Although each level of control is important and has its unique functions, the most important form of control is undoubtedly that on the local level. No outside agency can adequately control an institution that endeavors to employ devious practices to win games. The ideal in intercollegiate athletics is to have each individual college and university conduct its athletic affairs on such a high level that no outside regulation becomes necessary. There are many institutions that have such intercollegiate athletic programs.

The history of intercollegiate athletics is a story of a long struggle for control between the faculty and students and alumni. Intercollegiate athletics were first organized and controlled by students and alumni, but both groups proved unequal to the task of conducting the program on a satisfactory basis. So many abuses and vicious practices developed that the faculty finally had no alternative but to take over control. Experience throughout the years has repeatedly shown that students and alumni are incapable of administering intercollegiate athletics toward educational goals. Institutional control has gradually developed and today is accepted as the desirable standard.

When institutions decided to take over the control of intercollegiate athletics, various types of committees were created to administer the program. In those early days when professional physical education was not well advanced and professionally trained administrators were not available, this appeared to be the only solution. Some committees were composed entirely of faculty. Many institutions continued to give students and alumni a part in the control of the athletic program by including them on the executive committees. In such committees the faculty members usually outnumbered the combined student and alumni members to assure faculty control. In other institutions the students and alumni were loath to surrender any of their power to the faculty. As a result, the faculty was in the minority on many of the regulatory committees that came into existence.

The faculty-dominated committees were largely responsible for the improved standards that gradually developed in intercollegiate athletics. The committees exercised complete administrative authority over the entire athletic program. The athletic director administered the decisions and policies of the committee. The faculty members usually were unacquainted with athletic problems, but they did recognize educational principles and ideals and they strove steadfastly to attain them.

Over the years, the methods of administering athletics have gradually changed. Today, two major issues are involved in the institutional control of intercollegiate athletics. The first of these is concerned with the matter of whether intercollegiate athletics will be administered as an integral part of the overall physical education program or as a separate athletic department. The second issue involves the question of whether or not an athletic committee should be employed and, if so, what its relationship to the athletic program should be.

Athletics as part of the physical education program. In many colleges and universities, particularly the smaller ones, the program of intercollegiate athletics is a part of the overall physical education program. The director of physical education has the ultimate responsibility for the entire athletic program. He may direct the athletic affairs himself, or this responsibility might be delegated to a staff member. The policies for the athletic program may be developed either by the general faculty or the physical education staff. The athletic director is responsible to the director of physical education, who, in turn, is responsible to the president. The cost of the athletic program is included in the physical education budget. Any income is purely incidental and goes into the institutional treasury. Coaching duties are carried on by various physical education staff members.

Scott[2] has indicated the advantages of this type of administrative setup:

With *one* program there is likely to be more consistent adherence to the educational objectives of the institution and of the department.

With *one* department, narrow departmentalization and specialization are discouraged, and the activities of all phases of the program may be correlated in the interests of harmony, economy, and effectiveness.

With *one* executive, a single staff may be more economically and effectively assembled and assigned to perform the multiple functions required for the conduct of the broad program of physical education for all students.

With *one* staff, responsible to one administrative officer, there may be a greater sharing in the formation of policies governing all aspects of the unified program of physical education. This, in turn, may lead to a greater sense of sharing the responsibility for the successful operation of the whole program.

With *one* executive, facilities may be more effectively designed and constructed in the interests of all students, and more economically and equitably assigned to serve the needs of class work, intramurals, and recreational programs for both sexes, and for the accommodation of the program of competitive athletics.

With *one* executive, the equipment for the program may be more economically purchased, centrally controlled, and effectively distributed to meet the physical education needs of all students.

[2] Harry A. Scott, *Competitive Sports in Schools and Colleges* (New York, Harper & Row, Publishers, 1951), p. 239.

With *one* executive, the indoor and outdoor facilities and equipment may be more efficiently maintained and prepared for the multiple uses of the entire program of physical education for all students.

With *one* executive in a *single* department, with *one* staff housed together and responsible for the conduct of a *unified* program, there can be developed the same kind of group effort, group loyalty, group responsibility, and group morale among staff members as each of the instructors requires of each student who participates in athletic sport for which he is responsible.

Athletics as a separate department. This type of administrative pattern is one in which a separate athletic department is headed by a director who is directly responsible to the president or athletic committee. This type of organization is found more frequently in larger institutions. Such a method of administering intercollegiate athletics was not possible in the early days because well-trained administrators were not available. However, over the years a vast body of material relating to the administration of athletics has been built up. Today, many directors are available who have acquired the techniques and understanding necessary to administer an athletic program.

The advantage of a separate department is more obvious in a large institution. The size of the operation and the amount of money involved are factors that favor separation from the physical education department. It is admittedly more expensive to operate, but big-time intercollegiate athletics usually have the funds for separate facilities and personnel. In many of the larger institutions arrangements are worked out where certain personnel and facilities are shared with the physical education department. When athletic personnel are used in the physical education department, they should be scheduled during the terms when they are not under heavy coaching pressures.

Athletic committees. The second issue referred to above in administering intercollegiate athletics relates to the use of athletic committees. Practices are so varied in colleges and universities that it is difficult to describe a trend. Some institutions make no use whatsoever of such committees. In other colleges and universities these committees have complete administrative authority over intercollegiate athletics. This latter method of controlling athletics predominated when institutions first took over the conduct of the athletic program. In recent years it has been largely discarded because of its inherent defects. A committee is a poor administrative unit because it is constantly changing. The alumni and student members cannot profit from the experience because their terms are usually only one year in length. Moreover, the committee may ignore all the experience and training of the director. It hardly seems logical for an able, well-trained director to be told what to do and how to do it by a group whose members rarely have an adequate background and understanding of the problems involved.

The advisory athletic committee is probably the most extensively employed and popular type of such plans in use today. This is used both for the separate athletic department and for the unified department, which includes athletics. The person responsible for athletics possesses complete authority, but the advisory athletic committee recommends policies to him. Students, alumni, and faculty are usually represented on such committees. The advantage of an advisory committee is that all interested groups have a channel through which they can express their convictions about the program to the director. The director possesses complete power, but it is helpful to him to know the reactions of undergraduates, alumni, and faculty to his conduct of the athletic program. Such an advisory committee is objected to on the basis that other departments in the institution do not have them. The justification for their existence, however, is that students and alumni are more interested in the athletic program than in the academic activities of the institution.

Control of interscholastic athletics

Interscholastic athletics, like intercollegiate athletics, are controlled on three different levels, namely, the national, state, and local levels. All of these different aspects of control are closely interrelated and complement each other. Each will be discussed in turn.

Control on the national level

Interscholastic athletics are administered nationally by the National Federation of State High School Athletic Associations. This national organization was developed out of the state athletic associations. The beginning was made in 1920, when representatives of five nearby state associations met in Chicago to discuss problems that had resulted from high school athletic contests that were organized by colleges and universities or other promoters. The need was evident for a national organization that could operate in areas beyond the scope of the state athletic associations. In 1921, four states—Illinois, Iowa, Michigan, and Wisconsin—formally started the national organization. They were charter members, and the future development of the organization was due in large part to their leadership.

In 1922 representatives of eleven states attended the Chicago meeting. Since that time the National Federation has grown rapidly and, today, only Texas is a nonmember. By 1940 a national office with a full-time executive staff became necessary and was established.

The purpose of the National Federation [3] is stated in its Constitution:

The object of this Federation shall be to protect and supervise the interstate athletic interests of the high schools belonging to the state associations, to assist in those activities of the state associations which can best be operated on a nation-wide scale, to sponsor meetings, publications, and activities which will permit each state association to profit by the experience of all other member associations, and to co-ordinate the work so that waste effort and unnecessary duplication will be avoided.

Achievements of the National Federation

The National Federation has accomplished many notable achievements since it was originated. An understanding of these is basic to any discussion of interscholastic athletics.

Abolishment of national championships. In 1934 the National Federation took action to refuse to sanction any meet or tournament that is in the nature of a contest to determine a national high school championship. No such contest has been held since that time, although there have been many attempts to do so. The reasons for the stand of the National Federation were excessive travel and expense for the teams involved, too much interference with school work, and increased pressure upon players, the coach, the school, and community. Consequently, schools that were members of state high school athletic associations affiliated with the National Federation were prohibited from taking part in such competition. The National Federation took the position that there were no advantages to be gained in competition for a national championship but that there were many disadvantages. If any high school desired more competition, it would be a simple matter to schedule additional games locally.

Regulating interstate contests. The National Federation stipulates that in all interstate competition each school shall employ the rules of its own state athletic association. An interstate contest that involves a round trip exceeding 600 miles for one of the teams is prohibited unless both state athletic associations, through the National Federation, sanction it. Basketball tournaments that involve schools from more than one state are not sanctioned unless the tournament is for an area that is a natural community or when, because of mountain barriers, a small section of the state is isolated in such a way that competition across state lines is essential to the filling of a suitable schedule.

Recommendation of minimum eligibility requirements. After a

[3] National Federation of State High School Athletic Associations, *Handbook: 1964-65* (Chicago, 1965), p. 11.

careful review of all the eligibility requirements of the various state associations the National Federation has recommended what it considers the basic minimum requirements that should prevail. Because of the prestige of the National Federation and its relationship to the state associations, many of the latter groups have voluntarily adopted these minimum standards. This has done much to unify eligibility requirements in the various state athletic associations in the United States.

Opposition to all-star and postseason contests. The National Federation has been cognizant of the abuses that would develop if bowl, all-star, or charity games were to be permitted without limitation. In 1947 the following resolution was unanimously adopted: [4]

1. This group is unalterably opposed to the principle of all-star and out-of-season athletic contests in which high school students or high school graduates of the previous year are participants, because:

(a) Such contests do not harmonize with the generally accepted educational philosophy of high school athletics which emphasizes varied seasonal activities, broad participation, and school direction and supervision.

(b) There are few tangible values, apparent either to the individual or to the selected team as a whole, resulting from such contests.

(c) No practical or satisfactory method has been devised to date for the selection of members of all-star teams to insure that injustices are not perpetrated.

(d) There has been growing evidence of commercialism and exploitation of high school athletes through their participation in such contests. In too many instances such games have been the "market place" in which their "wares" have been displayed before the highest bidder.

(e) Further, it is the opinion of this group that the clothing of all-star and out-of-season contests in the garment of "sweet charity" is insufficient justification for their existence. Experience has revealed that often pitifully small proportions of receipts from such games have been realized for their avowed purposes.

(f) Such contests are likely to imbue immature and inexperienced high school students selected for them with the false idea that their athletic prowess is something upon which they should capitalize commercially, rather than its being an endowed talent that is theirs to use for the pleasure and satisfaction they may receive from athletic competition.

(g) In practically all all-star contests with which this group has been apprised, there have been insufficient and inadequate practice periods provided prior to the playing of the games. In football, particularly, it is impossible to condone a practice period of five or six days for a group of boys who, previously, have never played together, especially after a lapse of an eight or nine months' period since previous football competition. Most high school, college, and professional teams require a minimum pre-game practice period of fifteen days or more.

2. Further, it is recommended that states subscribing to the attitude of this group as indicated in (1) give consideration to the adoption of regulatory measures which will prohibit or discourage their member schools, administrative, coaching, or instructor personnel, and registered athletic officials from participation, management, supervision, player selection, coaching, or officiating in

[4] *Ibid.,* p. 23.

any all-star or out-of-season athletic contests in which high school students or graduates of the previous year are participants.

Formulating and publishing playing rules for interscholastic sports. Dissatisfaction with the football rules that were devised for college and university football led, in 1931, to the appointment of a National Federation Committee to draw up rules for interscholastic football. These were published in 1931 and used experimentally in Illinois, Iowa, and Wisconsin. The new regulations proved popular immediately, and more and more state associations adopted them. At the present time forty-three states are playing under the National Federation rules.

The National Federation publishes an edition of the Official Basketball Rules. These rules are made jointly by a committee that is composed of representatives of the National Collegiate Athletic Association, the Y.M.C.A., the A.A.U., Canada, and the National Federation. This edition contains much supplementary material that aids in the high school program.

The National Federation also maintains Six-Man Football and Soccer rules committees and publishes rule books for these sports. Track and Field and Baseball rule books (Federation edition) are also published. The various Federation publications now exceed 850,000 copies annually.

Adapting playing equipment and regulations to high school boys. Originally, high school athletic competition was patterned after intercollegiate athletics. The same type of equipment was used; the length of the playing periods and the dimensions of the playing areas were similar. It became evident with time that adaptations to younger, smaller participants were necessary. The National Federation took the lead in studying and experimenting with equipment, with the result that the size of footballs and basketballs was reduced, the high hurdle was lowered, the discus was made smaller and lighter, the low hurdle race was shortened, and a more satisfactory and less expensive basketball backboard was developed. Safety features were incorporated into football headgear, face, mouth, and tooth protectors, clothing, and shoes. Not only was the equipment better suited to the capabilities of high school boys and made safer but a considerable reduction in cost was effected.

Condemning solicitation of high school athletes. The National Federation [5] adopted the following resolution on solicitation in 1937:

The National Federation of State High School Athletic Associations assembled at New Orleans February 20, 1937: ⌣

Believes that solicitation of high school athletes by individuals and organizations representing institutions of higher learning is having a definitely detri-

[5] National Federation of State High School Athletic Associations, *Handbook: 1954-55* (Chicago, 1954), p. 16.

mental effect: (1) upon the boys so solicited; (2) upon the general high school student body; (3) upon the general public interest in the welfare of education.

Further, that this solicitation of athletes is seldom directed, stimulated, or fostered by those responsible for the management of the academic offerings of the institution of higher learning.

Further, that certain institutions of learning, both secondary and higher, have discriminated against the accepted standards of academic accomplishment in favor of the athletically inclined student, especially in regard to enforcement of entrance requirements by some of the institutions of higher learning.

Further, that this solicitation of athletes is different in nature and effect from that used to attract students interesed primarily in academic education.

It is resolved, that the National Federation hereby earnestly requests the co-operation of all representatives of institutions of higher learning in the elimination of all forms of solicitation of boys of athletic ability which differ in manner or form from the ethical practices used by said institutions in attracting all students.

It is further resolved, that the faculties of all such institutions are earnestly requested to hold the athletically inclined students to the same academic requirements imposed upon all other students of the institution, either at entrance or during residence.

It is further resolved, that each member state is requested to pass similar resolutions.

To assist in remedying the problem of college solicitation of high school athletes the National Federation, at the 1950 and 1951 annual conventions, approved Standard #10, which reads as follows: "The solicitation of athletes through tryouts and competitive bidding by higher institutions is unethical, unprofessional, and psychologically harmful to the boy. It destroys the amateur nature of athletics, tends to commercialize the individual and the program, the use of athletic skill for gain, and takes an unfair and unjust advantage of competitors."

The items below are suggested interpretations of Standard #10: [6]

1. The functions of guidance and advisement to assist a student in the selection of a higher institution should be performed by the principal, director or guidance, of designated advisers.

2. Interviews between accredited representatives of higher institutions and prospective applicants for admission should be arranged only through the school guidance department.

3. Tryouts of high school athletes should not be permitted, and the entertainment and transportation of boys to college campuses to display athletic prowess should be prohibited.

4. Transcripts of high school records should be sent only to the admissions office.

[6] National Federation of State High School Athletic Associations, *Handbook: 1964-65,* p. 34.

5. Standards for admission to higher institutions should apply to the athlete and nonathlete alike.

6. Only bona fide students who are satisfying recognized educational standards in high school or in college should be permitted to compete in athletics.

7. All financial aid to students should be based on demonstrated ability in high school subjects and activities.

(a) No athletic "scholarships" as such should be awarded.

(b) All scholarship aid must be administered by the institution itself and not by alumni, civic groups, or other individuals.

(c) Each institution should publish qualifications for all scholarships offered.

(d) Scholarships should be limited to actual expenses for tuition, fees, room, board.

(e) Payment for employment should be made only when services are rendered.

(f) No grant should be withdrawn because of failure to participate in athletics.

Effecting an agreement with organized baseball on the signing of high school players to professional contracts. The National Federation, since 1944, has negotiated with organized baseball to prevent high school players from signing contracts to play professional baseball before their eligibility for participation in high school athletics has terminated. The current agreement is as follows: [7]

1. No student of a high school shall be signed to a contract by a major or minor league club during the period the student is eligible for participation in high school athletics. In any instance where such eligibility has expired prior to the student's graduation from high school (a) because of the student's age; or (b) because he has completed the maximum number of semesters of attendance, he may thereafter be signed to a contract which does not obligate him to report for service prior to graduation of the class with which he originally entered high school, i.e., until eight semesters after his original entry into the ninth grade.

2. A student who drops out of high school prior to expiration of his athletic eligibility and continues to remain out for at least one year may thereafter be signed to a contract for immediate service provided his withdrawal from high school was not suggested, procured, or otherwise influenced by the club contracting with him, or by any official or employee of such club or of any of its affiliates.

3. Nothing herein shall be construed as prohibiting any major or minor league club, its officers, agents, or employees from talking to any high school student at any time concerning a career in professional baseball and discussing the merits of his contracting, when eligible therefor, with any particular club.

4. "Tryouts" to which students may be invited may be conducted during the school year, provided that (1) no student shall be permitted to participate in any such tryout unless the principal of his high school, if not employed by a major or minor league club, shall have approved such participation in writing, and (2) provided further that any such tryout must be limited to not more than five high school students.

[7] *Ibid.*, p. 35.

5. Any contract made in violation of this rule shall be declared null and void, and the offending club (and any club owned by or affiliated with such club) shall be prohibited from signing such player for a period of three years from date of declaration of voidance of such contract. In addition, such club shall be fined $500, by the commissioner in the case of a major league club, or by the president of the National Association in the case of a minor league club, and the official, scout or employee of the offending club who participated in the violation shall be subject to such penalty as the commissioner or the president of the National Association, as the case may be, shall impose.

Sanctioning procedures for international contests. Because of the increasing opportunities for international competition of high school athletes the National Federation [8] took the lead in establishing procedures and policies governing such competition. The following recommendations were approved:

1. The original contact in the United States be made with the state high school association of the state in which the competition is to be held.
2. Specific schools should be contacted only after high school association agreement and cooperation.
3. The state high school association will, if it approves of the plan and can arrange for the competition, apply to the National Federation for sanction.
4. The National Federation, upon receipt of the request from the concerned state association, will make application for approval with a United States member of the appropriate international body for the necessary action.

Wrestling weight control standards. Excessive weight loss resulting from "crash dieting" or "drying-out" has become a matter of serious concern in interscholastic wrestling. This practice represents a serious threat to the health of many of those who participate in it and it should be condemned. The National Federation [9] in 1963 adopted the following policies to control this problem:

Introduction:
Each school administrator shall certify the minimum weight class of all wrestling participants. It is recommended that each boy have certified a minimum weight based upon his body type and musculature. This minimum weight should be established in cooperation with the coach, parent and physician. It is further recommended that there be no weight reduction in excess of the normal off-season weight.

Minimum criteria:
1. Each participant shall have established his certified minimum weight on a date, at the beginning of the season as designated by the state association.
2. Each participant shall make his certified minimum weight at each weigh-in. Failure to do so will cause him to have established a higher minimum weight class. (Weight classes increase two pounds in January and one in February.)
3. Each state association shall set forth the procedure for supervising the weigh-in at which the minimum weights are established and for the recording of participant's certified minimum weights.

8 *Ibid.,* p. 19.
9 *Ibid.,* p. 30.

4. Weigh-ins must be conducted in accordance with the provisions of the National Wrestling Rules Publication.

5. The State Association shall formulate an enforcement policy that will minimize undesirable weight caused by crash-dieting (dehydration, use of laxatives and others).

6. Each state association shall have a regulation prohibiting use of any heat device used for dehydration purposes.

In addition to the above accomplishments, the National Federation has urged the development of athletic accident benefit plans by the state athletic associations. It has assisted in the development of a program of motion pictures for use in football, baseball, and basketball meetings and for use in school assemblies or service club programs. A national press service was inaugurated to aid editors of state association monthly bulletins. It has also recommended plans for the training, classification, and registration of high school officials.

Control of interscholastic athletics by state high school athletic associations

The history of interscholastic athletics is a story of a long, difficult struggle to place these activities on a sound educational basis. So many vicious, undesirable practices developed around the high school athletic competition that school administrators were forced to take steps to control them in order to preserve their educational values. School superintendents and principals organized state high school athletic associations to control interscholastic athletics because they were unable to solve the problems individually. These organizations deserve most of the credit for the present high plane on which interscholastic athletics are conducted.

The first state high school athletic association was formed in Wisconsin in 1896. Indiana followed in 1903, and Ohio in 1904. Today, every state has an organization to administer interscholastic athletics. Membership in these associations is usually permitted to any accredited public high school, although in some states any high school that meets the standards for memberhip is permitted to belong. For each member school the principal must be the responsible spokesman.

It should be noted that some of these state organizations are known as "school activities associations" rather than "athletic associations." This designation is used because in some of these state organizations responsibility for nonathletic activities comes under their jurisdiction. Supervision of contests in musical, dramatic, speech and other nonathletic activities is provided.

These associations are conducted by boards of control which range in size from three to sixteen members. Membership on the board of control is confined in most states to school administrators, but in some states teachers, coaches, school board members, and university professors are eligible for membership. The duties of the boards of control are usually to determine the general policies of the association, to decide the rules of eligibility, and to settle disputes referred to them by various districts or sections of the state into which the association is divided. Every state has an athletic commissioner or executive secretary who has full charge of the clerical, financial, and executive work of the association. Thirty-nine states have full-time executive secretaries; the remainder have part-time executive secretaries. The executive secretary conducts tournaments and meets, keeps detailed accounts of the competition, handles the finances, receives the scholastic records of the competing students, disseminates publicity, and performs other duties. The administrative authority, however, is usually vested in the board of control.

State athletic associations are classified into three types: (1) the voluntary, independent associations, (2) the associations affiliated with state departments of education, and (3) those affiliated with state universities. Approximately two-thirds of the associations are of the voluntary type. In the associations affiliated with state departments of education, the control resides with the department of education. In the voluntary associations, school administrators control the program. It is a common practice in these associations for the state director of physical education to be represented on the executive committee.

Functions of state athletic associations. State high school athletic associations vary in the functions they perform. The following functions are carried on by most state associations:

1. Sponsoring athletic-injury benefit programs
2. Conducting tournaments and meets
3. Establishing standards for interscholastic athletics
4. Registering and classifying officials
5. Sponsoring coaching clinics
6. Publishing bulletins and newsletters
7. Interpreting playing rules
8. Promoting summer athletic programs
9. Establishing contest regulations
10. Adjudicating disputes
11. Arranging and supervising competition in various nonathletic activities

Financing state athletic associations. A variety of sources of income is available to support state athletic associations. Most states have annual membership fees, with the majority assessing the fee on the basis of school size. Receipts from state tournaments and meets are the largest source of revenue in the great majority of states. Entry fees and fees for registration of officials are negligible from the standpoint of income production.

Local administration of interscholastic athletics

In the final analysis the activities of the National Federation and the state athletic associations are translated to local high schools. The efforts of the state and national organizations are designed to come to fruition in each individual school. However, what happens in the local schools depends to a large extent upon how the program is conducted. The standards which the state and national associations endorse can be defeated by poor local administration.

The superintendent of schools. The superintendent of schools is the individual ultimately responsible for the type of athletic program which is in operation in the schools under his jurisdiction. Although the school board has the final responsibility for all that happens in the schools, it is the superintendent who recommends policies to them. He is also the board's executive officer, and he is held responsible for the implementation of its policies. In his recommendations to the school board concerning personnel, facilities, and budget, he is instrumental in determining the type of program which will be in operation.

The superintendent should take the initiative in establishing a desirable athletic policy for the local schools. Unless he does so, undesirable elements in the community may develop an emphasis that would be educationally untenable. In every community there are individuals and groups who are more interested in victories and championships than in what happens to the participants. Constant vigilance and determination are necessary to keep the athletic program on a sound educational basis.

The principal. The principal is more directly concerned with the actual operation of the program. He is held accountable by the superintendent for the conduct of interscholastic athletics in accord with the stipulated policies. The conduct of the students at athletic contests is his responsibility. In schools that have athletic committees the principal is invariably a member, frequently the chairman. He possesses veto power over the actions of the committee. The principal should give evidence of his interest in the athletic program by attending various contests. The enforcement of the regulations and policies of the state athletic association is his duty.

The relationship of school administrators to the interscholastic athletic program requires that they be prepared to cope with the problems that develop. The principal and superintendent will make many costly mistakes in their relationships to the athletic programs unless they are familiar with the philosophy, principles, policies, and standards that should prevail. It is an unfortunate fact that few school administrators ever receive proper professional preparation in this important area.

The director of athletics. The director of athletics administers the details of the athletic program. He is responsible to the principal for the conduct of the athletic program in accord with the policies of the school and the state athletic association. He must discharge his responsibilities conscientiously and faithfully, regardless of his own reactions to the policies. (For duties of the athletic director, see p. 294.)

The athletic committee. Athletic committees constitute an important factor in the administration of athletics in many high schools. A study by Adams shows that the larger schools tend to make greater use of athletic committees than smaller schools. His findings are shown in Table 8-1.

Table 8-1. High schools with athletic committees.

	Large Schools	Medium Schools	Small Schools
Athletic Committee in Operation	132	84	54
Schools Without Committees	85	110	120

Source: Harry Bennett Adams, A Report on Current Practices in the Administration of Interscholastic Athletics in 591 Selected Secondary Schools of the United States. Unpublished master's thesis, University of North Carolina, 1950, p. 77.

The individuals generally serving on such committees are the principal, athletic director, coaches, faculty members, and students. In some schools the dean of boys, superintendent, and a member of the school board may serve. The faculty members, in most cases, are appointed by the principal. The student members are elected by the general student body of each class or appointed by the student council. The duties of athletic committees have been surveyed by Adams and are listed in Table 8-2.

MEDICAL SUPERVISION OF ATHLETICS

Protecting the health of athletes

In citing the values of athletics, coaches invariably mention the contribution that is made to health. There can be no doubt that ath-

Table 8-2. Duties of the athletic committee.

	SIZE OF SCHOOL		
	Large N-217	Medium N-195	Small N-179
The Duties of the Committee Are:			
Policy Making	93	57	24
Advisory Only	46	40	33
Veto Power over Actions of the Committee Exercised by:			
Principal	57	29	26
Board of Education	41	23	7
Superintendent	24	15	15
Athletic Director	1	2	3
The More Common Duties of the Committee Are:			
General Policies	32	22	10
Approve Budget and Finances	36	13	8
Approve Schedules	24	14	11
Approve Awards	26	12	10
Approve Purchase of Equipment	9	7	5
Approve Admission Prices	8	3	5
Determine Eligibility	4	4	2
Publicity	2	3	2
Advise and Help Raise Funds	1	2	4
Plan Rallies	2	3	1
Ticket Sales	0	4	1

Source: Harry Bennett Adams, A Report on Current Practices in the Administration of Interscholastic Athletics in 591 Selected Secondary Schools of the United States. Unpublished master's thesis, University of North Carolina, p. 80.

letics, if well conducted, will make a significant contribution to the health of the players. Unfortunately, however, in many schools, the health of the athlete is not given the consideration it merits. Outside of a few universities, colleges, and high schools, the method of conducting athletics from the health standpoint leaves much to be desired.

The medical examination. The medical examination is the first and most important measure to be considered in the proper health supervision of athletics. All athletic aspirants should be examined to determine their physical fitness for participation in athletics in general and also in any one sport in particular. The examination should be made by a physician who has the time and facilities to do his task properly.

The standard of a medical examination for participants in interschool athletics is generally accepted. Some small schools still do not require such an examination, but these represent a very small minority. Most of the state high school athletic associations require a medical examination prior to participation in interscholastic athletics. A similar practice is standard procedure in practically all colleges and universities.

The real problem with respect to the medical examination is to get an adequate one. A great many are merely cursory inspections of the heart. A five-minute examination in which the pupil does not even strip cannot be considered satisfactory. If the examination is to be thorough enough to significantly reduce possibility of injury, special attention should be devoted to the age, weight, nutrition, bones, feet, eyes, nose, throat, abdomen, glands, heart, lungs, and general health of every individual. This should include urinalysis and blood-pressure tests.

In colleges and universities the medical examination is usually given by the physician or physicians in the health service or by physicians engaged by the athletic department. Almost invariably, these examinations are provided without charge to the participants. The customary practice in secondary schools is to have either the school physician or a private physician employed by the school give the medical examinations. However, in many secondary schools the candidates are expected to obtain the examination from their family physician on special forms supplied by the school or the state athletic association. In this latter case, the cost of this service is borne by each student. Not infrequently, local physicians volunteer their services for the medical examination.

Treatment of athletic injuries. The team physician is the key man in the treatment and care of the injured athletes. It is preferable to have as team physician an individual who has had specialized training in orthopedics. Knowledge of athletic contests and their demands is also an important prerequisite. However, smaller institutions with limited funds are often forced to use the doctor they can afford. Many doctors volunteer or accept very small token payments for treating injured athletes because of their interest in the program.

Many schools have a trainer who serves as an adjunct to the team physician. He performs many valuable services, such as taping, bandaging, massaging, supervising the use of various therapeutic equipment, like the whirlpool bath and infrared lamp, administering first aid, and supervising special exercises which have been prescribed by the physician. The trainer in large colleges and universities is a full-time employee. In smaller colleges and in most high schools he is probably the coach or some other faculty member who has had special training for these duties.

The trainer is not a substitute for the physician. The physician should be the one to go upon the field to examine an injury and determine the advisability of continuing play. It is also the physicians' responsibility to decide when an injured student has recovered sufficiently to return to practice. It is essential that the trainer never invade the doctor's area of responsibility. He must studiously refrain from diagnosing injuries and prescribing treatment.

Larger and wealthier institutions can afford to have a physician attend all practice sessions as well as regularly scheduled games. Most schools cannot meet this standard, but they should at least have one in attendance at home games, particularly in football, basketball, wrestling, and other vigorous sports where there is a likelihood of injury. Adams [10] points out that 92 percent of the large high schools, 70 percent of the medium high schools, and 49 percent of the small high schools require the attendance of a physician at home contests.

The coach's contribution to health. Since the coach has so frequently proclaimed the health values of athletics, he should, to be consistent, conduct athletics with the health of the players constantly in mind. As health is an important objective of athletics, it is difficult to justify various unsanitary practices commonly associated with athletics, such as the practice of sliding a dirty towel across the floor for the use of an entire team or providing a common water bottle for a team. The continued use of filthy equipment merely for the sake of superstition is equally reprehensible. Neither are dirty floors, locker rooms, shower rooms, and wrestling mats in harmony with good health.

The coach can play an important role in the reduction of injuries by his emphasis upon physical conditioning. Although three weeks of practice before the first football or basketball game has become an accepted practice players should be well-conditioned when they report for practice. More and more football coaches are prescribing a conditioning program for all squad members during the month preceding the opening practice. To insure the accomplishment of this objective many coaches hold a mile run on the first day of practice.

The use of weight training has grown rapidly not only from the standpoint of strength development but also to prevent injuries. Research has revealed that a properly designed and conducted weight-training program is capable of reducing the incidence of injuries.

The football coach must exercise appropriate precautions to prevent heat cramps, heat exhaustion, and heat stroke. These conditions must be anticipated during the early weeks of the football season when

---

[10] Harry Bennett Adams, *A Report of Current Practices in the Administration of Interscholastic Athletics in 591 Selected Secondary Schools of the United States.* Unpublished master's thesis, University of North Carolina, 1950, p. 54.

high temperatures and high humidity are frequently encountered. Prevention of heat problems involves:

1. Conditioning. Players who are in excellent physical condition can adjust to excessive heat and humidity better than those who are not. This fact emphasizes the importance of all players reporting for the first practice in top condition.

2. Proper clothing. Short-sleeved, lightweight, loose-fitting jerseys are indicated when practices and games are conducted in hot weather (above 80° F.). Stockings should not be worn. Perspiration-soaked T-shirts should be exchanged during the half-time period of a game or midway in the practice period. These precautions will facilitate the loss of body heat by evaporation.

3. Water and salt intake. Players should be permitted to take sips of water at intervals during practice periods or games in excessively hot, humid weather. Salt tablets are also recommended during the first 2 or 3 weeks of practice. Players who lose considerable weight during a practice period especially need supplementary salt.

4. Practice schedules. Periodic rest periods are recommended when very great heat is accompanied by high humidity. When the temperature is above 80° F. and humidity is in excess of 70 percent the practice period should be rescheduled during a cooler period of the day.

Another cause of injuries is overmatching. A small institution with a limited squad should never schedule a football game with an institution that has a squad of such size that adequate substitutes are available. Likewise, individuals should not be matched against each other in contact sports if they vary appreciably in size, strength, ability, and experience. Courts have found coaches liable for negligence when injuries have occurred because of extreme mismatching.

The coach should insist upon equipment that provides a high degree of protection for the participants in body-contact sports. Much research has been done in order to develop equipment that will reduce the incidence of injuries. As a result of this research significant improvements have been made. The protection of the player should be the paramount concern as the purchase of equipment, particularly football equipment, is contemplated. Proper fitting of equipment is also an important consideration.

The many health implications of interschool athletics emphasize the importance of the professional preparation of the coach. The best preparation for coaching is found in physical education. The professional preparation of the physical education major is designed to prepare the individual to safeguard the health of the students in the many ramifications that occur in physical education and interschool athletics. The coach whose preparation has been as an academic teacher is not qualified for his many responsibilities in safeguarding and promoting the health of his team members.

Athletic accident benefit plans

Colleges and universities assume the cost of most of the athletic injuries that members of intercollegiate squads sustain.[11] A few of the larger high schools do likewise, but most schools assume no responsibility for the injuries incurred in interscholastic athletics. Within recent years state high school athletic associations have developed athletic accident benefit plans to reduce the financial burden upon the parents of the injured participant that the treatment of athletic injuries may impose. These athletic benefit plans have proven so successful that the efforts of the state associations in this regard are generally considered among their most significant undertakings.

The athletic accident benefit plans have produced the following beneficial results:

1. The cost of the medical and dental care of injured athletes to their parents has been greatly reduced. This has been accomplished by spreading the cost over all the participants. In addition, in some states earnings from other sources have been applied toward the reduction of this expense.

2. The athletic benefit plans have brought about a great increase in the number of schools that required a medical examination of all participants in interscholastic athletics.

3. Where necessary, immediate diagnostic and medical attention has been available. When the cost of medical care had to be borne entirely by parents, some with limited means were loath to incur medical expense.

4. The reporting of all injuries was required in the various accident benefit plans. Among the data requested was the cause of the injury. With these facts school men were able to eliminate some of the most hazardous features of the various sports by changing the rules. This has been particularly true of football.

Forty-five states operate some sort of athletic accident benefit plan. Three ways of administering these plans predominate. (1) The athletic accident benefit plan is administered as a function of the state high school athletic association. (2) Arrangements are made with a life insurance company to administer the plan. (3) Some state high school ath-

[11] The National Collegiate Athletic Association administers a group insurance program whereby member colleges can provide catastrophe medical coverage for athletes injured in practice, play, or transport. This plan provides coverage only for very serious injuries which require unusually heavy medical expense.

letic associations discovered that they were unable to operate a mutual benefit plan without incorporating as a benefit company. This was done by vote of the membership of the state associations. Officers were elected, and the companies are operated on a nonprofit basis.

In each athletic accident benefit plan coverage is provided for supervised practices and regularly scheduled interscholastic contests. Thirty-eight plans provide coverage for injuries sustained in intramural competition. Compulsory physical education classes are or can be covered in thirty-seven plans. Injuries received during transportation to and from contests and practices are covered by twenty-six plans, if the transportation is school provided or school approved and under the supervision of qualified school personnel. Thirty-two plans pay benefits for locker and shower room accidents. Fourteen of the plans provide for the inclusion of coaches in the coverage offered. In Wisconsin the coverage includes elementary school students and students in supervised athletic programs conducted during the summer months.

All of the plans pay medical, dental, and X-ray benefits for injuries suffered under conditions outlined by the terms of the plans. Almost all of the plans provide hospitalization benefits.

In Nevada an appropriation from the state legislature defrays the entire cost of the accident benefit plan, which is administered by a commercial company. In all other plans students are required to pay a premium. The cost of the premiums varies with the different plans. For example, in one state the student fee is $5 for football and all other approved sports, including physical education and intramurals. Excluding football, the fee is $2. Football requires a higher premium than any other sport. However, even for football the premium varies from $5 to $10.

In general, the private insurance companies charge a higher fee. Part of the fee, however, is absorbed by the schools in some states but not in others. In most of the state association benefit plans the member schools are charged a fee. In some states funds from state tournaments are used to help defray the expense of the accident benefit plan. These additional sources of revenue contribute to the lowered premiums of the state association plans. Because of the higher premiums the private insurance plans usually pay higher benefits and provide greater coverage for injuries.

Wisconsin Interscholastic Athletic Association Athletic Accident Benefit Plan. The Wisconsin Interscholastic Athletic Association has been the pioneer in the development of athletic accident benefit plans. Under the leadership of P. F. Neverman, executive secretary of the association, the first plan was initiated in 1930. Since that time the program has grown steadily, with a variety of new features being introduced from time to time. The benefit plans in many other states have been patterned after that in Wisconsin.

The Wisconsin Interscholastic Athletic Association Accident Benefit Plan includes a *Special Program* and a *Scheduled Program.* The major difference between these two programs is that the Special Program pays all medical, dental, and hospital bills up to a maximum of $2,000 while the Scheduled Program pays according to a Schedule of Allowances up to a maximum of $500. The rates for the various aspects of the two programs are given in Table 8-3.

Table 8-3.

	RATES PER PUPIL	
	Special Program	Scheduled Program
Part I. Pupil Coverage (No Interscholastic Athletics)		
Kindergarten-Grade 8	$ 1.45	$ .90
Grades 9-12	2.20	1.35
Part II. All Sports Coverage (Including Football)		
Individual—Grades 9-12	13.00	8.00
Grades 7-8	7.50	5.00
Group Rates (Based on Enrollment) also Available		
Part III. Limited Sports Coverage (Excluding Football)		
Individual—Grades 9-12	4.00	3.00
Grades 7-8	2.50	2.00
Group Rates (Based on Enrollment) also Available		
Part IV. Summer Activity Coverage		
Individual Enrollment	1.00	.50

Source: *1964-65 WIAA Accident Benefit Plan* (Steven Points, Wisconsin, Wisconsin Interscholastic Athletic Association).

The group rates are considerably less in cost per pupil than the individual rates. From 25 to 30 percent of the school districts pay the entire cost of the pupil coverage program. In the remaining school districts 50 percent of the premium is paid by the school district and 50 percent by the pupils. Twenty percent of the premiums of the summer activity coverage is paid by school districts and 80 percent by students. Approximately 50 percent of the school districts pay the entire premiums for the all sports coverage and limited sports coverage. In the remaining districts 75 percent of the premium is paid by the districts and the remainder by the students. These data make it evident that a great amount of accident protection is provided in Wisconsin at an exceptionally reasonable cost.

The 1964-1965 schedule of benefits for the Scheduled Program is indicated in Appendix B.

ELIGIBILITY REQUIREMENTS

Importance of eligibility requirements

Athletic associations and conferences have always been concerned with the eligibility requirements of those who take part in interschool competition. This problem was instrumental in the formation of these groups and is today one of their chief concerns. Standardization of eligibility requirements was necessary to equalize athletic competition. Our entire structure of interschool athletics is based upon uniform eligibility requirements. Equitable competition and educational outcomes would be impossible without common standards.

The amateur rule

The most frequently stipulated eligibility requirement is that each individual must be an amateur in order to compete against other schools. An amateur is defined by the National Collegiate Athletic Association as one who engages in sports solely for the physical, mental, or social benefits he derives therefrom and to whom the sport is nothing more than an avocation.

Amateur standing may be lost by:

1. Playing under an assumed name
2. Using knowledge for gain (officiating, coaching, tutoring)
3. Receiving money or board for playing
4. Competing with professionals
5. Competing for prizes
6. Selling prizes
7. Betting on competition
8. Issuing a challenge to compete for money
9. Playing on an outside team where admission is charged
10. Receiving money in excess of actual expenses
11. Signing a contract to play with a professional team
12. Receiving consideration for connecting oneself with any athletic organization

Many heated debates have been precipitated on the subject of amateurism in school athletics. There are those who protest bitterly against barring from school competition a boy who has been paid at some time for his athletic ability. They claim that the amateur code came to us from England, where it originated to preserve sports for the aristocracy by keeping out of competition those who had to work for a living. Such a code is out of place in a democracy, they aver. These opponents also point out that the amateur rule does not operate for the other school subjects, such as music, art, speech, or literature.

As a result of the amateur rule, much subterfuge has been resorted to for the purpose of evading it, in spirit if not in letter. The purpose of the rule, ostensibly, is to prevent the individual who has sufficient skill to command a price for his services from competing against others who do not have this degree of skill. The opponents of the rule advocate more modern and educationally sound means of classifying players and equalizing competition. There are some who protest against declaring an individual a professional in all sports if he is professional in one sport. If a boy should be paid for summer baseball or professional football, why should he be barred from basketball and track if he is eligible according to all other standards?

Colleges and universities have gradually been moving away from the strict interpretation of the amateur rule. In several conferences it is legitimate to provide tuition, board, room, and limited expense money for athletes. A certain amount of work is required for this financial assistance, although such work is not usually done during the competitive season.

High school eligibility regulations

In addition to the rule on amateurism other eligibility regulations for interscholastic athletic competition are:

Age. The trend in high schools is definitely in the direction of reducing the upper age limits at which boys may participate in interscholastic athletics. Not many years ago the upper age limit in most states was twenty-one years of age. Today, the upper age limit in thirty-three states is nineteen years. In thirteen of these states no further competition is permitted after the nineteenth birthday if it comes before September 1. Otherwise, students may compete during the balance of the school year. In the other twenty states a boy may compete in a sport season if his birthday occurs during the sport season. In fifteen states athletes become ineligible upon their twentieth birthday. In two states competition is permitted if the twentieth birthday is after September 20.

Attendance. Forty-eight states limit the amount of competition by any student in any sport to four years. The remaining two states set the limit at three years. All states consider the student ineligible after he has attended a four-year high school eight semesters or a senior high school six semesters. Attendance of fifteen days is regarded as a semester.

Entrance dates. In the great majority of states the period of enrollment ranges from ten days to three weeks after the opening of school, after which no student may enter and be eligible during that semester.

Residence and migration. All states rule that the student becomes ineligible for a year or one semester when he changes from one school to another, unless there is a bona fide change of residence. When the family actually moves into the new school district, the student usually becomes eligible immediately, providing he was in good standing at his original school. An exception to this occurs when evidence becomes available that undue influence was used to bring about the change in residence. This has become a problem of sufficient magnitude to cause some state associations to establish regulations against it.

Participation on nonschool teams. The great majority of state athletic associations have regulations that forbid a member of a school athletic squad to compete on a nonschool team during the season. Several states have the regulation that outside competition may be permitted if approved by the school principal. However, such permission would be granted only rarely.

Physician's examination. Thirty-three states require a physician's certificate stating that the student is physically fit to participate in interscholastic athletics. It is surprising that such an essential and universally recognized practice is not mandatory in all schools.

Scholastic requirements. The great majority of states require that the student must have completed with a satisfactory grade a designated number of courses—usually three—during the preceding semester. Nearly all states also require that the student be doing passing work in three full-credit subjects during the current semester. This eligibility regulation is based on the assumption that satisfactory achievement in the various academic courses is the primary purpose of the secondary school. Students are prevented from participating in other school activities until they can demonstrate adequate accomplishment in these essential courses. Participation in athletics is thus a reward for successful scholastic attainment. Students who fail to do passing work obviously need to spend more time and effort in study. Because athletics are time-consuming and strenuous, participation in them should be denied to those who cannot carry both programs successfully.

In 1938 New York eliminated the scholastic eligibility requirement on the ground that interscholastic athletics are an integral part of the physical education program and no student should be prevented from gaining the benefits of participating in them. This move eliminated in this state the distinction between curricular and extracurricular activities. In effect, it gave athletics equal status with the academic subjects. It eliminated the questionable practice of employing scholastic eligibility as a disciplinary measure. It recognized that athletic participation is just as important for a poor student as for a good one.

Other states have not followed the lead of New York in this direction. School men in general are satisfied with the academic eligibility requirement. They feel that it is simpler to administer uniformly than to follow the New York regulation. They have seen this requirement operate to the advantage of many athletes. The number of students who are prevented by this requirement from participating in athletics is negligible. Although the elimination of scholastic eligibility appears sound philosophically, school administrators are not convinced that it is a practical measure at the present time.

Awards. Twenty-four states stipulate that the utilitarian value of an award to any player may not exceed the stated limit, which varies from $1 to $5. Ten states restrict the award to a school letter. In two states the value of the award may not exceed $10.

Undue influence. Sixteen states have regulations that declare a student ineligible if it is proven that undue influence has been used to get the student to enroll in a particular school.

Parents' consent. Twenty states report that it is necessary for the student to obtain the consent of his parents in writing before he is eligible for participation in interscholastic athletic contests. Most states using this rule provide a special form for the student to take home for his parents' signature.

College and university eligibility regulations

The eligibility rules for intercollegiate competition are much the same as those for high schools. In the larger conferences, the freshmen rule is usually observed. Some schools, however, have interschool contests for freshmen, and others do not. This naturally limits the player to three years of participation on a varsity squad. This must be completed within a period of five consecutive years. Certain entrance requirements are maintained. There is not the uniformity of scholastic requirements in colleges that there is in the secondary schools. Most institutions require passing work in two-thirds to three-fourths of the normal student load, in both the previous and the present semesters. Normal progress toward the degree is required, and varsity athletes are expected to graduate with their class. Outside competition on teams not representing the institution is quite uniformly prohibited.

AWARDS

Value of awards

The practice of granting awards to those who compete in interscholastic and intercollegiate athletics is found in practically all schools. The custom is in accord with the universal practice of honoring successful or outstanding performance. In the schools, it corresponds to the honors, keys, pins, emblems, insignia, and the like, which are granted for meritorious achievement or service in either curricular or extracurricular activities. This practice has received considerable condemnation on the ground that the student should engage in an activity for itself rather than for any outside rewards. However, when the awards are intrinsically rather than extrinsically valuable, the objection to them is not so justifiable. When an award has only a sentimental value attached to it instead of a monetary or utilitarian value, it is unlikely that the award will become the sole goal of the activity. As an incentive to engage in worthwhile activities, it seems that an inexpensive award is perfectly justifiable.

The school letter has replaced the laurel wreath of the ancient Greeks as the award for athletic performance. In high schools the letter constitutes the customary form of award, although some schools also award a sweater with the letter. The majority of states follow the rule of the National Federation of State High School Athletic Associations and limit the cost of their awards to $5 or less. In colleges a sweater and letter are usually presented to the boy who qualifies. Some schools grant a sweater and letter for each achievement; others merely present the sweater and letter for the first award in a sport and only the letter in subsequent qualifications. Some universities and colleges permit a choice between a sweater and letter and a blanket carrying the school letter for the second award in the same sport. Many high schools having freshmen and class teams reward the qualifying players with class numerals. Numerals and sweaters are usually awarded to freshmen in institutions having the freshmen rule.

Major and minor awards

The advantages and disadvantages of major and minor letters have been much discussed. Some colleges and universities have no distinction between sports and grant the same letter for all sports. This is justified on the basis that a boy who has sufficient ability to represent his school is entitled to an award. The chief argument brought against this practice is that some sports, football particularly, demand much more from the boy than fencing, golf, tennis, and some of the other sports. The majority of colleges and universities grant the minor letter for those sports considered minor. However, a number of schools follow the practice of presenting major awards for outstanding performances in minor sports. An example would be winning the conference championship in golf or tennis.

The majority of high schools award the same letter to all who qualify, regardless of sport. However, many differentiate the sports into major and minor categories. This is done much more frequently in the larger high schools. In these schools the awards for minor sports are either a smaller monogram or the same size monogram as is awarded for the major sports but with a letter designating the minor sport.

The student managers of the various teams are usually awarded letters or insignia of different types. Frequently they are given the same type of award that the players receive. A more common award, however, is a major monogram with the designation "M" or "Mgr" on its face or directly underneath it.

Recommendations for awards are initiated by the coaches, usually on the basis of the established requirements. Generally, the coach's recommendations are acted upon by the athletic director or athletic council or both. The awards are ordinarily presented at some ceremony, such as a banquet or student assembly.

Requirements for awards

The requirements for letters differ greatly in different schools. The following are the major letter requirements for a number of colleges and high schools:

FOOTBALL

1. Participation in two conference games
2. Participation in three conference games
3. Participation in half of the quarters of major games [12]
4. Participation in half of the total number of quarters
5. Participation in six quarters of major games
6. Participation in six full quarters or their equivalent in time in major games
7. Participation in one full half in each of three major games and participation in one other game
8. Participation in two full halves with one or more specified teams
9. Participation for a total time equal to ten minutes per major game
10. The recommendation of one or more specified authorities for meritorious service
11. An award to seniors for loyal service during the three years of their eligibility upon recommendation of the coach.

BASKETBALL

1. Taking part in one half of major games
2. Playing a total of 60 minutes
3. Playing a time equal to ten minutes per conference game

[12] Major games are usually conference games or the equivalent.

4. Playing six full halves in conference games
5. Playing eight full halves in conference games
6. Playing in half the total number of halves
7. The recommendations of one or more specified authorities for meritorious service
8. An award to seniors for loyal service during the three years of their eligibility

TRACK

1. Winning a first in one or more specified meets
2. Winning second or better in one or more specified meets
3. Winning a third in one or more specified meets by seniors
4. Placing first in one or more specified meets (all members of a relay team)
5. Winning a place in the conference meet
6. Breaking a school record in competition
7. Winning ten points in conference competition and not all against same team
8. Winning eighteen points in two seasons
9. Winning twenty points in three seasons
10. The recommendation of one or more specified authorities for meritorious service
11. To seniors for loyal service during the three years of their eligibility

BASEBALL

1. Playing in 50 percent of total innings of all conference games
2. Playing in 50 percent of the conference or other specified games
3. Participation (four full innings) in at least two-thirds of the major games
4. Playing at least thirty innings and participating in at least five conference or other specified games
5. Pitching at least five innings in each of two conference games
6. Pitching (four full innings) in at least one third of the conference games
7. Pitching eighteen innings of conference games
8. Pitching at least three full games of major rank
9. Pitcher and catcher participating in 25 percent of all innings of conference games
10. The recommendation of one or more specified authorities for meritorious service

11. To seniors for loyal service during the three years of their eligibility upon recommendation of the coach

SWIMMING

1. Win second or better in the conference meet
2. To members of a water polo team winning a first in the conference or other specified meet
3. Breaking a school record in competition
4. To the members of the winning or second-place team in the conference
5. Winning ten points, including one first in major dual meets
6. Making an average of two points for conference dual meets

WRESTLING

1. Winning second or better in conference meet
2. Winning six points in dual meets
3. Winning two or more bouts with conference opponents
4. To all members of the team winning the conference championship provided they qualify for the minor letter
5. Granted at the discretion of a specified authority for performance of unusual merit
6. To seniors for loyal service during the three years of their eligibility

TENNIS

1. First place in the conference or other specified meet
2. Winning two conference matches, one of which must be singles
3. Winning three matches in singles or doubles during the conference season
4. Second place in the conference or other specified meet
5. Letter awarded for exceptionally meritorious work upon the recommendation of specified authority

GOLF

1. Winning second or better in conference or other specified meet
2. To members of team winning conference championship
3. For performance of unusual merit at the discretion of one or more specified authorities

THE ATHLETIC DIRECTOR

Athletic directorship usually a part-time position

In colleges and universities the director of athletics administers the athletic program. In large institutions this is usually a full-time position, but in most schools he will have other duties. In fact, some physical education directors also direct the athletic program. In small colleges the athletic director generally has coaching or teaching duties. In most secondary schools an athletic director administers the athletic program. Not uncommonly, however, a separate member of the faculty designated "Faculty Manager of Athletics" assumes the direction of the athletic program.

Responsibilities of the athletic director

The administrator of the interschool athletic programs is generally involved with the following duties:

1. Purchase and care of equipment
2. Preparation of budgets
3. Ticket sales and finances
4. Public relations
5. Preparation of facilities
6. Scheduling
7. Game contracts
8. Preparation of eligibility lists
9. Securing officials
10. Arranging team travel
11. Student manager system
12. Arrangements for scouting
13. Supervision of coaching staff
14. Administration of home athletic contests

A number of the above duties are considered in other chapters. The remainder will be discussed below.

Scheduling. The responsibility for scheduling falls upon the athletic director. In arranging schedules, close consultation with the head coaches of the various sports is necessary. Although it is not always possible to do so, the schedules should meet the approval of the coaching staff. In addition, the schedule should be approved by the athletic council or board. The school administrator—usually the principal, but in some schools the superintendent—gives final approval. In making schedules, the athletic director is guided by institutional policies and by league or conference regulations. The total number of games in each sport is determined in part by school policy and in part by conference or state athletic association regulations. Ordinarily, one half of the contests are played at home. Ideally, the home games and the games away from home are alternated. High school schedules are generally made a year in advance, but colleges and universities frequently arrange their schedules five or six years ahead. Schools that are in leagues or conferences have most of their schedules automatically filled. They may be able to play only one or two outside teams, if that many.

Athletic directors are expected to arrange schedules that will not conflict appreciably with school work. For this reason the weekends are preferred. Care must be observed in arranging team trips so that absence from classes will be held to a minimum. The schedule should not conflict with important school events that are held regularly. It is advisable for the athletic director to consult with the school administrator and the student council because many major events such as Homecoming, Dad's Day, and the like are built around the athletic schedule.

Game contracts. The great majority of interscholastic and intercollegiate athletic contests are confirmed by means of contracts. Most state high school athletic associations have standard forms, which the high schools in the state are expected or required to use. Each school has a signed copy of the contract, which specifies the date, time, place, and financial arrangements for the contest. It may also state the manner in which officials will be selected. The principal as well as the athletic director is supposed to sign the contracts for high school games.

Preparation of eligibility lists. A standard procedure in interscholastic athletics is for the competing schools to exchange eligibility lists prior to the game. This is required by most state associations. This list, which is certified by the principal, is usually exchanged about one week prior to the contest. The required data concerning each player varies from state to state. In some states merely the names of the eligible athletes are indicated. Others go into considerable detail and include such data as date of birth, year in school, number of semesters in athletics, and number of subjects passed the previous semester and passing the current semester. Most state athletic associations also require member institutions to submit an eligibility list to the association office.

Much the same procedure is followed in most colleges and universities. In some of the larger conferences the eligibility lists are sent to the conference commissioner, who checks the status of all players on the list.

Securing officials. Poor officiating cannot be condoned. There are so many capable officials, that there is no justification for securing poor ones. The practice of "trading games" has led to much poor officiating.

Instead of being selected on the basis of his ability, an official is chosen on the basis of his willingness to reciprocate. Furthermore, the practice of trading games leads to suspicions of favoritism. For the sake of the players and the game, good officials should be obtained.

The usual practice in selecting officials is for the two schools to agree upon certain individuals. The athletic director of the home institution initiates the matter by sending a list of approved officials to the athletic director of the visiting school. As soon as agreement has been reached, contracts should be sent to the chosen officials. Such contracts usually specify the date, time, place, assignment, and financial arrangements. The athletic council of the school should finally approve all officials selected. It is recommended that negotiations for officials begin early. The better officials are engaged many months in advance of the opening of the season.

To promote uniformity in the interpretation of playing rules, as well as to give school administrators the assurance that only qualified persons are in control of their contests, many states have established plans for the registration and classification of all persons who desire to become officials. Only men who meet these standards are permitted to officiate in interschool competition. As a result, the players, the schools, and the spectators benefit from a more efficiently handled contest.

Most states require all persons who desire to officiate in high school contests to register with the state association secretary. Member schools are required to use only registered officials. The officials must renew their registration annually. Ordinarily, officials are required to attend an annual rules interpretation meeting prior to the opening of the season. Because of deaths occurring during working hours, the Pennsylvania State Association requires that officials have annual physical examinations.

A number of states have a plan for the classification and rating of officials. Some states also have the officials rate the schools. These rating scales, judiciously used, will prove valuable in improving the conduct of interschool contests and raising the standard of officiating. The official rates the sanitation, lighting, and ventilation of the gymnasium, as well as the attitude of the coach, the principal, the players, and the spectators toward the opponents and officials. Rubin has developed an excellent rating scale, shown in Table 8-4, which might well be used by associations, conferences, and coaches to rate the ability of basketball officials.

Some colleges and universities secure their officials through the office of the conference commissioner, who makes the assignments from the list of approved officials. To get on the approved list the officials must pass rule examinations and demonstrate a satisfactory degree of competence in trial officiating. The larger conferences conduct rules interpretation meetings and carefully supervise the work of the officials. In

Table 8-4. Rating scale for basketball officials.

Official's Name..............
Home Team..............
Visiting Team..............

Preliminary Duties (10)

1 (a) Arrived at specified time
1 (b) Times and scorers acquainted with respective duties
1 (c) Determined upon signals to use to designate fouls and free shots
1 (d) Designated the official score book
1 (e) Scorers reminded to blow horn only when ball is dead
1 (f) Inspected timer's watch
1 (g) Length of playing periods determined
1 (h) Ground rules explained to visiting captains and given choice of baskets and balls
1 (i) Players given time to warm up
1 (j) Game begun on scheduled time

Score......

General Performance (75)

9 (a) Strict and correct interpretation of rules
9 (b) Decisions made consistently
9 (c) Impartial decisions
9 (d) Correct decisions; penalized those players who actually committed fouls, but appeared not to do so
9 (e) Game well controlled
9 (f) Fouls called closely
8 (g) Penalized infringement of rules by players not in possession of ball, as personal fouls in back court, unsportsmanlike conduct
4 (h) Used good judgement
9 (i) Anticipated movement of ball; kept close to ball; ahead of ball
1 (j) Ball skillfully handled in jump balls; ball tossed with a quick upward thrust perpendicular to floor with no advantage to either player
2 (k) Ball quickly put in play from out-of-bounds, after goals, jump balls
2 (l) Moved with uniform speed throughout game
1 (m) Decisions made in sharp, cleancut, decisive, and fearless manner
1 (n) Announced score at each half

Score......

Date of Game..............
Time Game Started..............
Time Game Finished..............

Personality (15)

5 (a) Uniform distinct from either team
3 (b) Cool, reserved, and confident
3 (c) Tactful
2 (d) Neat appearance
2 (e) Not pugnacious

Score......

Notes:

To be rated day after game—
Minimum score for each item—0
Maximum score—the score opposite each item
Referee should be rated according to his performance, getting either minimum score or any score between the two.
(Ex.: Correct decisions, etc. may be worth only 4)

Excellent	90-100
Good	89-90
Fair	70-79
Poor	0-69

Total Score......

Rating..............
Score..............
Score..............

Rated by..............
Position..............

Date..............
Source: Robert Rubin, "Rating Scale for Basketball Officials," Journal of Health, Physical Education, Recreation (January, 1936), p. 33.

many small colleges it is necessary to resort to the procedure of submitting a list of officials to the other institutions and deciding upon mutually satisfactory individuals.

Competent officials are necessary for women's athletic contests. Women, rather than men, should be in control of girls' and women's sports. They are better acquainted than men with the standard rules for women's athletics. In addition, they are more certain to be aware of special considerations, such as health safeguards, which may arise in the management of a woman's contest. The Division of Girls' and Women's Sports has an Officiating Rating Committee that certifies officials. The committee is organized in various sections of the country, and it is possible for any woman who desires to take the tests. Officials who have been approved by this committee are undoubtedly well qualified.

Arranging team travel. The athletic director must take care of a variety of details in connection with team trips. He should consult with the head coach on some of the important details, such as the menu, the time of arrival and return, the hotel, and the like. Many directors permit the team managers to handle most of these details, but the responsibility still remains with the athletic director. (For legal implications of travel, see p. 488.)

The squad should leave together, stay together after they arrive, and return home together. It is standard procedure not to permit players to return home with any other individuals except their parents. It goes without saying that the coach should always accompany his squad.

All details of the trip should be arranged in advance. All the players should know who is on the traveling squad and the time and place of departure. Parents should be notified of the details of the trip. Some coaches obtain the permission of parents for their son to take the trip. The hotel, transportation, and eating arrangements should be prepared well ahead of time.

Money should not be given to the players for expenses. It is better for the coach or manager to handle the funds on trips and defray all the expenses that are incurred. He should have sufficient cash available to meet all the expected expenses of the trip. He should receive receipts for all funds expended. He is expected to account for all expenditures upon his return. Ordinarily, the hotel and transportation costs are billed to the school.

It is standard procedure that the players assume responsibility for their personal equipment. Duffle bags are usually provided for this purpose. The remaining equipment, such as balls, first-aid supplies, helmets, and blankets, is the responsibility of the student managers. They also need to check the players carefully to see that they do not forget their personal equipment.

If the trip can be made in several hours it is preferable to make it on the day of the game. Not only is this policy less expensive but it is better for the players. They eat and sleep better at home and are more relaxed when they are in familiar surroundings.

Student manager system. Student managers render invaluable services to athletic directors and coaches. Practically all high schools and colleges and universities use student managers. When a good manager is available, he is a joy to both the coach and athletic director because he relieves them of many responsibilities.

The work of student managers is hard and time-consuming. In addition, it frequently appears to be thankless. However, the student stands to benefit from it in a variety of ways. He is recognized by his fellow students for his unselfish service and contribution to the team. In many schools the head managership is considered one of the most coveted positions. The manager learns how to work with a variety of people. He benefits from the responsibility he carries and from the lessons he learns by doing his job.

A good manager must be dependable, thorough, prompt, and resourceful. His personality is especially important because he must get along well with the players, coaches, the athletic director, and all others with whom he comes into contact. He must have a mind for details. It is essential that he be a good student because the job takes up much time and reduces the number of hours available to him for study.

The manager is generally appointed by the athletic director or coach of the sport concerned. Usually, the coach and athletic director have reached an agreement on the candidate beforehand. Frequently, the selection is made on a merit basis. This last method is preferred in the larger institutions where a number of candidates are available. It operates by having a number of sophomore managers from whom two junior managers are selected. One of the junior managers is then selected as senior manager. In smaller schools the athletic director and coach consider themselves fortunate if they have any volunteers.

Student managers perform a wide variety of duties. Some of the common ones are:

1. Recording the daily attendance
2. Bringing all the equipment to and from the practice field
3. Caring for the equipment during practice
4. Keeping a list of the addresses, phone numbers, locker numbers and combinations, and class schedules of all squad members
5. Officiating practice games

6. Checking on players' eligibility
7. Arranging for trips, meals, and hotels
8. Rendering a report of all expenditures after a trip
9. Packing various items of equipment for trips and making sure that the equipment is available
10. Checking that all players have their personal equipment on trips
11. Supervising the work of the assistants
12. Meeting visiting teams and rendering whatever assistance is needed
13. Meeting officials and taking care of their needs
14. Recommending his successor to the athletic director
15. Being available to assist the coaches and athletic director in any way they request

Arrangements for scouting. Scouting is accepted today as an essential part of interschool football and basketball. It is no longer regarded as spying and unethical but is approved and regulated. The scout, usually an assistant coach, calls for his tickets at the athletic department office and makes his presence known to the team he is scouting. He is provided with seats in the press box and is shown every courtesy. His purpose is to discover the basic offensive and defensive formations, the trick plays, and the abilities and peculiarities of the team. Some coaches exchange formations or films with each other in order to dispense with scouting. However, scouting, as it is conducted today, is the best assurance against suspicion. Most of the no-scouting agreements have been abrogated because of the difficulty incurred in preventing information concerning an opponent from reaching the coach and the players.

The chief problem with scouting today is to regulate it. There is a trend to scout each opposing team not more than twice. A further limitation is to permit only two representatives to scout a game at one time. Many coaches consider it unethical for coaches to make scouting reports, game films, and coaches' analyses of games available to other schools.

Supervision of coaching staff. The athletic director has the responsibility of conducting the athletic program in accordance with the policies of his institution and the regulations of the conference or league to which his school belongs. In addition, compliance with state and national athletic association regulations is required. He must be alert to the many policies and requirements and observe them in spirit as well as in letter. This involves, among other things, the supervision of the various members of the coaching staff.

Forty-seven state associations permit only certified teachers to coach in secondary schools. Most colleges and universities follow the same practice. Experience has demonstrated that it is easier to control athletics when the coaches are bona fide faculty members. Their professional preparation is such that they understand and appreciate the purposes of the school and the necessity for the various regulations to govern athletics.

The quality of the athletic program is determined more by the caliber of the coaches than by any other consideration. This fact makes their selection a vitally important matter. Unfortunately, coaches are too often chosen on the basis of their technical competence. The character and ideals of candidates receive too little attention. Ideally, the coach should understand his sport thoroughly. He should know boys and be an effective leader. He needs to be a skilled teacher, with the ability to develop sound fundamentals and well-coordinated offensive and defensive team play. He must realize that athletics are a part of school experiences and they must therefore be conducted to achieve educational objectives. He must appreciate that sports exist for the education and development of boys rather than that boys exist for the winning of games.

Good coaches are distinguished by their observance of the following principles: [13]

1. They recognize that coaching is teaching.
2. They make their work an integral part of the school program, giving special attention to its educational contribution.
3. They insist on the enforcement of all rules of athletic eligibility and seek no favor for athletes.
4. They are fair and unprejudiced in relationships with students.
5. They pay careful attention to the physical condition of players at all times.
6. They see to it that only competent game officials are selected and support their decisions.
7. They teach students to use only legitimate and ethical means in trying to win.
8. They counteract rumors of questionable practices by opponents.
9. They seek to prevent gambling, obscene language, and other offenses against honesty and decency.
10. They set good examples for boys to follow.
11. They help student athletes to understand that they are neither more nor less important than their fellow students.

Administration of athletic contests

One of the most important responsibilities of many athletic directors is the management of home athletic contests. This task must be done well because the public, students, and visiting team will resent and be critical of inefficient management. Poor administration of athletic contests will eventually result in reduced income from gate receipts.

The efficient management of a home game is dependent upon care-

---

[13] Educational Policies Commission, *School Athletics* (Washington, D.C., National Education Association and American Association of School Administrators, 1954), p. 61.

ful planning. Well-managed athletic contests do not happen accidentally
—they are as efficiently managed as they are planned. The chief difficulty in the administration of contests is to handle the multitude of details which is involved. These details are known but it is easy to forget
or to overlook some of them. For this reason some athletic directors employ a check list. Such a check list includes all the details that must be
handled in the management of a contest. After a detail has been discharged a check is made to indicate the fact. Such a scheme should
eliminate inefficiency in athletic contest management.

The following check list for football can be adapted to other sports.
This check list presupposes the completion of various arrangements
prior to the opening of the season. Such details as the engagement of
the officials, procurement of equipment, preparation of publicity materials—posters, schedules, programs, and the like. Procurement of equipment, arrangement for a physician, ordering of tickets and other necessary supplies, and repair and improvement of facilities must be taken
care of far in advance of a particular game.

CHECK LIST FOR FOOTBALL

1. *Week of Game*

    (a) Personnel

    ( ) (1) Secure student help and arrange to meet them at definite
    time and place on day of game: ( ) ticket sellers; ( )
    ticket takers; ( ) program sellers; ( ) concession sales-
    men; ( ) ushers; ( ) guards; ( ) parking attendants;
    ( ) scoreboard operators.

    ( ) (2) Complete arrangements for police.

    ( ) (3) Assign managerial duties (visiting team, officials, home
    team).

    ( ) (4) Arrange for physician.

    ( ) (5) Write officials and indicate when and where to report.

    ( ) (6) Arrange for scorer and timer.

    ( ) (7) Obtain announcer for public address system.

    (b) Publicity

    ( ) (1) Distribute advertising posters.

    ( ) (2) Provide daily press releases.

    ( ) (3) Submit program material to printer by Tuesday.

    ( ) (4) Complete press box arrangements.

    ( ) (5) Distribute complimentary tickets to press and radio.

( ) (6) Complete arrangements for band.

( ) (7) Complete arrangements for half-time entertainment (if any).

(c) Equipment

( ) (1) Send out laundry and dry cleaning (Monday).

( ) (2) Have laundry and dry cleaning returned.

( ) (3) Get game uniforms ready.

( ) (4) Get game balls (2) ready.

( ) (5) Get officials' accessories ready: ( ) gun and blanks; ( ) three whistles; ( ) two watches; ( ) yard markers; ( ) down markers; ( ) chain for linesman; ( ) scorebook.

( ) (6) Get medical supplies and stretcher ready.

(d) Facilities

( ) (1) Inspect facilities: ( ) game field; ( ) goal posts; ( ) bleachers; ( ) fences and gates; ( ) scoreboard; ( ) ticket booths; ( ) press box; ( ) canvas fence covers; ( ) toilets; ( ) concession booths; ( ) dressing rooms; ( ) water fountains; ( ) benches.

( ) (2) Have facilities cleaned and repaired.

( ) (3) Have field lined day prior to game.

( ) (4) Have decorations arranged.

( ) (5) Have bleachers erected (if necessary).

(e) Administration

( ) (1) Write visiting team to determine time of arrival and requirements.

( ) (2) Make arrangements to accommodate visiting team.

( ) (3) Get tickets and forms ready for ticket sellers.

( ) (4) Place tickets on sale (Monday) at appropriate places.

( ) (5) Request cash needs for ticket sellers, concessions, and program sellers.

( ) (6) Make arrangements for meals for home team.

2. *Day of Game*

(a) Personnel

( ) (1) Pick up change and tickets, and meet ticket sellers.

( ) (2) Distribute change to program sellers and concession sellers.

( ) (3) Meet and assign duties to other student help.

( ) (4) Check with physician.

( ) (5) Meet and assign duties to police.

(b) Publicity

( ) (1) Have public address equipment set up.

( ) (2) Have public address announcer information ready.

( ) (3) Provide spotter for press box.

( ) (4) Make available programs and starting line-ups for press.

( ) (5) Provide refreshments for press representatives (at half).

( ) (6) Check half-time entertainment (if any).

(c) Equipment

( ) (1) Issue game uniforms.

( ) (2) Provide towels and soap for visiting team.

( ) (3) Prepare first-aid kit.

( ) (4) Have sideline coats, blankets, etc., available.

( ) (5) Have officials' accessories available: ( ) gun and blanks; ( ) three whistles; ( ) two watches; ( ) scorebook; ( ) yard markers; ( ) down marker; ( ) chain for linesman.

(d) Facilities

( ) (1) Check to see that scoreboard and timer are functioning properly.

( ) (2) Check public address system.

( ) (3) Check facilities: ( ) toilets; ( ) drinking fountains; ( ) entrances and exits; ( ) bleachers; ( ) press box; ( ) benches; ( ) visiting team's dressing quarters; ( ) officials' dressing quarters; ( ) condition of the field.

( ) (4) Keys issued to: ( ) home managers; ( ) visiting managers; ( ) manager for officials.

(e) Administration

( ) (1) Make out checks for: ( ) visiting teams; ( ) officials; ( ) police; ( ) student help.

( ) (2) Check in receipts from: ( ) ticket sellers; ( ) concessions; ( ) program sellers.

( ) (3) Deposit funds.

( ) (4) Check on weather early on day of game and make any adjustments which are indicated.

PROBLEMS OF INTERSCHOOL ATHLETICS

The serious athletic problems

There are numerous problems facing interschool athletics. The most serious of these are emphasis on false values, bad athletic practices, championships and tournaments, player control, proselyting and subsidization, junior high school athletics, interschool athletics for girls and women, the academic teacher versus the physical educator as coach, public pressures, and overemphasis. Each will be discussed in turn.

Emphasis on false values. After an exhaustive study, the Education Policies Commission [14] has indicated that the emphasis upon false values is one of the major problems that mar interscholastic athletics in American schools today. Its statement on this issue is as follows:

When a high school student body attaches false values to the importance of interscholastic athletics, the entire school program is frequently disrupted. Under the guise of school spirit, waves of hysteria accompany frenzied preparation for an athletic contest. A conviction of the necessity for winning permeates the school, the community, the players, the coaches.

In such an atmosphere athletes are excessively revered and pampered. Members of the opposing team may be regarded as hated rivals and treated as invading enemies. Actions are encouraged that seek to injure, subdue, or humiliate an opponent. Game officials become targets for primitive, hysterical outbursts of derision, sometimes resulting in physical violence. Under these conditions, appreciation of the game is lost in the wildly partisan, unsportsmanlike manifestations of the crowd. After such a contest, victory elevates these partisans to high levels of ecstasy; defeat plunges them into the depths of frustration and despair.

Overemphasis on winning. Low standards of sportsmanship undermine a school's entire program of citizenship education. When interscholastic athletics place so much emphasis on victory that cheating, deceit, subterfuge, and unsportsmanlike acts are condoned, opportunities for citizenship training are sacrificed. Young people who are stimulated to believe that victory for the school team is more important than anything else are not learning to keep life values in perspective.

Glorifying star athletes. The star athlete on a successful team must be of strong character indeed to keep values in balance when he becomes the center of attention of school and community, flattered and publicized, and courted by scouts for college material. False values are distressingly evident when a boy who fails to make the team suffers despair or self-reproach, or when a player's game-losing mistake brings him the reproach of others.

Disparaging the nonathlete. In a teen-age society that has embraced athleticism as one of its supreme values, the boy who does not care very much about athletics loses status. Because of this and the attitude of some adults he may be pressured into taking part in distasteful and harmful physical activities. His lack of enthusiasm for the school team may provoke the taunts and derision of schoolmates. Desire to conform to an accepted pattern of behavior may lead to self-depreciation and inner conflict.

School games as public spectacles. It is bad enough for adult sports enthusiasts to demand that schoolboy games be staged for their benefit. It is worse when schools yield to this demand. False values are rampant when the notion prevails that school athletics exist primarily for public amusement. A school pro-

---

14 *Ibid.,* p. 6.

gram of public relations based on athletics provides, in the long run, an ineffective and unstable basis for good school-community relations.

Bad athletic practices. Many bad athletic practices are defeating the purposes of interscholastic athletics. The more common of these are: [15]

1. Overemphasis on the varsity. This practice leads to a disproportionate share of facilities, equipment, personnel, and funds being devoted to varsity teams. The inevitable result in most schools is that the students who most need athletics are deprived of the opportunity to engage in them.

2. Distortions in the educational program. Teachers are often under pressure to lower their standards for varsity athletes. In some schools they find it difficult to hold athletes to the same quality and quantity of work, attendance, and grading standards that they expect of other students.

3. Coaches under pressure. This is a familiar situation. In many communities the coach must win to hold his job. This pressure will inevitably cause some coaches to resort to vicious, unwholesome tactics in order to win games.

4. Financial woes. The failure of the school board to finance the interscholastic program adequately leads to a reliance upon gate receipts to keep the program functioning. When the athletic program must exist largely or entirely upon gate receipts, a variety of undesirable practices occur. The criterion becomes money rather than educational values. The result is overemphasis upon winning. Schedules are made with an eye to the income rather than the welfare of students. Individuals or groups in the community are solicited for financial assistance.

5. Farm teams. In order to obtain better material for high school teams a system of competition, beginning in the elementary grades, is carried on through the junior high school. The boys are prepared for the time when they are eligible for the high school team. No consideration is given to the welfare and desirable development of the boys. The program in some cities is analogous to the farm system of major league professional baseball teams.

6. Recruiting of players. Although recruiting on the high school level is not nearly as extensive as it is on the college level it still exists to such an extent that many state high school athletic associations have found it necessary to legislate against the practice. The most frequent offense is influencing parents to make a change of residence in order to place the athlete within the area covered by the school.

7. Neglecting the girls. With the varsity athletic teams monopolizing the facilities, there is little opportunity in most schools for girls to carry on intramural and recreational sports.

[15] *Ibid.,* pp. 7-10.

8. Recruiting by colleges. Aggressive recruiting tactics by colleges may interfere with the normal routine of a high school. In addition, there is excessive absence among star athletes because they are visiting various colleges and universities and, in some cases, participating in tryouts.

Championships and Tournaments. For many decades there has been much opposition to championships and tournaments. This opposition is not found as much in institutions of higher education because the problems are not as acute. The participants are more mature, and since they usually travel by plane there is less interference with the academic program. Likewise, there is little criticism of league or conference championships being awarded on the basis of percentage points. The prime targets have been high school state championship meets and tournaments. Particularly condemned were the state tournaments extending over three or four days preceded by regional, district, and sectional tournaments, each also spread over several days. It was not at all uncommon for a team to play 5 or 6 games over a three-day period.

The extent of state high school championships is represented in Table 8-5 from the data for the 1964-1965 school year.

Table 8-5.

Sport	States Determining State Championships	Sport	States Determining State Championships
Baseball	33	Skiing	4
Basketball	46	Soccer	4
Football	20	Softball	1
Six-or Eight-Man Football	7	Swimming	32
Golf	37	Tennis	40
Gymnastics	15	Track and Field	48
Indoor Track	10	Volleyball	4
		Wrestling	34

Source: National Federation of State High School Athletics, *Handbook: 1964-65* (Chicago, 1965), p. 72.

The advocates of reform of championships base their objection on the following points:

1. Championships rather than the game itself become the objects of play.
2. The schools involved become disrupted.
3. Participants lose much time from classes.
4. The importance of winning is overemphasized.
5. Tournaments are physically and emotionally harmful to participants.

6. The expense of engaging in tournaments is too heavy in some schools.
7. Communities expect too much of their teams.

In defense of state play-offs it should be pointed out that state athletic associations derive most of their income from this source. In addition, in some states the participating schools receive part of their tournament expenses from this income. Further, certain values have been attributed to championships, such as the benefits of travel, the crystallization of school spirit, increased community interest and pride, and the social values to the players. Finally, it should be recognized that if the schools did not provide such play-offs other agencies probably would. It is unquestionably better that schools conduct championship competition rather than private or commercial agencies.

Over the years the conduct of tournaments and meets, particularly at the high school level, has improved to such an extent that much of the criticism has abated. The credit for this improvement belongs primarily to the state athletic associations and the school administrators who direct them. These men have been very conscious of the undesirable features of state championships and they have made every effort to eliminate them. They have stopped the national championships. The three or four tournament stages preceding the final competition have been reduced or eliminated. Very helpful has been the creation of tournaments for schools according to their size. Thirty-one of the forty-six states that have state championships in basketball follow this practice. When the schools of the state are divided up into three or four separate tournaments the length of tournament structure is reduced and the number of games to be played by each school is sharply curtailed. As a consequence the schedule can be arranged to avoid the necessity of any team playing more than one game per day. In addition this arrangement is more equitable to the small schools.

It would be erroneous to assume that all opposition to tournaments has been dissipated. There are still some problems that have not been solved. Ten states hold championship play-offs for girls in basketball. One state conducts a state basketball championship tournament for junior high schools. Despite these and other problems, however, school administrators through their state athletic associations have made substantial progress in putting the championship competition on a sound educational basis.

Player control. On October 20, 1927, the Central Committee of the New York State Public School Athletic Association passed the famous "Regulation One," which was modified to its present form on December 27, 1927. In substance, this regulation recommended that after the contest began, the two coaches should sit together and permit the respective captains to direct the teams. The coach might attend to the physical injuries of his team, and he could order the withdrawal of a player from the game; but that was the extent of his authority. When a player was withdrawn, he was unable to reenter the game. His substitute was selected by the captain, who made substitutions as he chose. It was suggested that each coach send a representative to the other team's dressing room in order to prevent accusation of bad faith. The intention of the rule was to give every opportunity for the development of responsibility and resourcefulness on the part of the captain and of responsiveness to team-mate control, true loyalty, and team play on the part of the players.

There immediately arose a storm of favorable and unfavorable criticism concerning this radical departure from the traditional method of conducting athletic contests. Those who endorsed this reform felt that it was in harmony with the best educational philosophy. Ability to solve problems is best attained by practice in problem solving; leadership is best attained by practicing it. The domination of the coach during the contests destroyed the richest educational values of leadership, responsibility, and resourcefulness. There were some who believed that the pressure on the coach to win would be reduced with the boys themselves in control of the games. There is no doubt that the standard of performance would be lowered, but both teams would be equally affected.

The opposition to this proposal was very strong, particularly among the coaches. The opponents of the reform felt it was idealistic but impractical. They pointed to the early history of interschool sports when the faculty was forced to regulate these activities because of student mismanagement. Why abolish the coaches who have raised the standards of athletics from their poor position before the advent of the twentieth century? The coach today is far better qualified to conduct athletics on a high plane than the coaches of the past have been. Another argument used against player control was that many schools, particularly the small high schools, have no leaders who are qualified to handle this difficult assignment. Even with the coach on the bench, it is frequently difficult for the captain or team leader to control the team. The "Mexican generals" on athletic teams present a serious problem to many coaches. Athletic contests are filled with intense emotional situations, and the responsibility upon the captain in control would be tremendous. His mistakes would be magnified by his team mates, and hard feelings would be sure to result. He would be accused of playing his friends, whether or not he did. It is doubtful whether the captain could be entrusted with the physical welfare of his team mates, although the coach or a physician on the bench could manage this.

The sentiment in favor of "Regulation One" has practically disappeared. Few, if any, schools adhere to the recommendations of this regulation today. In recent years the trend has been away from player control. The unlimited substitution rule in college and high school football and the rule in basketball which permits the coach to talk to his players during a time out are steps in the opposite direction. However, even though present regulations increase coach control, good coaches will continue to make every attempt to develop leadership and resourcefulness in their athletes. There never was a good team without a good leader. By developing better leaders and thinkers, the good coach knows he is building a better team. He is unable to dominate every situation that occurs during the game, and the better he has developed initiative and leadership, the better will these situations be met. Furthermore, the interval between halves presents the coach with the most favorable educational opportunity he will ever have to inculcate the valuable lessons that can arise out of athletic competition.

Proselyting and subsidization. This is the most serious problem confronting intercollegiate athletics. Proselyting and subsidization do exist in high schools, but nowhere to the same extent as in colleges and universities. High schools are publicly supported local institutions, and the expense of attending them is very little. Furthermore, in many cities where there is more than one high school, the district in which the boy lives determines the school he must attend. The state high school athletic associations have vigorously combatted proselyting and subsidizing by passing regulations against them. But this does not mean to imply these evils do not exist in secondary schools. Financial aid is sometimes given to boys who would not otherwise be able to attend high school. Considerations of various kinds are used occasionally to persuade parents to move to another community in order that their son might participate in athletics in a certain school. On the whole, however, this problem is minor in comparison to what it is in colleges and universities.

The effort to control proselyting and subsidizing of star athletes in institutions of higher learning has a long history. College administrators have opposed it for many years. College athletic conferences and associations have attempted unsuccessfully to halt the practices. The Carnegie Foundation investigation of college athletics, which culminated in its 1929 report (Bulletin No. 23), revealed a shocking disregard for the athletic codes and educational standards. However, despite this revelation the flagrant abuses have continued. If anything they were accentuated, particularly after World War II. The basketball gambling scandals, in which a considerable number of players in seven different institutions were tried and found guilty of consorting with gamblers; the West Point episode, in which a large number of athletes violated the traditional honor code; and the Pacific Coast Conference explosion in 1956, in which many athletes of four universities were involved in wholesale violations of conference regulations, made this postwar decade one of the blackest pages in the history of intercollegiate athletics.

The evidence is clear that intercollegiate athletics in many institutions are permeated with hypocrisy, dishonesty, and deceit. Agreements that institutions have pledged to honor have been deliberately broken. Lack of respect for rules may be traced to an attitude of studied evasion, which amounts to a philosophy of the calculated risk. Institutional personnel, as well as alumni, have been involved in these sordid schemes against the regulations. The amazing feature about the matter is that colleges and universities are dedicated to truth, justice, honor, integrity, and other lofty virtues. Among the mottoes of American universities the word "truth" or its Latin equiavlent *veritas* appears more than any other. This inconsistency in what the school is aiming to achieve and what is actually happening in athletics must be eliminated.

Three groups of individuals are primarily involved in this problem. The first is comprised of the college and university administrators. In the last analysis, the president of the institution is responsible for what happens to it. If he has the power and is determined to have the athletic program in his school conducted in accord with the established regulations, it will be done. Many instances are available where this has been done. However, many presidents do not have the power, desire, or courage to cope with the situation. Alumni pressures, particularly, make it difficult for them to maintain desirable standards.

The coach is placed in an untenable position in many institutions. His uncertain tenure makes it imperative for him to win. The alumni constantly clamor for winning teams, and they are willing in many instances to supply the necessary financial assistance. The heavy financial obligations that many athletic departments have represent an additional pressure. In order to solve these problems good athletic material from high schools or junior colleges is a necessity. In this situation it is difficult for the coach not to succumb to the temptation of violating the regulations governing recruiting.

The alumni have proved the source of most of the difficulties in intercollegiate athletics. Their insistence upon winning teams has led to most of the evils which beset this program. They have been willing to spend much time and money to go after the prospects that the coaches have designated they want. Their activities have been almost impossible to control. They feel they are rendering a service to their alma mater and, at the same time, helping deserving students who could not otherwise afford to attend college. Perhaps the reason why they cannot see the wrong in violating athletic regulations is that little effort has ever been made to develop the proper attitudes among them.

Since the close of World War II the trend has been to liberalize the financial assistance given to athletes. A number of athletic conferences provide a full athletic scholarship—tuition, board, room, books, and a small amount for incidental expenses. This is justified on the basis that the athlete deserves this assistance because the time he would ordinarily use to earn his way is devoted to athletics. Moreover, he is making a worthwhile contribution to his institution. These scholarships are administered through the college or university and are expected to cover basic subsistence. The athletes are not permitted to accept other financial grants or to work. Whether or not athletic scholarships will solve the problem remains to be seen.

After a survey of opinions from institutional presidents, coaches, and alumni, Hickman made the following recommendations to solve the aforementioned problems: [16]

1. Each prospective football player in order to obtain an athletic scholarship must be qualified for admission the same as any other student. Some suggestions have been made that a national test should be given, such as the college board examinations, in order to standardize admissions. We feel that this is completely impracticable because of the varying degree of secondary school standards in different sections of the country and also the wide range of requirements for admissions at different institutions. Admission standards must be left to the individual institution, and in any case be no lower than the conference level.

2. The applicant must show economic need. It should be the duty of each institution to check thoroughly the financial status of the athlete's family and their ability to pay his college expenses. In no case should he be given more aid than needed.

3. Each player should receive through regular institutional channels, and only through these channels, sufficient financial aid to take care of his normal college expenses such as board, room, tuition and fees, books, laundry and dry cleaning. The individual college should make up a budget of necessary expenses of a regular student, and this criterion should be the amount of the athletic scholarship awarded. The amount in dollars and cents will vary from institution to institution and from conference to conference, but in any case it must not be above the actual expenses as certified by the college.

4. All other financial aid, except that outlined in No. 3, is prohibited. The prohibition includes promise of financial aid beyond the minimum time required for a student to complete his allowable athletic competition, and outside aid and outside jobs, except jobs during the summer and during the school vacations, for which the pay is not greater than that received by other people doing the same kind of work. Any outside rewards or inducements to athletes or prospective athletes, such as gifts of money, clothes, lavish entertainment, loans or acting as sureties for loans, shall be considered as excessive financial aid and be prohibited.

5. The acceptance of any aid, except that outlined in No. 3, shall result in immediate expulsion of the student involved. Assuming a conference and all of its members, or, so far as that goes, all the conferences and colleges, have adopted this scholarship plan, then there is no reason why this rule should be broken. When an institution guarantees the needed expenses of an individual, there are certain responsibilities that he must assume. This should be explained

[16] "Nine Points of Survival" (*Sports Illustrated* with Herman Hickman, Copyright 1956 Time Inc.).

to him in full by a regular faculty representative the day he registers. He should be asked to sign a pledge to this effect in order to receive his scholarship.

6. A fixed percentage of athletic scholarships—we suggest 75%—should be reserved only for boys in the conference territory of the college or university and its environs. This would avoid the widespread recruiting abuses which occur in the course of competition for players from other sections. Another point that might be well taken would be to put a limit on the number of athletic scholarships each institution could provide so as to keep the competition on the same plane within a conference.

7. To receive an athletic scholarship and remain eligible for it, the recipient must take a regular course of study, of his own choice, leading to a degree. He must take a normal load of academic hours and maintain a satisfactory average. Before the beginning of his third year he must have attained the proper number of credit hours and quality points to become a full-fledged member of the junior class or his scholarship will be withdrawn. If this rule was adopted and maintained by all institutions, most of the critics of college football would be hushed. Phony jobs and under-the-table pay are relatively unimportant compared to this phase. The maintenance of these standards does away with the stigma of "hired" athletes. The word "amateur" becomes real. In other words, strict observance of this rule places the proper connotation on the noun "proselyte."

8. The responsibility for proper practices of recruitment and subsidization of players should be placed squarely on the shoulders of the head football coach. The president of the institution and his faculty committee on athletics should demand that the coach be personally and directly responsible to the president and his committee for his actions. They should insure and assure him against undue pressure to win games at any cost. They should free him of financial worries about gate receipts, and they should fire him if he or any of his assistants directly or indirectly give, have given, promise, or condone any financial aid to players or prospective players beyond the regulations of the institution.

9. The "athletic dormitory" and the year-round training table should be abolished. We realize that the training table during the season, especially for the night meal after practice and the pre-game meals on Saturdays, is a must. But for better player-student relations the athletic dormitory should be done away with or divided with nonathletic students, and the training table abolished out of season. And, more important, all incoming freshman athletes should be mixed at the beginning with other members of the student body. This might be impracticable at some institutions and economically unsound at others, but it would improve the stature of college football immeasurably.

Junior high school athletics. The subject of interscholastic athletics on the junior high school level has been a red-hot issue among physical educators for the past twenty-five years. The American Association of School Administrators,[17] the American Medical Association,[18] the Educational Policies Commission,[19] and the Joint Committee (composed of

[17] American Association of School Administrators, *Health in Schools: Twentieth Yearbook* (Washington, D.C., National Education Association, 1951).

[18] American Medical Association, "Junior High School Athletics" (November 23, 1951). A news release.

[19] Educational Policies Commission, *op. cit.*

representatives of the American Association for Health, Physical Education, and Recreation, the Society of State Directors, Department of Elementary School Principals, and the National Council of State Consultants in Elementary Education) [20] have all come out in opposition to such competition. Despite the condemnation of all these national organizations, junior high school athletics have continued to flourish.

The arguments against junior high school interscholastic athletics have been summarized by Mitchell [21] as follows:

1. Physiological. Boys in the junior high school period are in the stage of very rapid growth. Growth is work. Consequently, boys of these ages should not be subjected to additional strenuous activities which are of long duration. In informal competition the boy alternates short periods of exertion and rest. But when he competes as a member of a school team, he will have to continue beyond the natural limits of his endurance. This is considered harmful.

2. Psychological. The junior high school boy is not ready emotionally for the mental strain, tension, and excitement engendered by the varsity-type competition. Participation in informal or intramural athletics does not develop the high pressures which competition before adult audiences does. The boy ought to be prepared gradually for the type of athletic program he will experience in the senior high school.

3. Sociological. Junior high school boys are too young to be regimented in the manner of high school and college athletes. They are at an age when they need to develop self-reliance, independence, and to make their own choices. It is contrary to normal growth patterns to subject his every decision, his every move to the dictation of adult-imposed orders.

4. Economic. Interschool athletics are expensive. The cost of equipment, facilities, coaching staff, medical care, travel, and other items is exceedingly heavy. Gate receipts in junior high schools cannot be counted upon to absorb a large part of the expense. Reliance upon school funds is necessary. This leads to the temptation to try to carry on the program with cheap equipment and inadequate facilities. The hazards of conducting football on such a basis are obvious. In addition, the available resources are concentrated upon a small number of students to the detriment of the remainder.

5. Educational. The junior high school period is one in which the students should explore a wide variety of interests. Specialization should come in the senior high school or later. It is too early for boys to concentrate on one or two sports and to miss the opportunity to try out many different activities.

Some support of the physiological argument against junior high school athletics comes from Lowman [22] who writes that "Dr. Mark Jansen of Leiden, Holland, years ago pointed out that fast-growing cells

[20] American Association for Health, Physical Education, and Recreation, *Desirable Athletic Competition for Children* (Washington, D.C., 1952).

[21] Elmer D. Mitchell, "The Case Against Interscholastic Athletics in the Junior High School," *University of Michigan School of Education Bulletin* (November, 1951), pp. 23-25.

[22] C. L. Lowman, "A Consideration of Teen Age Athletics," *Journal of Health, Physical Education, Recreation* (September, 1941), p. 398.

and tissues are most vulnerable, i.e., most liable to damage or injury. Skeletal structures, as well as organs, are in a stage of rapid growth just preceding and during adolescence. Accordingly the potentials of injury are greater at this age."

Wilton Krogman,[23] the noted anthropologist, bases his opposition to junior high school interscholastic athletics on the ground that children have only so much energy and when they are using it for growth, heavy additional demands should not be placed upon them. He states:

As a human biologist I hold it basically unsound to impose upon the rapidly growing organism excessive physical demands. The catch here is, of course, the definition of the word "excessive." In a sense the definition must refer to the skills, aptitude, and potential of the individual; this means a demand-evaluation based on the child's own growth progress. In a larger sense, however, this means that the *entire circum-pubertal period,* roughly 11-14 in girls, 12-15 in boys, is one in which maximum protection must be given to the growing child, for balance between energy-intake and energy-use (in function and in growth dynamics) is finely drawn—there is too often no reservoir of excess energy upon which to draw. By "protection" I mean that the child in such a growth surge should not be required to lavish energy upon various kinds and degrees of athletic performance.

I should like to point out that I am not in the least condemning. I am admonishing. I am certain that Physical Education as a discipline, will implement growth thinking into any and all programs of athletic skills, be they merely curricular (as gym classes) or competitive (as intramural or interschool). My thinking applies mostly to the latter, and especially to the vigorously aggressive contact sports. There is no profit it seems to me, in risking traumata—either morphological or physiological—at a time when the child, (especially the boy) is depositing all his energy in the bank of growth. It will yield him a high rate of interest in normal, healthy progress toward maturity. Why, then endanger the yield by a too-great withdrawal from the energy account?

Perhaps the most valid argument against junior high school interscholastic athletics is that in regard to the adequacy of the resources for the service and intramural programs as well as the interschool program. An interscholastic program should not be attempted unless it can be done without interfering with the instructional and intramural activities. The needs of the great majority of students must be met before a varsity program is initiated. This stipulation would eliminate the interscholastic program in most junior high schools because the facilities, equipment, and personnel are not adequate for all *three* programs.

Most physical educators would withdraw their reservations about junior high school interscholastic athletics if the service and intramural programs could be classified as excellent. It is an unfortunate fact that many junior high schools that sponsor interscholastic programs have

---

[23] Wilton Krogman, "Factors of Physical Growth of Children as They May Apply to Physical Education," *Proceedings: 1954 National Convention of the American Association of Health, Physical Education, Recreation,* p. 63.

intramural programs that could not even be considered mediocre. Even the quality of the service programs in some schools have been sacrificed in favor of an interschool athletic program.

The opponents of junior high school athletics claim that the main motivation for such teams is to prepare material for high school teams. This is an adult exploitation of the interest of boys and produces unfortunate results. At the same time a program does not produce a wealth of varsity material to the same extent as a comprehensive intramural program. The limitation of squads will automatically eliminate some boys who would later develop into varsity players. The phenomenon of puberty produces many amazing results, and the small, unimpressive boy in the seventh grade may be an outstanding athletic prospect in the senior high school. If strong varsity teams are desired for the senior high schools, the best way to attain them is to provide a comprehensive intramural program in the junior high schools.

The proponents of junior high school athletics argue that many of the criticisms of this program are unfounded. They point out that practices are shorter, fewer games are played, and the length of games is reduced to bring the competition within the capacities of the players. Research data are not available to demonstrate the physiological and psychological harm of such competition. Thousands upon thousands of junior high school boys have participated in interschool sports with no apparent ill effects. Walker [24] found an injury incidence of 5 percent in junior high school football in Texas as compared to a 10 percent incidence in senior high school football.

Insofar as the educational argument that the junior high school period is too early to specialize in one sport is concerned, supporters of the program point out that students have the opportunity to become acquainted with a variety of activities in the physical education service program. They also contend that only a small number of players participate in the varsity program in more than one sport.

To justify the varsity program in junior high schools it is pointed out that unless the school provides a program for the superior performers various agencies within the community will do so. Ordinarily, these agencies will not conduct the program on as high a level as the school will. It is a fact that many boys participate on several different teams during the same season. The possibility of deleterious consequences of this type of competition are decidedly greater than that involved with school teams.

The most far-reaching survey of junior high school interscholastic athletics was made in 1958.[25] The 2,312 junior high schools whose prin-

[24] Malcolm Walker, "Interscholastic Football in Junior Highs," *Athletic Journal* (February, 1951), p. 24.

[25] Reprinted by permission of the National Association of Secondary School Principals, 1958, copyright: Washington, D.C.

cipals participated in the survey represented 90 percent of the junior high school enrollment in the United States. Eighty-three and six tenths percent of the principals favored the interschool program and 16.4 percent were opposed. Eighty-five and two tenths percent of the junior high schools sponsored an interscholastic program. Of the 1,803 principals who favored the program, 494 reported that they supported it only if the competitions were within the school system. Seven hundred seventy schools scheduled games only within the school system. One thousand three hundred eighty-one engaged in athletic relations outside their own school system. Principals of 630 schools indicated that interscholastic athletics stimulated the intramural program; principals of 188 schools reported that the interscholastic program detracted from the intramural athletic program. The majority of the principals—1,522 —reported no clearly unfortunate experience with interscholastic athletics. The unfortunate experiences included:

1. Undesirable rivalry 143
2. Unsatisfactory player attitudes 99
3. Excessive cost to school 112
4. Unsatisfactory awards 20
5. Bodily injury or strain 129
6. Unsatisfactory night games 107
7. Detriment to pupils' studies 89
8. Yes, but no comment

The American Association for Health, Physical Education and Recreation opposed junior high school interscholastic athletics for many years. However, at the National Conference on Youth and Fitness [26] the following recommendation was approved by the conferees: "Except for boxing, interscholastic sports in grades 7-9, when properly organized, can make a significant contribution to total youth fitness. It is recommended that proper school authorities establish procedures which will allow these sports to be carried on with due consideration for safety, maturity, weight, height, speed, intensiveness of competition, number of games and length of schedule."

The authors support a junior high school interscholastic athletic program only if excellent service and intramural programs are already in existence. The needs of the majority of the students must have priority. If varsity teams are supported, they should be carried on in accordance with the various recommended policies. The playing rules and court dimensions should be modified to suit the capacities of the players. Shorter seasons, short practice periods, and reduced schedules are essential. Tournament play should be prohibited. Long trips should not

[26] Report of the National Conference on Fitness of Secondary School Youth, *Youth and Fitness* (Washington, D.C., American Association for Health, Physical Education and Recreation, 1958), p. 35.

be permitted. Good equipment, safe facilities, adequate medical super-vision and care, and, most important of all, professionally trained leader-ship should be available. The program should have no relationship to that of the senior high school. Any hint of influence of senior high school coaches should be avoided.

Interschool athletics for girls and women. The question of inter-school athletics for high school and college girls and women has been a very controversial one. Up until comparatively recently most women physical educators and the women's professional organizations were united in their opposition to such competition. Today, this opposition to such competition has moderated considerably, although women leaders still prefer intramural competition, play days, sports days, and telegraphic meets for girls.

Various reasons were advanced against extramural competition for girls. It was thought that strenuous athletic participation would affect adversely the reproductive function of women. Concern was expressed that the delicate female sexual organs might be damaged or displaced by violent exercise. In addition, it was felt that the narrow hips which are characteristic of many women athletes created special problems in childbirth.

This objection to vigorous exercise is rarely heard today. No sci-entific evidence has been produced to substantiate these claims. On the other hand, Jokl has presented evidence that completely refutes the claims that athletic competition has an adverse effect upon the repro-ductive organs of women. He has summarized two recent studies which reveal that insofar as major disorders during pregnancy, duration of labor, incidence of Caesarean section, and the use of outlet forceps, and fertility ratios are concerned, there is no appreciable difference between athletes and nonathletes. In fact, if any advantage was gained, it was by the women athletes.[27]

Another argument that has been advanced against interschool ath-letics for women is that girls would be handicapped during their menses. Jokl describes a study, done in 1930, on the effect of menstruation upon the performance of champion women track and field athletes.[28] The data revealed that participation during menstruation had no effect upon 63 percent of the performers, resulted in an improved performance in 29 percent of the performers, and produced a decrease in only 8 percent of the performers. Jokl also reported a similar investigation by Ingmam in the 1952 Olympic Games in Finland. One hundred seven female champions, consisting of nine swimmers, thirteen gymnasts, twenty-eight basketball and baseball players, fourteen skiers and skaters, and

---

[27] Ernest Jokl, "Some Clinical Data on Women's Athletics," *Journal of the Association for Physical and Mental Rehabilitation* (March-April, 1956), p. 48.

[28] *Ibid.*, p. 48.

forty-three track and field athletes, from 15 to 35 years of age, were involved in this study. All but four had participated in their sports during menstruation without experiencing any difficulty whatsoever. Of this group, twenty reported better than normal performances during menstruation; forty-five felt no effect of menstruation upon performance, and thirty-nine experienced poorer than normal results.

The statement of Hillebrandt and Meyer [29] also bears upon this same point:

Indirect evidence such as we now have is in favor of the continuous exercise as a sane regime for the normal female during menses. This policy, put into effect in England by the Council of Medical Officers of Schools Association, has met with approval. It has been associated with a marked reduction in the incidence of dysmenorrhea. Not only does it seem physiologically normal to continue exercise during menstruation but large scale experience with this policy as a mode of conduct for adolescent and young adult women has demonstrated it an intelligent prophylactic.

Another argument presented against interschool athletics for women was that it was unladylike, that it hardened the woman and made her aggressive and masculine. Today, however, the ideal girl is strong, healthy, and vigorous, but not without the desirable feminine characteristics. To consider athletic participation and feminity as incompatible is a mistake. Furthermore, as was pointed out earlier, women have a great need for training and practice in those desirable social qualities, such as cooperation, sportsmanship, loyalty, and emotional control, in which, it has been charged, they have been deficient in the past. No man or woman is born a poor sport, disloyal, or uncooperative. Women, given the same opportunities to practice and develop them, will have desirable social traits in the same degree as men. Woman, from time immemorial, has spent her life chiefly in the home, where she had no particular need or opportunity to develop these qualities under conditions of competition.

A woman has greater freedom today, however, than ever before. More and more, she is participating in the social, political, and economic life of the world. If she is to fit harmoniously into this different life, she needs a different training. A valuable part of this training will be gained through competitive sports.

Scott's observation [30] regarding the effects of interschool athletic competition upon women is pertinent:

If they are harmed in any way by their experience in these competitions, little evidence of that fact has been revealed. To those girls who object to participa-

---

29 Frances Hillebrandt and Margaret Meyer, "Physical Data Significant to Participation by Women in Physical Activities," *Research Quarterly* (March, 1939), p. 20.

30 Harry A. Scott, *Competitive Sports in Schools and Colleges* (New York, Harper & Row, Publishers, 1951), p. 455.

tion in games and sports in the belief that such activity will produce bulging, unsightly muscles, and coarsened features, the answer to their fears can be found in part by attendance at the moving picture theatre or various other places of amusement and entertainment where former sports champions appear in the role of glamorous performers in the theatre arts. It should, of course, be the ambition of every department of physical education to preserve and add to the desirable feminine qualities of girls and women. There is little evidence, however, that properly conducted athletic competition coarsens or renders women less attractive than they were when they chose to engage in competitive sports. It may be said, however, that a healthful vital appearance, skillful bodily movement, and a degree of poise in group relations, all of which may be gained through properly conducted competitive sports, are definite assets to the American ideal of womanhood.

A more valid argument against interschool competition for girls is that women leaders wished to avoid the undesirable practices that had been associated with interscholastic and intercollegiate athletics for boys. It is entirely logical that the women do not want overemphasis upon winning, overspecialization, undue publicity, public pressures, interference with classes, exploitation, and the like.

They have been particularly concerned about the conflict of interscholastic athletics with other programs that they believe should have precedence. They are determined—and properly so—that the needs of the majority will not be sacrificed to have a representative team. They recognize that few institutions have the facilities, equipment, and personnel to have interscholastic teams for girls without sacrificing other more important aspects of the program.

In addition to the service and intramural programs women physical educators use the term *extramural competition* to refer to competition with one or more other schools or organizations. Included in this category are: (1) play days and sports days, (2) telegraphic meets, (3) invitation meets, and (4) interscholastic or intercollegiate meets.

Play days and sports days are women's unique contributions to physical education. They represent the type of athletic competition that women developed as a substitute for intercollegiate and interscholastic sports. The women wished to avoid the abuses and defects that have characterized men's interschool competition. The play-day movement originated as an outgrowth of the meeting in 1923 of the National Amateur Athletic Federation when a group of women drew up their resolutions for women. The triangular play day for Mills College, Stanford University, and the University of California attracted considerable interest and led the way for subsequent play days, not only in colleges but in high schools as well.

A play day is defined as a day when girls from several schools or colleges meet and play with, rather than against, each other. They come together at the invitation of one of the institutions. The girls are divided into teams, each team representing no one school but a combination of all. In this way, there is an approximately equal number from each school on each team. Teams adopt the names of colors and are known throughout the day as blues, green, whites, and the like. The emphasis is on "sport for sport's sake" and "play with us and not against us." The customary number of activities is from five to seven, though more or fewer may be used. Experience has shown, however, that too many activities on the program are undesirable. Equally undesirable are long trips and widely diversified age groupings of the participants. Many schools have only one play day a year, but two or three appear to be the usual number.

A variation of the play day is the sports day. In this type of competition, several schools meet for the day; but the teams remain intact, and the players are not interchanged as in the play day. One or more sports may be included in the program. There is usually more than one team representing each organization participating in this form of competition. In both the play day and sports day, the activities are usually those in which the girls have been instructed in their physical education classes. A play day or sports day is not an occasion to teach new games, although it might be a good place to demonstrate a new one. Schools might be invited to bring their intramural championship team in a particular sport.

The advantages of play days and sports days are obvious. They offer particularly fine opportunities for social contacts. A large number of girls can engage in a wide variety of recreational activities. Excellent opportunities for leadership prevail. They successfully avoid the defects of interscholastic and intercollegiate athletics.

The philosophy of competition expressed by the Division of Girls and Women's Sports is that before interscholastic and intercollegiate sports are considered there should be excellent service, intramural and informal extramural (play days, sports days, telegraphic and invitation meets) programs. This philosophy is quite similar to that of most men physical educators with the exception that the *informal extramural program* has been interjected as having priority over interschool competition.

According to the philosophy expressed by the Division of Girls and Women's Sports the only type of approved competition for junior high school girls over and beyond intramural sports is occasional play days and sports days. At the senior high school level a broadening program of intramural and informal extramural competition is recommended to complement the service program. If these aspects of the program are not jeopardized a school may consider interscholastic competition. The policies suggested for the senior high school are also recommended for the collegiate level.

The majority of women physical educators will continue to oppose interscholastic and intercollegiate schedules for girls unless two conditions are met. The first of these concerns the conflict between varsity and intramural and informal extramural programs. They will never sacrifice the welfare of the majority of girls to have interschool athletics. The priority must be given to intramural and informal extramural programs (it is assumed that no conflict will be involved with the service program). If sufficient resources are available for varsity teams without any substantial interference with the intramural and informal extramural programs, a major objection will be removed.

The second condition is related to the conduct of interschool competition. Over the years women leaders have developed principles and standards for competitive athletics for girls and women. See Appendix E for the guidelines for competitive programs on the high school and college and university levels.

If interschool competition for girls could be conducted under the circumstances indicated above, the opposition of women physical educators would be materially reduced. The women recognize that it is a sound educational principle to make special provisions for the superior students. This is done in many other school activities, and the trend is definitely in the direction of providing special curricula, courses, and programs for those who are gifted. The following statement from the standards for athletics for girls and women developed by the Division of Girls' and Women's Sports [31] (this organization for girls and women is analogous to the National Federation for State High School Athletic Associations and the National Collegiate Athletic Association for boys and men) pertains to this point:

There is nothing in the creed of education which rules out the expert. There is no defensible reason why an educationally designed athletic program should either fear or fail to develop the maximum skill which an individual may possess. A well-conducted program of athletics will provide for the whole range of skill. This will be true not only in the matter of leadership and coaching provided but in the provision at every level of skill for competition between equals.

Women leaders are also cognizant of the fact that if they do not arrange interesting and challenging competition for the outstanding girls, other groups and agencies in the community will do so. Needless to say, such competition often leaves much to be desired insofar as the welfare of the girls is concerned.

Leyhe [32] investigated the opinions of over 800 women members of

[31] Committee on Standards of the National Section for Girls' and Women's Sports, "Standards in Athletics for Girls and Women."

[32] Naomi Leyhe, *Attitudes of Women Members of the American Association for Health, Physical Education, and Recreation toward Competition in Sports for Girls and Women.* Unpublished doctoral dissertation, University of Indiana, 1955, microcards.

the American Association for Health, Physical Education, and Recreation concerning competitive athletics for girls and women. She found that the great majority was opposed to national, state, district, and county tournaments for girls and women. However, in regard to conducting a schedule of varsity competition for girls under sound leadership and high standards a bare majority was opposed. The women were quite generally favorable to interschool competition in individual sports. The women who themselves had competed in interschool sports were much more favorable to such competition than were those who had not competed. The number of women opposed to intercollegiate competition was not so great as the number opposed to interscholastic competition.

Leyhe's data bear out that women physical educators have appreciably modified their opposition to interschool competition for girls in the past quarter century. However, the majority is not prepared to endorse such an athletic program until it can be conducted toward the best interest of all the girls. Since few schools have or will have in the near future the resources to conduct *both* an intramural and a full extramural program it will undoubtedly be many years before the present pattern is appreciably altered.

The academic teacher versus the physical educator as coach. The question of whether it is better to have an academic teacher rather than the physical educator do the coaching of varsity teams has been extensively debated. It is argued that if the physical educator teaches his classes as he should, he is likely to come to varsity practices devoid of the energy and the enthusiasm he should have. A much more serious disadvantage is the neglect on the part of physical educators of their duties in the instructional program. Because of the pressure to win and the inordinate demand upon their time, many physical educators who serve as coaches either stop teaching and become "ball tossers" in order to devote more time to preparation for their practices, or they exploit their students to seek out and develop material for their varsity squads. There is little doubt that instructional and intramural programs would be conducted on a much higher level if physical education instructors were relieved of their coaching responsibilities. The excellent programs conducted by women physical educators provide ample evidence of this fact.

On the other hand, the major advantage of the physical education teacher as a coach is that he is specifically prepared for this responsibility. There are three separate aspects of this preparation: (1) with his background of the philosophy and principles of physical education he can better appreciate the place and purposes of athletics in the total school program, (2) he will possess the physiological, anatomical, and health background necessary to protect and safeguard the health and welfare of the participants, and (3) he has a much broader and more diversified preparation for the actual coaching. Also, the closer acquaintance of the physical educator with all the boys in the school is a distinct advantage. Having these boys in his physical education classes gives him the opportunity to assess their athletic potentialities.

The academic teacher has several advantages. He is confined to the classroom all day and will profit greatly from the opportunity to participate in a vigorous activity program. This will provide a wholesome diversion that will not interfere with his teaching responsibilities because, ordinarily, academic teachers coach only one sport. The informal relationship with the students helps the academic teacher understand them better and gives him a prestige he could not otherwise obtain. It is highly beneficial to the morale of the school as a whole to have a number of academic men interested in and cooperating with the boys in athletics.

The only serious disadvantage of academic teachers as coaches is that ordinarily they do not have special preparation for this assignment. To play on a varsity team in college does not constitute adequate preparation for coaching. If the school administrator were fortunate to have some academic teachers with major or minor preparation in physical education, this disadvantage would not pertain.

Several considerations are involved in providing a solution to this problem. In the first place, most administrators must use a combination of physical education and academic teachers to meet the requirement of coaches. Considering the number of sports in which competition is conducted, the necessity of having second, or junior, varsity and perhaps even freshman teams, and the desirability of having more than one coach per team in certain sports, the school administrator is hard put to provide the necessary leadership. He has no other recourse but to use academic teachers.

The school administrator can go a long way in solving the problem by employing men as academic teachers who are adequately prepared to coach. He might be in a position to insist that these staff members obtain additional training in summer sessions. When academic teachers lack a suitable background they can be used advantageously as assistant coaches or as coaches of the milder, "nonpressure" sports. The school administrator must accept his responsibility of insisting that physical educators who do coach meet all their obligations insofar as the instructional and intramural programs are concerned. Finally, the entire athletic program should be directed by an individual with a good physical education background. His supervision will do much to reduce or prevent mistakes by untrained academic teachers.

Reducing overemphasis. Overemphasis in interschool competition is commonly seen in the heavy schedules and the overly long seasons of some teams. To reduce such overemphasis, many state athletic associations restrict both the number of games which can be scheduled in a sport and the length of the sports season. Twenty-seven state high school associations limit the number of football games, and thirty-five limit the number of basketball games in which member schools may engage. Restrictions are ordinarily placed only upon football and basketball schedules. Twenty basketball and nine or ten football games represent the average number of games permitted. Thirty-three states set definite dates for the beginning and end of the various sports seasons. Because of the varying climatic conditions, the dates of beginning and ending of the sports seasons will differ. In most states, the football season begins on the first day of September and terminates on the Saturday after Thanksgiving. The basketball season commonly extends from the first day of December to the last day of the state basketball tournament.

Thirty-two state athletic associations prohibit spring football practice. Some collegiate conferences have banned or reduced spring football. Thirty-eight state associations have eliminated all-star games. All national championship competition on the secondary school level has been prohibited.

Public pressures. Public pressures of various kinds are exerted upon educational administrators on both the secondary school and college and university levels when dissatisfaction develops about the interschool athletic program. Webber [33] identifies these pressure groups as:

1. Booster or Quarterback Clubs
2. Parents. In this group are those parents who are dissatisfied with the won–lost record of the team; those who have sons they feel should be playing more; and those who desire to exploit their sons' athletic ability.
3. Sports writers and announcers
4. Promoters of special events

These groups frequently assist the athletic program in a variety of ways. They may purchase and erect scoreboards, obtain additional seating capacity, provide funds for the purchase of needed athletic equipment, procure jackets for players and coaches, and arrange postseason banquets. However, Webber [34] points out some of the undesirable results of such pressure groups.

1. Overemphasis on winning
2. Public criticism of the coach
3. The use of key athletes, regardless of physical condition
4. Participation in championships or all-star games

[33] Robert Webber, "Public Pressures and Their Effect on Athletes," *Bulletin of the National Association of Secondary School Principals,* Vol. 44, No. 256 (May, 1960).
[34] *Ibid.*

5. Presentation of special awards to winning teams, outstanding players and successful coaches
6. Extensive publicity concentrated on a few athletes
7. Overemphasis on spectator sports

The solution to the problem of undesirable pressure groups has several facets. One of the most important of these is a clear, concise statement of athletic philosophy and the policies that will guide the conduct of the athletic program. This statement should be read annually at the first meeting of these pressure groups.

A second important consideration is the selection of the right type of coach. The coach who is selfishly interested in making a name for himself will make use of pressure groups in unacceptable ways. He can create serious problems for the institution and the athletic director by soliciting undesirable forms of assistance from outside groups. The preferred type of coach is one who is interested in the educational objectives of athletics and who subscribes completely to the athletic philosophy and policies of the school.

The athletic director and the educational administrator must stand behind the coach when criticisms come from pressure groups. Mistakes and defeats are inevitable but the solid support of the coach by his superiors will not only maintain the morale of the players and the coaching staff but will counter the undeserved judgments of critics.

The final measure to employ in dealing with pressure groups is to take the initiative in guiding their activities. They cannot be ignored. Rather than to become involved in controversy it has been found necessary to maintain good public relations with them. Meetings should be held and philosophy and policies explained. If proper rapport can be established with them such groups can become an asset rather than a liability to the athletic program.

Desirable trends in athletics

There are definite trends in intercollegiate and interscholastic athletics. Athletics, as they are conducted today, are far more acceptable educationally than they were thirty years ago. The direction in which they seem to be traveling augurs well for interschool athletics of the future. More and more of the objectionable features are being eliminated, and it is safe to predict that, in the not-too-distant future, athletics will be conducted to the satisfaction of educators and to the permanent enrichment of the educational program. Some of the trends toward more educationally significant goals are pointed out below.

Increasing power of athletic associations and conferences. The state associations are gradually expanding their powers and assuming more and more control of interscholastic athletics within their jurisdiction. Their original concern was eligibility, but now their functions have broadened to include athletic insurance, officials, awards, athletic equipment, the conduct of meets and tournaments, the classification of schools, and the development of high school standards for high school boys. This expansion of the powers and functions of the state associations is undoubtedly a step in the right direction. There can be no more effective agency in the state for raising the plane of interscholastic athletics to the high level upon which it should be conducted. College and high school athletic conferences may also become powerful forces for improving the standards of interschool athletics. Progress can be made only through the medium of well-organized groups.

Classifying schools and players. There seems to be a distinct trend toward classifying schools and players. Instead of having one state championhip, some states are conducting tournaments for two or three types of schools, depending upon their size. In Wisconsin, Class A schools are those with an enrollment of 500 or more, Class B from 160 to 500, and Class C under 160 pupils. This is a much more equitable method of conducting tournaments, and it has proved extremely popular. The small schools have an equal opportunity under this setup, and athletics have been stimulated in these schools. The practice of having "B" teams and lightweight teams is also an advancement over the single heavyweight team. Not only does this plan give more boys an opportunity to engage in interschool athletics, but the lighter boys, who would have no chance to make the heavyweight team, are able to obtain the benefits of competition. Educationally, the classification of schools and players is sound procedure.

Interschool athletics for all. There are many more boys today who are given the advantages of intercollegiate and interscholastic athletics than ever before. For years, football, baseball, basketball, and track were practically the only sports in which interschool competition was provided in most schools. In the decade of the thirties, there was a trend to schedule competition in many more sports. World War II has greatly accentuated this trend. The situation in secondary schools for the 1964-1965 school year is depicted in Table 8-6.

Increase in benefit and protection plans. State high school athletic associations have continued to improve their programs to take care of athletes who become injured in athletic competition. These plans have been so successful that they are gradually expanding in a number of ways. Not only are they providing more and better coverage to varsity athletes but they are now embracing students injured in the service and intramural programs.

Wider distribution of honors. The tendency for teams to elect co-captains and for the coach to appoint captains for different games is in

Table 8-6. Sports participation survey.

Sport	Number Schools	Number Participants
Archery	30	175
Badminton	214	1,956
Baseball	13,248	357,145
Basketball	19,112	639,755
Bowling	456	8,220
Cross-Country	5,390	101,773
Curling	581	5,393
Decathlon	25	75
Fencing	22	184
Field Hockey	2	40
Football: 11-Man	12,922	772,802
8-Man	1,060	25,241
6-Man	237	4,744
Golf	5,792	62,630
Gymnastics	613	13,091
Hockey	486	11,665
Lacrosse	59	1,500
One-Mile Team Race	105	840
Pentathlon	55	130
Riflery	270	4,210
Rowing	101	505
Rugby	10	192
Rugger	23	390
Skiing	400	6,479
Soccer	1,443	32,506
Softball	348	7,071
Swimming	2,042	60,216
Tennis	5,072	76,368
Track and Field	15,524	512,271
Track (Indoor)	646	8,322
Volleyball	3,488	44,012
Water Polo	106	4,367
Wrestling	4,237	126,862

Source: National Federation of State High School Athletic Association, *Handbook 1964-65* (Chicago, 1965), p. 58.

contrast to the practice in the past. This is a healthy sign that the opportunities for leadership are being distributed more liberally than heretofore. Another indication of the same tendency is the large number of awards that are granted to all teams. Substitutions are made much more frequently than they have been in the past. With "B" and lightweight teams, with limitation of participation, with more frequent substitution, and with a wider variety of sports, the ideal of "athletics for all" may more nearly approach "interschool athletics for all."

Reduction in school time lost. Much greater consideration is given today to the time lost from school by athletes. Long trips are things of the past for most high schools. Intersectional games were frequent a decade ago, but they are quite exceptional today in high schools. Forty-two state associations have adopted the policy of prohibiting postseason games of any nature. Schools are competing within their conferences and against local opponents. Emphasis on national championships has been eliminated, and there is considerable question as to the advisability of state championships. The trend in many high schools to refrain from playing contests on a day or night preceding a school day to avoid distraction from school work is another indication that athletics are being conducted more to the satisfaction of educators. Friday is the most popular day for interscholastic contests, but most colleges play on Saturday, although this practice is frequently reversed.

Extra pay for coaches. The practice of paying high school coaches an additional stipend for their coaching duties developed during World War II. Agitation for extra pay arose during the war when many other teachers were able to supplement their incomes by various types of employment in the afternoons after their school duties were over. Coaches felt they were entitled to additional remuneration because in most cases the time devoted to their coaching duties was over and above a full teaching load.

A survey by the National Education Association showed that coaches received additional amounts above their regular salaries in 157 of 197 cities. There is every reason to believe that in the years since this survey was made the percentage of coaches who received extra compensation has increased appreciably. This policy was adopted first in the larger cities. However, the practice has since spread to other cities and to smaller communities. The great majority of interscholastic coaches are now recipients of extra pay for their coaching duties.

Jack George [35] has described the arguments that the advocates of the extra pay philosophy use to support their point of view:

1. Since many school systems have established a single salary scale for grades K-12, teachers who assume the leadership in the after-school, evening, and weekend activities are giving additional time and effort as compared to those who do not.

2. Many teachers, especially those with family responsibilities, still find it necessary to seek additional sources of income. Extra pay for school activities makes it possible for school staff members to devote their time and efforts to the supervision and direction of school-sponsored programs.

[35] Jack George, "Extra Pay for Extra Services," *Administration of High School Athletics. Report of a National Conference* (Washington, D.C., American Association for Health, Physical Education and Recreation, 1962), p. 59.

3. Since compensated tutoring opportunities are becoming more available, a teacher cannot afford to conduct after-school activities without pay.

4. Many schools base salary increments on specified degrees and a number of graduate credits. Time devoted to after-school, evening, and Saturday activities may hinder a teacher from pursuing graduate work. These activities automatically limit the time they can devote to study during the school year, thereby decreasing and delaying earning potential.

5. Most teachers who have special ability or talent that is utilized in these activities spend considerable time attending meetings and clinics and reading appropriate journals and magazines. This self-improvement process is time-consuming and expensive and contributes to the objective of upgrading the skill of conducting the activity.

6. Since these teachers are often directly involved with the public, for example, in dramatics, band concerts, and sports, they become vital school public relations personnel. Reimbursement for services will create a more favorable teacher selection situation within a school.

7. While we like to believe that all teachers are dedicated, it is obvious that extra pay for extra services attracts better teachers.

The arguments against extra compensation are:

1. It is difficult to define "extra work." Virtually all teachers have responsibilities that extend beyond the normal teaching schedule. Preparation for classes, grading papers, conferring with students and rendering reports are examples of duties that academic teachers routinely perform. A problem is created about where to draw the line between those who receive extra compensation and those who do not.

2. Overloading any teacher is undesirable because eventually his teaching effectiveness will be reduced. Teachers carrying extra work will inevitably neglect some of their other duties. All too often the service program has paid the price of coaches who were overloaded with work.

3. Unlike workers in business and industry professional personnel are expected to meet the demands of their work without seeking additional remuneration. According to their ethical standards professionals are obligated to perform their services without regard to compensation for overtime.

To solve this dilemma some school administrators reduce the teaching load of coaches in order to eliminate an overload situation. This will, of course, require the employment of additional personnel. Rarely are the coaches satisfied with such an arrangement. In some communities coaches are granted additional compensation in only one sport. This has the effect of avoiding overloading the coaches for the entire academic year.

In some school districts only coaches receive compensation for extra services. This arrangement is not equitable. Faculty members involved in dramatics, student publications, musical organizations, intramural athletics, girls' athletic association, cheerleading, and the like believe they have as good a case for extra pay as the coaches. If extra compensation is to be provided it should be available to all who perform services over and beyond a normal day.

Certification of coaches. Sentiment in favor of requiring coaches to be better prepared professionally for these duties is increasing rapidly. Thirty-eight states require high school coaches to be certified teachers. However, in only several are special professional requirements imposed. While a majority of coaches are physical education majors or minors a substantial percentage have had no preparation whatsoever for such responsibilities. Such individuals are usually former college athletes who qualify as teachers by virtue of having a teaching major in an academic subject.

It is this latter group that presents the problem. They clearly lack most of the professional qualifications for coaching. According to Frost [36] the special competencies over and above those required for standard teacher certification are:

1. An understanding of the relationship of the interscholastic athletic program and the particular sport they are coaching to the total education program
2. A knowledge of first aid and the safety practices and techniques pertinent to the sport they are coaching
3. An understanding of the possibilities of legal liability as well as sound practices and preventive measures
4. A thorough knowledge and understanding of the biological, social, moral, emotional and spiritual values which may accrue from the activity and the best methods of bringing about these desirable outcomes
5. A knowledge of the most accepted principles of growth and development and their implications for the sport
6. An understanding of the best methods of developing and conditioning members of athletic squads
7. A knowledge of the basic principles in the care and prevention of injuries together with an understanding of the proper relationship of the coach to the school or team physician
8. The ability to speak in public so as to bring credit to the profession and the school and so as to more effectively inform the public of the educational possibilities of his sport
9. An understanding of the basic psychological principles of motivation, stress, play, emotion and group interaction
10. A thorough knowledge of the fundamentals, offenses, defenses, strategies and teaching methods involved in the particular sport. Included will be squad organization, coaching techniques, and sound motivational procedures
11. A knowledge and a sense of responsibility for local, state, and national rules and regulations

36 Reuben B. Frost, "Should Coaches Be Certified?" An address presented at the Third General Session of the 45th Annual Meeting of the National Federation of State High School Athletic Associations, June 29, 1964, pp. 12-13.

Many of those who support special certification for coaches would not insist upon it for coaches of such sports as tennis, golf, bowling, and volleyball. Sports usually thought of as needing certified coaches include football, basketball, wrestling, gymnastics, hockey, soccer, swimming, and track and field. The factor that differentiates these two groups of sports is the greater intensity of the latter category with the implication of danger to the participants.

City and state directors of physical education and executive-secretaries of state athletic associations are overwhelmingly in favor of professional certification for coaches. Those who have reservations about such certification are the high school principals. When they review their requirements for head and assistant coaches for varsity, reserve, and freshmen teams they become concerned about meeting their requirements if professional certification is required. To help solve this problem it has been suggested that certification should only be required of head coaches of the potentially hazardous sports.

In Indiana in senior high schools the varsity head football and basketball coach shall be "a licensed physical education teacher." All other coaches in seventh to twelfth grades shall be regularly licensed teachers with at least eight semester hours of approved college credit in first aid and in courses related to physical growth and development.

In Minnesota the following law [37] will go into effect for the 1966-1967 school year:

1. A teacher *in a secondary school* who is head coach in any of the following areas: football, basketball, track, hockey, wrestling, baseball, shall be certificated either through professional preparation in the physical education major or minor *program,* or through a special coaching requirement in physical education.

The special coaching requirement is acceptable when the approved preparing institution certifies to the commissioner of education that such person has completed, in addition to his regular teacher education program, not less than *nine* quarter hours in courses *of which Principles of Physical Education is required, and the remaining courses selected from at least two of* the following four areas:

Administration of Athletics
First Aid and Prevention & Care of Athletic Injuries
Human Science
Coaching and Athletic Techniques

2. Effective with the 1966-67 school year, such certification of new head coaches as stated above shall become mandatory. This requirement does not apply to teachers contracted for as head coaches prior to September 1, 1966.

Summer competition. One of the most recent innovations in interscholastic athletics is the continuation of athletic competition through

---

[37] *Administrative Manual for Minnesota Public Schools,* 1966, Code VI, Section 5076.6, Public School Athletic Coaches.

the summer months. Minnesota and Iowa have pioneered in this new development. In these states several hundred schools compete in baseball, swimming, tennis, and golf. Competition is first carried on within districts. The district winners compete for the state championship. Ten states now carry on summer baseball programs.

Competition throughout the summer is carried on in the same manner as it is during the school year, except that the students do not attend classes. The standard rules of the state athletic association govern all contests, and the coaches are regular members of the faculty. In many communities one or more of the regular coaches are retained on a twelve-month basis to supervise the summer activities. All students who were eligible during the second semester are eligible for summer competition. Practices are held in the late afternoons or evenings.

This new development appears to have great possibilities. In most states the sports program in the spring is always handicapped by inclement weather. The summer months are ideal for carrying on competition in such sports as baseball, swimming, tennis, and golf. Because many communities have outdoor pools, the number of schools that can compete in interscholastic swimming during the summer months far exceeds the number that can do so during the school year. Because of longer schedules and better facilities, summer interscholastic competition reaches more students over a longer period of time. In addition, these sports are splendid recreational activities at this time of the year. It is vitally important that as many students as possible be brought into the summer athletic program.

SELECTED REFERENCES

AAHPER, *Administration of High School Athletics* (Washington, D.C., American Association for Health, Physical Education and Recreation, 1962).

AAHPER, *Coaches' Handbook* (Washington, D.C., American Association for Health, Physical Education and Recreation, 1960).

AAHPER, *Current Administrative Problems* (Washington, D.C., American Association for Health, Physical Education and Recreation, 1960).

AAHPER, *Spectator Sportsmanship* (Washington, D.C., American Association for Health, Physical Education and Recreation, 1961).

AAHPER, *Values in Sports* (Washington, D.C., American Association for Health, Physical Education and Recreation, 1962).

Educational Policies Commission, *School Athletics* (Washington, D.C., National

Education Association and American Association of School Administrators, 1954).

Forsythe, Charles, *The Administration of High School Athletics,* 4th ed. (Englewood Cliffs, N.J., Prentice-Hall, Inc., 1962).

Forsythe, Charles, *The Athletic Director's Handbook* (Englewood Cliffs, N.J., Prentice-Hall, Inc., 1956).

National Federation of State High School Athletic Associations, *Handbook: 1964-65* (Chicago, 1965).

9

intramural athletics

Development of intramural athletics

Translated literally, intramural means "within the walls." Intramural athletics, therefore, may be defined as athletic activities carried on within the walls of an institution. Intramural athletics appeared in the schools long before anyone even thought of physical education and interschool athletics. The desire to play is universal, and some form of it has always existed. It seems inconceivable that this powerful urge could have been entirely suppressed in our first educational institutions. The beginnings of intramural athletics can undoubtedly be traced, then, to the informal sports and games that were indulged in by our first students in their leisure moments. This type of play, within the walls of the institution, may properly be considered intramural athletics, although it does not exactly resemble our intramural athletics of today.

There is ample evidence that boys participated in various sports in our early American schools despite the obstacles in the form of hostile teachers and the Puritan philosophy of the sinfulness and foolishness of play. As educational institutions multiplied and the school population increased, informal play activities among students expanded. The haphazard nature of these activities gradually gave way to better organization. Competition was organized between societies, fraternities, dormitories, and classes. The students conducted their activities by themselves. The faculty was indifferent. In 1859, the Yale undergraduate body was divided into twelve intramural boating clubs of twenty men each. These contests continued for nine years before giving way to a system of interclass crews. Baseball was organized as an intramural sport at Princeton in 1864. Field days for track and field sports were conducted on an in-tramural basis at Yale and Princeton about this time.

As the intramural program developed, students looked beyond the confines of their own institutions for competition. It is interesting that interschool athletics arose from intramural sports. But the development of interschool athletics had no deleterious effect on intramurals. The students continued to play among themselves with no faculty guidance or interference. The fact that these activities continued with unabated interest in the face of the bitter interschool rivalries is ample testimony to the vitality of intramural athletics. Those students who were not good enough to represent their school against other schools expressed their natural desire for play and competition against their fellow students. Intramural athletics, discovered by students and promoted by students, continued to expand and develop.

About the beginning of the twentieth century, some progressive physical educators began to take an interest in these intramural pro-grams. They saw in these activities unusual opportunities to broaden the scope of physical education. From 1907 to 1912 it became increas-ingly apparent that some authorized individual was needed to control and regulate these expanding activities. The athletic associations at Michigan and Ohio State made provision for departments of intramural athletics in 1913. Other schools soon followed their example. World War I gave a tremendous impetus to intramural sports. Athletic depart-ments were always favorably disposed, because they saw in intramural athletics a training ground for varsity material. In high schools the movement to adopt intramural departments came into full swing in 1925. A steady growth of intramural athletics continued in colleges and universities up to World War II. The development was considerably slower in the secondary schools. Because so many college men were drawn into the armed services, the intramural programs were greatly curtailed during the war.

As the previous war had done, World War II exerted a profound effect upon intramural programs. The war had clearly demonstrated the values of sports, and a general conviction prevailed that intramurals must be made available to all who were unable to make the institutional teams. A determined effort was made to provide more intramural services to more students. Programs were expanded, chiefly by including addi-tional activities. While the ideal "athletics for all" was not attained in most institutions, it was more nearly approximated than ever before.

The relationship of intramural athletics to required physical education and interschool athletics

Because intramural activities were originally initiated and con-ducted by students and were carried on outside of regular school hours on a voluntary, noncredit basis, they were considered extracurricular in nature. However, when the concept of the curriculum was broadened to encompass all the activities conducted under school auspices, both intramural and interschool athletics came to be considered legitimate curricular activities. Today, the intramural program is an integral part of the physical education program and justifies the expenditures and attention given to it.

The purpose of intramural sports is to supplement the curricular activities of physical education in order that the objectives of physical education may be more completely realized. Intramural activities have the same relation to required physical education as the school paper has to journalism and debating has to public speaking. The physical education curriculum functions mainly in developing the fundamentals of various sports and knowledges and of appreciations and desires in connection with them. An adequate amount of competition is not possible in the instructional classes. Specialization is impossible because of the small time allotment and the large number of activities which deserve consideration. Intramural athletics offer the opportunity for more competition and for specialization in preferred activities. The required program should develop the fundamental skills, techniques, and knowledge of golf, tennis, badminton, handball, swimming, volleyball, softball, wrestling, basketball, baseball, and other sports. To the greatest extent possible, an appreciation of these different sports and a desire to engage in them further should be established.

Each student will have individual preferences, which he should express in intramural athletics. By continuing his participation, he will develop more skill and realize more pleasure. An individual enjoys doing what he does well. With the increased skill and satisfaction comes a heightening of all the values, physical, mental, and social, which are attributed to physical education. Intramural athletics, arising out of the required activities, will not only result in the maximal function of the physical education curriculum but will bring about a more effective intramural program. The extension of the work of physical education into the informal activities of the intramural program naturally calls for a close cooperation between those in charge of both programs.

Interschool athletics represent the peak of the physical education pyramid. The poor and mediocre athlete expresses himself in intramural sports, but the place for the superior athlete is in interschool sports. The division of students into groups of approximately equal ability is endorsed by educators. Certainly, there are more educational values to be derived when the skilled athletes and the poor and mediocre athletes compete against opponents of equal ability. The greatest good of the greatest number should be the athletic ideal, and it can only be realized by a comprehensive, integrated physical education program, including the required, intramural, and interschool activities. Each of these phases of the total program should aid and supplement the others. The interschool program serves as an incentive to the required and intramural programs. Intramural athletics must not be conducted as a training ground for varsity athletics. There can be no objection, however, if out of the intramural activities varsity material is developed, provided this is incidental.

Organization of the intramural department

The intramural activities should be an integral part of the physical education program. As such, it should derive its financial support from regular school funds. Authorities are unanimous in their agreement in this matter, and it is fortunate that only a small percentage of high school and college intramural programs are administered and supported as a part of the interschool athletic program. Grambeau's survey [1] revealed that the department of physical education controlled the intramural athletic program in fifty-five of the sixty-seven colleges and universities studied. Figures 9-1 to 9-3 indicate recommended organizational relationships of intramural athletics in a college, a large high school, and a small high school.

The intramural director. The intramural department is usually headed by one individual, known as the director of intramural athletics. The plan of placing one person in full charge of intramural athletics is considered the most effective way of organizing and coordinating all the intramural activities. However, very few schools can afford a full-time director. In the majority of institutions, the intramural director has other duties to perform in addition to those connected with the administration of the intramural department. He may be the director of athletics or physical education. He is frequently a coach and just as often an instructor of physical education. Regardless of what his other duties may be, the intramural director should be the person best qualified for the position.

An essential criterion of the intramural director is enthusiasm. Regardless of other desirable qualifications, the director will not be successful in overcoming the difficulties and problems he will encounter unless he gives dedicated and resourceful leadership to the program. A desultory, disinterested attitude on the part of the director toward intramurals explains many weak programs.

Organizational ability is a prerequisite to success. Professional preparation in the organization and administration of intramural ath-

---

[1] Rodney J. Grambeau, *A Survey of the Administration of Intramural Sports Programs for Men in Selected Colleges and Universities in North America.* Ed.D. dissertation, University of Michigan, 1959, p. 166.

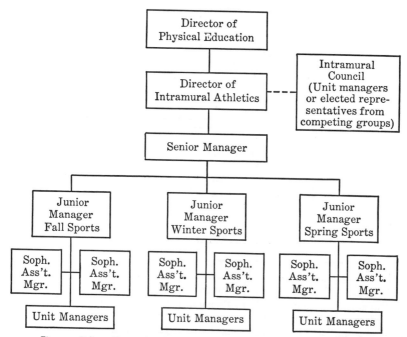

Figure 9-1. Organization of Intramural Program for Colleges.

letics is invaluable. He must have an understanding of the relationship between the physical education service program and intramurals.

The most readily available individual will not often be a successful director. Neither will an intramural department function properly when the various coaches of the different sports combine to administer the program. Nothing will do more harm to an intramural program than fluctuating leadership throughout the year. This is a weak administrative setup and should be avoided at all cost.

The custom of having coaches assist in the intramural department has been criticized on the grounds that the coaches are primarily interested in developing candidates for their respective teams and that this interest dominates their intramural duties. If coaches had adequate physical education backgrounds, there would be little objection to their work in intramurals. The intramural director requires assistance, and the coaches can be of great help in their various specialties or in their off seasons.

The practice of permitting students to control intramural athletics has serious disadvantages. The proper administration of the program requires more time than students can afford, and charges of politics and favoritism often result. Furthermore, students graduate after they

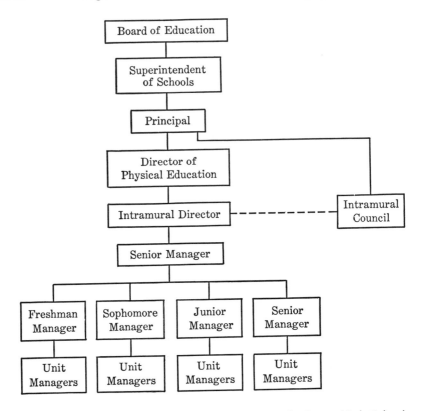

Figure 9-2. Organization of Intramural Program for Large High Schools.

have accumulated sufficient experience to handle the position capably. Fluctuating leadership means fluctuating policies. The mere fact that a staff member is the director does not indicate that all of the opportunities for valuable experience and training for students are eliminated.

Intramural councils. Many secondary schools and the great majority of colleges and universities make use of intramural boards, councils, or committees to help administer the program. It is usually made up of the intramural director, senior manager, representatives of the participating groups, a member from the student council, and interested faculty members. The functions of these boards include formulating policies, making eligibility rules and modifying the rules of various sports to meet local conditions, acting upon protests, deciding forfeits, and approving the budget.

Such a board is of great assistance to the intramural director. In addition, it provides an exceptional opportunity for students to exercise leadership. The democratic process also gives the program more vitality and appeal because the students feel they are a part of it.

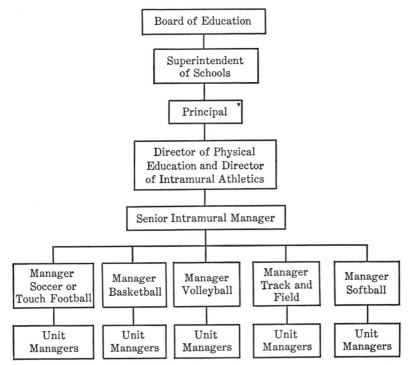

Figure 9-3. Organization of Intramural Program for Small High Schools.

Student managers. The student managers really perform most of the work of the intramural department. The number of managers varies from school to school, but in nearly every case there are fewer senior managers than sophomore and junior managers. A large number of sophomore managers try out during the year. They usually are assigned to one sport during a season, and they assist in conducting the competition in this activity. From this list two or four junior managers are selected on the basis of their service and qualifications. One senior, who is called the intramural manager, is chosen to cooperate with the intramural director in conducting the whole program. Oftentimes, the director serves in an advisory capacity and permits the manager to administer the program. The duties of the senior manager vary, but in general he is responsible for making out schedules, for notifying teams of their games and assignments, for promoting publicity, for assembling data on contests, for assigning duties to the sophomore and junior assistants, and for general supervision of the program. The many responsibilities and duties of the senior intramural manager combine to present an exceptional practical training in leadership and executive ability.

The senior manager is usually the only manager who is given an award, which is usually a school letter with or without a sweater. When a letter is awarded, it is usually modified in some way to distinguish it from the regular varsity letter. Some schools award gold medals, others numerals or special intramural insignia. In rare instances the senior manager is paid for his services. Some schools present the junior managers with an award. The sophomore managers are not given awards, but they receive valuable experience acting as officials, scorekeepers, and timekeepers, and handling other details.

Team managers. Each unit participating in the intramural program should be represented by a manager. This individual serves as the contact man between the intramural department and the unit. He usually acts in this capacity for the school year. He submits entries, eligibility lists, and protests, if any. He announces scheduled contests and assumes the responsibility of getting his team to the proper area at the correct time. He may also coach the team, although many units will appoint separate coaches. Some individual must assume the responsibility of the team when an intramural contest is being played. This may be the team manager, the coach, or the captain.

Intramural finances

Fortunately, intramural athletics are not expensive. Considering the large number of students who participate, the cost per capita is exceptionally small and the value received extraordinarily large. There are probably more benefits to pupils realized per dollar invested in a well-planned and well-directed intramural program of sports than in almost any other activity in which pupils participate.

High schools. In a survey of intramural programs in the high schools of Pennsylvania Krupa [2] found that the per pupil cost in small high schools (1-199 pupils) was 92 cents; for the medium school (200-499 pupils) 44 cents; for the large school (500-999 pupils) 32 cents; for the very large school (over 1000 pupils) 27 cents; and for all high schools 36 cents. The cost per student participant for the small schools was $1.86, for the medium schools $1.42, for the large schools $1.09, for the very large schools $1.20, and for all schools $1.24. These costs have undoubtedly increased since Krupa made this survey.

The money is expended upon awards, office supplies, labor, equipment, intramural handbooks, insurance, officiating, and salaries. The per capita cost of intramurals in high schools is not as great as in colleges. Where all the students are located in one building and are readily

2 Joseph H. Krupa, *A Study of Intramural Sports for Boys in the Public Secondary Schools of Pennsylvania.* Ed.D. dissertation, University of Pittsburgh, 1953, p. 54.

available, office expense is materially reduced. The high school awards are much less expensive also. The officials in high school intramurals are rarely paid, as compared to those in college intramurals. The equipment item may be greater or smaller, depending upon the extent to which equipment is furnished to the players. Intramural departments, as a rule, require the players to supply their personal equipment. Footballs, basketballs, soccerballs, volleyballs, nets, bases, and the like are usually provided. This equipment is ordinarily borrowed from the physical education department. Beuttler's study [3] in Iowa revealed that in 92.4 percent of secondary schools the equipment from the physical education program was used for intramural activities. A charge is assessed against the intramural program in some schools for the use of this equipment. The regular physical education facilities are used when available.

The physical education budget is the major source of intramural funds. In Krupa's investigation [4] it was revealed that 84 percent of the revenue for intramural athletics in Pennsylvania high schools came from physical education budgets. In Iowa this figure was 87.9 percent. This is as it should be. An admission charge to a special intramural event is a good source of revenue. Other sources are concessions, carnivals, entry fees, a student activity budget, and interscholastic athletics. The trend is definitely away from depending upon gate receipts from interscholastic athletics.

Colleges and universities. Scott,[5] in a survey of intramural programs in liberal arts colleges, found that the cost of intramural athletics in small institutions was $2.02 per male student, or $3.14 per student participant; in medium-sized colleges the cost was $1.79 per male student, or $3.07 for each participant; and in large colleges the cost was $1.35 for each male student, or $2.11 for each participant. The average cost for all institutions was $1.62 per student, or $2.64 per participant.

Another more recent study [6] revealed that the overall cost averaged $2.73 per student enrolled. In state institutions the average was $2.49 per student; in private colleges it was $3.49 and in denominational institutions it was $1.96. The range of amount spent per student was 12 cents to $5.12 in state colleges, 28 cents to $27.50 in private colleges and 63 cents to $3.79 in denominational institutions. It should be noted, however, that these costs do not reflect the expenses involved in facilities, staff personnel, and many items of equipment.

The major expenditures are for awards, office supplies, postage,

3 Fred C. Beuttler, "Boys' Intramural Athletic Programs in Iowa's Secondary Schools," *11th Annual Proceedings of the National Intermural Association* (1960), p. 32.

4 *Op. cit.*, p. 57.

5 Elmer B. Scott, *An Evaluation of Intramural Sports Programs for Men in Selected Liberal Arts Colleges*. P.E.D. dissertation, University of Indiana, 1954.

6 H. Spurgeon Cherry, *Survey Report on Financing College Intramurals* (University of Florida, 1965).

officiating, intramural handbooks, secretarial assistance, equipment, and salaries.

The physical education budget is the main source of support for intramural athletics in colleges and universities. However, in some institutions, the sole or major source of support comes from intercollegiate athletics. A number of colleges and universities use student activity fees to finance intramurals. Entry fees from the competing groups supply a portion of the necessary funds. There is much less reliance upon concessions, carnivals, plays, magazine sales, and other student efforts in college than in secondary schools.

Intramural finances in the colleges are handled by the athletic director, the business manager, the intramural director, and the head student manager. Student entry fees are usually collected by student managers. The intramural director approves all expenditures. The intramural director cooperates with either the athletic director or the head of the physical education department in developing the intramural budget.

Units of competition

Good units of competition contribute a great deal to the success of the intramural program. Selection of competing units is not a problem in the individual sports, for each individual is a unit by himself (though certain groups encourage their members to enter into individual competition). Strong units for team sports are necessary, however, inasmuch as teams tend to break up after several defeats. Homogeneous groups which are bound together by some common bond make the best competitive units.

College and university units. In institutions of higher learning, the fraternity is the most effective unit of intramural competition. Dormitories are also strong units, particularly if they are not too large. The trend to divide students into smaller dormitory groups will make for better competitive units. Both fraternity and dormitory students develop a strong group solidarity, and they are easily organized for intramural competition.

In the past, class units, that is, freshmen, sophomores, juniors and seniors, have been extensively employed. Interclass competition is especially successful in the smaller colleges. Divisions within the college or university, such as liberal arts, engineering, and education, are natural groups that might be used as bases of competition. In larger institutions, the various colleges can be divided into their different departments, such as civil engineering and mechanical engineering and further subdivided into freshman, sophomore, junior, and senior engineering. Other competitive groups may be military units (where ROTC programs are in operation), sports clubs, literary societies, and eating and boarding clubs.

The biggest problem of most intramural directors is to obtain sufficient participation of the unorganized, independent students. These students will participate satisfactorily in single and dual sports, particularly if the tournaments are well publicized and energetically promoted. The real difficulty is to secure participation in team sports. The independent students are not permanent and they have no basis for loyalty. They are hard to contact. The crucial factor is the leadership of these groups of students. All methods of motivating and promoting participation must be consistently and effectively employed to get a substantial percentage of independent students into the program.

A number of schools have discovered that the best way to organize the independents is to divide the entire student residential area into districts or zones. The zones are carefully worked out so that each contains approximately the same number of independent students. For example, at the University of Illinois, the campus is divided into 43 zones, each of which has approximately 175 students. Each zone operates under the leadership of an athletic manager who makes every effort to organize the students within his area for intramural athletics. In most larger schools the independents compete among themselves, but the winners meet the intrafraternity and dormitory winners for the championship of each sport.

Cumberland University has a unique system of organization which can work out well in a small institution. All students are assigned by lot to one of eight teams: (1) Red, (2) Green, (3) Yellow, (4) Black, (5) White, (6) Brown, (7) Orange, (8) Blue.

New students are assigned to the team having the fewest members on its roster. Once assigned to a team, a student remains a member as long as he attends the university.

High school units. Krupa, investigating the bases of competition for high school intramurals, found the most common units of competition to be as shown in Table 9-1.

Krupa's study revealed that the most frequently employed unit of competition was the grade or class in school, that is, freshman, sophomore, junior, and senior. In small schools this is a convenient unit. In larger institutions, however, the percentage of students who can participate is not large enough to justify using this plan; but this objection may be minimized by having two or three teams from each grade or class. Students in a grade are not so tightly knit and unified as they are in a home room; thus the home room has become a popular unit of competition in the larger secondary schools. This is a natural unit, which is usually permanent for the school year. Ordinarily, the students are in the same grade. They are together often enough to develop a

Table 9-1.

	Small Schools	Medium Schools	Large Schools	Very Large Schools	Total
Grades (Classes)	60	123	75	37	295
Home Rooms	30	76	84	36	226
Pick-up Groups	31	49	33	13	126
Physical Education Classes	26	44	22	17	109
Independent Groups	15	22	22	12	71
Clubs	5	13	11	9	38
Vocational Classes	5	12	3	7	27
Academic Classes	3	6	1	4	14
Boy Scout Troops	5	2	4	2	13

Source: Joseph H. Krupa, A Study of Intramural Sports for Boys in the Public Secondary Schools of Pennsylvania. Ed. D. dissertation, University of Pittsburgh, 1953, p. 61.

group spirit and loyalty. The membership of the home room is such that the majority of students will be able to participate during the year. Students in home rooms are also easy to organize. Communication poses no problems.

The study by Krupa indicates that physical education classes are frequently used as a basis of intramural competition. This does not mean that intramural competition should necessarily be carried on during class periods. What it does suggest is that the physical education period be used to stimulate interest in the intramural program and that teams be organized from the class members.

Competitive units for women. It is as important, if not more important, for women to have satisfactory bases of competition for their intramural activities. Girls and women do not enter into intramural activities as readily as boys and men do, and the most effective competitive units are desirable. College women commonly use sororities, classes, dormitories, boarding clubs, physical education classes, and arbitrary groups. Women's Recreation Association sports clubs are also excellent groups. High school girls employ classes, home rooms, physical education classes, residential districts, and groups classified according to height and weight. The age-height-weight classification has proven peculiarly unsuccessful for girls. The classification on the basis of age alone appears to be as good as any.

The program of activities

What is included in the intramural program is dependent largely upon the activities that are presented in the physical education service program. If intramural activities are to arise out of the curricular activities and return to enrich them, then the intramural program must be based essentially on the physical education program. This is sound procedure, for activities in which students have had very little training and experience would hardly be so acceptable as those with which they are familiar.

The intramural programs will naturally vary in different localities, just as the physical education programs will. Winter sports are extremely popular in the northern states, but they would be impossible in the south. In certain areas, soccer is more popular than any other fall sport. In other localities wrestling and boxing are more enthusiastically received than basketball. There are, however, certain activities that seem to be in demand everywhere. Basketball, touch football, softball, volleyball, tennis, track and field are almost invariably successful intramural activities. Girls prefer volleyball, basketball, swimming, softball, tennis, and golf. Country-wide, basketball is undoubtedly the most popular intramural activity. Practically all students are familiar with and enjoy the game. The number of players is small and can be readily assembled. Very little equipment is needed, and the game does not consume an inordinate amount of time. Sports that are familiar, do not need much time and equipment, and are free from long, arduous training periods are the most preferred intramural activities. Students engage in intramural sports for the joy and recreation that they receive and thus, for the most part, are unwilling to undergo hard work and punishment.

The range of activities naturally varies with the size of the school. The large university must provide a greater variety of activities than the small high school. Something for everyone all the time should be the goal of the intramural department. In order to provide for individual differences, several different activities should be available at all times. Sports in which little interest is demonstrated should be eliminated from the program after they have had a fair trial. There is a danger in having too many activities, but that is to be preferred to too few activities. The average number of intramural activities in small high schools ranges from three to six. In large colleges and universities, twenty-five to thirty activities are frequently offered.

The trend in education to make special provision for those students who are subnormal should be carried over into intramural athletics if it is at all possible. Some intramural departments have taken steps in this direction. In some schools, there are Class A and Class B teams, particularly in intrafraternity competition in college. It is desirable to have experienced and inexperienced classifications in certain individual sports, such as boxing, wrestling, and fencing. At the University of Illinois, tournaments are conducted among the students enrolled in the various physical education courses. This type of competition is par-

Table 9-2. Activities for high school and college boys.

Fall	Winter	Spring
Archery	Basketball	Archery
Cross-Country	Badminton	Baseball
Touch Football	Wrestling	Golf
Speedball	Swimming	Horseshoes
Soccer	Volleyball	Softball
Softball	Bowling	Swimming
Tennis	Foul Shooting	Tennis
Golf	Handball	Track and Field
Football Field Meet	Squash	Volleyball
Swimming	Table Tennis	
Volleyball	Skating	
	Indoor Track	
	Relay Carnival	
	Water Polo	

Table 9-3. Activities for high school and college girls.

Fall	Winter	Spring
Archery	Badminton	Archery
Deck Tennis	Basketball	Deck Tennis
Field Ball	Bowling	Field Ball
Field Hockey	Deck Tennis	Field Hockey
Golf	Fencing	Golf
Softball	Foul Shooting	Horseshoes
Soccer	Handball	Softball
Speedball	Shuffleboard	Soccer
Swimming	Skating	Speedball
Tennis	Swimming	Swimming
Volleyball	Table Tennis	Tennis
	Volleyball	Track and Field
		Volleyball

ticularly well adapted to the beginner, as the experienced performers are excluded.

The activities for the intramural program may be selected from those shown in Tables 9-2 and 9-3.

Eligibility for intramural competition

Very few schools set up school eligibility requirements for intramural participants. The opinion prevails that a student should be allowed to participate in intramural athletics, regardless of his scholarship, if he is permitted to remain in school. Little would be gained by barring players from intramural competition because of scholastic deficiencies. The intramural department is more interested in encouraging students to participate than in setting up barriers to their participation. The eligibility regulations are chiefly concerned with the amount of participation and the conduct of the players. Some of the common regulations are:

1. Varsity squad members are ineligible for all intramural activities during the varsity season. Any player who is dropped for ineligibility may not compete in that sport in the intramural program.
2. Letter men are ineligible to compete in the intramural sport in which they won their letter.
3. Freshmen squad members may not compete in intramural sports at the same time that they are on a freshmen squad.
4. A student who is barred from varsity or freshman athletics because of professionalism is not permitted to compete in the intramural sports in which he is a professional.
5. A student may play on only one team during a given season. He may engage in one or two individual sports, however, simultaneously with the team sport.
6. After playing in one contest with a given team, a player may not transfer to another team in that sport.
7. Any special student or any student taking less than half the normal work shall be ineligible for intramural competition.
8. Any student who is on probation for disciplinary reasons may not participate in intramural activities.
9. Any team using an ineligible player shall forfeit the contest or contests in which that player participated.
10. Any player who is guilty of unsportsmanlike conduct may be declared ineligible to compete in intramural sports.

Some criticism has been directed against the last rule. The critics point out that the individual may be taught sportsmanship if allowed to continue his competition, but if he is restrained from competing, he may engage in less wholesome activities. However, because of the inexperienced officials and the bad example set for other players, it seems desirable to have some effective method of controlling these players. The loss of the privilege of competing in intramural athletics is a penalty which few interested boys care to incur.

Medical examinations

If it is desirable for varsity athletes to undergo a thorough medical examination, it is equally desirable for intramural competitors to do so. Although intramural athletics are not so strenuous as interschool athletics, the varsity candidates undergo an organized, supervised conditioning program, which intramural athletes do not. Varsity players are provided with superior equipment, and they are given better, immediate attention in case of injury. Health may be seriously impaired in intramural competition, and the most essential safeguard is the required medical examination for all competitors. It was revealed in Grambeau's study [7] of intramural athletics in colleges and universities that forty out of sixty-seven institutions required a medical examination prior to participation in intramural athletics. It is reasonable to assume that the remaining twenty-seven institutions required such an examination at the beginning of the freshman year. Insofar as secondary schools are concerned, Krupa [8] found that only thirty-seven schools out of 471 required a medical examination other than the regular school examination for participation in intramural sports.

Accident insurance

Serious injuries in intramural competition create difficult financial problems for students who have no insurance. Many high schools have accident insurance policies available to cover students in physical education, intramural or interscholastic athletics. These policies are optional. In forty-two of the sixty-seven institutions of higher education surveyed by Grambeau [9] accident insurance was available. Some schools required such insurance.

Preliminary training periods

In order to safeguard further the health of the intramural contestants, preliminary training periods are advocated. The instances where boys have entered swimming and track meets and other strenuous sports, such as boxing, wrestling, speedball, soccer, basketball, and water polo, without a day of preliminary practice are far too numerous. The intramural department should make it impossible for a boy or a girl to engage in strenuous activities without an adequate conditioning program. This is more difficult to do in the team sports than in the individual sports. Each unit sponsoring a team should be urged to practice several times before the first contest. The schedule should be so arranged that this preliminary practice is possible. Students engaging in individual sports that call for considerable endurance should be required to practice a definite number of times. Unless a boy is able to

---

[7] *Op. cit.,* p. 169.
[8] *Op. cit.*
[9] *Op. cit.,* p. 170.

show that he is in excellent physical condition as a result of engaging in other activities, he should be denied permission to participate in strenuous activities if he has not practiced the required number of times. The intramural director and the various coaches should decide upon the minimum number of training periods that are needed to prepare adequately for competition in each sport. After the number of training periods has been set up, each entry should be required to report to the intramural manager or the coach of that sport. Thus, the boy who plans to enter the mile run in the intramural track meet should report to the intramural manager or track coach the required number of times. Such a plan will go a long way toward making intramural athletics, particularly wrestling, track, and swimming events physically wholesome.

Time periods

The best time for intramural contests is in the afternoon after the classes are over. Students prefer it, as do their parents. Faculty supervision is easier to obtain. For these reasons intramural contests should be scheduled at this time if it is at all possible. The major problem is the conflict with interschool squads regarding the use of facilities. This is usually more acute during the indoor season than in the fall or spring. A partial solution is to play intramural contests on the afternoons when the varsity basketball team plays games. Some schools arrange to practice the varsity team at night once a week in order to provide some opportunity for intramurals in the afternoon. In certain schools a period is provided for intramural competition before varsity practice starts.

In one school system the varsity basketball team practiced in the morning before classes started. The intramural athletic program was able to use the gymnasium immediately after the last class in the afternoon. The reasoning behind this arrangement was that only twenty students were involved on the basketball squad while hundreds participated in the intramural program. Further, it was felt that the motivation of the basketball players was so great that no serious problem was anticipated in the early morning practice period.

The noon-hour period is extensively used in high schools. In some situations it is possible to play off contests before the participants eat. Many intramural activities of a somewhat less strenuous type such as volleyball, softball, table tennis, horseshoes, and foul shooting, may be conducted after lunch. If the activity causes the participants to perspire, they should be required to shower and change clothes afterward.

A considerable number of schools schedule intramural contests during the regular physical education service classes. If a school had a daily period of physical education this might be justified. It is difficult to defend this practice in institutions where physical education is scheduled for only two or three periods per week. Under these circumstances sufficient time is not available to provide the instruction which is necessary in the service program.

Because of the lack of space, it is frequently necessary to arrange intramural competition at night. This is unsatisfactory because it interferes with the students' homework and necessitates an additional trip to school. Parents do not take kindly to night intramurals. Forfeits are much more frequent at night than in the afternoon. The problem of providing custodial services is created. If night play cannot be avoided, the schedules should be 'arranged so that no student will be required to spend more than one evening per week in intramural activities. An excellent time for intramurals is on Saturday mornings and, frequently, on Saturday afternoons. The physical education facilities are not being used, and the majority of students are unoccupied at these times.

The figures from Krupa's study in Table 9-4 show the time schedule for intramural sports in Pennsylvania high schools.

Table 9-4.

Time	SMALL SCHOOLS		MEDIUM SCHOOLS		LARGE SCHOOLS		VERY LARGE SCHOOLS		TOTAL	
	No.	Per-cent	No.	Per-cent	No.	Per-cent	No.	Per-cent	No.	Per-cent
Immediately after School	45	47	90	51	93	67	50	84	278	59
Noon Hours	55	58	88	50	63	45	13	22	219	47
Gym Classes	28	29	32	18	19	14	13	22	92	20
Evenings	11	12	25	14	22	16	8	13	66	14
Club Periods	9	9	23	13	12	9	7	12	51	11
Free Periods	19	20	13	7	10	7	7	12	49	10
Saturdays	4	4	10	6	26	19	6	10	46	10
Varsity on Trip	3	3	11	6	4	3	6	10	24	5

Source: Joseph Krupa, A Study of Intramural Sports for Boys in Public Secondary Schools of Pennsylvania. Ed. D. dissertation, University of Pennsylvania, 1953, p. 66.

Officials

Good officiating is one of the essentials of a successful intramural program. Poor officiating robs the sport of much of its pleasure. It also leads to many protests and, consequently, dissatisfaction. Good officials are difficult to obtain in small colleges and high schools. Varsity athletes are used extensively because of their prestige and competitive experience. Ineligible athletes offer a good source of officials. Members of the faculty usually officiate a large share of the contests. Varsity coaches provide excellent officiating when they have time for it. If plenty of student managers are available, they can be used. The intramural director and his assistants may need to serve as officials at times. As a final resort, each team may be forced to supply one of the officials. Volunteer students are usually available, and some develop into good officials.

Colleges and universities have found that special training sessions for officials are very helpful. In Grambeau's study [10] 82 percent of the intramural departments conducted such clinics. In twenty institutions written examinations were given to candidates for intramural officiating. Grambeau also found that better than 90 percent of the intramural departments required the officials to dress in a distinctive type of officiating uniform.

The problem of intramural officiating is facilitated in those colleges and universities that have a professional physical education program. Physical education majors make excellent officials, and they are often willing to volunteer their services for the experience they receive. In many institutions a course in officiating is required, and the laboratory part of the course consists of officiating in intramural contests.

Some institutions find it necessary or desirable to pay for intramural officials. This practice prevails widely in colleges and universities. When funds are available to do this, excellent officiating usually prevails.

Intramural officials associations have proven effective in raising the standard of intramural officiating in many colleges and universities. The objectives of such associations are to promote a higher degree of sportsmanship and fair play in all intramural sports, to control serious injuries through competent officiating, and to make the games more interesting and enjoyable to both participant and spectator. In one institution the intramural officials association meets three days a week throughout the season. Rating cards are sent in concerning each official's performance after each game. In many institutions the intramural officials association conducts sports clinics for various intramural sports. Such clinics are scheduled prior to the start of competition and include rules, interpretations, and discussion of ground rules. Sports clinics have the effect of facilitating officiating.

Protests

The customary ruling in regard to protests is that they be made in writing within twenty-four hours after the contest in question, accompanied by a small fee, which is returned if the protest is granted but

10 *Op. cit.,* p. 170.

kept if it is not. This gives the students time to cool off and reconsider their protest. Protests will be reduced if the intramural department has someone available at the various games to settle disputes. The protests that are filed with the intramural department are usually acted upon by the administrative board of control. No consideration should be given protests that involve mistakes in judgment by the officials. Legitimate protests are those based upon the question of ineligibility of players and mistakes involving interpretation of the rules.

Forfeits

Forfeits are the bane of the intramural director's existence. They present a problem for all intramural departments, although the better organized departments are less troubled in this respect than the poorly organized ones. If the students and organizations regard their intramural participation as a privilege, there will be fewer forfeits. Some departments place a heavy penalty upon forfeits, and this appears to reduce them. This penalty usually involves the loss of intramural points, although some departments deprive the forfeiting organization of all intramural privileges for the remainder of the year. This seems to be a heavy penalty, but it has worked to reduce forfeits. The cause of forfeits, in most cases, is discouragement following repeated defeats. If the competition is equalized to a reasonable extent, some of these forfeits can be prevented. The number of forfeits is appreciably diminished where the weaker organizations compete among themselves.

Intramural publicity

In order to arouse and maintain interest in the intramural program, the students should be kept informed constantly about the activities of the program. Continuous publicity will do much to stimulate additional students to enter into intramural sports and, at the same time, will serve as an added incentive to those who have been participating. Good publicity will also enable the intramural department to operate much more efficiently, as the students will be better informed of playing dates, playing locations, changes in schedules, entry dates, league standings, playoffs, and many other facts that should be known.

The best source of intramural publicity is the student newspaper. Space is usually easy to obtain, and if the intramural director makes effective use of it, he can stimulate great interest in the program. Items of unusual interest, noteworthy achievements, unique program features, league standings, schedules, and daily results should be publicized. The local newspaper has been found to be effective in publicizing the intramural program. This is particularly true of high school intramurals.

The bulletin board is an excellent means of informing the student body of the intramural program. Every intramural department should have at least one bulletin board. In some schools several boards are used to good advantage. The bulletin board should be strategically located so that the greatest number of students will see it. It should be well lighted and well maintained, with eye-catching, up-to-date announcements, posters, and schedules.

Announcements at student gatherings and in physical education classes are a frequently used method of conveying information to students. Homeroom announcements are very helpful in high schools. Mailing information bulletins to students has been effectively used in some institutions. A recommended procedure is to gather all entering freshmen and new students together and explain the program to them. Such a meeting may well be a part of the orientation sessions that many institutions provide new students. At this occasion intramural handbooks can be distributed and interest-finding questionnaires secured from all students.

Intramural handbooks should be available to all students if it is at all possible to afford them. Many high school and college intramural departments furnish handbooks and feel that the expense is well justified. Intramural handbooks give the student a clear picture of the intramural department, its organization, its administration, its rules and regulations, its leaders, the program of activities, the point systems, and additional facts with which the students should be familiar. The intramural director and managers will find that the handbook will save them many explanations and interpretations of the rules. The students will find that the handbook will give them a much clearer understanding of the operation of the intramural department and enable them to conduct their activities more intelligently.

Intramural coaching

A few institutions provide instruction for the intramural participants. The schools that give physical education credit for intramural competition frequently follow this practice. Such a plan has much to recommend it, but it has the disadvantage of overworking the already overworked physical education staff. When a varsity coach or a recognized authority coaches intramural contestants, considerable interest is aroused among the students. In some colleges and universities, students specializing in physical education may be used; but these students rarely have the prestige and influence to perform this task successfully. The desirability of coaching intramural participants is unquestioned; but until more assistance is given the physical education departments, the instruction will be confined to the physical education classes in most colleges and high schools.

Intramural awards

What has been said in the previous chapter in regard to awards may also be applied to intramural awards. Those who advocate the discontinuance of awards are attacking a universal practice. Awards are granted in all walks of life, and if a reform is desired, more would be accomplished by starting the proper training in infancy. Crusading physical educators would produce few worthwhile results if awards were abolished only in physical education and in no other lines of endeavor. The use of awards as incentives to intramural participation can be defended as long as they remain inexpensive. Intramural awards to individuals in the majority of high schools cannot be in excess of one dollar. The trend appears to be quite definitely away from the expensive prizes that were so characteristic a number of years ago. Intramural awards are becoming symbols of achievement and, as such, are justifiable.

The winners of individual competition may be awarded medals, cups, class insignia, or ribbons. Group competition is usually divided into leagues comprising the permanent groups, such as fraternities and dormitories, and the temporary groups, such as independents. The winning teams of the permanent group are awarded pennants, shields, plaques, or cups. The winning temporary groups would have no use for team trophies; so they are usually given emblems or medals. A larger, more pretentious cup is awarded to the permanent group and to the individual for the best all-year performance. Some institutions purchase the awards before the competition for them commences. This procedure is to be recommended, as the students have the opportunity to see the awards for which they are competing, and it insures prompt distribution of the awards after they have been won. An award that is granted six months after it has been won has lost much of its value to the student.

Intramural statistics

The intramural department ought to have careful records of student·participation in the activities of the program. These records are valuable within an institution itself, but they should not be used as a basis for comparison with other intramural departments. Some directors place great emphasis upon accumulating impressive statistics. They evidently harbor the belief that the success of the department is measured by the size of the participation statistics they amass. The progress shown by the department from year to year would be a better criterion of its success than would be a comparison of its participation with that of another institution.

In order to have a true picture of the intramural participation, the director will want to discover (1) the total number of students who have been reached by at least one activity, (2) the average number of sports in which each student participated, and (3) the average number of games played in each sport by each student or the participation hours of each student. The participation hours of every student in the separate activities is extremely valuable information to have, but more difficulty is involved in securing it. It is quite necessary that all of the above be compiled every year. The values of these participation records are as follows:

1. The gain or loss in intramural participation over the previous year can readily be ascertained.
2. The proportion of the entire student body participating in intramural sports will be discovered.
3. Whether the students are taking advantage of the intramural program throughout the year or are only participating sporadically will be disclosed.
4. The popular and unpopular activities will be discovered. The gain or loss in interest in the various activities from year to year will be evident.
5. The most successful units of competition can be ascertained.
6. Excessive participation on the part of some individuals can be checked.
7. The statistics may be used to show the need of greater financial assistance.
8. The success or failure of various administrative procedures may be checked.

In compiling participation statistics, a separate card should be kept for each individual. This card should give a complete picture of the intramural participation of the student. Only the actual games in which the student engages should be recorded. A record of the informal, unorganized play of each individual would be highly desirable, but practical considerations make it unfeasible.

Methods of organizing competition

Tournaments both for intramural and other school purposes are discussed in this chapter. They are not presented as the meat or basic elements of the intramural diet but as the trimmings, the excessive use of which may lead to recreational indisposition. In the past it has not been uncommon to consider tennis, for example, played just for the fun of it as something less than tennis played in an intramural tournament, chiefly because the competitors could not be included in the figures used to justify the intramural program. This necessity of presenting justifying evidence, imposed upon those sponsoring intramural activities, has led in some cases to undue emphasis on tournaments and to encouraging individuals to enter too many sports events in order to swell the totals as much as possible. Despite some cases of overemphasis, however, tournaments are still valuable, and a judicious use of them adds interest and enthusiasm to the program of activities.

The type of activity, the time available, student interest, the end in view, and similar modifying factors determine the type of tournament that should be used. All types presented below have strong and weak points, but some serve one purpose well and others serve another.

Elimination tournaments

This type of tournament involves the elimination of all competitors until only one winner remains. There are four types of elimination tournaments.

Single elimination. The single elimination tournament is the least desirable because it emphasizes the *elimination* of teams and players. For example, in this type of tournament one half of the competitors are eliminated after their first contest. Further, since a single defeat eliminates a contender, the eventual winner often is not the best team or player. Nor does the defeated finalist represent with certainty the second best team or player, since one of the teams or players in the other half of the bracket may be superior. However, despite these disadvantages, there is a place for the single elimination type of tournament. It is short and selects a winner quickly. It is interesting to watch and can be conducted with limited facilities and a large number of entries. The use of the single elimination tournament is justified when the time available is limited.

The first step in arranging a single elimination tournament is to draw for positions. The positions in the brackets are numbered, and each team or player takes the position indicated by the number drawn, as in Figure 9-4. In the tournament shown the location of each team was determined by the number that was drawn. Thus, the captain or representative of Team B drew #1; the representative of Team A drew #4, and so forth.

When the number of entrants is not an even power of two (that is, 2, 4, 8, 16, 32, etc.) "byes" must be arranged so as to avoid having an uneven number of teams or players left to compete in the semifinal or final rounds. All the byes must be placed in the first round. The competition is less intense in the first round, and a rest before play does not

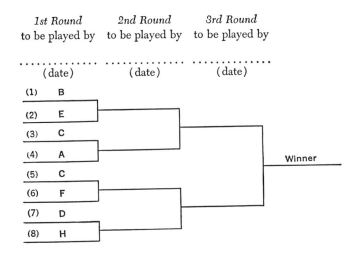

Figure 9-4.   Single Elimination Tournament.

provide the advantage of a rest after a game or two. The number of byes should be sufficient to assure a number of contestants for the second round that is an even power of two. This is accomplished by subtracting the total number of entrants from the next higher power of two. For example, with eleven entrants, subtract 11 from the next higher power of two, which is 16. This leaves 5, which is the number of byes. The total number of entrants (eleven) minus the five byes leaves six contestants to play each other in the first round. Three will lose, leaving eight contestants in the second round. As 8 is an even power of two, only two teams can now meet in the final round. The byes should be distributed as evenly as possible between the upper and lower brackets. Figure 9-5 shows a sample bracket for thirteen teams.

"Seeding" is a process employed to place the competitors who, by virtue of previous performance and reputation, are considered superior in separate brackets or as far apart as possible in the same bracket in order to minimize their chances of meeting in the early rounds. With two seeded entries one should be placed at the top of the upper bracket and the other at the bottom of the lower bracket. If four entrants are to be seeded the third should be placed at the top of the lower bracket and the fourth at the bottom of the upper bracket. If there are byes, the seeded players get them in the order of their ranking. Thus, number one gets the first bye, number two the second, and so on. No team or player ever receives more than one bye. Seeding should be employed only when the previous record of the teams or players justifies it.

The number of games in a single elimination tournament is always one less than the number of entries. Thus, with thirteen teams entered,

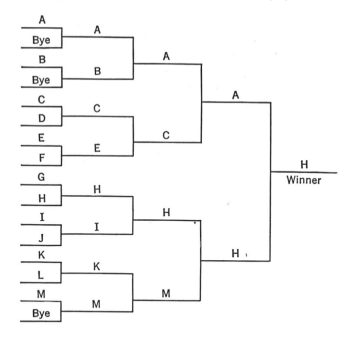

Figure 9-5. Single Elimination Bracket for Thirteen Teams.

12 games would be required to complete the tournament. The number of rounds required is equal to the power to which two must be raised to equal or exceed the number of entries. With thirteen entrants 4 rounds are necessary to complete the competition.

Consolation elimination tournament. This type of tournament is superior to the single elimination in that it permits each team to play at least twice. A good team that has been eliminated by the champion in the first round may continue to play with a chance to win secondary

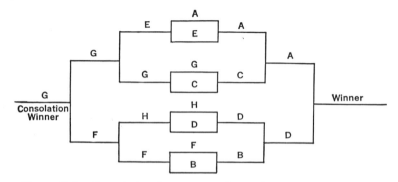

Figure 9-6. Consolation Tournament for Eight Teams (First Type).

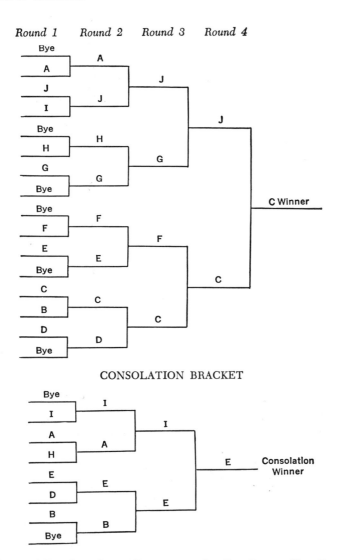

Figure 9-7. Consolation Tournament for Ten Teams (First Type).

honors. More games are involved, and greater player interest is engendered.

There are two general types of consolation elimination tournaments. In the first type all the losers in the first round (or those who lose in the second round after drawing a bye in the first round) play another single elimination tournament. The winner of this second tournament is the consolation winner. Figure 9-6 is an example of the manner in which a consolation tournament of this type with no byes is arranged.

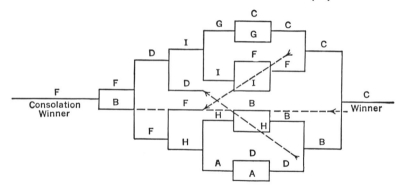

Figure 9-8. Consolation Tournament for Eight Teams (Second Type).

Figure 9-7 illustrates the manner in which a consolation tournament including byes may be arranged.

A second type of consolation tournament provides an opportunity for any loser to win the consolation championship, regardless of the round in which the loss was sustained. Figure 9-8 is an example of this second type of consolation tournament.

Double elimination tournament. This is a tournament in which a player or a team must be beaten twice to be eliminated; the play continues until all but one have been twice defeated. The double elimination tournament is a step in the direction of a round robin tournament and selects a more adequate winner. It provides for at least twice as much play as in a single elimination tournament and maintains maximum interest. A double elimination tournament of 8 teams will involve either fourteen or fifteen games (Figure 9-9).

Bagnall-Wild elimination tournament. This is a modified form of the elimination type of tournament. Its strong point is the selection of true second- and third-place winners; its weakness is the delay following the first round before those who are to try for second or third places can be matched. It should be used when second and third places are of particular significance or when a point system is in operation and points are awarded for these places.

First place is determined by means of straight elimination play. To determine second place all the competitors defeated by the champion previous to the final round compete against each other in an elimination tournament, the winner of which plays the defeated finalist for second place. In Figure 9-10, the defeated finalist (A) proves to be best among the teams defeated by the winner and wins second place. However, Team K (defeated by A) does not automatically become third place winner. One of the other teams defeated by A might be better than K. To determine this an elimination tournament is conducted among the

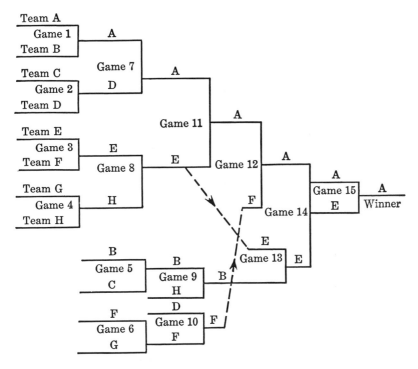

Figure 9-9. Double Elimination Tournament for Eight Teams.

teams defeated by A. The winner (second best team in the upper bracket) plays K (second best team in the lower bracket) for third place.

In the event the defeated finalist (Team A) should lose in the match for second place, Team K becomes second-place winner. This automatically leaves Team A the third-place winner.

The playoffs for second and third place should not await the playing of the finals match. As soon as it is determined that Teams A and H are to be the finalists the elimination competition between the teams defeated by each of the finalists should begin. Thus, before the finals, Teams B and F and G and I should play matches. This will reduce the amount of play after the winning finalist has been determined.

Round robin tournaments

If sufficient time and facilities are available, the round robin tournament is the best type of tournament to employ. It produces a true winner, ranks the other competitors, permits all participants to continue play until the end, and does not require one contestant to wait until others have played the next round.

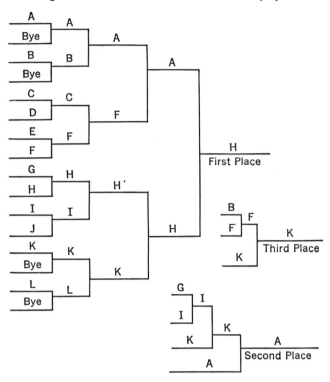

Figure 9-10. Bagnall-Wild Tournament for Twelve Teams.

Regular round robin. In the round robin tournament, each team or player plays each other competitor in the league. In a single round robin one game is played with each other team or player; in a double round robin two games are played with each of the opponents. In professional baseball, the major leagues use the round robin tournament, and each team plays eighteen games with each other team.

The positions of the teams at the end of a round robin tournament are determined by percentages. Each team's percentage is obtained by dividing the number of games won by the total games played. For example, if a team played eight games and won seven, its percentage would be .875. In cases of tie games, the customary procedure is not to count such contests as games played when the percentages are computed. A better plan is to count a tie as half a victory and half a defeat. Thus, a team that wins seven games, loses four, and ties one would have a percentage of .625 (7.5 ÷ 12).

The British and Canadian systems of determining team standings in round robin tournaments are somewhat different. In the Canadian system, two points are awarded for each victory and one point for each tie. Thus, if a team wins twelve games, loses three, and ties one, its total points would be 25. The team with the greatest point total is the winner. The British carry this one step further. They determine points as in the Canadian system, but the point total obtained is then divided by the total possible points (total games played multiplied by two). In the example just given, the team's percentage would be .781 (25 ÷ 32).

The formula for determining the total number of games to be played in a round robin tournament is $n(n-1)/2$ with n representing the number of teams in the tournament. Substituting for n in an eight-team league, the formula is $8(8-1)/2$ or twenty-eight games. Since there are eight teams involved, eight is used; since each team plays every team but itself, eight minus one is used; and since it takes two teams to play one game, it is necessary to divide by two.

To draw up a round robin schedule, place as many numbers as there are teams in two vertical columns. The numbers should be arranged consecutively down the first column and up the second. With each number representing a team, this arrangement provides the pairing for the first round. Thus, Team #1 plays Team #8; Team #2 plays #7; Team #3 plays #6, and Team #4 plays #5 in the first round. To obtain pairings for subsequent rounds, rotate the numbers *counterclockwise* around one of the numbers that remains fixed. In the example given in Table 9-5, number one is fixed with the other numbers rotated around it.

Table 9-5.

Round 1	Round 2	Round 3	Round 4	Round 5	Round 6	Round 7
1 vs. 8	1 vs. 7	1 vs. 6	1 vs. 5	1 vs. 4	1 vs. 3	1 vs. 2
2 vs. 7	8 vs. 6	7 vs. 5	6 vs. 4	5 vs. 3	4 vs. 2	3 vs. 8
3 vs. 6	2 vs. 5	8 vs. 4	7 vs. 3	6 vs. 2	5 vs. 8	4 vs. 7
4 vs. 5	3 vs. 4	2 vs. 3	8 vs. 2	7 vs. 8	6 vs. 7	5 vs. 6

When an uneven number of teams is entered the same plan is used. However, in this case the bye should be placed in one of the positions and the other numbers rotated about it. The number opposite the bye signifies the team that receives the bye in that particular round. In the example given in Table 9-6, the bye is placed in the upper left-hand corner and the other numbers are rotated *counterclockwise* around it. Another method of drawing up a round robin tournament is illustrated in Figure 9-11. Schedules for even numbers of teams follow one general plan; those for odd numbers of teams do likewise except that the schedule is drawn for the next greater even number and the last vertical column to the right represents the byes.

Table 9-6.

Round 1	Round 2	Round 3	Round 4	Round 5	Round 6	Round 7
Bye 7	Bye 6	Bye 5	Bye 4	Bye 3	Bye 2	Bye 1
1 vs. 6	7 vs. 5	6 vs. 4	5 vs. 3	4 vs. 2	3 vs. 1	2 vs. 7
2 vs. 5	1 vs. 4	7 vs. 3	6 vs. 2	5 vs. 1	4 vs. 7	3 vs. 6
3 vs. 4	2 vs. 3	1 vs. 2	7 vs. 1	6 vs. 7	5 vs. 6	4 vs. 5

The letters in Figure 9-11 represent teams, and the numbers playing days. Numbers at the intersection of the various vertical and horizontal columns indicate that the teams represented in the columns concerned play on the playing day indicated by the number. That is, 7 on

EIGHT TEAM SCHEDULE

	A	B	C	D	E	F	G	H
A		1	2	3	4	5	6	7
B			3	4	5	6	7	2
C				5	6	7	1	4
D					7	1	2	6
E						2	3	1
F							4	3
G								5
H								

NINE TEAM SCHEDULE

	A	B	C	D	E	F	G	H	I	Bye
A		1	2	3	4	5	6	7	8	9
B			3	4	5	6	7	8	9	2
C				5	6	7	8	9	1	4
D					7	8	9	1	2	6
E						9	1	2	3	8
F							2	3	4	1
G								4	5	3
H									6	5
I										7
Bye										

Figure 9-11.   Round Robin Schedules.

vertical F and horizontal C means F plays C on the seventh playing day; likewise E plays B on the fifth playing day. These relationships can be noted in the arrangement of the numbers in the schedule. All numbers are in regular order except those in the last column to the right (1 following 7 is in regular order when 7 is the largest number). The last column to the right starts with the largest odd number, then goes to the smallest even number and on up through the even numbers in order, then starts with the smallest odd number and continues through the remaining odds in order. The numbers in this last vertical column, except the first and the last, are always one less than the first number.

The Lombard round robin. The Lombard tournament is a unique form of round robin competition in which the entire tournament is competed in a day or several hours. This is accomplished by playing abbreviated contests. This type of tournament should not be thought of as a substitute for regular round robin competition. Rather it is a special type of tournament which can be used effectively under certain conditions.

In certain sections of the South, where outdoor facilities are ample and usable during the winter, this type of tournament is used for parish and sectional basketball play. In it the competitors are only away from home for a short time. This circumstance reduces the cost to the schools because no lodging need be provided and comparatively few meals need to be furnished. First, second, third, and fourth places are determined without putting an undue strain on any competitor.

Assuming a tournament of seventeen basketball teams and a playing time of 32 minutes, which is the customary length of high school basketball games, the tournament works as follows. Each team meets every other team or plays 16 short games. Therefore, divide 32 by 16 to give the length of time of these abbreviated games, which is exactly two minutes. Eight courts and sufficient officials to conduct 8 games at a time are required. Each team is assigned a scorer, who keeps a record of its scores for all games in one column and the scores of all opponents in another. All teams start play at one time, play two minutes, and then shift to another court to play another opponent until a complete round robin tournament of two-minute games is played. The scores for each team are totaled for the 16 games. The opponents' score is then subtracted from each team's own score. The four teams with the largest positive scores are selected to play a regular round robin to decide the winner and other ranking places if desired. In the event of a tie for fourth place after the first round robin of two-minute periods, the tying teams play for the right to enter the final tournament.

Since the players of the various teams have played only the equivalent of one full-time game, the first round of the final tournament of four teams can be played the day of the abbreviated round robin. Then all teams can go home, and the four remaining contenders can return the next Saturday to complete the tournament. This assumes that they live within a radius of forty or fifty miles.

During World War II the Lombard tournament, used somewhat differently from that indicated above, was extensively and effectively employed in the army. Its great value lay in the fact that an entire round robin tournament could be completed within a period of several hours. For example, a Lombard round robin tournament in basketball in a league of twelve teams (66 games) can be completed in less than four hours if two courts are available and six-minute games are played. If more courts are available the time may be further reduced. The Lombard tournament worked very successfully with from 6 to 12 teams playing on two or three courts. In this way, teams alternate playing and players have a chance to rest. For this reason, it is an excellent tournament for players who are not yet in condition to play full-length games. The best length of basketball games proved to be from five to six minutes.

To assist in scoring the Lombard tournament, a scoreboard such as indicated below has been found helpful. For each game played, two scores must be recorded, one for each team. A team's scores are recorded and added *horizontally*. If Team #4 defeated Team #1 by a score of 10 to 5, Team #4's score would be +5, and Team #1's score would be −5. If Team #2 defeated Team #3 by a score of 6 to 0, its score would be +6, and Team #3's score would be −6 points. These scores are recorded as shown in Table 9-7. The Lombard type of tournament

Table 9-7.

				Games				Total	Score
	#1	#2	#3	#4	#5	#6	#7		
Team #1	−5								
Team #2	+6								
Team #3	−6								
Team #4	+5								
Team #5									
Team #6									
Team #7									
Team #8									

can also be employed effectively for volleyball, speedball, soccer, touch football, cage ball, American ball, handball, badminton, squash, and tennis. When used for volleyball, handball, squash, badminton, and tennis, only one game or set should be played against each opponent.

Combination tournaments

An excellent tournament for intramural purposes should (1) provide for even or well-matched competition, (2) be neither too long nor too short, (3) exclude none from competition after a game or two, (4) require few or no competitors to play a great many more games than other participants, and (5) select a true champion. There are several forms of combined elimination and round robin tournaments that meet these requirements reasonably well.

For purposes of illustration, a combination elimination round robin elimination tournament is presented for 20 basketball teams in Figure 9-12. Two rounds of a double elimination tournament are played first to classify the competitors into four leagues. To do this, seed teams as well as possible and play the first round; then have winners play winners and losers play losers. Place those who won twice in the first league; those who won one and then lost one in the second

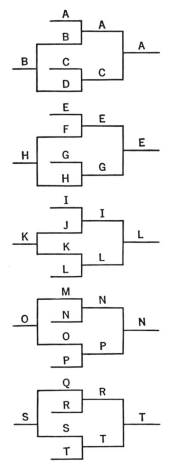

Key—First league: A, E, L, N, T; Second league: C, G, I, P, R; Third league: B, H, K, O, S; Fourth league: D, F, J, M, Q.

Figure 9-12. Elimination Bracket (for a Combination Elimination Round Robin Tournament).

league; those who lost one and then won one in the third league; and those who lost two in the last league.

Now that the teams are classified, play a round robin schedule for each league. Each team will then have played six games, two in classifying and four in its league. Place the first- and second-place winners of leagues one and two and the first-place winners in leagues three and four in the final championship tournament. This will discourage the practice of losing in the classifying rounds in order to gain a place in a weaker league. A double elimination tournament is recommended for these six teams; but if time is short, a straight elimination may be necessary. A round robin tournament may be used but is not to be recommended, since most of the teams are already eliminated, and the remaining six would need to play much more than the other teams.

An interesting method of providing even more participation is to group the place winners in each league together in single elimination tournaments. For example, put all first-place winners together as in the above example; do likewise with the second-place teams in each league. Similar tournaments are drawn up for the teams in third, fourth, fifth, and sixth places (see Figure 9-13).

Figure 9-13. Single Elimination Tournament for Finalists.

At times, the space and time available are not adequate to permit even an elimination tournament for a large number of entries. When this occurs in certain sports the number of participants can be quickly reduced by holding a qualifying round in which only the best performers qualify for the finals. Such sports as track and field, swimming, golf, bowling, and foul shooting are well adapted to the use of qualifying rounds. For example, in a golf tournament all the contestants may play a qualifying round and the sixteen players with the best scores thus play a single elimination tournament for the championship. To simplify tournament play the number of entries which qualify is usually a power of two.

Challenge tournaments

This form of tournament is desirable when the activity is such that it can be carried on by the players independently without formal schedules. It is used for single or dual competition rather than team sports. Tennis, golf, handball, squash, badminton, boxing, wrestling, horseshoes, and archery are the activities for which this type of competition is most commonly used.

A challenge tournament affords competition with contestants of near equal ability. It provides an opportunity for all competitors to continue play since none is eliminated. It is entered into with more zest in situations where all the players know each other. This type of tournament is useful in selecting team members in individual sports. When used this way, the players at the top of the ladder represent the institution in interschool competition. The ladder tournament is widely used by wrestling coaches to select the competitors in each weight each week.

There are two common types of challenge tournaments, the ladder and the pyramid (see Figure 9-14). Contestants' names are inscribed on cards that can either be placed in slots or hung on hooks. Placing the players on the ladder or in the pyramid in the order in which they sign up will furnish an incentive for all who are interested to sign up quickly; it will encourage competitors to do what should be done. Positions may also be determined by the various players drawing numbers from a hat. Only if the time is short is seeding to be recommended.

Rules governing play for the various forms will differ somewhat, and local factors will also modify them, but in general the following rules, with minor modifications, will suffice.

1. It must be definitely stated what constitutes a win.
2. Players may advance by challenging and defeating, or by gaining default from defending player (player challenged).

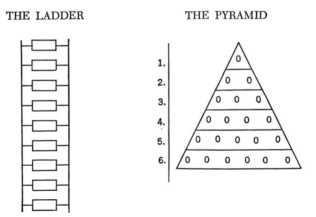

Figure 9-14.   Challenge Tournaments.

3. A player may challenge two players above him. That is, C may challenge A or B.

4. If the challenger wins, only players involved change places; if the defender wins, positions remain as before, and the defeated challenger may not challenge the same player again for a week.

5. Challenges must be met in the order that they are made.

6. After two contestants have played, they cannot play each other again until each has played once with another contestant.

7. In some challenge tournaments the rule exists that a player must defeat someone in his own horizontal row before he can challenge someone above him.

8. A defender must play within three days after receiving a challenge, provided he has not challenged above himself before receiving the challenge. If he has, he must meet the challenge within three days after his match, provided he is still in challenging range (three places) of the challenger. (As a substitute rule two challenge days may be selected each week, on one of which a player may challenge and on the other of which he must defend his position.)

9. There is no acceptable excuse, except inclement weather, for failure to play within the time limit stated in rule six; if defender cannot play within set limit, he must forfeit.

10. In case of difficulty concerning challenging and acceptance of challenges, set up a challenge board or require all challenges to be dated and handed to tournament manager, who will then post them.

11. In the pyramid form a player may challenge any player in the rank above; that is, any player in rank five may challenge any player in rank four, who may in turn challenge any player in rank three, and so on.

12. The player at the top of the ladder or pyramid at the end of a specified period of time is the winner.

The funnel tournament

The funnel tournament is a combination of the ladder and challenge type tournaments. It works best with activities like handball, bad-

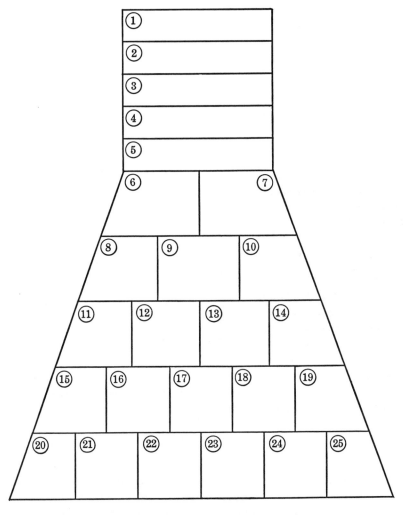

Source: Reproduced by permission of the Program Aids Company, 550 Fifth Avenue, New York, N.Y.

Figure 9-15. Funnel Tournament.

minton, table tennis, and horseshoes. It is played off in a manner similar to a challenge tournament. A player must defeat someone in his own horizontal row before he can challenge into the next row. The top five positions are played as a ladder tournament (see Figure 9-15).

The tombstone tournament

This is not a widely known tournament yet it has been used very effectively for group and individual competition. It involves a cumulative score, and the person or team that accumulates the best record over a specified period of time or achieves a predetermined goal in the shortest time is the winner. For example, in swimming, each entrant indicates on a chart the distance he has swum each day. At the end of the stipulated period of time the contestant who has swum the greatest distance is the winner. If the distance is established, such as 100 miles, the winner would be the individual who first negotiated this distance. A chart such as that shown in Figure 9-16 should be used to record the performance in this type of tournament.

100-MILE SWIM (8800 POOL LENGTHS).

Entries	June 1		June 2		June 3		June 4		June 5	
	Daily Record	Total Score	Daily Record	Total Score	Daily Record	Total Score	Daily Record	Total Score	Daily Record	Total Score
Jones, H.	44	5068	66	5134	22	5156				
Henry, B.	60	4896	60	4956	88	5044				
Brown. W.										
Marsh, M.										

Note—Scores are recorded in pool lengths.

Figure 9-16.

The above procedure may be used for competitions in hiking, chinning (one trial per day), pushups, situps, distance running, broad jumping, shot-putting, football punt for distance, and many similar events. For example, in basketball free throwing, it could be specified that each man was to take twenty-five throws each day. At the end of a month (or some other specified period) the player who has made the greatest number of baskets is the winner. In horseshoes, each player might play three games every day and record the total ringers made. After a definite number of rounds, the player with the most ringers is the winner. In archery each player might keep his daily score, and the winner would be that contestant who had accumulated the greatest number of points by a certain date.

In such events as the shot put, broad jump, and football punt each player may be given three or five trials, counting only his best performance. Additional practice each day is encouraged.

In all these events it is obvious that all competitors should compete under the same rules and conditions. When this type of tournament is conducted among widely separated units, it is necessary to select events that are little affected by varying weather conditions and facilities. The progress of the tournament in such a situation is made known to the various competitors either by telephone or mail.

The tombstone tournament may be used for group as well as individual competition. When the number of competitors in each group is the same, the group total may be computed each day until the end of the tournament. For example, to determine the winner in the standing broad jump each competitor would jump five times each day and count his best jump. If all the competitive groups were of the same size, the total distance jumped each day could be computed. At the end of the tournament, the group that had jumped the greatest distance would be the winner.

If the groups are not exactly the same size, it is necessary to obtain group averages. The group average would be scored every day, and the group with the greatest total at a set date would be the winner.

Point systems

Intramural point systems are used to determine the group of individuals who performed most or best or both throughout the entire year. Such scoring plans are very valuable in stimulating and maintaining interest in intramural activities for the entire year. Many organizations and individuals are inclined to enter only those activities in which they are proficient. A point system, however, encourages them to engage in a wide variety of activities. The group influences all its members to participate, and, incidentally, those who most need big-muscle play activity are persuaded to enter into various sports. Many students get their first experience with different activities in this manner. With individual and group point systems operating, the whole participation in the program becomes less haphazard and sporadic. Scoring plans will function effectively in both college and high school intramurals.

Group point systems. There are many different types of group scor-

Table 9-8.

Division I	Division II	Division III
Soccer	Track	Tennis
Volleyball	Swimming	Wrestling
Baseball	Cross-Country	Boxing
Playground Ball		Horseshoes
Water Polo		Free Throwing
Bowling		Golf
		Handball

ing plans. The Illinois plan is particularly noteworthy. All of the activities are divided into three divisions, as shown in Table 9-8. Achievement points are awarded as follows:

Division 1:

(a) Five points for every contest won.
(b) One point for standing at end of the league season; that is, one point for last place, etc., and leading team is given the number of points according to the number of places in the league.
(c) Twenty-five points for winning organized house championship.
(d) In case of a tie game, each team is given one half of the number of points it might have won.

Division 2:

(a) Each team will be awarded the total number of points won in an authorized meet.
(b) Ten additional points will be awarded the team winning the championship of each meet.

Division 3:

(a) One point will be awarded for winning a match or contest in tennis singles, handball singles, boxing, wrestling, horseshoes.
(b) Two points will be awarded for winning a match in tennis doubles, handball doubles, or golf.
(c) Five points shall be awarded for winning the championship in each sport in the division.

In the event that several teams are tied for one place at the end of the season in Division I sports, the points for tied places shall be evenly divided between the tied teams. If a team forfeits a game to an opponent, it shall have the number of points deducted that it would have received had the game or contest been won. If two teams have the same number of points at the end of the intramural season, the trophies shall be awarded to the organization having the highest scholastic average.

Whenever the number of competing units is small, each team may be awarded points according to the order in which it finishes in each sport. For example, in interclass competition, the team winning the league may be awarded 8 points; second, 6 points; third, 4 points; and fourth, 2 points. The major sports are usually given more points than the minor sports.

Some departments grant the various organizations points for varsity letter men, squad men, and freshmen squad members. The justification for doing this is that some groups will prevail upon their members to confine their activities to intramural rather than varsity or freshman competition. Some departments deduct points for poor sportsmanship. Scholarship is granted points in a few intramural departments.

Transylvania College has a unique scoring system. It is entirely individual and organizations get their points by adding together all the points of each person belonging to the group. For scoring there are three classifications, namely, team sports, intermediate sports (tennis, badminton, handball, and the like), and individual sports (table tennis, horseshoes, free throwing, and so forth):

1. Points for team sports:
   (a) Participation at least two minutes   6
   (b) Winning game   1

2. Points for intermediate sports:
   (a) Participation in each event or match   4
   (b) Each victory   2
   (c) Winning championship   10
   (d) Second place in tournament   8
   (e) Third place in tournament   5

3. Points for individual sports:
   (a) Participation in each contest   2
   (b) Winning each match   2
   (c) Winning championship   5
   (d) Second place in tournament   3
   (e) Third place in tournament   1

An interesting group scoring plan is employed at Ottawa University.

1. Team sports:
   The number of players required to make up a team is multiplied by 3 for each win and by 1 for each loss. The points for a tie game are determined by adding a win and a loss and dividing by 2.
   Example:

Points for each game played

	Won	*Lost*	*Tie*
Basketball	15	5	10
Volleyball	18	6	12

Thus, a basketball team which won ten games, lost four, and tied two would accumulate a total of 190 points.

2. Tournaments: *Points*
   - (a) Participation in doubles 1
   - (b) Participation in singles 1
   - (c) Each victory (doubles or singles) 2
   - (d) Loss 1
   - (e) Championship 5
   - (f) Second place 3
   - (g) Quarter-finalists 1

3. Meets:
   - (a) Participation in each event 1
   - (b) First place in each event 5
   - (c) Second place in each event 3
   - (d) Third place in each event 1

4. Championship:

   A championship in any team sport or meet will score twenty-five points for the championship team.

Individual point systems. Individual point systems are similar to group scoring plans. Every student has the opportunity of competing for individual honors. A simple method of scoring individual points is as follows:

1. Award five points to each player for every team victory in which he participated.
2. Award one point for competing in and not winning a team sport.
3. Award five points for each individual or doubles victory in tennis, handball, golf, horseshoes, boxing, wrestling, or foul shooting.
4. Award one point for competing in and not winning in the above sports.
5. Award each man the total number of points he won in a track, cross-country, or swimming meet.

Some departments grant points for varsity letters or squad membership. Sportsmanship and scholarship are also frequently rewarded by intramural points. There is a movement in high schools to include a large number of factors, such as participation in school activities, hygienic habits, sportsmanship, physical fitness tests, and the like, in determining the individual winner.

The individual point system has probably received more emphasis in the girls' intramural program than in that of the boys'. It has been especially popular in the high schools where it is usually fostered by the athletic associations. In addition to being awarded points for participation in all of the physical education activities the girls may also be granted points for health, posture, sportsmanship, and proficiency in the elements of various sports. The aim of such systems is to encourage all-round athletic ability. When the girl has accumulated a certain number of points she is rewarded with an award of some kind, a letter, emblem, pin, sweater, or blanket.

A point system can be of value in stimulating participation in a wide variety of sports. It loses its value when it becomes too complicated or replaces intrinsic interest in athletics. The following point system, which is in operation at Barnard College, is a simple, effective one.[11]

Honors shall be awarded to outstanding seniors in recognition of their participation in athletics, and contribution to the Athletic Association throughout their college course. These shall be awarded as follows:

Class A—gold A.A. pin, Requirements:
1. Very highest degree of versatility, proficiency, and leadership in athletics. Health and academic standards are automatically included in this, for a girl should not take part in a sport unless she meets the necessary health and academic requirements.
2. Definite contributions to A.A. other than participation in sports—as a manager, officer, committee member or the like
3. Dependability and regularity of participation
4. Habitual good posture. A girl receiving the Class A award should be of All Star standard in several sports and would have shown a contributive interest in A.A. activities during her college career.

Class B—silver A.A. pin, Requirements:
The same basis as for Class A, but lower standards of skill, versatility, and leadership.

Class C—bronze A.A. pin, Requirements:
The same basis as for Classes A and B, but lower standards of skill and less emphasis on versatility and leadership.

It should be pointed out that a problem exists in regard to individual point systems. The record keeping, particularly in programs that have large student participation is extensive. It is for this reason that many intramural departments do not make provision for an individual point system.

Intramural trends

In the postwar era many colleges and universities extended their intramural programs in response to the unprecedented demands

---

11 Agnes R. Wayman, *Education Through Physical Education* (Philadelphia, Lea and Febiger, 1934), p. 194.

brought about by the greatly expanded student bodies. Many new activities made their appearance. In addition to the traditional sports, such activities as archery, lawn bowling, ice skating, ice hockey, skiing, bicycling, crew, hiking, two-man volleyball, lacrosse, shuffleboard, weight lifting, codeball, aerial darts, and rugby football were being included in intramural programs.

Intramural departments in many institutions have definitely extended the scope of their services. The concept of intramurals has broadened and many programs have taken on a definite recreational aspect by providing competition in billiards, pool, bridge, chess, rifle shooting, roller skating, croquet, and dart baseball. Coeducational recreation is organized and conducted by some intramural departments for veterans and their families. Many intramural directors have assumed the responsibility for the informal, unorganized athletic competition in their schools and have developed and expanded these opportunities. Special efforts are made in a number of colleges and universities to bring faculty members into the intramural program.

Sports clubs. There has been a considerable development of sports clubs in colleges and universities since the war. These clubs are usually organized by groups interested in recreational sports, such as tennis, badminton, skiing, table tennis, archery, weight lifting, handball, and squash. At times these clubs are coeducational. In most cases they are organized and sponsored by the intramural department. These organizations usually have a constitution and officers. It is quite common for these clubs to compete in municipal and intercity leagues, as well as with other colleges and universities. Expenses of such competition are borne by the organization members. A limitation is usually placed on the number of outside contests. A common requirement is that a faculty member accompany the club team on all trips.

Informal athletic competition. Intramural directors have been giving increased attention to the spontaneous, informal athletic competition which exists in practically all institutions. There are always students who are anxious to play when the facilities and equipment are available. By setting facilities aside for such competition and publicizing the opportunity, many more students can be brought into such competition. The intramural department can extend this program by providing a match-making service for all sports. With such an arrangement any student could indicate the sport he would like to play and the time he has available. The amount of participation and the number of participants justifies the effort of the intramural department to promote this informal competition.

Faculty recreation. Some intramural departments have assumed the responsibility for promoting faculty recreation. The faculty has great need for recreational activities, and some provision should be made for those who desire to play The intramural department is the logical agency to assume responsibility for conducting faculty recreation.

Faculty leagues and faculty tournaments can be conducted in institutions with large faculties. In the smaller colleges and high schools, the best that can be done for the faculty members is to set aside a regular period for them and provide the necessary facilities and equipment. The intramural director or the staff member in charge of faculty recreation should keep the faculty constantly informed and encourage them to use all the recreational opportunities that the department has available.

SELECTED REFERENCES

Grambeau, Rodney, *A Survey of the Administration of Intramural Sports Programs for Men in Selected Colleges and Universities in North America.* Ed.D. dissertation, University of Michigan, 1959.

Krupa, Joseph H., *A Study of Intramural Sports for Boys in the Public Secondary Schools of Pennsylvania.* Ed.D. dissertation, University of Pittsburgh, 1953.

Leavitt, Norma, and Hartley Price, *Intramural and Recreational Sports for Men and Women* (New York, A. S. Barnes & Co., Inc., 1949).

Means, Louis, *Intramurals: Their Organization and Administration* (Englewood Cliffs, N.J., Prentice-Hall, Inc., 1963).

Mitchell, Elmer, and Pat Mueller, *Intramural Sports,* 3rd ed. (New York, The Ronald Press Company, 1960).

Sheerer, Wilham, *High School Intramural Program* (Minneapolis, Burgess Publishing Co., 1952).

10

student leaders in
physical education

Educational values of student leadership

Ours is a society in which everyone is granted the right to be a
leader in any line of endeavor for which he can prepare himself. We do
not select certain classes as the ruling or leading groups and arbitrarily
relegate others to the less desirable positions. We believe in giving and
taking, in following in some aspects of life while leading in others.

Modern educational philosophy accepts and sponsors the proposition that we learn to do by doing; that is, by actually practicing or living out an experience we require more knowledge of it than by just
hearing or reading about it. If the schools are to prepare students to
live enriched lives during both school life and adult life, many opportunities must be provided for practice of the elements of successful living. One of these elements, certainly, is leadership, around which can
be developed cooperation, loyalty, sociability, and many other desirable
social qualities. Few, if any, other school subjects provide the number
of leadership opportunities that are to be found in physical education.
The instructor who does not take advantage of the outstanding opportunities offered is failing to make use of the possibilities at his command; he is not putting to good use the talents that have been intrusted
to him by the community in which he teaches. The use of student
leaders does not provide an opportunity for the instructor to rest while
the students do his work; instead, it provides a more complete means of
educating through physical education, since it permits the students to
share in various aspects of leadership which the instructor directs.

Student leaders in class work

Since practically all students in the school are members of physical education classes for at least a part of their school career, the regular class work offers an opportunity to provide some type of leadership training for a large percentage of the students. The principles and procedures are essentially the same in junior high school, senior high school, and college. They can be applied below junior high school, but this involves more difficulties. Some minor modifications will need to be made at the various age levels, for the two sexes, and for different types of activity.

A specific class will be considered. In discussing the problem, the following assumptions are made: (1) That the class is composed of 45 10th grade boys, (2) that grades are given for the course in physical education, (3) that a variety of activities (speedball, softball, volleyball, formal work, and games of lower organization) are included, and (4) that the system of student leaders is being introduced for the first time in the school under consideration. Necessary modifications can be made in applying the following material to the other age, sex, and activity groups.

Presenting the plan. This should be done at the first meeting of the class. Some time might well be spent in pointing out the values and opportunities this type of procedure has for the various class members. The general setup and procedure of the plan should be explained, and in this connection the authority and responsibility of a leader should be clearly designated. As a means of overcoming the possible objection that one student should not have the right to tell another what to do, it should be explained that there can be no leaders unless there are followers; and that, in order to have followers when one's turn comes to lead, it is only fair that he serve as a follower for the other fellow's leadership.

Opportunities to lead. There are enough different leadership opportunities in a class of this type that each student should be able to find something in which he can lead reasonably well. Some of those opportunities are listed and discussed in brief:

1. Serving as a leader of squad or class group. There can be, quite conveniently, four or five such leaders in a class of this size. This is one of the better leadership possibilities, for students in this position take charge of their group, under the instructor's direction, for many of the activities.

2. Serving as an activity leader. Student leaders can be of invaluable assistance to the instructor by demonstrating activities in which they are competent and by giving individual help to students who need it.

3. Membership on rules committees. The chairmanship of this committee is an important position. These students present their recommendations to the class concerning local rules interpretation, ground rules for obstacles in the playing area, and matters of that type. The chairman presides during discussion and voting on proposed local rules and alterations. This committee serves as a standing committee to whom rule interpretation problems can be referred during the term. Three to five members are sufficient.

4. Leader of warming-up exercises. This should be passed around so that several class members have the chance to lead the group. These boys must display enthusiasm and assurances tempered with friendliness.

5. Spotters. Spotters are necessary in tumbling and apparatus activities. Students selected for this purpose should be among the most highly skilled in the group.

6. Officials. A class of this type should provide its own officials for the games that are to be played. Some of the better boys can act as chief officials and those less experienced as assistants. These boys should be granted the customary authority due officials of the game concerned.

7. Membership on equipment and grounds committee. The activity area should be in condition to use, but it should be checked by someone to be sure that it is. In softball the bases may need to be placed and taken up later; in volleyball the nets may need to be put up, and in practically every sport the equipment needs to be brought out before class and returned after class. This committee of five members takes care of the above and similar duties.

8. Leader for games of lower organization. Every student in the class should have his turn at presenting a game of this type and directing the remainder of the class in it.

9. Captain of all-star team. Two players can serve in this capacity for each sport. The members, elected by their classmates on the all-star team for the exhibition game at the end of the portion of term assigned to the sport in question, will elect their own captains.

Methods of selecting leaders. In most cases the advantages of participation will be distributed more evenly, and the whole plan will work out more smoothly if the instructor appoints leaders and thus apportions opportunities. This is particularly true concerning officials, committee members, leaders for warming-up exercises and for games of lower organization. However, group leaders should be consulted or given the right to appoint stunt leaders from time to time.

The matter of selecting group leaders presents a somewhat different problem, for these boys must conduct and manage their groups during a large portion of the class time. They must be the type that others will follow readily or the system will not function properly. For the first semester there will be but one-third to two-fifths of a normal class which can serve creditably as group leaders, and those are the boys who should act in that capacity. Later, many more can learn the essential techniques. At the first meeting of the class the instructor should appoint leaders to serve for about three weeks until the class members have an opportunity to know one another. It should be announced that these leaders are to serve three weeks. If the instructor knows few or none of the students, he should still appoint his first group of leaders at about the end of the first meeting. This can be done on the basis of size, general appearance, apparent confidence, extrovertive tendencies shown by speaking up when the opportunity is offered, and on the basis of hunches. On these bases some few will be appointed who do not possess adequate qualifications, but the same would be true if the appointments were made a few meetings later. There is no value in hesitating, for all are new, and a weak leader will probably get along better at first while all are learning the routine than he would later when the routine is established. When the three weeks are up, the class members should elect their leaders for the next division of time—probably five or six weeks. All class members except the first group leaders are eligible. Each member should vote for as many boys as there are to be leaders. The old leaders should count the votes in the presence of the instructor and announce only the highest candidates. If five leaders are to be elected, the five highest become group leaders for the next period. At the end of their service period others are elected as above, with only those who have not served as group leaders eligible for election. The class members can be trusted to elect only those whom they consider leaders, since the weight of group opinion will overbalance a few votes for personal friends. Those selected by the class are those whom the class will follow.

Methods of guiding leaders. This can be done in part by means of general instructions to all concerning the responsibilities and techniques of leadership, but it is done chiefly through leaders' conferences with the instructor. These may be group or individual conferences. For new leaders there should be group conferences at which the specific duties to be performed are discussed, additional suggestions are made, and questions are answered. As the leaders gain experience, the conferences should become less frequent and more individual in nature. A definite effort must be made to help the leader who needs help, but those who are having no difficulties need not be included in the later conferences.

Method of selecting group. Each leader should have the opportunity to choose his group. This should not be done in the presence of the rest of the class members, except for the first time, when the members do not know each other's abilities. Since the purpose here is to develop leadership instead of inferiority complexes, the poorer performers must be spared the depressing effect of being chosen from among the last. They need to have their confidence built up, not destroyed by being made to feel that they are the least desirable candidates. Except as stated above, the following method of selection is recommended. All class members' names except those choosing are written on the board. The right to choose first, second, third, and fourth (assuming four leaders) is determined by lot. On the second round the order is reversed, and he who chose fourth gets the chance to choose fifth; he who chose third chooses sixth; he who chose second chooses seventh; and he who chose first chooses eighth and ninth. This method is followed in order to provide for more equal competition. The choices granted each leader are given in Table 10-1. As a student is chosen, his name is marked off the

Table 10-1.

First	1	8	9	16	17	24	25	32	33	40	41	
Second	2	7	10	15	18	23	26	31	34	39	42	
Third	3	6	11	14	19	22	27	30	35	38	43	
Fourth	4	5	12	13	20	21	28	29	36	37	44	45

board and placed on the list of the man who chose him. The teams should be posted on the bulletin board with the names arranged in alphabetical order; then none will be reminded that he was chosen last or next to last.

Each new group of leaders will choose their squads from the class roll. This will tend to place the men each leader wants on his squad and give each class member a chance to become better acquainted with a larger percentage of the class.

Class control under leaders. Insofar as possible each leader should control and conduct the activities of his group. Only in extreme circumstances should the instructor step in and take charge of a group for control purposes, for when he does that he is destroying the confidence of the leader and the respect of his group for him. The instructor should provide control helps, but they should be more indirect. One of the soundest approaches to this is basing the grade in part on the social aspect of class work. Since one of the purposes of the school is that of developing good citizens, the acts of good citizenship should be rewarded and those of poor citizenship should be penalized. A serviceable device to use in developing better conduct is the "Can't Take It Club." The instructor pledges prospective members for this club on the basis of refusal to follow designated leaders. This refusal may include objecting to officials' decisions, failure to comply with group leader's requests, talking in rules meeting when not recognized by the chairman, and any other acts that provide evidence of not being willing to accept the requests of those in charge. When a student is pledged, the instructor announces his pledging at the next class meeting. Another offense makes him a member of the club. In some situations his squad may initiate him into the club by running him through the spanking machine or something of that type; in other situations the initiation should not be included. The first one to commit three offenses becomes president. Each additional offense carries with it some advanced degree in the "Can't Take It Club," and each advance in the club reduces the score that will be given in the social aspects of the work. If initiations are popular, each advance in the club may merit initiation. There will be few, however, who go any further than full membership in the club, and most of the group, under normal conditions, will not even be pledged.

Individual conferences with the chronic offender and with the leader who has control difficulties are often helps in improving control. Simply talking it over with the unadjusted student in private conference may clear up the matter for him. In the case of the leader, helpful suggestions and the building up of confidence are important.

In some cases the plan of making anyone who objects to an official's decision the new official helps the official to remain in control.

Student leaders in intramural activities

Historically, intramural activities furnished the outstanding opportunity for students to lead in physical education in the schools of this country. This still remains a particularly favorable area of operation for student leaders, under faculty guidance. Since student leadership forms an integral part of the discussion of intramural athletics, it has been presented more fully in Chapter 9.

Student leaders in varsity athletics

Interscholastic and intercollegiate athletics provide two distinct types of student leadership opportunities: those delegated to the students selected to direct their respective teams in action and those provided for managers and assistants. Captains of the various teams and other specific team generals, such as the quarterback in football, the catcher in baseball, and the coxswain in crew, are the leaders of the first type. The captains may be elected by the letter winners of the previous year or appointed by the coach for a season or for a single contest. Many coaches prefer to have the captain serve for a season, especially if there is one boy who is an outstanding leader, for this practice gives more stability to the team organization. If there is no boy who really stands out as a leader, the team may function as well or better with a different captain for each contest. If the practice of having a different captain for each contest prevails, the coach almost always appoints him. Specific team generals, other than captains, are appointed by the coach to fit the particular requirements of the position.

These positions of leadership in varsity athletics are some of the most desired and most valuable in the entire school. Consequently, it is not sound practice to permit one boy to serve as captain in 2 or 3 sports or for two years in one sport, since others should also have an opportunity to receive the benefits of this experience. It should also be remembered that student leaders should be under the direction of the coach. If there is any value in training and experience, the coach certainly is better qualified to direct than students are. If the coach cannot be trusted with matters of supervising leadership, the remedy does not lie in turning the responsibility over to students but rather in dismissing that coach and securing one who can take care of his normal responsibilities.

Opportunities for managers in varsity athletics (see page 299).

Leaders corps

Some schools have well-established leaders corps. They are somewhat differently organized and conducted than the student leader organization previously described. They represent an elite group in the school and membership is highly prized—in fact it may be considered one of the highest honors in the school.

Standards for membership are very high. Such criteria as the following are commonly established: (1) excellence in physical education activities, (2) a level of physical fitness which is appreciably above the average, (3) at least average academic achievement, (4) leadership ability, (5) good citizenship, and (6) interest and enthusiasm in physical education.

In a senior high school a common practice is to select only seniors for the leaders corps. They have the advantage of greater maturity and experience in this program. Ordinarily the selection is made in the spring of the year while the students are still juniors. All staff members should participate in the selection of the student leaders.

Members of the leaders corps wear a distinctive uniform, which sets them apart from other students in physical education classes. Likewise they wear a jacket or insignia in their academic classes, which identifies them as members of the leaders corps. Ordinarily, the students purchase their own clothing.

The duties of the members of the leaders corps are to assist the instructor in his physical education classes. To render more valuable assistance they usually go through several sessions per week with the intructor. These extra meetings are held at times when students have free periods such as during activity periods. The purpose of such sessions is to provide the student leaders with a thorough understanding of the next lesson and the manner in which they will perform their role. In addition, they will have the opportunity to perfect their own skills.

A leaders corps program is invaluable in strengthening the total physical education program. In addition to providing a valuable leadership experience for the students involved a leaders corps helps to recruit future physical educators. Many secondary school students have been stimulated to enter the field of physical education because of the interest engendered while they participated as a member of a leaders corps.

Another invaluable contribution of the leaders corps is that more individual assistance is available to students who need it. The instructor may have one or two student leaders in his class who can render assistance to those students who have difficulty mastering the skill that is being taught. Such individual attention is difficult to provide when the instructor is handling a class of thirty to forty students all by himself.

SELECTED REFERENCES

Hughes, William Leonard, Esther French, and Nelson Lehsten, *Administration of Physical Education for Schools and Colleges* (New York, The Ronald Press Company, 1962), pp. 206-210.

Kozman, Hilda Clute, Rosalind Cassidy, and Chester O. Jackson, *Methods in Physical Education* (Dubuque, Iowa, William C. Brown Company, Publishers, 1964).

11

budget making and finance

Importance of efficient financial management

The financial management of his department is one of the most important duties of the physical education administrator. Although the financial aspects of the service and intramural programs are not particularly difficult or time consuming, those of the interscholastic and intercollegiate athletic programs do entail considerable responsibility. Most physical education directors administer the interschool athletic programs and are therefore concerned with handling money, making all types of financial transactions, bookkeeping, and preparing budgets. In handling these financial matters, simple and effective procedures are available and should be used.

Any school official who receives and expends funds is expected to employ sound business methods. For him to do otherwise reflects adversely upon him. This situation prevails, regardless of the size of the institution or the amount of money involved. No teacher or administrator can afford to be careless or ignorant in handling public funds.

Another reason why efficient financial management is important is that maximum benefit must be secured from the revenue available. Most departments never have sufficient funds to provide all the desired services to students. Consequently, available resources must be wisely employed. Almost invariably those departments with the most serious financial problems use the most unbusinesslike procedures. This is particularly true of small high schools and colleges.

Despite the great importance of this phase of their duties, few directors are prepared for the efficient financial administration of the physical education department when they first undertake it. The great majority of administrators learn by the trial-and-error method. Experience may be the best teacher; but it is an expensive teacher, particularly where finance is concerned. Large universities and colleges emphasize the importance of special training when they employ an expert to handle the business affairs of the intercollegiate athletic program. The director is frequently selected for his business ability. The professional physical education programs should make some provision to prepare physical educators for the financial responsibilities that they will encounter in their positions.

THE PHYSICAL EDUCATION BUDGET

In the great majority of schools the budget for the service and intramural programs is prepared separately from the budget for interschool athletics. In an extensive study Adams [1] discovered that approximately 80 percent of secondary schools followed the practice of having a separate budget for the athletic program. In a more recent study Kingsbury [2] found that over 80 percent of the first class school districts had separate physical education and athletic budgets. When the physical education budget (including intramurals) is submitted separately from the budget for interschool athletics, it is much easier to prepare because it is not concerned with the estimation of income and it does not involve the amount or variety of expenditures. In such instances the physical education director's duties are not appreciably different from those of the head of the physics or chemistry department. The interschool athletic program is the factor that accentuates the financial responsibilities of physical education administrators.

Source of financial support

In most high schools and colleges and universities the usual practice is to finance the service and intramural programs from the institutional budget. The service program is considered a part of the curricular offerings and, as such, is almost invariably supported from the regular school funds. Similarly, the cost of facilities and personnel for

[1] Harry Adams, *A Report on Current Practices in the Administration of Interscholastic Athletics in Five Hundred Ninety-one Selected Secondary Schools in the United States.* Unpublished master's thesis, University of North Carolina, 1950, p. 35.

[2] Keith W. Kingsbury, *An Analysis of Budgetary and Financial Practices Utilized by Physical Education Departments in First Class School Districts of Washington State in 1963.* M.S. dissertation, University of Washington, 1963.

intramural athletics is almost always carried in the institutional budget. At times, however, the equipment and operating expenses come from the interschool athletic funds. This situation should not prevail because intramural athletics are an integral part of the physical education program and should be provided for all students as a desirable educational experience.

Steps in preparing the physical education budget

The major items involved in the separate physical education budget (including intramurals) are capital outlay, expendable equipment, and maintenance and repairs. These items should be included under these separate headings in the budget. The cost of capital equipment and maintenance and repairs is comparatively easy to estimate. Capital equipment includes all expenditures that increase the value of the school plant, such as additions of any kind to the grounds, buildings, or fixed equipment. A new backstop, tennis court, or shower room are examples of capital outlay. Maintenance and repair items include painting, refinishing, and repair of equipment.

The first step in determining the expendable equipment (balls, nets, shuttlecocks, bats, and the like) needed for the following year is to take an inventory of what is on hand. This should be done as late in the school year as possible because the equipment will continue in use until classes are terminated for the summer. Ordinarily, it will be necessary to take inventory three or four months before the end of the school year. In this case an estimate must be made of the amount of wear and tear of the equipment during the remainder of the school year. With experience this can be done quite accurately.

In making the inventory it is important to classify the condition of all items of equipment. Some equipment will be new or almost new; other equipment will be in moderate condition; some items will need repair; and others should be discarded. A careful inventory is of vital importance, since the request for new equipment is based upon it. It is not a responsibility to turn over to students, although students may assist with it.

The next step is to determine the total amount and type of equipment which will be needed during the next school year. Analysis of budgets for previous years will indicate the amount of equipment normally required. This amount can be used as the starting point for determining over-all requirements. Changes in the number of students, departmental policies, or the nature of the service and intramural programs will increase or decrease this amount. When the estimate of total equipment needed has been obtained, the amount of new equipment to be ordered will be the difference between what is required and what is left over.

In making the estimate of what is needed the administrator should be certain to order an adequate amount. It is better to err on the side of too much rather than too little equipment. This is not to suggest padding the budget, but to recommend liberal rather than ultra-conservative estimates. It is preferable to have a small amount of equipment left over at the end of the year rather than to run short.

In many secondary schools the physical education department is given a budget for supplies (balls, nets, rackets, bows, arrows, shuttle-cocks, etc.) based on a certain amount per student in school. All expendable items for the department for the year must be purchased from this budget. In regard to equipment items (trampoline, parallel bars, mats, baskets, etc.) usually the principal is allocated a lump sum for such items annually. All department heads then make requests to the principal for equipment items. His decisions are based upon what he considers the most urgent needs.

After the budget has received the necessary approvals the equipment should be ordered. Practice varies in this regard. In some schools the physical education administrator is free to order whatever equipment he prefers as long as his total spending does not exceed the money allocated. In other schools bids from several merchandisers must be invited. In this case the administrator must prepare detailed specifications of what he wants. When equipment is purchased in this manner, frequently, the type of equipment received is not what was wanted. Generally, the responsibility is the administrator's because he did not prepare the specifications in sufficient detail.

In a department with several staff members it is advisable to solicit their advice before ordering new equipment. The different staff members may have had more experience with certain items of equipment than the administrator, and their recommendations may be very helpful.

THE ATHLETIC BUDGET

Support of interschool athletics

Interscholastic and intercollegiate athletics are usually supported in part from the institutional budget and in part from gate receipts and other sources of income. Although most schools include the salaries of coaches from the regular institutional budget and provide for the maintenance and operation of the athletic facilities, few institutions go so far as to appropriate funds to meet the current expenses of the athletic program. In a study of 2,125 secondary schools, Hughes and Schooler [3] discovered that only 15 percent of the school districts were moving toward complete financing of the athletic program from tax funds.

Ideally, interschool athletics should be financed in the same way as any other school subject. The only justification for interscholastic and intercollegiate athletics is the significant educational experiences they provide. These experiences are so vital and important that they merit financial support from institutional funds. These values of athletics cannot be obtained if the program must be supported by gate receipts. Gate receipts and educational outcomes are incompatible objectives of interschool athletics. Experience has repeatedly demonstrated that athletics are conducted on a much higher plane if they derive their support from regular school funds.

The reason for the failure of many schools to finance athletics properly stems from the philosophy that only curricular activities are deserving of such support. Athletics originated as extracurricular activities and in many schools are still considered in that category. However, there is an increasing trend to regard athletics as an integral part of the school curriculum. In New York State, athletics by Board of Regents' action are a definite part of the physical education program of the schools, and boards of education are empowered to provide financial assistance from regular school funds.

The practice of expecting interschool athletics to be largely self-supporting has led to most of the problems that have developed. The amount of gate receipts is largely dependent upon the success of the teams. The effort to produce winning teams often results in undesirable educational practices. Most of these are involved in getting superior athletes into school and in keeping them eligible to play. The athletic program can never be educational in a desirable sense so long as it remains commercial.

The following statement by Hughes and French [4] relates to this matter:

So long as the program of competitive sports must depend for its very existence upon the direct financial support of the public, it is not unreasonable to expect that varsity athletics in such schools and colleges will reflect the public rather than the educational point of view. Where this is the case, it can scarcely be hoped that athletics will attain perfection in the imperfect society

[3] Otto Hughes and Virgil Schooler, *A Survey of Athletics in the Secondary Schools of the North Central Association*, Bulletin of the Indiana University School of Education, Vol. 32, No. 4 (July, 1956).

[4] William Hughes and Esther French, *The Administration of Physical Education for Schools and Colleges* (New York, Ronald, 1954), p. 309. Copyright ©, 1954, The Ronald Press Company. Reprinted by permission of the publishers.

which so profoundly influences their policies. If interscholastic and intercollegiate athletics are ever to reflect the educational rather than the public point of view, they must first achieve financial independence.

The Educational Policies Commission strongly recommends that the complete costs of the interscholastic athletic program be paid out of general school funds. In some states this cannot be done until permissive legislation is passed. Such legislation should be initiated in those states where it is needed.

The results of financing interscholastic athletics entirely out of tax funds in one city are reported as follows by the Educational Policies Commission: [5]

1. The high school program has ceased to be a commercial enterprise, dependent on gate receipts. Outside pressure for postseason, charity, all-star, and curtain raiser games have been eliminated.
2. More adequate health and safety protection is accomplished by having fewer games and contests, avoiding play during inclement weather, providing safe equipment and safe transportation, and valuing the health of the participant above the winning of the game.
3. Most football games are now played on week-end afternoons, with resulting decrease in such problems as vandalism and rowdyism.
4. All schools within a system are assured of equal quality of equipment and supplies. Through central purchasing savings can be had.
5. Some of the hidden costs of public high school athletic fees are reduced for the student.

Sources of athletic income in high schools

In a very extensive study Adams [6] found the five most frequent sources of income were: (1) gate receipts, (2) board of education, (3) student activity fees, (4) season tickets, and (5) athletic association membership fees. Each of these services will be discussed.

Gate receipts. Gate receipts are an important source of income in interscholastic athletics. Football and basketball are the chief income-producing sports, although even these are not operated at a profit in many small schools. The other interscholastic sports rarely produce a profit.

Gate receipts should come predominantly from the adult public. It is an accepted policy to keep admission prices for students at a minimum. Athletics are organized for the benefit of students, who should not be deprived of the opportunity to attend because of high admission prices. A small number of high schools admit all students free. Students should also be given priority when it is necessary to limit attendance

[5] Educational Policies Commission, *School Athletics* (Washington, D.C., National Education Association and American Association of School Administrators, 1955), p. 66.
[6] *Op. cit.,* p. 45.

at indoor athletic contests because of inadequate seating accommodations.

The philosophy that the interschool athletic program should be subsidized by the institution does not infer that gate receipts should be abolished. Although this measure has considerable merit it is too revolutionary to be practical at the present time. Gate receipts are not objectionable so long as they are incidental. Sufficient funds should be appropriated to insure the adequate operation of the program. The gate receipts would then revert to the institutional budget.

In many high schools all athletic income goes directly into the student activity budget. This includes gate receipts and guarantees that come from games played away from home. In this situation the costs for equipment, travel, medical care, scouting, advertising, towels, laundry, films, officials, and other operational expenses will be defrayed from the student activity budget.

Ordinarily high schools do not have guarantees. The usual procedure is for the home team to keep all gate receipts.

In many communities deficits will be paid by the school district or from the student body budget. In some school districts it is expected that deficits will be made up in the coming year. It is exceptional to require that the deficit be liquidated during the ensuing year. Some schools are fortunate enough to have a surplus at the end of the year. Such surpluses are either carried over to succeeding years, transferred to the student body budget, or turned over to the school district.

Student activity fees. Another important source of income is derived from the student activity fee. A substantial majority of high schools have adopted a student activity plan to provide support for all student activities. Under this plan each student pays a prescribed amount—usually from $5 to $8—which entitles him to admission to all home athletic contests and to all other school functions for which there is a charge, such as school plays, concerts, and operettas. In addition, the cost of the student newspaper and the school annual is defrayed in whole or in part. Most schools also admit students from the visiting institutions to athletic contests at a reduced rate upon presentation of the student body card. Students who do not belong to the student activity association are usually admitted to home contests at a reduced fee.

The income from student body fees is usually apportioned over the various student activities. The allocation may be made by the student council, a student activity board, or a committee that consists of representatives of the various activities.

Various arrangements are made to collect the student activity fee. In some schools the entire fee is collected in a lump sum early in the fall. In others the fee is paid on the installment basis, such as 15 cents per week for each week of the school year or 25 cents per week until the activity ticket is paid for. Experience has demonstrated that it is better practice to have the activity ticket completely paid for before the basketball schedule is completed. In the majority of schools the student activity plan is not compulsory. This plan, however, interests a larger percentage of students in the various activities than any other.

Student athletic association. In some schools each student is assessed a certain amount, which entitles him to membership in the student athletic association. The cost of membership in the athletic association varies from $2 to $5 per year and gives the student the privilege of attending all home games. Membership may be required or optional. This method was quite popular a number of years ago but has been replaced in many schools by the student activity plan.

Miscellaneous sources. Many high schools find it necessary to resort to additional methods of raising money. In the smaller institutions, the revenue from gate receipts, school board appropriations, and student fees is often insufficient to meet all of the expenditures. Funds may be raised by dances, operettas, concerts, carnivals, pageants, minstrel shows, a school circus, class socials, plays, magazine subscriptions, moving pictures, and picnics. These methods of raising money frequently prevent athletic deficits. Some schools find it necessary to use one or more of such methods annually. The chief objection to raising money in this way is that students spend too much time and effort upon the particular activity. At times, also, these activities take an undue amount of the teachers' time. If these money-raising ventures are overdone, the public becomes resentful.

Procedure in preparing the athletic budget

At the end of the season for each sport a careful inventory of the equipment and supplies is made. Based upon this inventory the head coach of the sport makes out a tentative list of the equipment that will be needed for the following year. This list and the estimated cost is reviewed with the athletic director who may or may not modify it in consideration of the anticipated funds. The coach and athletic director then discuss this budget with the principal. If it appears satisfactory to him he presents it to the Budget and Finance Committee of the Student Council. If it is approved there it will go to the Student Council for final approval.

Type of student tickets

Regardless of the manner in which students pay for their home athletic events, most schools provide some type of season ticket for them. In some institutions, a ticket is used that is punched in the appropriate space for each contest. Other institutions use a booklet made up of detachable slips that are consecutively numbered. The student's signature is on the cover of the booklet, and a space is provided on each slip for his signature. For each contest, a designated slip is detached from the booklet. For identification purposes, students may be asked to sign the slip, and the signature may be compared with that on the cover. Some schools attach small photographs to the season ticket or booklet to eliminate their use by others than students. Student tickets should not be transferable.

Sources of athletic income in colleges and universities

In the institutions of higher learning the chief sources of athletic income are gate receipts, student athletic fees, activity tickets, and institutional appropriations. Additional sources of revenue may be contributions, subscriptions, concessions, programs, parking fees, rentals, and radio and television broadcasting fees.

Contrary to the popular impression, intercollegiate athletics in the great majority of institutions are not self-supporting. Were it not for substantial support from institutional budgets, most intercollegiate athletic programs could not continue. The salaries of coaches and other personnel connected with athletics, as well as the expense of maintaining and operating athletic facilities, come from this source. It is generally expected that athletic income will be sufficient to cover such operating expenses as equipment, travel, medical care, laundry, and officiating.

It is only in a relatively small number of institutions that the income is sufficient to cover all expenses of intercollegiate athletics without assistance from the institutional budget. Even in these institutions a portion of the salaries of athletic personnel may come from the physical education budget if these staff members perform some services in the physical education department. In some of these schools the gate receipts are sufficient to purchase new buildings and facilities that are used for physical education and intramural as well as intercollegiate athletic activities.

A number of the wealthier private colleges provide for the complete support of intercollegiate athletics in the general budget. All expenses are covered by appropriations. The athletic income is purely incidental and reverts to the institutional budget.

Heavy reliance is placed upon gate receipts in colleges and universities. The bulk of these come from football and basketball. When these two sports must support themselves as well as most of the other sports and pay salaries and provide college buildings and equipment, a situation is created which invites overemphasis by those concerned with its direction and management. Intramural athletics are financed from the athletic budget in many institutions. Educators have been very critical of various uneducational aspects of intercollegiate athletics; yet they themselves are partially responsible for their existence. If the heavy burden on gate receipts could be lightened by adequate financial support, athletics would become more valuable as an educational agency.

Student fees help substantially in supporting the intercollegiate athletic program. Most schools find it necessary to require the students to purchase a season ticket or coupon book. The price varies from $10 to $20 for the school year. This fee permits the student to attend all home athletic contests and to purchase tickets for contests away from home at a reduced cost.

Concessions

The income-producing possibilities of concessions have rarely been appreciated in small schools and colleges. In these smaller institutions, where the financial need is the greatest, the concessions are frequently overlooked or, if they are used, they are inefficiently operated. Professional teams and large university athletic departments have discovered that there is substantial revenue in concessions if they are properly handled.

Concessions may be handled by the school itself or by an outside concessionaire. Within the school it may be operated by the physical education or athletic department, the athletic association, or by some student organization. When concessions are handled outside the school, the concessionaire should be selected after competitive bids have been received. In advertising bids the detailed specifications that will govern the concession should be stated and should become part of the concession contract. The concession specifications should require that the concessionaire sell no commodities and employ no persons of which the school may disapprove. Standards of sanitation and methods of vending should also be explicitly stated.

The contract should provide for payment of a percentage of gross receipts. The flat-sum arrangement may work a hardship on the institution or the concessionaire. Net income should not be used as the basis for determining percentages, as there is invariably the question of what costs the concessionaire will include in determining net proceeds.

For interschool athletic events that draw considerable attendance, the management of the concessions becomes a business operation of such size that high schools and colleges have difficulty handling it effectively. In these instances most of the institutions have found it advantageous to have a concessionaire handle them. Experience has shown that more income has been received from a concessionaire than from a school-operated concession.

Increasing gate receipts

The best way to increase gate receipts from high school and college athletics is to have winning teams. However, there are other methods of making athletic contests more attractive to the public. A season ticket sold at a reduced rate is one of the most effective methods of increasing gate receipts. Such a plan guarantees a definite income despite poor teams and bad weather. It also provides funds early in the season when they are needed to get under way. Adults are appreciative of the opportunity because it results in a saving to them. The price of a season ticket varies from 50 to 75 percent of the total cost of tickets to each home game. If season tickets are made transferable, they will prove more attractive to adults.

In many communities reserved seats will appeal to certain adults. Some individuals are willing to pay more if they are assured of a good seat. There are always individuals who are unable to arrive at the game in time to get a good seat, who would not attend if reserved seats were not available.

Well-coached teams appeal to the public. Public interest cools quickly when the players demonstrate poor fundamentals and appear disorganized. Many individuals will continue to support a team even in defeat if it gives the appearance of being well coached. In this connection, it is important to schedule opponents of approximately the same strength as the home team. Unevenly matched teams are not good attractions. In addition to being well coached, teams will appeal more to spectators if they are smartly attired.

One of the strongest attractions and most colorful features of athletic contests is the music, cheering, and pregame and half-time entertainment. Good officiating adds to everyone's enjoyment of a game. Attractive, accurate programs, a good scoreboard and a loud-speaker system with a capable announcer are all factors that provide satisfaction to the spectators.

Other factors that contribute to the comfort and enjoyment of spectators are good seats, convenient entrances and exits, and a sufficient number of clean, readily accessible restrooms. Having good parking facilities available near the athletic field or gymnasium is an important consideration. Contests should always be started at the time advertised.

There is no question whatsoever that night football produces substantially more revenue than afternoon contests. A large part of the adult public who find it impossible to leave their work or business in the afternoon are able to attend at night. There is, however, considerable opposition to night football from the standpoint of being less desirable for students.

The importance of good publicity in increasing gate receipts is well established. The entire matter of publicity is discussed in Chapter 13.

The control of finances

In the early days of interscholastic and intercollegiate athletics, the control of finances resided in the hands of the coach or graduate manager. These individuals were rarely called upon to account for the funds of the athletic department, and audits to check the athletic accounts were seldom used. Under these conditions, it is not surprising that a great deal of money was misused and misappropriated. Such financial practices naturally served to increase the evils of commercialization and subsidization.

High schools. More financially and educationally sound methods of handling interscholastic athletic funds have evolved in recent years. In general, the trend is for these moneys to be handled in the same manner as other school funds. Adams,[7] in an extensive study of interscholastic athletics, found that the persons responsible for the control of athletic funds in the order of frequency were: (1) the principal, (2) a member of the business department of the faculty, (3) the business manager of the school system, (4) the faculty manager of athletics, and (5) the superintendent.

The practice of having the treasurer or business manager of the board of education handle all athletic funds has much to recommend it. Such a plan centralizes all financial matters and insures a more businesslike procedure. In particular, a more accurate audit is likely to result. However, many boards of education hesitate to assume the responsibility for athletic funds because they are not tax moneys and do not come within the scope of their duties.

Adams' [8] data reveal that in the great majority of high schools all funds are handled within the school itself. The recommended practice is to use a centralized accounting system whereby the responsibility for all financial accounts is centralized in one individual, such as the principal, commercial teacher, or other designated person. A system whereby the various accounts are decentralized and handled separately leads to confusion and inefficiency.

In the centralized accounting system all athletic funds, along with all other activity funds, are deposited with the school treasurer. Records are maintained for all deposits. When purchases are to be made,

7 *Ibid.,* p. 69.
8 *Ibid.,* p. 71.

a purchase order in triplicate must be signed first by the athletic director and then certified by the school treasurer. One copy goes to the vendor, one copy is retained by the school treasurer, and the remaining copy is kept by the athletic director. Bills are not paid by the school treasurer until an invoice has been received from the vendor and checked by the athletic director or his representative that the materials received correspond with what has been ordered. At periodic intervals, probably once a month, the school treasurer submits a report to the athletic director and principal on the condition of the athletic budget.

The school treasurer should be bonded for the largest amount of money that he will be responsible for during the year. His accounts should be audited annually by a qualified auditor.

Colleges and universities. As the faculty assumed control of athletics, it undertook to remove the control of finances from the hands of those directly in charge of athletics. Although athletic directors still handle the funds in a number of institutions, the common practice today is to place the handling of athletic finances in the office of the general business manager of the college or university. A number of the larger universities have a business manager within the department. The most satisfactory plan, however, is to have the university treasurer or the university business officer in actual charge of the care and distribution of athletic funds. This individual is usually a highly trained businessman, well qualified to handle the funds of the athletic department. Under such a plan, the misuse of funds is reduced to a minimum.

Under this plan, the director may make out a requisition for any purchases he desires to make. This requisition is sent to the purchasing department, where two vouchers are made out and sent to the vendor. The vendor sends the equipment to the athletic department and returns the vouchers with the equipment as bills. The athletic department receives and checks the equipment and vouchers. One of the vouchers is kept on file and the other is sent to the business office, which then pays for the purchase. When the director desires cash, he makes out a requisition directly to the business office for the desired amount. Practically all institutions require receipts from the director or coach for his cash expenditures.

The above plan has much to recommend it. The director may make purchases as he sees fit, as long as he remains within his budget. He is not deprived of his authority to make expenditures. An unfortunate situation exists in some institutions where the business manager dominates the purchase of athletic equipment. If the director is unable to purchase wisely for his department, he is poorly qualified for his position. It would appear that his experience in this field and his knowledge of the specific use for which the purchases are intended should

make it desirable that he be at least consulted when purchases are made
for his department.

Special procedures in large cities

Interscholastic athletics in larger cities are usually coordinated
by an individual who functions from a central office, usually the superintendent's office. Methods of operation vary from city to city. A common
practice is to pool all gate receipts and to divide the total amount equally
among all schools. In one city all athletic funds are turned over to the
central office. Ten percent of each athletic department's gross receipts
is placed in a general fund. The remaining 90 percent of income is available to each school to use as it desires. The money in the general fund
is used to assist the poorer schools in financing their athletic programs.
In many cities the purchase of all athletic equipment is coordinated
through the central office. This results in greater economy and, at the
same time, insures each school a reasonable amount of equipment, with
no school having an advantage over any other. A central organization is
particularly desirable in those cities that have central stadiums and
armories or coliseums.

Oakland, California, provides an interesting example of a centralized
administration of interscholastic athletics.[9] In this city the school district
assumes the responsibility of providing for the coach and his salary, the
supervisory staff, and all facilities including their maintenance. The gate
receipts for all interscholastic athletic competitions are deposited in a
central fund. From this fund the director of physical education pays for
all transportation costs, officiating, all medical expenses, including physician's fees, and all other expenses of a general nature. Each spring each
school receives an identical allotment from the central fund. Schools are
not permitted to use student body or other funds to supplement this
allotment. Each school is also provided with a petty cash fund of $25
each semester for incidental expenses.

Athletic equipment is purchased on a centralized basis, although no
school is required to purchase any item it does not want. With respect
to pieces of equipment that can be standardized, such as balls of all types,
baseball bats, and shoulder pads, the coaches of the various sports reach
an agreement as to what they prefer. The specifications for these items
are set up and bids invited. Samples equal or superior to the standard
in quality, utility, and construction must be submitted. The coaches
meet to make the final selection. All equipment not meeting the specifications is eliminated. The lowest bidder receives the order for equip-

9 David Snyder, "Financing Interscholastic Athletic Programs," *California Journal of Secondary Education* (February, 1948), pp. 85-88.

ment meeting the standards. In the matter of athletic clothing for the various sports, each school decides upon the quality, pattern, and colors. Specifications are then set up and bids invited. Samples must be made available. Again, the lowest bidder whose samples are satisfactory receives the order.

When purchases are made the successful bidder is sent a purchase order. At the same time the school receives a duplicate purchase order. Upon receipt of the invoice from the seller and the duplicate purchase order from the school, properly signed and certifying that goods have been received in the quantity and quality as ordered, the bill is paid.

Snyder [10] enumerates the values of this equalization plan as follows:

1. It has provided an opportunity for school leaders to educate students on the basic outcomes of, and necessity for, equality of opportunity.
2. It has equalized standards and quality of equipment for all players.
3. It has permitted the less wealthy schools the use of other student body funds in about the same proportion per student as other schools.
4. It has eliminated special fund-raising events for purchase of equipment.
5. It has lowered the cost of equipment because of competitive bidding.
6. It has meant a real saving in that each school, knowing approximately its athletic budget for each year, can plan wisely over a period of years for its acquisition of equipment.
7. It has permitted each school to have adequate and safe transportation.
8. It has taken many of the burdens and time-consuming problems of athletics out of the hands of the coaches and department heads, thus permitting them more time for their physical education program.

Budget making

The first essential in the efficient management of any enterprise is to plan carefully in advance the income and the expenditures for a fiscal period. This process is essentially what is known as budget making. A budget is merely the complete financial plan, which is based upon the estimated expenditures to be made and the expected income. Budget making naturally originated in connection with business and governmental enterprises. The practice was found desirable and has since extended to most business enterprises and public service organizations, including the schools.

The safest way to avoid deficits in athletics is to adopt budgets that limit the appropriations to the income and then confine the expenditures to the appropriations. The budget results in planned spending. It is the best insurance of an equitable distribution of available funds to all the activities of the athletic department. Examples of the spending of too much money on one sport, resulting in the curtailment or elimination of other sports, are not hard to find. The antagonisms and embarrassment that may develop when this occurs could be eliminated if a budget were

10 *Ibid.,* p. 87.

set up and followed. By means of the budget, the director can show where the money was spent and thus prevent any suspicion of misuse of funds. The need for increased appropriations can be shown and justified more easily and effectively with a budget than without one. Extravagant and foolish buying will be checked, and comparisons with previous years and with other institutions can be made. The budget permits an analysis of the cost of the various sports and reveals where revision can be made, if necessary, with the least loss in the effectiveness of the department.

Procedure in making a budget

There are far more poorly constructed budgets than well-constructed ones, since few athletic departments construct them in accordance with the accepted principles of budgetary procedure. Every school presents an individual problem, but there are some fundamental principles that should be observed by any director who is constructing a budget. There is nothing mysterious about making one; nor is it necessary to be a business expert to do it. Any administrator can construct a satisfactory budget by carefully following a few fundamental principles.

Physical education and athletic budgets are ordinarily prepared in March or April. They are made out annually. The director of physical education has the responsibility for formulating the physical education budget. In colleges and universities the athletic director develops the athletic budget. This same situation prevails in the majority of high schools. However, the principal has this responsibility in many schools. The superintendent, particularly in smaller schools, frequently carries this assignment. Other groups or individuals with this responsibility are the athletic council and the faculty manager of athletics.

The steps in constructing a budget are: (1) collecting the necessary information, (2) classifying the information, and (3) presenting and adopting the budget.

Collecting the necessary information. The information the budget maker collects is concerned with the expected income and necessary expenditures. In estimating the income for the coming fiscal period, the director must consider carefully all the sources from which he may expect revenue. He will know what guarantees will be received for all contests away from home unless the guarantee is dependent upon gate receipts. In the light of past years, how much can be expected at the gate for each home contest throughout the year? Are there any factors during the coming year which will influence the gate receipts one way or another? Will the teams be particularly good or bad? Are colorful teams to be played? Are unusual attractions that will add to gate receipts to be provided? Are strong counterattractions occurring on the days of games? These are only a few of the questions that the director must consider as he estimates the anticipated revenue from gate receipts. He should be conservative in his estimates rather than optimistic. Weather conditions cannot be forecast for the coming year. Basketball is easier to estimate than football because weather conditions do not figure so heavily. In regard to student fees, the director will need to consider any factors that may affect enrollment and the students' desire and ability to purchase season tickets. The appropriation from the board of education or the board of trustees can be estimated from previous appropriations. The director is usually familiar with the board's policies and will probably know whether any changes in the appropriation are likely. If revenue is anticipated from any additional sources, the amount may be calculated on the basis of previous income from these sources.

The estimate of expenditures proceeds along similar lines. The guarantees to be paid opponents are already known unless the gate receipts are to be divided. The cost of transportation and other expenses of trips can be estimated quite accurately on the basis of previous trips. Approximately what will be the expense of each home game? Officials, student help, faculty help, policemen, publicity, tickets, and rent are some of the expense items to be considered in figuring the cost of home games. What purchases will have to be made? This is a difficult item to estimate. An inventory of the equipment on hand is necessary before any accurate estimate of future needs can be made. The cost of purchases may be secured fairly accurately by consulting the cost of the same items in the past. Investigation of the prices other schools are paying is also of assistance. Price trends and the probable future prices must be considered. An average of the past five years may be used to estimate the cost of other items, such as laundry, medical attention and supplies, scouting, awards, intramural activities, and equipment repairs. Office supplies, insurance, telephone, and telegraph expense can be estimated on the basis of previous years' expenditures. The director should never forget that the budget is no better than the time spent estimating it.

Information about these various items should be gathered and compiled continuously. All the needs observed should be noted throughout the year. The entire department should be encouraged to inform the director of present and future needs in order that he may know where new expenditures are needed most. The director should not fail to consult the various staff members who are in a position to assist in supplying needed information. He should keep in constant touch with the supply houses and read current catalogues on the cost of athletic equipment.

Some administrators resort to the practice of "padding" the budget on the assumption that the persons who finally approve it will make a reduction anyway. By including expenditures that are not really necessary or by overestimating the cost of certain items, these administrators hope to build up a cushion that will enable them to obtain the funds they actually consider necessary. Such a practice is dishonest and, in the long run, reflects adversely on the administrator. It breeds distrust and engenders suspicion. Administrators should present honest budgets and be prepared to justify them.

Classifying the information. After the information has been gathered it should be classified. This insures uniformity of presentation and provides for accuracy in planning. It facilitates the gathering and compiling of the data, and it makes easier the reviewing and revising of the estimates. The form the classification takes should resemble the form of the final budget. The information relating to capital outlays and maintenance and operation of the plant is not included in the budget. In high school and most college budgets salaries are not included. All the information is classified under two general heads: one dealing with the information concerning revenue and the other bearing on expenditures. Every item for which an expenditure is contemplated, even though it may amount to only a few dollars, should be reflected in the budget. These smaller items can be segregated under larger headings, but the detailed information should be available if requested. Sample classifications for physical education and athletic budgets are illustrated on pages 410-415.

Presenting and adopting the budget. In colleges the athletic budget is first approved by the athletic committe or board, which usually administers the policies of the department. If no such group exists, the president probably approves it. Final approval of the budget is usually made by the board of trustees or board of regents. High school budgets are first approved by the principal, then by the superintendent, and, finally, by the board of education. At times, the business manager of the college or high school approves the budget before it goes to the board of education or board of trustees. The budget should be adopted before any purchases are made or expenditures entered into for the next year. The fiscal period in use is frequently a factor in the success or shortcomings of the budget, and for this reason, it seems advisable to suggest July 1st as the first day of the fiscal year, because the latter will then approximately coincide with the school year.

Administering the budget

After the athletic and physical education budgets are adopted, they become the financial program of the department. Should they be followed rigidly? There are some who believe that after the budget has been adopted the expenditures should be made as directed. Others hold to the view that the budget should be reviewed again when the expenditures are actually to be made. The general practice, however, is to follow the budget figures fairly closely. The variation is usually from 3 to 5 percent in which the expenditures exceed or fail to match the appropriations.

Practically all budgets make provisions for readjustments. Emergencies are certain to occur, and the budget should be elastic enough to provide for them. There are several different plans that may be followed. An emergency or contingency fund may be set aside in the original budget. But if this fund is too small, the administrator may feel cramped in his efforts to adjust appropriations to unforeseen circumstances. If on the other hand, the fund is too large, it may encourage waste and carelessness and thus defeat one of the main purposes of budget making. The most common plan is to transfer funds from one budgetary item that appears likely not to need all the available money to the item on which the demand has unexpectedly increased. Such transfers, if appreciable,

Table 11-1. Physical education budget I.

Receipts

Football	(See Schedule I)	xxx.xx
Basketball	(Schedule II)	xxx.xx
Baseball	(Schedule III)	xxx.xx
Track and Cross-Country	(Schedule IV)	xxx.xx
Swimming	(Schedule V)	xxxx.xx
Golf	(Schedule VI)	xxx.xx
Tennis	(Schedule VII)	xxx.xx
Wrestling	(Schedule VIII)	xxx.xx
Gymnastics	(Schedule IX)	xxx.xx
Appropriations	(Schedule X)	xxx.xx
Donations and Subscriptions	(Schedule XI)	xxx.xx
Other income	(Schedule XII)	xxx.xx
Total Estimated Receipts		xxxx.xx

Expenditures

Football	(Schedule XIII)	xxx.xx
Basketball	(See Schedule XIV)	xxx.xx
Baseball	(Schedule XV)	xxx.xx
Track and Cross-Country	(Schedule XVI)	xxx.xx
Swimming	(Schedule XVII)	xxx.xx
Wrestling	(Schedule XVIII)	xxx.xx
Golf	(Schedule XIX)	xxx.xx
Tennis	(Schedule XX)	xxx.xx
Gymnastics	(Schedule XXI)	xxx.xx
Required Physical Education	(Schedule XXII)	xxx.xx
Intramural Athletics	(Schedule XXIII)	xxx.xx
General	(Schedule XXIV)	xxx.xx
Total Estimated Expenditures		xxxx.xx

however, must have the approval of the athletic board, the business manager, or perhaps, in a college, the president.

Proper records should be kept in order that the actual revenue and expenditures may be compared with the budget estimates. These records are invaluable to the administrator as he prepares his new budget. In addition, they are of value in making necessary adjustments where indicated in the current budget. The administrator should receive monthly reports so that he may know the relationship of income and expenses with the budget estimates. He needs to know whether actual income is in line with his estimates. Concerning expenditures he must always know the amount appropriated, the amount expended, commitments that must be paid but have not yet been received, and the unallocated balance. If income is much lower than anticipated during the first half of the fiscal period, it might be indicated that expenditures should be reduced in the second half of the period to prevent a serious deficit.

A practical budget

The physical education department may have one or two budgets, depending upon whether or not the athletic budget is separate. A combined budget, which may be used by a large university or modified to meet the needs of a small high school, is given in Table 11-1.

Each source of income is explained in greater detail in the actual schedule for that source. Expenditures are also itemized in greater detail in the schedules. The following schedules are illustrative:

Schedule I—Football receipts:

1. Game at	xxx.xx
2. Game at	xxx.xx
3. Game at	xxx.xx
4. Game at	xxx.xx
5. Game at	xxx.xx
6. Game at	xxx.xx
7. Game at	xxx.xx
Radio broadcast receipts	xxx.xx
Program receipts	xxx.xx
Concession receipts	xxx.xx
Total estimated football receipts	xxxx.xx

Schedule XIV—Basketball expenditures:

Office expense	xxx.xx
Printing and advertising	xxx.xx
Travel	xxx.xx
Wages	xxx.xx
Salaries	xxx.xx

Equipment and supplies	xxx.xx
Clearing and expenditures	xxx.xx
Awards	xxx.xx
Medical attention and supplies	xxx.xx
Officials	xxx.xx
Guarantees	xxx.xx
General	xxx.xx
Total estimated basketball expenditures	xxxx.xx

The various expenditure schedules may be itemized in greater detail. The following classification and codification are suggested as an aid in keeping a detailed, reliable record of expenditures in the physical education department:

CLASSIFICATION OF ACTIVITIES

A. Football
B. Baseball
C. Basketball
D. Track and cross country
E. Wrestling
F. Swimming
G. Golf
H. Tennis
I. Gymnastics
J. Required physical education
K. Intramural athletics
L. General

CLASSIFICATION OF ACCOUNTS

Office expense:
011 Dues and subscriptions
012 Stamps and postage
013 Telephone and telegraph
014 Freight, express, and cartage
015 General

Printing:
021 Tickets, yearbooks
022 Advertising—newspapers and magazines
023 Advertising—posters, schedules, etc.
024 Advertising—photographs and engraving
025 General printing

Travel:
031 Team transportation
032 Scouting
033 Local transportation
034 Hotel and lodging
035 Meals
036 General travel

Supplies:
041 Athletic supplies (not equipment)
042 Medical supplies
043 Grounds and pool supplies
044 General

Repairs:
051 Equipment repairs
052 General repairs

Wages:
061 Handling bleachers
062 Ticket takers and ticket sellers
063 Police
064 Assistants to medical supervisor
065 Auditing
066 Student help in equipment room, towel box
067 General

Equipment:
071 Equipment
072 General

Laundry and cleaning:
081 Towels
082 Dry cleaning
083 Laundry

Insurance:
091 Travel
092 Earnings
093 Public liability

Other expenditures:
101 Hospital and dental service
102 Medical attention

103 Awards
104 Guarantees
105 Officials—fees and expenses

In those institutions where salaries are paid from athletic revenue, a salaries account should be carried. This would include all salaries that are not paid directly by the institution. The preceding classification is used as follows: every expenditure made is allocated to some activity. Thus, if a telephone bill for football is paid, football is charged with the amount of the bill. Therefore, the item will be recorded as 013A. The 013 refers to telephone and telegraph expense and the A to football. Intramural awards would be recorded as 103K. A trip by the tennis squad would be recorded as 031H for the transportation expense, 034H for the hotel expense, and 035H for the meal expense. When all expenditures are classified in this manner as they occur, it is a simple matter to find out what the total expenditures for each activity have been. The coach himself may employ the above system of recording expenditures in order to know the cost of the various items and activities without having recourse to the business office or the school treasurer.

If a simpler, less detailed budget is desired, the example listed below may be followed. This budget, which was used in a small college, can readily be adapted to a high school.

PHYSICAL EDUCATION BUDGET II

Income

Student activity tickets	xxx.xx
Gate receipts, guaranties—football	xxx.xx
Gate receipts, guaranties—basketball	xxx.xx
Gate receipts, guaranties—baseball	xxx.xx
Gate receipts, guaranties—track	xxx.xx
Other income	xxx.xx
Total income	xxxx.xx

Expenditures

General items, office:

Calls and telegrams	xxx.xx
Stamps, stationery, and office supplies	xxx.xx
Student help (stenographer and secretary)	xxx.xx
Total	xxxx.xx

General items for all activities:

Organization—dues and assessments	xxx.xx

Expense for attending conference meetings	XXX.XX
Medical examination for varsity and freshman squad	XXX.XX
Medical and training supplies	XXX.XX
New towels	XXX.XX
Laundry of towels	XXX.XX
Laundry and repairs (general items)	XXX.XX
Lining materials for fields	XXX.XX
Total	XXXX.XX

Intramurals:

New equipment	XXX.XX
Trophies and medals	XXX.XX
Officials	XXX.XX
Total	XXXX.XX

Tennis:

Equipment	XXX.XX
Traveling expense	XXX.XX
Medical attention	XX.XX
Awards	XX.XX
Total	XXXX.XX

Swimming:

Equipment	XXX.XX
Traveling expense	XXX.XX
Medical attention	XXX.XX
Officials	XXX.XX
Awards	XXX.XX
Total	XXXX.XX

Cross-country:

Equipment	XXX.XX
Traveling expense	XXX.XX
Medical attention	XXX.XX
Awards	XXX.XX
Total	XXXX.XX

Golf:

Traveling expense	XXX.XX
Awards	XXX.XX
Total	XXXX.XX

Wrestling:

Equipment	XXX.XX

Traveling expense   xxx.xx
Medical attention   xxx.xx
Officials   xxx.xx
Awards   xxx.xx
  Total   xxxx.xx

Baseball:
Equipment   xxx.xx
Traveling expense   xxx.xx
Medical attention   xxx.xx
Officials   xxx.xx
Awards—varsity   xxx.xx
Awards—freshmen   xxx.xx
Miscellaneous (games)   xxx.xx
  Total   xxxx.xx

Track:
Equipment   xxx.xx
Traveling expense   xxx.xx
Medical attention   xxx.xx
Officials   xxx.xx
Awards—varsity   xxx.xx
Awards—freshmen   xxx.xx
Miscellaneous (meets)   xxx.xx
  Total   xxxx.xx

Basketball:
Equipment   xxx.xx
Traveling expense   xxx.xx
Medical attention   xxx.xx
Officials   xxx.xx
Publicity and advertising   xxx.xx
Rent of floor   xxx.xx
Cleaning and repairing equipment   xxx.xx
Awards—varsity   xxx.xx
Awards—freshmen   xxx.xx
Miscellaneous (games)   xxx.xx
  Total   xxxx.xx

Football:
Equipment   xxx.xx
Traveling expense   xxx.xx
Medical attention   xxx.xx
Officials   xxx.xx

Publicity and advertising   XXX.XX
Cleaning and repairing equipment   XXX.XX
Awards—varsity   XXX.XX
Awards—freshmen   XXX.XX
Miscellaneous (games)   XXX.XX
   Total   XXXX.XX
   Total expenditures   XXXXX.XX

The accounting procedure

The proper functioning of the budget and the success of budgetary procedures depend largely upon an adequate accounting system. Although the director is rarely in charge of the accounting procedure, he should have some conception of it. It would be impossible for the director to conduct his department on a businesslike basis without the help of the accounting system. It serves to restrict the expenditures to income. Unanticipated tendencies in cost and income will be revealed in time to revise the budget. The director secures much of the information for drafting the budget from the accounting records. The accounting method protects the director or the coach from charges of carelessness and misuse of funds. Upon the information supplied by the accounting records, the director can base his request for further financial assistance from the board.

The individual in charge of the athletic finances is interested in current income and expenses. The accounting method classifies revenue on the receipts side of the budget. However, the recording of current expenditures is more complex. Pittenger [11] states that there are four essential parts in recording expenditures:

1. Original records of every transaction involving expenditure of funds are preserved. These records are almost indispensable when the time comes to audit the physical education accounts.

2. Some form of day book or journal record of expenditures is often useful to serve, on the one hand, as a guide to the original record files, and on the other, as the basis from which to post the regular ledger accounts. This feature is omitted, however, in the smaller high schools, where the ledger pages are posted directly from the original records of financial transactions.

3. The heart of the system is the classified ledger record in which the completed expenditures are regularly posted against the budgetary appropriations in order to reveal the amount expended and the amount remaining for each and every budgetary item at any time.

4. The final state of the accounting procedure is reached in the periodical reports, balance sheet, and revenue statement from the accounting officer to the director of physical education setting forth the current financial situation.

11 B. J. Pittenger, *An Introduction to School Finance* (Boston, Houghton Mifflin Company, 1935), p. 113.

The annual audit. Provisions for frequent, regular audits must be made if the budget is to function properly as an instrument of fiscal control. An audit serves as a check on the manner in which the director administers the budget and gives assurance that the budgetary provisions are being carried out. The audit should be made by competent auditors who are not directly connected with the administration of the school funds. The great majority of schools follow this practice. The head of the commercial department often makes the audit. The audit should be made annually, because the work involved is less confusing and a closer check can be made than when it is delayed. Good budgetary procedure requires an external, independent, annual audit.

Expense reports

Following a trip by a school athletic team a report should be made of the expenses that were incurred. Receipts should be obtained for all expenditures for which cash is paid. Most of the larger institutions employ a form similar to the one used by the University of Pennsylvania (see Figure 11-1). The use of such a form facilitates the accounting of the expenses and is a more businesslike procedure than that followed in schools which do not use any forms.

Interschool financial agreement

Practically all colleges and large high schools sign contracts with each other for all interschool contests. The practice of making verbal financial agreements still persists in some of the smaller high schools. Such a procedure is hardly businesslike, and it naturally lends itself to misunderstanding and mistakes. In order to make financial agreements between schools more understandable, more explicit, and more binding, regular contracts should be signed by both schools for all contests. These contract forms are supplied by the state associations or conferences.

Handling school funds

Schools are frequently careless in their management of gate receipts. The large sums of money which often are involved should call forth all precautions to insure against loss. Another argument for the sale of tickets in advance of the game is that it prevents the accumulation of large sums of money. Theft insurance is carried by all large schools, and the game manager is usually bonded. Plenty of police protection should be provided, particularly when the funds are collected and taken from the ticket offices. Unless the amount is very small, ar-

EXPENSE REPORT FORM.

UNIVERSITY OF PENNSYLVANIA
Division of Intercollegiate Athletics
EXPENSE REPORT

UNIVERSITY OF PENNSYLVANIA

VS.

Opp. _____ _____

_____ Game   Played at _____ Date _____

Time of Departure _____ Date _____

Time of Return _____ Date _____

Name of Transportation Co. _____

Received from Intercollegiate Division .... $ _____

Cash Returned to   "   " .... $ _____

Total Cash Expenses, ... $ _____

Expenses by Orders, ... $ _____

                Total Cost of Game, ... $ _____

Total Receipts from Game, ... $ _____

University of Pennsylvania Share, ... $ _____

University of Pennsylvania Profit/Loss on Game, ... $ _____

EXPENSES, TRANSPORTATION, ETC.	REMARKS
No. of Men Taken on Trip... _____	_____
" " Coaches " " " .... _____	_____
" " Attendants " " " .... _____	_____
" " Managers " " " .... _____	_____
_____ Railroad Fares .... $ _____	_____
_____ Bus Hire .... $ _____	_____
_____ Sleeping on Pullman ... $ _____	_____
Hotel Accommodations(Rooms) $ _____	_____
_____ Breakfast $ _____	_____
Meals _____ Luncheon $ _____	_____
_____ Dinners $ _____	_____
Tips .... $ _____	_____
Taxi Hire .... $ _____	_____
Telephone Charges .... $ _____	_____
Baggage " .... $ _____	_____
Freight " .... $ _____	_____
Incidental Expenses ...... $ _____	_____
(Specify)	_____

_____ Manager

_____ Checked

_____ Approved

Figure 11-1.

417

rangements should be made to deposit the gate receipts in a bank or police station after the game.

It is a cardinal principle in schools as well as in business organizations that all financial transactions should be recorded in some tangible way. It is for this reason that receipts for all purchases are necessary. By the same token, when money is received receipts should be given and carbons retained. Such receipts are essential when the accounts are audited. An accurate record must also be available of ticket sales at athletic contests. Ordinarily this is done by recording the number on the roll prior to and following the game. These data are also necessary for the auditors.

Game reports

In many schools the athletic director is expected to provide game reports after each contest. This report includes such items as attendance (according to such categories as children, students, general admissions, and so forth), gate receipts, complimentary tickets, expenses, other income, weather conditions, and the score. These reports serve as a valuable record for future use, especially in the preparation of future budgets.

Petty cash fund

It is an established business procedure for the administrator to have a small petty cash fund of approximately $25 from which he can make small purchases. It is much simpler to make purchases of less than $2 directly rather than to make out a purchase requisition. Receipts for all purchases should be obtained. When the petty cash fund is exhausted, the receipts should be submitted along with the request for an additional appropriation.

SELECTED REFERENCES

Bucher, Charles A., *Administration of School Health and Physical Education Programs* (St. Louis, The C. V. Mosby Co., 1963), Chap. 5.

Forsythe, Charles E., *The Administration of High School Athletics* (Englewood Cliffs, N. J., Prentice-Hall, 1962), 4th ed., Chap. 10.

Howard, Glen, and Edward Masonbrink, *Administration of Physical Education* (New York, Harper & Row, Publishers, 1963), Chap. 6.

Hughes, William Leonard, Esther French, and Nelson G. Lehsten, *Administration of Physical Education For Schools and Colleges* (New York, The Ronald Press Company, 1962), 2nd ed., Chap. 15.

12

the purchase and care
of equipment

Importance

The purchase and care of equipment was not an important responsibility of those in charge of the first interschool teams, for the players furnished their own equipment. As interscholastic and intercollegiate athletics grew, schools undertook to equip the players. For a number of years the equipment item did not assume large proportions because little equipment was needed. The athletic program was limited to a few sports, the squads were small, and the players were not equipped so elaborately and completely as they are today. Furthermore, the cost of athletic equipment was considerably less than it is at present.

Today, the purchase and care of equipment constitutes one of the director's most important responsibilities. Most athletic departments feel obligated to protect the members of the teams to a reasonable extent with adequate equipment. Not only are the injuries reduced but well-equipped, well-dressed teams appeal more to the public than unattractive teams. Equipment expense has become one of the largest items in the athletic budget and a great deal of money may be wasted unless equipment is purchased carefully and cared for properly. A great deal has been learned about buying and caring for equipment in recent years. Directors have purchased equipment more wisely and have cared for it more carefully since the beginning of World War II. Many of the expense items in the budget do not lend themselves readily to reductions, but directors have found numerous ways by which they can reduce the expense of equipment without appreciably impairing its effectiveness and appearance. It is essential that every director know equipment thoroughly and be acquainted with the policies, methods, and techniques by which equipment might be bought and cared for most economically.

Provision of equipment by school

Practically all schools provide the playing equipment for the service and intramural programs. The student is expected to furnish his own uniform. Many schools provide towels and towel service at no cost to students; but many make a charge for this service. In still other schools the provision of clean towels is the responsibility of the student. This means that he must bring his own towel and take it home for laundering. This practice is not recommended because of the problems involved in administering it.

For interschool athletics it is highly desirable to have the school furnish most items of equipment, including uniforms. Adams[1] study revealed that in 60 percent of large high schools, 48 percent of medium-sized high schools, and 34 percent of small high schools, all personal equipment was furnished to squad members. In approximately 62 percent of the small high schools and 45 percent of the medium-sized high schools, shoes were not furnished by the school. Many high schools rent shoes—particularly football shoes—to the players. An appreciable percentage of small and medium-sized high schools do not furnish socks or gloves. Virtually all schools provide playing uniforms, but it is exceptional for a school to furnish such specialized and personal equipment as golf clubs and tennis rackets.

Students should not be required to provide all or part of their uniform, because, inevitably, some will be unable to afford to become candidates for teams. Equally undesirable is the practice of using cheap, ill-fitting equipment that has been borrowed or handed down year after year. Some parents will purchase football shoes that are too large with the hope that they will last the student three years. The provision of most items of athletic equipment by the school is a standard toward which all physical education departments should work.

Purchasing equipment

The coach should always be consulted in the purchasing of athletic equipment for his squad. He knows the specifications, he understands what materials are needed and how they are to be used, and he

1 Harry Adams, *A Report on Current Practices in the Administration of Interscholastic Athletics in Five Hundred Ninety-one Selected Secondary Schools in the United States.* Unpublished master's thesis, University of North Carolina, 1950, p. 15.

sees them tried and tested. He comes into contact with the problems that are presented by the equipment. This practical experience with athletic goods enables the coach to make valuable suggestions and recommendations.

The athletic director also plays an important role in the purchase of equipment. He may have far more experience with equipment than the coach, and if this is the situation, he should tactfully guide the coach in his recommendations. He must also determine that the equipment request is in line with the budget and that the amount and type of equipment ordered can be justified.

In high schools the principal usually has the responsibility of approving purchases of athletic equipment. The superintendent also does this frequently, particularly in the smaller schools. The athletic council, board of education, and business manager of the school may also have this responsibility. In colleges and universities the approval of the athletic director is usually all that is necessary. However, the athletic council or the business manager may also give approval.

The inventory. Before athletic equipment is purchased the need for it should be carefully considered. This will necessitate an itemized inventory of the equipment room covering both the amount and the condition of the materials on hand. Some directors can be rightly criticized for being unable to justify amounts of equipment purchased. The inventory is the best insurance against overbuying on some items and underbuying on others. The director and coach should always have firsthand information concerning the amount and condition of the stock on hand, and an accurate idea of team personnel and requirements for the coming season.

Purchasing policies

After the needs have been determined the director is prepared to buy. But the purchase of athletic equipment involves much more than merely buying goods to the limit of the budget. Every director is anxious to obtain the best service and the longest life in equipment per dollar spent. In order to attain this objective there are some recognized policies of buying which might be followed. Purchasing athletic equipment is a business proposition, and it should be conducted on a businesslike basis. There are certain procedures that are recognized as sound in any business. Although each school presents separate problems, there are certain fundamental principles of buying which will operate successfully in most situations.

Standardization of equipment. "Standardization of equipment" is a common expression among directors. By this term is meant the adoption, by a school, of a certain color, type, and style of equipment which is maintained over a period of years. There are advantages in buying certain consistent types of equipment, usually from the same firm. It allows for replacement of the equipment in whole or in part. It maintains quality of material and color. The end result is uniformity over a period of years. Economy is practiced in that items can be matched in varied quantities without having to purchase a complete new outfit each season. Parts and replacements are easily obtained and repairs can be made more successfully. The uniformity of equipment for team members adds color to the organization and strengthens the team morale. There is no question that lack of uniformity may be interpreted as bad buying. The director must be alert to the rapid changes in equipment, however, in order that he will not be found with a large store of obsolete or extinct types on hand.

Quality merchandise. It is the consensus of informed opinion that, as a policy, the purchasing of the better grades of equipment is best. The most expensive equipment is not always the best, but it must be recognized that good material will be more expensive than cheap material. It has been proved on numerous occasions that quality merchandise fits better, looks better, wears longer, and can be repaired more advantageously than cheap items. The director must not go to the extreme in paying prices to the point that teams go unequipped on a limited budget, but experience has shown that in the majority of cases, low-cost materials are low-grade materials. The practice of purchasing cheap merchandise for reserve and freshmen teams has not proved to be economical. It is far better to pass down from the varsity squad quality material in good repair than to provide a cheap grade of equipment that may last for the season but gives little promise of being suitable for reconditioning.

Buy within range of ability to pay. This is a sound policy in any business. Credit is easily obtained, and many directors have gone heavily into debt as a result of unrestrained purchasing. Even though many schools operate on a budget, it is possible to spend more for equipment than can be afforded. Buying too much and too expensive equipment has plunged many athletic departments into debt. Buying too much equipment is not so serious a mistake as buying too expensive equipment, because the surplus can be used later. Many coaches and directors have been overanxious to equip their teams with the best and have gone to extremes in their buying. Although quality merchandise is advocated, small high schools cannot afford to buy the same grade of equipment that large universities use. When a director overpurchases equipment, the operations of the entire department may be curtailed, and his ability as an administrator is questioned. Frequently, schools buy recklessly after financially successful years. As a long-term policy, consistent, regular buying is to be preferred.

Early ordering. The director should not overlook the advantages of ordering equipment early. These advantages include:

1. Early delivery. This is an advantage because opportunity is still available to correct mistakes, make size adjustments, and order additional items, the need for which could not be foreseen when the original order was submitted.

2. Better equipment management. When equipment is delivered early ample time for marking and storing is available.

3. Better equipment. An early order is more likely to result in exact equipment carefully made to specifications by unhurried craftsmen.

Early buying also aids the manufacturer. He is better able to estimate the expected volume of business and prepare for it. He can produce better materials at a better price if the labor is spread out over the entire year instead of being accumulated during certain intervals. In addition, the reputable manufacturer has the opportunity to replace materials that are defective or not up to standard.

Concerning ordering equipment for interschool athletics the Athletic Goods Manufacturers Association recommends the schedule presented in Table 12-1.

Table 12-1.

	Take Inventory	Order Equipment	Delivery	Mark Equipment
Football	November	December–March	July	August
Basketball	March	April–July	September	October
Baseball	June	October–January	March	April
Track and Field	June	November–January	September	October

Source: Athletic Manufacturers Association, *How to Budget, Select, and Order Athletic Equipment* (Chicago, Athletic Goods Manufacturers Association, 1962).

The best interests of the school should guide purchasing decisions. Not infrequently some sporting goods dealers, in order to obtain a school's equipment business, have offered gifts to the coach or administrator. A set of golf clubs, a rifle, jacket, fishing tackle or a tennis racket have been given to obtain a favorable decision. Such inducements should never be accepted; it is a violation of professional ethics to do so. Decisions about equipment purchases should be based upon the best interests of the school rather than the personal gain of the individual making the decision.

Purchase from reputable concerns. It is essential to deal with companies that have a proven reputation for sound business policies. A reputable dealer will service his account. Service to a buyer is an integral part of the manufacturer's product. Reliable companies also guarantee the excellence of their products and this guarantee is worth paying for.

Few directors are accurate judges of textiles, leathers, and other materials used in the manufacture of athletic equipment. Cheaper grades of fabrics, fiber, padding, and leather can be made to look like better grade materials. Unless the director knows equipment thoroughly, he must rely upon the integrity of the companies with which he deals. He has no other recourse. Every administrator will discover that buying from reputable firms will prove more satisfactory and more economical as a long-term policy.

This does not mean that all goods should be bought from the same firm year after year. There are tendencies to form too strong an attachment for a particular manufacturer, which should be avoided. The quality and price of his goods may change to advantage or disadvantage. New materials and new processes may enable one firm to excel temporarily in certain items. It is better to keep an open mind regarding the products of different manufacturers.

Take advantage of legitimate discounts. Many discounts that are offered to prospective buyers are, in reality, no discount at all. The amount of the discount is added to the original selling price in order that it might be taken off to attract purchasers. "Two percent within ten days" is, however, a legitimate discount. The seller can afford to offer this discount for the advantage of being paid within ten days after the goods are billed. Practically all firms offer this discount and the director can save his department considerable money by taking advantage of it. Many of the larger institutions buy in the spring, but on a September 30th dating. The discount period carries up until October 10th, by which time football gate receipts are available to pay the bill and still take advantage of the discount.

Legitimate discounts may be secured if large quantities of athletic equipment are purchased at one time. The director should take advantage of this discount if his purchases are large enough to obtain it. Frequently, the larger universities ask various reliable companies to submit bids for supplying the athletic equipment. Considerable savings may result by this method of buying, as manufacturers are willing to reduce their selling prices for a larger volume of business.

Official equipment

Practically all games or sports have certain items of equipment that must be manufactured to specifications and are commonly marked "official." The specifications may call for a definite weight, length, relative dimensions, certain types of maerial, or the exclusion of certain materials. The purchaser should be acquainted with such specifications or any changes that may occur from year to year or season to season. Cases have occurred where competitors have been ruled out of an athletic event or records have been refused on the grounds that the implements used were not "official." This may have come about through the ignorance of the purchaser or the misrepresentation of a salesman.

How to buy

The best buyers study market conditions for proper values. Equipment prices fluctuate and the director who knows when to buy and when to refrain from buying can save his department money. Although prices are fairly uniform among sporting goods houses, excellent values are frequently offered on certain items by the various companies. If the director records and files the prices of equipment of the different firms, he can compare them when he is ready to buy.

It is a fact that the most expensive materials are not always the best. The most effective way to discover how equipment stands up is to use it and check the results. Some universities use spring football and freshmen teams as proving grounds for football equipment. If equipment rooms are properly managed, they should serve as laboratories to check the results of purchasing decisions. It is a simple matter to tag equipment and check it from time to time to see how it wears. The form in Figure 12-1 is used at the University of Iowa for this purpose. Not only does such a check on the equipment show how it wears but it also indicates the amount of shrinkage of the items tested.

Local dealers

Preference should be shown to local dealers if they can provide the needed items of equipment at prices that are comparable to those of out-of-town firms. A policy frequently practiced is to buy from local dealers if their prices do not exceed those of outside merchants by more than 10 percent. This assumes, of course, that the quality of the merchandise is identical.

Ordinarily, the local dealer is in a position to provide better service within the community. In addition, he pays taxes that help support

EQUIPMENT CHECKING FORM.

Manufacturer or Dealer	Style No.	Identification No.	Price	Size	Measurements						Choice or Grade (1, 2)	Article:
					Original	After First Wash	After Second Wash	After Third Wash	After Fourth Wash			Remarks

Note—"Identification number" means a number stencilled on each item to distinguish it from the next. The columns under the heading of "Measurements" are divided into two merely for illustration. In the case of undershirts (quarter-sleeves or T-shirts), there might be three or four columns depending on the amount of information needed, i.e., sleeve length, body length, chest measurements, etc.

Figure 12-1.

the local schools. He is also called upon to carry ads in the school paper, to sell tickets for local athletic contests, and to support the local physical education programs in many other ways. These considerations justify dealing with local firms as long as the difference in price and quality of the merchandise is not excessive.

Purchasing in a small school

The greatest need for wise buying is in the small schools. Peculiarly enough, most of the poor purchasing occurs in the institutions that can least afford it. Service is the major factor to be considered in the small schools because the equipment must be used year after year.

Very seldom are complete outfits bought for an entire first team or squad; instead, a few uniforms or parts of uniforms are bought. The best solution to the problem is to standardize the equipment and then purchase an excellent grade of material. Fancy, high-priced merchandise is impracticable for the small institutions. The small high schools cannot expect to equip their teams with the same grades of materials as those used by the universities, but the manufacturers have supplied strong, serviceable equipment that is well suited to their needs.

Approval of equipment by the national federation

The National Federation of State High School Athletic Associations has taken a step to make the sale of unreliable equipment by dishonest companies more difficult. A joint committee of the National Federation and a number of leading sporting goods concerns have worked out a plan to establish certain standards of safety and to label approved equipment. Each of the firms agrees to make up a line of merchandise which meets the standards set up by the joint committee. Under the supervision of the committee the materials and types of construction are tested in a United States government testing laboratory, and only those articles that satisfy rigid tests are approved. The approval is indicated by a federation tag and label, which guarantee that the materials are exactly as they are represented. The National Federation approval is withdrawn from any article that is found to be inferior. In case dishonesty on the part of the manufacturer is indicated, approval will be withdrawn from all products of that manufacturer.

Ordering equipment

In any type of school, large or small, order blanks should be used in purchasing equipment. To order verbally is a poor policy. If the director or purchasing agent orders goods verbally he will probably fail to make a record of the transaction. When the merchandise arrives it cannot be checked accurately, and in case of a dispute the buyer will not be able to show just what goods were ordered.

If the director makes a practice of ordering goods by letter he should keep a carbon copy of his letter. Order blanks are preferable, however. They are uniform in size and can be filed systematically. Furthermore, it is desirable to use an order number that will check with the invoice number. The director who uses order blanks and keeps them filed will have a complete record of his purchases from which he can easily make reports for the season or year.

The samples in Figures 12-2 and 12-3 are suggested as guides in

EQUIPMENT VOUCHER.

ATHLETIC DEPARTMENT

Name of School

City————————State

VOUCHER

To be returned to the Purchasing Agent

ALL BILLS MUST BE RENDERED IN DUPLICATE ON THIS FORM

Our order No._____Date_____
 Must be shown on all voucher forms.

Dr. To. _____Name of Firm_____

Address of Firm

_____
 Street   City   State

Terms_____ Your Order No._____ Your Invoice No._____

Quantity	Material	Unit Price	Total Price	Trade Disc.	Net Amount

Appropriation_____Approved_____

Rec'd O.K. _____ Date_____

Figure 12-2.

printing order blanks and vouchers. The usual letter size, $8\frac{1}{2}$ by 11 inches, is commonly used.

The original copy of the purchase order is sent to the firm with two voucher forms, and the duplicate purchase order, which should be printed on colored stock, is filed until the goods are received. With the duplicate order blanks on file, the purchasing agent or director may

EQUIPMENT ORDER BLANK.

ATHLETIC DEPARTMENT

Name of School

City————State

PURCHASING ORDER

Date_____

To._____

_____

_____

Please deliver the following articles to the athletic department:

Quality	Article

Please follow directions exactly

I.

Address every package of goods to

Director_____

Athletic Department_____

School_____

City   State

Order No._____

Ship Via._____

II.

Please bill us goods on the attached voucher forms, returning both the white copy and the duplicate pink copy. Be sure to indicate our purchase order number on all voucher forms.

Purchasing Agent._____

Approved by._____

Figure 12-3.

readily check up at any time to ascertain when the goods were ordered. When the bill is paid, the duplicate purchase order may be filed with the receipted voucher. When possible, goods should be ordered by catalogue numbers.

Most schools use voucher forms that have proved satisfactory. The original or white form is filed with the copy of the purchasing order to show payment, and the duplicate is returned to the shipper with the check to show that the bill has been paid. Some firms will return their own voucher forms along with the voucher that was attached to the purchasing order. The vouchers provide for a statement of terms. When orders are placed a number of months or weeks in advance, it is well to state that goods are to be billed at a certain date.

At the lower left-hand corner of the sample voucher the word "Appropriation" is marked. This space should be used for indicating the sport or department to which the goods should be charged. The line marked "Rec'd O.K." is to be used when the goods are received by one person and the voucher is approved by another. At times, there will be mistakes in shipping, and when this is the case the fact will be noted in this space after the goods are unpacked.

There is a difference of opinion regarding the value of purchase order blanks and voucher forms in the smaller institutions. The volume of business in the larger schools necessitates purchase order blanks and vouchers, but there is a need for system and businesslike procedure even when purchasing on a small scale. The cost of printing the forms is really insignificant when distributed over a period of years.

Considerations in selecting athletic equipment

The Athletic Goods Manufacturers Association [2] has recommended some basic *considerations in selecting athletic equipment.*

1. Design and material. The design must be practical while the material must be thoroughly serviceable. One should be skeptical of a dressed-up item where basic design and playability may be sacrificed for eye appeal. Many times the extras and frills serve no functional purpose.

Each year many new fabrics and materials, made from new synthetics and plastics, are introduced. These may or may not be an improvement over an older fabric or material. The physical education administrator cannot afford to have a closed mind and should not hesitate to experiment with new materials.

2. Utility and cost of maintenance. Equipment should be purchased on the basis of utility—that is, it should meet specific game and safety needs. Also, the equipment should be of such quality and construction that it is easy and inexpensive to maintain.

In considering the utility and cost of maintaining equipment be sure to check

---

[2] Athletic Goods Manufacturers Association, *How to Budget, Select, and Order Athletic Equipment* (Chicago, Athletic Goods Manufacturers Association, 1962), pp. 14-17.

(a) Are there frills on the equipment, making it difficult to maintain?
(b) Will the equipment clean up easily and well?
(c) Does the equipment have to be repaired and reconditioned after normal use?
(d) Is the equipment too costly to maintain for effective use?

3. Safety factor in protective equipment. In purchasing protective equipment the first consideration must be the safety of the wearer. It is inexcusable to sacrifice the safety of students in order to save a few dollars.

4. Quality and workmanship. There is no substitute for quality in athletic equipment. The materials from which the equipment is made must be of excellent quality. The workmanship is equally important.

5. Source of supply. See "Purchase from Reputable Concerns," p. 425.

6. Price. It is never wise to sacrifice quality for price. Chances should not be taken with untested low-cost equipment. Athletic equipment should never be purchased on the basis of price alone.

Purchasing specific items of equipment

In this section the discussion will center on some specific items of equipment and those features of each which the purchasing agent should bear in mind when making his selection.

Fabrics. A wide variety of fabrics is available for physical education and athletic garments. In addition to cotton and wool and such synthetics as nylon and rayon many new synthetic and plastic fibers are available. These can be combined into an endless variety of fabric materials. Virtually all of these possess certain advantages for specific situations and uses.

One of the problems encountered with fabrics is shrinkage. "Sanforized" garments have been tested for shrinkage in accordance with United States Government-approved tests. They are guaranteed not to shrink more than 1 percent in width or length.

Colorfastness is one of the desired and necessary qualities of many fabrics. Since garments are subjected to sunlight, perspiration, and frequent washings, the best dyes to use to maintain the color are those known as "vat-dyes."

Football shoes. The shoes are very important items of equipment. It is a sound principle to purchase the best shoes that the budget will permit, because, in the long run, it will prove economical. Since there are so many different types of leather, tannages, and construction features involved in the manfacture of shoes, it is particularly important to rely upon shoes from reputable manufacturers.

The Goodyear welt construction has been proven by long experience to be excellent for all-around serviceability. Because it is built around a leather insole this type of construction assures a good foundation for the shoe. This will enable it to take wear and tear, mud, water, and perspiration without losing its shape. Moreover, it is always repairable.

Kangaroo leather—either yellow or blue-black—is the preferred material for shoe uppers because of its light weight, great strength, moisture resistance, pliability, and durability. However, this is the most expensive leather. Calfskin also makes an excellent leather for the uppers. Horsehide is a less expensive material for uppers. It does not possess the advantages of kangaroo or calfskin, but it is serviceable and stands up well. Cowhide makes the best sole leather for football shoes because it is tough, water resistant, and does not readily scuff or crack.

Fiber substitutes for leather should be avoided. Good leather that has been saturated with water will not become mushy or lose its original shape. Shoes with detachable rubber cleats have almost entirely replaced shoes with attached leather cleats. The cleats (male) which screw into the sole are preferable to those (female) which screw into a fixture mounted on the sole.

A critical consideration in regard to shoes is that they fit properly. Correct size is probably more important in shoes than in any other item of football apparel. The consequences of improperly fitted shoes could be extremely serious.

Helmets. Because of the serious nature of injuries to the head the football helmet is the most important piece of protective equipment. The protection afforded rather than cost, weight, or appearance should be the guide in purchasing this piece of equipment. As soon as helmets do not offer complete protection to the head they should be discarded. Such helmets should never be used for practice or handed down to reserve or freshmen teams.

Helmets are made of a hard, outer shell, usually leather or plastic, which is capable of absorbing the hardest blows without denting. The shell should be well padded on the inside, preferably with sponge rubber. A web suspension in the crown has become popular because it distributes the shock throughout the helmet. "Helmets which have a canvas, leather, or rubber padding, regardless of their thickness, attached directly to the fiber or plastic shell, furnish less protection to severe jarring than those with an air space between the foundation and the shell." [3]

Football pants. Football pants are made of a variety of materials. Canvas of eight-ounce weight per square yard has been a very popular

[3] Virginia Bourquardez and Charles Heilman, *Sports Equipment: Selection, Care, and Repair* (Englewood Cliffs, N.J., Prentice-Hall, Inc., 1950), p. 118.

material for this piece of equipment. It is a strong, durable material that can be cleaned readily. It is not so expensive as other materials. Whipcord and gabardine cloth are good materials for football pants. If whipcord is heavy enough, it will not pick up water as readily as canvas; it will last longer, take color better, and keep its bright appearance and sheen. The purchase of satin, silk, or balloon-cloth pants is not recommended if service is desired. They are flashy, but mud and lime, when allowed to dry in them, take out the color and weaken the fabric.

Nylon cloth is being used increasingly for football pants. This material wears exceedingly well, holds its sheen indefinitely, cleans easily, is resistant to moisture, retains shape well, and, at the same time, weighs less than most other materials. Nylon pants are expensive, but in the long run they are economical.

As a rule, the purchase of shell pants will prove more economical if good materials are used. Many schools still use the regular pants with the hip pads attached. This type of pants is wasteful in that it will wear out much more quickly than the pads. It is advisable to buy shells and get good pads for them. The pads will outlast many pairs of pants.

The knees are the weak spots on almost all pants. It pays dividends to buy them with large leather knee pads. The leather should extend almost from seam to seam and come down close to the bottom elastic. The use of an elastic two-way stretch in the back of the pants reduces the strain on the knees and at the same time improves the fit. The crotch also should be reinforced because it is subject to hard wear. Eyelet stays are also important. Stays should be faced with leather because laces will wear out the best cloth eyelet holes, and when this happens the pants keep sliding off the hips.

Basketball pants. Basketball pants are usually made from tackle twill (rayon), satin, and cotton. Nylon is not used extensively for this item of equipment. When it is used, however, pants should be lined because of the translucency of the material.

Jerseys. Nylon fabric has become very popular for football jerseys. It is usually combined with wool or Durene for this item of equipment. When it is used with wool, the great strength of nylon is combined with the absorption and warmth qualities of wool. It fits well, is elastic, durable, and holds colors well. The Durene-nylon combination provides a lightweight but very strong jersey. It cleans easily, is elastic, and holds its color exceptionally well. Woolen jerseys are warm in cool climates and hold their shape well. They fit well and can be made up attractively in a variety of color combinations. It is a delicate fabric to clean. It is not durable. Like nylon, woolen jerseys are expensive. Knitting mills weave woolen in various grades and mixtures with other fibers in order to combine the best qualities of each.

Cotton football jerseys are used by some schools during the warm weather early in the fall. In the South most of the schools wear the lighter jerseys, usually made up of the high-grade cotton or Durene, which is dressed-up cotton. As cotton is much cheaper than nylon or wool, some schools use cotton jerseys for practice, if handed-down woolen or nylon jerseys are not available. Cotton jerseys are considered best for track.

Rayon is extensively used for track and basketball jerseys. It is usually combined with cotton. It is an inexpensive jersey, holds colors well, is of medium weight, and is easy to clean. Rayon is not a good material for football jerseys because it lacks durability.

White football jerseys are not advisable because they are difficult to keep clean. In addition, they are not so strong as other fabrics since bleaching weakens the fibers. White may be satisfactory for basketball and track but not for football. The raglan jersey, which is designed to fit over shoulder pads without stretching and strain, is favored by many coaches.

In purchasing jerseys of all kinds and T-shirts, it is very important to obtain neck sizes which are large enough. When the neck sizes are too small the jerseys and T-shirts are easily torn as the players pull them over their heads.

Shoulder pads. Shoulder pads have been greatly improved in recent years. Kapok and foam rubber have replaced felt and rubber as padding. Both are excellent from the standpoint of protection. The foam-rubber pad is considered the best, but it is also the most expensive. It is not so durable as the kapok padding because perspiration causes it to lose its resiliency. For this reason, if foam rubber is used it should be adequately treated for moisture resistance. Kapok is easier to recondition.

The fiber part of shoulder pads (and hip pads) should be waterproofed. Fiber is composed largely of wood pulp and is susceptible to water, just as a piece of stiff cardboard is. Unless the fiber is waterproofed, it will break down if exposed to moisture and will no longer provide protection.

Both types of shoulder pads—the flat and the cantilever—have their advocates. Manufacturers claim that either type will afford equal protection. The fit of the pad is an important consideration. When the pad is placed on the shoulders it should fit snugly. The pads should fit down well over the chest and there should be a strap from the chest to the back protector to keep the pad snug.

Hip or kidney pads. Hip pads must be carefully purchased if they are to fit properly, provide adequate protection, and still not hinder various movements. They must protect the coccyx, the heading of the femur, and the anterior-superior spine of the ilium. They are padded like shoulder pads with kapok and foam rubber.

Inflated balls. Rubber balls of all types have been greatly improved in recent years, and since they are appreciably cheaper than leather balls, they have supplanted the latter in many instances. Rubber balls are used extensively in service classes and intramural athletics. Some interscholastic and intercollegiate teams employ them at times for practices. Rubber balls are durable, will not lose their shape, and will not pick up moisture. Because of this resistance to moisture, rubber balls are especially valuable for football or soccer practices which are held in the rain or on a wet field. Rubber basketballs, volleyballs, and softballs are also available.

Almost all leather inflated balls are made of cowhide, which does not stretch as much as horsehide. The difference in prices of footballs, basketballs, volleyballs, and soccerballs is due largely to the grade of leather that is used. The choice section of any hide is called the *bend,* which comes from the middle of the upper back of the animal. The section immediately surrounding the bend is termed *back* and is considered the second best part of the hide. The fibers in these two sections of the hide are more closely knit, stronger, and more firm than other types of leather. The third best leather is rump, and grouped together as the poorest types are shank, flank, and neck. These sections have fibers of varying lengths and are usually spongy and coarse. The best balls, with close, small, tight, and firm fibers, will keep their shape, but cheaper balls, of inferior leather, will not. One good ball will give greater service than two inferior balls.

Rackets. Rackets are made of a variety of materials. The preferred material for both tennis and badminton frames is well-seasoned, second-growth ash. Both types of frames are laminated. Steel tennis and badminton rackets are available, but apart from their durability, and thus reduced expense, they have no other advantage. Aluminum and fiberglass frames have just been made available, but further experience is needed before they can be properly evaluated. Plastic badminton rackets have also recently appeared, and these seem to be very promising.

Rackets are strung chiefly with gut and nylon. Gut is preferred, but its cost limits it to the most expensive rackets. Nylon has almost entirely supplanted silk for badminton and tennis strings. It stands up well, is not affected by moisture, and is relatively inexpensive. Tennis rackets are strung with 15- and 16-gauge strings; badminton with 19- to 20-gauge strings. By stringing badminton rackets with 16- to 18-gauge strings considerable saving is effected because these heavier strings rarely break.

Shuttlecocks. Plastic shuttlecocks have been sufficiently developed so that they are satisfactory for all but expert players. They are much less expensive than shuttlecocks made with goose feathers. The development of plastic shuttlecocks has been a boon to badminton. Many schools have been able to introduce badminton into the service and intramural programs because of the greatly reduced cost of the shuttle-cocks.

The care of equipment

A good equipment room is the first essential in the proper care of athletic equipment. A carelessly kept supply room can take a greater toll on the life of athletic equipment than many hours of hard service on the playing fields because athletic equipment spends most of its life in the equipment room. The equipment room must be conveniently located adjacent to the locker and training rooms. It should be large enough to store all of the equipment of the department adequately and provide sufficient space for the handling and repairing of it. Proper lighting and heating are important. The equipment room ought to be well ventilated, dry, free from sweaty walls and pipes, and protected against moths, roaches, rats, and other rodents. The equipment room should be so constructed that shelves and bins can be built against the walls in order to have articles readily accessible for issue. Fairly deep shelves that will accommodate cartons and bulky articles are necessary. Narrower shelves for shoes and smaller articles are desirable. Enough shelves should be available so that nothing need be dumped in the corners or on damp floors. Steel bins and shelves are recommended. A cage-door, sliding type of window with a counter is necessary.

Every athletic department needs a drying room in conjunction with the equipment room. In almost all gymnasiums there is a corner in which an inexpensive drying room can be built. Placing wet uniforms in a locker after practice or a game will tend to rot the material and to rust the lockers. With the use of a drying room this problem will be solved, and the department will save a considerable amount of equipment. In addition, the drying room is a necessity if the department hopes to launder its own equipment and towels.

A room 3 feet deep, 10 feet wide, and 8 feet high, lined with thin-gauge galvanized iron, can be equipped at a small cost. Galvanized iron pipe is the most satisfactory material for hangers. It is wise to construct a protective shelf of galvanized pipe and wire about 3 feet above the floor to prevent articles from falling on the heating unit. A 7-foot heater, equipped with six equally spaced 600 watt, 220 volt, screw-type electric elements, will supply adequate heat. Excellent ventilation may be assured by cutting eight 3-inch holes in the doors 4 inches from the floor, and constructing the top of the room in a cone shape, with a small power fan installed in a 6-inch pipe that discharges the air currents out of doors. The fan should run only when the heat is turned on.

A drying room of this size will accommodate training shirts, shoulder harness, sweaters, pants, and socks for thirty-six football players or the entire uniform, exclusive of training pants, for fifty basketball players.

Equipment room management

An equipment room manager is indispensable to the director and coach whose presence is required on the practice field or in the training room when equipment is most wanted by students. Universities and large colleges employ a full-time equipment room manager. A few large high schools can afford a full-time manager, but smaller institutions cannot. A part-time custodian may be employed or the janitor may take charge of the equipment. In most high schools the coach must assume responsibility for the equipment room. A common practice, however, is to appoint students to manage the equipment room. In some institutions the students are paid, but in many the students receive a manager's award for their service. Student managers are rarely as capable and proficient as full-time managers, but if they are carefully selected and trained, they will discharge their responsibilities satisfactorily.

If the equipment room manager requires assistance, he may be assisted by the managers of the various sports or by the student assistants. No other students should be permitted in the equipment room. If the equipment manager is to be held responsible for all of the equipment, he and his assistants should handle it alone. When everyone has access to the equipment the manager faces a hopeless task in preventing loss and preserving order.

Issuing equipment. Every piece of equipment issued should be accounted for. A very desirable method of keeping a record of equipment is through the card system. Each student signs a card on which is recorded the equipment issued to him. Every sport has a special card of a different color. On each card are listed the equipment items that are issued for that sport. The football cards may be yellow and the basketball cards white. After each card is signed it is filed alphabetically according to its color. Figure 12-4 is an example of a card that might be used.

At the beginning of the school year the equipment manager should assign all lockers, issue equipment to the students upon request of the director or coaches, and handle the daily routine task of managing the towel service. In the course of a season the equipment manager should inspect the playing equipment from time to time. This is done for the purpose of culling all equipment that is beginning to wear and of saving the athlete from possible injuries. The material that has been culled should be sent to the repair shop immediately. This means of checking and repairing often saves the department considerable money.

At the end of the playing season the equipment manager and his

EQUIPMENT RECORD.

FOOTBALL

Name_____

Address_____

Date_____

Class_____

Practice	Out	In
Pants		
Shoulder Pads		
Jersey		
Under-shirt		
Sox—Inner		
Sox—Wool		
Supporter		
Stockings		
Shoes		
Special Pads		
Towel		
Sweat-shirt		
Game		
Pants—Rain		
Pants		
Jersey		
Shoes		
Shoes—Rain		
Sox		

Locker
No._____
Combination

_____

Checked out by_____

Checked in by_____

Figure12-4.

helpers check in all equipment. This can be done far better by cleaning
the lockers than by having each player check in his own equipment to
the stockroom. There are always some players with more equipment
than is charged against them, and this is the best method of securing it.
Each piece of equipment, when checked in, should be tagged with its
size and with the former player's name. This saves the manager time
the following season in giving it out to the returning players. Each
article should be closely inspected, and those needing cleaning and repairing should be cared for at once. An inventory can be taken at this
time in order to determine the equipment consumed during the season.
A check can be made at the close of the season to see how the equipment
has stood up in comparison with other makes during the previous years.

Some schools check each player's equipment into the equipment
room daily. Every player is given a number that is the key to the control of this system. This number appears upon the locker to which

the player is assigned. It is marked upon each piece of his equipment except the towel, quarter shirt, supporter, and socks, which are called white equipment. The number is also marked on the equipment rack above each player's hook in the equipment room where his equipment is kept at all times. Only the white equipment is retained in the lockers. On reporting for practice, the player comes to the window of the stockroom and gives his number to the equipment manager, who goes to the rack and brings the player all the equipment placed under that number. At the close of practice every evening the player returns his practice equipment to the window and the manager replaces it upon the rack. The senior manager checks the equipment displayed under each number daily and, if any pieces are missing, he endeavors to locate them. If any of the equipment is in need of repair, it is attended to immediately. The night before a game the practice equipment is removed from the racks and temporarily stored. Game equipment is substituted in its place upon the racks, and the player follows the same routine on the day of the game as he does for the practice sessions. This is an excellent system of handling athletic equipment, and it is recommended if a large equipment room is available.

All equipment that is taken from the equipment room must be accounted for in some way. Coaches or their managers and instructors should sign for the equipment they use. Students who check out balls and other equipment for free play should sign for them. Ordinarily, they are requested to return the equipment within a certain time and never to keep it overnight. The practice of students signing for equipment and then permitting other students to return it later should be discouraged. This frequently results in lost equipment. In some schools each student checking out an article for free play exchanges it for one of his street shoes, which is not returned to him until the borrowed items are returned. All equipment should be numbered and each student should then sign for a numbered item.

Use of equipment. The development of the proper attitude among all students regarding their athletic equipment is the most important consideration in the care of equipment. Much equipment is lost or damaged by carelessness or destructiveness. Frequently, varsity athletes do not feel an obligation to treat equipment carefully. Unless all students have a respect for property and are indoctrinated with a desire to care for their equipment properly, considerable damage and loss will be incurred. Students must appreciate the fact that athletic equipment is loaned and not given to them and that they are responsible if it is lost. Petty thievery can best be combated by making each player accountable for everything checked out to him.

Marking equipment. All pieces of athletic equipment of an institution should be marked in some way in order to identify them. The usual way of doing this is to stencil or stamp the name or initials of the school on the equipment. In addition, athletic clothing should have the sizes clearly indicated on them. The identification of the school on athletic clothing does not suffice; the items issued to each player should be numbered and the numbers recorded in the equipment room. This is additional bookkeeping, but it helps to trace missing articles. When this system is known to all the students within a school, it reduces the amount of stealing.

Cloth articles may be successfully marked with a stencil and stencil paint or an India ink stamp. Leather goods can be stamped. In some institutions initials are burned into leather goods, but unless this is done carefully, the leather will be damaged. Wooden items of equipment can be marked by burning initials at some convenient spot. Identification labels can be sewed into some articles. Many items of equipment may be purchased already marked. An additional charge is usually made for this service. It has been found, however, that it is more economical to purchase sweat socks with some mark of identification than to mark them in the equipment room.

Care of specific types of equipment

It stands to reason that not all athletic equipment can be treated, cleaned, or stored in the same way. The materials from which the equipment is made—leather, rubber, fabric, wood, and so forth—require different methods of care. If the persons using it are to get the maximum service from the equipment he orders, the athletic director and his assistants must be familiar with the manner of caring for the various types of apparatus on hand.

Leather balls. The vulnerable part of any leather ball is the stitching. The stitching can be protected by relieving the pressure inside the ball between seasons. Slowly drying the ball when it is wet rather than forced drying will also protect the stitching. When inflating a ball with a rubber core valve, always moisten the needle, preferably with glycerin. If the needle is moistened with the mouth, remove the moisture from the needle after using it. A rusty needle will injure the core of the valve. The needle should be inserted with a gentle, rotary motion. A pressure gauge should always be used to insure correct inflation. A chart should be available next to the pump or on the wall to indicate the desirable air pressure for the different types of balls. Overinflation should be avoided, inasmuch as it strains the fabric lining and thus affects the shape and life of the ball.

A ball that has been used in the mud should be wiped clean with a damp cloth and then dried at the normal room temperature. Leather balls should never be placed near a radiator or hot-air register. To clean

Table 12-2. Care of textile fabrics.

General Considerations for All Fabrics	Cotton	Covered Rubber Thread	Nylon	Rayon	Wool
Regular Hang in cool, dry place when not in use (woven fabrics). Apply deodorants (if used) some time before garment is worn. Use shields to protect shirts, jackets, dresses from deterioration and fading.					Brush frequently, especially cuffs, neckline, etc. Air frequently; dust and dirt adhere easily.
Laundering Launder or clean after every wearing (ideal). Check for spots and tears before laundering. Test small, inconspicuous section for color fastness. Close slide fasteners. Use mild, pure soap flakes (preferable to soap), and soft water. Dissolve soap flakes first. Avoid rough handling and rubbing; squeeze suds through garments. Wash colored fabrics separately (in absence of color fast guarantee); do not soak these garments. Rinse in clear warm water; do not wring or twist. Remove excess water.	Wash in HOT water if necessary. Use any good laundry soap; cotton resists strong alkalis well. Bleach white fabrics if increased whiteness is desired. Rinse thoroughly after bleaching.	Wash in WARM water.	Do not use boiling water. Use any good laundry soap. Avoid strong bleaches. Remove some dirt and spot stains by simply rubbing with a damp cloth.	ACETATE Use mildly warm water. This rayon melts easily. Choose soap carefully; alkalies dull. Use bleaches carefully if at all; bleaches cause saponification. REGENERATED Wash very carefully; these rayons very weak when wet	Measure before washing (unless shrink-proof). Wash as follows: Soak in warm sudsy water about ½ hour; change water and wash in warm soap solution. Rinse well; leave small amount soap in garment to prevent felting. Do not use chlorine or strong bleaches. NOTE: Avoid sharp changes in temperature in washing, rinsing, and drying.

Hang in shade (unless garment is white) as sunlight is often harmful to color.

Hang on smooth surface; hooks, knobs, etc. may damage.

Ironing

Check small, inconspicuous section for correct ironing temperature if this is unknown.

Dampen slightly (most fabrics).

Use smooth, even pressure.

Use a HOT iron if necessary.

Use a warm not hot iron (rayon temperature for ironing is suitable).
Do not use bleaches.
Dry in natural heat, NOT in hot oven.

Iron with warm not hot iron. (Rayon ironing temperature is suitable)

Use warm not hot iron. Iron on wrong side.
Iron when nearly dry except: rayon-wool, iron when dry; rayon-other fibers, iron when damp; rayon shark-skin, iron when noticeably damp.

Iron through a cloth placed on wrong side of garment.

Storage

Remove starch unless starch is guaranteed not to weaken.
Be sure garments are clean and dry.
Inspect for moths and other insects.
Store in cool, dark place, protected from dust and dirt.
Spray storage area occasionally with effective mothproof agent.

Store in relaxed position, not under tension

Treat with mothproof agent before storage unless garment is mothproof.

Special Considerations for Knitted Fabrics

Repair runners at once
Measure before laundering (unless garments are shrink-proof).
Dry on a flat surface (do not hang up).
Do not use pins on these fabrics.
Lay flat when storing.

Special Considerations for Pile Fabrics

Do not iron some pile fabrics (unnecessary).
Expose reverse side of corduroy and velvets to steaming water. When dry brush pile side in direction of pile.

Source: Virginia Bourquardez and Charles Heilman, *Sports Equipment: Selection, Care, and Repair*, © 1950. Reprinted by permission of Prentice-Hall, Inc., Englewood Cliffs, N.J., pp. 275, 276.

a ball that has been discolored commercial cleaners or saddle soap are recommended. When the leather of a ball has become harsh and rough because of repeated exposure to moisture, an application of a commercial leather dressing or a light mineral oil will prove helpful.

Leather balls should be partially deflated when stored away between seasons. They should be stored in a cool, dry place without objects of appreciable weight upon them.

Rubber balls. The chief enemies of rubber are direct sunlight, heat, grease, and oil. With regard to sunlight and heat, all that can be done is to avoid exposure when possible. Grease and oil should be removed with soap and warm water. Dry-cleaning fluids should never be used on rubber goods. Rubber balls should be stored in a cool, dry bin or box away from heat or sunlight.

Textile fabrics. Bourquardez and Heilman have made a thorough study of the care of textile fabrics. Their recommendations are indicated in Table 12-2.

All woolen items must be protected against moths. Moths will not attack nylon or cotton fabrics. After jerseys are cleaned, they should be stored away by sizes. They should not be stored in open bins where dust will collect but in closed containers with moth repellent.

Leather goods. The most common sources of trouble with leather goods are high temperatures and excessive moisture. There are three types of formations which accumulate on leather, only one of which is harmful. This is green mold, which rots leather. In order to prevent green mold rot, leather articles should be kept in a cool, dry place. When wet, leather equipment should be dried immediately, but the action should not be forced. The article should be dried at normal room temperature without the use of artificial heat. Sun drying and air streams or pressure should never be used.

The proper care of leather shoes is especially important. They are subject to dampness due to perspiration, rain, or snow. This condition tends to remove the tanning oil from the leather, causing it to dry out and crack. In addition, shoes if worn when very wet become misshapen. In caring for wet shoes, lime and mud should first be removed. Warm water should be used if necessary. Oil or grease should then be applied and worked into the leather. Castor oil is especially recommended. If the oil is warmed before application, it is more efficacious. Oil should be applied to the uppers, and wool grease to the soles. It is important to keep oil and grease away from rubber cleats. Wearing football, baseball, and track shoes on stone or concrete floors should be discouraged.

Before leather shoes are stored away after the season they should be cleaned and oiled. They should be oiled again about the middle of the year. The toes should be stuffed with paper to help the shoe retain its shape. The shoes should be stored in special compartments to promote air circulation and to avoid crushing.

Wooden equipment. Wooden equipment, such as bats, golf clubs, hockey sticks, javelins, bows, and lacrosse sticks, are built to last for long periods of time and will do so when properly handled. Moisture is the main source of difficulty. It will damage the wood where the finish has worn away. Consequently applications of warm linseed oil are recommended whenever the finish of the wood requires it. Javelins and vaulting poles should be stored in such a way that warping is prevented. Storage of wooden equipment in a cool, dry place is recommended.

Nets and rackets. Nets that are exposed to dampness will rot. Nets that are used outdoors should be tarred. If they are dipped in creosote every year, their life will be prolonged. They should be taken in during bad weather, kept dry, and repaired at the first indication of damage. If space is available, it is better to hang tarred nets on pegs in a cool, dry area rather than to fold or roll them. Badminton and tennis rackets should always be kept in presses when not in use. Restringing is much less expensive when it is done immediately after a string has been broken. Probably the greatest source of racket problems is too great string tension. This condition greatly increases string breakage and the loss of shape of the frames. At the same time it does not improve the performance of the poor and average players. Expert players use tightly strung rackets, but such equipment is neither necessary nor desirable in physical education and intramural activities. A tension of from 50 to 60 pounds is adequate for such use.

Badminton shuttlecocks. Badminton shuttlecocks should be kept in a moist environment. The feathers lose their oils in a dry atmosphere. A humidifier is recommended for the storage of a considerable number of shuttlecocks. The greatest damage to shuttlecocks comes through careless use. Students should not be permitted to abuse this fragile equipment. Shuttlecocks are also saved when students are prevented from smashing and swinging vigorously until they have developed proper skill and timing.

Archery tackle. All bows should be unstrung when not in use. On the archery range the bow should be hung on the ground quiver between rounds. When not in use, the arrows should be racked in a dry place. The rack should be so constructed that there are three pressure points on the arrow—one two inches from either end, and one in the middle—to prevent warping.

Helmets. Helmets should be cleaned before they are stored away. Dirt and hair oil should be removed by using saddle soap or a commercial ball cleaner. In storing helmets the important consideration is to maintain their shape. Throughout the year they should be carefully stored on special racks, or they may be stuffed with newspaper with head trees on the inside and suspended from wires close to the ceiling. They should not be hung by the chin strap. Helmets should not be crushed by having heavy objects placed upon them or by having individuals sit upon them. Throwing of helmets should also be prevented. The common practice of carrying helmets in a duffle bag is not recommended.

Hip and shoulder pads. These items of equipment should be cleaned and repaired before being stored. Hip and shoulder pads can be washed with warm water and soap if care is used to avoid getting too much water into materials, such as kapok, which absorb it. Leather parts should be lightly oiled after cleaning. Special forms upon which shoulder pads may be stacked are easily made. Stacking pads more than five or six high will spread the arches of the bottom pads to the point where they lose their body-conforming shape. If space is available, open wooden racks to accommodate not more than two pads to each space is the ideal arrangement. Hip pads should be hung by the belt loop.

Mats. The two common practices that are harmful to gym mats are rolling or bending them in any way and dragging them on the floor. Mats should always be kept flat. When they have to be moved they should be carried by the handles or transported on a mat truck.

Canvas mats should be cleaned once a month with a vacuum cleaner. If they are heavily used and become grimy, they should be cleaned with a commercial mat cleaner. Tears in the body or the handles and broken tufts should be repaired immediately. When the mat cover is beyond repair, it is less expensive to have it re-covered than to purchase a new mat.

Track equipment. Metal shots should be cleaned with steel wool and oiled before being stored away. Steel tapes should be treated similarly. Discuses should be cleaned and shellacked, then placed in a rack, and stored in a room that is not overheated. Javelins should always be hung from a height with the point downward to prevent warping.

Cleaning uniforms

The great majority of institutions must rely upon commercial cleaners to launder their athletic uniforms. This is a specialized type of work which requires trained personnel and proper facilities. The athletic director would be well advised to seek a cleaner who specializes in this type of cleaning.

Athletic uniforms are among the most difficult-to-clean garments known to the cleaning industry. They are subjected to dirt, perspiration, rough usage, and a variety of stains—grass, blood, resin, iodine, and adhesive tape. In addition, practically all items of the uniform consist of two or more fabrics, each of which may require separate handling.

Excessive heat whether in the wash water, rinse water, or in drying will shrink the garment. Generally lukewarm water (100° F.) is recommended. In any case, the rinse water should be the same temperature as the wash water. Automatic tumble dryers and certain forced air methods are dangerous because of the heat.

White garments should always be washed alone. Different colored garments should not be mixed. Colored garments are not adversely affected by water at a lukewarm temperature. High temperatures can be very harmful to colored items. Any bleaching agent will have a serious effect on the fastness of color and therefore should be restricted to white or natural cotton garments.

For certain fabrics, especially brushed and woven wool, dry cleaning is the only safe method. It may also be used successfully to remove dirt and ordinary stains from other garments. However, dry cleaning normally is not sufficient to combat perspiration and perspiration stains. Wet cleaning must be used in such instances.

Any garment, such as two-way stretch football pants, that contains rubber yarn or elastic in the knit fabric should never be dry cleaned. The cleaning fluid will dissolve the rubber threads. The same holds true for water-repellent garments.

Sporting goods manufacturers recommend that the athletic director take a complete uniform to the cleaner in advance of the season to prepare him for the type of cleaning it will require. If the cleaner knows the fabrics involved in the various parts of the uniform, whether or not rubber is used, and the color fastness of the garments, he is much more likely to clean it properly.

Repairing equipment

Athletic directors would profit by investigating thoroughly the possibilities of repairing their own equipment. The extent to which it should be repaired depends upon the size of the school and amount of athletic equipment handled. In some of the larger institutions the stockrooms are so completely equipped that all athletic equipment can be repaired. The practice in the majority of schools is to make simple repairs and to send the remainder to local repair companies or national reconditioning concerns. Many schools could cut their equipment bill appreciably by enlarging their repairing facilities.

A sewing machine that can sew leather as well as textile materials is indispensable in the equipment room. Such a sewing machine will more than pay for itself in a short time by mending the rips and tears that occur so frequently in all types of athletic materials. Special facilities for sewing footballs, basketballs, and baseballs by hand should be available also.

The repair of shoes is important. The shoes should be inspected frequently in order that damage may be detected at its beginning. Detachable cleats should be shifted around so that they will wear evenly and be of uniform height on all shoes. When the cleats are shifted, the fixtures should be checked to ascertain that they are tight. The old cleats should be used on the practice shoes and the new ones placed on the game shoes. It frequently occurs that when one shoe is useless for further wear, its mate is still in fair condition. These odd shoes should be saved for replacements.

Common sense must be used in repairing equipment. Up to a certain point it is good economy to recondition athletic materials, but beyond that it is a waste of money. Some directors make the mistake of repairing old equipment that will not give them enough service to pay for the repairs made. It is more advisable at times to sell old equipment to cleaning and reconditioning firms and use the money to buy new equipment.

In the great majority of schools only minor repairs can be made on athletic equipment. The practice has developed of sending all equipment in need of repair to special equipment reconditioning companies. A number of these have developed in all sections of the country. Originally, many of these firms were not adequately prepared to do effective work, but most of those that have survived have developed the personnel, the specialized equipment, and the technical skill to do a superior job of reconditioning athletic equipment. It is the experience of most athletic directors that in the long run it is more economical to turn over the bulk of the repair work to reputable concerns of this type.

School laundry

The great amount of laundry service which physical education departments need every year, particularly for towels, runs into large sums of money. More and more schools are finding they can reduce this expense considerably by installing laundry units and doing their own laundry. All that is necessary is the purchase of a good washing machine and dryer. The work of laundering the equipment can be done by the equipment manager, the custodian, or student help.

SELECTED REFERENCES

Athletic Goods Manufacturers Association, *How to Budget, Select, and Order Athletic Equipment* (Chicago, Athletic Goods Manufacturers Association, 1962).

Bourquardez, Virginia, and Charles Heilman, *Sports Equipment: Selection, Care, and Repair* (Englewood Cliffs, N.J., Prentice-Hall, Inc., 1950).

13

public relations in physical education

What is public relations?

The modern concept of public relations has emerged from the term *publicity*. Schools have been concerned with publicity for many years, but experience has shown that much more than publicity is needed to secure public understanding and support. Public relations is much broader than publicity. Although publicity is its major tool, public relations is concerned with *all* the impressions that people receive rather than those obtained only through the various publicity media. Fine [1] points this out in his definition: "Public relations is more than a set of rules—it is a broad concept. It is the entire body of relationships that go to make up our impressions of an individual, an organization, or an idea."

In addition to the information that is transmitted via newspapers, radio, films, television, annual reports, and demonstrations, public relations for physical education involves all the relationships that the various staff members have with students, parents, other teachers, administrators, school board members, and the general public. It also involves the impressions obtained from the secretary, custodian, equipment room manager, and any other personnel associated with the physical education department. It even includes the visual, auditory, and olfactory impressions received from the athletic fields, gymnasium, swimming

1 Benjamin Fine, *Educational Publicity* (New York, Harper & Row, Publishers, 1943), pp. 255-256.

pool, and locker and shower rooms. As Fine has indicated, it involves "the entire body of relationships" associated with physical education.

Purposes of public relations in education

Inasmuch as the public schools are supported by taxation an obligation exists on their part to give an accounting of their activities to the public. The schools belong to the people. The public invests heavily in education, and the citizens are entitled to know what is being accomplished with their money. In addition to discharging this responsibility to the public, the schools find it necessary to keep the people informed about their activities in order to obtain the kind of support needed to maintain a high level of efficiency. The cost of public schools is the largest item in municipal budgets, but as long as public confidence and support are maintained this expense is cheerfully borne. Harral[2] points out:

Administrators and others must strengthen their public relations programs. Education will meet current needs only as the masses of people—the throngs who keep the wheels of society moving—understand the schools and take an active interest in supporting them. Upon the attitudes of the public and its willingness and ability to provide the revenues, the development of education in this country depends. As long as education justifies itself in the minds of those who are instrumental in financing it, the financing will continue. These are bedrock considerations.

Still another purpose of public relations is to rectify mistakes, to clear up misunderstandings, and eradicate negative and antagonistic attitudes. These conditions always exist in the general public, and they are powerful deterrents to good will. It is particularly important to influence these individuals favorably, because they might otherwise become leaders of attacks upon the schools.

Purposes of public relations in physical education

The purposes of public relations in physical education do not differ from those of the entire field of education. The following statement of detailed purposes of public relations in physical education by Davis and Wallis[3] further clarifies the meaning of this term:

1. To create good will with all pertinent publics (pupils, parents, school personnel)
2. To help pertinent publics understand the reasons for and values of physical education

2 Stewart Harral, *Tested Public Relations for Schools* (Norman, Okla., University of Oklahoma Press, 1952), p. 4.

3 Elwood C. Davis and Earl L. Wallis, *Toward Better Teaching in Physical Education,* © 1961. Reprinted by permission of Prentice-Hall, Inc., Englewood Cliffs, N.J.

3. To inform pertinent publics of present programs and planned changes in programs, policies, etc.

4. To inform pertinent publics of services rendered by the department, and its willingness to serve

5. To inform pertinent publics of events that have occurred and will occur

6. To encourage participation in suitable activities related to the program and in the use of available facilities

7. To inform the publics of the expenditure of funds (probably through the superintendent's annual report)

8. To enlist assistance in suitable projects and other help

9. To encourage and publicize activities that are as self-supporting as possible

10. To show reasons for greater financial support if needed (and if approved by the school administration)

11. To rectify mistaken ideas, remove misunderstandings, erase negative attitudes

12. To guide and promote public opinion in favor of worthy programs of physical education

Need and importance of public relations in physical education

It has been pointed out previously that an obligation exists on the part of all public agencies to report periodically to the community. It was also pointed out that continued public support depended heavily upon an effective public relations program. As Harral [4] says: "public relations seeks to bring about a harmony of understanding between any group and the public it serves and upon whose good will it depends."

Of all areas of public schools, physical education, particularly, needs to bring about "a harmony of understanding" among parents, teachers, school administrators, and other citizens in the community. This need stems from the fact that the philosophy, activities, and methods in physical education have changed so greatly in the past three decades that few adults understand and appreciate present-day programs. Most people react in terms of their own experiences. When they recall the physical education they themselves endured, they are not disposed to tax themselves heavily for it.

Far too few physical educators have concerned themselves with reporting and interpreting physical education to the public and school administrators. They have only themselves to blame when the public is unwilling to provide adequate financial support for this phase of the school curriculum. During the depression years of the thirties physical education was eliminated or greatly curtailed in hundreds of communities. School boards and school administrators, when confronted with the problem of operating on reduced budgets, too often considered physical education as a "fad and frill" and acted accordingly.

As education faces unparalleled expansion in the years ahead be-

[4] Stewart Harral, *Public Relations for Churches* (New York, Abingdon-Cokesbury, 1945), p. 7.

cause of the skyrocketing enrollment, physical education faces a challenging situation. When school costs are increasing so enormously, all items in the educational budget are being scrutinized with great care. Any program or service that cannot be justified in terms of its contribution to the welfare of school children will have difficulty in surviving.

Physical educators must justify their existence. It is unfortunately a fact that physical education facilities are the most expensive "class rooms" in our schools. School administrators, school boards, parents, and the general public must be convinced that the funds expended upon physical education pay rich dividends. When these groups understand what physical education can contribute to children in terms of health, vitality, physical fitness, citizenship, sportsmanship, and happiness, adequate support will be forthcoming. Parents will pay for what they want for their children. They always want the best and will unstintingly support what they are convinced is desirable. But they must be convinced.

Responsibility for public relations

The physical education administrator is responsible for the public relations of his department. In fact, this is one of his most important responsibilities. Whether he wills it or not, he and the other faculty members, the school secretary, custodian, and equipment room manager are all involved in public relations in their every contact with other people. Since these contacts have significant implications for the department, it is the responsibility of the administrator to concern himself with them and to do everything within his power to assure that the over-all effect will be favorable and enhance the program. Good public relations aid and abet the physical education program; poor public relations damage and, in some cases, bring about the elimination of the program.

Although the central authority for public relations must reside with the administrator, every worker within the department must share in the responsibility. In his associations with others each staff member is creating attitudes in their minds toward physical education. One staff member is capable of doing more damage to public relations than can be overcome by all the remaining staff members. A good public relations program must be a team effort.

Principles of public relations in physical education

In this section we shall list and discuss six principles that constitute a sound basis for any public relations program in physical education that is going to be effective.

1. The public relations program must be based upon truth. All

facts, data, and interpretations that are reported to the public must be presented impersonally, unselfishly, and honestly. By the very nature of public relations any misrepresentation will inevitably create adverse public opinion.

2. The best foundation for good public relations is a sound program. The most elaborate public relations program cannot cover the basic defects of a poor program. It should never attempt to do so. The first step in successful public relations is a physical education program that is making a genuine contribution to the lives of students. A limited, poorly taught program can have no other result than bad public relations. The following statement emphasizes this point: [5]

When the public relations program of a school system rests on a foundation of sound classroom accomplishment, it is like a house built upon a rock. Storms of ill-founded criticism and innuendo will not overwhelm it. Its foundations are sure. On the other hand, the most systematic and skillfully devised publicity cannot maintain the public's confidence or win its approval for a school program that is fundamentally unsound. No shoring up "interpretation" can permanently conceal the shortcomings and failures of misdirected or ineffective teaching. Public relations, under such circumstances, is built on shifting sands. The public cannot hear what is said because it is so acutely aware of what the school program is—or is not.

In this connection it should be pointed out that the program can be far from ideal and still develop good public relations. In schools that have limited facilities, equipment, and time, and large classes, no one expects the physical educator to accomplish what could be done under ideal circumstances. The criterion, however, is how effective is the program *under the circumstances?* In any given situation a superior teacher will produce better results than a poor or mediocre teacher. Many physical educators have obtained improved facilities, equipment, and time allotment because of the excellent public relations that developed from a program that was as good as it could be under unfavorable circumstances.

3. The public relations program should be continuous. Unfortunately, very few physical educators have any definitely planned public relations program for their departments. What few programs do exist are usually of the campaign type, which are not considered as effective in molding public opinion as is a continuous program. The common practice has been to neglect the public relations program until an emergency arises and then to conduct an intensive campaign to secure public support. Although this procedure has some value, it so resembles propaganda that the public develops a more suspicious, defensive attitude than it would if it were supplied regularly with information. Campaigns are

[5] American Association of School Administrators, *Public Relations for America's Schools: Twenty-eighth Yearbook* (Washington, D.C., 1950), p. 59.

more successful if the public has been educated by a continuous program of public relations.

4. Public relations is a two-way process between the community and the schools. The concept of public relations wherein everything originates within the schools and flows to the public is a limited one. The public is capable of providing more than mere financial support, as important as that is. The trend is toward genuine cooperation in planning and working for good schools, with the public giving as well as receiving the ideas. Mutual understanding and teamwork between the community and the school give laymen greater confidence in their schools. In addition, parents are led to a better understanding of the role of the home, the community, and the school in the whole program of education.

A committee of fourteen school administrators made the following observation about public participation in school affairs.[6]

The significance of public participation in educational planning is that it represents one of the most effective means of helping people talk through the problems of education. Citizens come together to explore, plan, and think through and solve educational problems in co-operation with the board of education and the professional staff. In this manner, by digging deeply into the rich strata that are basic to good education, the individual will grow in experience and knowledge. His view of education will be more complete. From these co-operative experiences will come understandings which lead to better support for the schools and an improved school program.

One of the most promising trends in physical education is the development of physical education advisory committees. In some communities such committees are in operation for a variety of school areas. The committees are considered school board committees, and each member is invited to serve each year, by a letter from the chairman of the school board. The decision concerning membership of the various committees is made after consultation by the superintendent of schools, the supervisor of the area concerned, and the chairman of the board. The membership consists of from twenty to thirty members, one third of whom are school personnel. The lay members are men and women and represent a cross section by occupation and geographical area throughout the system. The school people also represent a cross section of school personnel, that is, men and women, elementary and secondary teachers, and administrators. One school board member is assigned to each committee. The supervisor of the area is secretary for the committee and provides leadership and direction. The chairman is elected by the group.

The physical education advisory committee is informed of the work of the past committees and the needs and problems of the physical education service, intramural, and interscholastic athletic programs in

---

6 *Public Action for Powerful Schools*, Metropolitan School Study Council Research Studies No. 3 (New York, Teachers College Bureau of Publications, 1949), p. 4.

all the schools. Problems are discussed, study groups formed, resolutions passed, and the minutes provided for the superintendent, who transmits the committee's resolutions and recommendations to the school board.

5. A knowledge of what the public thinks about the schools is essential. The more school personnel know about the level of understanding and attitudes of the public in regard to the schools, the more intelligent and effective will be the public relations program. Thus, schools have been making increasing use of opinion polls. The advantages of knowing the areas of ignorance and misinformation in the community, the prevailing opinions and attitudes on educational matters, the views of particular groups, and the obstacles that need to be overcome before certain proposals can be implemented are obvious.

This principle has particular implications for physical education. Because of the great changes in philosophy, objectives, programs, procedures, and evaluative techniques in the past twenty-five years, it is probably true that the adult population has a more erroneous impression of physical education than any other subject area within the schools.

6. The effective public relations program involves all school personnel. Schools could learn some valuable lessons from business organizations regarding the orientation of all personnel in their public relations responsibilities. The most successful stores devote much effort in training clerks, secretaries, floor walkers, elevator operators, and other personnel to work successfully with people, yet in most schools there is an assumption that everyone will automatically practice good public relations. Good public relations do not happen in the normal course of events; they are the result of a well-planned program, intelligently and continuously executed. The quality of the public relations program is commensurate with the effort put into it.

Relatively few physical education departments have a planned public relations program. Only rarely is this subject discussed in staff meetings or included in departmental policies. Seldom is an organized effort made to familiarize the teaching staff with desirable public relations procedures. Even though there is abundant evidence to the contrary, the presumption apparently exists that the teaching personnel always practices good human relationships. The nonteaching personnel, such as the stenographer, clerk, secretary, custodian, and equipment room attendant, is also important from this standpoint; yet few efforts are made to assure that it treats students, faculty, and the general public in a courteous, dignified, and friendly manner. A brusque secretary or telephone operator, a dirty or unshaven custodian, an uncouth and inconsiderate equipment room clerk can damage the reputation of the physical education department.

Nevertheless, the overall impression of the public toward physical education depends much more upon dedicated, superior teachers than upon any other consideration. The impressions received by students from their teachers are gained over a much longer period of time, and they are more intimate, dynamic, and vital. They relate to matters of much more crucial concern to students. The favorable public image created by the teacher may be adversely affected by discourteous secretaries or custodians; on the other hand, the finest possible impressions created by nonprofessional personnel cannot begin to compensate for an incompetent, selfish, disinterested teacher.

Planning and organizing the public relations program

A number of factors need to be considered in establishing a public relations program within a physical education department. These factors will depend upon the size of the department and upon the existence of an on-going program for the entire school system as well as the specific school. The most important considerations involved in planning and organizing a public relations program are:

1. The specific purposes of the program should be indicated. These purposes should be discussed and approved by all members of the staff. Unless there is unity and support for the program by all staff members, there is not much point in initiating such a program.

2. The past and present policies and procedures need to be evaluated in terms of the effects that they have had upon the public relations of the department. Data should be collected from students, alumni, parents, faculty, and other groups regarding their reactions to these policies and procedures. Factors that produced misunderstanding and resentment must be eliminated.

3. In the larger departments the best-qualified person should be designated to assume the responsibility for the program. In the smaller departments the physical education administrator must undertake this assignment himself. There are specific duties that must be regularly performed and others that occur at irregular intervals. When one individual has these duties as part of his responsibility, they are more likely to be done promptly and efficiently. Often everyone's responsibility becomes no one's responsibility.

4. If the school or school system has a definite public relations program, the efforts within the physical education department must be integrated with it.

5. The facts to be emphasized in public relations should be determined. In making this selection a public opinion poll might prove very helpful. The decisions concerning features to be emphasized should be made by all staff members.

6. All media for disseminating information should be employed.

The various groups within the general public of greatest concern to physical education should be reached by the most appropriate means of communication.

7. The results of the public relations program should be checked from time to time. Such an evaluation is necessary to guide future efforts and to assess what has been accomplished.

8. The entire staff—nonteaching as well as teaching personnel—must be "public relations conscious." Each should know his responsibilities and limitations in the program.

Multiple publics

There is no one public. Formerly, the idea was held that a school or department had relations with a "public." We know now that there are many publics differing in size, organization, interests, methods of communication, and systems of control or guidance. Every religious, political, service, social, and professional organization constitutes a public. Every individual is, ordinarily, a member of several publics.

This concept of publics is important in public relations because the approach to a specific group depends upon its nature and interests. A successful approach to one group may prove ineffective with other groups. One of the lessons which specialists in public relations have learned is that the various media of communication must be planned for specific groups—a shotgun approach is of dubious value.

Concerning physical education, the important public consists of students, parents, other teachers, school administrators, school board members, press, radio, and television personnel, and representatives of related governmental and social agencies. Each of these groups will be considered in greater detail.

Students. By all odds, the most important group from the standpoint of public relations is the student body. Two reasons exist for this situation. In the first place, student reactions to physical education powerfully affect the opinions and attitudes of parents, other members of the family, and friends. Each pupil is a daily reporter on what happens in his physical education relationships. What he thinks and says about his school work and his teachers is extremely important. If he is happy and successful in his relationships, he is a booster for the program. No more effective approach could be made to his parents. Even though his parents might have had a negative or antagonistic attitude toward physical education, they become ardent supporters when his reports are enthusiastic and favorable. The instances are legion where parents, convinced of the importance of physical education for their children, have used their influence to bring about improved facilities, equipment, class size, and time allotment. The correlation between *pupil approval* and *public approval* of physical education is very high.

The second reason why students represent such an important group is that they are tomorrow's public. They eventually become the parents, doctors, lawyers, businessmen, school administrators, congressmen, politicians, public officials, college presidents, school board members, and the like. Their attitudes toward physical education are conditioned largely by their own school experiences. Individuals who strongly support physical education and others who are bitterly prejudiced against it are found in every community. To some physical educators belongs the credit for the friends and supporters who have been created; others are responsible for the enemies.

Unfortunately, much harm has been done to physical education in various states and communities by individuals who were antagonistic to it. Some of these individuals obtain positions of power and influence which they employ to the detriment of physical education. Behind the defeats and setbacks that physical education has suffered is the failure of one or more physical educators. Every student who is slighted, neglected, humiliated, or otherwise mistreated, who is frustrated and unhappy in his experiences in physical education, has been adversely affected. When he graduates from school, if the sum total of his impressions is negative, he can hardly be expected to be an enthusiastic supporter.

Parents. The importance of this public has already been emphasized. It has also been pointed out that the support of parents can be obtained by providing them with an excellent program while they are in school and by contributing positively to the health, fitness, skill development, social adjustment, and recreational competencies of their children. Additional ways of increasing the understanding and appreciation of parents are also available to the physical educator and should be utilized.

Administrators have learned that much more needs to be done to educate citizens about their schools. Many of the problems with which education is confronted are due to the ignorance or misinformation of people. Increasingly schools are teaching students about their schools in simple, nontechnical terms—their place, values, organization, operation, and sources of support. Units of study about the school itself merit consideration, along with units on other community agencies and institutions. Children should be educated to understand and appreciate the services of teachers no less than those of policemen, firemen, and postmen.

Such a program would be valuable insofar as physical education is concerned. If high school and college students were taught something of the nature and purpose of physical education, it would do much to spread understanding about this aspect of the curriculum. They would not only communicate what they learn to their parents but they would also acquire a greater appreciation of its benefits which would carry over into adulthood.

Parents can also be educated via reports, visits to school, demonstrations, parent-teacher meetings, and various types of publicity. The features that are reported are dependent upon what the people want to know about physical education and what they should know. They should know that modern physical educational philosophy no longer conceives of the school as being concerned only with the "three R's" or preparation for a vocation. They should realize the increasing need for physical education—a need that cannot be adequately served by any other agency in the school. Once they have been convinced of its indispensability, they should know how it fulfills its purpose in an educational institution. In other words, parents should be educated to know the objectives of physical education and the means by which they may be attained. They should know about physical education operating at its best.

The major interest of parents in physical education revolves about their children. They are eager to know the progress and achievement of their boys and girls. If a student is not making satisfactory progress, his parents want to know why and what might be done to remedy the situation. They are interested in the course of study and the values of the different activities to their child. They might have questions about the teaching procedures and methods of evaluation which are employed. The health and physical fitness of their boys and girls is a matter of vital concern to all parents.

It appears that what parents want to know about physical education corresponds very closely to what they should know. The following items, which are based on the parents' interest and need for information about physical education, are suggested as being of most value for publicity purposes:

1. The progress and achievement of their children
2. Methods of instruction
3. Health and physical fitness of their children
4. The program of activities
5. Need for physical education
6. The objectives of physical education
7. Intramural athletics
8. Teachers of physical education
9. Physical education facilities
10. Attendance and behavior of pupils in physical education

Other teaching personnel. Another important public for physical education consists of the other teachers within the school system. Good public relations with this group pays valuable dividends. When they comprehend the nature and purposes of the program and are sympathetic, they can be very helpful in interpreting it to students, parents, and the general public. In their advising and counseling functions they can be more helpful to both the students and the physical education department. Also, if they are favorably disposed toward physical education, they are unlikely to vote for school policies and regulations that are inimical to it.

Physical educators can win the support of the other teachers in a number of ways. The most important step toward this end is the development of an educationally respectable program—one which merits a place within the schools. Teachers usually obtain from their students a fairly accurate impression of the physical education program. An excellent program will gain their respect. Other teachers admire physical educators who are educators—who exert a wholesome influence upon their students. They lose their respect for physical education when questionable practices, which teach youth undesirable lessons, are tolerated.

Physical educators must also play their role as teachers. They should attend faculty meetings, PTA meetings, and other school functions. They should demonstrate interest in all school activities and should avoid conveying the impression that they are a group set apart from the other faculty. The more they associate with other teachers professionally and socially, the better will their public relations be with this important group.

The support of all faculty members for the interscholastic and intercollegiate athletic program is invaluable, and the cooperation of most of them can be easily gained if the athletic director and coaches demonstrate interest in and support of the purposes of the school. If every effort is made to conduct the athletic program on an educational basis the respect of most of the faculty will be forthcoming. However, faculty members resent pressure from coaches to grant unwarranted concessions to athletes. They dislike overemphasis upon winning, with its concomitants of poor sportsmanship, excessive demands upon the time of the students, and the debasement of academic standards. Other faculty members admire and support the coaches who attend faculty meetings and other staff functions, who consider themselves a part of the school team and cooperate with school policies and purposes, and who are always more concerned about the welfare, character, and ideals of their athletes than anything else.

School administrators and school board members. This is a small but very important public. The status of physical education within a school or a city system can be drastically affected by this group. When the individuals involved become convinced that physical education merits an increased time allotment, more teachers, an additional gymnasium or swimming pool, the improvements are usually forthcoming.

Physical educators can win the support of their principals and superintendents if they become part of the team in trying to accomplish the purposes of the school. School administrators want loyalty and cooperation from their teachers. They do not want teachers who are apparently working toward objectives that have no relationship to those of the school system.

School administrators and school board members are sensitive to public opinion. The best way to win their support is to have favorable information come to their attention from students, parents, other teachers, and the various publicity media. The combination of a good program and good public relations will usually produce the desired results. It is also helpful if the physical educators conduct an effective program of evaluation with which they can demonstrate objectively how the children in the program have developed. An annual report that cites the progress and present status of the program and indicates the needs and problems is invaluable in interpreting the program to this particular public.

Members of the press, radio, and television. The importance of these publicity media emphasizes the necessity to work cooperatively with their representatives. The publicity they can disseminate is invaluable, and the only cost is the time required to cooperate. Physical educators should take full advantage of this opportunity and assist the representatives of these communication media in every way possible. Another important consideration is to treat all individuals concerned impartially. The surest way to damage public relations with personnel of the press, radio, and television is to show preference to one or another.

Representatives of government and social agencies. Good public relations should exist between physical educators in the schools and those in other agencies in the community, such as the Y.M.C.A., Y.W.C.A., boys' clubs, and the municipal recreation department. It is mutually advantageous to all to work cooperatively with each other. Facilities, equipment, and personnel may be shared on occasions. Programs may be cooperatively arranged. Most important of all, perhaps, is the banding together of all professional people when certain emergencies arise. When physical education in the schools is under attack, the personnel of other community agencies can be of invaluable assistance.

The teacher's role in public relations

In the daily interaction of pupil and teacher the most lasting and vital public relations are undoubtedly built. Certainly the teacher has the most associations with pupils, and he works more directly and intimately with them than do nonteaching personnel. Consequently, the intrinsic value of teacher-pupil relationships is a major factor in the school's public relations.

Physical education teachers have exceptional opportunities to contribute to the wholesome development of their pupils. The activities are exciting and challenging, and students are enthusiastic about them. The goals—health, physical fitness, skills, wholesome recreation, social adjustment—are vitally important and esteemed by parents and pupils alike. With these advantages, physical education teachers are strategically situated to develop outstanding public relations.

Unfortunately, these opportunities are often ignored. Not at all uncommon in physical education are certain undesirable teaching practices and procedures. Among those faculty members who may irrevocably damage the department's public relations are the following:

1. The teacher who tosses out a ball and leaves the area
2. The teacher who offers the same activities year after year without progression or change
3. The teacher who ignores the weak and inept to concentrate upon the superior performers
4. The teacher who never teaches systematically
5. The teacher who exploits his physical education classes to locate and develop varsity performers
6. The teacher who is sarcastic, abusive, disparaging, and impatient
7. The teacher who concentrates upon only one objective of physical education to the exclusion of the others
8. The teacher who is dirty, unshaven, or slovenly in appearance
9. The teacher who shows dislike or bias toward students because of their physical or mental disabilities, or their racial, social, or religious backgrounds

Such teachers have a devastating effect upon public relations. Students, parents, other teachers, school administrators, board members, and the general public have nothing but scorn and disrespect for these types of physical educators.

Studies have been made which show the characteristics that students most esteem in their teachers:

1. They like a teacher to be fair and firm, with no favoritism to any pupil or group. They resent teacher bias. Often teachers are adjudged unfair because of an inadequate understanding of their motives. Teachers should be alert in discovering and remedying misconceptions that occur.

2. They like a teacher to be sincere. It is impossible to teach successfully what one fails himself to practice. Courtesy will not result if the teacher is discourteous. Good sportsmanship cannot be expected if the

teacher or coach endorses an illegal play or unsportsmanlike tactic. Pupils quickly discover whether a teacher sincerely believes in and practices such virtues as honesty, courtesy, loyalty, good sportsmanship, and charity.

3. They like a teacher who has an interest in them. They resent being ignored or "brushed off." The informal relationships in physical education provide an ideal setting for students to talk with their teachers about their daily work, studies, future problems, or hobbies. Physical educators can be very effective counselors if they are willing to take the time to talk to their students.

4. They like teachers who make learning interesting. They prefer teachers who motivate learning, who have patience and give them additional assistance, who help them evaluate their progress. They like teachers who are considerate of the opinions of students and who make learning a joint endeavor.

5. They like teachers who know their subject. They quickly discover the teacher who is poorly prepared, and they soon lose respect for him.

Some physical education teachers confine their human relations to the classroom. They hold themselves aloof from the community and its various organizations and groups. This is unfortunate from a public relations standpoint. A community likes a teacher, particularly a physical education teacher, to participate in community activities. The people want the teacher to fit in, to observe their customs and traditions. That a teacher's private life is his own is largely fiction. Teachers, especially those new in a community, should be sensitive to the behavior codes that differentiate one community from another. They should not necessarily be enslaved to local customs, but they should have an appreciation of prevalent traditions and a consideration for them within the limits of good taste and good sense.

There is also an obligation on the part of all citizens to participate in community enterprises, and every teacher should do so. In most communities physical education teachers are expected to engage in youth activities that relate to their field. The Boy Scouts and Girl Scouts, Y.M.C.A. and Y.W.C.A., service clubs, churches, civic and fraternal groups, and many other community organizations offer many opportunities for physical educators to broaden their community contacts.

Physical education teachers have been unflatteringly stereotyped over the years. They are envisioned as overdeveloped muscularly, attired in sweat clothes, uncouth in their use of language, lacking in the social amenities, and uninterested in scholarly and cultural attainments. By their actions physical educators must invalidate these impressions. They must be aware of these concepts and make a particular effort to eradicate them.

In summary, the role of the physical education teacher in the public relations program is accomplished through good human relations. The value of tact, courtesy, and friendliness toward all with whom he comes into contact cannot be overestimated. A dedication to the welfare of all his students is essential.

Public relations techniques and media

In addition to *staff* and *program* there are many other public relations techniques and media that can be used. These include newspapers, radio, television, films, filmstrips, slides, graphic and pictorial materials, public addresses, demonstrations, school publications, and annual reports to parents. So many media are available that a problem is presented in making a selection of the ones to use.

The obvious criterion to employ in determining what media to use is that it should be the best one available for the specific purpose. The particular public or publics for whom the information is primarily intended is another important factor. Expense, time, facility of preparation, and availability are other considerations.

The newspaper. The local newspaper is a powerful factor in molding public opinion. As it reaches practically everyone in the community, it becomes an invaluable means of informing people about physical education. Because of the public's interest in its schools, newspapers are very liberal with space for school news. The only cost for this is the time required to cooperate with the press. Physical educators should take full advantage of this opportunity and assist the representatives of the local papers in every way possible. They should furnish the newspapermen with news regarding physical education in the school and undertake to learn themselves what constitutes news, what are news values, and how news stories are prepared. Such a background is highly desirable, for most physical educators find it necessary to write news stories frequently. In only the larger institutions is there a separate publicity man whose sole duties are to assemble and prepare the news stories. In the great majority of schools, the individual in charge of physical education must prepare the material himself and either place it in the hands of those responsible for school publicity or give it directly to the newspapers. It is a mistake to depend entirely upon the visits of the reporter in order to get physical education news into the local papers.

When the director prepares his own stories they fall into one of three different types. *News stories* are reports of the events as soon as they are over. They must contain the six basic elements of all newspaper leads: who did what, when, where, why, how. *Advance stories* are notices given out in advance of events, stating in future tense the basic elements. The more important the events, the greater the number of advance stories. *Feature stories* are those in which the writer explains, interprets, describes, and develops in popular form some interesting subject for the purpose of informing, entertaining, or giving practical guidance. The feature story generalizes over many events and a long time, whereas news and advance stories usually treat of one specific event at a specific time.

Harral [7] gives the following valuable suggestions for preparing news stories.

1. State facts only, not personal opinions.
2. Tell your story briefly in simple language, then stop.
3. Answer the questions who, what, where, when, and why early in the story.
4. Make the report accurate and coherent.
5. Paragraph and punctuate properly.
6. Be especially careful about names, titles, hours, and subjects.
7. Avoid abbreviations, slang, adjectives, wordiness, and involved sentences.
8. Omit headlines.
9. Submit clean typewritten copy, double spaced.
10. Always get your story in on time.

To this advice we might add that the news story should be written in the third person and should not include too many superlatives.

Harral [8] also makes the following suggestions for effective press relations:

1. Play fair with newspapers if you expect them to play fair with you.
2. Establish personal contacts with members of the newspaper staff.
3. Lose no opportunity to be of service to reporters and editors.
4. Do not send the editor thinly veiled school propaganda or advertising.
5. Since newspapers attempt to mirror life, do not expect them to publish only favorable stories.
6. Newspaper space is valuable. Don't expect too much space to be devoted to news of education.
7. Evaluate your news through the eyes of the editor.
8. Never be too busy to see a reporter.
9. Don't play favorites. Treat all reporters alike.
10. Be as eager to help the reporter to get the details of an adverse story as you would a favorable one.
11. If an editor has been generous in giving space to news of school affairs, don't strain your relationship by continually demanding more.
12. Express your appreciation to reporters and editors.
13. Invite representatives of the press to banquets, receptions, or special occasions.
14. Do not evade or side-step a reporter's questions. He may think you have something to hide.
15. Remember that a reporter seeks facts, not hearsay or rumor.
16. Don't be condescending. Reporters deal with all types of people.

7 Stewart Harral, *Tested Public Relations for Schools* (Norman, Okla., University of Oklahoma Press, 1952), p. 127.
8 *Ibid.,* p. 135.

17. Plan for dull days by having several tips for feature stories.
18. Don't ask the reporter for favors. He isn't the editor.
19. Don't expect the impossible. Trust the editor to know news values.
20. Keep an ideal file of potential news stories, features, and pictures.

Radio and television. Radio and television are powerful communications media because of the large number of people they reach. They have been effectively used to interpret physical education and to provide the public with essential information. Both of these media welcome programs from the schools and are usually cooperative in making their facilities available.

All commercial radio and television stations are required to devote a certain amount of time to public service programs. Many schools have a regular program scheduled on this basis. Physical education has the opportunity, along with other school activities, to participate. In addition to these sustaining programs, information and announcements may be broadcast by means of spot announcements and newscasts. Many of the same materials prepared for newspapers can be used on newscasts if they are rewritten.

When physical educators have opportunities to present programs over the radio or television, they must seek technical assistance. Ordinarily, the individual with this responsibility for the school system will render this assistance. Radio and television personnel are also available for this purpose.

Films, filmstrips, and slides. These visual aids are being increasingly used by schools to present ideas, activities, and needs. The public has few opportunities to observe the work of the schools, and these media are usually more effective than verbal descriptions.

The production of a film is an expensive undertaking and requires careful planning and experienced direction. A number of the larger school systems have produced excellent films that have justified the expense and effort. Some physical educators have made films of their departmental activities with the assistance of volunteers who possess the technical competence required. Even though they are silent films, they are of value.

Slides and filmstrips can be developed from any good photographs. They are inexpensive to make and can be quite effective, particularly if they are in color. Ordinarily, these aids are used in conjunction with a talk on some phase of the school activities.

Other graphic and pictorial materials. Photographs, charts, graphs, and diagrams are included in this category. The Chinese proverb, "A picture is worth a thousand words," emphasizes the importance of these media.

Photographs tell a story and arouse interest. If they are well done, they interpret, dramatize, inform, and explain. They can be used for reproduction in newspapers and reports, for bulletin boards, exhibits, and window displays. For best results photographs should have a good background, show action, and involve small groups only.

Charts, graphs, and diagrams are valuable in presenting various types of statistical data. Data on budget, school growth, and participation in school activities, as well as comparisons of various types, are much more effectively portrayed by these visual aids than by words.

Public speaking. Physical educators have frequent opportunities to speak before groups. They receive invitations to address P.T.A. groups, service and fraternal clubs, and social civic organizations. All of these invitations should be accepted because they present opportunities for developing good public relations. It goes without saying, however, that the effect of an address depends upon how well it is presented.

The fact that an invitation to speak has been extended indicates that the group has an interest in what the physical educator has to say. Nevertheless, much careful preparation is indicated. There are, of course, a few individuals who can give an excellent address with little preparation, but they are the exception that proves the rule. In general, the quality of the speech will correspond to the amount of time devoted to its preparation.

Mastery of subject matter and interest in it are two prerequisites to effective speaking which the physical education teacher should possess. Sincerity and enthusiasm are other essentials. Speech authorities urge that speakers make an outline of the major points they wish to cover rather than write the speech out in detail and memorize it. Reading a speech is also considered poor practice. Another common mistake is to try to cover too much in one talk. Practice in delivering the speech is recommended.

Student publications. The student newspaper, the school annual, and the student handbook are important communications media that can be utilized to advantage by the physical educator. These projects are vital to the students, who are grateful for whatever assistance and cooperation they receive from the faculty. Student reporters should be treated courteously and extended all the assistance they require. The student publications can be of great help in giving the students, particularly those working on them, an understanding of physical education.

Annual reports. Many school systems publish an annual report that describes the status, progress, activities, and needs of the schools. In his yearly report to the school administrators and the school board, the physical education administrator should present a fair and honest summary of what has been accomplished in his department and indicate what its important needs are. His presentation is made stronger when he can provide objective evidence rather than personal opinion to support his recommendations. For example, if he can present objective data that show that local children do not compare with other children or with recommended standards, he is much more likely to secure favorable action.

Demonstrations. Demonstrations are extensively used by physical educators to promote understanding and support. Correctly used, these media provide an unusually effective means of interpreting physical education to parents and the general public. It is easy to get the public to attend, and it is not difficult to create the understandings that lead to favorable public opinion. In addition to the public relations value, demonstrations are of exceptional educational value to students and teachers alike.

Demonstrations are placed before the public on special occasions, such as Parent-Teachers Night, Open-House Night, Field and Play Days, or whenever the occasion indicates the desirability of one. They should be made annual occasions rather than a device to use only when physical education is in trouble. As an integral part of the physical education program they deserve the time, space, and personnel which are required for their proper execution.

Demonstrations should represent the regular program to the public. They should involve all or as many students as can be used rather than only the outstanding performers. Preparation for the demonstration should not interfere appreciably with the regular program of instruction. The primary purpose is to *inform* the public, not to entertain it. Physical education has outgrown the practice of spending weeks preparing for an exhibition. Experience has shown that this approach damaged public relations rather than improved them. The demonstration should endeavor to present a representative cross section of the program and, at the same time, interpret it to the observers.

Public relations by national, district, and state organizations

The national, district, and state physical education organizations should initiate and carry out a definite plan of public relations. In fact, this represents one of their major functions. They supplement the work of local personnel and perform certain services on the national and regional levels which could not be done by individual teachers. The total public relations effort requires an effective program not only on the local level but on the wider state, district, and national levels.

The public relations functions of the national association are directed by a professionally trained individual. He is assisted by other paid personnel, as well as by the national officers. On the district level the public relations efforts must be spearheaded by the officers or special committees of the district association. The state director of physical education, assisted by state association officers, conducts the program on this level.

The functions of these individuals are limited by the funds at their disposal and the needs of their organizations. Some of the things that national, district, and state organizations can do to further the public understanding and support of physical education include:

1. Disseminate and suggest public relations ideas and methods to members of the organization in the field.
2. Prepare and disseminate appropriate material for release to newspapers, radio and television programs, and speakers.
3. Establish cooperative relationships and mutual understanding with related national organizations, such as the American Medical Association, Parent-Teachers Association, American Public Health Association, National Recreation Association, American Legion, and Veterans of Foreign Wars.
4. Publicize conventions, meetings, and speeches.
5. Gather and pass on to members in the field information regarding the newest developments and best practices in physical education.
6. Study all bills that come before the Congress of the United States and state legislatures to ascertain their possible effect on physical education.
7. Take the lead in developing the strategy to be used in promoting certain bills and opposing those detrimental to physical education.
8. Promote an international relations program.
9. Provide a plan and means of getting physical education literature published in educational and other periodicals serving professional groups.
10. Prepare films, books, and brochures that will interpret physical education.
11. Conduct a research program to gather data on important needs and problems.
12. Conduct national and regional conferences on specific areas of physical education, such as facilities, teacher education, and athletics, to solve problems and upgrade the profession.

Public relations in interscholastic and intercollegiate athletics

Basically, all that has been stated heretofore in regard to physical education public relations applies with equal force to interschool athletics, which constitute one of the important aspects of physical education. Every contact, impression, or relationship that people have with the athletic program of an institution will mold public opinion positively or negatively. Because of the powerful interest of the public in athletics and its tendency to overemphasize winning teams, it is particularly important to cultivate as much good will as possible by effective public relations. In addition, public attendance and support of the athletic program need to be solicited.

Public relations with the general public

Some of the factors that are instrumental in developing favorable public relations are as follows:

1. Strong teams
2. Well-coached teams
3. Well-dressed teams
4. Opponents of approximately even strength
5. Good officiating
6. Band and other entertainment
7. Good accurate programs
8. Field and equipment attractively set up
9. Games started at time advertised
10. Good seats for spectators
11. Clean, ample, convenient rest rooms
12. Convenient entrances and exits
13. Loudspeaker system and capable announcer
14. Good scoreboard
15. Reserved seats
16. Popular admission prices
17. Good parking facilities adjacent to the field or gymnasium
18. Courteous ushers, parking attendants, and ticket sellers
19. Knothole club for children

The general public does not like to see unsportsmanlike conduct exhibited by the home team or fans. There are always some rabid spectators who want to win at any price, but these do not represent the attitude of the majority of adults. They prefer their teams and coaches to conduct themselves in a gentlemanly manner and do not like to see players who are unable to lose gracefully. They are critical of poor cheering by the students, halfhearted singing after defeat, reprisals against the officials. Rallies and after-game celebrations that are characterized by vandalism and irresponsible behavior are obviously ruinous to public relations. Experience has shown over and over that the coach with high ideals and exemplary sportsmanship, which he imparts to his players, the student body, and the fans, will invariably develop better public relations than one whose won-and-lost record may be better but whose ethics are questionable.

Public relations with newspapers, radio, and television personnel

An extremely important consideration is the relationship of the athletic director and coach with sportswriters, publishers, and representatives of radio and television. Publicity through these various media, if translated into dollars-and-cents value, would be infinitely more than an athletic department could afford to pay. Yet, practically the only cost of this publicity is the time and effort required to cooperate with the personnel.

It pays to be honest with the sportswriters. There are times when it is desirable to suppress information. On these occasions, more will be gained by taking reporters into confidence and requesting their cooperation than by trying to deceive them or hide the facts from them. Frequently, stories will break which the coach may not wish to have published. If the confidence of sportswriters has been cultivated, they will communicate with the director or coach and, if he desires it, refrain from publishing the story. Many coaches make the mistake of trying to build up a belief in the weaknesses of their squad in order to establish a ready alibi for a possible defeat or to gain greater glory for a supposedly unexpected victory. Others go to the other extreme and boast of victories before the game is played. Some coaches are constantly seeking personal publicity. Sportswriters soon see through such tactics, and lose respect for the coach and the team, who thereby lose a powerful source of support. No athletic director or coach can afford to alienate sportswriters.

In those communities that support more than one newspaper, the coach must be careful to be impartial to the representatives of each. Much rivalry naturally exists between the various papers, and the coach may lose the support of all the papers by showing partiality to one. The same situation applies to relationships with representatives of the different radio and television stations in the community.

It is poor economy to be stingy with complimentary tickets for newspaper, radio, and television personnel. When they come to cover a contest, special conveniences should be provided for these representatives. Good seats are essential. If a press box is available, it should be equipped so that the writers and broadcasters get the game information first. This may be done by telephone from the field or by messenger boys. The press box, naturally, should be equipped with telephones to the outside. The larger universities have a representative from each team in the press box to identify the players and supply pertinent information. Many institutions serve hot coffee and sandwiches to the representatives of the various publicity media. In short, every effort should be made to anticipate the needs of these individuals and to assist them in doing their jobs.

Public relations with alumni and parents

In recent years many coaches have endeavored to develop effective public relations by weekly letters to alumni, supporters, faculty, parents, and other interested individuals. Other coaches have weekly meetings with local groups. Some coaches write letters to parents. All these methods are of value in transmitting correct information to interested groups, and if they are well done, supporters are gained. Much of the antagonism toward coaches and teams is the result of misinformation.

Public relations with opponents

Contrary to the opinion of some coaches and rabid fans, opposing teams represent a public with whom good relations are essential. Fundamentally, the Golden Rule should apply in all relations with teams from other institutions. They appreciate courteous, hospitable treatment, and every consideration should be shown to them as guests. Some of the recommended courtesies to be shown visiting teams includes:

1. Providing refreshments after the game
2. Providing official hosts. These individuals—usually managers—should endeavor to provide for every need of the visitors
3. Providing satisfactory dressing and showering facilities
4. Accepting all decisions of officials in a gentlemanly manner
5. Avoidance of rough tactics by home players
6. Exemplary behavior of fans of home team
7. Writing letters of commendation for outstanding qualities exhibited by the visiting team

Athletic publicity

Publicity for school athletics should stress the educational purposes and true values of these activities. Many undesirable practices and pressures persist in athletics because the public has never been educated to anything else. The following statement is pertinent: [9]

The challenge ahead lies in interpreting and promoting the sound educa-

[9] Clifford L. Brownell, Leo Gans, and Tufie Maroon, *Public Relations in Education* (New York, McGraw-Hill Book Company, 1955), p. 154. Copyright, © 1955, by McGraw-Hill Book Company, Inc. Reprinted by permission of the publisher.

tional values inherent in sports. The public has to cultivate the desire to exert its influence in making sound athletic policies stick. The people in the community can be the strongest force in determining that athletics should be conducted chiefly for the good of the players. The right kind of sound, interpretive publicity—and plenty of it—is the crying need. If the schools and teachers and an informed public would fight intelligently the evils in sports practices, it would not take long to remove the evils and to establish athletics as a worthwhile educational activity of value to participants, to school morale, and to community welfare.

The public has been educated to a wrong sense of values largely through the medium of the printed word. This same medium must be used to provide the proper perspective about athletics. This can be done by feature stories primarily. These cannot achieve the desired purpose if they are written in a pedantic style. The human interest stories involved in athletics can be written in simple, everyday language and can bring out incidents involving sportsmanship, sacrifice, teamwork, courage, loyalty, integrity, idealism, leadership, self-discipline, and unselfishness. Every athletic squad has many incidents which, if represented in nonacademic terms, illustrate the educational values of sports.

Athletic publicity in large universities is handled by a special individual or department having that specific duty. In smaller colleges and high schools this function is handled in a variety of ways. Sometimes, capable students may be assigned to take charge of athletic publicity. A few schools have part-time publicity men. A member of the faculty with journalistic training may assume the responsibility for the publicity program as part of his duties. Frequently, the director or coach must perform this service himself. It is very important that someone who is responsible to the director or school administrator be assigned to this work if the public is to develop the proper attitude toward school athletics.

Much of the publicity in athletics is directed toward increasing the attendance at games. The following are effective media to use in this connection:

1. Daily newspapers
2. School newspapers
3. Radio and television
4. Popular periodicals
5. Moving pictures
6. Posters
7. Athletic periodicals
8. Souvenir programs for events
9. Windshield stickers

10. Tire covers
11. Signs and billboards
12. Direct mail and circulars of information
13. School annuals
14. School and departmental catalogues
15. School and departmental bulletins
16. Reports
17. Talks by athletic leaders

The practice has grown up in recent years for all college and high school athletic departments to prepare a "dope sheet," which is made available to all local sportswriters and sportscasters in the area. This brochure contains pertinent publicity material about the team. The names of all squad members, with data concerning the age, height, weight, experience, position, and potential of each, are given. The previous season's record and the outlook for the present season are indicated. The names, experience, and achievements of the coaching staff are also included. Other information includes the schedule, type of offense and defense employed, school colors, nicknames, and the like. The value of such data from the publicity standpoint is obvious.

School athletic games and contests may be effectively advertised in a number of ways. The media listed above are well known. Some of the less known, economical, yet effective methods are herewith suggested:

1. Ladies' day or ladies' night. Admit all ladies free of charge to some particular game or games. This has proved very effective in increasing attendance and gate receipts at professional baseball games, and there is no reason why it should not be successful in interscholastic and intercollegiate contests.

2. Knothole clubs. Admit all children under twelve years of age to all home games, excepting perhaps the homecoming game, for from 10 to 25 cents. This creates a favorable attitude toward the school on the part of the public. Many adults come to the game because they wish to be with their children and take care of them after the game. The knothole club is segregated in a special section and kept there until the game is over. This greatly reduces the problem of watching the fences and gates to prevent the children from stealing into the games.

3. Post card, direct mail campaign. Organize a mailing list of prospective customers, usually alumni. Three days before the game, mail a post card with an appropriate picture on it to all of the mailing list. This card should convey anything of important informational value. The following items are suggested:

(a) Pregame information on opponents

(b) Names and numbers of outstanding players
(c) Dates and starting time
(d) Seating facilities
(e) Record of opposing team if significant
(f) Any significant advertising features pertaining to the coming game; for example: the coach of the opposing team, comparative scores, scores of this game in previous years, and all-star players and high-score men

4. Telephone campaign. Organize a group of volunteer students and have each call ten prospective spectators the day before the game. Divide the list of prospects, usually alumni, among the students, and have them call these people and briefly announce a few pertinent facts about the game.

5. Parents', fathers' or mothers' day. Allow the whole family to come for the price of one ticket. This is a valuable means of introducing the sport to the students' parents. They may find they enjoy it and return on later occasions.

6. Game coupons. Sell four-game coupon books at the start of the school year at reduced prices. These coupons should be transferable and good for any athletic contest during the entire school year. A campaign may be conducted to sell season passbooks to the public at the same rate that students pay. This means a considerable saving to interested individuals and will greatly stimulate attendance among the general public.

7. Advance sale of tickets at reduced prices. This is a sound procedure in advertising the game and increasing sales. Every ticket purchaser becomes a medium of advertising. It also insures a fair crowd and gate in the event of bad weather.

8. Loudspeaker advertising vehicles. Theaters and other enterprises are now using special automobiles fixed with display signs, amplifiers for announcements, and musical devices. This appears to be an effective method of advertising games on the day before and the day of the game. It is of greater value in larger cities.

9. Ticket-selling contests. Ticket-selling contests between campus or school groups have been used successfully to promote sales. For a small trophy or prize, much advertising can be secured and ticket sales materially increased.

10. Posters. Attractively designed posters should be placed in strategic locations. Store windows, theater lobbies, restaurants, hotels, and other places that are certain to attract public attention should be utilized. An excellent plan is to post the announcements of the game on all hotel bulletin boards for the benefit of out-of-town visitors.

Radio and television

The radio has proved to be one of the most effective media for athletic publicity. When interschool athletics were first broadcast, many directors felt that the radio would keep large numbers of spectators from attending the contests. There was even agitation in certain collegiate conferences to ban broadcasts of football games. However, experience has proved beyond the question of a doubt that the radio has greatly increased the number of followers of interschool sports. Many individuals now believe that television will reduce attendance, particularly at small college and high school contests. In fact, data are available to show that attendance has been materially reduced when contests are played at the same time that feature college games are telecast. Many smaller colleges and high schools have been forced to schedule their games on Friday afternoon or evening or Saturday evening to avoid the direct competition with major attractions.

The proposal to eliminate televising athletic contests has been seriously discussed. At the present time the National Collegiate Athletic Association is controlling the amount of telecasting of contests. Whether television will eventually increase attendance at athletic events as radio has done remains to be seen.

SELECTED REFERENCES

Brownell, Clifford, Leo Gans, and Tufie Maroon, *Public Relations in Education* (New York, McGraw-Hill Book Company, 1955).

Bucher, Charles A., *Administration of School Health and Physical Education Programs* (St. Louis, The C. V. Mosby Co., 1963), Chap. 10.

Davis, Elwood Craig, and Earl L. Wallis, *Toward Better Teaching in Physical Education* (Englewood Cliffs, N.J., Prentice-Hall, Inc., 1961).

Harral, Stewart, *Tested Public Relations for Schools* (Norman, Oklahoma, University of Oklahoma Press, 1952).

Hughes, William L., and Esther French, *The Administration of Physical Education* (New York, A. S. Barnes & Co., Inc., 1962), Chap. 5.

14

legal liability for injury

Importance of knowledge concerning legal liability

Physical educators have become increasingly concerned about the legal implications of injuries that occur while students are participating in the physical education program. It is well established that more injuries occur in physical education classes, intramural athletics, and varsity sports than anywhere else within the school. In 1941 Poe discovered that of the 168 legal court cases involving public school pupils, the highest number by far involved injuries received while participating in physical education. Table 14-1 indicates the number of reported legal cases in the different school areas.

The fact that accidents frequently occur in physical education situations has several implications for physical educators. In the first place they are always personally liable for their own negligent behavior when it results in injury to someone else. They must always face the possibility that careless conduct might take every cent they possess. In the second place, a successful suit against the school may eliminate or seriously emasculate the program. Accidents happening in tumbling and apparatus in particular have resulted in the widespread elimination of these activities from junior and senior high school physical education programs. School boards are not inclined to retain activities that juries have regarded as dangerous.

Finally, physical educators have a moral obligation to conduct their programs in such a way as to protect the welfare of their students. When they understand the legal implications of their work, they should be-

Table 14-1. Causes of reported legal cases involving public school pupils.

Causes	Number
Dangerous or Defective Condition of School Buildings	24
Industrial Arts	16
Health and Physical Education	76
Transportation of Pupils	35
Miscellaneous	17
Total	168

Source: Arthur Poe, *School Liability for Injuries to Pupils* (New York, Teachers College, Bureau of Publications, 1941), p. 5.

come more sensitive to their responsibilities. Eventually, they should devise procedures that would prevent or at least reduce the frequency of accidents.

Administrative responsibility

It is the physical education administrator's responsibility to conduct his program in such a way that there will never be an occasion for legal action against his staff members, himself, or the school district. This can be accomplished by eliminating the basis for suits for legal liability, namely, negligent behavior. It is a difficult assignment for the administrator to attain the objective of having all staff members carry on their duties of all times without ever being negligent. Nevertheless, this is the objective.

In this connection it is imperative that the director be thoroughly familiar with all pertinent aspects of legal liability. Since state laws vary in regard to the liability of teachers and school districts he must be conversant with the situation in his state. He needs to be alert to the policies of his school district in this regard. Acquaintance with the concept of negligence and the implications this has for his program is essential. He needs to know the legal precedents that have been established regarding physical education and interschool athletics.

Once he has an adequate background the administrator must acquaint his staff members with the implications in regard to their duties. His objective must be to make his personnel knowledgeable and sensitive to the types of behavior which may be interpreted as negligent. Together with his staff members the administrator should establish policies and procedures that are designed to prevent injuries and consequent legal action. Such policies and procedures would include: (1) supervision, (2) appropriate activities, (3) environmental safeguards, (4) health procedures, (5) transportation, (6) first aid, and (7) accident reporting.

Negligence

There can be no legal liability for injury unless two conditions prevail. The first of these is that negligence must be shown. Negligence is considered the failure to act as a reasonably prudent person would act under the circumstances. Courts interpret a reasonably prudent person to be one who would foresee danger of an accident. Negligence is gauged by the ability to anticipate danger. If such foresight is reasonable, failure to seek to prevent danger is negligence. The second condition is that negligence will not arise unless there is a duty toward the person which is disregarded. The law imposes such a duty upon all teachers. It is clear that the physical educator as a teacher has such a duty. After all, the pupils are forced by law to attend school; physical education is compulsory in most states and schools, and when they are in school, pupils are under the authority of teachers. Under these circumstances the law imposes upon physical education teachers the obligation of acting as a reasonably prudent, careful, and well-trained teacher would act under the circumstances.

Negligence has two aspects. The first of these involves doing something that a prudent, reasonable person would not do under the circumstances because he foresees the risk of injury to others. The second aspect relates to the failure to do something that a prudent, reasonable person would foresee as necessary for the protection or assistance of another individual to whom he owes a duty.

Harper's outline [1] of negligent behavior reveals in more specific terms the nature of negligence. An act may be negligent because:

1. It is not properly done; appropriate care is not employed by the actor. Example: the instructor who permitted a student to use the trampoline without spotters.

2. The circumstances under which it is done create risks, although it is done with due care and precaution. Example: two softball games are played on opposite ends of an area which is not large enough to avoid overlapping outfielders.

3. The actor is indulging in acts which involve an unreasonable risk of direct and immediate harm to others. Example: the physical education instructor placed a boy at a certain position to mark where the shot-put landed. The instructor put the shot which hit the boy's head.

4. The actor sets in motion a force, the continuous operation of which may be unreasonably hazardous to others. Example: the school board selects a candidate to teach physical education who is unqualified by training and experience for his duties.

[1] Fowler V. Harper, *A Treatise on the Law of Torts* (Indianapolis, The Bobbs-Merrill Co. Inc., 1938), pp. 171-176.

5. He creates a situation which is unreasonably dangerous to others because of the likelihood of the action of third persons or inanimate forces. Example: instructor permitted a student to ride a bicycle on a playground which was crowded with other pupils. This resulted in an injury to another student.

6. He entrusts dangerous devices or instrumentalities to persons who are incompetent to use or care for such instruments properly. Example: instructor permits students to use fencing foils without supervision.

7. He neglects a duty of control over third persons who, by reason of some incapacity or abnormality, he knows to be likely to inflict intended harm upon others. Example: failure of instructor to supervise and control the conduct of a bully on a play area.

8. The actor fails to employ due care to give adequate warning. Example: instructor who was responsible for supervision absented himself from the area. Another example was involved when a student was struck by a car when crossing the street between the gymnasium and the athletic field. Negligence was found because no crosswalk was provided, no safety instruction was given to the students, and no warning signs for motorists were posted.

9. Of a failure to exercise proper care in looking out for persons whom the actor has reason to believe may be in the danger zone. Example: the physical education teacher who did not clear the students from the area directly behind the batter in a baseball game.

10. The actor fails to employ appropriate skill to perform acts undertaken. Example: inability to perform first aid when it should have been administered.

11. He fails to make adequate preparation to avoid harm to others before entering upon certain conduct where such preparation is reasonably necessary. Example: the instructor permitted students to use horizontal bar without a mat underneath.

12. He fails to inspect and repair instrumentalities or mechanical devices used by others. Example: the failure to inspect flying rings and other hanging equipment periodically.

School board liability

The liability of a school district for damages growing out of negligent behavior is very different from the liability of a private individual. The reason is that the school district is performing what is considered a governmental function. In the exercise of a governmental function, a municipality is generally held to be exempt from liability suits for the negligence of its servants. This freedom from suit stems from the legal doctrine that "the king can do no wrong." This doctrine goes back many centuries in the legal traditions and practices of England. There, on the theory of the divine right of kings, "the king can do no wrong" and, therefore, cannot be sued. When we won our independence, the governmental units in this country, federal, state, and local, succeeded to the legal status formerly employed by the king of England. Thus, the state or any of its subdivisions, such as a school district, "can do no wrong" when it is performing a governmental function, no matter how careless or negligent it may be.

Two other reasons have been advanced by the courts for the immunity of school districts and their boards from suits. One of these is that the boards of education have no authority to divert funds that have been raised for school purposes to other ends, such as paying for damage suits. The other is that it is in the interest of public policy to have immunity. It is obvious that if school boards could be readily sued for damages because of negligence of school personnel, the entire educational program could be halted or disrupted if heavy damages were awarded to a plaintiff.

Trends in regard to governmental immunity

The justice of governmental immunity has been questioned increasingly in recent years. Through no fault of their own some pupils sustain serious injuries in physical education classes. The cost of medical care and hospitalization may amount to many thousands of dollars. In some instances, the student may be permanently handicapped.

These innocent victims of negligent behavior have no recourse in states where school districts have governmental immunity except to bring suit against the teacher. This is not a promising alternative because teachers ordinarily do not possess the financial resources to pay large damage suits. As a consequence, the parents must bear the loss or a major part of it.

The obvious injustice of such cases has resulted in considerable agitation to correct such situations. Even though school districts in the great majority of states still enjoy immunity against suits resulting from the negligence of school personnel the trend is definitely in the other direction. Courts are critical of the wrongs perpetuated under the doctrine of governmental immunity and increasingly are rendering decisions favorable to injured students.

For this reason many more school districts are taking out liability insurance. The availability of such insurance has obviated the argument that exposure to liability would be ruinous to public school systems. There is a growing recognition that injuries suffered in school should be compensated and the loss distributed either by insurance or taxation.

Statutory imposition of responsibility of school districts

As mentioned above, the immunity of federal, state, and local governments from damage suits has received considerable criticism because injustice is done to individuals at times. To mitigate these inequities a few states have passed statutes that waive, in whole or in part, the governmental immunity from such suits. In California the state legislature has fixed responsibility for injuries upon school boards for their officers or employees, just as private individuals or companies are liable. In Washington a statute waives the immunity of schools for accidents due to negligence but retains it if the accident occurred on a playground or in a field house or involved athletic apparatus. Thus, in Washington, the effect, so far as accidents occurring in physical education and athletics are concerned, is the same as in the states where governmental immunity is observed.

Three states—New York, New Jersey, and Connecticut—have what are known as "save harmless statutes." These statutes permit the payment from school funds of damages arising out of injury sustained by pupils or other persons through the negligence of teachers or other employees of the school district. Thus, in these states, the teachers are protected from financial loss arising out of a judgment against them. In Iowa, the Iowa supreme court once handed down a decision that teachers are not liable for damages while carrying on a governmental function, even though they are guilty of negligent conduct.

Several states have what are known as "safe place statutes." This legislation requires schools to provide safe facilities for the pupils. This involves both the construction and maintenance of the facilities. When accidents occur because of improper construction and maintenance, school districts in several states are liable. In most states with this type of legislation school districts are immune to damage suits.

Some injured persons have sought recovery from school districts on the claim that a nuisance was maintained. A nuisance is a condition or situation that is inherently dangerous. An attractive nuisance is a facility or piece of equipment that is appealing to a child but that, if left unguarded, might prove dangerous to him. Even though a child or a pupil might technically be considered a trespasser, the courts have considered the presence of such attractions as holding out an invitation to children to play with them. Even though negligence cannot be demonstrated, the existence of a nuisance may result in a successful suit against a school district. The courts in different states are divided, however, in their interpretation of such cases. A physical education teacher might be found guilty of negligence for not properly safeguarding a dangerous allurement. Thus, the teacher who forgot to lock up the swimming pool was found negligent when students used the pool and one of them was seriously injured.

Liability of private institutions

Private schools and colleges are generally immune from suits that are the results of negligent behavior on the part of institutional personnel. It is apparent that private institutions cannot be regarded as performing a governmental function. The basis upon which the immunity of private schools and colleges is established is that they are charitable institutions. If a school can demonstrate that it exists for the public benefit and not to make a profit, it will be immune to damage suits. Tuition charges do not disqualify a school, since they are usually necessary to help defray the institutional expenses.

Liability of teachers

As has been indicated previously teachers themselves are always personally liable for their own negligence. The courts have consistently ruled that teachers, supervisors, administrators, and other school employees are liable when they have been negligent. The immunity of the school district from liability because it is performing a governmental function does not extend to protect the individual who committed the negligent act (except in Iowa). When the teacher is not negligent, there is no liability, regardless of the seriousness of the injury. A teacher is also liable to the school district for any loss that his negligence has caused. However, it is rare that the school district would seek to recover damages from a teacher.

Liability insurance

As pointed out previously, many school districts now purchase liability insurance to protect themselves or their teachers from damage suits. In some states where education is regarded as a governmental function and school districts enjoy immunity, the purchase of insurance is not permissible on the ground that the school board insure itself against a liability that does not exist. No school district may purchase insurance of any type in the absence of statutory authorization.

To protect themselves against liability suits many physical educators purchase their own liability insurance. Such policies are relatively inexpensive and they relieve the instructor of concern about a heavy damage suit. The American Association for Health, Physical Education and Recreation has worked out arrangements whereby members may, at very little cost, obtain liability insurance, which will provide protection up to $10,000 and also cover defense costs.[2]

Defenses against negligence

It should be clear that there are many accidents in which negligent behavior is not involved. Pure accidents are those that occur without carelessness on the part of some other person. There are many such accidents that are completely devoid of negligent behavior.

It should be understood that to warn a pupil of dangerous places and actions is *not* an adequate defense if a suit is brought for negligence. This is not regarded as sufficient care to relieve teachers of legal responsibility for damages in the possibility of an accident. Neither does it suffice to put up written instructions regarding proper conduct to avoid accidents. Such instructions are valuable from the standpoint of reducing accidents, but when one does occur, they do not relieve the instructor from liability if he has been otherwise negligent.

However, a teacher is not always liable when an accident occurs, even though he has been negligent. There are four different legal defenses that might be employed by the teacher to avoid losing a suit. These are:

1. Proximate causes of injury. The negligent behavior must be what is known as "the proximate cause of the injury" before a jury will sustain a damage suit. This means that the negligent action of the teacher was the direct and immediate cause of the injury. If the accident were only indirectly or remotely due to the careless behavior of the teacher, the latter would not be liable. The negligent conduct must be a substantial factor in causing the injury, or the claim will be disallowed.

2. Contributory negligence. If the injured student failed to act as a reasonably prudent individual should have acted under the circumstances and if this negligence contributed to the accident, any negligent conduct on the part of the teacher is cancelled. The student is expected to employ a reasonable standard of self-protection. When contributory negligence can be demonstrated, the law makes no effort to apportion the wrong between the student and the teacher.

It should be recognized, however, that what is reasonably prudent conduct on the part of an adult might not be so construed for an adolescent or child. The standard of behavior expected of a child is that which other children of the same age, intelligence, sex, and background would ordinarily demonstrate under the circumstances. If the child does not exercise the degree of care that normally would be expected of

2 *Journal of Health, Physical Education, Recreation* (January, 1960), p. 45.

such a child for his own protection, his contributory negligence would cancel any negligence on the part of the teacher.

3. Assumption of risk. When individuals voluntarily engage in activities they take upon themselves the risks involved in such participation. This applies particularly to intramural and interschool athletics. Both players and spectators assume the normal risks involved in participating in or witnessing athletic contests. The spectator at a baseball game who is struck by a foul ball assumes this risk when he comes to the game. The spectator who was injured at a football game when some of the players fell out of bounds voluntarily assumed this risk when he attended the game. The player who is injured in a football game understood that when he tried out for the team he was taking a risk of injury. It should be pointed out, however, that players have the right to assume safe equipment, safe facilities, and qualified leadership when they become candidates for school teams.

4. An act of God. Where an uncontrollable act of the elements occurs and there is an injury, no liability is attached to the teacher, even though he might have been negligent.

Sources of suits in physical education

The most common sources of accidents in physical education which may lead to liability suits are unsafe facilities, defective equipment, transportation, failure to provide proper instruction, and improper supervision. Slippery floors (especially following dances), holes or ruts in outdoor areas, dangerous obstructions on play areas, bleachers without guardrails, the playing of basketball games on adjacent courts which have the same or overlapping sidelines, outdoor areas which are lined with unslaked lime, the use of streets to which automobiles have access for physical education classes and activities are common examples of unsafe facilities. The items of equipment which are most often defective are springboards, flying rings, diving boards, and horizontal bars. One student was injured by a flying bat in a baseball game because the instructor permitted the batter to use a bat that did not have a knobbed end. The failure to use mats on the floor for apparatus and tumbling activities, or on the wall at the end of the gymnasium where races are run, have led to successful liability suits. A mat not firmly fixed on a slippery floor, a piano improperly supported, a climbing rope not periodically inspected, gymnasium lockers not securely fastened to the floor, and radiators improperly padded have all produced injuries that subsequently led to damage suits.

If an accident occurs when the physical education instructor is absent or obviously not supervising his class, he is negligent. Courts have ruled that it is negligent to use a janitor, student teacher, or student assistant to supervise physical education facilities and activities in the absence of the regular instructor. When he is supervising, he must actively control the pupils rather than stand by as a passive observer. In particular, he must prevent pupils from harming others. However, if the area is too large or the number of pupils too great, the negligence will be that of the school district rather than that of the instructor. In California a jury held a school district guilty of negligence when the plaintiff's leg was broken in a fight on a playground where only one supervisor was assigned to supervise approximately 150 pupils.[3]

Failure to lock up facilities to prevent their use during the absence of the instructor has led to successful damage suits. Supervision also involves the inspection of equipment and facilities to be certain they are in safe condition. Failure of the instructor to report hazardous conditions has led to successful suits against school districts and the instructor. Unnecessary delays in repairing faulty facilities or permitting their use before repairs have been made are likewise negligent behavior.

Physical education teachers have been found negligent in not providing adequate instructions to their pupils and in permitting students to engage in activities that were beyond their ability to perform safely. "It is readily understood that no physical education teacher or coach would intentionally injure a pupil. But the physical education teacher who does not instruct a pupil as to the proper method of using a dangerous apparatus in the gymnasium has omitted a specific legal duty and, if harm ensues, is liable for tort through negligence." [4] Thus, in New York a pupil was injured in boxing. The teacher was held liable because the student was untrained and not warned of the dangers of this sport.[5] A pupil was injured in performing a head stand. The state was declared liable because the teacher in a normal school had failed to provide proper instructions.[6] A physical education teacher was found liable for the injuries incurred when a student attempted to perform a running front somersault in a tumbling class. The basis of the negligence was that the activity was beyond the level of skill of the student.[7] A physical education teacher was declared liable for a damage suit that developed when a large, poorly coordinated boy was injured in a shuttle relay race in which he was required to run at full speed toward a brick wall and return. In California it was ruled that physical education teachers are liable if they assign an exercise to a pupil which is beyond his level of ability.

[3] Charonnat v. San Francisco Unified School District, 56 Cal. App. (2d) 840, 133 p. (2d) 643 (1943).

[4] Marc Guley, "The Legal Aspects of Injuries in Physical Education and Athletics" (Unpublished Ed.D. dissertation, Syracuse University, 1952), p. 54.

[5] LaValley v. Stanford, 70 N.Y.S. (2d) 460 (1947).

[6] Gardner v. State of New York, 22 N.E. (2d) 344 (1939).

[7] Govel v. Board of Education of Albany, 60 N.E. (2d) 133 (1944).

Physical education teachers must be constantly alert to anticipate student behavior that may lead to accidents. They must understand students well enough to guard against their pranks and irresponsible actions. The alert, experienced teacher knows his pupils so well that he can sense what they will do in specific situations. This is invaluable in preventing pupils from injuring themselves from careless activities.

Public institutions have immunity from suits that arise out of negligence in transporting students unless there is a statute that waives the immunity. It is sound procedure to have institutional athletic teams travel in a school bus or a bonded public common carrier. Public carriers always have their own liability insurance against accidents. Private cars are commonly used to transport team members, but this practice is not recommended. When this is done, both the owner of the car and the school should be familiar with the public liability laws that are involved. Liability insurance should be carried by the driver and the owner of the car. If it is not available, it should be taken out by the school. The athletic director would be seriously negligent in permitting students to travel in a private car unless both the car and the driver were completely insured. It is not recommended that student drivers be used. In California a tennis coach arranged to have team members ride home in a car driven by a pupil known to be a reckless driver. The car was in poor condition with defective brakes. The school district was held liable when an accident occurred in which one boy was killed and another seriously injured.[8]

Another area of lawsuits involves permitting players to return to practice or to a game after they have suffered an injury. Such decisions should never be made by the coach. Medical approval should always be obtained. In the widely publicized case of Welch v. Dunsmuir Joint Union High School District[9] in California, the court upheld an award for $206,804 to a football player hurt in a scrimmage whose injuries were aggravated by the negligent manner in which he was removed from the field.

Liability in first-aid and medical treatment

When a student is injured, the school nurse or a physician should be called immediately. If neither is available and the pupil is obviously in need of first-aid treatment, the physical educator should administer it. For him not to do so is negligence. However, this is as far as he should go. He will be liable for negligence if he continues treatment of an injury. His responsibility extends only to the administration of emergency treatment. Teachers are also expected to exercise sound

[8] Hanson v. Reedly Joint Union High School District, 111 P. (2d) 415 (1941).
[9] 326 P. (2d) 633 (Cal. App. 1958).

judgment in summoning medical assistance or in transporting the injured student to his home or to a doctor.

Value of releases and waivers

Many high schools follow the practice of requiring all candidates for athletic squads to procure from their parents signed statements releasing the school from any claim for injury that might be incurred while participating in the sport. Such releases or waivers are valueless if a suit for negligence is instituted. They have no validity before the law because a parent has no authority to waive a claim accruing to his child for personal injury. However, such waivers and releases might be used because most parents think they have waived their legal right to bring suit.

Policies and procedures to reduce accidents

It was previously suggested that the administrator and his staff develop policies and procedures that would reduce injuries and thus minimize the possibility of lawsuits. The following list is suggestive:

1. Supervision:
   (a) Always be careful and alert when students are under your supervision—an ounce of prevention is far better than a pound of cure.
   (b) Under no circumstances leave a class without supervision. Students, custodians, and student teachers are not considered appropriate supervisors.
   (c) An instructor should not be called from class to answer the phone or to speak to a visitor.
   (d) Anticipate the possibility of accidents. Particularly anticipate the negligence of students which might cause injury to other students.
   (e) Request additional supervision if the group is too large.
   (f) Make certain that facilities are inaccessible to students when no supervision is available.

2. Environmental safeguards:
   (a) All apparatus and hanging equipment must be inspected annually and a report submitted.
   (b) Students must not be permitted to use equipment or apparatus that is in need of repair.
   (c) Request in writing that apparatus and equipment be repaired as soon as the defective condition has been noted.
   (d) Make certain that rules and regulations governing use of apparatus are posted.

(e) Do not line outdoor areas with unslaked lime. Such lines should be made with gypsum or slaked lime.

(f) Adequate space should be provided for all vigorous activities. Overcrowded conditions produce many accidents.

(g) Use floor and wall mats and other protective equipment whenever they are necessary.

(h) Holes in outdoor areas should be promptly filled and dangerous obstructions removed.

3. Medical procedures:

(a) Students taking physical education or participating in interschool athletics who have been ill or injured must have medical approval before they resume activity.

(b) Do not treat injuries or prescribe treatment.

(c) Administer first aid when necessary if a doctor or nurse is not available.

4. Appropriate activities:

(a) Do not permit students to participate in potentially hazardous activities until they have received proper instructions and have had adequate practice.

(b) In body contact activities such as football, boxing, and wrestling match students who are reasonably comparable in weight, strength, and experience.

(c) Require that students have appropriate protective equipment in sports where indicated.

5. Transportation:

(a) Travel in school bus or public carrier whenever possible.

(b) The use of private cars for transportation should be discouraged. Under no conditions should they be used unless the driver and the owner of the car are insured.

(c) Faculty supervision of students on trips is mandatory.

Accident reports

Accident reports should be required in all schools. They not only focus attention upon the causes of accidents but they also may aid the school personnel and district in liability suits that develop from student injuries. Such reports are basic to a safety program in the school. They also protect the school and staff members from undesirable publicity. Since lawsuits for legal liability may not be tried in court for many months a complete and accurate accident report is far superior to human memory in presenting the facts in the case.

The accident report should include the name and address of the

STANDARD STUDENT ACCIDENT REPORT FORM.

Part A. Information on ALL Accidents

1. Name: _____ Home Address: _____
2. School: _____ Sex: M ☐ : F ☐ : Age: ____ Grade or Classification: _____
3. Time accident occurred: Hour _____ A.M.: _____ P.M. Date: _____
4. Place of Accident: School Building ☐   School Grounds ☐   To or from School ☐   Home ☐   Elsewhere ☐

| 5. NATURE OF INJURY | Abrasion ____
Amputation ____
Asphyxiation ____
Bite ____
Bruise ____
Burn ____
Concussion ____
Cut ____
Dislocation ____
Other (specify) ____ | Fracture ____
Laceration ____
Poisoning ____
Puncture ____
Scalds ____
Scratches ____
Shock (el.) ____
Sprain ____ | **DESCRIPTION OF THE ACCIDENT**
How did accident happen? What was student doing? Where was student? List specifically unsafe acts and unsafe conditions existing. Specify any tool, machine or equipment involved. ____
_____
_____
_____
_____
_____ |
| PART OF BODY INJURED | Abdomen ____
Ankle ____
Arm ____
Back ____
Chest ____
Ear ____
Elbow ____
Eye ____
Face ____
Finger ____
Other (specify) ____ | Foot ____
Hand ____
Head ____
Knee ____
Leg ____
Mouth ____
Nose ____
Scalp ____
Tooth ____
Wrist ____ | _____
_____
_____
_____
_____
_____
_____ |

6. Degree of Injury: Death ☐   Permanent Impairment ☐   Temporary Disability ☐   Nondisabling ☐
7. Total number of days lost from school: _____ (To be filled in when student returns to school)

Part B. Additional Information on School Jurisdiction Accidents

8. Teacher in charge when accident occurred (Enter name): _____
   Present at scene of accident: No: _____ Yes: _____

9. IMMEDIATE ACTION TAKEN
   First-aid Treatment ____ By (Name): _____
   Sent to School Nurse ____ By (Name): _____
   Sent Home ____ By (Name): _____
   Sent to Physician ____ By (Name): _____
   Physician's Name: _____
   Sent to Hospital ____ By (Name): _____
   Name of Hospital: _____

10. Was a parent or other individual notified?   No: __ Yes: __ When: _____ How: _____
    Name of individual notified: _____
    By whom? (Enter name): _____
11. Witnesses: 1. Name: _____ Address: _____
    2. Name: _____ Address: _____

| 12. LOCATION | Specify Activity
Athletic field _____
Auditorium _____
Cafeteria _____
Classroom _____
Corridor _____
Dressing room _____
Gymnasium _____
Home Econ. _____
Laboratories _____ | Specify Activity
Locker _____
Pool _____
Sch. Grounds _____
____ Shop _____
Showers _____
Stairs _____
Toilets and Washrooms _____
Other (specify) _____ | Remarks
What recommendations do you have for preventing other accidents of this type?
_____
_____
_____
_____
_____ |

Signed: Principal: _____ Teacher: _____

Read Carefully   *Instructions*   *Fill in Completely*

A. Use Part A of the Form to report *all* student accidents. Injuries requiring a doctor's care, or keeping a student out of school one-half day or more, should be reported regardless of where the student was when injured (on school property, en route to or from school, at home or elsewhere).

B. Use Part B of the form to report additional information on injuries to students while under the jurisdiction of the school. School jurisdiction accidents, however slight, should be reported promptly. Unless otherwise defined by administrative ruling or court action, school jurisdiction accidents are those occurring while students are on school property, in school building and on the way to and from school.

Important: In order that maximum use be made of accident reports, it is essential that the accident be described in sufficient detail to show the unsafe acts and unsafe conditions existing when the accident occurred. The description should answer such questions as: What was the student doing at the time of the accident? (Playing tag or football, operating lathe, cutting lawn, etc.) Was he using any apparatus, machine, vehicle, tool or equipment? How was he using it? Would it have been safer to do it some other way? Was another person involved in the accident in any way?

(For further information on the preparation of the original accident report and the monthly summary sheet, see *Safety Education Memo No. 3* —"Student Accident Records and Analysis.")

Source: Reprinted by permission of the National Safety Council, 425 North Michigan Avenue, Chicago 11, Illinois.

Figure 14-1.

student, the activity in which the injury occurred, the date, hour, place of accident, person in charge, medical attention provided, and circumstances causing the accident (see the Standard Student Accident Report Form recommended by the National Safety Council in Figure 14-1). It is very helpful to obtain signed statements from witnesses. If witnesses declare that they know nothing about the accident, it is desirable to obtain their written statements to that effect. Any statements of witnesses regarding contributory negligence on the part of the injured person is valuable evidence.

SELECTED REFERENCES

Bucher, Charles A., *Administration of School Health and Physical Education Programs*. 3rd ed. (St. Louis, The C. V. Mosby Company, 1963).

Harper, Fowler V., and James Fleming, Jr., *The Law of Torts* (Boston, Little, Brown and Company, 1956).

Leibee, Howard C., *Liability for Accidents in Physical Education, Athletics, Recreation* (Ann Arbor, Michigan, Ann Arbor Publishers, 1952).

National Commission on Safety Education, *Who Is Liable for Pupil Injuries?* (Washington, D.C., The National Education Association, 1950).

15

office management

Importance of efficient office management

Every physical education administrator needs to understand the essentials of efficient office management. This need is obvious in large departments, where secretaries, clerks, telephone operators, and receptionists are available to provide a variety of services for the public and the department personnel. However, the same functions must be carried on in a one-man department, where no secretary or office equipment is available. Regardless of the size of the department, correspondence must be carried on, reports rendered, materials duplicated, equipment ordered, materials filed, and records maintained. Whether the department is large or small, the internal requirements are the same. The only difference is that in the small department the administrator must do more things himself, and in the large department the various duties are delegated to others to perform.

An effective office operation is important to the success of the department. The work of the administrator and the staff members is assisted materially by office personnel. Faculty members are relieved of a variety of duties that can be better performed by office employees. Services to students and the general public are improved. Communications are enhanced. As a consequence, better public relations are engendered.

There are proper and improper ways of performing all the office details in a physical education office. To do them correctly saves both time and money. The efficient operation of a department requires sound office procedures. Such procedures have been tested and proved in business and industry and may be readily adapted to school situations. No administrator can afford to fail to use them.

Office unit orientation

The administrative offices should be centrally located so as to be accessible to all who have business with the director or any of the staff members. Almost invariably the office is located near the entrance of the gymnasium or the physical education building. Staff offices should be located adjacent to the central office and close to the classrooms.

The desirability of having a large central office serving as a work room for the secretarial and clerical staff, as a repository for departmental records, and as a reception room for visitors is evident. In addition, a conference room should be available for staff and committee meetings, conferences, and as a place for the entertainment of guests. However, neither of these facilities will be found in most high schools.

Office functions and practices

The size of the physical education office usually varies with the size of the institution and the extensiveness of the program. In some very small secondary schools the physical education administrator is fortunate to have an office. In many other small schools, if he has an office, it is one that he shares with several other staff members. Office personnel, if any is available, usually consists of a part-time secretary or volunteer student secretary or clerk. At the other extreme are the physical education administrators in large colleges and universities who have several secretaries, a telephone operator, and perhaps even a receptionist—all housed in commodious offices with the latest types of equipment.

Regardless of the size of the office staff and facilities, there are many functions that are common to practically all offices. These are: (1) answering and placing telephone calls, (2) receiving visitors, (3) answering correspondence, (4) filing, (5) duplicating materials, (6) keeping appointments and meeting obligations and (7) providing services to staff members. Each of these functions will be discussed briefly.

Answering and placing telephone calls. In larger offices telephone calls will be placed and answered by the secretary or telephone operator. The administrator without office assistance must perform this function himself. In either case standard telephone technique and courtesy should be observed. Favorable or unfavorable impressions of the department are readily created by the manner in which telephone calls are received. The proper procedures do not accidentally occur—they must be taught and insisted upon by the administrator.

The individual answering the telephone must be as friendly and as cordial as if the caller were a visitor in the office. Courtesy and helpfulness are essential. Good public relations are created when the receiver of the call demonstrates a willingness to do whatever is required. Sincerity of purpose and desire to be of service to people is the key to good telephone relationships. Since emotions are readily reflected in one's voice, care must be exercised not to show anger. When it is necessary to give a negative answer the caller must have the feeling that he has been courteously treated.

The telephone should be answered promptly. The department should be identified immediately. The name of the person receiving the call is frequently given. For example, "Department of Physical Education, Miss Smith speaking." Such terms as "Hello" and "Yes" are not used in answering telephone calls in a business office.

A pencil and telephone pad should be available to take messages or telephone numbers that are to be called. If the administrator is not available, the secretary may be able to provide the desired information herself. If the administrator is occupied, the secretary should have an understanding with him regarding interruptions. When the administrator leaves the office, he should let the secretary know where he can be located and when he expects to return. When he is out of his office, a form similar to the one given in Figure 15-1 should be used to indicate that a call has been received in his absence. If the person called is not

FORM FOR RECORDING TELEPHONE CALLS.

Date_____19_____ Name_____
While you were out, there was a personal telephone call today.
Time_____ o'clock
From Mr._____
Of_____
Who said_____
Telephone number is:_____
Signed_____

Figure 15-1.

in, the secretary should always offer to take a message. It is helpful to get the name of the caller if he does not identify himself. In such instances the questions "May I have him call you?" or "Mr. ——— is not in. Is there a message?" are in order.

Receiving visitors. Every member of the clerical staff should be well versed in the common courtesies of greeting visitors as they call at the office. Needless to say, all visitors should be made welcome. They should be cordially greeted, and every effort should be made to meet their needs. In the event the caller has no appointment, the purpose of his visit should be determined. If it is necessary to wait to see the administrator, the caller should be comfortably seated. Something to read should be offered him. If the administrator is not available, either an appointment should be arranged or an effort made to have someone else provide the assistance the visitor desires. Visitors with appointments or important visitors should be announced immediately. A courteous procedure should be worked out whereby the secretary interrupts an unnecessarily long interview with a visitor, especially when other visitors are waiting. She can enter the office and announce, "Mr. Smith is here for his ten o'clock appointment." When there are no callers, an effective procedure is to summarize what has been discussed and to inquire if there are other matters to be considered.

Answering correspondence. One of the quickest ways for an administrator to gain a poor reputation is to be negligent or careless about answering his correspondence. Some administrators have a policy of answering every letter within twenty-four hours after it has been received. Although this may not be possible in all cases, it is a sound practice to answer correspondence promptly. Not only should the answer be prompt but it should be complete as well. All questions should be answered carefully and in good English. Needless to say, *all* letters should be answered.

Many letters that the administrator receives can better be answered by some other member of the department. A form is usually employed, requesting the appropriate action by the staff member. Many letters of a routine nature can be answered directly by the secretary. This will save the valuable time of the administrator. In larger institutions letters of the same type are commonly received. These may be answered by a standard form reply.

It is standard procedure to proofread all outgoing letters to detect mistakes. The address should be checked for accuracy. Carbon copies are necessary, and they should be filed with the related correspondence. When the letter contains enclosures, its weight should be determined to insure proper postage. Each letter should be examined to determine whether it has been signed. Unless the letter is neatly and correctly executed it should not be forwarded. No administrator can afford the unfavorable impression which a smudged, carelessly written letter will produce.

In many small schools the administrator will have no secretarial help whatsoever. In these situations he must handle his own correspondence. If he is unable to type, his only recourse is to write out his letters longhand. The other extreme occurs where a full-time or part-time secretary is available to take shorthand. In between these extremes are the schools in which dictaphones are available. Dictaphones have several advantages. They can be taken home and letters dictated at night or over the week end. Administrators who have part-time secretaries can dictate at any time and have the completed cylinders available for the secretary when she arrives. When the administrator is constantly interrupted during dictation, or if he has difficulty composing a letter, he can save the time of his secretary by using the dictaphone.

If the administrator has a student or an inexperienced secretary, he must remember to dictate slowly. In addition, he should have the secretary read back to him the material that he has dictated. He should also check the letter carefully before he signs it. The administrator should save the time of his secretary by having everything in readiness for dictation. If any reference data are necessary, they should be obtained prior to summoning the secretary. It is poor economy to have a secretary unoccupied because she is waiting to take dictation.

Filing. An effective filing system is essential in any office. All of the correspondence, records, budgets, and reports must be filed in such a way that they can be located quickly. It is not difficult to locate recently filed material, but on occasions several years may elapse before it is needed. Reference to filed material is constantly necessary, and when it cannot be located, delay, inefficiency and, at times, embarrassment result. Filing is more accurately done when only one person does it.

A variety of filing systems are known, but in schools the alphabetical system is used almost invariably. The material to be filed is classified according to name, subject, or a combination of name and subject. Large physical education offices will probably use both a name and a subject file, but the great majority will use the combination system.

The name file refers to names of people or organizations with whom correspondence or business is carried on. Individuals are filed under their surnames. The alphabetizing is continued through as many letters as are necessary to differentiate the names. Prefixes such as De, Di, Mac, Mc, von, and O' are part of the name they precede. In this system a folder is made for each name or correspondent if there is sufficient material to justify starting a folder. From three to ten papers justify starting a folder. A lesser amount is filed in a *miscellaneous* folder. A miscellaneous folder is made for each letter of the alphabet and is located behind the last name folder under the particular letter. Any material for which there is no separate name folder is filed in the miscellaneous folder, alphabetically rather than by date.

Subject filing refers to filing the material according to the subject matter with which it deals. The subject headings must be specific, significant, and technically correct. Nouns are generally used to refer to the subject. Subheadings are used in subject filing. A miscellaneous folder is also used in subject filing. The papers in a subject folder are arranged by date, with the latest date on top. When subject files are used, the maintenance of a separate alphabetical list or card index of the subjects is recommended. This will prevent filing material under a new heading when a folder is already available.

A subject file is necessary in any physical education office because of the nature of its operation. Items such as budgets, schedules, contracts, equipment orders, records, and reports must be filed according to subject. Since there are many more items that would be filed under subjects than under names, most physical education offices should file by subject into which names are incorporated. This may be done by including correspondence in the miscellaneous folder in a special correspondence folder. However, if extensive correspondence is carried on, a separate name file should be maintained.

In any filing system cross references are necessary to locate various documents. This is useful when reference is made to a specific document that might be filed under several headings. The material should be filed under the most logical heading, and a cross-reference form should be placed in the folder under the related designation. The cross-reference form should be mimeographed on 8½ by 11½-inch paper that is colored. It should allow for (1) the correspondent's name, and (2) data to indicate to what letter or document reference is made.

When a file is removed from the filing cabinet for any length of time an "out" slip or guide should be inserted. Regular "out" guides have pockets for the cards that indicate the location of the missing file. When individual papers are removed from the files, an "out" slip should be substituted. An "out" slip should be wider than regular paper in order to clearly show above the edges of the other papers within the folder. When folders or papers are not returned promptly to the files but are kept at various desks, the filing system is soon disrupted. Secretaries must keep their filing up to date. When they are busy, there is a tendency for a considerable amount of unfiled material to accumulate on their desks.

In setting up a filing system for a medium-sized school, the first step should be to segregate the total program into specific subjects, such as: (1) physical education, (2) intramural sports, (3) health education, and (4) interscholastic sports. Each drawer of a four-drawer filing cabinet would refer to a specific area with the subareas listed in alphabetical order.

The physical education drawer could be subdivided into the following areas:

1. Annual reports. A folder for each annual report should be included.
2. Budget. A folder for each annual budget for each of the past five years should be maintained.
3. Committees. A folder for each committee should be filed.
4. Correspondence. Folders should be arranged alphabetically under this heading. All carbons and original copies of communications should be filed in the appropriate folder.
5. Departmental policies. The departmental policy file should be included in a folder. If desirable, a number of folders might be used with each including the policies in different areas.
6. Equipment. A folder should be included listing the equipment, excepting that included in the interscholastic athletic inventory. The new equipment on order should also be noted.
7. Financial matters. Duplicate copies of all requisitions and duplicate vouchers submitted for payment can be filed under this heading.
8. Personal records. A folder for each student should be available. This should include his medical examination records, correspondence with family physician, parents, and others. Excuses and the anecdotal record of student achievement and conduct can also be filed in this folder.
9. Service program. A folder for each activity taught should be available. This might include lesson plans, rules, syllabus, examinations, and teaching aids, such as clippings from newspapers and magazines. In addition, a folder for the program and schedule for each year for the past three years should be included.
10. Student help. Records for all part-time and student help should be kept in this folder.
11. Test data. Complete data on physical fitness and other tests should be filed in folders according to the school year in which they apply.

The intramural sports drawer could be subdivided as follows:

1. Intramural activities. A folder for each sport included in the program should be available. These should include rules governing that activity. In addition, it might include past records and schedules.
2. Officials. A folder with the names, addresses, telephone numbers, and qualifications of all officials used in the program should be available.
3. Programs. A folder should be available which would contain the

details of each year's program for a period of five years. The details should cover such items as the participants and teams in each sport and the results of all the competition.

4. Publicity. A folder should be retained which has all the posters, announcements, news stories, and other publicity materials.
5. Schedules. This folder should contain schedules for all intramural activities for the current year.

The health education drawer might be arranged as follows:

1. Administrative policies. A folder under this heading should be included for each of the following areas: communicable disease control, emergency care and injuries, excuses, health of school personnel, and scheduling.
2. Health services. A folder under this subject heading should be included for each of the following areas: health examinations and followup, screening, counseling, communicable disease control, and sanitation of the school plant.
3. Health instruction. A separate folder under this subject heading should be available for each of the following areas: personal health, weight control, vision and hearing, dental health, communicable and noncommunicable disease, first aid and safety, family life education, nutrition, exercise, rest and recreation, health services and products, community health, narcotics and alcohol education, mental health and personal adjustment, and smoking.
4. Healthful school living. A separate folder under this subject heading should be included for each of the following areas: school lunch, seating, heating, lighting, ventilation, swimming pool sanitation, and locker and shower room sanitation.

The interscholastic sports drawer might be subdivided as follows:

1. Budget. A folder should be filed for the interscholastic athletic budget for each year for the past five years.
2. Contracts. A folder is desirable for each sport that involves contracts.
3. Eligibility lists. For each sport, a folder should be available in which there is an eligibility list.
4. Equipment. A folder for each sport should be available in which data concerning equipment is filed. These data should include an equipment inventory plus a listing of new equipment that has been ordered.
5. Game reports. A folder for each sport should be included which would contain game reports for home games. The game reports should include such data as attendance, weather, gate receipts, opponent, and score.

6. Officials. All data relating to officials should be filed under this heading in folders arranged according to sports.
7. Schedules. Schedules for all sports in the current year should be included in a folder. Folders for previous years should also be maintained. In some schools a folder for future schedules is needed.
8. Sports. A folder for each interscholastic sport should be maintained. Included in such a folder will be squad personnel, current records, lesson plans, scouting reports, coaching aids, and the like.
9. Transportation. A folder should be developed for each sport. Every folder should contain all arrangements for travel by the respective team.

From time to time the files should be checked and obsolete material removed. It does not take long for the files to become cluttered with useless documents unless they are cleared at periodic intervals, annually or semiannually. Some of the material can be discarded completely; other papers may be transferred to an inactive file. How long various documents are retained depends somewhat upon the nature of the material and the space available in the filing cabinets.

Duplicating materials. A constant need exists in a physical education office to have materials duplicated. In addition to the requirements in instructional classes for objective examinations, reading lists, syllabi, instructional materials, and outlines, coaches may wish to have plays duplicated for their players, and the intramural director will require numerous copies of rules and schedules. The administrator will also need to have various materials duplicated, such as departmental regulations, announcements, minutes of committee meetings, and instructions to staff members and students.

In most high schools and colleges the materials are mimeographed or dittoed in a central office. However, when the volume justifies it, the physical education department has found it advantageous to possess its own duplicating equipment. Dittoing equipment, particularly, is inexpensive to purchase and to operate. Although the ditto and mimeographing machines are simple to operate, it is advisable to restrict their use to authorized individuals only. On staffs where little if any office personnel is available, staff members can learn how to operate the duplicating machine. They can then reproduce their own materials.

Keeping appointments and meeting obligations. On many occasions physical education administrators must make appointments to speak to people or to perform some task by a certain stipulated time. To meet these obligations the administrator must have some infallible system of reminding him of these events. He must use the techniques that have proven successful in all types of offices. He simply cannot afford to miss or to be late for an appointment, forget details, or submit tardy reports.

The establishment of regular office hours facilitates the making and keeping of appointments. When staff members, students, tradespeople, and others know what the regular office hours are, they can usually arrange to see the administrator at a mutually convenient time. He must keep his secretary informed concerning any changes in his office hours, especially when he knows he will be absent or late.

When the necessity of performing a task occurs, many administrators endeavor to take care of it immediately. If the administrator is free for an immediate appointment, or can make a telephone call, write a letter or prepare a report at once, rather than defer it, there is no possibility of forgetting it. If the matter cannot be immediately disposed of, a notation should be made concerning it. Calendars are essential in any office to assure that appointments are kept and obligations met. The administrator needs a desk calendar with 15- or 30-minute time designations. All appointments and obligations should be noted on the calendar. Every office has a number of recurring items every year, and these should be noted on the calendar at the beginning of the school year.

The administrator also needs a pocket appointment book. This should include all the notations that are on his desk calendar. He will make appointments when he is away from his own office. He will also need to know of his office appointments when he is elsewhere. It is essential that the appointments on his desk calendar and pocket calendar coincide.

If a secretary is available, she should also maintain a desk calendar. It is her responsibility to see that her calendar and those of the administrator are accurate, identical, and up to date. She must be careful to learn of the appointments that the administrator makes when he is away from his office. She must see that the administrator meets all his appointments and obligations. To remind her employer of a task he should do, the secretary should place the file on his desk. If it is obvious that he has overlooked a call or appointment, she should remind him of it. It is a sound practice to spend the first few minutes each morning with the secretary, discussing the daily schedule. Some secretaries place a typed schedule of the administrator's appointments on his desk every morning. Whenever the administrator leaves the office, his secretary should be aware of where he might be reached and when he expects to return. When he leaves his office at the end of the day, he should check his calendar to see whether he has any early appointments the following day.

It is a mistake for the administrator to rely upon his memory for the conduct of his daily affairs. It has been said that "the shortest pencil is better than the longest memory." Everything that cannot be taken care of immediately should be written down in such a way that it will not be forgotten.

A very helpful office device that may be combined with a desk calendar is known as the office tickler. The tickler carries reminders for certain routine activities. There are in every department many duties that recur each year. These can be indicated on the office tickler in advance. The tickler file usually consists of a box built to hold 3- by 5-inch memorandum cards. A tabbed guide for each month and thirty-one tabbed guides for each day of each month are needed. Each activity that is to be performed at a future date is noted on the appropriate card. The cards are filed according to dates. The tickler file should be checked every morning. Certain items that occur frequently throughout the year can be handled by a single card. Thus, if the payroll must be completed on the last day of each month, the same card may be used each month, rather than making twelve separate entries.

Another task that can be handled by the secretary is making travel arrangements. The secretary should know the approximate time of departure and return, the mode of travel, accommodations desired, appointments, and hotel preference. With this information, she is able to make all the arrangements and save considerable time for the administrator.

In larger offices secretaries make the necessary arrangements for committee meetings. To work out a convenient time and place for a number of people to meet is frequently a time-consuming process.

Providing services to staff members. A major function of the physical education office is to provide various services to staff members. There are a variety of ways in which the work of staff members is assisted by office personnel. The most important of these is to type examinations, reading lists, course outlines, reports, speeches, and letters. In many secondary schools such assistance is not available and the staff member must either do the typing himself or get along without it. Neither alternative is desirable. The time of staff members is too important to be spent laboriously typing essential materials. On the other hand, if typed materials are not available, the performance of the staff member may be diminished.

The secretarial personnel may also assist staff members by arranging appointments, gathering travel information, maintaining student personnel records, recording test data, contacting students, and the like. The more staff members can be relieved of these essential details, the more time will be available for them to perform their teaching, supervisory, and advisory functions.

Office management in a small high school

The heavy load of the administrator in a small school makes good organization and efficient methods of office management particularly necessary. He should have one period set aside every day for the conduct of his departmental affairs. If such time is not provided, he will need to use his free period or time before or after school.

Whatever assistance the administrator has will come from students. Fortunately, in most high schools it is possible to obtain senior students interested in office work who will volunteer their services to gain experience. It is not difficult to find students who can type and some are capable of taking shorthand. The administrator will probably have to use several students to accomplish all the necessary duties. In this way the duties that require special skill can be reserved for the period when the student with that skill is available.

It is relatively easy to teach the student clerks how to use the telephone, to receive visitors, to file materials, to use the mimeograph or ditto machines, to maintain records, and to perform the essential housekeeping duties of the office. They can render invaluable service if they are used wisely. They must be given recognition for their services, and care must be exercised not to exploit them.

In the small high school office equipment is usually limited. The minimum items in any office should consist of:

1. One desk for each teacher
2. Desk tools (ink stand, paperweight, paper cutter, scissors, ruler, paste, blotter, pens, pencils, paper, stapler, and clips)
3. Calendar and memorandum ad
4. A large work table for student assistants
5. Extra chairs for guests
6. A four- or five-drawer filing cabinet with lock
7. Several card files of different sizes
8. Bookshelves
9. Magazine stand

A typewriter and a typewriter table are very important items that are often unavailable in small high schools. If this equipment is not available, access to some other typewriter within the school should be obtained. If a telephone cannot be procured, the office telephone may be used.

Office management in a medium-sized high school

In a medium-sized high school the physical education administrator has the same duties as the administrator in the small school. However, he is much more likely to be allocated time for his administrative duties. He may be relieved of one or two teaching periods per day for this purpose. More office equipment will probably be available. He will undoubtedly have more people to whom he can delegate various duties. It might be possible to use the principal's clerical staff for dictation, typing, and mimeographing. Student assistants will continue to be needed. For part-time and student secretarial help, a specific job description will be helpful. If they can have recourse to written instructions and policies concerning their various responsibilities, they will avoid many mistakes. A typewriter and typewriter table and a telephone and an alphabetical index to common telephone numbers should be available in the administrator's office.

Office management in a large institution

In a large school where one or more clerical personnel are available the role of the administrator is that of office manager. All the activities carried on in the office are his responsibility. The duties of the different individuals are assigned and supervised by him.

A standard procedure in large offices is to develop a job description for each member of the clerical staff. This lets the employee know specifically what is expected of him and that he or she is held responsible for demonstrating competence as it applies to these responsibilities. This does not mean that each employee is restricted from assuming other duties in the office as circumstances require.

In a large office a definite organizational structure might be necessary for the office personnel. Responsibility must be vested in some individual—usually the most experienced, the most mature, and the highest-ranking member. The administrator will not have the time to concern himself with the details of managing the office. The assignment of duties, distribution of work, and supervision of the work of all office personnel should be delegated to this person.

The administrator is responsible for the development and maintenance of high morale and *esprit de corps* among the office personnel. He accomplishes this by creating pleasant working conditions, by establishing reasonable standards of accomplishment, by providing suitable working tools, and by friendly, helpful supervision.

In large schools the matter of communication within the office and among the staff is a problem. The accepted practice is to use written interstaff memoranda. Special forms are available for this purpose. These memoranda are time saving and have the advantage of fixing responsibility. In addition, they reduce the risk of misunderstanding and error.

The secretary [1]

An important asset that many administrators overlook in planning their work is a capable secretary. By working with an intelligent

[1] The authors are indebted to Miss Eleanor Metheny of the Division of Physical Education, University of Southern California, for the material in this section.

secretary and learning to delegate to her all the responsibility that she is capable of assuming and by leaving in her hands many time-consuming routine matters, the administrator will find that he has much more time for creative work and will thereby be of much greater value to his profession. The wise administrator, then, should know what a good secretary is, what she can do, and how to make the best use of her abilities.

It may seem a bit obvious to state that intelligence, personality and character are the three general personal qualifications of a good secretary, but the lack of any one of these dooms many an otherwise promising girl to the rank of the automaton who "takes dictation."

Her intelligence should be practical and analytical, not merely abstract, and she should be able to comprehend the factors in any situation and make some reasonable decision about it, with sound logic to back up her judgment. Her intelligence must include a capacity for detail and an ability to deal with the almost endless routine matters that arise in any administrator's office. And if this intelligence is to function to the best advantage for the secretary and the administrator, back of it must be a real interest and pride in the activities, welfare, and progress of the department. If she is desultory and detached regarding her duties and performs them mechanically, she will be no particular asset. When an administrator has a secretary who is dedicated to her position and takes a deep personal interest in the success of the department, he is indeed fortunate.

The personality of the secretary is of critical importance. She constantly encounters students, staff members, other faculty, and visitors, and it is vital that she create a favorable impression. Since the administrator will spend from one third to three fourths of his working hours in her company, it is axiomatic that her personality be an important consideration to him. The pleasant, cheerful, and sensible girl is not only easier to work with than the temperamental one but will usually accomplish much more in the same amount of time.

The caller's first impression of the administrator comes from the front office, where he is received by the secretary. She is the office hostess and, as such, should have all the prerequisites of any hostess—graciousness, cordiality, interest, and tact. By her own well-bred manner and well-groomed appearance, she should convey the impression of the well-run office where all demands are given courteous attention. She should meet people easily and pleasantly and attend to their wants as effectively as possible, making no obvious display of efficiency, but quietly accomplishing what needs to be done. She will need endless poise, good humor, and diplomacy in dealing with the many who come to the office, and she must also exercise discrimination in determining which of them have legitimate business with her employer and which of them do not. In a word she must be efficient, but charmingly so.

Her telephone voice and manner should be as pleasant as her office personality. She should be able to convey to the person who calls that he is talking to a capable and willing person who, in most cases, can supply him with the information he needs without troubling the administrator about it. To assume the somewhat belligerent "who wants to talk to him?" attitude is as rude as it is inexcusable.

The secretary who really becomes a part of the organization must be extremely adaptable and ready and willing to do whatever must be done, no matter how far it may seem to fall out of her sphere of activity. She must remember that her position exists because she can be of service to the administrator, and that service is never limited to the mere mechanics of letter writing.

If she is to rise above the ranks of the typists, she will find herself sorely needing a sense of humor to enable her to keep proper perspective on herself, her job, and those around her. She must be able to talk easily and entertainingly on occasion, but above all, she must learn to be a good listener and to take an active interest in the discussions of the plans of the present and future which her employer will want to talk about to someone who understands what it is all about but who can be trusted to keep his confidence.

To be worthy of the name, the secretary must be absolutely reliable in all situations so that her employer may trust her as completely as he does himself. Her loyalty to him must be absolutely unquestionable. In the course of her day's work a secretary learns many things that are not for publication, but no matter how prone she may be to gossip about her friends and neighbors, she will never under any circumstances gossip about office information, however trivial it may be. The necessity for personal integrity is too obvious to need statement.

The training of the good secretary should be more than a matter of shorthand, typing, filing, and office practice, although these, of course, are essential. Most important is a knowledge of the English language and its correct use, which must include spelling and diction. Since she will compose numerous letters that will go out over the signature of her employer, she should have an appreciation of style and form in composition in order to make her letters convincing. She should know the essentials of order and have a systematic way of getting her work done, not only in the quickest way but in the best possible way. She should sense the relative importance of each task and learn to do first things first.

It is desirable but not essential that she have some training in the field in which her employer is interested. If this is not feasible, she should acquire at an early date a very real interest in that field and keep herself reasonably well informed about it. This will not only add to her enjoyment of her work but will increase her value to her employer.

Having hired a secretary, many an administrator seems to feel that his responsibility is ended, and from then on it is up to her. If he takes that attitude, he will soon find that he does not have a capable secretary but just one more girl working in the office. It is important that as soon as she begins working, he should see to it that she has all possible information concerning the work that is to be done. In any organization there is almost endless red tape with which the secretary becomes entangled in the course of her day's work, the workings of much of which she will eventually learn by trial and error. But a knowledge of the regulations will save her endless time and trouble. Do not expect her immediately to assume charge of all the routine matters that will arise. Give her time to learn. But gradually, as she proves herself capable, delegate to her all the responsibility she is able to handle. This is the point at which most administrators fail. They cannot bear to see authority to act on matters, however trivial, placed in hands other than their own. Remember that she is an intelligent adult and treat her as such; and having given her responsibility, trust her with it and let her feel that you do trust it. Her judgment may soon be almost as good as your own in those situations that are covered by previously determined policies.

Much has been written of loyalty of the secretary to her employer, but much more might be written about the loyalty of the employer to the secretary. She is, presumably, intelligent and capable of handling her job, and she should be backed up by her employer in any reasonable situation, not made the scapegoat for all the mistakes that occur in the office. To humiliate her in order to inflate one's ego before important callers is, of course, an inexcusable but not uncommon practice. A feeling of mutual loyalty and respect helps to create an office morale that makes the secretary feel that she is an integral part of the organization and that she is working not *for* but *with* a wise and understanding man, not for a salary but for the good of the profession. It is this feeling that turns a stenographer into a secretary and makes her a real asset to her employer.

SELECTED REFERENCES

Bucher, Charles A., *Administration of School Health and Physical Education Programs* (St. Louis, The C. V. Mosby Company, 1963), Chap. 4.

Hughes, William Leonard, Esther French, and Nelson G. Lehsten, *Administra-*

tion of Physical Education for Schools and Colleges (New York, The Ronald Press Company, 1962), Chap. 14.

Neuner, J. W., *Office Management: Principles and Practices* (Cincinnati, Southwestern Publishing Co. 1959).

Strong, E. P., *Increasing Office Productivity* (New York, McGraw-Hill Book Company, 1962).

16

evaluation

Importance of evaluation

Evaluation is a major responsibility of the physical education administrator. The need for evaluation is present in any viable, dynamic organization. For only when outcomes are measured against original purposes or stated goals will the administrator be able to judge progress. With the resources at his command he is expected to accomplish the objectives for which his organization was created. He is not unlike the football coach who constantly evaluates the strengths and weaknesses of his team and endeavors to augment the strengths and to eliminate the weaknesses.

The administrator's goal is the greatest possible accomplishment of his organization's objectives. This requires the maximum contribution of all staff members. It is imperative that the physical education administrator evaluate the achievements of his staff members individually and collectively to determine how successful they have been and how their future efforts may be improved.

The importance of evaluation is aptly expressed by Williams: [1] "Occasionally an administrator or teacher contends that the practical affairs of his work leave no time for attention to *evaluation*. In a sense evaluation is like bookkeeping in business; it indicates direction, and shows degrees of accomplishment. The worth of administrative pro-

[1] Jessie F. Williams, Clifford L. Brownell, and Elmon L. Vernier, *The Administration of Health Education and Physical Education* (Philadelphia, W. B. Saunders Co., 1964), p. 319.

cedures . . . remains obscure or unknown unless their effects are evaluated."

Aspects of evaluation

Evaluation has many aspects. Most of the people who are related or involved with a high school or college physical education program will probably evaluate it. Many parents evaluate the effects of the program on their children. Students evaluate their teachers and the program. The teachers evaluate student achievement. Other faculty members evaluate the physical education department. The department chairman is evaluated by his superior as well as by his own staff members. He in turn evaluates the performance of his staff members. Finally, the administrator should evaluate himself.

All of these aspects of evaluation are important but there is one that transcends any of the others. This is the evaluation of student achievement. The schools exist primarily for this purpose and their success or failure depends upon how well this objective is accomplished. In reality, if student achievement comes up to expectations the evaluations of the physical education department by parents, students, other faculty and the school administrator are likely to be favorable. Likewise, an appropriate level of student achievement reflects excellent teacher performance. If student and faculty performance are excellent it is quite likely that the administrator himself is performing successfully.

Knowledge of standards essential

Basic to the administrator's evaluation of the performance of the different aspects of his organization is the knowledge of the standards these aspects should attain. If he is to evaluate an intramural program he should have in mind what an excellent program should be. His appraisal of the teaching effectiveness of a staff member should be based upon the concept of what a superior teacher would do and be under the circumstances. One of the reasons why so many poor programs exist in our secondary schools and colleges and universities is that the administrator does not have in mind what the program could or should be. He has no valid target in mind toward which to aim. He is not familiar with the standards that have evolved over the decades in such areas as curriculum, intramural athletics, interschool athletics, facilities, equipment, evaluation, and staff. Knowledge of these standards is indispensable to the physical education administrator.

Purposes of evaluation

Cowell and France [2] outline some specific purposes of evaluation:

1. To help teachers, parents, and pupils examine the values they want to achieve from the physical education program
2. To give strong encouragement to administrators, teachers, parents, and students to evolve certain policies, blueprints of goals and direction, as basic agreements of educational purposes against which to validate their educational procedures
3. To provide a periodic check on the degree to which specified objectives are attained for an individual or group of individuals
4. To improve counseling methods by providing basic information and new insight into the needs of individual students
5. To encourage teachers to adjust and improve the teaching process and methods to aid in the achievement of objectives
6. To give administrators, teachers, parents, and students certain psychological security and a feeling of accomplishment
7. To form the basis for sound public relations by helping the taxpayer to realize that his money is contributing toward healthy and happier children today and better citizens tomorrow
8. To stimulate greater professional growth in teachers

Evaluation must be continuous

For the administrator evaluation is a continuous process. Decisions such as those involving personnel or budget may be made only once a year but they are based upon judgments that extend over many months. As the administrator carries out his responsibilities he is constantly making appraisals of every aspect of his operations. This is a desirable situation because evaluations that are based upon many impressions made over an extended period of time are apt to be sounder than those that are hastily made.

EVALUATION OF STUDENT ACHIEVEMENT

The physical development objective

The physical development objective cannot be evaluated with a single test because it involves a variety of components. A test battery with different tests for each of the various components is needed. A

---

[2] Charles C. Cowell and Wellman L. France, *Philosophy and Principles of Physical Education* (Englewood Cliffs, N.J., Prentice-Hall, Inc., 1963), p. 178.

number of valid test batteries are available. Various states such as California, Oregon, Washington, New York, Indiana, and Minnesota have developed excellent test batteries. Many universities have done likewise. All of the armed services likewise have carefully designed physical fitness test batteries.[3]

Probably the most extensively used physical fitness test is that developed under the sponsorship of the American Association for Health, Physical Education, and Recreation.[4] The AAHPER Youth Fitness Test was first published in 1958 and revised in 1965. It consists of seven test items for boys and girls. The tests and the component of physical fitness which each measures are given in Table 16-1.

Table 16-1.

Component	Girls	Boys
Arm Strength	Flexed-Arm Hang	Pull-Up
Abdominal Strength	Sit-Up	Sit-Up
Speed and Agility	Shuttle Run	Shuttle Run
Leg Power	Standing Broad Jump	Standing Broad Jump
Speed	50-Yard Dash	50-Yard Dash
Arm Power	Softball Throw for Distance	Softball Throw for Distance
Endurance	600-Yard Run-Walk	600-Yard Run-Walk

Source: American Association for Health, Physical Education and Recreation, *Youth Fitness Test Manual* (Washington, D.C., AAHPER, 1965).

National norms are available for each test for boys and girls from the fifth through the twelfth grades. Norms are also available for college men and women.

This AAHPER Youth Fitness Test possesses a variety of advantages. It requires little equipment, the test items are those with which teachers and students are familiar. The battery can be easily and quickly administered, with one exception the items are the same for boys and girls, and the tests can be given from the fifth grade through college. The availability of national norms is a very great advantage to the administrator. He is able to compare the performances of his students with those of other children of the same ages. In this way he can evaluate the effectiveness of the physical education program. If his

---

[3] These state, university, and armed services test batteries are described in the following references: H. Harrison Clarke, *The Application of Measurement to Health and Physical Education*, 4th ed. (Englewood Cliffs, N.J., Prentice-Hall, Inc., 1966). Carl Willgoose, *Evaluation in Health Education and Physical Education* (New York, McGraw-Hill Book Company, 1961).

[4] AAHPER, *Youth Fitness Test Manual* (Washington, D.C., American Association for Health, Physical Education, and Recreation, 1965).

students are unable to meet the national standards he must determine the reason or reasons. Perhaps the time allotment or facilities are inadequate. The cause might be poorly qualified teachers or the lack of emphasis upon the physical development objective.

The availability of these national standards gives the administrator a powerful lever in his effort to correct the deficiencies of his program. Parents and the general public do not want their children to be appreciably below the level of children throughout the country in the various aspects of physical fitness. It is much easier for the administrator to secure what he needs to strengthen his program when he can demonstrate unfavorable comparisons of local children and youth with the national norms.

If the administrator prefers not to use an already established test battery to evaluate the physical fitness of his students he has another alternative. He may use separate tests for each of the various components of physical fitness. Cardiovascular, strength, endurance, and agility tests are available. Table 16-2 gives specific tests of each type.

Table 16-2.

Cardiovascular Tests	Strength Tests	Endurance Tests	Agility Tests
1. Schneider Tests	1. Physical Fitness Test	1. Runs of Various Distances	1. Burpee Tests
2. McCurdy-Larson Organic Efficiency Test	2. Strength Index	2. McCloy Endurance Ration	2. Jack Spring
3. Harvard Step Test	3. Cable Tension Strength Tests	3. Drop-Off Index	
4. Tuttle Pulse Ratio Test	4. Kraus-Weber Tests		
	5. Larson Muscular Strength Tests		

The motor skill development objective

To evaluate motor skill development requires more than one test. In fact, a battery of tests is required to assess skill in one sport adequately. Skill tests in a wide variety of physical education activities have been developed over the years. Some of these are excellent tests but many have limitations that preclude their use. Their validity coefficients may not be high enough; they may require too much equipment; they may take too long to administer; their reliability may be too low; norms may be lacking; they may have too limited applicability; they may not be capable of differentiating abilities at all grade levels.

Some of the well-known sport skills tests include:

1. Hyde Archery Achievement Tests
2. French-Stalter Badminton Skill Tests
3. Lockhart-McPherson Badminton Test
4. Miller Wall Volley Test (badminton)
5. Kelson Test (baseball)
6. Leilich Basketball Test for Women
7. Stroup Basketball Test
8. Johnson Basketball Test
9. Knox Basketball Test
10. Phillips-Summers Bowling Norms
11. Schmithals-French Field Hockey Tests
12. Borleske Touch Football Test
13. Brace Football Achievement Tests
14. New York State Football Tests
15. Cornish Handball Test
16. New York State Softball Test
17. O'Donnell Softball Skill Test
18. New York State Soccer Test
19. McDonald Soccer Test
20. Hewitt Swimming Achievement Scales
21. Table Tennis Backboard Test
22. Dyer Tennis Test
23. Broer-Miller Tennis Test
24. Russell-Lange Volleyball Test
25. Brady Volleyball Test

The American Association for Health, Physical Education and Recreation has undertaken a project that will greatly assist in the evaluation of motor skill development. The Sport Skills Project involves the development of batteries of skill tests for each of the following activities: archery, badminton, baseball, basketball, football, golf, gymnastics, field hockey (women), soccer, softball, tennis, volleyball, lacrosse (women), swimming (women), track and field (women), and bowling. Test batteries for other sports will eventually be developed.

Each test battery measures the principal skills of the sport. The tests were designed to measure performance level. Each one of the tests for a particular sport is intended to measure a single fundamental skill of the sport. The skills selected for each sport were determined by expert consultants. All of the tests met the criteria of validity, reliability, objectivity in scoring, administrative feasibility, standardization of instructions, and variability.

While standardized tests in many of the academic disciplines have been in existence for many years such tests have never been previously available in physical education. These norms possess the great advantage of providing the administrator and his staff with standards with which the performance of their students may be compared. Previously they had no way of knowing whether the performance level of their students in the various sport skills was good, bad, or indifferent as compared to that of other students of the same ages throughout the country.

The national norms for sport skills can benefit the administrator in the same way that national physical fitness norms do. When the lack of adequate resources of time, facilities, or personnel results in poor performance of his students in the various sports the administrator now has objective evidence of this fact. Previously he lacked such data to prove the need for greater time allotment, better facilities, or more personnel. The lack of resources always affects adversely the performance of students but now the administrator can make his case with objective data rather than with merely personal opinion.

The knowledge and understanding objective

Physical educators have used knowledge tests for many decades. These tests have usually been of the objective type. The tests may have been constructed by the instructor himself or they may have been published tests that have been statistically validated. The tests may include any or all of the following areas:

1. Knowledge of skill performance
2. Rules
3. Strategy or activity patterns
4. Protective requirements
5. Conditioning procedures
6. Effects of activity upon health
7. Codes of etiquette appropriate to the activity
8. Understanding of effective utilization of the organism in movement
9. Factors affecting performance such as age, sex, drugs, nutrition, fatigue, alcohol, and tobacco

There is no dearth of physical education knowledge tests that have been constructed. Such tests are available for archery, badminton, basketball, bowling, golf, canoeing, handball, field hockey, folk dancing, ice hockey, riding, softball, tennis, soccer, volleyball, stunts and tumbling, swimming, and track and field.[5]

[5] For further information on these tests see H. H. Clarke, *Application of Measurement to Health and Physical Education,* 4th ed. (Englewood Cliffs, N.J., Prentice-Hall, Inc., 1966).

Unfortunately, none of the above tests have national norms. They would not enable the administrator to evaluate the performance of his own students against that of a larger population. However, the American Association for Health, Physical Education and Recreation has underway a project to serve this purpose. The Project on the Measurement of Understandings in Physical Education will soon be completed and it will make available standardized knowledge tests over the entire field of physical education, including the activities, the effects of activities on the human organism and factors modifying participation in activities. When these tests and standards are available the administrator will be able to make comparisons with a wider popular on this important dimension.

The social development objectives

How can the administrator evaluate how much progress the students at his institution have made in regard to the social development objectives? Apparently, physical educators do much less evaluation of this objective than they do of physical development, motor skills and knowledge and understanding. Probably, also, they do much less planning for this objective than the others. The idea is widely prevalent that social development is a concomitant of the physical education program and does not require careful planning and specially designed programs.

Several different types of tests have been used to measure social adjustment. One of the most commonly used measures is the behavior rating scale whereby observers rate the frequency with which certain types of behavior have been observed. The Blanchard Behavior Rating Scale is representative of this type of device (see Figure 16-1). Another approach to the assessment of progress toward the social objective is by means of a social acceptance determination. These instruments involve students rating their fellow students on the basis of their social acceptance. One type developed by Cowell is called the Cowell Personal Distance Scale (see Figure 16-2). Each individual's score in a class or group is obtained by adding the total weighted scores given by all the participants and then dividing by the number of participants. The lower the index, the greater the degree of acceptance by the group. Sociometric techniques involving the use of the matrix chart and sociogram are also of value in determining the most popular and the isolated students.

Measures of general social adjustment may also be used to advantage. A number of excellent instruments such as the Washburne Social Adjustment Inventory, The Bell Adjustment Inventory, The Minnesota Multi-phasic Personality Inventory, and the California Psychological

Name:_____ Grade:_____ Age:_____ Date:_____

School:_____ Name of Rater:_____

BEHAVIOR RATING SCALE

Personal Information	No Opportunity to Observe	Never	Seldom	Fairly Often	Frequently	Extremely Often	Score
Leadership							
1. Popular with classmates...............		1	2	3	4	5	
2. Seeks responsibility in the classroom.......		1	2	3	4	5	
3. Shows intellectual leadership in the classroom		1	2	3	4	5	
Positive Active Qualities							
4. Quits on tasks requiring perseverance.......		5	4	3	2	1	
5. Exhibits aggressiveness in his relationship with others...........................		1	2	3	4	5	
6. Shows initiative in assuming responsibility in unfamiliar situations................		1	2	3	4	5	
7. Is alert to new opportunities..............		1	2	3	4	5	
Positive Mental Qualities							
8. Shows keenness of mind.................		1	2	3	4	5	
9. Volunteers ideas........................		1	2	3	4	5	
Self-Control							
10. Grumbles over decisions of classmates......		5	4	3	2	1	
11. Takes a justified criticism by teacher or classmate without showing anger or pouting...		1	2	3	4	5	
Cooperation							
12. Is loyal to his group.....................		1	2	3	4	5	
13. Discharges his group responsibilities well....		1	2	3	4	5	
14. Is cooperative in his attitude toward his teacher...........................		1	2	3	4	5	
Social Action Standards							
15. Makes loud-mouthed criticism and comments		5	4	3	2	1	
16. Respects the rights of others..............		1	2	3	4	5	
Ethical Social Qualities							
17. Cheats...............................		5	4	3	2	1	
18. Is truthful............................		1	2	3	4	5	
Qualities of Efficiency							
19. Seems satisfied to "get by" with tasks assigned.............................		5	4	3	2	1	
20. Is dependable and trustworthy............		1	2	3	4	5	
21. Has good study habits...................		1	2	3	4	5	
Sociability							
22. Is liked by others.......................		1	2	3	4	5	
23. Makes a friendly approach to others in the group.............................		1	2	3	4	5	
24. Is friendly.............................		1	2	3	4	5	

Source: B. E. Blanchard, "A Behavior Frequency Rating Scale for the Measurement of Character and Personality in Physical Education Classroom Situations," *Research Quarterly* (May, 1936), p. 56.

Figure 16-1. Blanchard Behavior Rating Scale.

Grade

I would be willing to accept him:

What to do	Into my family as a brother	As a very close pal	As a member of my gang or club	On my street as a next-door neighbor	Into my class at school	Into my school	Into my city
If you had full power to treat each student in this group as you feel, just how would you consider him? Just how near would you like to have him to your family? Every student should be checked in some one column. Circle your own name and be sure you check every student in one column only.	1	2	3	4	5	6	7
1. Stanley Whitaker							
2. James Southerlin							
3. Parvin Schriber							

Source: Charles C. Cowell and Hilda M. Schwehn, *Modern Principles and Methods in High School Physical Education* (Boston, Allyn and Bacon, Inc., 1958), p. 307.

Figure 16-2. Cowell Personal Distance Scale.

Inventory [6] have been frequently and successfully used in physical education.

EVALUATION OF STAFF

The best way for the administrator to evaluate the effectiveness of his staff is to determine the extent to which the departmental objectives are being achieved. If evidence is available that student performance on standard tests for the various physical education objectives has attained a satisfactory level the administrator is justified in believing that his staff as a whole has met the most important criterion. This is not to say, however, that perfection has been attained. It is quite likely that an even better performance of students might be obtained. Likewise, some staff members are probably more effective in accomplishing the objectives than others. Consequently, the administrator must constantly evaluate the performance of every one of his staff members.

Criteria of an effective staff

Some of the criteria of an effective staff are:

1. An adequate number of staff members are available to cover all assignments without being overloaded or without classes being too large.
2. Staff members meet the recognized standards of professional preparation.
3. Specialists are available for all positions requiring specialized preparation.
4. Each staff member has a mastery of the subject matter for which he is responsible.
5. Staff morale is high. Staff members are all loyal to each other and the department.
6. The staff is enthusiastic, neat, punctual, and dedicated to welfare of students.
7. The staff members are respected by other faculty members; they command admiration and respect in the community.
8. The staff members are progressive; they keep abreast of the literature and research; they belong to the appropriate professional organizations and they regularly attend professional meetings.

---

6 For further details concerning these inventories see Carl Willgoose, *Evaluation in Health Education and Physical Education* (New York, McGraw-Hill Book Company, 1961).

9. Each staff member is conversant with the various methods of presenting his subject to his students and is consistently successful in the methods he employs.
10. Staff members use appropriate evaluative procedures.
11. Student interest and participation is enthusiastic. Absences, excuses, and disciplinary problems are at a minimum.

Supplementing the above criteria is the statement by Nyman,[7] the principal of Lafayette School, Salt Lake City, in which he describes what he expects of his physical education teachers:

1. Professional enough to serve his fellow workers in their improvement
2. Kind enough to win young folks to his leadership
3. Doctor enough to heal the heartbreaks and soul injuries common to a big school
4. Cultured enough to be a model in taste and language
5. Creative enough to be able to put art into physical education activities and appreciate originality in others
6. Big enough to overflow into the lives of other teachers in the school to keep them balanced and encouraged
7. Wholesome enough to set the mental health climate of the school
8. Religious enough to be secure, clean, optimistic, and courageous
9. Skillful enough to provide practices in wholesome, constructive group living
10. Adaptable enough to make a physical education and health program in spite of weather, interferences, and lack of equipment
11. Young enough to catch new ideas

Appraising staff members

The best way for the administrator to assess the performance of staff members is through personal observation. His supervisory responsibilities require that he observe the various individuals on his staff teach their classes from time to time. This is particularly needed for new staff members. He will, of course, be conversant with the details of the professional preparation and experience of his associates but in the appraisal of teachers there is no substitute for actually observing them in action.

In the normal associations in and about the department the administrator will gain many impressions of his colleagues. Such factors as personal appearance, punctuality, thoroughness, attention to detail, cooperativeness, professional attitude and the like will be revealed to the observer.

The administrator receives information about his staff members from a variety of sources. From parents, students, other faculty members, and citizens in the community will come unsolicited reports that

7 Emil Nyman, "What I Expect of My Physical Education Teachers," *State Journal,* Iowa Association for Health, Physical Education and Recreation (Fall, 1959).

may reflect favorably or unfavorably upon the performance of his teachers. Students will spread information about their instructors and not infrequently some of this comes back to the administrator. Some administrators solicit the opinions of students by means of anonymous questionnaires.

PROGRAM EVALUATION

Undoubtedly the best measure of the quality of a physical education program is the extent to which it achieves its goals. If the evidence indicates that the physical education objectives are being effectively attained the administrator is justified in believing that he has a good program. Likewise, if the standards that are recommended for staff are met by his own staff members it is almost inevitable that the program will be excellent.

Despite these considerations, however, the administrator must evaluate his overall program. As has already been pointed out the administrator must always be endeavoring to obtain greater pupil progress and increased staff effectiveness. As the Olympic motto "Citius, Altius, Fortius" meaning "Swifter, Higher, Stronger" symbolizes a constant striving for perfection so must the administrator aspire constantly to do better.

Chapter 4 has already considered the standards that are recommended for the physical education service program. Chapter 8 has covered the standards for the interschool athletic program and Chapter 9 the standards for the intramural athletic program. Standards for physical education facilities were reviewed in Chapter 7. Consequently, at this time, only a summary of program evaluation will be presented.

Evaluative instruments

Over the years a number of instruments, rating scales or criteria have been developed to evaluate the program of physical education. Daniels [8] has constructed a detailed instrument to assess a secondary school physical education program. The Division of Health, Physical Education and Recreation of the New York State Department of Education [9] has produced some excellent evaluative check lists. The Evaluative Criteria [10] has been one of the most popular and extensively used

8 Arthur S. Daniels, *Evaluative Criteria for Physical Education: A Self-Appraisal Check List for Ohio Secondary Schools* (Columbus, Ohio, The Ohio State University, 1954).

9 State Department of Education, Division of Health, Physical Education and Recreation, *A Check List for Physical Education* (Albany, New York).

10 Cooperative Study of Secondary School Standards, *Evaluative Criteria* (Washington, D.C., Cooperative Study of Secondary School Standards, 1960).

instruments to evaluate a secondary school physical education program. The Bureau of Health Education, Physical Education and Recreation, California State Department of Education has coordinated the development of an excellent set of criteria to assess the quality of a secondary school program of physical education. The criteria are presented in Appendix C. At a national conference on physical education for college men and women criteria to appraise the instructional program were developed. They are outlined in Appendix D.

SELF-EVALUATION

Many administrators never think of evaluating their own leadership. They evaluate everyone else in their organization but for some reason they forget themselves. Yet from the standpoint of the success of the department there is no one whose performance is more important. It is vital that they objectively appraise the manner in which they are administering the unit.

Criteria for self-evaluation

If the department is successful in accomplishing its objectives, if the staff is excellent and if the program and facilities meet recommended standards there is every reason to believe that the administrator is successful. However, regardless of the success he has enjoyed every administrator knows that perfection has not been attained. He can see areas in which improvement can be made. In fact, if he becomes complacent he is committing a serious error.

Criteria that emphasize important aspects of administration are listed below:

1. The administrator has been successful in eliciting 100 percent effort from each member of the organization.
2. The administrator has been successful in securing a fair share of the budget and the resources available.
3. High morale prevails among all staff members.
4. The department enjoys high respect within the school and in the community.
5. Staff members are loyal to each other and to the departmental objectives.
6. The administrator is fair and impartial to all staff members.
7. The administrator personally sets an example of the values for which the department stands.

8. Consistency characterizes the administrator's decisions and actions.
9. Regular staff meetings are held.
10. The administrator never violates the chain of command.
11. The administrator solicits and respects the opinions of staff members and students.
12. Curriculum development is a cooperative process.
13. The physical education program is accepted on an equal basis with other departments in the school.
14. The organizational objectives are being accomplished.

SELECTED REFERENCES

Clarke, H. H., *The Application of Measurement to Health and Physical Education,* 4th ed. (Englewood Cliffs, N.J., Prentice-Hall, Inc., 1967).

Cowell, Charles C. and Wellman L. France, *Philosophy and Principles of Physical Education* (Englewood Cliffs, N.J., Prentice-Hall, Inc., 1963), Chap. 2.

Havel, Richard, and Emery Seymour, *Administration of Health, Physical Education and Recreation for Schools* (New York, The Ronald Press Company, 1961), Chap. 15.

Howard, Glen, and Edward Masonbrink, *Administration of Physical Education* (New York, Harper and Row, Publishers, 1963), Chap. 8.

Oberteuffer, Delbert, and Celeste Ulrich, *Physical Education. A Textbook of Principles for Professional Students* (New York, Harper and Row, Publishers, 1962), Chap. 2.

Willgoose, Carl, *Evaluation in Health Education and Physical Education* (New York, McGraw-Hill Book Company, 1961).

Williams, Jessie F., Clifford L. Brownell, and Elmon L. Vernier, *The Administration of Health Education and Physical Education* (Philadelphia, W. B. Saunders Co., 1964), Chap. 24.

standards in athletics for boys in secondary schools[1]

1. The program of athletics should be developed with due regard for the health and safety standards.

(a) A health examination should be required previous to participation, preferably on a seasonal basis with an annual examination a minimum.

(b) A physician should be present at all contests involving activities where the injury hazard is pronounced.

(c) A contestant who has been ill or injured should be readmitted to participation only on the written recommendation of a physician.

(d) A contestant upon returning to participation after illness or injury should be carefully observed, and if there is any doubt as to his condition he should immediately be referred to a physician.

(e) The coach (faculty member in charge) should be competent in first aid and thoroughly versed in sports conditioning and training. It is also strongly recommended that all players be given basic instruction in first aid.

(f) In case of head, neck, or spine injury or suspicion thereof, the player should be removed from play, placed at rest, and be given the immediate attention of a physician.

(g) Every school should have a written policy regarding the responsibility for injury incurred in athletics, and this policy should be known to all participants, their parents, and other responsible adults. Arrangements should be made for obtaining and paying for medical and hospital care of injured participants, in accord with local policy.

[1] Joint Committee Report, "Standards in Athletics for Boys in Secondary Schools," *Journal of the American Association for Health, Physical Education, Recreation* (September, 1951), p. 17.

(h) Competition should take place only between teams of comparable ability, and playing seasons should be limited to reasonable duration.

(i) The best obtainable protective equipment should be provided for all participants, and special attention should be given to proper fitting of such equipment.

(j) No preseason games should be played until players are well drilled in fundamentals and have had a minimum of two weeks of physical conditioning.

(k) Play fields should meet standard requirements for size of area, playing surfaces, and facilities for safety, and all reasonable precautions should be taken to prevent accidents.

(l) Contests should be selected, and rules and lengths of playing periods should be such that they are not overtaxing the physical abilities of high school students.

2. Good citizenship must result from all coaching and from all interschool competition. The education of the youth of the nation fails unless it creates the proper ideals and attitudes, both in the game and off the field.

(a) The contribution of athletics to citizenship—indeed, to life itself—will be judged according to the contribution they make to fine living.

(b) Athletics should contribute a feeling, on the part of the athlete, of personal worth, excellence in performance, self-respect, and desirable personal and social growth and development.

(c) Educationally, winning is not the only important item. While the will to win within the rules of good sportsmanship is an important attribute to good citizenship, there is always a tendency to overdo the importance of winning in athletics. Other important contributions are those desirable changes made in skills, habits, and attitudes of the participants.

(d) Athletics are responsible jointly with education for establishing among boys and girls those standards of behavior that represent the best in good citizenship. Athletics must contribute to those virtues which are socially sound for a democracy, such as truthfulness, fair play, honesty, modesty, give and take, courtesy, self-discipline, courage, generosity, self-restraint, and loyalty to team, state, and nation.

3. The ten cardinal athletic principles are accepted as expressing the policies of our organization, and it is urged that these be displayed in the literature of our organization. To be of maximum effectiveness, the athletic program will:

(a) Be closely co-ordinated with the general instructional program and properly articulated with the other departments of the school.

(b) Be such that the number of students accommodated and the educational aims achieved justify the use of tax funds for its support and also warrant the use of other sources of income.

(c) Justify the time and attention which is given to the collection of "other sources of income" which will not interfere with the efficiency of the athletic program or of any other departments of the school.

(d) Confine the school athletic activity to events which are sponsored and supervised by the proper school authorities so that any exploitation or improper use of prestige built up by school teams or members of such teams may be avoided.

(e) Be planned in such a way as to result in opportunity for many individuals to explore a wide variety of sports and to set reasonable season limits for each listed sport.

(f) Be controlled in such a way as to avoid the elements of professionalism and commercialism which tend to grow up in connection with widely publicized "bowl" contests, barnstorming trips, and interstate or intersectional contests which require excessive travel expense or loss of school time or which are claimed to be justified by educational travel values.

(g) Be kept free from the type of contest which involves a gathering of so-called "all stars" from different schools to participate in contests which may be used as a gathering place for representatives of certain college or professional organizations who are interested in soliciting athletic talent for their teams.

(h) Include educative exercises to reach all nonparticipating students and community followers of the school teams in order to insure a proper understanding and appreciation of the sports skills and of the need for adherence to principles of game ethics.

(i) Encourage a balanced program of intramural activity in grades below the ninth to make it unnecessary to sponsor contests of a championship nature in these grades.

(j) Engender respect for the rules and policies under which the school conducts its program.

4. All schools shall use reasonable care in avoiding any participation in a contact sport between participants of normal high school age and participants who are appreciably above or below normal high school age.

Senior high school competition should be limited to participation in games, meets, and tournaments between participants enrolled in grades 9 through 12. Junior high school competition should be limited to participation in games, meets, and tournaments between participants enrolled in grades 7 through 9. These games, meets, and tournaments should be approved and conducted by appropriate secondary school authorities.

(a) All school personnel should utilize every precaution and procedure to assure competition in secondary school athletics on the basis of comparable parity.

(b) A significant phase in the growth of a living organism is maturity. Wide differences in the maturity places in jeopardy the well-being of athletic competitors. School personnel should permit competition between teams composed of comparable maturity.

(c) Certain stages of maturity can be distinguished and should be utilized as one of the bases for determining parity in athletic competition.

(d) Outstanding features of adolescence are insecurity, awkwardness, and excessive competitiveness. One can adjust himself to these factors of environment only by becoming more mature, wiser, and more self-reliant. These are additional evidences that parents and school personnel should use protective procedures in setting up competition between individuals and groups of preadolescent and adolescent age.

(e) A high school pupil or team should not compete with members of a college or university, a preparatory school, or other school which includes postgraduates on its teams, or against any independent team sponsored by an "outside" organization.

(f) A junior high school pupil or team should not compete with members of a team representing a senior high school, elementary school, or an outside organization. This would not, however, exclude the participation of ninth-grade pupils as a member of a senior high school team if the ninth grade is under the administrative direction of the high school principal and if the other conditions stated above are met.

(g) Appropriate secondary school authorities consist of legally certified teaching, supervisory, and administrative personnel directly under the superintendent of schools. These personnel should see that the items noted above are observed.

5. All schools shall fully observe and abide by the spirit and letter of established eligibility requirements which have been democratically developed by each of the state athletic associations.

6. Each state athletic association should attempt to secure the cooperation which would provide a plan of continuous eligibility from high schools to college.

7. For competition in which only one state is involved, no school shall participate in a meet or tournament involving more than two schools unless such contest has been approved by its state high school association or its delegated constituent or allied divisions.

8. The use of school facilities or members of the school staff shall not be permitted in connection with any postseason or all-star contest unless such contest has been sanctioned by the state athletic association.

9. A school shall not permit any employee or official to encourage or collaborate in any negotiations which may lead a high school athlete to lose his eligibility through the signing of a professional contract.

10. The solicitation of athletes through tryouts and competitive bidding by colleges and universities is unethical, unprofessional, and psychologically harmful. It destroys the amateur nature of athletics, tends to commercialize the individual and the program, promotes the use of athletic skill for gain, and takes an unfair and unjust advantage of competitors.

11. In all interstate athletic contests, each athlete shall compete under

eligibility rules which are at least as restrictive as those adopted by the state high school athletic association of his state, except in the case of nonmember schools which are not eligible for membership in their state associations.

12. No school shall compete in any of the following contests unless such contest has been sanctioned by each of the interested state high school athletic associations through the National Federation:

(a) Any interstate tournament or meet in which three or more schools participate.

(b) Any interstate two-school contest which involves a round trip exceeding 600 miles.

(c) Any interstate two-school contest (regardless of the distance to be traveled) which is sponsored by an individual or an organization other than a member high school.

13. No basketball tournament which is purported to be for interstate high school championship shall be sanctioned, and no basketball tournament involving schools of more than one state shall be sanctioned unless the tournament is purely community in character.

14. No contest which is purported to be for a national high school championship in any sport shall be sanctioned.

Wisconsin interscholastic athletic association medical allowances[1]

SCHEDULE ALLOWANCES (DENTAL)

Code

(71)	Fractures of enamel				$3.00

(Requiring treatment and polishing only)

(72)	Replacing broken facing				5.00
(73)	Recementing loosened crown or inlay				2.00
	Recementing loosened bridge				4.00
(74)	Fractured tooth—required fillings				

		Silicate	*Plastic*	*Amalgam*	*Gold*
	1. 1 surface restoration	$5.00	$5.00	$3.00	$12.00
	2 surface restoration		7.00	6.00	23.00
	3 surface restoration			9.00	30.00

	2. Requiring a ¾ crown gold restoration		$30.00
	3. Requiring a gold crown		30.00
	4. Requiring an acrylic or porcelain jacket crown		50.00
	5. Requiring kadon crown or jacket or chrome crown		12.00
	6. Open Face Crown		15.00
	7. Requiring a crown with veneer window		30.00
(75)	Loss of one or more anterior or posterior teeth		
	requiring bridge work, per tooth		
	Pontic—A Steel Facing		20.00
	B Tru pontic		25.00

[1] *1964-65 WIAA Accident Benefit Plan* (Steven Point, Wis., Wisconsin Interscholastic Athletic Association), pp. 25-28.

(76) Injury requiring an upper or lower partial denture
     acrylic, or acrylic and metal with clasps, $50.00
     for first tooth, $5.00 for each additional tooth,
     Maximum allowance   80.00

(77) Injury to tooth requiring pulp removal and root filling   15.00
     Apioectomy—including root canal filling   30.00

(78) 1. Repairing dentures or partial dentures
       broken but no teeth involved   10.00
     2. Replacing broken teeth on dentures or partial
       dentures, first tooth   10.00
       Each additional tooth   2.00
     3. Adding teeth on denture or partial denture to
       replace extracted natural teeth, first tooth   15.00
       Each additional tooth   2.00

(79) Extraction   3.00

(80) Maximum for chipped teeth for one accident   10.00

(81) Maximum for one dental injury   100.00

(82) Fractures
     (Item 7 of Medical Regulation applies to these fractures)
     1. Simple fractures of superior or inferior
       maxilla not requiring wiring or splints,
       including X rays and care   37.50
     2. Simple fractures of superior or inferior
       maxilla, reduction, fixation, postoperative
       care and including X rays   75.00
     3. Compound or comminuted fractures of superior
       or inferior maxilla, reduction, fixation,
       postoperative care and including X rays   100.00

(83) Where permanent type restoration is not used
     (allowances for treatment listed in this section are
     NOT compensable unless there is no permanent
     type restoration rendered within one year from
     date of injury):
     1. Palliative treatment—per treatment   2.00
       Maximum allowance   6.00
     2. Temporary crowns, bands or similar appliances
       Maximum   10.00
     3. Treatment appliances (including treatment partial) 25.00
       Each additional tooth   5.00

(84) X rays—first X ray $2.00 each additional $1.00
     Maximum X ray allowance   5.00

(85) Miscellaneous
     Consideration will be given for treatment rendered
     other than outlined in the Schedule of Allowances,
     such consideration and subsequent payment to be
     determined by Executive Committee and Dental
     Advisor of the Plan.
     No allowances for orthodontic appliances or treatment.

ALLOWANCES FOR FRACTURES, DISLOCATIONS, AND X RAYS.

	FRACTURES			DISLOCATIONS			X RAYS
	No Reduction	Closed Reduction	Open Reduction	No Reduction	Closed Reduction	Open Reduction	
1. Ankle Joint (One or All Malleoli)	$ 25.00	$ 60.00	$ 90.00	$ 10.00	$ 35.00	$100.00	$ 5.00
2(a). Clavicle	15.00	25.00	50.00				5.00
(b). Inner Joint				25.00	25.00	75.00	5.00
(c). Lateral Joint				15.00	50.00	75.00	5.00
3. Coccyx	15.00	25.00	50.00				10.00
4. Colles–Radius, Ulna	20.00	50.00	75.00				5.00
5(a). Elbow–T. Fracture	35.00	50.00	100.00		35.00	75.00	5.00
(b). Medial Epicondyle	20.00	35.00	75.00				5.00
(c). Lateral Condyle	20.00	35.00	75.00				5.00
(d). Radial Head	20.00	35.00	75.00				5.00
6. Femur (Shaft)	40.00	100.00	135.00				10.00
7(a). Forearm–Radius (Shaft Only)	20.00	50.00	75.00				5.00
(b). Ulna (Shaft Only)	20.00	50.00	75.00				5.00
(c). Radius and Ulna Shaft	30.00	60.00	100.00				5.00
8(a). Hip–Intertrochanteric	40.00	100.00	150.00		60.00	75.00	10.00
(b). Intracapsular	40.00	100.00	150.00		60.00	75.00	10.00
9. Humerus	35.00	50.00	100.00				5.00
10. Maxilla-Inferior, Superior or Zygomatic	32.50	70.00	95.00	10.00	10.00	75.00	5.00
11. Metatarsal–Single	10.00	20.00	30.00		25.00	40.00	5.00
(Each Additional)	3.00	5.00	12.50		20.00	30.00	
12. Nose	10.00	25.00	75.00				5.00
13. Patella	20.00	25.00	110.00		20.00	75.00	5.00

Note: These allowances are under the Scheduled Program. The Special Program allows all medical expenses up to $2,000.

534

No.	Fracture						
14.	Pelvis	$30.00	$60.00	$110.00	$	$ 60.00	$150.00	$10.00
15.	Rib (One or More)	15.00	15.00					10.00
16.	Scapula	25.00				25.00		10.00
	Shoulder		50.00	100.00		25.00	75.00	10.00
17.	Skull and/or Cerebral Hemorrhage	50.00						10.00
	Skull—No Cerebral Damage	25.00						
18.	Spine (Vertebral Body Compression One or More)	30.00	75.00	150.00	25.00	75.00	150.00	10.00 / 20.00 entire
19.	Sternum	10.00	25.00	50.00				5.00
20.	Tarsal Os Calcis	25.00		75.00				5.00
21.	Tarsal (Excluding Os Calcis)	20.00	50.00	75.00		35.00	75.00	5.00
22.	Tibia (Involving Knee Joint)	30.00	75.00	110.00				5.00
23.	Tibia or Fibula Shaft or Both	25.00	60.00	75.00				5.00
24(a).	Toe—Great	10.00	15.00	15.00		5.00	10.00	5.00
(b).	Other Toe	5.00	10.00	10.00		5.00	10.00	5.00
(c).	(Each Additional)	3.00	5.00	5.00				
25.	Transverse Process	10.00						10.00
26(a).	Wrist and Hand—Carpal	25.00	25.00	75.00		35.00	75.00	5.00
(b).	Metacarpal (Single)	10.00	20.00	25.00		15.00	25.00	5.00
(c).	(Each Additional)	3.00	5.00	10.00		10.00	10.00	
(d).	Finger	5.00	15.00	25.00		5.00	15.00	5.00
(e).	(Each Additional)	3.00	5.00	10.00		5.00	10.00	

criteria for evaluating the physical education program

SENIOR OR FOUR-YEAR HIGH SCHOOL

			QUALITY OF PRACTICE		
Questions	*Yes*	*No*	*Good*	*Fair*	*Poor*
1. Is there a workable plan to acquaint members of the community with the physical education program?					
2. Are channels provided for utilizing laymen's suggestions for improving the program?					
3. Does the physical education program have community approval?					
4. Is there a written up-to-date course of study?					
5. Is the course of study available upon request?					
6. Are there written school policies that govern the operation of the physical education program?					

[1] California State Department of Education, *Criteria for Evaluating the Physical Education Program, Senior or Four-year High School* (Sacramento, Calif., California State Department of Education, 1960).

			QUALITY OF PRACTICE		
Questions	*Yes*	*No*	*Good*	*Fair*	*Poor*
7. Are the policies kept up to date?					
8. Are the rules and regulations jointly developed by students and staff?					
9. Are the rules and regulations essential to carrying out the policies kept up to date?					
10. Is opportunity provided for teacher participation in the planning or improvement of physical education facilities?					
11. Are the results of a physical examination available for each student?					
12. Is there a follow-up on the recommendations from the physical examination?					
13. Are students grouped according to grade level?					
14. Are students grouped according to ability?					
15. Are students grouped at each grade level according to ability?					
16. Does the program include an orientation unit designed to facilitate a smooth transition from elementary or junior high school to high school?					
17. Is the program related to those of the schools from which most of the students come?					
18. Are written tests given on course content, such as strategy, terminology, and rules of the activities?					
19. Are physical performance tests used to determine individual expectancy?					
20. Are physical performance tests used to determine individual placement?					
21. Is the California Physical Performance Test or a similar one used?					
22. Are physical ability or skill tests used to help determine achievement?					
23. Are the students helped to understand					

Questions	Yes	No	QUALITY OF PRACTICE		
			Good	Fair	Poor
how their achievement is appraised and reported through marks?					
24. Are parents informed regarding the meaning of the marks used to indicate student achievement?					
25. Are the teachers, other than those in physical education, informed regarding the meaning of the marks used to indicate student achievement?					
26. Are the administrators kept informed regarding student achievement?					
27. Do students have opportunity to help plan the physical education program?					
28. Do students have opportunity to help evaluate the program?					
29. Does the program foster student leadership?					
30. Are students prohibited from substituting other activities for regular physical education?					
31. Are the physical education classes 40 or less in size?					
32. Is the class teaching time of the teachers of physical education the same as that for other teachers?					
33. Is the physical education period devoted solely to physical education activities?					
34. Does the school district provide an accident insurance plan for all physical education activities?					
35. Are students given opportunity to participate in intramural activities at times other than during the physical education period?					
36. Are students given opportunity to participate in a wide variety of intramural activities?					
37. Are students given instruction in the ac-					

| | | | QUALITY OF PRACTICE | | |
Questions	*Yes*	*No*	*Good*	*Fair*	*Poor*
tivities involved in the intramural program prior to their participation in it?					
38. Does the program provide for a majority of students to participate in extramural events, such as playdays, sports days, and invitational meets?					
39. Are games conducted in physical education properly officiated?					
40. Are games in intramural programs properly officiated?					
41. Do students participating in interscholastic athletics participate also in a well-rounded physical education program?					
42. Is there close co-operation between boys' and girls' programs in the use of facilities?					
43. Are boys' and girls' programs planned to provide for coeducational activities?					
44. Are the boys' and girls' programs coordinated so that both programs may operate successfully during inclement weather?					
45. Is there a plan, acceptable to all concerned, for procedures, such as handling of towels, gym uniforms, locks, lost and found, care of equipment?					
46. Does the plan ensure efficiency in procedures, such as handling of towels, gym uniforms, locks, lost and found, care of equipment?					
47. Are opportunities provided for the development of advanced skills?					
48. Does the program meet the physical needs of each student, including the physically handicapped?					
49. Does the program contribute to the development of desirable and suitable family type recreational activities?					

Questions	Yes	No	QUALITY OF PRACTICE		
			Good	*Fair*	*Poor*
50. Are suitable activities offered in coeducational physical education?					
51. Is the program designed to assist students who plan to become elementary school or physical education teachers?					
52. Does the program contribute to the development of physical fitness?					
53. Does the program emphasize the importance of maintaining physical fitness?					
54. Has the school a plan for periodical appraisal of the physical education program?					

INSTRUCTIONAL AREAS FOR BOYS IN SENIOR OR FOUR-YEAR HIGH SCHOOL

1. Is approximately 30 percent of the instructional time devoted to a variety of individual and dual activities, such as archery, badminton, bowling, golf, crosscountry, tennis, track and field, handball, and skiing?					
2. Is approximately 25 percent of the instructional time devoted to a variety of team games, such as basketball, touch or flag football, soccer, softball, speedball, speedaway, and volleyball?					
3. Is approximately 10 percent of the instructional time devoted to gymnastics, such as light and heavy apparatus, free exercise, tumbling, and weight training?					
4. Is approximately 8 percent of the instructional time devoted to combative activities, such as, wrestling, combative stunts, and basic instruction in boxing?					
5. Is approximately 10 percent of the instructional time devoted to rhythms, such as folk dance, square dance, social dance, and modern dance?					

			QUALITY OF PRACTICE		
Questions	*Yes*	*No*	*Good*	*Fair*	*Poor*

6. Is approximately 12 percent of the instructional time devoted to aquatic activities such as swimming, water safety, diving, water polo, and water stunts?

7. Is approximately 5 percent of the instructional time devoted to family recreational activities, such as table tennis, deck tennis, horseshoes, shuffleboard, bowling, quoits, croquet, hiking, fly casting, rifle marksmanship, and party activities?

Are conditioning exercises and movement fundamentals (body mechanics) stressed in the instruction given in each area of physical education?

INSTRUCTIONAL AREAS FOR GIRLS IN SENIOR OR FOUR-YEAR HIGH SCHOOL

1. Is approximately 30 percent of the instructional time devoted to a variety of individual and dual sports, such as archery, badminton, bowling, golf, roller skating, skiing, tennis, and track and field events?

2. Is approximately 20 percent of the instructional time devoted to a variety of team games, such as basketball, hockey, soccer, speedball, speedaway, softball, and volleyball?

3. Is approximately 15 percent of the instructional time devoted to movement fundamentals and gymnastic activities, such as stunts and tumbling, free exercise, and rebound tumbling?

4. Is approximately 20 percent of the instructional time devoted to rhythmic activities, such as folk dance, square dance, modern dance, and social dance?

5. Is approximately 10 percent of the instructional time devoted to aquatic ac-

Questions	Yes	No	QUALITY OF PRACTICE		
			Good	*Fair*	*Poor*
tivities, such as swimming, water safety, diving, synchronized swimming, and water stunts?					
6. Is approximately 5 percent of the instructional time devoted to family recreational activities, such as table tennis, horseshoes, bowling, quoits, rifle marksmanship, fly casting, shuffleboard, croquet, hiking, and party activities?					
Are conditioning exercises and movement fundamentals (body mechanics) stressed in the instruction given in each area of physical education?					

APPENDIX D

criteria for appraisal of college instructional programs

PHILOSOPHY AND OBJECTIVES

1. The educational philosophy of the department has been formulated in writing and is subscribed to wholeheartedly by the instructional staff.
2. The departmental philosophy is in harmony with the over-all educational philosophy of the college or university as stated in the appropriate publications of the institution.
3. The departmental philosophy is compatible with the principles set forth in the Report of the President's Commission on Higher Education as they relate to the education of college men and women.
4. The major objectives of the instructional program have been formulated in writing, and these specific objectives are compatible with the over-all educational philosophy of the department and the institution.
5. The major objectives of the instructional program cover the potential contributions of physical education in the area of:

    (a) effective movement;
    (b) skill in specific activities;
    (c) physiological function;
    (d) human relations;
    (e) knowledge, insights, understandings.

[1] American Association for Health, Physical Education and Recreation, *Physical Education for College Men and Women,* Washington Conference on Physical Education for College Men and Women (Washington, D.C., 1954), pp. 36-40.

6. In the development and conduct of the programs of physical education the administrator is committed to action through a democratic process which includes both faculty and students.
7. The department is guided by a sound philosophy of physical education. A concerted attempt is made to interpret a broad concept of physical education to faculty, students, administration and community.
8. The administrator gives consideration to the problems of men and women in regard to policy, budget, use of facilities, equipment, scheduling of classes, intramural programs and makes provision for instruction in coeducational activities.
9. The standards in the institution relating to staff qualifications, teaching load, size of classes, retirement, academic rank, and salaries apply equally to staff members in the physical education department.
10. The department promotes continuous in-service education to stimulate professional growth and improved service to students.
11. The basic instructional program is co-ordinated with other areas. (Intramural athletics, intercollegiate athletics, teacher education, etc.)
12. The source of financial support for the physical education program is the same as that for all other instructional areas of the institution.
13. Instruction in physical education, properly adapted, is required of all students throughout their undergraduate college careers.
14. All entering students are given a thorough physical and medical examination by home or staff physician prior to participation in the physical education program. (Followed by periodic exams.)
15. Exemption from participation in the physical education program for medical reasons is predicated upon the carefully co-ordinated judgment of the medical and physical education staff.
16. Students are permitted to substitute freshman and varsity sports in season for the purpose of meeting their physical education requirement but return to class at the end of their sport season.
17. It is the policy of the department not to accept veteran experiences, military drill, ROTC, band, and other extracurricular participation for the required instructional program of physical education.
18. Credit and quality or grade point value is granted on the same basis as any other area in the educational program.
19. Facilities and equipment are adequate with respect to quality and quantity.
20. Guidance and counseling of students is an integral part of physical education program.
21. Adequate supervision is provided for teaching done by graduate students and teaching fellows.
22. Comprehensive and accessible records are maintained to indicate student accomplishments within the program.
23. The department of physical education conducts a program of organized research.

PROGRAM

24. The program provides instruction in activities for every student.
25. The program provides for orientation of each student with regard to purposes, policies, and opportunities in physical education. (This may be accomplished by orientation week programs, medical and health examinations, courses, group printed materials, and demonstrations.)
26. The program offerings are well rounded, including body mechanics, swimming, team games, rhythms, individual and dual acitivies, with basic requirements for each student being set up according to his needs.
27. The program provides specific counseling and guidance (planned and incidental, group and individual) on a very definite pattern with appropriate referrals to other campus agencies (student health, counseling bureau, etc.).
28. The activities selected make full use of accessible community facilities.
29. The activities selected make full use of local geography and climate.
30. The program provides opportunities through coeducational classes for teaching men and women to develop skills and to enjoy together those activities which bring lifelong leisure-time satisfactions.
31. The activities selected offer opportunities for creative expression and for the development of personal resources.
32. The program provides instruction for efficient body movement in physical education and daily living.
33. The activities selected promote healthful functioning of organs and systems of the body within the limits of present physical conditions.
34. Some of the activities selected encourage all students to develop relaxation skills and to understand their importance, and provide specific opportunities for relaxation and rest where such is indicated.
35. The physical education instruction program provides a means of introducing students to the activities of the intramural program and encourages them to participate in it.
36. The physical education instruction program introduces students to, and encourages their participation in, the various recreational activities of the campus and community.
37. The physical education instruction program is integrated with other college programs and services concerned with health education.
38. Teaching methods provide progressive learning experiences through which each student derives the satisfaction in achievement which is essential for continued participation after college.

EVALUATION

39. The philosophy and objectives of a department are reviewed and re-evaluated periodically.
40. All the objectives, viz., skill, knowledge, attitudes, habits, etc., are included in

(a) the evaluation of the program;

(b) the final rating (or grade) given a student. The objectives are weighted according to the emphasis given in each course.

41. Selection and use of evaluation techniques are co-operatively planned within the department.

42. Evaluative measures are selected in the light of probable psychological and physiological reactions and result in stimulation of faculty and student interest and enthusiasm.

43. Evaluation of student status and progress are determined at the beginning, during and at the termination of the course.

44. Evaluative procedures are used to determine strengths and weaknesses of individual students and class groups and lead to guidance and help for the individual student.

45. Evaluative procedures are employed to determine strengths and weaknesses of the program

(a) for the college student;

(b) for post-college life.

46. Evaluative measures are employed only if the results are to be used in some way.

47. Objective measurement is used whenever possible.

48. If objective measurement is not possible, subjective judgment is used for purposes of appraisal.

49. Teachers are familiar with the best available evaluation techniques and use research findings insofar as possible.

50. All students and faculty participating in a course participate in the evaluation of student accomplishments and learning, teaching effectiveness, and course content.

competition for girls and women[1]

GUIDELINES FOR HIGH SCHOOL PROGRAMS

Principles

Competitive sports are an important part of the total physical education program for high school girls. A program of intramural and extramural participation should be arranged to augment a sound and inclusive instructional program in physical education. The interscholastic program should not be promoted at the expense of the instructional or the intramural programs.

As the interscholastic program is expanded, the State High School Athletic Association will be the regulatory body for its member schools. For schools that are not members, a regulatory body may need to be formed. The State Department of Education should be involved.

1. Existing legislative and administrative bodies for interscholastic athletic programs will retain ultimate control of the total program for girls within the state. However, a women's advisory board composed mainly of women high school physical educators will be formed to propose policies to these administrative and legislative groups and to review policies approved by them.

2. Total responsibility for the administration and supervision of the local interscholastic athletic program is vested in the local school administration and the appropriate persons designated by the administration.

3. The responsibility for leadership of the local girls interscholastic program should be delegated to the women physical education teachers. The school

1 Division of Girls and Women's Sports, "DGWS Statement on Competition for Girls and Women," *Journal of Health, Physical Education, Recreation* (September, 1965), pp. 34-37.

administration should delegate to them the major responsibility for planning, organizing, coaching, and supervising the program with the understanding that the ultimate authority remains in the hands of the administration.

4. The program, based on the needs and interests of the girls, should include those individual and team activities for which qualified leadership, financial support, and adequate facilities are available.

5. The entire financing of the girls' sports program should be included in the total school budget. Any monies collected should go into the general fund.

6. DGWS approved standards should be used in all sports. It is strongly recommended that DGWS rules be used in those sports in which DGWS publishes rules.

7. The administration should provide a healthful, safe, and sanitary environment for all participants.

Standards

Participants

1. Participants must be bona fide students of the high school which they represent. They shall not have attended high school for more than eight semesters after entering the ninth grade. They must be successfully carrying full academic loads. Students under temporary suspension or probation for disciplinary reasons should not be allowed to participate.

2. Participants must have amateur standing in the interscholastic sports in which they participate.

3. Written permission of the parent or guardian is required for all participants.

4. A physician's certification of a girl's fitness for participation shall be filed with the administration prior to the first practice in a sport. The examination must have been made within the time period specified by local regulations. Written permission by a physician should be required for participation after a serious illness, injury, or surgery.

5. Participants should carry some type of accident insurance coverage that protects them during athletic competition.

Leadership

1. The interscholastic program should be directed, coached, and officiated by qualified women whenever and wherever possible. No program should be expanded past the ability of the girls department of physical education to direct it.

2. All coaches should be certified teachers employed by the local board of education. If teachers other than trained women physical educators are used to coach, they should work closely with the girls department.

3. A woman faculty member appointed by the principal shall accompany and supervise girls teams at all contests.

4. Officials should hold a current intramural or above DGWS rating or an equivalent rating in the specific sport and should be registered with the appropriate administrative or regulatory bodies.

5. A doctor should be on call for all contests, and someone who is qualified in first aid procedure should be in attendance.

6. In case of question as to fitness for play, the official has the right to overrule the coach for the protection of the welfare of the girl.

Administration

1. All games and contests in which school teams participate must be under the direct sponsorship and supervision of the schools involved. No postseason games for teams or individuals should be permitted.

2. Girls may participate on only one interscholastic team during a season. They may not take part in a contest on any out-of-school team until the school sport season is completed. A girl is considered a member of a team when she participates in her first contest.

3. Competition should be limited to a geographical area which will permit players to return at reasonable hours. Safe transportation should be assured.

4. The maximum length of a sport season should be twelve weeks, with the first three weeks devoted to training and conditioning. The participant should take part in no more than five participation periods per week including games or contests. There should be no more than two games per week, which should not be played on consecutive days. Standards for specific sports are listed in the current DGWS guides.

5. Interscholastic competition should be limited to those sports for which DGWS publishes rules and standards, and they should be used in administration of program.

6. Awards when given should be inexpensive tokens of a symbolic type, such as ribbons, letters, and small pins. The giving of other types of awards as well as fund-raising for expensive or elaborate awards is considered a violation of this guideline.

GUIDELINES FOR COLLEGE AND UNIVERSITY PROGRAMS

Administration

The intercollegiate athletic program should be specifically designed for women, and its administration and organization should be the responsibility of the department of physical education for women. It is also the responsibility of the physical education faculty women to recommend and formulate policy for the expanded program to be submitted to the appropriate policy-approving authority of the institution.

Budget

The budget for women's intercollegiate athletics should be part of the budget of the institution so that the program is assured. A separate budget item should be specifically designated for this program. (This does not preclude the use of state monies, student fees, gate receipts, and other sources of income, but the program should not depend solely on fluctuating sources of income.)

The budget should be administered by the women's physical education department as part of overall administration.

Scheduling

Contests should be scheduled among schools having players of comparable ability in order to equate competition. In order to make this possible, scheduling in each sport need not be with the same institutions each season.

Scheduling with collegiate institutions is recommended. However, when budget is inadequate for travel, limited scheduling with outside organizations (i.e., church, industrial leagues, etc.) in the local area may be desirable. Scheduling should allow opportunities for participants of intercollegiate teams to meet on an informal social basis.

Health and Safety

Adequate health and insurance protection should be provided by the institution for all members of athletic teams. First aid services and emergency medical care should be available during all scheduled intercollegiate athletic events.

Tournaments

Problems surrounding the development of regional and national tournaments are so varied that the matter of intercollegiate tournaments needs further study. At this time it is recommended that tournaments be confined to participation within limited geographic areas.

Leadership (teachers, coaches, and officials)

1. Good leadership essential to a desirable sports program. The qualified leader meets the standard set by the profession through an understanding of (a) the place and purpose of sports in education, (b) the growth and development of children and youth, (c) the effects of exercise on the human organism, (d) first aid and accident prevention, (e) understanding of specific skills, and (f) sound teaching methods. It is desirable that, when possible, leaders of women's sports have personal experience in organized extramural competition. The leader should demonstrate personal integrity and primary concern for the welfare of the participant.

2. The program should be under the direct supervision of the women's physical education department. Qualified women should teach, coach, and officiate wherever and whenever possible, and in all cases the professional background and experience of the leader must meet established standards of the physical education profession.

3. It is strongly recommended that an official's rating be considered a prerequisite for coaching in order to enhance the coach's understanding of the official's role.

4. Intercollegiate events should be officiated by DGWS nationally rated officials. In those sports where DGWS does not rate officials, an equivalent rating is acceptable.

5. If a nonstaff member is teaching or coaching, a woman member of the physical education faculty should supervise and chaperone the participants. Cooperative institutional efforts should be devoted toward preservice and inservice programs and clinics for leaders and teachers.

6. DGWS-approved rules should be used in the conduct of all intercollegiate sports events.

Participation

1. Intercollegiate participation should not interfere with primary educational objectives.

(a) A student may not participate as a member of an intercollegiate athletic team and at the same time be a member of a team in the same sport outside her institution.

(b) Local policy-making groups may wish to qualify this policy for occasional individual students.

2. The athletic schedule should not jeopardize the student's class and study time.

(a) The length of the season and the number of games should be established and agreed upon by the participating schools.

(b) The length of the season will vary according to the locale and sport but should not exceed twelve weeks, including at least three weeks of preliminary conditioning and instruction.

(c) Standards for specific sports concerning number of practices and/or contests per week are found in the DGWS guides.

3. Women should be prohibited from participating

(a) on a men's intercollegiate team;

(b) against a men's intercollegiate team;

(c) against a man in a scheduled intercollegiate contest.

4. To be eligible to participate in intercollegiate athletics, the individual must be a full-time student of the institution and maintain the academic average required for participation in all other major activities. Undergraduate students only are eligible to participate in the intercollegiate athletic program. For the purposes of eligibility, an undergraduate student is defined as one who has not received the B.A. degree or its equivalent.

5. Transfer students are immediately eligible for participation following enrollment in the institution.

6. A medical examination is a prerequisite to participation in intercollegiate athletics. This examination should be given within the six-month period prior to the start of the sports season each year. Where health examinations are done by the family physician, a covering letter explaining the program of activities and an examination which would include the information needed is suggested. Written permission by the physician should be required for participation after serious illness, injury, or surgery.

7. A participant in intercollegiate athletics maintains amateur status if she has not received money other than expenses as a player, instructor, or official in any sport.

8. There should be no scholarships or financial assistance specifically designated for women athletes. This does not preclude women who participate in the intercollegiate athletic program from holding scholarships or grants-in-aid obtained through normal scholarship programs of the institution.

athletic field and court layouts[1]

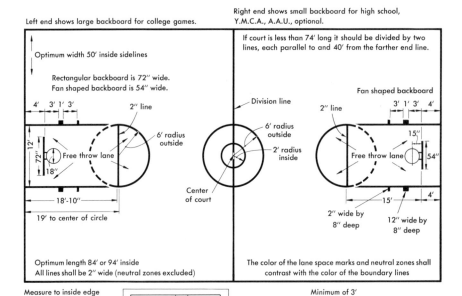

Left end shows large backboard for college games.

Right end shows small backboard for high school, Y.M.C.A., A.A.U., optional.

Optimum width 50' inside sidelines

If court is less than 74' long it should be divided by two lines, each parallel to and 40' from the farther end line.

Rectangular backboard is 72" wide.
Fan shaped backboard is 54" wide.

Fan shaped backboard

4'   3' 1' 3'   2" line

Division line   2" line   3' 1' 3'   4'

12'   6' radius outside   6' radius outside   15"

72"   2' radius inside

Free throw lane   Free throw lane   54"

18"

18'-10"   Center of court   15'   4'

19' to center of circle   2" wide by 8" deep   12" wide by 8" deep

Optimum length 84' or 94' inside
All lines shall be 2" wide (neutral zones excluded)

The color of the lane space marks and neutral zones shall contrast with the color of the boundary lines

Measure to inside edge of boundary lines.

3'

Minimum of 3'

Preferably 10' of unobstructed space outside. If impossible to provide 3', a narrow broken 1" line should be marked inside the court parallel with and 3' inside the boundary

BASKETBALL COURT

[1] Courtesy of Wilson Sporting Goods Company.

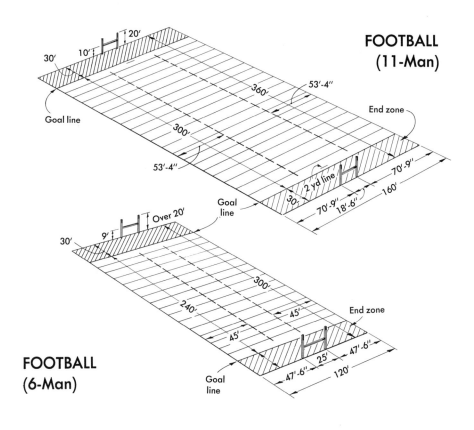

FOOTBALL
(11-Man)

30' 10' 20'

Goal line

53'-4" 360' 53'-4"

300'

End zone

Goal line

2 yd line 70'-9" 18'-6" 160' 70'-9" 30'

FOOTBALL
(6-Man)

Over 20'

30' 9'

Goal line

240' 300' 45' 45' End zone

47'-6" 25' 47'-6" 120'

Goal line

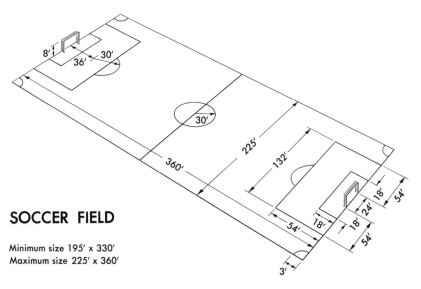

SOCCER FIELD

Minimum size 195' x 330'
Maximum size 225' x 360'

8' 36' 30' 30'

360' 225' 132'

54' 18' 18' 24' 18' 54'

18' 24' 18' 54' 54'

3'

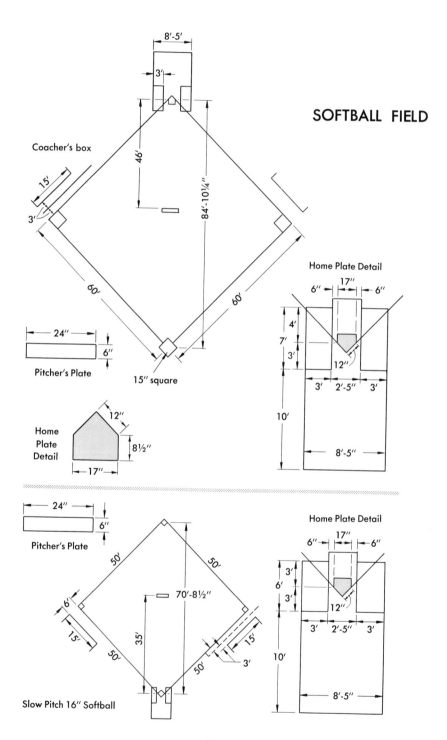

SOFTBALL FIELD

8'-5'

3'

Coacher's box

46'

84'-10¼"

15'

3'

60'

60'

Home Plate Detail

6" 17" 6"

24"

6"

Pitcher's Plate

15" square

4'

7'

3'

12"

3' 2'-5" 3'

10'

8'-5"

12"

**Home
Plate
Detail**

8½"

17"

24"

6"

Pitcher's Plate

Home Plate Detail

6" 17" 6"

50'

50'

3'

6"

3'

70'-8½"

12"

35'

50'

50'

15'

15'

3'

3' 2'-5" 3'

10'

8'-5"

Slow Pitch 16" Softball

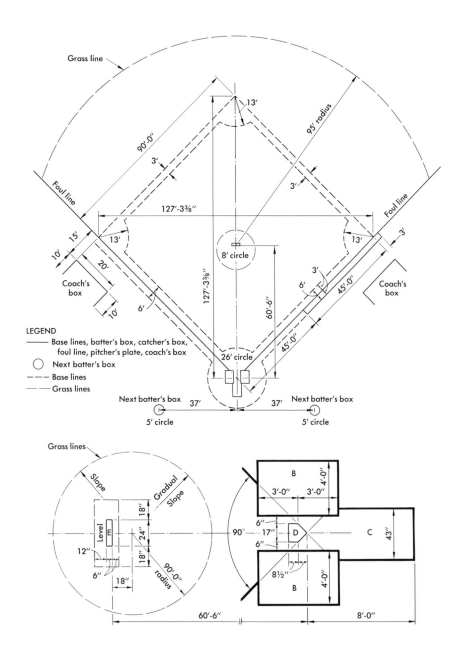

Grass line

13'

95' radius

90'-0"

3'

3'

Foul line

127'-3⅜"

Foul line

15'

13'

8' circle

13'

3'

10'

20'

Coach's box

127'-3⅜"

60'-6"

3'

6'

45'-0"

Coach's box

10'

6'

45'-0"

LEGEND

—— Base lines, batter's box, catcher's box, foul line, pitcher's plate, coach's box

○ Next batter's box

- - - Base lines

— - — Grass lines

26' circle

Next batter's box

37'

37'

Next batter's box

5' circle

5' circle

Grass lines

Slope

Gradual Slope

18"

90°

B

4'-0"

3'-0"

3'-0"

Level

E

24"

6"

17"

D

6"

C

43"

12"

18"

6"

90'-0" radius

8½"

B

4'-0"

6"

18"

60'-6"

8'-0"

BASEBALL DIAMOND

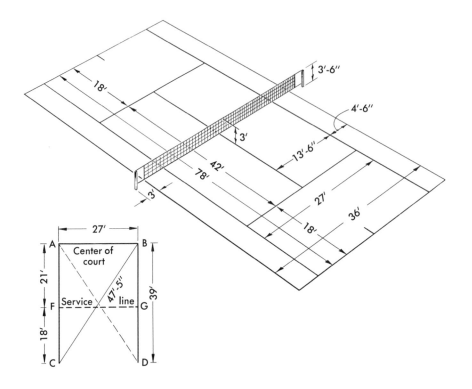

LAWN TENNIS Singles and Doubles

HOW TO LAY OUT A TENNIS COURT

First spot place for net posts, 42 feet apart. Measure in on each side 7½ feet and plant stakes 27 feet apart at points A and B in diagram.

Then take two tape measures and attach to each peg—one tape 47 feet 5¼ inches, the other 39 feet. Pull both taut in such directions that at these distances they meet at point C. This gives one corner of the court. Interchange the tapes and again measure to get point D. Points C and D should then be 27 feet apart. Put in pegs at C and D and measure 18 feet toward net and put in pegs to denote service lines.

Proceed in same way for the other half of court and add center line from service line to service line—distance 42 feet. Then add 4½ feet on each side for alleys. Alleys should then be 2 feet inside posts on each side. Put in permanent pegs to mark all corners.

Measure to outside edge of boundary lines.

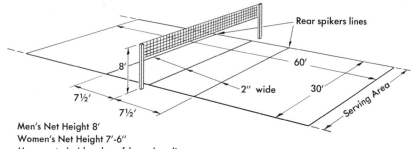

Men's Net Height 8'
Women's Net Height 7'-6"
Measure to inside edge of boundary lines.

VOLLEYBALL COURT

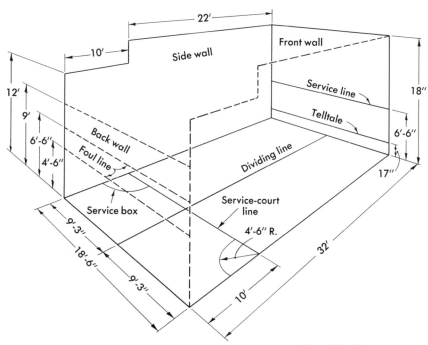

SQUASH COURT

Doubles Court
45' x 25' x 20'

Front Wall—20' High
Side Walls—20' x 31'
Back Wall Telltale Line—7'
Service Line—15'

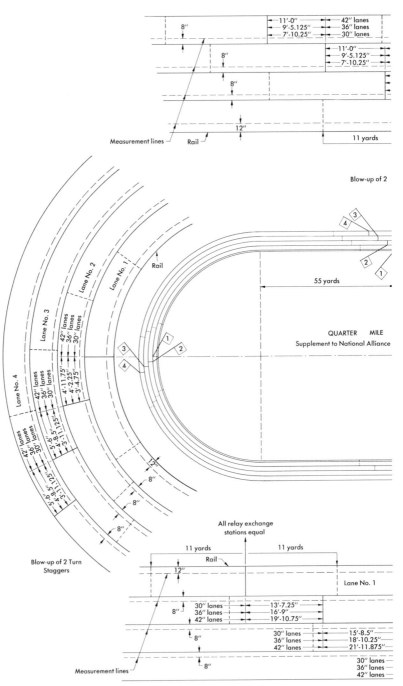

8"
←—11'-0"——→ 42" lanes
←—9'-5.125"——→ 36" lanes
←—7'-10.25"——→ 30" lanes

8"
←—11'-0"——
←—9'-5.125"——
←—7'-10.25"——

8"

12"

Measurement lines — Rail — 11 yards

Blow-up of 2

55 yards

QUARTER MILE
Supplement to National Alliance

Lane No. 1

Lane No. 2

Rail

Lane No. 3

42" lanes
36" lanes
30" lanes

4'-11.75"
4'-2.25"
3'-4.75"

Lane No. 4

42" lanes
36" lanes
30" lanes

5'-6.5"
4'-8.5.125"
3'-11.25"

42" lanes
36" lanes
30" lanes

5'-6.5.1.25"
4'-9.5.125"
3'-11.25"

12"

8"

8"

8"

Blow-up of 2 Turn
Staggers

All relay exchange
stations equal

11 yards   11 yards

Rail

Lane No. 1

12"

8"
30" lanes ⊢—13'-7.25"——
36" lanes ⊢—16'-9"——
42" lanes ⊢—19'-10.75"——

8"
30" lanes ⊢—15'-8.5"——
36" lanes ⊢—18'-10.25"——
42" lanes ⊢—21'-11.875"——

8"
30" lanes —
36" lanes —
42" lanes —

Measurement lines —

Blow-up of 2 Turn Staggers

558

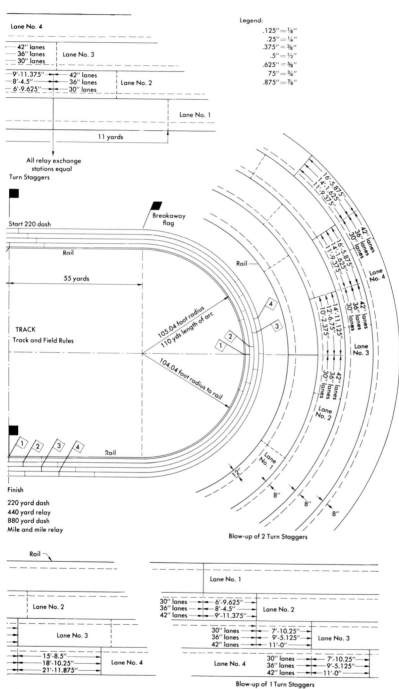

Lane No. 4

- 42" lanes
- 36" lanes
- 30" lanes

Lane No. 3

- 9'-11.375" — 42" lanes
- 8'-4.5" — 36" lanes
- 6'-9.625" — 30" lanes

Lane No. 2

Lane No. 1

11 yards

All relay exchange stations equal

Turn Staggers

Legend:
.125" = ⅛"
.25" = ¼"
.375" = ⅜"
.5" = ½"
.625" = ⅝"
.75" = ¾"
.875" = ⅞"

Start 220 dash

Breakaway flag

Rail

55 yards

Rail

TRACK

Track and Field Rules

105.04 foot radius
110 yds length of arc

104.04 foot radius to rail

4
3
2
1

Lane No. 4

42" lanes
36" lanes
30" lanes

16'-5.875"
14'-1.625"
11'-9.375"

16'-5.875"
14'-1.625"
11'-9.375"

42" lanes
36" lanes
30" lanes

14'-11.125"
12'-6.75"
10'-2.375"

42" lanes
36" lanes
30" lanes

Lane No. 3

42" lanes
36" lanes
30" lanes

Lane No. 2

Lane No. 1

12"

8"

8"

8"

1 2 3 4

Rail

Finish

220 yard dash
440 yard relay
880 yard dash
Mile and mile relay

Blow-up of 2 Turn Staggers

Rail

Lane No. 2

Lane No. 3

- 15'-8.5"
- 18'-10.25"
- 21'-11.875"

Lane No. 4

Lane No. 1

30" lanes — 6'-9.625"
36" lanes — 8'-4.5"
42" lanes — 9'-11.375"

Lane No. 2

30" lanes — 7'-10.25"
36" lanes — 9'-5.125"
42" lanes — 11'-0"

Lane No. 3

Lane No. 4

30" lanes — 7'-10.25"
36" lanes — 9'-5.125"
42" lanes — 11'-0"

Blow-up of 1 Turn Staggers

and break at flag after first turn with start from
chute or without chute

559

QUARTER-MILE TRACK

Approved by the National Federation of State High School Athletic Associations

Handicaps—When races, run in lanes, start on the straightaway and relay exchanges are made on the straightaway, the "staggered" distance may be determined from the following tables. These figures apply to all tracks that are laid out with semicircular turns, regardless of the number of laps to the mile.

For 30-Inch Lanes

No. of turns to run	4	3	2	1
Hdcp., Lane 2 over 1	27' 2½"	20' 4⅞"	13' 7¼"	6' 9⅝"
Lanes 3, 4, 5, 6, 7, and 8 over next inside lanes	31' 5"	23' 6¾"	15' 8½"	7' 10¼"

For 36-Inch Lanes

No. of turns to run	4	3	2	1
Hdcp., Lane 2 over 1	33' 6"	25' 1½"	16' 9"	8' 4½"
Lanes 3, 4, 5, 6, 7, and 8 over next inside lanes	37' 8⅜"	28' 3¼"	18' 10¼"	9' 5⅛"

For 42-Inch Lanes

No. of turns to run	4	3	2	1
Hdcp., Lane 2 over 1	39' 9½"	29' 10⅛"	19' 10¾"	9' 11⅜"
Lanes 3, 4, 5, 6, 7, and 8 over next inside lanes	43' 11¾"	32' 11⅞"	21' 11⅞"	11'

For 48-Inch Lanes

No. of turns to run	4	3	2	1
Hdcp., Lane 2 over 1	46'	34' 6"	23'	11' 6"
Lanes 3, 4, 5, 6, 7, and 8 over next inside lanes	50'	37' 6"	25'	12' 6"

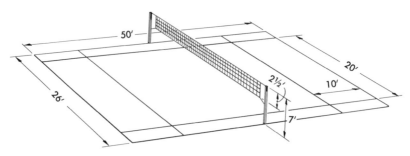

AERIAL TENNIS DART

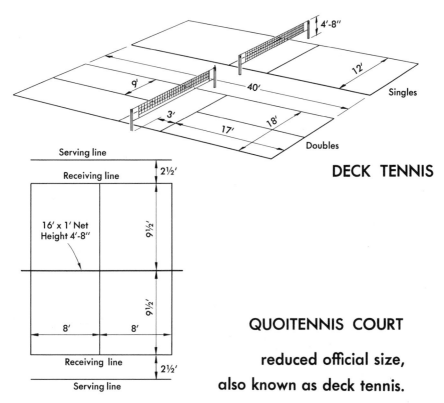

DECK TENNIS

QUOITENNIS COURT

reduced official size,
also known as deck tennis.

(Different size courts are sometimes used for similar games
of Quoitennis and Deck Tennis.)

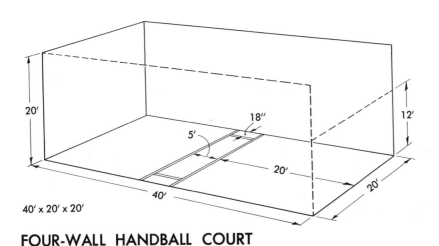

40' x 20' x 20'

FOUR-WALL HANDBALL COURT

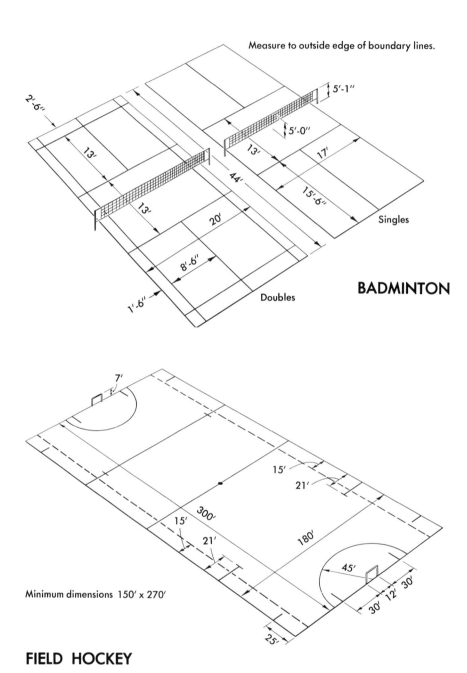

Measure to outside edge of boundary lines.

5'-1"

2'-6"

5'-0"

13'

13'

17'

44'

13'

15'-6"

20'

Singles

8'-6"

BADMINTON

1'-6"

Doubles

7'

15'

21'

300'

15'

180'

21'

45'

Minimum dimensions 150' x 270'

30' 12' 30'

30'

25'

FIELD HOCKEY

index

A.A.U., 271
Accidents, benefit plans, 283-285
Activity fees, student, 396-397
Adams, Harry, 391, 401, 421
Adams, Henry Bennett, 281
Administration, 1-17
　disciplinary action, 87-88
　processes, 48-90
　　controlling, 83-90
　　coordinating, 79-83
　　directing, 77-79
　　organizing, 66-77
　　planning, 48-66
Administrators, qualifications, 7-9
Aerial tennis dart, 560
Alcohol education, 208
All-star contests, opposition to, 270-271
American Association for Health, Physical Education and Recreation, 21, 24, 85, 114, 149, 164, 314, 317, 323, 484, 514-515, 516, 518
American Association of School Administrators, 313
American Medical Association, 33, 313
American Physical Education Association, 21
Anatomical structure, and athletics, 109-110
Anderson, C. L., 178, 202
Annapolis Conference on Fitness, 96

Annual Reports, 468-469
Appointments, 502-504
Archery tackle, care of, 445
Armed forces, 177-178
　physical fitness tests, 92-93, 95-96
Associations, athletic, 262-264, 268-275; see also specific organizations
Athletic director, 294-304
Athletic Goods Manufacturers Association, 431-432
Athletic programs, European, 259, 260
Athletics, history, see Interschool athletics
Automation, and physical development, 27-28, 34-36, 103-104
Awards, athletic, 290-293, 356

Badminton courts, 562
Bagnall-Wild elimination tournament, 362-363
Baldwin, Bird T., 110
Bartky, John, 66
Baseball, award requirements, 292-293
Baseball, high school, 273-274
Baseball diamond, 555
Baseball fields, 250-252
Basketball, award requirements, 291
　court, 552
Bates, Aubrey, 167
Beuttler, Fred C., 343
Bond, Marjorie, 159

Bookwalter, Karl W., 92n., 96
Breckenridge, Marian E., 39
Browning, Robert, on physical education, 26
Bucher, Charles, 7
Bureau of Health Education, Physical Education and Recreation, California State Department of Education, 523

"Can't Take It Club," 386-387
Cardinal Principles of Secondary Education, 18, 19
Carnegie Foundation, 310
Ceilings, in physical education plant, 228
Central Purpose of American Education, The, 20
Championship, high school, 307-308
Character building, 42-44, 108-109
Chase, Francis S., 10
Clifton, Marguerite, 159
Coach, and health of athletes, 281-283
Coaching staff, 300-301, 329-332, 355-356
Coefield, John R., 30
College Committee on Physical Education and Athletics, 149-150
College Physical Education Association, 149
College programs, 71-73, 144-155, 548-550
  characteristics of students, 150-151
    physical, 150
    psychological, 151
  coeducational, 155
  criteria for appraisal, 155
  orientation, 148-149
  proficiency requirement, 148
  required courses, 145-147
    nature of requirement, 146-147
  survey courses, 149
  time requirement, 147-148
  waiver of requirement, 149-150
Combination tournaments, 368-371
Commission on the Reorganization of Secondary Education, 18
Community, physical education programs and, 60-61
Community health programs, 209
Concessions, 399-400
Conferences, athletic, 61-62
Consumer health education, 209
Contests, administration, 301-302
Control, of players, 308-310
Correspondence, 497-498
Cowell, Charles, 39, 44, 513, 518

Cowell Personal Distance Scale, 518
Cureton, Thomas, 119
Curriculum, 39-41
  diversity of, 58-59
Cuspidors, 232
Custodial facilities, 233

Davis, Elwood C., 451
Deck tennis, 561
Delegation, of authority, 73, 75-76
Demonstrations, 469
Dewhurst, Frederick, 27
Dimock, Marshall, 2, 7, 11, 14
Division of Girls' and Women's Sports, 321, 322
Division of Health, Physical Education and Recreation, New York State Department of Education, 523
Doors, in physical education plant, 228-229
Drinking fountains, 232
Drying rooms, 231
Duplicating materials, 502

Education, purposes of, 18-21
Educational Lessons from Wartime Training, 93
Educational Policies Commission, 19-21, 313, 395
Educational system, and physical education, 62-63
Eisenhower, Dwight D., 35-36
Elementary school, programs in, 113-117
  core of program, 116-117
  importance of, 114-117
Elimination tournaments, 358-363
Environmental hazards, 209
Equipment, 59-60, 271, 420-449
  approval, 428
  care, 437-438, 441-446
  laundry, 448
  local dealers, 426-427
  method of buying, 426
  official, 426
  ordering, 428-431
  provision, 421
  purchasing, 421-426, 431-437
  repairs, 447-448
  room management, 438
  in small schools, 427-428
  uniforms, cleaning, 446-447
Evaluation, 511-525
  program, 523-524, 542-545

Evaluation—*Continued*
  self, 524-525
  staff, 521-523
  student achievement, 513-521, 535-541
Evaluative criteria, 523
Extramural competition, defined, 320
Fabrics, 432
Federal Security Agency, 177
Field hockey, 562
Filing, 498-502
Films, 467
Finances, 390-419
  accounting procedures, 415-416
  administering budget, 407-408
  athletic budget, 393-419
  budget making, 404-407
  control, 401-403
  expense reports, 416
  game reports, 418
  interschool agreement, 416
  in large cities, 403-404
  petty cash fund, 418
  physical education budget, 391-393
  practical budget, 408-415
  school funds, 416-418
Fine, Benjamin, 450
Floors, in physical education plant, 225-228
Football, award requirements, 291
  check list, 302-303
  fields, 251-252, 553
France, Wellman L., 513
French, Esther, 394
French, John R., 173
Frost, Reuben B., 331
Funnel tournament, 373

Game contracts, 295-296
Garfield, James A., 156
Gate receipts, 395-396, 398, 400-401
George, Jack, 329
Girls and women, 318-323
Golf, award requirements, 293
Goodyear Company, 433
Grambeau, Rodney J., 338, 350, 353
Grieder, Calvin, 9
Griffiths, Daniel, 5, 8, 10-11
Gutteridge, M., 39, 44
Gymnasium, *see* Physical education plant

Hale, Creighton, 118
Handball court, four-wall, 561
Harper, Fowler V., 480

Harral, Stewart, 451, 452, 466
Health, and Physical fitness, 32-34
Health, *see* School health education
Health careers, 209; *see also* Staff
Hein, Fred V., 33
Helmets, 443, 445, 446
Hetherington, Clark W., 26-27, 102
Hickman, Herman, 312
High school athletes, solicitation of, 271-272
High school programs, guidelines, 546-548
High schools, physical education organization, 70-71
Hillebrandt, Frances, 319
Hip pants, 435-436
Hirschborn, Kurt, 33
Hirschland, Ruth, 94
Hollman, Wildor, 29-30
Hughes, Otto, 394
Hughes, William, 394
Hunsicker, Paul, 93, 94, 95

Immunization programs, 195-196
Injuries, 59, 280-281
Insurance, liability, 484-485
Intercollegiate Athletic Association, 257, 262
Intermediate grades, programs in, 123-128
  characteristics of children, 123-125
    physical, 124
    psychological, 124
  implications of, 125-128
  importance of, 123
International contests, sanctioning procedures, 274
International health activities, 209
Interschool athletics, 255-334
  athletic director, 294-304
    part-time, 294
    responsibilities, 294-301
  athletics and physical education, 258-260
  awards, 290-293
    requirements, 291-293
      baseball, 292-293
      basketball, 291-292
      football, 291
      golf, 293
      swimming, 293
      tennis, 293
      track, 292
      wrestling, 293

Interschool athletics—*Continued*
colleges and universities, 256-258
control, 261-278
intercollegiate, 262-268
local, 265-268
national, 262-264
regional, 264
interscholastic, 268-269
local, 277
control—*Continued*
national, 268-269
state high school athletic associations, 275-277
eligibility requirements, 286-289
amateurs, 286-287
college, 289
high school, 287-289
age, 287
attendance, 287
awards, 289
entrance dates, 287
parents' consent, 289
participation, 288
physician's examination, 288
residence and migration, 287-288
scholastic requirements, 288-289
undue influence, 289
importance, 286
medical supervision, 278-285
accident benefit plans, 283-285
protection, 277-283
objectives, 260-261
problems, 304-333
academic teacher as coach, 323-324
athletics for girls and women, 318-
325
bad practices, 306-307
championships and tournaments, 307-
308
false values, 305-306
junior high school, 313-318
player control, 308-310
proselyting and subsidization, 310-
314
public presures, 325-326
reducing overemphasis, 324-325
standards, 261
trends in athletics, 326-333
Intramural athletics, 335-381
competition units, 344-346
college and university, 344-345
high school, 345-346
women, 346

Intramural athletics—*Continued*
eligibility, 348-349
finances, 342-344
colleges and universities, 343-344
high schools, 342-343
organization, 338-342
councils, 340
director, 338-340
student managers, 341-342
team managers, 342
point systems, 375-379
group, 375-378
individual, 378-379
program, 346-348
accident insurance, 350
awards, 356
coaching, 355-356
forfeits, 354
medical examinations, 349
officials, 352-353
preliminary training periods, 350-351
protests, 353-354
publicity, 354-355
statistics, 356-357
time periods, 351-352
relationship to required athletics, 336-
338
trends in, 377-381
faculty recreation, 380-381
informal athletics, 380
intramural, 379-381
sports clubs, 380
tournaments, 358-375
challenge, 371-373
combination, 368-371
elimination, 358-363
funnel, 373
round robin, 363-368
tombstone, 374-375

Jarman, Boyd, 31
Jerseys, 434-435
Jewett, Ann E., 116
Johnson, Lyndon B., 35-36
Jokl, Ernest, 318
Jones, Harold E., 32, 44
Junior high school, program in, 128-133,
313-318
characteristics of students, 128-129
physical, 128
psychological, 129
implications for, 129

Kapovich, Peter V., 92
Katz, Robert, 4
Kennedy, John F., 31, 35, 36
Kenney, Harold, 152
Kingsbury, Keith W., 391
Knuttgen, Howard, 94
Koontz, Harold, 84
Kraus, Hans, 33, 94
Kraus-Weber test, 94
Krogman, Wilton, 315
Krupa, Joseph H., 342, 343, 345, 346, 352
Kuhlen, Raymond, 39, 44

Larson, Leonard A., 92, 95
Laundry, school, 448
Lavatories, 232
Lawther, John, 37
Leather balls, care of, 441-444
Leather goods, care of, 444-445
Lee, Beatrice J., 39, 44
Lee, Mabel, 29
Legal liability, 478-493
    accident reduction, 489-490
    accident report form, 491-492
    accident reports, 490
    administrative responsibility, 478
    insurance, 484-485
    in medical treatment, 488-489
    negligence, 480-481, 485-486
    of private institutions, 484
    releases and waivers, 489
    of school board, 481-482
    of school districts, 483-484
    sources of suits, 486
    of teachers, 484
    trends, 482
Leyhe, Naomi, 322, 323
Lies, Eugene T., 107
Lighting, in physical education plant, 229
Locker rooms, 233
Lockers, 232-233
Lockhart, Aileene, 159
Logan, Gene A., 40
Lowman, C. L., 314

McCollum, Robert H., 30
McKee, Robert, 39, 44
McKinney, Wayne C., 40
Mats, care of, 446
Means, Louis, 94
Medical examination, 279-280
Meyer, Margaret, 319
Miller, Dona Mae, 159

Mitchell, Elmer D., 314
Motor skill tests, 515-516
Motor skills, 36-39

National Amateurs Athletic Federation, 320
National championship, high school, abolishment of, 269
National Collegiate Athletic Association, 257, 262-264, 265, 271, 322
National Conference on Fitness of Secondary School Youth, 137
National Council of State Consultants in Elementary Education, 314
National Council on Schoolhouse Construction, 246
National Council on Youth and Fitness, 317
National Education Association, 329
National Federation of State High School Athletic Associations, 268-275, 277, 293, 322, 428
National Safety Council, 211, 491
National Society for Prevention of Blindness, 211
National Society for the Control of Cancer, 211
National Tuberculosis Association, 211
Nets, care of, 445
Nevada, benefit plan, 284
Neverman, P. F., 284
Newman, William H., 50-51, 64-65, 66, 75, 77, 86
Newspapers, *see* Press, the
New York, scholastic requirement, 288
New York State Public School Athletic Association, 308
Nixon, John E., 117
Nixon, Richard N., 96
Nutrition and weight, 209
Nyman, Emil, 522

O'Donnell, Cyril, 84
Office management, 494-510
    functions and practices, 495-496
    size of school and, 504-506
    unit orientation, 495
Officials, 252-253, 295-298
Oxendine, Joseph, 146, 147

Pacific Coast Conference, 310
Pants, basketball, 434
    football, 433-434

Pennsylvania State Association, 296
Physical education, defined, 17-18
  objectives, 17-46
Physical education plant, 214-255
  indoor facilities, 217-236
    apparatus, 235-236
  indoor facilities—*Continued*
    arrangement, 222-223
    auxiliary gymnasium, 220
    location of building, 220-221
    locker unit, 233-234
    materials and construction, 224-225
    room dimensions, 221-222
    surface materials, 225-233
    traffic control, 223-224
  outdoor activity areas, 246-253
    general features, 247-253
    play areas, 247
    site selection, 247
  problems of, 214-215
  swimming pool, 236-246
    construction features, 239-241
    cost factors, 241-242
    indoor versus outdoor, 236-237
    pool supervision, 245-246
    preliminary planning, 237-239
    water circulation, 242
    water treatment, 242-245
  teaching stations, 215-216
Physical Education Service Program, 91-
  155
  curriculum development, 97-101
    administrative provisions, 100
    educational philosophy, 99
    evaluation, 101
    nature of children and, 100
    selection of activities, 100
    social philosophy, 98-99
    statement of objectives, 99-100
  inadequacies, 91-97
  selection of activities, principles for,
    101-109
    physiological, 101
    psychological, 101
    sociological, 102
    see also Physical Education Service
    Program, curriculum development
  sex differences and, 109-111
  time allotment of, 111
Physical examination, 57
Physical fitness indices, 31
Pictorial materials, 467-468
Pittenger, B. J., 415

Plumbing, in physical education plant,
  230-231
Point systems, in intramural athletics,
  375-379
Popp, James, 31, 44
President's Council on Physical Fitness, 95
Press, the, 465-467
Primary school, program in, 117-123
  characteristics of children,
    physical, 117-118
    psychological, 118-119
  implications for program, 119-123
Professional Preparation Conference, 159,
  162, 164
Prudden, Bonnie, 33
Public relations, 60-61, 450-477
  alumni and, 473
  athletic publicity, 473-477
  community and agencies, 462
  defined, 450-451
  and general public, 471
  in interscholastic and intercollegiate
    athletics, 470-471
  and media personnel, 472-473
  media used, 465-469
  multiple publics in, 458-462
  need and importance of, 452-453
  with opponents, 473
  with organizations, 469-470
  with other teachers, 460-461
  with parents, 459-460, 473
  planning and organizing, 457-458
  and press, 462
  principles, 453-457
  purposes, in education, 451
  purposes, in physical education, 451-
    452
  responsibility, 453
  and school administrations, 461-462
  student aspects, 458-459
  teacher's role, 462, 465
Public schools, organization for physical
  education in, 67-68
Public speaking, 468
Publicity, 473-477
Pullias, Earl, 159

Quarter-mile track, 558-560
Quoitennis court, 561

Rackets, 436
Radiators and heating, 230-231
Radio and television, 467

Rarick, Lawrence, 39, 44
Rodgers, Elizabeth, 117
Rosenstengel, William Everett, 9
ROTC, 149
Round robin tournaments, 363-368
Rountree, Colonel, 93
Rubber balls, care of, 44
Ryan, Allan J., 33
Schedule allowances, dental, 531-534
Schneider, Elsa, 114
School health education, 176-215
  healthful school living, 182-186
    daily organization, 184-186
    environment, 183-184
    food, 185
    meaning, 182-183
    teacher-pupil relationship, 185-186
    teacher's health, 186
  instruction, 198-213
    basic principles, 202-203
    conceptual approach, 209
    importance, 199-200
    meaning and purpose, 198-199
    methods, 210-212
    scope, 203-209
      correlation, 203-204
      elementary school instruction, 204-209
      health course, 204
    teacher, 200-201
    time allotment, 201-202
  objectives, 178-179
  organization, 179-182
    coordinator, 180-182
    personnel, 182
    scope, 182
  services, 187-198
    communicable disease control, 195-197
      attendance, 196-197
      common cold, 196
    emergency care procedures, 197
    excuses, 198
    follow-up program, 194-195
    health appraisal, 187-194
      periodic dental examination, 189-190
      periodic medical examination, 187-188
      psychological examination, 190
      screening tests, 190-191
    nature and scope, 187
    outlook, 177-178

School health education—*Continued*
  services—*Continued*
    relation to physical education, 176
    responsibility of educators, 176-177
    supervision of personnel, 197-198
School Health Education Study, 205, 209
School Health Education Survey, 200
School system, organization for physical education, 70
Schooler, Virgil, 394
Schram, Wilbur, 28
Scott, Elmer B., 343
Scott, Harry A., 266, 319
Scouting, 301
Secretary, 506-509
Senior high school, program in, 133-144
  block program, 140-141
  characteristics of students, 133-134
    physical, 133-134
    psychological, 134
  graduate achievement, 138-140
  flexible scheduling, 141-142
  homogeneous classes, 141
  implications for, 134-138
  preparation of curriculum, 144
  substitution for physical education, 143
  summer session, 144
Services, 91-155, 187-198, 504
Sex education, 209
Shoes, football, 432-433
Shoulder pads, 435, 446
Showers, 231
Shuttlecocks, 436-437, 445
Skills, in administration, conceptual, 4
  human, 4
  technical, 4
  see also Motor skills
Sliepcevich, Elena, 199, 200, 207, 208
Smoking, 209
Snyder, David, 403, 404
Soccer field, 553
Social development objectives, 41-44
  contribution to, 42-44
  obligation to, 44
Society of State Directors of Health, Physical Education and Recreation, 24, 314
Softball field, 554
Squash court, 557
Staff, 156-175
  morale, 172-173
  qualifications, 157-167
    experience, 165-166
    health, 166-167

Staff—*Continued*
  qualifications—*Continued*
    interview, 167-168
    personality, 157-159
    preparation, 159-165
  selection, 167-169
    activities, 168-169
    college transcripts, 168
    observation, 167-168
    personal interview, 167
    philosophy, 168
    skills, 169
    sports participation, 168
    written examination, 169
  teaching load, 169-170
  training in service, 170-172
Standards, 512, 526-530
"Standards in Athletics for Boys in Secondary Schools," Joint Committee Report, 526-530
Stoodley, Agnes, 21
Student Athletic Association, 397
Student leaders, 382-390
  class work, 383-387
  intramural activities, 387
  leader corps, 388-389
  varsity athletics, 387-388
Student manager system, 299-301
Student publications, 468
Subsidization of athletics, 310-314
Summer competition, 332-333
Swimming, award requirements, 293
Swimming pool, 236-238
Syracuse University, 31

Teaching versus administration, 5-8
Tead, Ordway, 2, 7, 13
Team travel, 297-298
Telephone calls, 495-497
Tennis, award requirements, 293
  court, 556
Textiles, care of, 444

Tickets, student, 397-398
Toilets, 232
Tombstone tournament, 374-375
Tournaments, 358-375
Track, 252-253
  award requirements, 292
  equipment, 446
Troester, Carl, 34
Tryon, Caroline, 39, 44

United States Military Academy (West Point), 30
United States Office of Education, 96
University of Illinois, 152
University of Oregon, 31

Venereal disease education, 209
Ventilation, in physical education plant, 229
Visiting teams, receiving of, 62
Visitors, 497
Vincent, E. Lee, 39
Volleyball court, 557

Wagner, Miriam, 29
Walker, Malcolm, 316
Wallis, Earl L., 451
Wayman, Agnes R., 379
Webber, Robert, 325
Weiss, Raymond A., 92
Welch *v.* Dunsmuir Joint High School District, 488
Williams, Jessie Fiering, 44
Wisconsin Interscholastic Athletic Association Athletic Accident Benefit Plan, 284-285
Women, *see* Girls and women
Wrestling, award requirements, 293
  standards, 274-275

Young Men's Christian Association, 271